4 31

D0213193

DATE DUE

GOVERNMENT
AGENCIES

The Greenwood Encyclopedia of American Institutions

Each work in the *Encyclopedia* is designed to provide concise histories of major voluntary groups and nonprofit organizations that have played significant roles in American civic, cultural, political, and economic life from the colonial era to the present.

1. *Labor Unions*
Gary M Fink, Editor-in-Chief

2. *Social Service Organizations*
Peter Romanofsky, Editor-in-Chief

3. *Fraternal Organizations*
Alvin J. Schmidt

4. *Political Parties and Civic Action Groups*
Edward L. Schapsmeier and Frederick H. Schapsmeier

5. *Research Institutions and Learned Societies*
Joseph C. Kiger, Editor-in-Chief

6. *Private Colleges and Institutions*
John F. Ohles and Shirley M. Ohles

7. *Government Agencies*
Donald R. Whitnah, Editor-in-Chief

The Greenwood Encyclopedia of American Institutions

Government Agencies

editor-in-chief
DONALD R. WHITNAH

GREENWOOD PRESS
Westport, Connecticut • London, England

Library of Congress Cataloging in Publication Data

Main entry under title:

Government agencies.

  (Greenwood encyclopedia of American institutions,
ISSN 0271-9509 ; no. 7)
  Bibliography: p.
  Includes index.
  1. Administrative agencies—United States. I. Whitnah,
Donald Robert, 1925-   . II. Series.
JK421.G65   1983   353.04   82-15815
ISBN 0-313-22017-4 (lib. bdg.)

Library of Congress Catalog Card Number: 82-15815
ISBN: 0-313-22017-4
ISSN: 0271-9509

First published in 1983

Greenwood Press
A division of Congressional Information Service, Inc.
88 Post Road West
Westport, Connecticut 06881

Printed in the United States of America

10 9 8 7 6 5 4 3 2 1

FOR MY DAUGHTERS, VICKI AND TARA

CONTENTS

C ——————————————————————

D ——————————————————————

E

F

G

H

I

J

L

M

N

O ——————————————————————————————

P ——————————————————————————————

R ——————————————————————————————

S

T

U

V

W

Y

CONTRIBUTORS

Graham Adams, Jr., Professor of History, Mount Allison University, Sackville, New Brunswick, Canada, has written *Age of Industrial Violence: The Commission on Industrial Relations, 1910-1915* (1966).

Paul D. Addis, graduate student in the history of medicine at the University of Maryland, has work experience with the AFL-CIO and includes a number of oral history materials in his appropriate research on the Occupational Safety and Health Administration.

Thomas G. Alexander, Professor of History and Director, Charles Redd Center for Western Studies, Brigham Young University, has written *A Clash of Interests: Interior Department and Mountain West, 1863-1896* (1977).

Dean C. Allard, Head, Operational Archives Branch, Department of the Navy, Naval Historical Center, Washington, D.C., is coeditor of *U.S. Naval History Sources in the United States* (1979).

Kent Anderson, Lecturer in History, University of Arizona, is the author of *Television Fraud: The History and Implications of the Quiz Show Scandals* (1978).

William D. Bajusz, Manager, Intelligence Applications Analysis, the BDM Corporation, was formerly with the Arms Control and Disarmament Agency, serving in policy planning and coordinating.

Howard Ball, Professor and Head, Department of Political Science, University of Utah, has written: *The Warren Court's Conceptions of Democracy* (1971), *The Vision and the Dream of Justice Hugo L. Black: An Examination of a Judicial Philosophy* (1975), *No Pledge of Privacy: The Watergate Tapes Litigation, 1973-1974* (1977), and *Judicial Craftmanship or Fiat? Direct Overturn by the United States Supreme Court* (1978).

Andrew H. Bartels wrote his dissertation in history on the Office of Price Administration, 1940-1946. He later was employed by the Council on Wage and Price Stability.

Richard A. Bartlett, Professor of History at Florida State University, has published widely on the U.S. frontier. He has edited *Rolling Rivers: An Encyclopedia of America's Rivers* (in press) and is author of *Great Surveys of the American West* (1962), *Nature's Yellowstone* (1974), and *The New Country: A Social History of the American Frontier, 1776-1890* (1974).

Daniel R. Beaver, Professor of History, University of Cincinnati, has written "Newton D. Baker and the Genesis of the War Industries Board, 1917-1918," *Journal of American History* (1965) and *Newton D. Baker and the American War Effort, 1917-1919* (1966).

Larry Berman, Associate Professor of Political Science, University of California, Davis, has written *The Office of Management and Budget and the Presidency, 1921-1979* (1979).

Robert H. Bremner, Professor Emeritus, Ohio State University, has written widely in social history including editing *Children and the Youth in America: A Documentary History* (1970-1974), *The Public Good: Philanthropy and Welfare in the Civil War Era* (1980), and *American Philanthropy*(1960).

D. Clayton Brown, Associate Professor of History at Texas Christian University, has among his writings published the book *Electricity for Rural America: The Fight for REA* (1980).

Harold L. Burstyn, Historian, Geological Survey, U.S. Department of Labor, has written a number of articles in the history of science.

Ronald E. Butchart, Associate Professor, State University of New York, College at Cortland, specializes in U.S. social and intellectual history. He is the author of *Northern Schools, Southern Blacks, and Reconstruction: Freedmen's Education 1862-1875* (1980) and a number of articles and reviews.

Robert G. Carey, Professor of English, Montgomery College (Maryland), has written *The Peace Corps* (1970).

David Chalmers, Professor of History, University of Florida, has written *Neither Socialism nor Monopoly: Theodore Roosevelt and the Decision to Regulate the Railroads* (1976) and *The Muckrake Years* (1974).

Marilyn Sara Cohen, President of MSC Associates, consulting for museums, exhibits, and publications, has previously been employed by the National Bureau of Standards and the Smithsonian Institution.

Paul K. Conkin, Professor of History, Vanderbilt University, has written numerous articles and books on U.S. intellectual topics, including *FDR and the Origins of the Welfare State* (1967), *The New Deal*, 2d ed. (1975), and *Tomorrow a New World: The New Deal Community Program* (1959).

Robert J. Cressman, Ships Histories Branch, Naval Historical Center, and formerly a historian with the U.S. Marine Corps, has contributed other articles to journals and anthologies on military history.

George H. Daniels, Department of Social Sciences, Michigan Technological

University, has written *American Science in the Age of Jackson* (1968) and *Science in American Society: A Social History* (1971).

Roger Daniels, Professor and Head, Department of History, University of Cincinnati, specializes in social and immigration history, and has coauthored *American Racism: Exploitation of the Nature of Prejudice* (1970), edited *Anti-Chinese Violence in North America* (1978), and written *Concentration Camps U.S.A.: Japanese-Americans and World War II* (1971).

MacArthur Darby, Assistant Vice-President for Academic Affairs, University of Louisville, is a historian and has experience in affirmative action matters.

Grant M. Davis, Oren Harris Professor of Transportation, University of Arkansas, has written *The Department of Transportation* (1970) and numerous articles on all phases of transportation.

Ralph F. de Bedts, eminent Professor of History Emeritus, Old Dominion University, has written *The New Deal's SEC: The Formative Years* (1964), *Recent American History*, 2 vols. (1973), and is completing a book manuscript on Kennedy and American Appeasement.

Lieutenant Colonel Drue L. DeBerry, Air Force Historical Office, has research interest in military history, especially Air Force history.

Lieutenant Colonel W. Scott Dillard, Associate Professor of History, U.S. Military Academy, wrote his Ph.D. dissertation on "The United States Military Academy, 1865-1900: The Uncertain Years" (1972).

John M. Dobson, Professor of History, Iowa State University, has written "Six Decades of Stalemate: The Changing Mandate of the U.S. Tariff Commission," *Midwest Review of Public Administration* (1980) and previously served as a Foreign Service Officer at the Department of State. He is the author of *Politics in the Gilded Age: A New Perspective on Reform* (1972).

A. Ross Eckler, employed for many years at the Bureau of the Census, has written *The Bureau of the Census* (1972).

J. Merton England, Historian, National Science Foundation, is completing a book manuscript on the NSF history for 1945-1957 and writes articles on the history of science.

George Q. Flynn, Professor of History, Texas Tech University, has written *The Mess in Washington: Manpower Mobilization in World War II* (1972). He is now writing a biography of Lewis Hershey, former head of the Selective Service System.

Wayne E. Fuller, Professor of History, the University of Texas at El Paso, has written *The American Mail: Enlarger of the Common Life* (1972) and *R. F. D.: The Changing Face of Rural America* (1964).

Philip J. Funigiello, Professor of History, College of William and Mary, has written *Toward a National Power Policy* (1973) and *The Challenge to Urban Liberalism: Federal-City Relations During World War II* (1978).

Herbert Garfinkel, Professor of Political Science and Vice-President for Academic Affairs, University of Louisville, has written *When Negroes March: The March on Washington Movement in the Organizational Politics for FEPC* (1959).

John D. Garwood, Professor of Economics and Vice-President for Academic Affairs Emeritus, Fort Hays State University, has written with W. C. Tuthill, *The Rural Electrification Administration: An Evaluation* (1963).

James A. Gross, Professor, New York State School of Industrial and Labor Relations, Cornell University, has written *The Making of the NLRB: A Study in Economics, Politics and the Law* (1974) and *The Reshaping of the NLRB: National Labor Policy in Transition* (1981).

Frederick Gutheim, Consultant, Dickerson, Maryland, and Professor of American History and Urban Planning, Department of Urban Regional Planning, George Washington University, has written *The Federal City, Plans and Realities* (1976) and *Worthy of the Nation* (1979).

James L. Harwood, Archivist, Records Disposition Division, National Archives and Records Service, has long experience in documents pertaining to loans and debts of the various states, particularly for the pre-federal period.

Jordan Jay Hillman, Professor of Law, Northwestern University, is the author of *The Parliamentary Structuring of British Road-Rail Freight Coordination* (1973) and *The Export-Import Bank at Work: Promotional Financing in the Public Sector* (1982).

Robert F. Himmelberg, Professor of History, Fordham University, is the author of *The Origins of the National Recovery Administration: Business, Government, and the Trade Association Issue, 1921-1933* (1976).

Abraham Hoffman, Department of History, Los Angeles Valley College, has written *Unwanted Mexican Americans in the Great Depression* (1974).

Hope K. Holdcamper, Archivist (retired), National Archives and Records Service, has compiled, with Carmelita S. Ryan, "Preliminary Inventory of the General Records of the Department of the Treasury, Record Group 56" (1977).

R. Gordon Hoxie, President, Center for the Study of the Presidency, New York, and editor of *Presidential Studies Quarterly*, is the author of *Command Decision and the Presidency* (1977) and editor of *The White House: Organization and Operations* (1971) and *The Presidency of the 1970's* (1973).

Frank Hoy is Director of Research and Experiential Education, Small Business Development Center, the University of Georgia. He is now working on a number of topics including the Small Business Administration.

Clyde E. Jacobs, Professor of Political Science, University of California, Davis, is coauthor of *The Selective Service Act: A Case Study of the Governmental Process* (1967).

D. Clayton James, Professor of History, Mississippi State University, and 1980-1981 Morrison Professor, U.S. Army Command and General Staff College, is the author of *The Years of MacArthur*, 2 vols. (1970-1975).

Renée M. Jaussaud, Archivist, Legislative and Natural Resources Branch, National Archives, has compiled an inventory of materials in the National Archives and Records Service relative to the U.S. Fish and Wildlife Service.

Rhodri Jeffreys-Jones, Professor of History, University of Edinburgh, Scotland, has written *American Espionage: From Secret Service to CIA* (1977) among other publications on U.S. history.

William A. Jordan, Professor of Economics, York University, Ontario, Canada, has written *Airline Regulation in America: Effects and Imperfections* (1970), *Performance of Regulated Canadian Airlines in Domestic and Transborder Operations* (1981), and numerous articles on aviation regulation.

Lane C. Kendall, Commander, U.S. Maritime Service, on the faculty of the U.S. Merchant Marine Academy, and with vast experience in the operational side of shipping, is the author of *The Business of Shipping* (1976, 1979).

Ramunas A. Kondratas is Assistant Curator at the National Museum of American History, Smithsonian Institution. He has published articles on the history of clinical medicine and public health in Europe and the United States. He is currently writing a survey history of public health in the United States.

Linda J. Lear, Adjunct Associate Professor of History, George Washington University, is working on a full-length biography of Harold L. Ickes. The first volume has already been published: *Harold L. Ickes: The Aggressive Progressive* (1981).

Carole Levin, Visiting Assistant Professor of History, the University of Iowa, has published articles in the fields of both English history and women's studies in various journals, including the *International Journal of Women's Studies*.

Tom Forrester Lord, Consultant and Architectural Expert, Adjunct, Rice University, has written *Decent Housing: A Promise to Keep* (1977).

Richard Lowitt, Chairman and Professor of History, Iowa State University, is the author of *George W. Norris*, 3 vols. (1963, 1971, 1978) and has edited *America in Depression and War* (1979).

Thomas G. Manning, Professor of History Emeritus, Texas Tech University, has written widely in the history of science, including *Government in Science: The U.S. Geological Survey, 1867-1894* (1967).

Harvey C. Mansfield, Sr., Ruggles Professor Emeritus, Department of Political Science, Columbia University, is the author of a book on the earlier period of the General Accounting Office, *The Comptroller General: A Study in the Law and Practice of Fiscal Administration* (1939).

Alfred A. Marcus, Battelle Human Affairs Research Center, Seattle, has written *Promise and Performance: Choosing and Implementing an Environmental Policy* (1980) and "The EPA," in James Q. Wilson, ed., *The Politics of Regulation* (1980).

George T. Mazuzan, Chief Historian, Nuclear Regulatory Commission, has done extensive research on the Nuclear Regulatory Commission and related matters and is coauthor with Roger Trask of *An Outline History of Nuclear Regulation and Licensing, 1946-1979* (1979).

Donald R. McCoy, University Distinguished Professor of History, the University of Kansas, includes among his many writings, "The Beginnings of the Franklin D. Roosevelt Library," *Prologue: The Journal of the National Archives* (Fall 1975) and *The National Archives: America's Ministry of Documents* (1978).

George T. McJimsey, Professor of History, Iowa State University, specializes in several areas of American history, including research on Harry Hopkins and the Works Progress Administration.

R. Michael McReynolds, Archivist, Judicial and Fiscal Branch, National Archives, has completed research on a number of aspects pertaining to the Department of Justice.

Clark Mitze, Consultant in the Arts, Sacramento, served formerly as a program officer with the National Endowment for the Arts in addition to further experiences with arts councils in Illinois, Missouri, and California.

Walton S. Moody, Historian, Office of Air Force History, has conducted a number of research projects in aviation and Air Force history.

William T. Moye, Historian, Bureau of Labor Statistics, Department of Labor, has published articles in the *Monthly Labor Review* and *Industrial and Labor Relations Review*. Presently, he is writing a history of the Bureau of Labor Statistics.

Daniel M. Nelson, Professor of History, the University of Akron, is the author of *Unemployment Insurance: The American Experience, 1915-35* (1969).

Hugh S. Norton, Johnson Professor of Economics, University of South Carolina, includes among his writings *The Employment Act and the Council of Economic Advisers* (1977).

James S. Olson, Associate Professor of History, Sam Houston State University, has written *Herbert Hoover and the Reconstruction Finance Corporation, 1931-1933* (1977).

Keith W. Olson, Professor of History, University of Maryland, is the author of *The G. I. Bill, The Veterans, and The Colleges* (1974).

William E. Pemberton, Professor of History, University of Wisconsin-La Crosse, is completing a book on the First and Second Hoover Commissions and research on an agency recommended by them, the General Services Administration. He has also written *Bureaucratic Politics: Executive Reorganization During the Truman Administration* (1979).

Neal H. Petersen, Acting Deputy Historian, Department of State, has publications in the field of U.S. diplomacy.

Harold T. Pinkett, Consulting Archivist and (retired) former Chief, Legislative and Natural Resources Branch, National Archives, has written widely in agriculture and forest history and is the author of *Gifford Pinchot: Private and Public Forester* (1970).

Joseph A Pratt, Associate Professor of History, Texas A & M University, has been a visiting scholar at the Department of Energy and has published *The Growth of a Refining Region: Twentieth Century Growth of the Houston Area* (1980) and several articles in business history.

Harry Howe Ransom, Professor of Political Science, Vanderbilt University, has written *The Intelligence Establishment* (1970).

Wayne D. Rasmussen, Chief, Agricultural History Branch, Department of Agriculture, with Gladys L. Baker, has written *The Department of Agriculture* (1972) and has published a number of articles in agriculture history.

William D. Reeves, Research Consultant, New Orleans, has completed his history Ph.D. dissertation, "The Politics of Public Works 1933-1935" (1968) and has published "PWA and Competitive Administration in the New Deal," *Journal of American History* (September 1973).

Malcolm J. Rohrbough, Professor of History, University of Iowa, has written *The Land Office Business: The Settlement and Administration of American Public Lands, 1789-1837* (1968).

Alex Roland, Associate Professor of History, Duke University, writes on military history and the history of technology. In press is his *A History of the National Advisory Committee for Aeronautics, 1915-1958*.

Mark H. Rose, Department of Social Sciences, Michigan Technological University, has written *Interstate: Express Highway Politics, 1941-1956* (1979).

John Salmond, Professor of American History, La Trobe University, Bundoora, Victoria, Australia, has published *The Civilian Conservation Corps, 1933-1942: A New Deal Case Study* (1967) and is writing a book on the National Youth Administration.

Richard L. Saunders, Associate Professor of History, Clemson University, has written *The Railroad Mergers and the Coming of Conrail* (1978).

Robert L. Scheina, Historian, U.S. Coast Guard, has published a large number of articles on American naval history, ship design, maritime disasters, the Coast Guard, and naval history pertaining to various other nations.

Paul J. Scheips, Historian, General History Branch, Center of Military History, Department of the Army, has edited *Military Signal Communications*, 2 vols. (1980) and has written his Ph.D. dissertation on "Albert James Myer, Founder of the Army Signal Corps: A Biographical Study" (1966).

F. M. Scherer, Professor of Economics, Northwestern University, has written *Industrial Market Structure and Economic Performance*, 2d ed. (1980), which includes material on patent-system economics.

William F. Sherman, Archivist, Judicial and Fiscal Branch, National Archives, has compiled two valuable, unpublished guides, "Preliminary Inventory of the

Records of the Bureau of Engraving and Printing" and "Preliminary Inventory of Records of Accounting Officers of the Treasury Department."

Michael Sherraden, Assistant Professor, the George Warren Brown School of Social Work, Washington University, has done extensive research on Department of Labor work programs for youth, including the Job Corps.

R. Elberton Smith, Professor of Economics Emeritus, California State Polytechnic University, has written *The Army and Economic Mobilization* (1959) in the official historical series U.S. Army in World War II.

Morton Sosna, Associate Director, Stanford Humanities Center, Stanford University, and former program officer, Division of Fellowships, National Endowment for the Humanities, has collected material on NEH history and has written *In Search of the Silent South: Southern Liberals and the Race Issue* (1977).

O. Glenn Stahl, formerly with many federal agencies including the Tennessee Valley Authority, Federal Security Agency, Civil Service Commission, U.S. Department of Agriculture, and Agency for International Development, and Visiting Lecturer at many universities, has published *The Personnel Job of Government Managers* (1971) and *Public Personnel Administration*, 7th ed. (1976).

James A. Steed, Assistant Archivist, Smithsonian Institution Archives, has specialized in a number of research projects for the Smithsonian and is coauthor of a memoir of Dr. Alexander Wetmore to be published in the *Biographical Memoirs of the National Academy of Sciences* (forthcoming).

Jeffrey K. Stine has been conducting detailed graduate research on the U.S. Army Corps of Engineers.

Paul Stuart, Assistant Professor, Department of Social Work, University of Wisconsin-Eau Claire, has published *The Indian Office: Growth and Development of an American Institution, 1865-1900* (1979) and "United States Indian Policy: From the Dawes Act to the American Indian Policy Review Commission," *Social Service Review* (September 1977).

Jack Sweetman, Assistant Professor of History, U.S. Naval Academy, is the author of *The U.S. Naval Academy: An Illustrated History* (1979) and "The Civilian Faculty: 1845-1960," *Shipmate* (January-March 1981).

Athan Theoharis, Professor of History, Marquette University, has written *Spying on Americans: Political Surveillance from Hoover to the Huston Plan* (1978).

Roger R. Trask, Deputy Historian, Office of the Secretary of Defense, is coauthor of *An Outline History of Nuclear Regulation and Licensing, 1946-1979* (1979). He has compiled and coedited *A Bibliography of United States-Latin American Relations Since 1910* (1968) and has written *The United States Response to Turkish Nationalism and Reform, 1914-1939* (1971).

David A. Walker, Professor of History, University of Northern Iowa, has written *Iron Frontier: The Discovery and Early Development of Minnesota's Three Ranges* (1979) and other scholarly works on business and frontier history.

Donald R. Warren, Professor and Chairman, Department of Education Policy, Planning, and Administration, University of Maryland, has written *To Enforce Education: A History of the Founding Years of the United States Office of Education* (1974) and *History, Education, and Public Policy* (1978).

Richard Hume Werking, Collection Development Librarian and Assistant Professor of History, Trinity University, is the author of *The Master Architects: Building the U.S. Foreign Service, 1890-1913* (1977).

Robert Craig West, Bank Standards Division, Federal Reserve System, Kansas City, has written *Banking Reform and the Federal Reserve, 1863-1923* (1977).

Gerald T. White, Professor of History Emeritus, University of California, Irvine, has written *Billions for Defense: Government Financing by the Defense Plant Corporation During World War II* (1980).

Donald R. Whitnah, Editor-in-Chief of *Government Agencies*, is Professor and Head, Department of History, University of Northern Iowa, and has also published *A History of the United States Weather Bureau* (1961) and *Safer Skyways: Federal Control of Aviation, 1926-1966* (1966, 1967).

Allan M. Winkler, Assistant Professor of History, University of Oregon, has written *The Politics of Propaganda: The Office of War Information, 1942-1945* (1978).

James Harvey Young, Candler Professor of History, Emory University, includes among his many publications in the history of science *The Toadstool Millionaires: A Social History of Patent Medicines in America Before Federal Regulation* (1961), *The Medical Messiahs: A Social History of Health Quackery in Twentieth Century America* (1967), and *American Self-Dosage Medicines* (1974).

PREFACE

The cynics among us today might well question just why anyone would waste any time studying about agencies of the federal government. After all, the current attack on every nondefense-related governmental budget is but a culmination of the bipartisan clamor originating in the mid-1970s to deregulate transportation, oil, and natural gas—indeed, to emasculate a number of additional federal programs that loomed unpopular at the time. But this tune rings familiar to scholars of past administrative history. As Professor Ralph de Bedts states in concluding his article in this book on the Securities and Exchange Commission* (SEC) "those businesses which are regulated and which depend on the public for their profitable existence . . . no longer could envision doing without agencies . . . which by their regulatory discipline have ensured them public confidence and public patronage." It is true that most of the agencies, departments, bureaus, corporations, commissions, or quasi-agencies included in *Government Agencies* have in their history suffered through the peaks and gorges of appropriations as Congress and the President have blessed or damned them, or, in some instances, the Supreme Court has ruled them out of existence.

Similar to the foregoing, the agencies—used here to include all federal entities—have chalked up notable achievements, disappointing failures, and in-house and external squabbles, in addition to an occasional scandal. In all fairness to government at all levels, this record probably rates fully as well or poorly as business and industry of the private sector. Yet the worn-out cliché, big business and big labor lead to big government, strikes a resonant chord here. As the United States progressed from a predominantly agricultural to a heavy industrial economy late in the nineteenth and early twentieth centuries, government, through its multiplicity of agencies, was called upon to promote industry as well as to regulate the seamy side of life, because numerous individuals in the private sector possessed not an iota of fairness or decency toward the millions of other

*An asterisk (*) after a title indicates that there is an article on that agency in this work.

Americans they exploited. Historians argue heatedly over the merits of reform-
oriented movements, such as Populism, Progressivism, the New Deal, and the
post-World War II examples, judging in each instance just how radical or conservative were the reformers and examining their results as to lasting value.

Big business necessitated the SEC, while burgeoning labor and its troubles
with business resulted in the National Labor Relations Board* (NLRB). A hasty
glance at the Contents informs the reader of the wide range of activities covered
in *Government Agencies*. Several categories of service come to mind, embracing
as they do a number of entities already in existence late in the eighteenth century
and the agencies that have originated only in the present century. Twelve arbitrary
examples are: Communications, Defense, Domestic (Internal) Protection, the
Economy and Employment, Education and the Arts, Environmental Growth and
Resources, Governmental Housekeeping, Health and Welfare, Individuals and
Groups, the International Scene, Science and Technology, and Transportation
(see Appendix 4 for lists of agencies that fit into these categories). Certainly
these groupings make as much sense as the meaningless tampering of the politicians in reassigning agencies among departments or granting independent status.

A foremost purpose in compiling *Government Agencies* is to stimulate interest
in the study of the federal government and the wealth of significant opportunities
scarcely tapped in ascertaining the what, why, and how of these organizations'
roles in the nation's economy. Each of the more than 100 articles attempts to
give the serious student of government a better understanding of these example
agencies, their problems, tasks, successes and failures, and of how they relate
to the individual.

A second purpose involves the nonscholar, the general reader with an interest
in government and how it affects the individual. *Government Agencies* provides
the nonspecialist with a ready reference to locate in adequate detail exactly what
these many federal agencies purport to accomplish in addition to the accompanying evaluations of their past activities.

The selection process revealed several rather startling dilemmas. First, a number of agencies have been the subject of numerous books and articles of scholarly
quality; others have little or nothing recorded about them. Second, the several
entities created in the very recent past offered scant perspective for meaningful
reflection. Third, enlisting the support of authors and deciding on the inclusion
of agencies presented uneven results. Agencies about which scholarly books or
articles existed, by authors who could contribute to *Government Agencies*, are,
of course, included. Several present governmental agencies, however, are not
included for the mechanical reasons detailed above. Others the reader will locate
subsumed under the appropriate department or other larger category (see Appendix 3 for a listing of umbrella agencies). Keeping pace with federal agency
reorganization—from the Cabinet level on down to the smallest bureau or commission—defies the patience of the most astute researcher. *Government Agencies*
attempts to strike a compromise by including the vast majority of existing agencies, while at the same time stressing the role of a select group of former agencies

and guiding the reader to additional sources of reading—both secondary and original sources whenever appropriate—allowing for further study and specialization. Usually, authors of articles mention the significant reorganizational changes pertaining to their own agencies. In addition, Appendix 1 presents a chronology of government agencies from 1776 to 1979, and Appendix 2 provides the reader with a genealogy of agency names. The reader will also notice the inclusion of several famous New Deal entities—the Works Progress Administration* (WPA), Public Works Administration* (PWA), Civilian Conservation Corps* (CCC), National Youth Administration* (NYA), and the National Recovery Administration* (NRA), all of which no longer exist. Likewise, interesting and essential wartime boards and commissions inform the reader about emergency planning, for example the War Industries Board* (WIB) of World War I and the World War II examples: War Manpower Commission* (WMC), War Production Board* (WPB), Office of War Information* (OWI), Office of Price Administration* (OPA), and the Defense Plant Corporation* (DPC).

Another key to selection focused on the services provided and the wide range of interests of reader-constituents considered therein: economic, political, diplomatic, social, intellectual, and military, to name several areas of concern. Again, types of agency ranged, for example, from traditional Departments of State, Labor, and Treasury to Bureaus of the Census, Indian Affairs, and Mines to the two famous Hoover Commissions, the corporations including the Tennessee Valley Authority* (TVA), to such quasi-agencies as the National Railroad Passenger Corporation* (AMTRAK) and the Smithsonian Institution.* All official titles used in *Government Agencies* were adjusted to the listings in the *United States Government Manual* (1981-1982). Through common usage, most scholars and nonscholars insert "United States" or "U.S." in front of agency names; this is done in this book only when it is officially part of the agency name. Abbreviations and acronyms popularly used or which appear in the *Government Manual* are also utilized here. The prefix "the" is omitted from agency names.

The many contributors to this work represent a large variety of academic backgrounds—and training and experience—enabling them to qualify eminently for the assignments. University professors, government historians and archivists, and research consultants in private enterprise are included. Historians predominate, but there are also a number of agency specialists in the fields of political science, economics, sociology, social work, law, English, professional education, and business administration. The reader is referred to these names in the Contributors section. Both mature writers and relative newcomers appear in the list.

Authors were asked to stress achievements, failures, administrative structure, in-house and external squabbles, and other features appropriate to the individual essay. At all times the author's individuality has been maintained and encouraged. To assist the reader, a very brief annotated bibliography was requested to conclude each entry. Naturally, some articles in this anthology are more interesting than others; various agencies recorded vastly more conflict and crisis than others. An overall suggestion to the reader interested in further study would be to contact, first, the agency involved and, second, the National Archives and Records Service* for possible older holdings of materials. Moreover, public and private libraries would have a number of the secondary works cited. Complicated restrictions exist on access to government documents, in particular those pertaining to the military and Department of State,* which might deny the scholar or reader the right to obtain materials for several decades. If working through the agency or National Archives fails, the only redress is through bureaucratic details of the Freedom of Information Act, which is not always successful. Again, in locating an agency, the *Government Manual* (latest edition) proves invaluable.

When Arthur Stickney of Greenwood Press first requested that I become Editor-in-Chief of this book, my immediate reaction was one of bewilderment: where would one begin in picking authors and agencies? Past experience with federal documents and agency histories assisted but could in no way overcome the sheer magnitude of the logistics. Naturally, I assume all blame for any shortcomings we allowed in *Government Agencies*. However, a number of people assisted me in numerous ways to make the task easier and to improve the final product. At Greenwood, Stickney, James Sabin, Susan Baker, Betty Pessagno, and especially Cynthia Harris showed patience and extended valuable hints from their successful experience with the previous titles under this series, *The Greenwood Encyclopedia of American Institutions*. Thanks to all the other contributors, the vast majority of whom judicially submitted their entries on time, suggested other possible authors, and supported the project in other important ways. All of the reference librarians at the Library of the University of Northern Iowa, as usual, provided expeditious and accurate service. The Graduate College and my colleagues at Northern Iowa helped me with a leave and other material assistance. The encouragement of several colleagues, here and elsewhere, in the selection process deserves special mention: David A. Walker, James Harvey Young, Hope Holdcamper, Richard Kirkendall, the late Walter Rundell, Jr., and Richard Lowitt. Over the past three years the research duties of Mark Williams, Robert Tecklenburg, Errol J. Olson, and Daniel Moody, all graduate assistants, were invaluable.

The voluminous correspondence and recordkeeping generated by the project could not have been handled without the cheerful and efficient services of Judith Dohlman, our departmental secretary. Thanks also to other history staff members and to Beth Jackson and Steve Moon. In every research and writing project, major or minor, I have been the beneficiary of the expert assistance and moral support at each stage of the project from my wife, Florentine Whitnah.

DONALD R. WHITNAH

GOVERNMENT AGENCIES

_A_

AERONAUTICS AND SPACE ADMINISTRATION. See National Aeronautics and Space Administration.

AGENCY FOR INTERNATIONAL DEVELOPMENT (AID). Congress established the Agency for International Development in 1961 to administer the economic development component of U.S. foreign assistance. AID, created as an autonomous agency within the Department of State,* represented the consolidation of the grant aid functions previously discharged by the International Cooperation Administration, the loan operations of the Development Loan Fund, and certain credit programs of the Export-Import Bank.* The agency, which recently celebrated its twentieth anniversary, has had a controversial and often uncertain term of existence. Reflecting contradictory and fluctuating public and congressional attitudes toward foreign aid, it has been the object of high expectations and the target of persistent critics.

Instances of U.S. foreign assistance may be found throughout the nation's history. In 1812, Congress appropriated $50,000 for the relief of earthquake victims in rebel-held areas of Venezuela. Thus did humanitarianism and political concerns exist from the onset. During World War I the United States provided substantial loans to its allies, which it attempted to collect during the interwar period to the detriment of international stability. Prior to and during World War II, America extended vast quantities of arms and financial aid to its allies, particularly Britain and Russia. It also provided limited technical assistance in the Western Hemisphere through the Institute of Inter-American Affairs. Immediately after the war, the United States was the leading contributor to the United Nations Relief and Rehabilitation Administration.

With the onset of the Cold War, the United States accepted the challenge of the Truman Doctrine to support by military and economic aid the independence of nations threatened by Communist aggression, first Greece and Turkey, and then by extension other nations of Europe and beyond. The Marshall Plan, providing for massive aid to promote the economic recovery of Western Europe, was launched in 1947. Congress created the Economic Cooperation Administration (ECA) to conduct the program.

ECA (1948-1951) proved to be the first in a kaleidoscopic succession of aid organizations, including the Mutual Security Agency (1951-1953), the Foreign Operations Administration (1953-1955), and the International Cooperation Administration (1955-1961). In addition, the Technical Cooperation Administration existed in the early 1950s to execute President Harry S Truman's Point IV operations, and the Development Loan Fund was established in 1957. The State Department maintained some manner of responsibility for the coordination of the economic and military components of foreign assistance through these administrative gyrations. Throughout, economic, developmental, and technical aid were extended basically in support of military aid.

Nevertheless, the concept of aid to the less developed nations on humanitarian grounds, and because it furthered interests of the United States that transcended opposition to Communist expansionism, was seldom absent. The Point IV program of 1949 was the result of a coming together of White House desire to make a democratic statement to the world and the promotion of technical aid by the State Department and its Office of Public Affairs. President Dwight D. Eisenhower frequently also spoke out in favor of assisting the poverty-ravaged peoples of the non-Western world.

In his inaugural address, President John F. Kennedy stated, "To those people in the huts and villages of half the globe struggling to break the bonds of mass misery, we pledge our best efforts to help them help themselves for whatever period is required—not because the Communists may be doing it, not because we seek their votes, but because it is right." He immediately appointed an expert task force, advised by eminent diplomats and scholars, to prepare enabling legislation for a coordinated and expanded development assistance program. Congress largely adopted its recommendations in the Foreign Assistance Act of September 4, 1961, an act to "promote the foreign policy, security, and general welfare of the United States by assisting the peoples of the world in their efforts toward economic development and internal and external security." Pursuant to the act, President Kennedy created AID by Executive Order, effective November 4, 1961.

Born in an atmosphere of idealistic enthusiasm, AID seemed destined to preside over a "decade of development." President Kennedy's personal interest in and effective promotion of development assistance and the end of an era of chaotic expansion and administrative turmoil provided promise for the future. Fowler Hamilton, a New York lawyer with some wartime experience in economic warfare, became the first AID administrator. He was succeeded within a year by David E. Bell, an international economist and expert in development assistance who had served in the Truman White House and as an adviser to the government of Pakistan.

Under Kennedy, the new agency achieved administrative stability and enhanced professionalism. Development assistance received high priority. Although an instrument of U.S. foreign policy, as illustrated by its position within the State Department, AID by design was accorded a degree of separateness that somewhat insulated it from day-to-day political concerns and permitted it more effectively to pursue long-term development goals. It was organized into regional bureaus roughly corresponding to State organization, but its legislative format under the Foreign Assistance Act of 1961 was by type of assistance, appropriations for grants and loans being considered separately. Perhaps the showcase area of AID assistance under Kennedy was the Alliance for Progress, with the agency administering the U.S. contribution to a long-term multilateral regional development program intended to transform the least developed areas of the hemisphere.

Other notable features of AID policy during the early 1960s included emphasis on recipient self-help and a continuation of the trend of the 1950s away from aid to European-developed countries to less developed nations of the Third World. In addition to outright grants and loans, the basic tools of assistance were the assignment of American specialists abroad and the training of host-country leaders in the United States. AID concluded arrangements as well with U.S. government agencies such as the Departments of Agriculture*; Health, Education and Welfare (Health and Human Services*); and Labor,* providing for the employment of their services and expertise for purposes of development abroad. AID also made extensive use of nongovernmental resources for technical assistance and economic growth: U.S. business, universities, foundations, and charitable organizations. By the end of 1962, AID was deploying perhaps five thousand regular and contract employees abroad, and financing the training of some eight thousand host-country individuals, mainly in the United States.

Despite the focus on long-range development, AID programs also supported the Cold War nation-building and counterinsurgency themes of the Kennedy years. AID's Office of Public Safety instructed local security forces, for example. In his Foreign Aid message of March 1962, the President asserted that all the atoms and armies of the Free World would be of little avail if nations were unable to stave off threatening forces within their own borders.

AID professionalism, expertise, and institutional stability continued to grow during the Lyndon B. Johnson presidency. Agency expenditures amounted to about $2 billion per year during the period, with two-thirds of all aid by 1965 aimed at economic and social progress in the underdeveloped world. Loans came to replace grants as the dominant form of assistance. Nearly half of AID-financed technicians were employed in development programs and worked in the fields of agriculture, education, and health. Family-planning programs commenced in 1967 with begrudging congressional acquiescence. AID administered U.S. narcotics-control programs abroad. Other developed nations and international organizations gradually joined the United States as important donors.

AID counted many successes in the 1960s. Missions came to be stationed in some seventy countries. Some programs, such as that in Formosa, were terminated on the grounds that development objectives had been achieved. The agency became engaged in disaster relief operations, to which it has channeled billions of dollars in hundreds of tragic situations over the years. Total AID employment reached a level of about fifteen thousand by mid-decade. The agency attained symbolic maturity with the naming of a General Advisory Committee chaired by the president of Cornell University in March 1965.

AID became increasingly involved in programs to combat subversion—public safety (local security), civic action (nation-building), rural and community development, labor and youth programs. Its commitments were especially extensive in Vietnam, with some $550 million of its 1967 fiscal year appropriations earmarked for that nation. The agency, with the Department of Defense,* administered the Vietnam Civil Operations Revolutionary Development Support Program.

As support for the war in Southeast Asia waned, with concomitant public questioning of America's pervasive role aboard, AID experienced rising criticism. Opponents of the Vietnam War often saw the agency as an instrument of misguided interventionism. Many across the political spectrum questioned its effectiveness. Disillusionment replaced enthusiasm, as the Alliance for Progress stalled despite the U.S. extension of $1 billion over a decade. The infusion of aid failed to stimulate the anticipated "take-off" of primitive economies or improve the lot of the common people.

In 1966, Congress enacted Title IX, amending the Foreign Assistance Act to specify that emphasis should be placed on assuring maximum popular participation in the development process. In 1967, the statute was amended to define the purposes of development assistance: popular participation, food self-sufficiency, education, health, and other specific activities. In the late 1960s, Congress slashed foreign-aid appropriations and passed the entire program by ever narrower margins. The advent of the Richard Nixon Administration, which itself had serious doubts about the utility of development assistance as previously administered, provoked AID's most serious crisis. While requesting large sums for military and military-support assistance in order to prosecute and wind down in orderly fashion the war in Southeast Asia, the administration also commissioned a study that recommended the dispersal of AID into its grant, loan, and insurance functions. Congress refused to approve dismemberment, but in 1971 for some months refused to vote funds for the continuation of the agency. Administrator John Hannah, former president of Michigan State University, convinced employees to persevere until Congress finally provided appropriations for continued operations in March 1972. Nonetheless, during the Nixon years AID experienced a series of budget cuts, continuing resolutions, and survival votes.

The Nixon Administration reaffirmed the importance of economic development and security assistance, but consonant with the gradual withdrawal from Southeast Asia and the "Guam Doctrine" insisted upon greater local self-reliance. The legislative aid proposals of the period were more clearly divided between International Security Assistance and International Development and Humanitarian Assistance. Pursuant to White House recommendations, AID reduced its official presence abroad to the lowest level since its establishment. Technical assistance was reshaped in the direction of more developing nation participation, concentration of priority projects, greater exploitation of U.S. research and scientific capabilities, and maximum use of the private sector. AID scrutinized its activities, attempting to enhance efficiency. Major areas of concentration included support for the Vietnamese economy to permit the orderly withdrawal of American troops and famine relief for millions whose lives were disrupted by war and unrest in the Indian subcontinent.

With the diminution of presidential power and traditional beliefs regarding U.S. involvement abroad in light of the Vietnam tragedy and Watergate, Congress effected a far-reaching reorientation of foreign assistance in 1973. Liberal members of the House, drawing on the expertise of AID professionals, the recommendations of a task force appointed by Hannah the previous year, and private advice, restructured the Foreign Assistance Act toward a sectoral approach to aid and away from country programs with their political linkage. This new approach also eliminated the loan and grant categories of authorization and appropriation and substituted new sectors of population planning and health; education and human resources development; selected development problems; and selected countries and organizations. The 1973 legislation redefined the target population as the poor of recipient countries and modified development strategy to stress popular participation rather than economic development per se. Funds were to be directed more toward agriculture, health, and education rather than to industrially oriented capital expenditures. The new format of foreign assistance separated entirely development assistance from military and military-support assistance. This distinction contributed to new, overwhelming congressional support for development assistance—and AID.

In the mid-1970s, AID personnel strength declined to about 6,000—down from 18,000 in the late 1960s, but this is attributable in part to the end of the war in Southeast Asia. The scope and impact of its programs remained enormous. In addition to continuing to conduct development activities, it serviced the needs of refugees from areas as diverse as Indochina and Angola. AID administered the "baby lift" from Vietnam in 1975. In support of the quest for peace in the Middle East, it engaged in some of the largest programs of its history, particularly in Israel and Egypt. Circumstances dictated that AID place heavy emphasis on Africa: relief for refugees in Somalia, eradication of smallpox, and help for the drought-stricken Sahel region.

The Jimmy Carter Administration made special efforts to direct aid to fulfilling "basic human needs," pursuant to the legislation of 1973, and toward ensuring that U.S. assistance promoted the cause of human rights and other social ends such as the participation of women in development. It gave minimal attention to ideological concerns. The United States was first to grant reconstruction aid to Marxist Zimbabwe. In 1979, pursuant to an adminstration recommendation, Congress created the International Development Cooperation Administration

(IDCA) to serve as a focal point within the U.S. government for economic matters affecting relations with developing countries. IDCA coordinates the activities of AID, the Overseas Private Investment Corporation, and the Trade Development Program.

In the 1970s, Congress encumbered the extension of foreign assistance with provisions designed to promote human rights, nuclear nonproliferation, narcotics control, and exclusively defensive employment of U.S. military equipment. Nonetheless, a new consensus in support of foreign aid existed. AID began fiscal year 1977 with an appropriation instead of a continuing resolution for the first time in its history. Serious appropriations battles and hiring freezes did return toward the end of the decade.

The Ronald Reagan Administration modified many development trends of the 1970s. AID's Bureau for Private Enterprise seeks to promote development by furthering cooperation between the private sectors of the United States and less developed nations. Emphasis has reverted to expanding industry and agriculture rather than providing industrial goods and food to the poorest of the poor. AID under Reagan's administrator, M. Peter McPherson, evinces less concern for egalitarian concerns, but insists upon more effective economic policies in the recipient countries. Programs are more often designed to support specific U.S. goals, such as the stability of Jamaica, Egypt, or Israel, than to promote world-wide development for its own sake. AID under Reagan is less likely to channel unconditional contributions into multilateral development organizations. The agency, of course, continues to administer many grant and loan programs for technical assistance and development in the more traditional mode. Congress has facilitated the new trends by removing many of the legislative constraints upon foreign aid imposed during the 1970s.

For all the praise and condemnation, the administrative twists and turns, and philosophical changes that it has endured since 1961, AID remains in the front lines as an implement of U.S. foreign policy and a positive presence in the world. Its projects have touched the most remote areas of the globe. In the 1980s, it continues to represent simultaneously a fundamental means whereby the United States can influence events abroad and transmit American humanitarian concern into action.

FOR ADDITIONAL INFORMATION: Robert E. Asher, *Development Assistance in the Seventies: Alternatives for the United States* (1970), presents the case for an upgraded foreign assistance program and supplies considerable information on the progress, problems, and prospects of AID's first decade, along with an excellent bibliography. Ellen Ziskind Berg, "The 1973 Legislative Reorganization of the United States Foreign Assistance Policy: The Content and Conflict of Change" (M.A. thesis, George Washington University, 1976) provides detailed analysis of the 1973 legislation in historical context. For proposals from an AID assistant administrator under Johnson and Nixon, see Paul G. Clark, *American Aid for Development* (1972). AID's first deputy administrator, Frank M. Coffin, in *Witness for AID* (1964) describes getting the agency off the ground. See also John H. Esterline and Robert B. Black, *Inside Foreign Policy: The Department of*

State Political Systems and Its Subsystems (1975), especially Chapter 8, "AID: Evolution of Foreign Assistance Programs," and Chapter 9, "The Politics of Economic Assistance."

Front Lines (1961-), the internal biweekly publication of AID, constitutes a running history of the agency, containing information on policy programs, procedures, and administration. The issues of November 4, 1976, and October 22, 1981, contain anniversary articles on AID's accomplishments over the years. AID, *Foreign Assistance: Source Book for Debaters* (1966) is a compilation of extracts from official publications, speeches, and statements.

NEAL H. PETERSEN

AGRICULTURE DEPARTMENT. See Department of Agriculture.

AIR FORCE. See Department of the Air Force.

AIR FORCE ACADEMY. See United States Air Force Academy.

AMTRAK. See National Railroad Passenger Corporation.

ARCHIVES AND RECORDS SERVICE. See National Archives and Records Service.

ARMS CONTROL AND DISARMAMENT AGENCY. See United States Arms Control and Disarmament Agency.

ARMY. See Department of the Army.

ARMY CORPS OF ENGINEERS. See United States Army Corps of Engineers.

ARMY SIGNAL CORPS. See United States Army Signal Corps.

ARTS ENDOWMENT. See National Endowment for the Arts.

ATOMIC ENERGY COMMISSION. See Nuclear Regulatory Commission.

AVIATION ADMINISTRATION. See Federal Aviation Administration.

_B_

BUDGET BUREAU. See Office of Management and Budget.

BUREAU OF ENGRAVING AND PRINTING. The Bureau of Engraving and Printing began with a handful of employees in the Office of the Secretary of the Treasury, occupying space in the basement of the Treasury Building, and for a period was under the technical control of the comptroller of the Currency. It became a major component of the Treasury Department* with broad responsibilities, a complex of buildings of its own, and a staff (as of 1929) in excess of four thousand employees.

At the start of the Civil War, when there was a great need for bonds, notes, and other obligations for financing the conflict, most engraving and printing of financial instruments for the government were done by private bank note companies (chiefly the American and Continental Bank Note Companies and, later, the National Bank Note Company) under contract with the Treasury Department. This lucrative business for the companies, not always to the financial advantage of the government, was destined to continue through the mid-1870s. When Congress authorized the preparation of additional notes in July 1862 (12 Stat. 532), the law gave the Secretary of the Treasury discretionary authority to have some of the work done in the Treasury Department, and to hire the necessary people and obtain the necessary machinery and supplies to carry out his decision. In February 1863 (12 Stat. 665), the National Currency Bureau was established in the Treasury Department under the supervision of the comptroller of the Currency, to have plates engraved and notes printed and issued to qualifying national banks for circulation. The unit which was to become the Bureau of Engraving and Printing was designated as the First Division of the National Currency Bureau. Many of the bank notes authorized by the act continued to be done by contract with the bank note companies, with the approval of the Secretary of the Treasury. When fractional currency, however, was issued as a temporary circulating medium, it apparently was made in the bureau under the supervision and controls established by Spencer M. Clark. In response to a suggestion by the Secretary of the Treasury, Congress included a provision in an act of June 1864 (13 Stat. 218), making it illegal for notes to be issued with engraved signatures and requiring that signing and sealing be done at the time of issue. This provision applied to Treasury notes as well as to national bank notes. In early 1867, Congress ordered that most engraving and printing for the government be done under the supervision of the Public Printer, but in July 1867 (15 Stat. 13), the act was amended to provide that the Treasury Department could continue to do printing using its own personnel. It was stipulated, however, that the department could hire no new employees for providing printing services.

In January 1869, the Bureau of Engraving and Printing unofficially became a separate entity. Its letterheads read, "Bureau of Engraving and Printing," and not (as formerly) First Division, National Currency Bureau. The Secretary mentioned the new division for the first time by name in his report on the state of the finances for the year ended June 30, 1869, and Congress also mentioned the bureau by name in an appropriation act (15 Stat. 312) for the first time. Although the reports of the Secretary of the Treasury for the early 1870s indicated his feeling that the bureau was capable of doing engraving and printing of high quality and on better terms than the contracts with bank note companies, Congress nevertheless required, in an appropriation act of March 3, 1875 (18 Stat. 373), that the contract system be continued. The act required that three plates be used in the printing of each note—two being under contract, and the final one to be applied in the bureau. At about the same time, it was also required that the notes be delivered to the Office of the Treasurer unsealed. The plates, rolls, and dies used by the National Currency Bureau were turned over to the Secretary of the Treasury for the use of the Bureau of Engraving and Printing in the processing and issue of the national bank notes. During the 1876-1877 fiscal year, the Secretary of the Treasury finally got permission to cancel the contracts with the bank note companies provided the bureau could do the same work as cheaply, and the contracts were accordingly canceled. Thus, the bureau had complete charge of the preparation and issue of Treasury notes and bonds, the printing and distribution of most classes of internal revenue stamps, and a great deal of miscellaneous printing for other government departments and agencies. The bureau did this work on a reimbursable basis. Thus, by the late 1870s, the parameters of the bureau's work were nearly complete except for the printing of postage stamps (added to the bureau's functions in 1895).

Personnel administration for the bureau was handled through the Appointment Division of the Secretary of the Treasury's Office, as was common to many of the Treasury bureaus at that time. Early recommendations for employment came chiefly from members of Congress; later employees were primarily nominated by the chief of the Bureau of Engraving and Printing. Many of the employees were women; many were either unemployed or the widows or dependents of Civil War soldiers. It appears there was no attempt to make appointments on the basis of race, although the records show that allegations were made that black women were being replaced unfairly by white employees. Women were mostly appointed to positions of printer's assistants and operatives, while skilled positions were occupied, in general, by men. The salaries of skilled positions were set by crafts, and those of unskilled positions by the Secretary of the Treasury. The application of civil service rules to the employment at the bureau did not seem to have a significant impact on employment patterns. The bureau kept detailed records showing the work assignments of its employees and changes of assignment; in addition, weekly reports were made to the Appointment Division of the Secretary's Office showing names of persons hired, dismissed, or whose job had been changed. Employment statistics at the bureau varied considerably, chiefly as a result of technological developments and the bureau's expanding workload. Major reductions occurred in 1877 (583 persons) and 1885 (259 persons). Typical figures for the mid-1880s follow: 1884 (1,145); 1885 (886); 1886 (824). In 1888, the number rose by 169 employees, and in several years the employment figures rose by 10 to 15 percent a year because of increasing demand. The peak employment was reached in October 1928, when the force stood at 4,676 employees. Many times overtime and second shifts were required to meet the demands for Treasury notes, due to lack of space for the necessary presses. The workload became especially heavy when silver certificates and Federal Reserve Notes went into circulation, and during financing of the Spanish-American War and World War I.

A frequent problem of the bureau was lack of space for carrying on its rapidly expanding activities and for housing operations such as the laundry, which were necessary adjuncts to its printing operations. The bureau soon outgrew its quarters in the basement and attic of the Treasury Building, and a new building was constructed for it in 1880. Further construction followed as space again became inadequate, and another building was constructed in 1891. Even with that building, the Secretary's Annual Reports in the 1890s and early 1900s called attention time after time to the need for more room for the bureau's operations. In the early 1900s, some ancillary functions were still conducted in wooden structures, which the bureau officials considered to be fire hazards both to the bureau and to its neighborhood.

Because of the technical nature of the bureau's operations, it was frequently involved in the invention, testing, or development of equipment such as power-operated presses needed to improve productivity. When Congress decided, for example, in 1889, that the use of power presses should be discontinued because of a disagreement with the manufacturers over royalties to be paid for notes produced on the presses, it was necessary to acquire over two hundred hand-operated presses to take up the slack in productive capacity, and hire and train many additional persons to operate them. Eventually some power equipment was reinstated in the bureau's operations.

The bureau's operations have usually been financed on three levels: (1) appropriated funds are used for expenses associated with specific products, such as for engraving and printing bank notes; (2) salaries of employees are appropriated; and (3) the bureau performs services for other agencies or bureaus on a reimbursable basis. This system, as far as can be determined from official records and reports, appears to have worked to the bureau's satisfaction.

The basic organizational structure of the Bureau of Engraving and Printing is functional. In 1928, the organization consisted of a director and two assistant directors—one for administration and the other for production. Divisions reporting to the assistant director for administration were Order, Accounts, Personnel, Mail and Files, Purchases, Storage, Issues, Disbursing, Hygiene, Watch, Buildings and Grounds, Plate Vault, Federal Reserve Vault, Engineering and Machinery, Garage, and Press Register. Divisions reporting to the assistant director for production were Engraving, Wetting, Plate Printing, Examining, Numbering, Postage Stamp, Surface Printing, and Ink Making. Each of these divisions had various subdivisions, called sections, responsible for various phases of its operations. The Engraving Division, for example, consisted of these sections: Clerical, Designing, Engraving, Transferring, Plate Cleaning, Proving, Hardening, Electrolytic, Machinists, Photolithographic, Steel Stock Cage, Stock Distributors, Pantograph, Hammering, and Place Haulers. The Accounting Division consisted of the Supervisory, Appropriation and Paper Control Records, Cost Accounts, Payroll, Timekeeping, Injury Records, Stock Control Accounts, and Messenger sections. Published information on the organizational structure of the Bureau of Engraving and Printing at other periods during its history is much less complete. In 1979, for example, the chief officials of the bureau were listed as a director, deputy director, assistant director for administration, assistant director for research and engineering, and assistant director for operations.

One of the bureau's most notable innovations, the introduction of smaller-sized currency, took over twenty years to materialize in 1929. Treasury Secretary Franklin MacVeagh, under President William H. Taft, favored the idea without gaining its implementation. Democrat Secretary William G. McAdoo supported the plan but was too engrossed with instigating the new Federal Reserve System* to give the currency scheme enough priority. By the mid-1920s, Secretary Andrew W. Mellon resumed the study, which culminated in the appearance of smaller currency within four years. Treasury officials conducted a vigorous campaign to advertise the change, which featured pictures of presidents on the bills.

Engraving and Printing employees faced cutbacks during the Great Depression largely in the form of furloughs or reduced total hours of work, which lasted for six years and reached the worst point in 1934. By the last quarter of fiscal year 1936, full production had again been resumed. Meanwhile, several new demands faced the agency. Panic-caused bank withdrawals led to the issuance— with scarcely two days of advance notice—of new Federal Reserve Bank Notes. The hasty deliveries, eventually reaching a total of $460 million, could be accomplished by utilizing existing stocks of blank engraved national bank currency. The New Deal efforts at relief, recovery, and reform called for gigantic check-writing chores on the part of the bureau for other agencies, for example, with barely a week's notice for the Federal Civil Works Administration's creating

4 million new jobs. U.S. Savings Bonds, nicknamed Baby Bonds and introduced in 1935 as an appeal to the small investor, each contained a President's portrait. During this period also, the great seal of the United States was first affixed to our money.

Bureau policy never encouraged the large-scale printing of foreign currency, but on occasion special orders were accepted, beginning with 10 million pesos for Cuba in 1934. Later, money was printed for Siam in 1945 and South Korea in 1947.

Technological advancement in the issuing of U.S. postage stamps materialized with electronic perforating of printed rolls, the first deliveries coming in 1935. President Franklin D. Roosevelt displayed a continuing keen interest in both currency and stamps. The bureau started its famous issue of the presidential series of stamps in 1938, followed by other series pertaining to scientists, poets, inventors, educators, composers, authors, and artists.

The World War II era witnessed a frantic but well-coordinated scramble to comply with a variety of new demands at home and abroad. Orders for printing, mostly from the War and Navy Departments, reached a dramatic increase already by late 1940. Hiring sufficient employees proved to be a major crisis, the peak number reaching 8,398 in 1943. Sixteen former employees gave their lives in the military service. Perennial shortages slowed production; especially scarce were nails, cheesecloth, soap, and wax.

War financing created the greatest demands on the bureau. War Savings Bonds rolled off the presses at a peak rate of 2 million bonds per day compared with 500,000 World War I Liberty Bonds each day. In 1941-1945, the plate-subject size was increased from two to five bonds to meet the demand of 27 million persons buying $500 million worth of bonds per month, mostly within the popular payroll savings plan. Elsewhere, the bureau printed for the Post Office* over 8.1 billion war postal savings stamps. In addition, wartime currencies for use in foreign nations were issued for our military—first, the Hawaiian dollars and then the "yellow seal" dollars for the invasion of North Africa (1942). Allied military currency was also printed for occupied areas. One interesting request called for worn-looking currency for our guerrillas in the Philippines. With assistance from the National Bureau of Standards,* the bills were aged by tumbling them in a mixture of sand, floor sweepings, and soggy coffee grounds. At the end of the war, countries overrun by Axis forces received postage stamps printed by Engraving and Printing. One of the most controversial of all bureau transactions ensued with the shipment of dry colors amounting to 5,516 pounds to the Soviets for their later alleged misuse in printing Allied Military Marks in Germany at the end of the war. The decision was not popular with bureau personnel but was apparently forced upon it by military and diplomatic pressures.

A number of technological breakthroughs have augmented bureau activities since World War II. Improved, nonoffset inks were introduced in the early 1950s for printing currency backs, and hand polishing gave way to a polisher mechanism. By the 1960s, sheet-fed dry printing had taken over one-half of the issues.

Meanwhile, the series of postage stamps kept pace with the inaugural of the space age, for example, Alan Shepard and Project Mercury as well as John Glenn's "U.S. Man in Space."

While the level of employees tapered off to approximately three thousand, administrative improvements also were recorded. Throughout the years, the bureau invoked the most stringent security measures against pilfering of materials and money. Until the middle of the present century, employees were automatically forced to pay for lost sheets in the currency process. Finally, the rules allowed for losses caused by mechanical or other nonemployee errors. Attempted thefts still occurred. For example, in 1954, an employee intended to steal two packages of $20 bills ($160,000). Replacement, dummy packages were discovered, and the guilty checker-distributor was tried and convicted. Bureau operations gained more flexibility when the so-called business-type budget was instigated in 1951 in an effort to minimize strict adherence to an exact annual budget.

Public fascination with the bureau persists even today; it has long remained one of the prime tourist attractions in the capital city.

FOR ADDITIONAL INFORMATION: Brookings Institution, *The Bureau of Engraving and Printing: Its History, Activities, and Organization*, Brookings Monograph No. 53, (1929), is a very good source of information on early administrative history and legislation affecting the bureau. Hope K. Holdcamper and Carmelita Ryan, comps., *Preliminary Inventory of the General Records of the Department of the Treasury (P.I. NO. 187)* (1977), contains significant records relating to the bureau and includes letters to the Secretary of the Treasury from the chief of the bureau, relating chiefly to personnel, as well as application and recommendation files of bureau employees, in the records of the Secretary's Appointment Division. National Archives and Records Service, *Guide to the National Archives of the United States* (1974), presents an overview of records relating to the bureau; see especially the articles on General Records of the Treasury Department (RG56) and Records of the Bureau of Engraving and Printing (RG318). William F. Sherman, comp., *Preliminary Inventory of Records of Accounting Officers of the Treasury Department* (unpublished manuscript), includes settled accounts of bank note companies for work done for or cooperatively with the bureau; accounts for reimbursing the bureau for its work; accounts for constructing the building for the Bureau of Engraving and Printing; and contracts for supplies. William F. Sherman, comp., *Preliminary Inventory of the Records of the Bureau of Engraving and Printing* (NC-14) (unpublished), includes personnel application and appointment registers, detailed registers of work assignments, and correspondence relating to the design and issue of notes and postage stamps. Superintendent of Documents, *Checklist of U.S. Public Documents, 1789-1909* (1911), is a convenient reference source for citations to Treasury and congressional documents relating to the bureau and to investigations of its activities and operations. Treasury Department, *History of the Bureau of Engraving and Printing, 1862-1962* (1964), is an excellent history, especially good on the bureau's formative years and on technological developments. Treasury Secretary, *Annual Reports on the State of the Finances* (various dates), deal with the bureau's activities and problems, its financial needs, and other matters, and beginning with 1884-1885, include extracts from the Annual Reports of the director of the bureau.

WILLIAM F. SHERMAN

BUREAU OF INDIAN AFFAIRS. Although Congress gave the Secretary of War responsibility for overseeing the nations's Indian relations in 1789 (1 Stat. 49), no separate bureau for Indian affairs existed during the nation's early years. The Secretary received reports directly from government officials in the field, over whose activities he exercised nominal supervision. Between 1806 and 1822, the United States operated trading houses or "factories" for the Indian trade; the superintendent of Indian trade, an official in the War Department,* acted informally as a coordinator for all Indian affairs, although his official responsibilities were limited to the supervision of the trading house system.

Indian affairs were dominated by trade, diplomacy, and the purchase of Indian lands by the government during these early years. In 1819, Thomas L. McKenney, Indian trade superintendent after 1816, persuaded Congress to establish an annual appropriation of $10,000 to promote the "civilization" of the Indians (3 Stat. 516). The appropriation, which Congress did not repeal until 1873 (17 Stat. 461), was used to encourage religious groups to establish Indian schools. Two years after Congress ended the government trading system, Secretary of War John C. Calhoun established a Bureau of Indian Affairs in the War Department, placing McKenney in charge. McKenney called the agency the "Office of Indian Affairs" in his reports, and that name was used somewhat consistently until 1947, when "Bureau of Indian Affairs" was again adopted.

Despite McKenney's support of the Indian Removal Act of 1830 (4 Stat. 411), which authorized the removal of Eastern tribes to areas west of the Mississippi River, he was removed by President Andrew Jackson. In 1832, Congress created the Office of Commissioner of Indian Affairs. The commissioner was to have the direction and management of all Indian affairs, and of all matters arising out of Indian relations, under the direction of the Secretary of War (4 Stat. 564). Two years later, the act to provide for the organization of the Department of Indian Affairs (4 Stat. 735) reorganized the field staff of the Indian Office by establishing a number of agencies and superintendencies.

In the Indian Intercourse Act of 1834 (4 Stat. 729), enacted on the same day as the act providing for the organization of the Indian Office, Congress defined the Indian country and specified the powers of government officials therein. In part restating provisions of earlier acts, the Intercourse Act provided for the licensing of traders, the removal of undesirable non-Indians from the Indian country, the prohibition of liquor sales to Indians, and criminal jurisdiction in the Indian country. The transfer of the Indian Office to the new Department of the Interior* in 1849 (9 Stat. 395) had no effect on these laws, except to place the agency under the supervision of the Secretary of the Interior.

Nineteenth-century superintendents were presidential appointees and had charge of Indian affairs within a defined geographic region. As territories were organized, the territorial governor often served as Indian superintendent for the territory. This gave the official dual—and often conflicting—responsibilities, since governors often conceived their responsibility as the promotion of territorial development, and Indian superintendents were supposed to fulfill the government's treaty obligations and protect Indian interests.

Indian agents, also presidential appointees, lived among the Indians. They became the most important functionaries in the Indian service as the removal of Indians and their concentration on defined reserves resulted in the development of a reservation system after the middle of the nineteenth century. Until 1878, agents appointed their own subordinates, including interpreters, clerks, skilled craftsmen, and often teachers and physicians.

The westward expansion of the white population and the Civil War resulted in a decade of Indian warfare in the 1860s. In 1869, President Ulysses S. Grant announced that he would support any plan that would bring "civilization" to the Indians and lead to their citizenship. In the Indian Appropriations Act of 1869 (16 Stat. 40), Congress created an unpaid ten-man commission to oversee Indian Office activities. Like the contemporary state boards of charities and corrections, the Board of Indian Commissioners was supposed to monitor expenditures and recommend means for improving administration. The board was active during the Grant Administration, although both the commissioner of Indian affairs and the Secretary of the Interior resisted its efforts to influence the Indian Office. President Franklin D. Roosevelt abolished the board in 1933, long after it had ceased to be a force in Indian affairs. President Grant attempted to end the political appointment of agents, by appointing first Army officers and later the nominees of religious denominations as agents. The denominations were encouraged to build schools on the reservations, resulting in some expansion of efforts to educate the Indians. In 1871, Congress ended the practice of making treaties with the Indian tribes and limited the power of noncitizen Indians to make contracts (16 Stat. 544, 566).

Grant discontinued most superintendencies during his administration; agents reported directly to Washington rather than through an intermediate official. The reservations were to become "schools for civilization," and agents devised a number of expedients during the 1870s to enhance their control of reservation life. Indian police forces would enable agents to maintain control without calling on the Army for assistance; the division of reservation lands into allotments assigned to individual Indians would isolate the Indian and motivate him to "get ahead"; and the leasing of grazing lands to ranchers would provide the agent with a source of funds to supplement inadequate appropriations.

The boarding schools established for freedmen following emancipation provided a model for Indian education. Seventeen Indians were admitted to Hampton Institute in 1878. An Indian boarding school modeled on Hampton was established in Carlisle, Pennsylvania, the following year, and the Indian Office established a number of other off-reservation boarding schools during the 1880s. Between 1880 and 1890, expenditures for Indian schools increased tenfold, when measured in constant dollars.

The allotment of reservation lands became national policy with the passage of the General Allotment Act in 1887 (24 Stat. 388). The act allowed the President to order the allotment of any Indian reservation: upon receiving his land, title to which was to be held in trust by the government for a period of twenty-five years, the Indian became a citizen of the United States. After each tribesman had received an allotment, the "surplus" was made available to white purchasers. The framers of the act expected that Indian owners would farm their allotments, but in the 1890s Congress permitted the leasing of allotments to whites under the supervision of the Indian Office, and this practice became widespread. In the Indian Appropriations Act of 1885, Congress gave federal courts jurisdiction over major crimes in the Indian country. Land, education, and law enforcement dominated the agency's activities during the remainder of the nineteenth century.

Congress established an inspection service for the Indian service in 1873 (17 Stat. 463). Inspectors, responsible to Washington rather than to regional officials, visited the agencies periodically to insure compliance with a growing body of Indian Office regulations. By the early twentieth century, inspectors who specialized in education, agriculture, and medical services were appointed and were frequently given supervisory as well as monitoring responsibilities. Agency personnel were brought into the civil service system during the administration of President Benjamin Harrison (1889-1893). Harrison's commissioner of Indian affairs, Thomas J. Morgan, also began to replace agents with school superintendents, appointed under civil service rules. By 1909, all of the Indian agencies were under the control of civil service superintendents. These developments resulted in increased attention to personnel matters and greatly increased the influence which Washington officials could exert over developments on the reservations.

During the twentieth century, the Indian Office added the development of Indian resources to the goal of educating and "civilizing" the Indians. Land sales resulting from allotment had diminished the Indian land base, while the Indian population was clearly increasing. The Burke Act of 1906 (34 Stat. 182) made the allottee's "competency" the criterion for ending the period during which title to an allotment could be held in trust. This provision made possible the indefinite survival of the Indian Office as a service and protective agency. Congress made all Indians citizens of the United States in 1924 (43 Stat. 1255), but this action did not alter the Indian Office's trust responsibility. Appropriations for the irrigation of Indian lands increased substantially during the first two decades of the twentieth century, as did appropriations for hospitals.

In 1928, an independent survey of Indian administration, the Meriam Report, found widespread poverty among American Indians and an ineffective Indian Office. The report, which was influential during the administrations of Charles J. Rhoads (1929-1933) and John Collier (1933-1945), called for increased appropriations for health and education, for better personnel and planning, and for increased attention to economic development. Collier hoped that the Indian Office would become a consultation agency, providing technical assistance to self-governing Indian tribes. The Indian Reorganization Act of 1934 (48 Stat. 984), a first step toward this goal, allowed tribes to establish governments with limited powers, subject to the approval of the Secretary of the Interior. In the Johnson-O'Malley Act of 1934 (48 Stat. 596), Congress authorized the Indian Office to contract with state governments for a broad range of social, health, and educational services, resulting in a substantial increase in Indian enrollment in public schools. Collier was also successful in negotiating agreements with the Department of Agriculture,* the Public Health Service,* and a New Deal agency, the Civilian Conservation Corps,* to provide services to Indian groups.

After 1937, Collier's relations with Congress deteriorated, and appropriations for tribal economic development were cut during World War II. Congress increased funding for educational and health services, however. After the war, the Indian Delegation Act of 1946 (60 Stat. 939) established a number of area offices with jurisdiction over Indian reservations in specific geographic areas. The act permitted substantial delegations of authority from the Secretary of the Interior to the commissioner of Indian affairs and from the commissioner to the area directors, bringing decision-making "closer to the Indian people," in the words of Commissioner Dillon S. Myer (1950-1953).

In an effort to terminate federal responsibility for Indians, in the 1950s, Congress transferred responsibility for Indian health to the Public Health Service (68 Stat. 674), permitted the states to assume criminal and civil jurisdiction over Indian lands, and removed federal prohibitions against the sale of liquor to Indians. Congress terminated federal supervision of a number of tribes during the 1950s. The termination acts also removed special social, health, and educational services which had been provided to the members of the terminated tribes by the Bureau of Indian Affairs.

During the 1960s, the Office of Economic Opportunity and other "Great Society" programs of the administration of President Lyndon B. Johnson established special Indian divisions. This change strengthened the tribal governments established under the Indian Reorganization Act of 1934, by providing funding for tribal projects. The goal of termination faded during the 1960s; late in the decade, both Presidents Johnson and Richard M. Nixon rejected termination in favor of the "self-determination" of organized Indian communities. The Indian Self-Determination and Education Assistance Act of 1975 (88 Stat. 2203) greatly increased the powers of tribal governments to contract with federal agencies, including the Bureau of Indian Affairs, to provide services and programs to their members.

Attempts to transfer the Bureau of Indian Affairs from the Interior Department to the Federal Security Agency in the 1940s and to the Department of Health, Education, and Welfare (Department of Health and Human Services*) in the 1960s were not successful. The bureau was thought to be at a disadvantage in Interior, since the department was oriented towards land management rather than social services. In addition, some charged that the commissioner, who reported to an Assistant Secretary, lacked access to the Secretary of the Interior. In 1977, the American Indian Policy Review Commission recommended separating the bureau from the Department of the Interior and making it an independent agency. However, in 1980, President James E. Carter abolished the position of commissioner of Indian affairs and placed an Assistant Secretary for Indian affairs in charge of the bureau, presumably giving the agency director better access to the Secretary.

FOR ADDITIONAL INFORMATION: The latest in a series of studies of the administration of the Bureau of Indian Affairs, Warren King and Associates, Inc., *Bureau of Indian Affairs Management Study* (1976), was commissioned by the American Indian Policy Review Commission and is summarized in the commission's *Final Report*, Vol. 1 (1977). Earlier studies include Lewis Meriam and Associates, *The Problem of Indian Administration* (1928); Laurence F. Schmeckebier, *The Office of Indian Affairs: Its History, Activities, and Organization* (1927); and Bureau of Municipal Research, "Administration of the Indian Office," *Municipal Research*, No. 65 (September 1915). The *Report of Board of Inquiry Convened by Authority of the Secretary of the Interior of June 7, 1877, to Investigate Certain Charges Against S. A. Galpin, Chief Clerk of the Indian Bureau, and Concerning Irregularities in Said Bureau* (1878) provides an unusually detailed account of Indian Office administration in the nineteenth century.

Francis Paul Prucha's *Bibliographical Guide to the History of Indian-White Relations in the United States* (1977) is an excellent guide to the primary and secondary sources on the Bureau of Indian Affairs. Prucha covers nineteenth-century Indian policy in *American Indian Policy in the Formative Years: The Indian Trade and Intercourse Acts, 1790-1834* (1962) and *American Indian Policy in Crisis: Christian Reformers and the Indian, 1865-1900* (1976). Paul Stuart, in *The Indian Office: Growth and Development of an American Institution, 1865-1900* (1979) concentrates on the Indian Office; his "United States Indian Policy: From the Dawes Act to the American Indian Policy Review Commission," *Social Service Review* 51 (September 1977): 451-463, traces twentieth-century developments in Indian policy.

The records of the Bureau of Indian Affairs are held by the National Archives and Records Service,* in the National Archives Building in Washington, D.C., and in a number of Federal Records Centers, in Record Group 75. In addition, much Indian material is collected in the *American State Papers: Indian Affairs*, 2 vols. (1832-1834), in the Serial Set of Congressional Documents, and in the Annual Reports and other publications of the Bureau of Indian Affairs. Robert M. Kvasnicka and Herman T. Viola, eds., *The Commissioners of Indian Affairs, 1824-1977* (1979), provides biographical sketches and bibliographical information on each of the agency's chief executives.

PAUL STUART

BUREAU OF INVESTIGATION. See Federal Bureau of Investigation.

BUREAU OF LAND MANAGEMENT. The General Land Office, established by Congress in 1812 as a bureau of the Treasury Department,* was charged with the administration of the public domain. The law of April 25, 1812, amended in 1849 (9 Stat. 395), specified that its chief officer, the commissioner, should "superintend, execute, and perform all such acts and things, touching or respecting the public lands of the United States." The enumerated functions included the issue of land warrants and grants, the schedule of sales, the collection of monies from purchasers, the preparation and issue of patents and deeds, and the maintenance of complete records of such transactions. It was a solemn charge that testified to the land system initiated and amended by the Congress but only hinted at the significance of the subject in American life. Land was a question of overriding importance in the Anglo-American colonies and the new independent American nation. It was the center of economic life, the basis of political democracy (according to Thomas Jefferson), and the litany of political figures for more than a century. The opportunity to acquire land was the principal reason for immigration to the New World, and, accordingly, the land system touched all citizens of the Republic.

The roots of an administrative system for the public domain lay in the colonial period, when land grants from the Crown had to be located and recorded in an orderly fashion. At the close of the American Revolution, the new, independent American nation took steps to make the land and its management her own. The first significant step was the creation of the "public domain," wherein the lands in the West claimed by several states (principally New York and Maryland) were ceded to the nation as a whole to be held in trust for the distribution to and benefit of all. Next came the question of the terms and conditions under which the land would be sold. Finally, an administrative system had to be established to survey, sell, and record. The Congress of the Confederation met these needs in the Ordinance of 1785. The Land Ordinance (as it came to be called) provided for a rectangular survey system before sale, a public sale with all citizens given the right to purchase, a good clear title in fee simple to the purchaser, and a central administrative system. This administrative seed would eventually flower into an elaborate recordkeeping apparatus, stretching over lands from the Appalachians to the Pacific, from the Canadian to the Mexican borders, and would become the instrument of ownership for millions by countless individual land transactions of varying sizes and complexities.

With the organization of the federal government under the new Constitution of 1789, the Treasury Department took over the outlines of this administrative structure. Subsequent legislation and executive decision over the next quarter-century enlarged the administrative apparatus and made it more responsive to new laws for the disposition of the public domain. Of lasting significance was the decision that the nation should run a retail as well as a wholesale business where land was concerned. These principles received official form in the Land Law of 1800, which established four district land offices in the Territory Northwest of the Ohio and reduced the minimum tract that might be purchased to 320 acres. Thus, Congress extended administrative services to the edge of the advancing frontier and offered tracts for individual farmers as well as speculators. Congress subsequently established additional district land offices as they were needed over the next century. The purchase of the Louisiana Territory in 1803 introduced another feature of the administration of the public domain in the first half of the nineteenth century, namely, the settlement of disputes concerning private land claims. Albert Gallatin, Secretary of the Treasury under Thomas

Jefferson, supervised the growth of this administrative structure to accommodate new land laws, the acquisition of new lands, and an increasingly large and far-flung bureaucracy concerned with the public domain. It was a demanding task, which Gallatin carried out with skill and integrity. By 1811, sales of the public lands had reached 1.2 million acres annually at eighteen district land offices, and the adjustment of private claims had become an important and time-consuming aspect of the land business. It was in response to these growing burdens that Congress established the General Land Office in 1812, concentrating in one bureau duties formerly carried out by the Departments of Treasury, State, and War.

The establishment of the General Land Office and the close of the War of 1812 coincided with a period of enormous physical expansion. This growth reflected population increase, both natural and by immigration; its principal manifestation was the occupation of the trans-Appalachian West. This immigration across the mountains was predominantly agricultural—farm families taking up land for cultivation—and the General Land Office found itself at the center of this maelstrom of movement, purchase, cultivation, and speculation. During the 1820s, the General Land Office was much occupied with administering a series of Relief Acts, and in 1830, Congress passed the first of a series of preemption laws; these laws were of special significance because of the long and cumbersome administration procedures that preemption demanded of the land offices. Congress responded to this large-scale immigration with increasing liberality in the form of smaller tracts and more district land offices to serve the frontier. When Congress passed a law in 1832 to reduce the minimum tract size from eighty to forty acres, it doubled the number of separate land transactions. Such legislation combined with a frenzied speculation in the years 1816-1819 and 1833-1836 to produce a veritable "land office business."

With this astonishing growth of the land business, the General Land Office began to fall in arrears. By 1832, it had to issue 40,000 patents a year to stay abreast of land purchasers; by 1834, it was 110,000; in 1836, 320,000 patents. In spite of frantic requests for clerical assistance, Congress refused to provide the means to administer the land system that it so freely amended. Pleas for help fell on parsimonious Jacksonian ears. In 1836, the General Land Office still had only seventeen clerks, the same number allowed in 1812. The large sales of 1835 and 1836, reaching an annual figure of 20 million acres, finally compelled Congress to undertake a wholesale administrative reorganization. In 1836, a Reorganization Act expanded the operations of the General Land Office by adding responsibility for surveys. It also retained the district land offices which now numbered sixty-five. The law specified divisions of responsibility that indicated those areas of principal congressional concern: private land claims, public land claims, surveys, records, and adjudication. The addition of a recorder and solicitor was recognition of the time-consuming nature of private claims. The act was an inflexible one. Instead of recognizing the cycles of the land business and the new duties associated with congressional whims, the act laid down a structure of organization and duties in excessive detail. Thus, it spoke to what needed to be done in 1836, but it did not provide for expansion of the General Land Office in the years ahead.

For the General Land Office, the quarter-century from the Reorganization Act of 1836 to the Civil War was marked by expansion of the public domain, more complex private land claims in response to this expansion, and new congressional legislation that offered public lands under ever more liberal conditions. The expansion of the area of the public domain included the Oregon Treaty of 1846 (183 million acres), cessions in the War with Mexico enumerated at the Treaty of Guadalupe Hidalgo in 1848 (338 million acres), and the Gadsden Purchase of 1853 (another 19 million acres). In 1843, the commissioner had complained that the private claims under British, Spanish, French, and Mexican grants, as well as Indian treaties, had brought land transactions in several places to a standstill. His problems were compounded by these new national acquisitions. To these duties must be added new congressional legislation in the form of a general Pre-emption Act (1841), the Graduation Act (1854), and, finally, the Homestead Law (1862). Each of these pieces of legislation had its own administrative burdens. Finally, Congress passed a series of military bounty acts, originally for veterans of the Mexican War but eventually expanded to include anyone who had served on active duty from the earliest Indian wars; and distribution of swamp lands to the states in which they lay (eventually 64 million acres). The incorporation of the General Land Office into the newly established Department of the Interior* (1849) did not seem to provide any more means to carry out these several responsibilities. In 1855, the commissioner reported that the office was four years in arrears, and three years later, he noted that some of the unfinished business included private land claims filed fifty years earlier. The number of district land offices reached eighty-five in 1861.

With the close of the Civil War, the citizens of the nation once again took up the public lands in great quantities, in this last generation of free land. So numerous were the entries that the General Land Office soon fell far behind in issuing patents. At the same time, Congress gave it new duties that testified to the changing nature of the public domain. Among these changes were mining laws, railroad land grants, and the beginnings of the conservation movement. Large-scale mining in the American West dated from the discovery of gold in California in 1848 and the great overland migrations of the '49ers. The first comprehensive mining act was passed in 1866, however, and amending legislation in 1870 and 1872 made the post-Civil War years the period of mining land law for the entire West. The land grants for transcontinental railroad construction dated from 1862, when Congress passed a series of laws for the purpose of construction, operation, and maintenance of railroad lines and a telegraph system. The General Land Office had much responsibility for a complex system of grants (eventually totaling seventy-five grants for 165 million acres) with innumerable conflicts among prior claimants. The beginnings of the conservation movement may be dated from 1877, with a law passed that year to set aside forest reservations. Conservation expanded with the establishment of the United States Geological Survey* under Clarence King in 1879. The famous Public Land Commission of that year (associated with a report by Thomas Donaldson, *The Public Domain*) laid the foundation for improved resources management. Congress attempted to deal with the delay in private land claims by the establishment of a Court of Private Land Claims in 1891. The court lasted only three years, and the adjudication work continued for another generation, especially for claims in Louisiana, Arizona, New Mexico, and California. In 1890, the date celebrated by Frederick Jackson Turner for the close of the frontier, the number of district land offices peaked at 123.

With the close of the frontier, the duties of the General Land Office increasingly shifted from surveys and sales to conservation, land management, and resources. In 1891, a law authorized the President to withdraw and reserve public lands for national forests, and six years later, subsequent legislation gave the General Land Office responsibility for the administration, conservation, and management of large areas of public lands with forests under the title National Forest Reserves. The conservation movement received great impetus early in the twentieth century from the work of President Theodore Roosevelt, who appointed a Public Lands Commission in 1903 and used its report in 1905 as the basis for much of his conservation work. In this quarter-century, the General Land Office found itself charged with the administrative work associated with the withdrawal of these lands from the public domain and the adjudication of the many disputes that arose over it. Aside from the continuing struggle to deal with private land claims, another source of work was the execution of the Dawes Severalty Act of 1887, under which Indian reservations were distributed in severalty to members of the several tribes. The opening of remaining Indian lands to white settlement, such as in Oklahoma in 1889 and 1893, and in the "West River" areas of the Dakotas in this century, provided a kind of benediction to the closing of the frontier presided over by the administrators of the General Land Office. In 1912, on the centennial of its founding, the General Land Office had 530 Washington staff, 102 district land offices with 415 land officers, 275 surveyors, and additional personnel to bring the entire total to 1,420.

In the course of the next half-century, the commissioners of the General Land Office presided over a diminishing empire. In 1925, Congress reduced the number of district land offices from eighty-four to forty-four, combining the duties of register and receiver into a single office. As a result, by 1928, the bureau's strength had been cut in half to 700. Two important changes of direction under the New Deal—the Taylor Grazing Act and the Indian Reorganization Act (both 1934)—involved the administrative services of the General Land Office. A major new departure was the establishment of the Bureau of Land Management (1946), incorporating the General Land Office. The new Bureau of Land Management grew rapidly, with a staff of 2,267 by 1956, more than 90 percent of it in the field. In 1960, the Public Lands Administration Act improved the efficiency of land management, authorized studies for future direction uses of the public domain, and set new fee schedules. On the occasion of the 150th anniversary of the founding of the General Land Office, fifteen district land offices functioned within the Bureau of Land Management, and the bureau's duties reflected the changing priorities in the administration of the public domain: recreation, wildlife, conservation of forest and mineral resources, and protection of what remained of the public domain.

The General Land Office came into existence in 1812 to administer the public domain in ways that seemed clear at the time. The object was to prepare lands for sale, sell them impartially to the highest bidder at a public auction, collect monies, give good and clear title, and keep complete records. Very rapidly, the Land Office became involved in interpreting and administering a complex, ever changing set of rules that involved more liberal ways of distributing lands to the public (preemption, graduation, and homestead), the use of lands as a public subsidy (canals, railroads, land-grant colleges), and a variety of ways to use lands (agriculture, mining, lumbering, grazing, recreation). For a century and a half, Congress filled the Statutes at Large with legislation concerning the public domain, and the General Land Office administered these laws. As the administrative arm of the national government concerned with the public domain, the General Land Office stood at the center of American growth during the nineteenth century. Its officials witnessed at first hand the occupation and exploitation of the American frontier in all its varied forms. It was a unique vantage point. In the twentieth century, Congress turned more and more to the preservation of the public domain, and, once again, the General Land Office carried out congressional wishes insofar as it was able to do so. That it was not always able to meet expectations throughout its long service lay in the parsimonious attitude displayed by Congress, especially in the nineteenth century. In spite of its heavy administrative burdens, Congress often refused to give it the necessary support to carry out its legislation charge.

FOR ADDITIONAL INFORMATION: The literature on the public domain and its administration is enormous. Roy M. Robbins, *Our Landed Heritage: The Public Domain, 1776-1970*, rev. ed. (1976), is a good general history. An important study is Paul Wallace Gates, *History of Public Land Law Development* (1968). Items especially useful for the General Land Office are Milton Conover, *The General Land Office: Its History, Activities, and Organization* (1923); Harold H. Dunham, *Government Handout; A Study in the Administration of the Public Lands, 1875-1891* (1941); Malcolm J. Rohrbough, *The Land Office Business; The Settlement and Administration of American Public Lands, 1789-1837* (1968); and Francis Harding White, "The Administration of the General Land Office, 1812-1911" (Ph.D. dissertation, Harvard University, 1912).

MALCOLM J. ROHRBOUGH

BUREAU OF MINES. In December 1907, the country was shocked to hear about a series of coal mine explosions. Newspapers reported 500 dead in two mines at Monongah, West Virginia; 250 in the Darr Mine of Jacob's Creek, 49 dead at Monongahela Valley, and 60 trapped in Fayette City, all in southwestern

Pennsylvania; and 75 buried alive in Yolande, Alabama. The outpouring of grief and the public and private demand that the situation never be repeated led directly to the establishment of the Bureau of Mines.

For several decades, however, the federal government had been expanding its relationship with various mining activities. From its inception in 1879, the United States Geological Survey* had established close ties with mineral industries through periodic investigations and publication of technological processes and a geologic map of the nation. Demand for special recognition and support grew in both the metal mining regions of the West and in eastern bituminous coal areas. Late in 1898, California Senator George C. Perkins, upon the recommendation of Survey Director Charles D. Walcott, introduced a resolution calling for the creation of a separate mines and mining division within the Geological Survey.

Although this initial effort failed, in February 1905, Congress appropriated $30,000 to analyze and test coal and lignite deposits. The following year, financial support was increased to $227,000 and the work extended to cover all fuels and structural materials. Quickly, other branches of the government turned to the Survey for advice, and the preparation of specifications and testing of fuels and materials became a standard feature of its responsibilities.

The initial work with fuels had been carried out in 1903-1904 during the Louisiana Purchase Exposition at Saint Louis under the direction of James A. Holmes. A graduate of Cornell University and former professor of geology and natural history at the University of North Carolina, Holmes had most recently served as North Carolina state geologist. When the Exposition closed, Holmes moved the testing facilities to several locations before selecting a permanent base at Pittsburgh in 1907. In April, the Secretary of the Interior established a Technologic Branch within the Geological Survey under Holmes's leadership.

Mine disasters in December 1907 laid a capstone on a deteriorating situation. Between 1890 and 1906, a total of 22,840 coal miners had been killed in the United States; the number of fatal accidents had nearly doubled in the preceding six years. Then in 1907, 3,200 were killed, one-half in Pennsylvania. The frightening carnage was blamed on the lack of reliable information concerning the safe use of explosives, on the presence of gases and flammable dust in mines, on the increasing number of miners sent to greater depths, and on the lack of proper and enforceable mine regulations.

Several major elements of the dominant Progressive spirit came to the forefront to meet this challenge: conservationists saw mining operations wasting a non-renewable resource at an appalling rate, the dominant industrialized sector of the American economy rested on vast mineral wealth, and, finally, Progressives abhorred the dismal working conditions that underground miners faced.

Congress responded by providing the Technologic Branch with $150,000 for protecting the lives of miners and for conducting investigations as to the causes of mine explosions with a view to increasing mining safety. The government turned to scientific research in order to meet an urgent problem. Although the initial appropriation applied to mines in the territories and in the District of Alaska, Congress quickly concluded that investigations could not be conducted by either states or individual companies. The problem was too large and too complex, the endless and costly duplication would produce conflicting results that might hinder the industry, and, if carried out under private auspices, the results would be subject to suspicion. Mine owners agreed that state legislation was chaotic; laws should be based on knowledge which only the federal government could supply.

Director Holmes and the Technologic Branch continued testing fuels and structural material and began investigating mine explosions and developing safety techniques. They trained personnel in first aid and rescue methods and then established several rescue stations at key locations in the coal fields and metal-mining regions. The emphasis of Holmes's operations clearly tended toward the engineering rather than the geologic aspects of the mineral industry. The next step, recognizing the need for mining operations to have direct representation in the government, was permanent administration and fiscal separation from the Geological Survey.

Congress established the Bureau of Mines, directed by James A. Holmes within the Department of the Interior,* effective July 1, 1910. The bureau was to assume the three areas of responsibility inherited from the Technologic Branch, but was to emphasize the safety of miners, improvement of working conditions, prevention of accidents, and proper use of explosives and electricity.

Holmes quickly established a model, experimental mine at Bruceton, Pennsylvania, near Pittsburgh. There he staged a series of spectacular test explosions, proving to mine owners that coal dust remained extremely dangerous even without the presence of gases. The director also organized and convened the first in a series of national mine-safety meetings. Before Holmes died of tuberculosis in July 1915, the bureau began certifying explosives safe for coal mine use and testing electrical equipment that would continue to function in a gas-filled environment.

Despite a positive beginning, the bureau's function was somewhat restrained, and its operation curtailed. The Bureau of Standards* assumed the task of testing clay, cement, and other structural materials. The desire to conduct wide-ranging studies outside the coal industry into western metal mining rarely evolved beyond the planning stage. Early appropriations often reduced rather than encouraged an emphasis on mine safety. Finally, the initial legislation prohibited bureau employees from inspecting or supervising any mine or metallurgical plant; that function remained with state authorities.

To meet negative reaction to several of these concerns, in 1913, Congress extended the bureau's responsibilities and clarified its position on research programs. These now involved the entire range of mining, metallurgy, and mineral technology. Investigations were to emphasize improving health conditions, increasing safety, efficiency and economic development, and conserving resources. Prevention of waste had been placed on an equal level with mine safety.

The bureau quickly launched into new fields of research and carried its services into Western regions. A Petroleum Division, with no regulatory power, offered production research to an expanding industry that had not undertaken similar activities within the private sector. Following a practice already operating in the Department of Agriculture* and in the Forest Service,* Congress funded the establishment of mine-safety and mining experiment stations throughout the country. The bureau could now make investigations and publicize the results closer to the mineral regions. These facilities were frequently created on university campuses, and their personnel worked closely with engineering departments.

The changing relationship between the federal government and the business sector during the 1920s and 1930s carried over into the Bureau of Mines's organizational structure. Secretary Herbert Hoover's Commerce Department* acquired control of most bureau functions in July 1925. The Coolidge Administration justified this action on the grounds that the federal agency had already established close ties with industry and should be controlled by a more appropriate body. In March 1934, however, President Franklin D. Roosevelt transferred the Bureau of Mines back to the Interior Department as Commerce became a prime target for contraction.

Mine-safety inspections, especially in coal-producing regions, became a bureau responsibility in 1941. Congress authorized federal agents to enter coal mines for the first time looking for health and safety problems. Their sole weapon, however, consisted of the right to publish inspection reports. Five years later, after Interior Secretary Julius A. Krug and United Mine Workers (UMW) President John L. Lewis helped settle a coal strike, the bureau issued a safety code and reported violations directly to Krug. In addition, union-selected mine-safety committees were empowered to inspect mines, recommend changes to management, and order miners out of hazardous sections.

In 1952, Congress expanded the bureau's authority by creating the Federal Coal Mine Safety Board of Review. Federal inspectors were to make annual visits to each mine unless a state safety program had been approved. These government officials could order the immediate abandonment of any area within a mine judged unsafe. The legislation specified safety violations covered by the law, established penalties, and offered operators an appeals procedure through the Safety Board.

During the 1940s and 1950s, mine leader Lewis used his political influence to express the union's position on tougher safety rules and to seek sympathetic federal administrators. In the late 1940s, for example, Lewis vigorously opposed the appointment of James Boyd as director of the Bureau of Mines. Although dean at the Colorado School of Mines and a metal-mining expert, Boyd had no knowledge of or experience with coal operations. Despite political clout that delayed the confirmation, Lewis lost this struggle. But in 1953, the active union leader experienced success. President Dwight D. Eisenhower nominated Tom Lyon, mining engineer and Anaconda Copper executive, to direct the bureau.

Unfortunately, at his Senate hearings, Lyon not only announced that he had received a $5,000 annual pension from Anaconda, but also declared his opposition to recently passed safety regulations. Lewis was especially upset that the director would be responsible for enforcing a law he believed should never have been passed. The UMW leader put pressure on supportive congressmen and forced the withdrawal of Lyon's nomination.

While the struggle over leadership ensued, an Interior-appointed survey team, composed of copper, coal, and oil company officials, recommended major changes in the Bureau of Mines. It hoped to reduce the administrative structure and centralize policy and program responsibility in the Washington office; separate health, safety, and inspection activities from scientific and technical research; terminate any production activities, especially the successful conversion of coal to synthetic liquid fuel at a Louisiana, Missouri, facility; and strengthen and unify data collection and statistical analysis. Despite congressional opposition, the reorganization was approved in the fall of 1954.

Once again a disastrous explosion aroused public indignation that ultimately resulted in a major legislative breakthrough. In late November 1968, seventy-eight men were killed inside a coal mine near Farmington, West Virginia. This tragedy prompted John Corcoran, Consolidated Coal Company president and chairman of the National Coal Association, to depart sharply from a century-old industry position. He publicly conceded that much stricter health and safety regulation was needed. Individual states could not deal with the problem in any uniform manner, and the industry had a poor safety record. On the other hand, Corcoran denied that operators placed production and profit ahead of safety. Describing the Farmington operation as a "safe, modern mine," he concluded that the most profitable companies possessed the best safety records.

The Federal Coal Mine Health and Safety Act of 1969, passed by a nearly unanimous Congress, provided the most comprehensive and far-reaching occupational health and safety legislation in American coal-mining history. Covering practically every coal mine and operator in the nation, the new statute called for much tighter and more frequent federal inspections; provided civil and criminal penalties for violations; established stricter controls over methane gas and electrical equipment and wiring; prohibited underground smoking or the use of open-flame lights; and mandated costly improvements in mine-ventilation systems and shelters containing food, water, and air. Congress delegated its rule-making authority to the Secretaries of Interior and Health, Education and Welfare, hoping to bring swifter action against violators. The legislation also required all coal mines to begin reducing the amount of respirable microscopic dust in underground operations. This regulation was designed to curb the spread of pneumoconiosis, commonly known as black lung, identified as a disabling hazard of epidemic proportions.

Despite warnings from the National Coal Association that the new standards were unreasonable and would force the closing of thousands of mines precipitating a national power shortage, Congress persisted. President Richard M. Nixon openly supported provisions in the law designed to eliminate health and accident hazards but expressed a concern over the tremendous cost of implementing the new rules. He objected to the fact that the federal government, not the states, assumed workmen's compensation responsibility for black lung victims, that the act created inconsistency among federally sponsored disability programs, and that administrative difficulties would necessitate corrective legislative changes. Despite these reservations, the law was seen as a monumental achievement in industrial safety and health legislation.

In 1973, Secretary of the Interior Rogers Morton announced a thorough reorganization of the department bureaus and offices. Central to this change, the Bureau of Mines retained its traditional control over energy, metallurgical, and mining research but lost its responsibility for mine health and safety enforcement and education and training functions. These activities were placed under the control of a new Mining Enforcement and Safety Administration (later called the Mine Safety and Health Administration). The transfer was a reaction to long-standing criticism that the bureau promoted mineral production and profitability at the expense of fair and vigorous enforcement of safety regulations. Opposition to Morton's action came from the UMW, which described the shift as mere bureaucratic reshuffling that would not improve conditions for individual laborers. Congress reacted negatively, expressing apprehension about the fact that safety matters still resided within the "industry-supporting" Interior Department.

This bureaucratic, conflict-of-interest charge and continuing devastation of life and property in mining regions eventually resulted in the passage of the Federal Mine Safety and Health Act of 1977. The new law combined all mine workers under a single, strong legislative umbrella by bringing together both the Coal Mine Health and Safety and the Metal and Non-Metallic Mine Safety acts. In addition to raising the standards, strengthening the inspection system, and mandating a safety-training program at every mine, the statute transferred the Mining Enforcement and Safety Administration from the Interior to the Labor Department.* Congressional supporters and UMW leadership called the measure a long overdue elimination of the basic conflict of interest between mineral production and enforcement of mine safety.

Additional responsibilities long associated with the Bureau of Mines were also transferred to other agencies. In 1974, Congress created the Energy Research and Development Administration and assigned to it bureau activities relating primarily to fossil-fuel research and development. Then, three years later the newly formed Department of Energy* absorbed bureau control over coal and fuel supply, demand analysis, and data gathering.

The 1970s proved to be a time of trial and testing for the Bureau of Mines. Reduced responsibilities combined with increased demand for the world's mineral resources forced bureau personnel to reevaluate and reorganize. As their work entered the present decade, however, they intended to remain the principal government agency for minerals problem analysis, for testing policy alternatives, and for assessing the mineral potential of federal lands. But research remains the primary function and represents the largest component of the budget (77.6 percent of the fiscal 1981 appropriation). This activity is centered around mineral technology in three areas: basic resources, environmental restoration, and health and safety.

For seventy years, the Bureau of Mines attempted to provide a supply of minerals that would meet national needs. Through the years this government agency worked closely, although not always harmoniously, with private industry, politically influential interest groups, and the academic community. In some areas, such as post-World War II synthetic fuel production, it operated in advance of contemporary needs; in other areas, such as coal mine safety, it too often reacted only after severe tragedy. As the bureau encounters the 1980s with a redefined legislative mandate, its personnel face new challenges to meet mineral and energy demands.

FOR ADDITIONAL INFORMATION: Sources related to a history of the Bureau of Mines are diverse, scarce, and widely scattered. Fred W. Powell, *The Bureau of Mines; Its History, Activities and Organization* (1922, reprint 1974), offers a brief outline of the agency during its first decade. The only other broadly focused summary was prepared by the Congressional Research Service of the Library of Congress in September 1976; see Allen F. Agnew, "The U.S. Bureau of Mines," Senate Committee on Interior and Insular Affairs, 94 Cong., 2d Sess. (1976). A. Hunter Dupree, *Science in the Federal Government, A History of Policies and Activities to 1940* (1957), reviews the bureau in the context of a government-private sector relationship. Specific activities and several prominent individuals are the subject of articles in such varied publications as *Dictionary of American Biography, Science, Business Week, Petroleum Engineer, School Life,* and *California Journal of Mines and Geology.* Appropriate issues of the *New York Times* closely follow most of the important events and controversies. Recently, the bureau's association with the production of synthetic liquid fuels has been the focus of a team of Texas A&M University scholars and Richard H.K. Vietor, "The Synthetic Liquid Fuels Program: Energy Politics in the Truman Era," *Business History Review* 54 (Spring 1980): 1-34. The bureau's publications are highly technical and demonstrate little concern for historical analysis or narrative. It has conveniently compiled a "Legislative History of the Bureau of Mines," which includes public laws, orders, and proclamations from 1910 to 1975. Current and future plans are outlined in Bureau of Mines, *Mining Research Review* (February 1980).

DAVID A. WALKER

BUREAU OF PUBLIC DEBT. The basic objective of all Treasury Department* policies is to maintain public confidence in the credit of the U.S. government. It is and will continue to be a cornerstone of financial soundness of the country, and a vital factor in the defense of the Free World. That the people of the United States have confidence in their national government should not be surprising. The United States has never failed to pay a lawful fiscal instrument.

During the early twentieth century, the administrative work of the public debt function was largely handled by two units of the Office of the Secretary of the Treasury: the Division of Loans and Currency and the Office of the Register.

The administrative and technical aspects of the public debt have been handled separately from the policy function, which has remained in the immediate Office of the Secretary.

The management of great sums of money requires considerable organization. While significant increases in administrative duties can be absorbed to an extent by existing agencies, there is a limit to the flexibility of any institution. The great increase of administrative work arising from the expenditures of World War I was handled by the Division of Loans and Currency and the Office of the Register of the Treasury. Both offices cooperated with one another. They consolidated procedures and eliminated as much duplication of effort as possible. Nevertheless, by the end of the war, the managers of the Treasury thought that centralized authority over public debt administration would insure better control over issue and retirement of the debt, avoid duplication of effort, and provide for proper administration of the public debt service. The expectation of continuity with a career manager brought the probability of further savings in time and money. The position of commissioner of public debt was created by order of the Secretary of the Treasury on November 11, 1919. The commissioner was responsible to the fiscal Assistant Secretary. The initial organization received official congressional recognition in the appropriation acts of fiscal year 1921.

As the public debt increased twentyfold during the war, so did the number of employees in Washington. The commissioner's new office added few people to the payrolls; the basic functions of issue and withdrawal accounted for most new hiring. The public debt administration would have expanded more but for the establishment of the Federal Reserve System* in 1914. During World War I, the Federal Reserve banks were made headquarters in their districts for handling subscriptions to the several loans, delivering securities against payments, and conducting of transactions in securities subsequent to their actual delivery.

The occupants of the commissioner's office have been long term. Only four men have held the post in seventy-one years, and all of them have served for ten years or more. There has been little turnover in the lower ranks of leadership, and promotions in the agency are usually made from within. There have been few reorganizations of the agency.

The agency was known as the Public Debt Service until 1940. The list of offices, divisions, and branches of the Treasury Department order of August 1921 made it clear that the agency was responsible for the instruments of public debt from the creation of the paper on which they were printed until that paper was destroyed.

Postwar retrenchment is reflected in the employment statistics. As the volume of debt instruments declined, so did the need for large numbers of employees. The Division of Loans and Currency was about 1.5 times the size of the Register's Office, which was about one thousand. The audit and accounts function needed about 130 people. Within a few years, the number of employees would fall to less than one-half the total. Most of the work of the Register's Office dealt with interest coupons and recording, auditing, and filing of coupons from either redeemed or canceled securities.

Only one scandal since 1919 has touched the agency. An accusation of fraud was made by J. W. McCarter of South Dakota, who had been Assistant Register of the Treasury during the war years. After he left office, he made his charges public against the Treasury administration. They were investigated by C. B. Brewer, special assistant to the Attorney General over a thirty-month period from 1921 to 1924. Reports were submitted to Congress by both the Treasury and Justice Departments,* and a congressional investigation resulted. The only conclusive evidence of fraud was the discovery of certain retired certificates received in the Register's Office and illegally paid twice. During the pressure of wartime bond drives, some certificates were issued with the same numbers, but all of the money due was received. Human error was proved but not fraud. The Secretary refuted the charges in the fiscal year 1925 Annual Report. No Treasury Department employees were prosecuted.

The retirement in fiscal year 1927 of the securities of the Second Liberty Loan, issued during World War I, saw the first use of radio as an advertising and communications medium by the Treasury Department. The radio announcement through National Broadcasting Company facilities covered the eastern part of the country. Treasury employees in Denver and San Francisco made similar broadcasts. The effort was successful; the early retirement of the Second and Third Liberty Loans saved the United States $74 million in interest.

Unfortunately, administrative planning for the redemption process was not so good. The Register's Office reported a considerable overload and backlog of work. In the Division of Loans and Currency, there was a very large turnover of staff: over 70 percent resigned or transferred. The rate the next year was lower but still nearly 50 percent because of the redemption activities.

The treasury saw several problems in its funding program, which needed solutions: (1) broaden the base of participation to include as many small, private investors as possible by removing surtaxes, except estate and inheritance taxes; and (2) make the Treasury system responsive and flexible to coincide exactly with Treasury needs. In 1929, federal surtaxes were removed on the principal of and interest from U.S. securities. In addition, the first issue of Treasury bills was made as a new type of short-term security, usually for ninety days, sold at a discount rate fixed by competitive bidding. The removal of surtaxes saw an oversubscription of Treasury bonds in 1929, with the public debt going to the smaller investor of $1,000 or less.

The approval of an amendment of the Second Liberty Loan Act on February 4, 1935, saw Savings Bonds authorized for issue. This would increase participation by the smaller investor in the public debt and avoid an inequity of the World War I issues. Because the Liberty Bonds were bearer securities, which could only be sold on the open market before maturity, the smaller investor in need of money was at the mercy of the market. This unfortunate circumstance saw many smaller investors getting as little as eighty-two cents on the dollar for their investment. The terms under which the new "Baby Bonds" were issued remedied this problem.

Reorganization Plan No. 3, June 30, 1940, established the Fiscal Service, under the direction of the fiscal Assistant Secretary, to include all functions pertaining to financing and fiscal activities. The agency was formally designated as the Bureau of Public Debt. For a short time this plan placed the Division of Savings Bonds under the commissioner of public debt.

As U.S. involvement in World War II grew closer, the significance of the Savings Bond program grew in the work of the bureau as well as for the entire Treasury funding process. In 1941, income taxes were again imposed on Savings Bonds. Through post offices, Defense Savings Stamps were sold which were intended to be converted into Savings Bonds. Over the six-year life of the renewed issuance of Savings Bonds, the sum of $6 billion in maturity value was subscribed. Less than 40 percent were redeemed before the end of the six years; the majority were held to maturity.

Early in 1941, the Defense Savings Staff was established in the Office of the Secretary. The staff would be in charge of the promotion of the sale of Savings Bonds. The program was to be expanded into a nationwide volunteer system. The bureau retained part of the functions of the old Division of Savings Bonds. It would continue to handle mailing lists and distribute promotional materials. In the spring of 1942, the Savings Bond program functions were moved to Chicago, Illinois. The volume of mail and printing had overtaxed the capabilities of the Washington area. As a shipping and publishing center, Chicago was in a better position to handle this division's large volume of work. In fiscal year 1942, the bureau's Division of Savings Bonds handled some 600 million pieces of mail.

The great volume of investment by the small holder of government securities was made more efficient by the payroll savings plan. By June 1942, a total of 108,000 firms were participating, nearly all of the large corporations, and 75 percent of all companies employing 100 or more persons.

During the war years, the bureau made increasing use of keypunch and tabulating equipment. The great number of registered securities required the adoption of machine-readable technology. Nevertheless, the number of prewar personnel in the bureau rose from about twenty-five hundred to over twelve thousand by 1945.

In 1949, a joint accounting project was established to improve federal accounting and reporting. The interagency development of government-wide accounting continues into the 1980s. This midcentury beginning marked the first time since 1921 that officials of the Treasury Dertment, the General Accounting Office,* and the Bureau of the Budget* adopted a formal program to improve basic accounting systems throughout the government.

The 1950s saw economical changes by the bureau in operating procedures and techniques and organization. The remaining functions of the Division of Savings Bonds were transferred to the U.S. Savings Bonds Division. The issue and redemption of Savings Bonds continues to be the bureau's largest administrative burden. In 1953, the Federal Reserve banks and branches assumed the bureau's responsibilities of auditing redeemed U.S. paper currency and the supervision of its destruction. New administrative and technical procedures adopted by the bureau involved an increasing amount of microfilming bulky, voluminous records and the use of machine-readable technology for the issuance and redemption of securities. In 1957, the decision to issue Savings Bonds in punchcard form was adopted. A new processing center was established in Parkersburg, West Viginia.

Adoption of new technology to the special needs of the bureau continued in the 1960s. Pilot studies in 1964 established the feasibility of using magnetic tape and microfilm to replace paper records. Issuing agents could use electronic computers to inscribe large volumes of Series E bonds. A further step in the reduction of paper work and the handling of discrete individual pieces of paper was the institution in 1968 of procedures for book entry of Treasury securities at the issuing Federal Reserve bank. This eliminated the possibility of lost, stolen, or strayed transferrable securities being held as government investment. In the 1970s, these procedures were extended to issuing agents of Savings Bonds. In 1980, 48 percent of the total items reported and 54 percent of the payroll sales were submitted on tape.

Seventeen years after its establishment, the Parkersburg center in 1974 received all of the functions of the old Chicago office. All microfilm records were located in a nearby West Virginia community. Two years later, a new computer system was installed at Parkersburg, which increased efficiency by using one computer language and machine to replace five different machines and three languages.

The Bureau of Public Debt has adopted management techniques developed by the American Management Association. The bureau has enjoyed a high rate of employee participation in its suggestion program, the adoption of flextime for improved employee morale, and the development and promotion from within its own staff of employees slated for senior management positions. Bureau reorganizations are typically made on the basis of well-planned pilot programs which test the change before it is imposed on the functions of the agency.

FOR ADDITIONAL INFORMATION: The principal deposit of records of continuing value is located in the Judicial and Fiscal Branch, Civil Archives Division, Office of the National Archives,* at the main building, Washington, D.C. They are identified as records of the Bureau of Public Debt, Record Group 53, and cover the period 1775-1918. Some series extend beyond World War I, but the bulk of the records of indebtedness end before 1917. There are no plans to accession indebtedness records for the later twentieth century. Important data files of policy and procedure will be accessioned along with important correspondence, speeches, publicity plans and documents, and audiovisual materials.

U.S. Department of the Treasury, Annual Reports of the Secretary of the Treasury, issued annually since 1801, reveal the statements of the secretaries, the review of each year's operations (calender year to 1842, fiscal year afterwards), the special exhibits and reports on public debt operations, taxation developments, international financial and monetary developments, the addresses and statements on general fiscal and other policies, together with the current and historical statistical data contained therein. They provide excellent background, as well as current information, on all aspects of government finance. William F. DeKnight, *History of the Currency of the Country and of the Loans of the United States from the earliest period to June 1900*, prepared . . . under the direction of J. F. Tillman, Register of the Treasury, 2d ed. (1900), is a useful source to understand the terms and technical aspects of the public debt. No subsequent publication covers the more modern operations. R. M. Robertson, *The Comptroller and Bank Supervision: A Historical Appraisal* (1968), is a useful discussion of banking policy, which helps explain some general Treasury functions and decisions that impinge on the public debt.

C. C. Abbott, *The Federal Debt, Structure and Impact* (1953), provides a useful discussion to aid the understanding of Treasury policy. The work will not provide information on technical aspects of the bureau's work. R. A. Love, *Federal Financing: A Study of the Methods Employed by the Treasury in Its Borrowing Operations* (1968 reprint of the 1931 edition), gives some information on the technical operations at the bureau level, but it, too, concentrates on the policy function in the Office of the Secretary of the Treasury.

JAMES HARWOOD

BUREAU OF RECLAMATION.   The Bureau of Reclamation was created in 1902 in the spirit of the Progressive Era. For years crusaders for irrigation of arid Western lands had argued for a federal reclamation law and the creation of a federal reclamation agency. It was felt that, through the reclamation of marginal lands, such a program could improve the economies of Western states and territories, relieve population pressures in cities through resettling people on the land, and benefit the cause of conservation. The proposal had met with considerable opposition from Eastern and Midwestern congressmen who felt such a program was overly preferential to one region of the country. They argued it would prove financially extravagant and would violate state rights. When Theodore Roosevelt became President in 1901, he gave strong support to the passage of a reclamation law. Under the guidance of Representative Francis G. Newlands of Nevada, the Reclamation Act became law on June 17, 1902, signed with wholehearted approval by President Roosevelt.

The Newlands Act, as the Reclamation Act was also called, seemed to provide something for everyone. It called for a reclamation fund into which settlers who took reclaimed lands would pay for the costs of improvement, thus alleviating the concerns of critics who saw such projects as pork-barrel legislation. The farmers who participated in this program would be drawn from Eastern cities to revive the sense of America's pioneer heritage while relieving pressure on crowded city slums. To implement the program's goals, the act created a Reclamation Service as an agency within the Geological Survey* of the Department of the Interior.*

As an agency created from whole cloth, the Reclamation Service required a staff that could offer some degree of expertise and perspective on Western water needs. Secretary of the Interior Ethan A. Hitchcock appointed Frederick H. Newell as chief engineer of the new agency. Newell had headed the Hydrographic

Branch of the Geological Survey, and his immediate superior in the chain of responsiblity was Charles A. Walcott, director of the Geological Survey, to whom Newell would continue to report. Newell drew much of his experienced personnel from the Hydrographic Branch, hiring men who had spent years investigating the water resources of the country's arid regions. As assistant chief engineer Newell hired Arthur Powell Davis, nephew of John Wesley Powell, the noted explorer who had earlier headed the Geological Survey.

The fledgling Reclamation Service soon discovered that it faced formidable challenges in the task of carrying out its assigned duties. To obtain passage, supporters of the Reclamation Act had been compelled to accept compromises and loopholes that invited criticism. The Reclamation Service was expected to survey the Western states and territories for feasible reclamation projects. However, the act's provisions required that funding for such projects heavily depend on the sale of public lands in each state or territory. Thus, it was possible for a state or territory to acquire more projects than it needed, while other regions with fewer land sales obtained fewer projects, even though the need for reclamation might be greater.

A major weakness in the act, which the Reclamation Service soon encountered, was the philosophical rationale which insisted that any person could attempt to farm reclamation land regardless of personal qualifications or lack of them. Within a short time, many farmers who took up reclamation land failed to make a success of their farms, and thereby became disappointed and bitter at having been misled. Moreover, the requirement that farmers repay the cost of the projects invited fraud, delays, and postponement.

Many of the program's shortcomings did not become immediately apparent. The first task of the Reclamation Service was to survey locations in the seventeen Western states and territories for possible reclamation projects, including the construction of dams and channels for the storage and distribution of water. Basic data were available from earlier surveys conducted for the Geological Survey, the information often having been obtained by the same men who were now employees of the Reclamation Service. By the summer of 1903, preliminary surveys were under way in all areas of the West. Because of the newness of the agency, Chief Engineer Newell soon found his engineers reporting back with differing procedures and methods of operation. In order to maintain consistency in the surveys, Newell called a conference of the Reclamation Service engineers at Ogden, Utah, in September 1903. He asked for reports on the preliminary surveys then under way, and he explained the need for regularity in making out contracts and vouchers.

As the surveys progressed, Newell realized that available funds would not be sufficient for the construction of all the proposed projects. He was forced to inform his engineers that neither experimental proposals nor projects that suggested a lack of profitability could be considered. Of seventy-nine irrigable areas investigated between 1902 and 1907, only twenty-five were selected initially for development.

In meeting the challenge of large-scale dam and canal construction, the Reclamation Service in its first years achieved some notable successes. High standards for safety and construction meant that Reclamation Service dams gained quick recognition for their quality. Roosevelt Dam on the Salt River in Arizona, Elephant Butte Dam on the Rio Grande, Pathfinder Dam in Wyoming on the Platte River, and other storage facilities captured public attention by their size and innovative design. Smaller dams predominated, however, particularly earth rather than concrete and masonry works, along with canals and tunnels.

The reservoirs built by the service soon brought other benefits besides water for irrigation. Electric power, recreational opportunities, and conservation activities such as tree planting enhanced the environment and improved the quality of life for settlers on reclamation land. Settlement of reclaimed lands was not without pitfalls, however, as the Reclamation Service found itself criticized for not considering the social needs of settlers. By considering itself as primarily an engineering agency, the Reclamation Service ignored some inevitable political issues. Most notable among these was the lack of qualifications some settlers brought to their new farms. Land speculators obtained some reclamation lands in hopes of turning quick profits. Continual pressure was placed on the agency by real estate interests and local chambers of commerce which hoped to attract a federal reclamation project to their region. Engineers were hard pressed to find time to survey adequately all the suggested sites. Some regions expressed great bitterness at losing proposed sites to other localities, a problem the Reclamation Service could do little about. Complaints arose from Owens Valley in Inyo County, California, when the service backed down in the reclamation of the Owens River in favor of the city of Los Angeles's ambitious aqueduct construction project. Owens Valley's anger threatened a major scandal because of the inadvertent involvement of a Reclamation Service official in the city's quest for additional water supplies.

Beyond such controversies lay the grievances of settlers who complained of the limited time for repayment, the excessive costs, and the stubborn refusal of Newell and other leading reclamation officials to compromise. Matters came to a head in the Woodrow Wilson Administration. Unhappy water users and hostile congressmen vented their discontent on the Reclamation Service in hearings during May 1913, and their complaints received support from Secretary of the Interior Franklin K. Lane. In August 1914, President Wilson signed an Extension Act extending the repayment period from ten to twenty years, a clear victory for the farmers. Newell found his authority undermined and his position as director of the Reclamation Service eventually abolished by Lane. Despite the protests of former President Roosevelt and leading engineers and conservationists, Lane remained adamant. In May 1915, Newell resigned from government service, somewhat bitter over how politics had become so involved with a government agency.

Newell's successor as director of the Reclamation Service was Arthur Powell Davis. For nine years Davis endured the buffeting of organizational revisions, appeals by farmers for repayment relief, problems in the agricultural sector of the economy, and criticisms of his emphasis on the engineering side of the service's programs. By 1922, less than 10 percent of the $135 million that the federal government had invested in reclamation had been repaid by farmers. Although the Reclamation Service was not involved in the scandals of the Harding Administration, Davis became a scapegoat for the agency's problems.

In June 1923, Secretary of the Interior Hubert Work created major changes in the structure of the Reclamation Service, acting in the name of bureaucratic efficiency. Work fired Davis, reorganized the Reclamation Service as the Bureau of Reclamation, and installed business-oriented David W. Davis as the bureau's first commissioner. The abrupt dismissal of A. P. Davis provoked considerable adverse comment from civil engineers. Work ignored the complaints and instituted such reforms as stressing the human and economic factors resulting from government reclamation projects; scientific classification of existing project lands; and an equitable plan for repayment by farmers.

Following a brief tenure as commissioner, D. W. Davis was replaced by Elwood Mead, an internationally known expert on water resources. Mead accepted the proposals of the Committee of Special Advisors on Reclamation that had been formed by Work and, following passage of the Second Deficiency Act in 1924, put them into action. Among the changes in program policy were determination of project feasibility prior to approval of the project, a sliding scale of repayment that varied with the productivity of the land, and the setting of qualifications for prospective farmers. Detailed land surveys were undertaken, and the government agreed to write off obligations on unproductive lands. Until his death in 1936, Mead campaigned actively on behalf of bureau programs and the efforts of farmers to achieve success on Reclamation-irrigated lands.

The earlier emphasis on construction of water storage and diversion facilities gave way to new perspectives in the 1930s. During the Great Depression, the Bureau of Reclamation came to stress multiple-purpose planning in its programs, incorporating electric power projects, flood control, and planning for entire river basins rather than just limited areas. The Boulder Canyon Project, encompassing the construction of Hoover Dam, Parker Dam, the All-American Canal, the Colorado Aqueduct, and the building of power transmission lines, proved the most ambitious public works project involving the Bureau of Reclamation prior to World War II. Franklin D. Roosevelt's New Deal provided a fivefold increase for the bureau's budget, making possible the authorization and construction of California's Central Valley Project, the Columbia Basin Project, and other grand constructions. Mead's immediate successors continued the commitment to major public works construction; projects were built according to the multiple-purpose definition that brought a human dimension to the concrete monuments.

In half a century, the Bureau of Reclamation had compiled a notable record of successful projects that had resulted in the development of Western water resources and the creation of public electric power for millions of people. Under Dwight Eisenhower's presidency, new definitions arose for the bureau which greatly modified its long-standing commitment to scientific and nonpartisan development of the nation's resources. The Republican party inaugurated a policy inimical to the bureau's philosophy, calling for "partnership" in projects between the public and private sectors, and greater control by states of their own water resources. The result of these pressures was reduction of the bureau's developmental plans and a drastic decrease in its budget. Despite the restrictions, accomplishments were noted in this era such as the linkage of power transmission lines from the Columbia River Power System to southern California, at a cost of $700 milliion, a program for full-scale development of the Missouri River Basin, and similar projects of significance.

In the 1960s, the Bureau of Reclamation encountered dramatic changes in the public's view of the environment. Whereas the agency had been founded by supporters of a utilitarian philosophy calling for development of resources to benefit the greatest number of people, those same alleged beneficiaries now actively opposed further tampering with the landscape. From the earlier isolated protests against such projects as Echo Park Dam in the 1950s, conservationists now led a growing public desire against projects that environmentalists contended were economically and environmentally unsound. Water projects came under attack from such a broad base of protest that President Jimmy Carter early in his term recommended termination of a number of authorized reclamation projects.

The Bureau of Reclamation now functions in an era of environmental consciousness. Once considered beyond reproach for its quality of dam design and engineering capabilities, the bureau suffered a major setback in the failure of the Teton Dam in eastern Idaho on June 5, 1976. The widespread destruction caused by the tragedy and the public uproar that followed prompted a review of all dam safety practices and procedures. Despite the tragedy and the criticism of recent years, the bureau's record of 320 storage reservoirs, thousands of miles of canals, pipelines, and tunnels, and over sixteen thousand miles of transmission lines speaks for a transformation of the West from arid desolation to conservation and utilization of vital resources.

FOR ADDITIONAL INFORMATION: Helpful introductions to information on the Bureau of Reclamation are Lawrence B. Lee, *Reclaiming the American West: An Historiography and Guide* (1980), and Michael C. Robinson, *Water for the West: The Bureau of Reclamation, 1902-1977* (1979). William E. Warne, *The Bureau of Reclamation* (1973), offers an institutional history by a former assistant commissioner of reclamation. William E. Smythe, *The Conquest of Arid America* (1969), was a pioneering study of the reclamation movement; the 1969 reprint edition includes a perceptive introduction by Lawrence B. Lee. The *Pacific Historical Review* of November 1978 presented a special issue on reclamation in the West. Many books have featured aspects of reclamation activity and controversy. Examples include Philip L. Fradkin, *A River No More: The Colorado River and the West* (1981); Abraham Hoffman, *Vision or Villainy: Origins of the Owens Valley-Los Angeles Water Controversy* (1981); and Norris Hundley, Jr., *Water and the West: The Colorado River Compact and the Politics of Water in the American West* (1975). **ABRAHAM HOFFMAN**

BUREAU OF REFUGEES, FREEDMEN, AND ABANDONED LANDS.

The emancipation of some 4 million Afro-Americans in 1863 suddenly confronted the nation with overwhelming moral obligations. Having participated or acquiesced in slavery, and having enjoyed the fruits of an economy heavily dependent upon Southern slave production, both North and South faced a debt far beyond mere humanitarian aid. The moral imperative of emancipation in a democratic society entailed the guarantee of rights and liberties, the protection of persons, and the promotion of economic security for the freed people.

In early 1862, even before emancipation, the North had begun responding to the problems created by black freedom as slaves fled to Union lines. The civilian response was the formation of freedmen's aid societies to organize philanthropic relief; the governmental response, after some confusion and contradiction, was generally to use the ex-slaves, then considered contraband of war, to further the war effort either directly in fatigue labor and later as soldiers, or indirectly in cotton production, the proceeds of which went to the government. Those responses, however, only addressed military necessity and minimal humanitarian demands. They were inadequate to meet the moral imperative facing the nation.

In 1863 and 1864, Congress considerd more systematic approaches to the freedmen, debating bills by Representative Thomas D. Eliot to create a Bureau of Emancipation and a Bureau of Freedmen's Affairs. Meanwhile, the American Freedmen's Inquiry Commission, created by the War Department,* began laying the foundation for a formal freedmen's agency. The Northern freedmen's aid societies, awed by the immensity of the aid problem compared to their philanthropic resources, lobbied for governmental aid and coordination. Finally, in March 1865, Congress created the Bureau of Refugees, Freedmen, and Abandoned Lands, known popularly as the Freedmen's Bureau.

The bureau as established in 1865 embraced more war-related issues than its supporters originally envisioned. In addition to providing for all subjects relating to the freedmen, the new bureau was given the duty of looking after the needs of Southern white Unionist refugees. The agency was also given control over all abandoned and confiscated Southern property, including substantial holdings of the Confederate government and Confederate leaders. Central to the 1865 legislation was a provision authorizing the distribution of land in forty-acre plots to freedmen and refugees.

Congress established the bureau within the War Department, thereby making it essentially a military organization. It was manned primarily by Army personnel, organized along the lines of a military bureaucracy, and followed military procedures. Even its civilian agents were subject to military discipline. The original legislation appropriated no funds for the bureau, expecting it to operate out of revenues generated by the rental and sale of lands, and expecting as well that, as a part of the military, it would draw on military supplies and facilities for transportation, buildings, medicine, rations, supplies, and the salaries of its military personnel.

Despite the efforts of the more liberal freedmen's aid societies and abolitionists to assure that bureau leadership fell to someone with antislavery antecedents, the post of commissioner went to General Oliver Otis Howard, a career Army officer with no known commitment to Afro-Americans. Commissioner Howard organized the bureau by assigning an assistant commissioner to each of the Southern states under military jurisdiction. (Delaware and West Virginia had no regular bureau office; they were occasionally served by the assistant commissioners of either the District of Columbia or Maryland. The bureau was active in Missouri for only a few months in 1865.) Howard provided himself and his assistant commissioners with small staffs of subordinates responsible for inspections, medical affairs, disbursements, education, land, claims, and similar matters. By May 1865, the Freedmen's Bureau was in operation, taking over the relief work of the Army, beginning to develop cooperative arrangements with the civilian aid organizations, and preparing preliminary plans for the distribution of abandoned and confiscated lands.

The bureau's early efforts to meet the legislative mandate to distribute Confederate property terminated abruptly, however, when, on May 29, 1865, President Andrew Johnson issued his Proclamation of Amnesty. The amnesty, and subsequent pardons given liberally to those excluded from it, restored civil rights and property to the rebels, thereby removing from bureau control nearly all confiscated property. The remaining property was inadequate to provide even a small percentage of freedmen with the promised forty-acre holdings.

The original legislation creating the bureau authorized it for only one year. It was apparent to many that by the end of its first year the bureau would have hardly begun the minimal work necessary. Thus, early in 1866, Congress passed a new bill extending the agency. President Johnson's veto of the bill marked the first blow in the rupture between Johnson and Congress over Reconstruction. Congress passed a second measure over another veto, authorizing two more years of service and appropriating about $7 million for expenses. Bowing to the presidential pardon, the bureau bill of 1866 made no mention of land redistribution.

The Freedmen's Bureau focused its energies on six distinct concerns: relief, land, labor, justice, moral reform, and education. Most pressing at the bureau's inauguration was relief for the masses of freedmen and whites displaced by the war. During and immediately following the war, many former bondsmen migrated to the freedmen's camps organized by the Army and the aid societies; others congregated in cities or towns, or moved about the South in search of families or as expressions of their newfound freedom. The disruption of Southern agriculture and the general collapse of the Southern economy left these refugees, as well as some still on plantations, utterly destitute and without prospects for employment. Many white refugees shared their plight. They required food, clothing, and medicine to relieve the suffering. As soon as it was capable, the bureau took over the government's share of this work.

From the first, the bureau sought to terminate its relief work as early as possible, fearing that the dole would create dependency and pauperize the freedmen. Howard and the assistant commissioners moved quickly to break up the freedmen's camps and to force blacks out of the cities and towns and back onto plantations. Rations for white refugees were similarly scheduled for early termination. A prostrate economy and disastrous drought, flood, and insect devastation of crops for three successive years after the war, however, rendered futile the efforts to end relief work in much of the South. Rations for both blacks and whites continued to be issued as late as 1868.

Beyond immediate relief, the freedmen's greatest need—and the one thing most clearly demanded by the ex-slaves—was land. The redistribution of Southern land would have given the Afro-Americans independence, an economic stake in the society, and a measure of protection from Southern whites. Realization of the congressional promise of forty-acre tracts would also have gone far toward satisfying the nation's moral debt to its former bondsmen. However, Johnson's pardon of ex-Confederates left the bureau with no means to meet its legislative obligation. Howard instructed his officers to inform the freedmen that there would be no redistribution and to convince them to return to the plantations. Thereafter, the bureau's land policy embraced a feeble attempt to promote black settlement on homesteads provided by the Southern Homestead Act of 1866—a largely futile effort since the federal property in the South opened by the bill was inaccessible and often of poor quality. In the following decade most would-be homesteaders, white and black, failed to win title to their claims.

In the absence of land redistribution or any other means of establishing black economic independence, and ever mindful of the grave concerns of Northern businessmen and Southern planters to reestablish the cotton economy, the Freedmen's Bureau devoted a major portion of its energy to returning blacks to their antebellum role as the South's agricultural labor force. Bureau agents sought to regularize the new free-labor status of the freedmen through labor contracts between planters and workers, and much of the agents' time was devoted to drawing up and registering contracts and adjudicating contract disputes. Remuneration took a variety of contractual forms, ranging from simple wage labor, in gangs or individually, to a share of the crop and tenantry forms. Recent studies of the bureau have concluded that, quite indirectly, the Freedmen's Bureau contributed to sharecropping's eventual domination of Southern agriculture as the sequel to slavery.

The military had first begun experimenting with postslavery forms of black labor, acting under the constraints of military necessity. The bureau, acting under the constraints of North-South accommodation and economic recovery without significant economic change, adopted the Army's forms with little alteration. Labor policy became the keystone of the bureau's work. It doubtlessly contributed significantly to restoring major features of Southern antebellum productive relationships. On the other hand, it also established the principle that blacks were free laborers entitled to sell their labor in the market. That principle was deeply compromised in subsequent years, but the property relationship of slavery was inexorably changed to an employer-employee relationship.

Black freedom also entailed altered legal relationships in the South. The Southern legal system discriminated against blacks, however, both through discriminatory laws and discriminatory administration of justice. Discrimination was deepened with the Black Codes of 1866. Commissioner Howard and other bureau officials were aware that the freedmen needed legal protection. They established bureau courts to adjudicate disputes involving freedmen, claiming jurisdiction whenever it appeared that local courts would not recognize the legal equality of black citizens.

While potentially a service second only to land redistribution in fostering black freedom, the bureau's efforts to promote justice were limited and short-lived. President Johnson managed to restrict the struggle for legal rights to a single issue: the acceptance of freedmen's testimony in local courts. As soon as the states agreed to allow blacks to testify in court against whites, the bureau abolished its own courts. By late 1866, the bureau had ended most of its legal activity except for its efforts to obtain black veterans' bounties and other claims against the military. The South eased discrimination in its laws sufficiently to regain control of its courts, but discrimination in the administration of justice generally remained untouched. The bureau courts made inroads into the Southern system of justice, at least promoting the principle that the Afro-Americans were citizens with civil rights. But they were probably only moderately successful in enforcing their own decisions and had jurisdiction over so few cases for so short a time that their value was sharply circumscribed.

If the bureau abandoned its efforts to obtain land and justice for the freedmen relatively early, it was indefatigable in its quest to promote their moral reform. In speeches and private counsel, bureau officials linked the restoration of agricultural labor with the moral virtues of hard work and honest labor, while inveighing against vagrancy and infidelity to contracts. The bureau authorized its agents to give slave marriages civil sanction. A freedmen's temperance union, organized by the bureau, bolstered the preachments of officials and missionaries. And, although the Freedmen's Savings and Trust Company was not legally connected with the Freedmen's Bureau, the bureau promoted the bank vigorously to provide a practical outlet for its encouragement to thrift.

The major instrumentality for the moral reform of the freedpeople, however, was the bureau's work in freedmen's education. While the bureau did not support its own schools, it provided coordination, data-gathering services, buildings for schoolhouses, transportation for teachers and supplies, and other forms of aid for the numerous Northern benevolent agencies working in freedmen's education. Reverend John W. Alvord served as general superintendent of education in the Freedmen's Bureau from 1865 to 1870, assisted by subordinate superintendents in each Southern state.

Bureau aid to freedmen's schools was not insubstantial. Materially, the bureau expended over $5 million in aid to school endeavors, a portion of which was instrumental in the creation of many Southern black colleges. Ideologically, by favoring the American Missionary Association (AMA) over other aid societies, the bureau lent support to the AMA's efforts to give Southern black education a conservative character. The very existence of black education in the postbellum South is due in part to the bureau; it may be argued that the emergence of public education generally in the South has indirect roots in the Freedmen's Bureau's support for black schooling.

The bureau's educational emphases reflected and reinforced other aspects of the bureau's work. Knowing the freedpeople's great thirst for education, bureau agents used the schools in their efforts to move the freedmen back to the plantations. The greatest aid went to those Northern agencies whose schools echoed the bureau's emphasis on moral reform over civil rights. Bureau officials sought to convince skeptical blacks that schooling was more essential for their freedom than landholding and economic independence.

In 1868, Congress ordered the Freedmen's Bureau to drop all of its activity as of January 1869, except for its education and bounty offices. Those functions were allowed to continue until 1872, but they were inadequately provided for. Bureau staff was reduced sharply. As officers were mustered out of the Army, the bureau lost experienced superintendents and suffered discontinuities. Supervision, coordination, and aid to black education declined. The state offices closed in late 1869 and 1870. The tenth, and last, *Semi-Annual Report on Schools for Freedmen* appeared in July 1870. Superintendent Alvord resigned four months later. With few functions still intact, the bureau ceased operations in June 1872.

The Bureau of Refugees, Freedmen, and Abandoned Lands was fully operational for less than four years. Its efforts contributed moderately to establishing minimal civil rights for the freedpeople and to easing somewhat their transition to freedom. Clearly, the bureau was neither radical nor a tool of Congressional Radicals, contrary to traditional interpretation. Its agents were expressly forbidden to engage in any partisan activity. Assistant commissioners with strong sympathies for the freedmen were quickly removed and replaced with officials more solicitous of the interest of planters and other whites. The bureau's policies in land, labor, and education served to blunt, not promote, the revolutionary implications and the moral obligations of emancipation. In the final analysis, the Freedmen's Bureau served primarily to sort out the flotsam of war, while leaving virtually untouched the nation's debt to the Afro-Americans.

FOR ADDITIONAL INFORMATION: The standard source for the history of the Freedmen's Bureau is George R. Bentley, *A History of the Freedmen's Bureau* (1955). His argument that the bureau was radical and anti-South, however, has been sharply revised by a number of subsequent studies of bureau activity at the state and local level; see, among others, Martin Abbott, *The Freedmen's Bureau in South Carolina, 1865-1872* (1967); Joe M. Richardson, *The Negro in the Reconstruction of Florida, 1865-1877* (1965); and Howard Ashley White, *The Freedmen's Bureau in Louisiana* (1970). Continuity between military and bureau policies toward the freedmen can be traced by comparing these studies with Louis Saxton Gerteis, *From Contraband to Freedmen: Federal Policy Toward Southern Blacks, 1861-1865* (1973).

Other researchers, taking black freedom rather than white prerogative as the standard against which to judge Reconstruction, argue that the bureau was eminently conservative, maintaining much of the Southern status quo; see especially William S. McFeely, *Yankee Stepfather: General O. O. Howard and the Freedmen* (1968); and Ronald E. Butchart, *Northern Schools, Southern Blacks, and Reconstruction: Freedmen's Education, 1862-1875* (1980).

RONALD E. BUTCHART

BUREAU OF STANDARDS. See National Bureau of Standards.

BUREAU OF THE CENSUS. For nearly two hundred years, the Bureau of the Census and a series of ad hoc predecessor agencies have been responsible for much of the information regarding the U.S. population and its economic and social institutions. A decennial enumeration was prescribed by the Constitution to apportion seats among the several states in the House of Representatives. In view of the magnitude of the operation in a rapidly growing country, it is surprising that the first twelve censuses were conducted by purely temporary organizations. This situation persisted until 1902, despite the fact that during the last half of the nineteenth century many officials testified to the inefficiency of the temporary offices, and attention was repeatedly directed to the fact that a number of other countries had created permanent bureaus.

The expansion of the bureau's programs may be seen in a number of developments since 1790. For many years this took the form of gradual changes in the number and types of inquiries included in the decennial censuses. Thus, information on occupations was added in 1840, and in the next fifty years growing concerns with economic and social problems led to other additions—some of them temporary—literacy, school attendance, value of real estate and personal estate, number and types of handicapped persons, and unemployment. Modern labor force and income questions were not added until 1940.

Another direction in which the bureau's program evolved was the addition of new censuses. Thus, the growing interest in measuring economic progress led to the initiation of a census of manufactures in 1810, and of agriculture and mining in 1840. The first census of governments was taken in 1850. The years from 1930 to 1965 brought the censuses of distribution, service trades, construction, housing, and transportation.

A third phase in the evolution of the bureau's program is to be found in the development of current statistics, that is, statistics generated by programs other than the periodic censuses. The two major components of current statistics are intercensal statistics (collected between periods of regular census taking) and foreign trade statistics. Intercensal statistics, accounting for most of the current statistics total, consist of annual, quarterly, and monthly series of data, and provide information on changes between the five- and ten-year benchmarks furnished by the periodic censuses. Most of the intercensal statistics were established after World War II. They may be regarded as a direct response to the growing demand for up-to-date information for decision-making by government and private industry.

The creation of a program of current statistics (other than foreign trade) was greatly advanced by three developments in the 1940s and later. The first was the advance in sampling theory and application that made it possible to develop valid sampling frames at reasonable cost in all the fields covered by the periodic censuses and in many others. The second development was the transfer to the census in 1942 of a labor force survey initiated by the Works Progress Administration (WPA)* in 1936. This survey provided the basis for the Current Population Survey, operated on a monthly basis after the early 1940s. It paved the way for many of the current census data on population and met many data needs of other agencies.

The third element essential for the full development of a program of current statistics was provided by Public Law 671, enacted in 1948, which gave strong support to current statistical surveys. Current data could henceforth be requested annually from business concerns on a mandatory basis, provided (1) the inquiries were similar to those included in complete censuses; (2) adequate advance public notice was given; and (3) a determination of public need had been made.

The fourth phase of the evolution of the bureau's program is to be seen in the great expansion of reimbursable work performed for other agencies. Such a development would have been impossible prior to the establishment of the permanent organization in 1902 and would have been much slower without the transfer of the field organization from WPA in 1942. The bureau's service work expanded greatly after World War II to a level well above the entire program of current statistics and often exceeded the expenditures for the periodic censuses. In these service contracts, the sponsoring agency retains control of the scope, content, and interpretation of the data collected, while utilizing the technical skills of the bureau in survey design, collection, processing, and tabulation. It may, in fact, be regarded as an intermediate position between the decentralized statistical organizations of some countries and the centralized systems of others, such as Canada.

During the period of program expansion, the organization of the bureau underwent a series of appropriate modifications. The planning and design of censuses and surveys, with associated research and development, are now carried out in a number of separate divisions, organized along subject matter lines. These subject matter divisions have long been grouped into demographic and economic areas, reflecting the fundamentally different problems of data collection and processing. The operations involved in assembling the bureau's statistics, including collection, processing, and tabulation, have all been centralized in specialized divisions in order to handle fluctuating workloads more efficiently and to assure that full use is made of technological advances in all parts of the program.

Certain legislative developments were particularly important in clearing the way for the notable program expansion of the bureau after 1900. The permanent

Census Act of 1902 created a continuing organization essential for the programs of current statistics and service work. The second development was the institution of strict rules on the confidentiality of census returns, first established in the law for the 1900 Census and subsequently strengthened further. These laws have historically given the Census Bureau a unique position among federal agencies by furnishing strong specific statutory protection to all information collected from the public. The unblemished record of maintenance of confidentiality has helped the bureau achieve a high rate of response to questions that are widely perceived as personal.

It is easy to speculate on the possibility that the Census Bureau program might have evolved as in certain other countries, for example, Canada, with the result that the United States would have had a centralized system rather than a group of independent statistical agencies, each representing special areas of concern, such as labor, agriculture, and housing. Indeed, the reports of some statistical commissions included recommendations that would have led to a greater degree of centralization, and many predicted such a change. In the 1920s and the 1930s, however, the bureau lacked a strong proponent of centralization, and the emergence of strong departmental agencies, all well able to defend their turf, made unlikely a consensus for centralization.

The tasks performed by the Census Bureau every ten years have been so different from those performed elsewhere that commercial equipment and methods have often not been adequate. Two outstanding breakthroughs in large-scale data processing—first, the punched card system and, later, electronic computers—both received initial impetus from inside the Census Bureau.

The beginning of the punched-card era can be traced to the cooperation between Herman Hollerith, a young man employed as a census special agent, and Dr. John Shaw Billings who was in charge of the Division of Vital Statistics. The most generally accepted account of the origin is that Billings suggested to Hollerith in the early 1880s that there ought to be some mechanical way of tabulating the results of a census. Hollerith became interested in the idea, left the government in 1883, and by the time of the 1890 Census had developed and tested a tabulating machine. This machine had its first large-scale application in that census and with only minor modifications was used also in the 1900 Census and for a part of the work in 1910. With the creation of a census engineering laboratory in 1907, the bureau developed the unit counter, designed in light of its unique requirements. This equipment met a large part of the bureau's tabulating needs for the decennial censuses of 1920 to 1940.

A later development, one of great national significance, was the bureau's pioneering in the development of Univac I, the first electronic computer designed for data processing, which was ready for bureau use in 1951. The more advanced computers and auxiliary equipment acquired by the bureau in the following years brought enormous gains in speed and reductions in cost. In addition, the new methods increased the accuracy of the data by sophisticated procedures for editing and for estimating incompletely reported data, expanded the amount of area and subject detail, and met the needs of many new data users through release of summary tape decks or through special tabulations. These advances have been valuable not only to government at all levels, but also to private enterprise.

In the years since 1940, truly great scientific advances have been made in the areas of sample design, response research, survey design, and systems analysis. The use of multistage stratified samples, clustering, varied rotation patterns, and the applications of collateral data to the estimating process have served to decrease unit costs very significantly, to spread the reporting burden more equitably, and yet to take full account of administrative feasibility. Research into the measurement and control of errors of response has resulted in very significant changes in decennial census procedures which are reflected in part in increased productivity and quality and, in part, in lower relative costs.

With the rapid growth in knowledge about both sampling and nonsampling errors, it is natural that statistical production began to be regarded as an integrated process in the 1960s, from the original planning of content and methods to the final system for the delivery of data to the consumer. It had become clear that many different factors affect the quality of the output and that some can be dealt with more readily than others. There are also many routes to increasing efficiency in the production process, some of which are capable of more rapid realization than others. With so many alternative courses of action, it became clear that much research would continue to be required to approach the optimum output with fixed resources.

An important result of the work done in research and development was the shift from the collection of census data by direct enumeration to collection by mail. In the case of the economic censuses, this shift was greatly facilitated by the use of administrative records (Social Security Administration* and Internal Revenue Service*) to furnish the needed mailing lists. In the case of the demographic censuses, extensive mail collection started with the 1960 Census, after a series of research studies had shown that the shift would improve the quality of the information collected, and also reduce the amount of underenumeration.

One distinguished demographer has observed that census data are so widely used that their source is frequently not recognized. This universality of use is not surprising since the data gathered by the bureau cover all U.S. inhabitants, the homes they live in, the factories and service trades that account for their total supply of goods and services, the farms and mines producing foods, fibers, fuels, and other commodities, and the retail and wholesale trade establishments that provide the flow of goods to ultimate consumers. Knowledge about some or all of these statistical universes is essential to decisions involved in planning, administration, and evaluation—regardless of whether the decisions are to be made by government, by business, or by nonprofit organizations. There are, of course, major difficulties in identifying, listing, and evaluating all these uses. The importance of a particular use is difficult to measure, and the exact role played by an individual figure is often unknown.

One specific use of data from the population census has grown notably in recent years, with the enactment of legislation providing for the use of population in the distribution of federal and state funds among political subdivisions. Hence, population figures enter into the calculations underlying the distribution of over $50 billion each year. Since this use, unlike other uses of census figures, depends upon exact totals, there have been strong demands for improved coverage and for adjustments to correct deficiencies, particularly in congested areas of large cities where undercounts are known to be more serious.

In the history of the Census Bureau, three controversies stand out, all of them concerned with the content and procedures of the decennial population census. Two of them were initiated and promoted by a member of Congress with strong personal convictions and the ability to rally considerable support for his views. The third arose in connection with the 1980 Census, mainly as the result of extensive concern that the expected undercount of certain groups would penalize some areas.

The first of these controversies arose over the inclusion in the 1940 Census of the first questions on personal income. Senator Charles W. Tobey of New Hampshire denounced these questions and introduced a Senate resolution calling for their deletion from the questionnaires which had already been printed. Thousands of letters came to the Senator, who was joined by seven other members of Congress in support of his resolution. Support also was voiced by a number of citizens groups, hearings took place in the Congress, and the extensive newspaper stories were predominantly favorable to the Senator. The drive lost its impetus, however, as the Census Bureau announced its plans to give citizens the option of sending their information directly to Washington. Although 15 million forms were printed and made available, only 200,000 were actually used.

In a work published in 1969, Hyman Alterman referred to the 1970 Census as the "Census of Controversy." Several years before the 1970 Census, Congressman Jackson E. Betts perceived the popular appeal of a proposal to place all census inquiries on a voluntary basis except for the few needed to validate the count of the population. Legislation to effect such a change was introduced in 1967, and, over the next two years, the number of congressmen who aligned themselves with Betts reached 145, or one-third of the members of the House. However, support for retaining mandatory census authority for the entire schedule rose gradually, as more and more important users recognized the seriousness of the threat to census statistics represented by the Betts legislation. Finally, the controversy was brought to an end by the enactment of a new bill, which retained mandatory authority for all census questions, but eliminated jail sentences for failure to comply, and required the Census Bureau to submit questions for legislative review.

The 1980 Census, even more than 1970, could be called the "Census of Controversy." The controversy in 1980 did not center on a single issue, however, and no one person was responsible. Perhaps the dominant feature in 1980 was the initiation of a series of legal actions to enjoin the Census Bureau from carrying out its work. The legal injunctions granted in a number of instances reflected the judiciary's growing willingness to intervene in what must have been comparatively unfamiliar territory. For example, the start of the census was almost postponed by virtue of an injunction, which would have forced the bureau to get a count of illegal aliens, in complete disregard of the testimony of bureau officials regarding the impossibility of making such a count. A number of other legal actions were based on the belief that the census procedures would give results unfair to the interests of minority groups in large cities, where undercounts have been relatively serious. One injunction was granted, which would have made it impossible for the bureau to release the 1980 totals at year's end as required by law. This injunction was lifted at almost the last possible moment for the bureau to meet its deadline. It is noteworthy that, despite the controversy over the 1980 Census procedures, the response to the mail inquiries was somewhat above the expected level, and the percentage of the population covered was the highest in recent decades.

It is likely that the decennial census will continue to be a subject of controversy, because so many public and private programs depend heavily on the results. The increasing cost (over $1 billion in 1980) also makes the census a good target for attack by those seeking to hold down public expenditures. Furthermore, an undertaking that calls upon every household in the nation to furnish mandatory replies to a number of personal questions will continue to be attacked by legislators and others who are ready to disregard the many needs served by census data.

FOR ADDITIONAL INFORMATION: Hyman Alterman, *Counting People: The Census in History* (1969); A. Ross Eckler, *The Bureau of the Census* (1972); Charles P. Kaplan, Thomas L. Van Valey, and associates, *Census '80: Continuing the Fact Finder Tradition* (1980); Laurence F. Schmeckebier, *Congressional Apportionment* (1941); Irene Barnes Taeuber and Conrad Taeuber, *People in the United States in the 20th Century* (1971); U.S. Bureau of the Census, *Bureau of the Census Catalog, 1790-1972* (1974); U.S. Bureau of the Census, *Statistical Abstract of the United States: 1980*, 101st ed. (1980); and Carroll Davidson Wright, *The History and Growth of the United States Census* (1900).

A. ROSS ECKLER

C

CAPITAL PLANNING COMMISSION. See National Capital Planning Commission.

CENSUS BUREAU. See Bureau of the Census.

CENTRAL INTELLIGENCE AGENCY (CIA). The Central Intelligence Agency was established by Congress in 1947 as part of a larger reorganization of the national security system, which also created a National Security Council* (NSC) and unified the defense establishment under a Department of Defense.*

The purpose of the CIA was to be the central clearinghouse for all strategic intelligence pertaining to foreign affairs. Intelligence was to be collected primarily by existing departments and agencies, such as the Department of State* and armed services. World War II experience with intelligence and covert operations had a major organization and doctrinal impact on postwar intelligence structures. During that war, the Office of Strategic Services (OSS) was established and U.S. intelligence was organized on a government-wide basis for the first time. The CIA was created in 1947, in part, out of elements of the wartime OSS and to some degree in the image and spirit of the OSS.

The 1947 statute specified CIA functions: to advise the National Security Council, including its chairman, the President, on foreign intelligence activities; to coordinate, evaluate, and disseminate to top decision-makers the best information on foreign affairs available within government; and to perform intelligence and related functions that could best be performed centrally for the national government. From this general statutory charter, which can be seen to contain some ambiguous assignments of function and which delegates specific implementing authority to the NSC, have flowed operational guidelines. These have been set in secret NSC intelligence directives that clarify the CIA's roles and delineate the jurisdictions and missions of other government intelligence agencies.

In 1949, Congress legislated further regarding the CIA, adding statutory provisions permitting the agency to use abnormally secret fiscal and administrative procedures and, in fact, exempting the CIA from usual limitations on the expenditure of public funds. CIA funds were allowed to be hidden in the budgets of other departments and then transferred to the agency without the normal restrictions. The 1949 statute further exempted the CIA from having to disclose its "organization, functions, name, officials, titles, salary, or numbers of persons employed." By this act Congress locked the door of secrecy on the CIA and gave the key to the CIA director. Congress has slowly been regaining entry to CIA secrets ever since.

Since 1947, the CIA has come to have three major functions, and the main features of its contemporary organization represent this tripartite division of work: foreign strategic intelligence, counterintelligence, and covert political action, including psychological warfare. Because there is common confusion and misunderstanding regarding these terms, it will be useful to pause for basic definitions, even if they have lost precise meaning in common usage. Accurate usage is to refer to intelligence as information gathering, analysis, and communication by a variety of means, only one of which is espionage. Intelligence, then, is a term that should be applied only to the informational function. Counterintelligence is a police and security function, designed to protect the security of one's own secret operational activities. It is primarily a negative function, although the counterintelligence process in capable of producing "positive" information of strategic value. A third function all too commonly subsumed under the "intelligence" label is covert political action, subversion, and a variety of secret operations, including paramilitary adventures and major intervention in the political events of other nations.

This terminological confusion is compounded by the incorporation of all three functions under the administrative roof of the Central Intelligence Agency, even though its original charter seems to demonstrate a congressional intent to create an intelligence agency only.

The CIA is headed by a director and deputy director, only one of whom can be a military professional. The earliest directors of the CIA were from the armed services. Directors and deputy directors are subject to Senate confirmation. In the turbulent years after Watergate, the CIA in one period had five different directors in a five-year period. The CIA director, in fact, wears two hats. He is both head of the agency and the President's principal intelligence adviser, thus carrying the title "Director of Central Intelligence." Theoretically, this makes him the head of the entire U.S. intelligence system, which some like to call the "community." In reality, the intelligence system in its over thirty years of existence has been one of proliferating, sometimes competing, intelligence units, some of which exceed in personnel size and resources those of the CIA. Leading members of the system include the Defense Intelligence Agency, separate intelligence units of each of the three armed forces, the National Security Agency (whose annual budget and personnel far exceed those of the CIA), Department of State intelligence, as well as Federal Bureau of Investigation,* Treasury,*

Energy,* Drug Enforcement, and a number of other agencies with intelligence functions.

The major subdivisions of the CIA are those for intelligence production, covert operation, science and technology, and administration. The annual budget of the CIA, as well as its total number of employees, have always been official secrets, but estimates have placed its annual budget in recent years as something under but approaching $1 billion and its personnel total as something under but approaching twenty thousand. Only a few members of Congress and of the Office of Management and Budget* are privy to exact figures. It has been a matter of intense debate in recent years as to whether disclosure of budget totals would harm national security.

The intelligence division, said to be the largest, produces intelligence reports in various forms, ranging from news items rapidly transmitted to long-range encyclopedic surveys or national intelligence estimates. While the CIA has the general image as the home of "spooks and spies," many, perhaps most, of the CIA's employees work a 9-to-5 routine day as research analysts, much as in a university research institute or in a modern "think tank."

In contrast, the operations directorate, which once masqueraded under the label of "Plans" division, has carried out missions over the years that earned it the nickname of "Department of Dirty Tricks." During the mid-1950's, this branch of the CIA became the dominant one. Under its direction, the CIA manipulated the politics of Iran, Guatemala, and the Congo (Zaire) and intervened with money, technical skills, and weapons of violence in political systems around the world. Some of this covert activity was designed to control political events; other activities were for the purpose of espionage: stealing, buying, or otherwise obtaining information its holders wished to keep secret. Some covert operations were successful; some were not. Many will never be disclosed. But some of those that failed dramatically, such as the U-2 flight over the Soviet Union in May 1960, the Bay of Pigs fiasco in April 1961, and paramilitary missions in Laos began to create questions in the minds of various observers about the efficiency of the intelligence system and the adequacy of its command and control apparatus. But it was not until the Vietnam War and the events which came to be called "Watergate" in the early 1970s that Congress and the mass media began the aggressive questioning of CIA's policy organization and control mechanisms.

The CIA's science and technology division is responsible for developing new techniques for intelligence gathering and for monitoring the technological developments in other nations as they pertain to U.S. national security. CIA's administration division concerns itself with routine administrative housekeeping functions as well as with recruitment, training, archival and library services, and other management functions.

Beginning in the mid-1970s, a major reform effort was under way to change the policies, organization, and controls over the U.S. intelligence system. The CIA bore the brunt of adverse criticisms when post-Watergate exposures revealed that the agency had been involved in assassination plots against foreign leaders, interference in the domestic politics of Chile (and scores of other nations), spying on Americans at home in clear violation of its legislative charter prohibiting internal security functions, mail openings in defiance of federal law, and a variety of other scandals.

President Jimmy Carter based his 1976 campaign in part on a promise to deal with alleged CIA inefficiencies and abuses. Reorganizations had, in fact, taken place in the administrations of Presidents Richard Nixon and Gerald Ford. These were designed primarily to enforce more internal controls over intelligence operations. Reform had been accomplished primarily by Executive Order. And Congress, in its effort to reassert legislative oversight regarding foreign policy, amended the Foreign Assistance Act of 1974 to require that the CIA be used overseas only for intelligence-gathering purposes unless the President should notify appropriate committees of Congress that the national security required covert action and supplied these committees with details. But the most significant congressional reform action was the creation in both houses of special investigating committees in the mid-1970s. The Senate Committee, headed by Frank Church (Democrat, Idaho) and the House Committee, headed by Otis Pike (Democrat, New York), created an extensive record of hearings and reports, putting on public record far more details than ever before disclosed, and making extensive recommendations for reform of the intelligence system. But the most significant outcome of all of this legislative activity was the creation in both houses of permanent committees with substantial staffs to oversee intelligence activities. This was the most important single outcome of the years of controversy involving the intelligence system.

Yet after five years, many of the more basic issues remain unresolved. As of this writing, Congress and the executive branch remain locked in controversy and confrontation over intelligence policy. The winds which once blew heavily in the direction of reforms that would sharply circumscribe intelligence activities began to change direction in the late 1970s, and measures to protect the secrecy and security of intelligence operations came to the forefront. It was once widely assumed that the executive and Congress would hammer out a comprehensive "charter" that would spell out CIA's roles, functions, and restrictions.

Briefly, the major issues that have been raised over the intelligence question are as follows:

Congressional Supervision. A previously mentioned 1974 statute, known as the Hughes-Ryan amendment, required the President to notify Congress before the CIA engaged in any covert operations abroad. The law specified only the foreign affairs committees of the House and Senate, but six other congressional committees demanded consultation. Ultimately, a consensus evolved that eight potential watchdogs were too many. In the Intelligence Accountability Act of 1980, Congress reduced the number of committees to two: the House and Senate Intelligence Committees. This was perhaps the most important reform since 1947, for in 1980 Congress regained what it had given away—the statutory right of access to full information about secret intelligence activities. Ambiguities remain, to be sure, on the question of timing and completeness of presidential consultation with Congress, but the principle of accountability was clearly reestablished.

Presidential Responsibility. Should the President be required to approve personally all covert operations? The 1974 statute did so require, but efforts are under way to modify this law to require advance approval only for covert operations involving "substantial" risks and consequences. Hidden in this controversy is whether the traditional principle of "plausible denial" should be continued, a doctrine that in the past has allowed the executive branch to undertake secret operations—such as assassination of foreign leaders—and later deny the existence of such operations because they lacked official approval at the highest level. At issue is whether the principle of accountability should be reinstituted.

Freedom of Information. The Freedom of Information Act requires the CIA to respond to public requests for certain categories of information in CIA files. The CIA retains authority to withhold information about covert operations. Whether the CIA should have more complete authority to withhold information has remained at issue, and it appears that Congress remains unconvinced that it should grant such complete discretion.

Names of Agents. Widespread agreement has developed in Congress that CIA employees, past and present, should be prohibited, with criminal penalties, from revealing the names of secret agents. But many have wanted to extend penalties to anyone for revealing names or related information about secret operations. Such an extended liability would cover journalists and scholars, even if the information were obtained from nonsecret sources. This issue has aroused such controversy that compromise is likely.

Investigating Americans. By Executive Order in 1978, the President imposed restrictions on the CIA's authority to investigate Americans abroad and reiterated prohibitions against the CIA performing any internal security functions. Some have argued that these constraints are too narrow and have sought permissive legislation to allow, in some cases—with U.S. court orders—the CIA to spy on Americans, as well as others. This, too, has been a roadblock to enactment of comprehensive "charter" legislation for the CIA at the end of 1980.

Role of CIA Director. The CIA director is both head of the CIA and, as "director of central intelligence," the President's principal intelligence adviser. At issue for some years has been whether the director's powers should be increased so that he would, as the President's agent, be an intelligence "czar" over the entire system, with effective control over policy, requirements, resources, and estimates. At issue is whether the loose confederation of multiple, autonomous, intelligence agencies should come under more centralized direction. One suggestion has been to strengthen the power of the CIA director. Another has been to separate the CIA management from presidential advice and to create within the White House an intelligence "czar" who would oversee the best intelligence system for the President. The idea of an intelligence "czar" has lacked widespread support, and the continuation of the present CIA director's role seems likely, even if it promises a continuing struggle between civilian (CIA) elements and military (Department of Defense) forces for the control over resources, collection, and interpretation of information.

The CIA has confronted the United States with an organizational dilemma. Security for some intelligence operations requires a deep secrecy. Democratic government requires accountability and disclosure. Reconciling these conflicting requirements has proved to be so difficult in recent years that public policy has tended to be stalemated. Whatever solution is achieved will inevitably be a delicate balance between secrecy and disclosure.

FOR ADDITIONAL INFORMATION: Paul W. Blackstock and Frank L. Schaf, Jr., eds., *Intelligence, Espionage, Counterespionage and Covert Operations*, Vol. 2 in the International Relations Information Guide Series (1978), an annotated bibliography; Ray S. Cline, *Secrets, Spies and Scholars* (1976); William E. Colby and Peter Forbath, *Honorable Men: My Life in the CIA* (1978); Tyrus G. Fain, Katherine C. Plant, and Ross Milloy, eds., *The Intelligence Community* (1977); Morton H. Halperin, Jerry J. Berman, Robert L. Borosage, and Christine Marwick, *The Lawless State: The Crimes of the U.S. Intelligence Agencies* (1976); Thomas W. Powers, *The Man Who Kept the Secrets* (1979); Harry Howe Ransom, *The Intelligence Establishment* (1970); and U.S. Congress, Senate Select Committee to Study Governmental Operations with Respect to Intelligence Activities, *Final Report* (1976).

HARRY HOWE RANSOM

CHILDREN'S BUREAU. The idea of a federal government bureau dedicated to the welfare of children originated around 1903 with Lillian Wald, head of the Nurses' (later Henry Street) Settlement in New York City. Florence Kelley, secretary of the National Consumers' League, drew up a statement of the work the agency would do, and the National Child Labor Committee spearheaded a campaign for its establishment. Bills to found the bureau were first introduced in 1906; another bill introduced in 1909 was strongly endorsed by the White House Conference on Dependent Children and was recommended for passage by President Theodore Roosevelt. It was not until 1912, however, that a measure introduced by Senator William Borah of Idaho establishing a Children's Bureau in the Department of Commerce and Labor* passed both Houses of Congress and was signed into law by President William Howard Taft. The act directed the bureau to investigate and report upon "all matters pertaining to the welfare of children and child life among all classes of our people, and . . . especially [to] investigate the questions of infant mortality, the birth rate, orphanage, juvenile courts, desertion, dangerous occupations, accidents and diseases of children, employment, and legislation affecting children in the several States and Territories." In 1913, the Children's Bureau became a part of the new Department of Labor.* The statutory responsibilities assigned it in 1912 have never been repealed.

Julia Lathrop, chief of the bureau from 1912 to 1921, began operations with a staff of fourteen and an annual budget of $25,640. Low appropriations continued to be a problem throughout the terms of Lathrop and her successors,

Grace Abbott (1921-1934), Katharine Lenroot (1934-1951), Martha Eliot (1951-1957), and Katherine B. Oettinger (1957-1968). In 1935, when the bureau had been in existence for more than twenty years, Senator Gerald P. Nye pointed out that the annual appropriation for the Children's Bureau amounted to about one-thirteenth of the sum authorized by Congress for maintenance of horses owned by the National Guard. A decade and a half later, at the start of the 1950s, when appropriations for research in agricultural methods and techniques were at an all-time high, Congress decreed that the Children's Bureau could fill only one in every four positions vacated by resignation or retirement.

Infant mortality was the first question investigated by the bureau. The inquiry reversed the usual method of studying infant mortality, beginning with birth rather than death records and following each child through the first year of life or such portion of it as the baby lived. The first investigation, made in Johnstown, Pennsylvania, and published in 1915, was followed by similar studies in nine other industrial towns and cities. Each examined the social and economic circumstances of the babies' families, and all indicated a close connection between high infant mortality rates and low earning, poor housing, large families, and mothers' employment outside the home. The studies also assembled data on successful methods of reducing infant mortality.

In addition to scholarly monographs, the bureau published popular bulletins on prenatal care, infant care, child care, and related subjects. *Infant Care*, used as a guide by many parents, was first issued in 1914 and proved to be the Government Printing Office's best selling publication. By 1963, 48 million copies of *Infant Care* had been distributed. It was periodically revised to incorporate changing professional knowledge in areas such as child development, nutrition, and mental health. Comparison of the different editions provides an overview of twentieth-century attitudes toward child rearing.

In 1917, Lathrop advocated use of federal grants to states as a basis of federal-state cooperation in reducing maternal and infant death rates in the United States. Under the Sheppard-Towner Act enacted in 1921, the Children's Bureau administered federal grants-in-aid to the states for promotion of state programs for infant and maternal health. After the Sheppard-Towner Act lapsed in 1929, measures to restore the program were introduced in each session of Congress from 1930 to 1935. Efforts in the late 1920s to transfer the health activities of the Children's Bureau to the United States Public Health Service* failed in part because of strong support for the bureau demonstrated by delegates to the 1930 White House Conference on Child Health and Protection.

In 1934, Katharine Lenroot and Martha M. Eliot, chief and assistant chief, respectively, of the Children's Bureau, working with the bureau's Advisory Committee on Child Welfare, prepared a staff report called ''Security for Children'' for the President's Committee on Economic Security. The report contained three major program recommendations: (1) revival of the federal-state programs for maternal and child health but on a broader base than in the Sheppard-Towner Act and including services to crippled children; (2) federal grants to the states for the purpose of establishing, extending, and strengthening child welfare services for the protection of homeless, neglected, and dependent children and children in danger of becoming delinquent; and (3) a federal-state program of aid to dependent children who, without a breadwinner in the home, would not be benefited by economic recovery, unemployment insurance, or work relief programs. The third proposal was similar to the mothers' pension programs in effect in some states, but it required the program to be statewide and to be administered in a nondiscriminatory manner. Most of the recommendations contained in "Security for Children" were accepted by the Committee on Economic Security and incorporated in Titles IV and V of the Social Security Act, but the act assigned responsibility for administering Aid to Dependent Children to the Social Security Board rather than the Children's Bureau.

During and immediately after World War II, the Children's Bureau administered the Emergency Maternity and Infant Care (EMIC) Program, which provided payments for maternity care for wives of servicemen in the the four lowest pay grades (about three-fourths of the armed services) and medical, nursery, and hospital care for their infants up to one year of age. Between 1943 and 1949, when the program ended, care had been extended to approximately 1.5 million maternity and infant cases. At its peak, EMIC covered one out of seven births taking place in the United States. In assessing the program, in a 1949 issue the *American Journal of Public Health* declared that EMIC had not only benefited the mothers and infants it served, but had also raised the level of maternal and child care in entire areas of the country.

In 1945 and 1946, the Children's Bureau strongly backed the maternal and child welfare bill sponsored by Senator Claude Pepper (Democrat, Florida), which would have authorized larger grants to the states than available under Title V of the Social Security Act for maternal care, medical care for children, services for crippled children, and child welfare services. Congress failed to approve the Pepper bill but nearly doubled both authorization and appropriations for the Title V programs administered by the Children's Bureau. Authorizations for these programs were again increased in 1950, 1958, and 1960, but, in the 1950s, appropriations seldom approached the sums authorized to be expended.

Government reorganization plans of 1946 and 1953 moved the Children's Bureau first from the Department of Labor to the Federal Security Agency and then to the Department of Health, Education and Welfare (Department of Health and Human Services*). The changes placed the Children's Bureau on a lower administrative level and left the chief without direct contact with a Cabinet-level official. The 1946 reorganization also transferred responsibility for administering the child labor provisions of the Fair Labor Standards Act of 1938 from the bureau to the Department of Labor.

Beginning in 1948 and continuing until 1970, the Children's Bureau published *Research Relating to Children*, compiled annually by the Clearinghouse for Research in Child Life. During the 1950s, the bureau gave particular attention to juvenile delinquency; it held symposiums, issued reports, and conducted studies of many aspects of the problem. The Division of Juvenile Delinquency Services, established in 1954, assisted state and local agencies with technical services and review of care and treatment of delinquent youth in detention facilities and training schools, juvenile court and probation services, police services relating to juveniles, and training programs for careers in the field of treatment and prevention of juvenile delinquency. By the 1960s, in addition to preparation of manuals and reports on a wide variety of subjects relating to children and youth, the bureau sponsored numerous research and development projects in child welfare and supported service—as well as research-oriented project grants in maternal and child health.

During World War II and for a number of years thereafter, the Children's Bureau took the view that the first duty of a mother, especially one with young children, was in the home. Even under the pressure of demand for women workers in defense plants and war industries, the bureau continued to maintain that decisions as to the care of young children should be made in the light of the children's needs and that these needs should always be given primary emphasis.

In the 1960s, the Children's Bureau's insistence on the needs of children as paramount to all other considerations, its determination to consider the interest of the "whole child" rather than particular problems relating to one aspect of child behavior, and its allegiance to a strategy of helping families and children by providing services rather than simply by income assistance came under increasing attack from many sources. Both liberals and conservatives found fault with what critics called "the aging bureaucrats in the Children's Bureau." Others contended that the bureau had become so involved in program operations that it was no longer serving its original purpose as a staff agency concerned with problems of child life and promotion of new programs to meet them.

In 1969, the Nixon Administration transferred the Children's Bureau's operating functions in maternal and child health, child welfare, and delinquency services to other agencies. A new agency, the Office of Child Development (in the Department of Health and Human Services), received the remnants of the bureau and its continuing obligation to discharge the investigative and reporting functions outlined in the act of 1912. Subsequent reorganizations pushed the bureau lower in the administrative hierarchy. In 1981, the bureau consisted of only a small staff headed by an associate chief in the Administration for Children, Youth, and Families, which in turn was located in the Office of Human Development Services. The Children's Bureau continued to investigate and report on matters relating to the welfare of children, but it no longer exercised an important role in developing national policies for children.

FOR ADDITIONAL INFORMATION: Julia Lathrop's prospectus for the Children's Bureau appears in *Proceedings of the National Conference of Charities and Corrections, 1912* (1912), pp. 30-33. Concise accounts of the bureau's history appearing at different stages of its development are Grace Abbott, *Ten Years Work for Children* (1923); Dorothy E. Bradbury, *Five Decades of Action for Children, A History of the Children's Bureau* (1962); and Frederick Green, et al., eds., "Anniversary Issue: Sixty Years of Service to

Children: Children's Bureau 1912-1972," *Children Today* (March-April 1972). U.S. Children's Bureau, *The Story of Infant Care* (1963), relates the history of the bureau's most famous and popular publication. William Schmidt, M.D., ed., *Children's Bureau Publications* (1974), reprints and briefly assesses the importance of some of the bureau's landmark investigations of infant mortality, nutrition, and mental health. Katharine F. Lenroot and Martha M. Eliot, "Security for Children," in U.S. Committee on Economic Security, *Social Security in America* (1937), outlines the Children's Bureau recommendations for programs to be included in the Social Security Act. Robert H. Bremner, et al., eds. *Children and Youth in America, A Documentary History*, 3 vols. (1970-1974), contains numerous documents relating to the bureau's origin and activities. Gilbert Y. Steiner, *Social Insecurity: The Politics of Welfare* (1966), and *The State of Welfare* (1971), are representative of works critical of the Children's Bureau in the 1960s and 1970s.

ROBERT H. BREMNER

CIVIL AERONAUTICS BOARD (CAB). The Civil Aeronautics Board was founded on August 22, 1938, under the provisions of the Civil Aeronautics Act of 1938 (52 Stat. 973). Initially, the CAB was part of the Civil Aeronautics Authority which consisted of the board itself, an administrator, and a three-member Air Safety Board. Together, they were responsible for the economic and safety regulation of air commerce and transportation, the establishment and operation of airways and other navigational facilities, the development of airports, and issuance of airman, aircraft, and air-carrier operating certificates.

Presidential Reorganization Plans No. 3 and 4, effective June 30, 1940, changed the name of the Civil Aeronautics Authority to that of the Civil Aeronautics Board, abolished the Air Safety Board, and reassigned the administrator to the Department of Commerce* as head of the Civil Aeronautics Administration. In the process, the CAB retained its responsibilities for regulating economic activities, prescribing air safety regulations, and revoking and suspending safety certificates. In addition, it gained the Air Safety Board's responsibility for accident investigation.

The Federal Aviation Act of 1958 (72 Stat. 731) made no substantive changes in the board's economic regulatory responsibilities, but effective December 31, 1958, it transferred to the Federal Aviation Agency* (formerly the Civil Aeronautics Administration) the CAB's power to prescribe air safety regulations, and to revoke and suspend safety certificates. Furthermore, the Department of Transportation* Act (80 Stat. 931) transferred the CAB's accident investigation responsibilities to the newly created National Transportation Safety Board,* effective April 1, 1967. Thus, only the economic regulation of air transportation has been the responsibility of the CAB throughout its whole existence.

Following important hearings in early 1975 before the Subcommittee on Administrative Practice and Procedure of the Senate Committee on the Judiciary, several bills were introduced in Congress proposing changes in airline regulation as practiced since 1938. Considerable debate took place during 1975-1978, both within Congress and in other forums, concerning the actual economic effects of CAB regulation and the desirability of maintaining the existing regulation as opposed to decreasing or terminating regulation. The first change in government policy resulting from this debate occurred on November 9, 1977, with the enactment of Public Law 95-163 (91 Stat. 1278). Sections 16-18 of that act essentially eliminated regulatory barriers to entry into domestic and intraterritorial all-cargo operations, and substantially reduced the CAB's jurisdiction over air freight rates. Furthermore, Section 9 allowed the intrastate carriers operating wholly within California or Florida to interline (exchange) traffic with interstate and foreign air carriers, and to file joint fares and rates for such through service.

The second, and more pervasive, change in government policy occurred on October 24, 1978, with the adoption of the Airline Deregulation Act of 1978 (92 Stat. 1705). This act served to decrease regulation and to adopt competition as the major means of achieving policy objectives in air transportation. Not only was the board instructed to be permissive, rather than restrictive, in responding to airline initiatives regarding fares and entry/exit, but its regulatory powers were scheduled to be phased out over the following six years, with the board itself to be abolished, effective January 1, 1985. As a result, the CAB has achieved the distinction of being the first major federal regulatory commission to be legislated out of existence.

The Airline Deregulation Act of 1978 (ADA) clearly established a watershed in CAB regulation, with the procedures, policies, and effects of regulation being quite different during the forty years from 1938 to 1978 than they have been since 1978. Because of this major change, the next portion of this article will emphasize the 1938-1978 period. Then, after the board's achievements during this major portion of its existence have been described, the provisions and the initial effects of the ADA will be outlined.

The CAB has always consisted of five members, including the chairman, who is responsible for the board's overall operation, a vice-chairman, and three members. Members are appointed to six-year terms by the President, with the consent of the Senate, and no more than three can belong to the same political party. In recent years, the board has been supported by a staff of around eight hundred individuals who, during most of the 1970s, were organized into the following six major bureaus: Accounts and Statistics, Fares and Rates, Enforcement, International Aviation, Operating Rights, and Administrative Law Judges. In addition, there have been a number of staff units such as Comptroller, Personnel, Administrative Services, Equal Employment Opportunity, Secretary, General Counsel, Information, and Community and Congressional Relations.

The CAB, in common with other federal regulatory commissions in the United States, is considered to be an arm of Congress, charged with the expert and detailed implementation of the general policies contained in the enabling legislation. During most of its history, the board has had considerable latitude in its interpretation and implementation of this legislation. This independence, however, has not been limitless. Congress has been able to influence CAB practices on an ongoing basis through its power to review the board's budget proposal and to appropriate funds for CAB operations. Senate review of new appointees has been another source of congressional influence, and, of course, board members and staff have been required to appear before congressional committees to answer questions regarding board policies and actions.

The executive branch of the federal government has been able to exercise influence over the board through the President's power to appoint members and to designate the chairman each year. In addition, the President submits the board's annual budget to Congress only after it is reviewed by the Office of Management and Budget.*

Finally, the judicial branch of government has also influenced the CAB because board orders may be appealed to the federal courts of appeal, and "the court shall have exclusive jurisdiction to affirm, modify, and set aside the order complained of, in whole or in part, and if need be, to order further proceedings by the Board . . . " (72 Stat. 795).

Since 1946, all federal regulatory commissions, including the CAB, have operated under the provisions of the Administrative Procedures Act (60 Stat. 237). Consistent with the provisions of this law, the CAB established formal procedures similar to those of a court. A case of any importance was generally heard publicly by an administrative law judge, with formal presentation of evidence, rebuttal evidence and testimony, and with full cross-examination of witnesses. The recommended decision of the administrative law judge was then subject to written exceptions by the parties and intervenors participating in the case. The case was then submitted to the board, briefs and oral arguments presented, a written decision issued, petitions for reconsideration filed, and, finally, the termination of the case with the board's acceptance or rejection of those petitions (14 CFR 302, Subpart A). But then, as already mentioned, board decisions can be appealed to the federal courts of appeal. From start to finish, proceedings have commonly extended over a period of two or three years, and some cases have lasted as long as six years.

Since 1977, the CAB has been experimenting with expedited procedures utilizing such devices as show-cause orders and the direct submission of case records to the board without a recommended decision by an administrative law judge. In addition, the ADA has established various time constraints and abbreviated hearing procedures designed to decrease the elapsed time between application and final decision. In general, however, most cases of importance have been subject to long, intense, and repeated scrutiny by all interested parties prior to final decision.

Between 1938 and 1978, the CAB sought to promote air transportation while protecting the existing regulated airlines by limiting entry into the industry, setting or approving fares and rates that had to be adopted by all carriers, authorizing antitrust exemptions for intercarrier discussions and agreements, and paying direct subsidies to carriers serving points generating little traffic. The board was particularly successful in protecting the twenty-two airlines originally certificated under the "grandfather" provisions of the 1938 act. As of 1978, twelve of those airlines still existed, and the ten that terminated service did so solely through merger with (or acquisition by) one of the other original carriers. No CAB-regulated airline went bankrupt during those years.

An indication of the CAB's success in protecting the "grandfather" carriers while U.S. air transportation was enjoying great growth is provided by the following revenue data. In 1938, the original airlines accounted for 100 percent of the $58 million in total operating revenues earned by the industry, while during 1978 the twelve surviving carriers still accounted for 82.8 percent of the $19.7 billion total operating revenues earned that year by the CAB-regulated airlines plus the intrastate carriers. The remaining 17.2 percent of total revenues was divided among thirty-four other airlines that managed to enter the industry by offering specialized services or by serving small communities of little interest to the original carriers. Included in these airlines were the local service, all-cargo, supplemental, Alaskan, regional, helicopter, intrastate, and "other" carriers, plus a second Hawaiian carrier.

Estimates of the economic effects of CAB regulation have been obtained by comparing the performance of the CAB-regulated interstate airlines with that of the relatively small intrastate carriers that operated within California, Florida, and Texas through 1978. Because these intrastate carriers did not operate across state boundaries, they were not subject to CAB regulation, but they were subject to the limited or permissive regulation of state regulatory commissions. Since, however, the CAB-regulated airlines operated rival service between most of the city pairs served by the intrastate carriers, a regulatory duopoly existed within those states in contrast to the regulatory monopoly of the CAB over interstate, overseas, and foreign air transportation. As a result, there were two important differences in the economic environments within California, Florida, and Texas as opposed to the rest of the country. First, new carriers were able to enter and provide scheduled service with large aircraft that was fully comparable to the service operated by the CAB-regulated airlines. Second, price competition was possible because fares authorized by the state regulatory commissions could be (and were) lower than the nationwide fares that the CAB required all of its regulated airlines to adopt.

Major differences developed between the performance of the CAB-regulated airlines and that of the intrastate carriers. With regard to entry, new carriers did enter in each of the states, thereby indicating that CAB regulation served to reduce the number of carriers in existence within the United States. Furthermore, while some of these intrastate carriers were successful, others were not. In sharp contrast to the CAB-regulated airlines, however, none of the failing intrastate carriers was merged with or acquired by a surviving carrier. Some simply terminated operations and sold their assets. Others went bankrupt. This lack of merger or acquisition implies that from 1938 through 1978 the possession of a CAB certificate awarding operating rights over specified routes was the unique asset of an airline that was sufficient to guarantee acquisition or merger (rather than bankruptcy) if the carrier was unsuccessful.

With regard to fares, all of the CAB-regulated airlines adopted coach and first-class fares based on CAB-authorized fare formulas that yielded very high fares-per-mile for short distances and lower fares-per-miles for long trips. These CAB-authorized fares were as much as 100 percent higher than the fares-per-mile of the intrastate carriers for comparable service in identical city pairs. Furthermore, consistent with their high basic fares, the CAB-regulated airlines offered many more promotional fares than did the intrastate carriers, whose low general fares greatly reduced the profit-making potential of lowering fares on a discriminatory basis.

The operating expenses of the CAB-regulated airlines have also been much higher than those of the intrastate carriers. Therefore, despite their higher fares, the profits of the CAB-regulated airlines have been very similar to those of the successful intrastate carriers. During the hearings by the Subcommittee on Administrative Practice and Procedure, the CAB-regulated airlines argued that the differences in their performance and that of the intrastate carriers were due to special circumstances that benefited the intrastate carriers. The subcommittee's staff undertook a careful study of their explanation and concluded that, at best, the items specified by the CAB-regulated airlines could account for only a very small portion of the cost differences.

A recent comparison of the operating expenses of regulated airlines with those of the intrastate carriers found that the large cost differences resulted from major differences in labor, fuel, and aircraft utilization, together with differences in average payments to labor. With regard to labor, during 1978 the revenue ton-miles (RTM) per employee produced by the successful intrastate carriers were from 40 to over 100 percent higher than the average of regulated airlines, after adjusting for the effects of distance. Furthermore, the intrastate carriers' average payments per employee were generally 25 percent lower than those of the large, regulated trunk carriers. Combined, these two factors yielded operating expenses per employee for the successful intrastate carriers that were 35 to 63 percent lower than the average for the regulated airlines, again, after adjusting for the effects of distance. Since employee expenses accounted for about 39 percent of total operating expenses in 1978, these very much lower employee expenses contributed significantly to the intrastate carriers' lower total operating expenses.

In contrast to their lower average payments to employees, the intrastate carriers paid 1 to 2 percent more for fuel than was paid by the CAB-regulated airlines. However, even though they operated the same types of aircraft, they managed to produce from 5 to 32 percent more RTM per gallon of fuel than the average for the regulated airlines due, in part, to achieving appreciably higher load factors. Therefore, after adjusting for the effects of distance, their fuel expenses per RTM ranged from about 4 to 30 percent lower than the average for the CAB-regulated airlines. Since fuel expenses accounted for around 21 percent of total operating expenses in 1978, this was another important source of lower operating costs.

The greater utilization of inputs continued with aircraft. Not only did the intrastate carriers install up to 25 percent more seats in the identical aircraft than the CAB-regulated airlines, but they managed to fill between 62 to 71 percent of those seats with passengers, while the annual load factors of the CAB-regulated airlines generally fluctuated between 50 and 60 percent. Combined, higher seat densities and higher load factors increased aircraft utilization by around 35 percent, with an associated reduction in operating expenses per RTM.

The CAB-regulated airlines' lower utilization of employees, fuel, and aircraft can partly be attributed to the board's inability to allocate traffic among the regulated airlines. Over the years, in response to repeated applications by the existing carriers, the CAB authorized between two to ten of these carriers to operate in each of a large number of city pairs. However, because both the 1938 and 1958 acts specifically prohibited the CAB from controlling schedules and equipment (52 Stat. 973 and 72 Stat. 754), it had no effective way of allocating traffic among the rival carriers. Since all the carriers had to charge the same CAB-authorized fares, their efforts to achieve larger traffic shares turned to service-quality rivalry. As a result, each carrier purchased large numbers of ever newer aircraft which were then operated at high-schedule frequencies and low-seat densities until annual load factors fell to breakeven levels. Similar examples of cost-increasing carrier rivalry can be found in inflight services, ground handling, advertising, and so forth. Thus, operating expenses escalated together with fares, so that profits were generally no higher than normal profits elsewhere in the economy, including those of the low-fare intrastate carriers.

The provisions of the ADA demonstrate that by 1978 a majority of senators and congressmen believed the overall fare and service performance of the intrastate carriers was preferable to that of the CAB-regulated airlines, and that similar performance would develop nationwide with the reduction of regulation and the expansion of competition. Thus, the ADA included the following major provisions:

1. A new declaration of policy emphasizing competition as the means of achieving increased efficiency, greater innovation, lower prices, and a wider variety of price/service offerings to the public.

2. Liberalized entry, both of existing carriers into new routes and of new carriers into the industry. The termination of service was also made easier, but with provisions for the retention of "essential air service" for ten years (with subsidy if need be) at all points that were certificated to receive service on the date of the ADA's enactment. The board's authority over domestic routes was to be terminated effective December 31, 1981, leaving only questions of carrier fitness as its responsibility over entry.

3. Fare flexibility within a "zone of reasonableness" ranging from 50 percent below to 5 percent above the CAB's authorized standard industry fare level (SIFL). The board was allowed to expand this zone, and it did so in September 1980 with the elimination of the lower limit and with the upward boundary set at $15 above the SIFL level, plus 30 percent (CAB Regulation P-98). The board's authority over domestic fares expired on January 1, 1983.

4. Reduced antitrust authority over mergers, acquisitions of control, interlocking rela-

tionships, and agreements was more like that applicable to other industries. The power to grant immunity from antitrust laws was also reduced and was made discretionary rather than automatic. The power over mergers and interlocking relationships was to be transferred to the Department of Justice* effective January 1, 1983.

5. Termination of the subsidy program for local service carriers effective January 1, 1986, with modifications to the program allowed starting after January 1, 1983. In the meantime, a new subsidy program was to be established to guarantee the ten years of "essential air service" to all existing certificated points. This new subsidy program was designed to provide the essential air service while promoting competition among the carriers applying for the subsidy. This was in contrast to the existing subsidy program, which paid the residual operating expenses of the local service carriers in return for their providing monopoly service to a number of small points.

6. Finally, the "sunset" provision of the ADA terminates the board effective January 1, 1985, unless Congress takes action to continue its existence. On that date, the board's residual powers are to be transferred to the Departments of Justice, State,* and Transportation, and to the Postal Service.* As this is being written, proposals for an earlier phaseout of the CAB have been submitted to Congress, with the CAB itself suggesting termination effective October 1, 1983.

These provisions apply to domestic and overseas (territorial) air transportation. Foreign transportation was largely unchanged by the ADA, but the fundamental pro-competition policy of the ADA has since been applied to foreign air transportation through the International Air Transportation Competition Act of 1979 (94 Stat. 35), adopted February 15, 1980. Of course, all actions in the international arena are subject to agreements negotiated between the United States and individual foreign countries, so that entry, fares, and other factors will generally be more constrained in foreign than in domestic operations.

Full adjustment to the fundamental changes instituted by the ADA will take years to achieve. Therefore, the early performance of the CAB-regulated airlines (now including the former intrastate carriers) should not be considered a clear indication of the ultimate effects of airline deregulation. So far, the transitional performance of the domestic airlines has been mixed. The price competition allowed under fare flexibility has occurred largely in the form of short-term "sale" prices adopted by carriers entering new city pairs, and in the form of a multitude of discriminatory discount fares. These latter fares have been designed to attract discretionary travelers while requiring the nondiscretionary traveler to pay higher general coach fares which have risen substantially in most city pairs where service is still being provided by the original CAB-regulated airlines. The city pairs enjoying decreased coach fares tend to be those where new scheduled carriers have inaugurated service. These include the transcontinental city pairs now served by former supplemental carriers, and short-haul city pairs served by such new airlines as Midway (out of Chicago), New York Air (from New York), and People Express (from Newark), as well as by the expanded interstate operations of Southwest Airlines (out of Dallas). Of course, the effects of deregulation on fares have been obscured by the roughly 150-percent increase in fuel prices that occurred in the two years following the decontrol of aviation fuel prices in February 1979.

There have also been substantial changes in the route structures of the existing airlines. Many of these carriers have moved into new city pairs and have changed their levels of service in other city pairs, while terminating service at small communities with low traffic volume. The termination of service at small communities is not a new phenomenon, however, having been a frequent occurrence under CAB-regulation as the introduction of larger aircraft made service to small communities unprofitable to the trunk and local service carriers, thereby causing these carriers to apply for service suspensions. Furthermore, the large increase in fuel prices has reinforced this move away from serving small communities with large aircraft. At the same time, replacement service by commuter carriers operating smaller aircraft has also occurred. In most cases, such service replacement has taken place without resort to federal subsidies under the "essential air service" program.

It is unusual to be able to review the life of a government agency from its inception to virtually its termination, but this can now be done for the CAB. Existing evidence demonstrates that the main effects of CAB regulation from 1938 to 1978 were to promote the interests of the original "grandfather" carriers and to decrease the entrance of new carriers into this rapidly growing industry. The resulting high fares, high service quality, and high operating costs were judged to be less desirable than the more efficient, lower-quality service produced by the intrastate carriers at much lower fares. The performance of the intrastate carriers is expected in time to spread among the other U.S. carriers under the pro-competitive policy of the Airline Deregulation Act.

With the enactment of ADA, Congress instigated a major experiment that will identify the effectiveness of deregulation. The experience of the U.S. airlines under deregulation will doubtless have a major impact on the degree of regulation to which other industries will be subjected in the future, both in the United States and in other countries.

FOR ADDITIONAL INFORMATION: George W. Douglas and James C. Miller III, *Economic Regulation of Domestic Air Transport: Theory and Policy* (1974); and William A. Jordan, "Airline Performance Under Regulation: Canada vs. the United States," *Research in Law and Economics* 1 (1979): 35-79, *Airline Regulation in America: Effects and Imperfections* (1970), and *Performance of Regulated Canadian Airlines in Domestic and Transborder Operations* (1981).

Useful governmental publications include: U.S. Civil Aeronautics Board, *Aeronautical Statutes and Related Material*, Revised June 1, 1954 (1954); *Civil Aeronautics Board Reports to Congress*, Fiscal Years 1968-1978 (1968-1979); *Handbook of Airline Statistics*, 1973 ed. (1974); *Report on Airline Service, Fares, Traffic, Load Factors, and Market Shares, Service Status on February 1, 1981*, 14 (April 1981); *Supplement to the Handbook of Airline Statistics*, 1977-1978 ed. (1979); and U.S. Senate, *Civil Aeronautics Board Practices and Procedures*, Report of the Subcommittee on Administrative Practice and Procedures of the Committee on the Judiciary of the United States Senate (1975).

WILLIAM A. JORDAN

CIVILIAN CONSERVATION CORPS (CCC). The Civilian Conservation Corps was created in March 1933, during the initial frantic "hundred days" of Franklin Delano Roosevelt's New Deal. It was the first of a number of agencies designed to cope with one of the most urgent and poignant of the social problems caused by the Great Depression, that of massive unemployment among youth. It is impossible to gauge with any accuracy just how many young Americans were without jobs in the first months of 1933, but the best estimate would be that more than 50 percent of young people between the ages of fifteen and twenty-four, and who were in the labor market, were either totally or partially unemployed. Of these, more than 250,000 had given up all pretense of a settled existence and were simply drifting about the country—the boy and girl tramps of America, as the writer Thomas Minehan called them. Millions more were mired in poverty, apathy, and hopelessness. The new President, who had talked so much in his recent election campaign of his faith in the future, would clearly have to do something to prevent further scarring of the generation that would inherit it.

There was need, too, to deal with scars of a very different kind, the havoc which generations of waste and ill-usage had wreaked on the American landscape. Wanton forest destruction and the resultant soil and wind erosion had created a problem of extreme seriousness, one which the new President, with his life-long interest in conservation, was determined to check. The Civilian Conservation Corps, then, was in one sense a catalyst: two wasting resources, young men and land, were brought together in an attempt to save both.

The idea of putting young men to work in the woods was scarcely a new one. The philosopher William James had advocated it, and various European governments had established conservation camps for the unemployed. Yet, of all the New Deal agencies, it bore President Roosevelt's personal stamp on it, expressing both his profoundly Jeffersonian belief that a rural existence was the best of all possible worlds, and his concern to stop the destruction of America's natural resources. He outlined his plans during the election campaign, and, immediately upon inauguration, moved to put them into effect. The enabling legislation quickly passed both Houses of Congress, and, on March 31, the bill was signed into law. The CCC was born.

The organizational structure of the new agency was extremely simple. Because the prime need was for speed to meet the emergency, it was decided to work as far as possible through existing federal departments, rather than set up a completely new line structure. The young men selected were required to come from relief rolls and to be between eighteen and twenty-five years of age; they were to be enrolled in camps of 200 each. They were to be put to work on conservation tasks and would be paid $30 monthly, $25 of which would be sent home to their families. Their initial period of enrollment was to be six months, renewable for up to two years. The Department of Labor* was given the job of selecting the enrollees, the War Department* of transporting them to the camps and administering these, and the Departments of Agriculture* and the Interior* of supervising the actual work projects. Coordinating the enterprise was a director and a small central office staff. In his search for someone to head the new agency, the President was somewhat circumscribed by the fact that the American Federation of Labor had evinced disquiet at the proposed wage scales. Anxious to mollify this body, he decided to appoint a prominent labor leader to the top position, and the man eventually selected was Robert Fechner. Fechner, a Southerner, a long-time member of the International Association of Machinists and a vice-president of the AF of L, held the position until his death, in 1939, and was succeeded by his deputy, James J. McEntee, also of the Machinists Association. A self-educated man, Fechner had little in common with the bulk of Roosevelt's advisers and department heads, but, in general, he ran the enterprise well.

Quickly, the various departments began their tasks. There were the inevitable teething troubles and administrative confusions; yet, given the scale of the enterprise, the initial mobilization proceeded with surprising smoothness. By July 1, a total of 274,375 young men had been enrolled and were already at work in 1,300 camps throughout the land. The provisions of the CCC had been extended, too, to two special groups in the population. On April 14, it was decided to enroll 14,400 American Indians in the corps, and a month later Roosevelt directed that 250,000 World War I veterans should also be included, regardless of their ages. President Herbert Hoover had dispersed the "Bonus Army" of 1932 with guns and bayonets; the approach of the new President was different. When the second "Bonus Army" arrived in May, its members were offered, rather than violence, the chance to work in the woods. Then, it had also been agreed that local woodsmen should be attached to the various camps, partly because their experience was needed but partly, also, to avoid trouble from them. Nearly twenty-five thousand were so employed.

After the hectic first months of organization, the succeeding period of the corps's existence was one of consolidation. Certain significant policy developments occurred, however, easily the most important of which was the decision to develop an educational program for the enrollees. This program arose initially from discussions between presidential adviser Louis Howe and George F. Zook, federal commissioner for education, and, though opposed at first by the Army authorities, it eventually became a going proposition. A director of CCC education was appointed in December 1933, responsible for the organization and administration of a thoroughgoing education program in the camps. It was hard work; yet, its success can be measured by the fact that within three years 35,000 illiterates had been taught to read and write, and 1,000 high school diplomas and 39 college degrees had been issued. CCC education was a success.

It came as no surprise, given the CCC's initial successes and his own commitment to it, that the President decided in January 1934 both to continue its operation and to permit some expansion. This was to be the pattern over the next two years. The corps grew steadily in size, reaching its highest point in September 1935 with 502,000 enrollees in 2,514 camps. From then on the numbers were reduced, mainly because of the creation in that year of a second youth organization, the National Youth Administration* (NYA), but also because the President, concerned at the cost, wished to make some reductions in the interests of economy. He was not always able to do so, however, often through congressional pressure. The CCC had very quickly become a congressional favorite. The camps were generally popular in the areas where they were established, and any suggestion of closing them usually resulted in pressure on the local Representative, which in turn became pressure on the President. In March 1936, for example, Democratic House leaders prevented a proposed reduction by petitioning Roosevelt, and there were similar protests whenever camp closings were suggested.

Such congressional pressure was one manifestation of an obvious fact. The CCC had clearly become, in the words of Rexford Tugwell, too popular for criticism. Almost alone of the New Deal agencies it enjoyed wide, bipartisan support. The reasons were many. It was obviously popular with the enrollees themselves and with their families, for it put flesh on young bones, enlarged horizons, and put money in people's pockets. Then, as has been stated, it was popular in the camp locality. The camps were normally established close to a village or small town, and their very presence was an economic shot in the arm for such communities. Each camp spent between $5,000 and $10,000 monthly in the local market and made some use of local labor. Thus, the economic "booster," which the CCC gave, could be crucial to the economic recovery of these places and explains the protests at camp closings. It explains, too, congressional determination to prevent these whenever possible. The CCC, however, was also popular with millions of ordinary Americans who would probably never see a camp or receive any direct benefits from it. They liked its image, they could easily accept the value of the work performed, and the idea of young men going out to work with their hands in the wilderness appealed to the romantic and nostalgic imagination of a nation whose President had recently announced that the last frontier had been closed. Though not everyone favored the corps— some liberals, for example, profoundly distrusted the military presence in the camps—it remains true that of the myriad New Deal creations, it was easily the most popular.

Within its frame of reference, it was also extraordinarily effective. Though associated in the public mind with tree planting, the CCC enrollees were involved in much more than simple reforestation. CCC youths fought fires, developed camping grounds and trails, improved grazing lands, developed soil-erosion projects, protected wildlife, constructed flood-control schemes, and even preserved and restored historical sites. Nevertheless, reforestation was the CCC's most important single function, and it is difficult to overestimate its contribution here. Indeed, of all the trees planted on public lands from 1776 to 1942, more than 75 percent were planted by the corps. If it was best known for its reforestation work, the reason is in this single statistic. But the CCC conserved human beings, too, as well as the landscape. The enrollees overwhelmingly benefited physically from the experience, but they also returned home with a far greater knowledge of their country—many of them, after all, traveled halfway across the continent to go to camp as much of the work was done in the West—and new hope for the future. The experiment clearly had proved a resounding success.

Despite the corps's popularity and its proven effectiveness, there were some areas of concern. The desertion rate, which normally ran around 10 percent, was too high. Most who left did so in their first few days in camp, no doubt because of homesickness and the unfamiliarity of a disciplined existence, and in that sense there was little that could be done to prevent them from going. Nevertheless, the problem was one of continuing bother to corps officials. There was some concern, too, about the agency's cost. It took $1,004 to keep an enrollee in a CCC camp for a year as opposed to $314 annually for an NYA enrollee. The cost factor was the main reason why Roosevelt, despite his great pride in the agency, tried from time to time to reduce its size. Then, there were inevitable points of disagreement between the cooperating federal departments, especially between the Interior and Agriculture, the product of a long history of interdepartmental rivalry. These, however, never seriously disrupted the CCC's work.

To many, the CCC's most serious shortcoming lay in its treatment of black enrollees. The act of March 1933, which gave it legal existence, contained a clause that there should be no discrimination "on account of race, color or creed" in the selection of enrollees. Yet, within a few weeks it was distressingly clear that its provisions were being systematically ignored by Southern selection agents. Blacks, probably the most desperately poor group in the United States and the group most in need of relief, were simply being passed over in county after county. It took a lot of pressure from Department of Labor officials before Southern relief directors moved reluctantly to select some blacks. Moreover, local communities were more often than not less than happy to have a black camp stationed near them—and this was a national and not merely a Southern problem. Indeed, what glimpses of moderation there were on this issue tended to come from the South. Gradually, a policy evolved. There was to be strict segregation in the CCC, blacks were not to be sent out of their home states, black camps were not to be forced on reluctant communities, and blacks were to be selected according to their ratio in the general population, 1 in 10. Fechner, himself a Southerner, had no desire to use his agency as an agent of social change, and though many blacks clearly benefited from their time in the corps, it never provided them with the degree of relief their general economic condition might have suggested was their due. Blacks within the corps were not allowed the latitude of movement accorded white enrollees, command in black camps was firmly retained in white hands, and there was never any attempt, in contrast with the corps' sister agency, the NYA, to move against prevailing racial attitudes. For this, its Southern-born director was primarily responsible.

In January 1937, President Roosevelt, acting on a campaign promise, recommended that the CCC become a permanent agency of government, and in

March legislation to that effect was introduced. The hearings on the bill revealed a strong body of bipartisan support for the agency, but an equally strong reluctance to grant it permanency. Eventually, it was extended for three years only, an action that was interpreted as a slap in the face for the President, given his personal involvement with the agency, and that, in part, might have reflected congressional disenchantment with Roosevelt's plan to reform the Supreme Court, then the dominant issue of the day. The CCC was never to attain the permanent status which FDR so desired, and, indeed, from 1937 on, the corps began slowly to lose importance. Finally, presidential attempts to reduce its numbers succeeded. By 1939, its strength had declined to 300,000 men in 1,500 camps, and this trend was accelerated once the outbreak of World War II and the resultant demand for munitions and materiel began at last to soak up the vast pockets of unemployment, which had stubbornly persisted throughout the 1930s. Although McEntee, who succeeded Fechner as director in 1939, moved aggressively to mesh the CCC's activities in with the nation's defense needs, its continued existence began to be called into question, especially after Pearl Harbor and the need to justify all government spending in terms of its relevance to winning the war.

In 1941, Congress created a Joint Committee on Non-Essential Federal Expenditures and charged it with recommending the elimination of all federal agencies not considered essential to the war effort. One of the first to come under its purview was the CCC. In late December 1941, the committee recommended its abolition, and though the President fought hard for what was always known as his "pet project," the mood for economy was too strong to resist. In June 1942, after a floor fight, the Senate concurred in an earlier House resolution to provide no further funds for the agency. The CCC was dead.

Dead it may have been, but forgotten it certainly was not. In eulogizing it, the *New Republic* said that through its soil and forest conservation it had added to the national wealth far more than the sums spent on it, even if one overlooks the benefits on the health and morale of otherwise jobless young men. In its nine-year existence, nearly 3 million young men passed through this makeshift, temporary organization. Given the fact that the United States was now at war, they had received valuable experience of military life on which the Army was able to build in the critical years ahead. More importantly, in the billions of trees they planted or protected, the parks and recreation areas they developed, the millions of acres they saved from soil erosion or flooding, they had provided a legitimate contribution to the heritage of every American. Arthur M. Schlesinger, Jr., once wrote of the CCC that it had left its monuments in the preservation and purification of the land, the water, the forests, and the young men of America. The judgment was apt.

FOR ADDITIONAL INFORMATION: In addition to the CCC official records in the National Archives,* the reader should consult Charles P. Harper, *The Administration of the Civilian Conservation Corps* (1939); Kenneth Holland and Frank E. Hill, *Youth in the CCC* (1942); George P. Rawick, "The New Deal and Youth: The Civilian Conservation Corps, the National Youth Administration and the American Youth Congress" (Ph.D.

dissertation, University of Wisconsin, 1957); John J. Saalberg, "Roosevelt, Fechner and the CCC—A Study in Executive Leadership" (Ph.D. dissertation, Cornell University, 1962); John A. Salmond, *The Civilian Conservation Corps 1933-1942: A New Deal Case Study* (1967); and Conrad L. Wirth, *The Civilian Conservation Corps Program of the United States Department of the Interior* (1944).

JOHN SALMOND

CIVIL SERVICE COMMISSION. See Office of Personnel Management.

COAST AND GEODETIC SURVEY. See National Ocean Survey.

COAST GUARD. See United States Coast Guard.

COMMERCE COMMISSION. See Interstate Commerce Commission.

COMMERCE DEPARTMENT. See Department of Commerce.

COMMISSION ON CIVIL RIGHTS. See United States Commission on Civil Rights.

COMMISSION ON INDUSTRIAL RELATIONS. See United States Commission on Industrial Relations.

COMMISSION ON THE ORGANIZATION OF THE EXECUTIVE BRANCH. See Hoover Commissions, Commissions on the Organization of the Executive Branch of the Government, 1947-1949, 1953-1955.

COMMITTEE ON FAIR EMPLOYMENT PRACTICES (FEPC). The Committee on Fair Employment Practices was the first federal agency authorized to implement a government-wide policy of nondiscriminatory employment and training. It was established shortly before U.S. entry into World War II by President Franklin D. Roosevelt (Executive Order 8802, 6 Fed. Reg. 3109, June 25, 1941). The order declared it the policy of the United States "to promote the full and equitable participation of all workers in defense industries, without discrimination because of race, creed, color or national origin."

The significance of the FEPC extends much beyond its nominal five-year life span. Its underlying principle of equal opportunity differed from current affirmative action policies and practices, but the FEPC initiated and fostered federal and then state governmental actions on behalf of fair employment for minorities. And the organizational politics which reshaped the historic Negro protest in forming the movement for FEPC presaged a new phase in the efforts to weld American blacks into a cohesive force on behalf of their civil rights.

The defense period just prior to American entry into World War II is fundamental, because it was then that Negro political activity was forced into independent action. During the Great Depression of the 1930s, Negro politics were essentially New Deal politics. With the defense boom Negroes were left behind by the general white citizenry. Negroes remained unemployed and on relief in large numbers for some time after the general economic situation markedly improved, and former allies, the white liberal organizations, became preoccupied with the war crisis along with the Roosevelt Administration. Under these circumstances, a new phenomenon appeared—the spontaneous involvement of large numbers of blacks in successful political protest without the collaboration of whites. Following the war, the Negro-white liberal alliance was reconstituted, but the earlier period of independent action profoundly altered that collaboration and from its seed grew contemporary assertions of Black Power.

Pressure politics strongly influenced President Franklin D. Roosevelt to issue Executive Order 8802 as interest-group tactics have impacted on policymakers throughout American history. However, the threat to rally black Americans for a mass march on Washington marked a departure from conventional lobbying methods. True, "direct action" demonstrations were not unique, as earlier evidenced by the 1932 Bonus Army march on Washington of World War I veterans. Similarly, the struggle for women's suffrage had been marked by marches and other militant tactics to dramatize that movement's pressure politics. Nonetheless, A. Philip Randolph's stirring call was notable.

Randolph, head of the Brotherhood of Sleeping Car Porters, evoked a strong response both from those on whom he called to join the march as well as from the targeted Roosevelt Administration. Randolph's bold threat was made during the early stages of World War II when Negroes, after years of depression, sought to share in the "defense-period's" expanded employment opportunities. America's self-proclaimed posture as the "Arsenal of Democracy" in arming the free world for its defense against the Nazi juggernaut seemed hypocritical in the face of discriminatory practices against its own ethnic minorities. The official organ of the National Association for the Advancement of Colored People (NAACP) editorialized in its March 1941 issue that its readers questioned whether "there is a great deal of difference between the code for Negroes under Hitler and the code for Negroes under the United States of America—the leading democratic nation in the world."

The context for desperate feelings of alienation from their country at a time of national emergency went beyond exclusion from defense jobs. The indignities of racial segregation cut deeper than ever, especially in the armed forces, at a time when democratic principles were emphasized. Negro morale was desperately low, and they made little effort to hide their dissatisfaction. Randolph's call for a national march on Washington "for jobs and justice" met with a growing response, and his claimed response of 10,000 potential marchers escalated to 50,000 and then to 100,000.

How many black marchers would in fact have descended on Washington will never be known. The march was called off when President Roosevelt established the first Fair Employment Practices Committee less than a week before the march was to take place. Thus, an international embarrassment was averted and a unique governmental agency was established.

As always, the conflict between organized interests favoring and opposing governmental action on behalf of civil rights did not cease with the establishment of the FEPC. And, too, apart from the continuation of conflicting group politics, especially in the Congress, the Roosevelt Administration was necessarily interested in preventing disruptions unfavorable to a united war effort. There were limits beyond which the administration could not press recalcitrant legislators from districts and regions opposed to governmental action on behalf of civil rights. In accepting its Final Report, President Harry S Truman complimented the FEPC for having performed an important war service task of great difficulty and delicacy, capably even under a continuous barrage of criticism and harassment. Proclaimed equality of opportunity in employment became something more than platitudinous piety as the FEPC began its difficult administrative assignment in 1941.

Such authority as the first national FEPC had derived from the constitutional powers of the presidency. The wartime crisis in which President Roosevelt issued his Executive Orders establishing and charging the FEPC brought added weight to presidential directives, particularly where governmental officials and contractors were the objects of compliance. Yet, even in a national emergency, presidential power is limited. Reflecting on the five years of FEPC endeavors to implement its assignment, Chairman Ross urged President Truman to work for a legislatively sanctioned agency. "Executive authority is not enough to insure compliance in the face of stubborn opposition. Only legislative authority will assure compliance in the small number of cases in which employers or unions or both refuse after negotiation to abide by the National policy of nondiscrimination" (FEPC, *Final Report*, 1946, p. v).

Without statutory sanctions, the FEPC's ability to influence the employment practices of government agencies and defense contractors depended on moral suasion, negotiation, public hearings entailing possibly embarrassing publicity, and citations of uncompromising offenders to the President. Under the 1941 Executive Order, the first FEPC was empowered to investigate complaints, to take undefined "appropriate steps" to resolve the problem, and to make recommendations to governmental agencies. A staff of eight members was located in the Office of Production Management. No regional offices were established, though the committee, appointed on July 19, 1941, moved rapidly with its first public hearing in Los Angeles (October 20-21, 1941). Subsequent hearings were held in Chicago (January 19-20, 1943), New York (February 16-17, 1943), and Birmingham, Alabama (June 18-20, 1943).

But on July 30, President Roosevelt placed the FEPC under the jurisdiction of the War Manpower Commission (WMC). The mythical independence of the FEPC, now an "organizational entity" within the WMC, collapsed when the WMC chairman, Paul McNutt, exerted his "supervisory" authority and "indefinitely postponed" the FEPC's scheduled hearings on discriminatory employment policies by the railroads. It is not coincidental that A. Philip Randolph's colleague in the Brotherhood of Sleeping Car Porters, Milton Webster, was chairman of the FEPC subcommittee, which had summoned the railroad companies to respond publicly to charges of racial discrimination in their hiring practices.

Negro leaders were dismayed, and resignations by several committee and staff members highlighted a renewed and vigorous protest. President Roosevelt responded with a new directive reconstituting the FEPC in the Executive Office of the President (Executive Order 9346, 8 Fed. Reg. 7183, May 27, 1943). A full-time paid chairman and six part-time members representing industry, labor, and the public were appointed. Its purview was broadened from "defense" industries to all government contractors, plus governmental agencies involved with war-production training and employment. Union membership, as well as job discrimination, was also covered. Moreover, it was not limited to resolving complaints brought by specifically aggrieved individuals. The Executive Order empowered the FEPC to conduct hearings, make findings of fact, and take appropriate steps to eliminate such discrimination. Substantially enlarged funding enabled the committee to open 15 regional offices and to employ some 120 staff professionals.

During its five years, the FEPC settled nearly five thousand cases by negotiation, including some forty racially triggered strikes. In the last year of the war, it held 15 public hearings and settled 1,191 out of 3,485 cases without public controversy. About 25 percent of the caseload involved alleged discrimination by governmental hiring officials. Most complaints concerned black workers, but discrimination against Mexican Americans and Jews was also significant. The purview of the wartime FEPC did not extend to discrimination on grounds of sex.

Although subsequent Executive Orders were aimed at discrimination in the federal Civil Service and by contractors with the government, it was not until 1964 that Congress enacted fair employment legislation. State FEPC laws, first established in New York in 1945, also became increasingly common. But recent federal efforts on behalf of equal employment opportunities for minorities, women, and other historically disadvantaged groups have transformed public policy and its administration. Earlier concepts of equal opportunity for all derived from a "color blind" Constitution (in Justice John M. Harlan's phrase, dissenting from the court's "separate but equal" doctrine in *Plessy* v. *Ferguson*, 1896). Currently, government pursues and requires "affirmative action" to eliminate patterns of discrimination measured by statistical evidence of disproportionate representation of historically excluded minorities and females in an occupational grouping. (See article on Equal Employment Opportunity Commission.*)

FOR ADDITIONAL INFORMATION: Of the voluminous sources available, the reader might consider these selected titles. For socioeconomic issues: H. R. Cayton and G. S. Mitchell, *Black Workers and the New Unions* (1939); L. J. Greene and C. G. Woodson, *The Negro Wage Earner* (1930); Dale L. Hiestand, *Economic Growth and Employment*

Opportunities for Minorities (1964); Herbert Hill, "The Racial Practices of Organized Labor—In the Age of Gompers and After," *New Politics* 4 (1965): 26–46; and Leslie H. Fishel, "The Negro in the New Deal Era," in Bernard Sternsher, ed., *The Negro in Depression and War* (1969).

Protest politics could be studied in Jervis Anderson, *A. Philip Randolph* (1972); Brailsford R. Brazeal, *The Brotherhood of Sleeping Car Porters* (1946); Herbert Garfinkel, *When Negroes March: The March on Washington Movement in the Organizational Politics for FEPC* (1959); Louis C. Kesselman, *The Social Politics of FEPC* (1948); and August Meier and Elliott Rudwick, *Along the Color Line* (1976).

Many additional sources exist among the FEPC reports, congressional hearings, and law journals.

HERBERT GARFINKEL

COMMUNICATIONS COMMISSION. See Federal Communications Commission.

CONRAIL. See United States Railway Association and Consolidated Rail Corporation.

CORPS OF ENGINEERS. See United States Army Corps of Engineers.

COUNCIL OF ECONOMIC ADVISERS (CEA). The Council of Economic Advisers was created in 1946 when President Harry S Truman signed the legislation (Public Law 304, Seventy-ninth Congress) which created it. The intent of the legislation was as follows:

The Congress declares that it is the continuing policy and responsibility of the Federal Government to use all practicable means consistent with its needs and obligations and other essential considerations of national policy, with the assistance and cooperation of industry, agriculture, labor, and State and local governments, to coordinate and utilize all its plans, functions, and resources for the purpose of creating and maintaining, in a manner calculated to foster and promote free competitive enterprise and the general welfare, conditions under which there will be afforded useful employment opportunities, including self-employment, for those able, willing, and seeking to work, and to promote maximum employment, production, and purchasing power.

The legislation provided for the appointment of a three-person council to advise the President and to assist him in preparing the *Economic Report of the President*, a major state paper.

SEC. 4. (a) There is hereby created in the Executive Office of the President a Council of Economic Advisers (hereinafter called the "Council"). The Council shall be composed of three members who shall be appointed by the President, by and with the advice and consent of the Senate, and each of whom shall be a person who, as a result of his training, experience, and attainments is exceptionally qualified to analyze and interpret economic developments, to appraise programs and activities of the Government in the light of the policy declared in section 2, and to formulate and recommend national economic policy to promote employment, production, and purchasing power under free competitive enterprise. The President shall designate one of the menbers of the Council as Chairman.

Although, of course, the President had been free to seek advice and counsel on economic matters from any source he chose, the Employment Act, as a new departure, formalized the machinery for this purpose. To be sure, the President is not required to listen to the council, much less act on its advice, but in a complex world such services have proven useful.

While the legislation required the President to appoint persons who by training and background would be suited for such a task, no specific requirements were laid down. One of the members is designated chairman and thus acts as spokesman for the group and as executive officer. In the early years, there was some difficulty as to the precise authority of the chairman, but the adoption of Reorganization Plan No. 9 in 1953 clarified the issue. The more than thirty persons who have served as council members since 1946 have represented varying views. None has failed to win confirmation, and the council menbers have worked in a generally harmonious fashion.

The act requires the President to issue in January each year an economic report (prepared by CEA), and this document is transmitted to the Joint Economic Committee (JEC), also created by the act of 1946. The JEC reviews the report and makes congressional response, holds hearings, and so on. Thus, the legislative branch has input into the process, a fact that has proven to be of great value. The *Economic Report of the President* has wide circulation and is much commented on by the press and widely read by the business community.

The council has a relatively small staff and makes maximum use of data produced by other federal agencies and private research groups. By its nature, the council is closely related to the presidency and has over the years reflected the fortunes and misfortunes of the various administrations. Some controversy arose in the early years as to how strongly the council should support or advocate administration policies as opposed to restricting itself to confidential advice. In fact, this problem led to the resignation of the first chairman, Edwin G. Nourse, in 1949. More recently, this question has faded and for the most part has not troubled those involved.

The council has no monopoly on economic advice or control over policy-making. The senior administration officials in the economic area, the Secretary of the Treasury,* the chairman of the Federal Reserve Board,* and the director of the Office of Management and Budget,* for example, are line officers who play at least as important a role as that assumed by the CEA chairman.

Personal rapport has been a large factor. Presidents have little time for discourse, and advisers who manage to get the presidential ear are apt to be those with whom he is personally compatible. Each President, of course, chooses the members of the council so as to reflect his (or his advisers') economic views, and most of the members come from the ranks of academic economists. The council is one of the smallest federal agencies, with a total staff of no more than twenty or thirty persons. Most observers agree that the council and the Joint Committee have been effective during the years of their existence, and that while there have been high points and low points, the Employment Act has been a successful piece of legislation.

While most of the attention has been focused on the council, the JEC has played a major role. One of the most important functions of the JEC (which has to some degree evolved more or less by accident) is that of public education. Over the years, the JEC has held countless hearings on economic issues, reviewed the *Economic Report*, and issued hundreds of economic studies. These have enjoyed wide circulation and have been of considerable value in informing the public (and, indeed, the Congress) on complex issues.

For an act in force for thirty years, the Employment Act has been surprisingly durable. Few suggestions for change have been made, and still fewer changes have been enacted. In 1949, the Hoover Commission* recommendations for administrative change were made (lodging more authority in the chairman), but the act was not changed in any basic way. From time to time, it has been suggested that the goal of "reasonable price stability" be incorporated into the act. So far organized labor has successfully opposed this proposal.

In 1966, amid the wage-price guidepost difficulties, Representative Henry S. Reuss of Wisconsin proposed that the guideposts be codified and that the CEA would be required to transmit them each January 20th to the Joint Economic Committee for approval. The CEA figures would remain in effect unless Congress changed them. At this time, there was also some consideration of a permanent type of wage-price agency. Neither idea survived.

In the early part of Richard Nixon's second term, his domestic counsel, John Erlichman, suggested an executive branch reorganization, which would create several "super Cabinet" posts, including one devoted to economics. This proposal was lost in "Watergate," but apparently it would have interposed a layer of authority between the CEA and the President.

In the Ninety-fourth Congress, Senator Hubert H. Humphrey of Minnesota and Congressman Augustus F. Hawkins of California introduced legislation to define unemployment at 3 percent of the labor force and to provide public jobs for those unable to obtain private employment. This proposal was adopted after a great deal of "watering down" in 1978. Otherwise the act remains little changed.

FOR ADDDITIONAL INFORMATION: Stephen K. Bailey, *Congress Makes a Law* (1950); Edward S. Flash, Jr., *Economic Advice and Presidential Leadership* (1965); and Hugh S. Norton, *The Employment Act and the Council of Economic Advisers* (1977).

HUGH S. NORTON

CUSTOMS SERVICE. See United States Customs Service.

_D_

DEBT BUREAU. See Bureau of Public Debt.

DEFENSE DEPARTMENT. See Department of Defense.

DEFENSE PLANT CORPORATION (DPC). The Defense Plant Corporation was one of the significant innovations in the emergency government prior to and during World War II. It was the brainchild of two imaginative Reconstruction Finance Corporation* (RFC) lawyers, Clifford J. Durr, an assistant general counsel, and his younger colleague, Hans Klagsbrunn. During the early months of 1940, they were members of an interagency team set up to devise a means of financing industrial facilities in the United States to support the British war effort. Both men were passionately opposed to Nazism which they saw as a threat to humane values. Both recognized that the United States would need to enlarge vastly its industrial facilities, especially after President Franklin D. Roosevelt, in May 1940, called for the production of at least 50,000 planes yearly. Both Durr and Klagsbrunn also recognized that private businesses, frightened by the huge amounts of overcapacity during the depression, were not likely to provide much capital to create more capacity unless they were the beneficiaries of risk-proof loans or other guarantees offered by the national government.

If government provided the ultimate source of capital, Durr and Klagsbrunn believed the public interest would be better served if government built and held title to the new plants. The plants could be leased to manufacturers who received government supply contracts, or the plants could be operated for the government on the basis of management-fee contracts. Late in May 1940, when Klagsbrunn helped draft an amendment permitting RFC to participate in defense financing, he was able to persuade Jesse Jones, RFC's former chairman and the powerful Federal Loan administrator, to include a provision permitting RFC to organize one or more corporations to construct, expand, and equip industrial plants for the manufacture of arms, ammunition, and implements of war if that should prove desirable. A year later, this power was expanded to include facilities for the manufacture of such basic materials as iron and steel to help further expand the volume of war goods.

DPC was one of four RFC defense subsidiaries (Rubber Reserve Company, Metals Reserve Corporation, Defense Supplies Corporation) set up during the summer of 1940. Of these, DPC was by far the most important and, for a time, the most controversial. DPC owed its origin to Durr's criticism of an aircraft-engine facilities contract, which Jesse Jones had offered the Wright Aeronautical Corporation at the request of William S. Knudsen, former president of General Motors and industrial commissioner for the National Defense Advisory Commission. Durr criticized the contract because it would have permitted the Wright Aeronautical Corporation to acquire eventually the large plant to be financed by RFC as a gift free of all taxes. He vigorously denounced the terms as grossly favorable to Wright and adverse to the interest of government.

Emil Schram, chairman of the RFC board and the only board member not dominated by Jones, was impressed by Durr's argument. On August 22, 1940, he organized the Defense Plant Corporation to use the power granted RFC earlier in the summer to construct, expand, equip, and hold title to industrial facilities for the purpose of defense production. Schram served as president. For executive vice-president, he chose John W. Snyder, the highly capable manager of RFC's Saint Louis agency. Durr became general counsel, and Klagsbrunn one of the two assistants general counsel.

At first, DPC focused on building and equipping plants for the manufacture of airplane engines and parts and for the assembly of aircraft. Because DPC held title to the property, the contractor operating the facility under lease could load no charge for depreciation into the price of the product. In cases where all of the production was going to the government, DPC charged only a nominal rental in order to keep down the cost of the product. In such cases, DPC required a downpayment on the facilities from the armed services ranging from 40 to 60 percent of the cost of the facilities and a promise to pay the balance out of future appropriations by Congress. In cases where only a part of the plant's production would go to the government, DPC charged a substantial rental based on the volume of sales that would repay DPC for its investment, plus interest, over a five-year period. Both lease forms included an option permitting the contractor to purchase the facilities under a standard formula designed to be fair to the government and the contractor.

Initially, DPC had heavy going, for it was resisted and resented in the private sector. Government title, despite the purchase option, smacked of socialism. Moreover, every plant built and paid for by government diminished the opportunity for moneymaking by investment bankers. During DPC's early months, a committee of the National Defense Advisory Commission was working on a plan (the Emergency Plant Facilities [EPF] contract), which would open the door wide for private financing supported by government guarantees. But DPC refused to concede priority of use for the EPF contract for commercial-type facilities at the more attractive nonstrategic locations, and the contract itself proved so complex and cumbersome for both contractors and the armed services that it was little used.

After RFC's powers were enlarged in the summer of 1941 to include constructing and equipping facilities for manufacturing basic materials, the scope of DPC activity similarly expanded. DPC entered into numerous contracts for facilities to manufacture synthetic rubber, magnesium, aluminum, iron and steel, and other needed wartime products. These contracts moved more slowly because Jones took a hand in the negotiations. Instead of the standard forms of contract used earlier, making for speed and equality of treatment, Jones insisted on separate negotiations for large projects. As a result, DPC's principal architect, Durr, left in a huff over terms he believed were too favorable to the Bethlehem Steel Corporation. Jones maneuvered Schram off the RFC board and into the chairmanship of the New York Stock Exchange in order to tighten his control over DPC. Several of the negotiations had dragged on for months before Pearl Harbor put an end to all delays.

DPC entered into no project unless the project was recommended by a sponsoring agency. The most frequent sponsor was the War Department.*

Dollar Value of DPC Authorizations, by Sponsoring Agency, August 22, 1940-December 31, 1945

SPONSOR	AMOUNT AUTHORIZED
War Department	$4,156,536,000
War Production Board* (and predecessors)	2,396,612,000
Rubber Reserve Company	836,304,000
Navy Department*	694,119,000
Petroleum Administration for War	525,713,000
Office of Defense Transportation	155,099,000
Maritime Commission*	104,823,000
Twelve other agencies	103,326,000
Total	$8,972,532,000

At the Washington headquarters, DPC was chiefly an organization of lawyers, for the principal activity was drawing up the terms of contract. In the field, at the level of the project, engineers and accountants were the principal DPC representatives. Because DPC mushroomed at a time when skilled personnel were at a premium, many accountants and engineers left a good deal to be desired, but no major evidence of malfeasance was ever uncovered.

DPC's authorizations for the construction and equipment of facilities crested at $2.6 billion during the first quarter of 1942; thereafter, the dollar amount of these authorizations speedily declined. By the end of 1945 in 2,300 projects scattered across the nation, DPC had disbursed the following sums:

**DPC Financing of Defense and War Facilities,
as of December 31, 1945**

FIELD OF INVESTMENT	DISBURSEMENTS (in millions)
Aviation	$2,614
Iron and steel	951
Synthetic rubber	740
Aluminum	684
Magnesium	428
Transportation	301
Ordnance	285
Aviation gasoline	237
Metals and minerals	138
Ships and parts	132
Other	472
Total	$6,982

In addition, DPC operated a machine-tool pool, guaranteeing a market for fully half ($1.9 billion) of the machine tools manufactured during the war and backing its orders with a 30-percent cash advance. On June 30, 1945, DPC was dissolved into RFC's Office of Defense Plants. At that time, it owned 96 percent of the nation's synthetic rubber capacity, 90 percent of magnesium, 71 percent of aircraft and aircraft engines, 58 percent of aluminum metal, and 50 percent of aluminum fabrication capacity, and had significant ownership in several other industries.

At the conclusion of the war, the nation faced the problem of disposing of these plants. The purchase option in the DPC lease, from which much had been hoped, proved of little use. The cost of most plants had ballooned as a result of such wartime practices as round-the-clock construction, involving overtime, the substitution of less desirable construction materials, and costly delays, with labor idle because of shortages of materials. The plants had also suffered hard wear in war production. But these plants and their equipment represented the most valuable part of the government's postwar surplus.

In general, the plants and equipment that were sold earliest brought the highest rate of return. DPC's two big pipelines from Texas to New Jersey, sold to a firm seeking outlets for natural gas along the East Coast, brought a return sufficient to permit the governmment to recapture the approximate total cost of both lines. The government enjoyed a similar satisfying outcome from the sale of its synthetic rubber plants, made competitive with natural rubber by the discovery of the "cold rubber" process after the war. In most other industries, however, the results were much less favorable. Shortcomings in DPC accounting practices during the war make any judgment dubious, but probably the average rate of recovery was no more than about 35 percent.

Most DPC plants made the transition from public to private title, adding their increment to the nation's production capacity. For at least three industries— aluminum, synthetic rubber, and natural gas—the DPC investment brought about significant change. The DPC aluminum plants ended Alcoa's monopoly by providing the means of entry for two strong competitors, Reynolds and Kaiser. DPC nurtured the synthetic rubber industry through its infant years until the necessary technological developments permitted the industry to stand on its own feet. DPC's big pipelines helped the natural gas industry to widen its market to the mutual benefit of Texas producers and East Coast consumers.

But DPC did not contribute to diminishing the extent of economic concentration in industry. The bulk of its investment was in large plants operated by large companies. These large plants, some located more for strategic than economic reasons, proved more difficult to sell than the smaller plants after the war. Large surplus plants were usually bought by large companies, and small plants by smaller firms.

The DPC plants accelerated the pace of industrialization in some regions, particularly the South and West. Early in the war, these facilities were disproportionately located away from the heavily industrialized Atlantic Coast because of fear of possible enemy attack. The presence of a larger labor pool in agricultural areas further to the west was also a factor. So was the presence of natural resources: bauxite for aluminum, imported chiefly from the Caribbean; rivers capable of generating cheap electric power in the Pacific Northwest for aluminum reduction and fabrication; magnesite for magnesium in Nevada; rich iron ore and coal deposits in Utah; and, above all, petroleum in Texas and Louisiana for aviation gasoline, and for butadiene and styrene for the manufacture of synthetic rubber.

Since World War II, few attempts have been made to draw on this wartime precedent. In 1948, when steel capacity was being taxed to the limit and steel companies were unwilling to build new facilities, the suggestion was made within government and labor circles that the government should build additional steel plants. A slightly watered down version of their suggestion became the most controversial point in President Harry S Truman's "Fair Deal" State of the Union message to Congress on January 5, 1949.

During the Korean War, an organization of aging New Dealers, Americans for Democratic Action, urged that the DPC pattern be reestablished to help bring about any necessary increase in industrial capacity, but its voice was almost alone. The situation existing at the time of the Korean War was different from that at the time of World War II. Since World War II, the nation had experienced several years of prosperity marked by substantial industrial expansion. Moreover, a new spirit of optimism permeated the business sector. Business was no longer so afraid of excess capacity. It also cared little for the DPC pattern with its taint of socialism. Instead, it was able to reestablish through legislation the pattern of tax amortization, also used in World War II, which allowed business a freer hand and at the same time protected firms from loss in case the facilities built during the war proved of limited or no postwar value. The only DPC activity revived during the Korean War was the use of some machine-tool pool orders beginning in 1951 to speed the flow of tools to war plants.

Thus, since World War II the precedent set by DPC has received little attention. But the DPC experience is a part of the record. It can be drawn on again whenever ventures of great public consequence seem too risky to be undertaken by private firms unless the terms of contract are so favorable as to be adverse to the interest of government. Perhaps the struggle to surmount the energy crisis, sooner or later, may bring about such an outcome.

FOR ADDITIONAL INFORMATION: The best source of information on the Defense Plant Corporation is Gerald T. White, *Billions for Defense: Government Financing by the Defense Plant Corporation During World War II* (1980). Three books that deal with the relations of DPC and particular government agencies are R. Elberton Smith, *The Army and Economic Mobilization* (1959); Robert H. Connery, *The Navy and Industrial Mobilization in World War II* (1951); and Frederic C. Lane, *Ships for Victory: A History of Shipbuilding Under the U.S. Maritime Commission in World War II* (1951). The Clifford Durr manuscript on the early history of DPC, "The History of the Defense Plant Corporation," in the possession of Mrs. Virginia Durr, Wetumpka, Alabama, has been substantially published in Harold Stein, ed., *Public Administration and Policy Development* (1952), except for the section relating to synthetic rubber. A thoroughgoing audit of DPC was carried out by the comptroller general of the United States, *Report on Audit of Reconstruction Finance Corporation and Affiliated Corporations for the Fiscal Year Ended June 30, 1945: Defense Plant Corporation*, 80th Cong., 1st Sess., H. Doc 474 vol. 4 (1947). Jesse H. Jones and Edward Angly, *Fifty Billion Dollars: Thirteen Years with the RFC, 1932-1945* (1951), grossly exaggerates Jones's role in DPC. An excellent finding aid for DPC records is *Preliminary Inventory of the Records of the Reconstruction Finance Corporation, 1932-1964* (1973) prepared by a staff member of the National Archives and Records Service.*

GERALD T. WHITE

DEPARTMENT OF AGRICULTURE (USDA). The United States Department of Agriculture was established on May 15, 1862, by a law signed by President Abraham Lincoln (12 Stat. 387). The new department was "to acquire and to diffuse among the people of the United States useful information on subjects connected with agriculture in the most general and comprehensive sense of the word." In carrying out his duties, the commissioner of agriculture was authorized to conduct experiments, collect statistics, and collect, test, and distribute new seeds and plants. This law, very broad in scope, has remained the basic authority for the department to the present time.

Proposals for an agricultural branch of the national government had been made as early as 1776. George Washington recommended the establishment of such an agency in 1796. Elkanah Watson later advocated a related plan, and the Secretary of the Treasury gave the idea support in 1819 by asking consuls and naval officers abroad to send home seeds and improved breeds of domestic animals.

In 1836, Henry L. Ellsworth, commissioner of patents, on his own initiative undertook to distribute seeds obtained from abroad to enterprising farmers. Three years later, Congress appropriated $1,000 of Patent Office* fees for collecting agricultural statistics, conducting agricultural investigations, and distributing seeds. By 1854, the Agricultural Division of the Patent Office employed a chemist, a botanist, and an entomologist, and was conducting experiments. During this period many farm editors, agricultural leaders, and officers of the numerous county and state agricultural societies continued to urge that agriculture be represented by a separate agency, although many Southern farm leaders were opposed. The United States Agricultural Society assumed leadership of the movement, and its efforts, combined with the pledges of the Republican party in 1860 for agrarian reforms that would encourage family farms, led to the establishment of the department.

The first commissioner of the new department (it was headed by a commissioner rather than by a Cabinet-level Secretary until 1889) was a Pennsylvania dairyman, Isaac Newton. In his Annual Report for 1862, Newton outlined a substantial research and information program which set the pattern for specific lines of work within the department for a number of years. The first experimental crop plots were on Washington's Mall, between the Capitol and the then unfinished Washington Monument. Newton was particularly interested in some imported varieties of wheat. When a sudden thunderstorm threatened the crop late in July 1866, Newton left his office and ran towards the Mall. He suffered a sunstroke and died of its effects some months later.

Research work expanded steadily but slowly during the rest of the century. Emphasis was upon developing more productive seeds and animals, with some effort to make the nation self-sufficient in such commodities as sugar, tea, and silk. Then, in 1897, a new era began with the appointment of James Wilson as Secretary. Wilson, known as "Tama Jim," was to serve as Secretary for sixteen years, under four presidents. He had been director of the Iowa State Agricultural Experiment Station and had served three terms in the U.S. House of Representatives.

During the sixteen years he was in office, Wilson made the department one of the great research institutions of the world. By 1912, both employees and expenditures were nearly seven times what they had been in 1897. Most of this increase was in research, including farm management, although both farm demonstration and regulatory activities were becoming prominent.

Scientific research in the department under the leadership of Wilson stressed increases in production on land under cultivation and efficiency in livestock production. For the most part, such research related to plant and animal life, soils, nutrition, and agricultural chemistry.

Wilson organized a number of new bureaus, headed for the most part by well-known, aggressive scientists. Many of the bureaus operated as virtually independent organizations, without regard to the activities of other bureaus. The new bureaus included Plant Industry, Entomology, Chemistry, Statistics, Soils, Biological Survey, and Forestry. The Forest Service* was established in 1905, after Gifford Pinchot, then head of the Bureau of Forestry, persuaded President Theodore Roosevelt to transfer custody of the national forests from the Department of the Interior* to Agriculture.

The department and the land-grant colleges entered into formal cooperative agreements, after the passage of the Smith-Lever Agricultural Extension Act in 1914, to carry the results of research in the department and the state colleges and experiment stations directly to farmers. This work resulted in the establishment of the Cooperative Extension Service, one of the most widely copied abroad of all U.S. governmental organizations.

The department's research activities provided a basis for regulatory functions, with the two often carried out in close relationship to each other. The Bureau of Animal Industry was created in 1884 after outbreaks of contagious animal diseases and the barring of American meat from some European markets focused attention upon the problem of animal plagues. Authority given the bureau to control the movement of livestock in interstate commerce was the first regulatory activity undertaken. In 1906, the department was given responsibility for two new laws—the Meat Inspection Act and the Food and Drugs Act. Although responsibility for the Food and Drugs Act was transferred from the department in 1940, it still carries out meat and poultry inspection and grading.

The development of federal standards and grades for farm products began with grain and cotton in 1916 in an effort to provide standard regulations for trading purposes and to protect farmers when their products were sold by grade. Since then, compulsory standards have been fixed for a number of commodities, while permissive standards have been issued for others. The quality of some fruits and vegetables going to market is controlled through marketing orders and agreements. All grain for export is inspected under authority of the Grain Standards Act of 1976.

In 1921, Congress passed the Packers and Stockyards Act, which prohibits unfair, deceptive, discriminatory, and monopolistic marketing practices, in livestock, poultry, and meat marketing. In addition to market regulation, the department protects both animals and plants by attempting to stop the importation of foreign pests or diseases. The department also cooperates with the states and the farmers in controlling diseases and pests within the United States.

The economic dislocations caused by World War I and declines in farm prices led to an intensification of statistical and economic research that would aid farmers in meeting market needs. The Bureau of Agricultural Economics was established in 1922. The department also encouraged farmers to organize cooperatives, particularly for marketing their products.

The emphasis upon research, regulation, and marketing, however, was not enough to restore farm incomes to comparable earlier levels. The depression of the 1920s, culminating in the Great Depression of 1929, led to the New Deal and to what has been called "the new Department of Agriculture."

The new department took shape under the leadership of Secretary Henry A.

Wallace, Iowa farm editor, geneticist, and hybrid seed corn breeder, and son of a former Secretary, Henry C. Wallace. When, on May 12, 1933, President Franklin D. Roosevelt signed the Agricultural Adjustment Act, the new direction was under way. With this law, the department was assigned, for the first time, responsibility for administering a program providing economic assistance directly to farmers.

The same economic circumstances that led to the passage of the Agricultural Adjustment Act led to programs that emphasized better rural credit facilities, soil conservation, aid for poverty-stricken farmers to acquire farms, and loans for rural electrification. Each of these programs led in turn to a new agency responsible for its administration. In the five years from 1932 to 1937, the staff of the department increased from 27,000 to 106,000 (in both 1950 and 1980, the total was 85,000 employees).

Most of the new programs were aimed at farmer welfare and farm production. The depression, however, affected city dwellers as well. Many of them were unable to purchase sufficient food, even though the farmers were told they raised a surplus that could not be marketed profitably. The department, working with welfare agencies, set up programs for distributing surpluses to the needy in both cities and rural areas, and began to emphasize marketing and distribution as contrasted with the production of farm products. The other side of the distribution program became important during and after World War II, when the War Food Administration, which was part of the department, allocated scarce foods among our allies, the armed forces, and the civilian population.

After World War II and the Korean War, the department gave particular attention to marketing problems, and to providing technical assistance to the less developed nations. During the 1960s and 1970s, attention was turned to seeing that every American had sufficient food, with emphasis on the Food Stamp Program to enable poorer families to buy needed food. Programs to reach poor rural people were developed, while the problems of commercial agriculture still were given attention.

Emphasis upon different problems and the gradual addition of functions have led to reorganizations of the department from time to time. During the late 1970s, a number of changes were made to give greater emphasis to programs for the consumer. The major change in organization, however, since the 1930s, came in 1953, when the traditional one Assistant Secretary of Agriculture was replaced by five.

The department in 1981 was headed by the Secretary of Agriculture, Deputy Secretary, and six Assistant Secretaries. The department agencies are divided into eight major groups, each headed by an Assistant Secretary or director. In addition, the Office of the General Counsel, the Judicial Office, the Office of Governmental and Public Affairs, the Office of the Inspector General, and the Office of Energy report to the Secretary.

The Food and Consumer Services group includes the Food and Nutrition Service and the Food Safety and Quality Service. The Economics, Policy Analysis and Budget group is made up of the Office of Budget, Planning and Evaluation, the World Food and Agricultural Outlook and Situation Board, and the Economics, Statistics, and Cooperatives Service. The Rural Development group includes the Farmers Home Administration, the Rural Electrification Administration,* and the Rural Telephone Bank.

The Marketing and Transportation Services Group consists of the Agricultural Marketing Service, the Animal and Plant Health Inspection Service, the Federal Grain Inspection Service, and the Office of Transportation. The International Affairs and Commodity Programs group includes the Agricultural Stabilization and Conservation Service, the Commodity Credit Corporation, the Federal Crop Insurance Corporation, the Foreign Agricultural Service, the Office of the General Sales Manager, and the Office of International Cooperation and Development. The group for Natural Resources and Environment consists of the Forest Service, Soil Conservation Service, and Office of Environmental Quality. Science and Education includes the Science and Education Administration. Finally, the administration group includes the Board of Contract Appeals, the Office of Administrative Law Judges, the Office of Equal Opportunity, the Office of Operations and Finance, the Office of Personnel, the Office of Safety and Health Management, and the Office of Small and Disadvantaged Business Utilization.

The names of agencies and duties assigned, as well as the configurations of agencies reporting to the different assistant secretaries, undergo frequent changes. However, the basic duties of the department stay much the same. In 1971, President Richard M. Nixon proposed abolishing the Department of Agriculture, while in 1977, President Jimmy Carter proposed transferring some of its functions to other departments. Neither happened. Over the years, even as the farm population was declining from half of the total in 1862 to 4 percent today, the department continued to represent a continuing national interest in food and agriculture.

FOR ADDITIONAL INFORMATION: Gladys L. Baker, "And to Act for the 'Secretary': Paul H. Appleby and the Department of Agriculture, 1933-1940," *Agricultural History* 45 (Oct. 1971): 235-258; Gladys L. Baker and Wayne D. Rasmussen, "Economic Research in the Department of Agriculture: A Historical Perspective," *Agricultural Economics Research* 27 (July-October 1975): 53-71; Gladys L. Baker, et al., *Century of Service: The First 100 Years of the United States Department of Agriculture* (1963); John M. Gaus and Leon O. Wolcott, *Public Administration and the United States Department of Agriculture* (1940); Ernest G. Moore, *The Agricultural Research Service* (1967); Robert J. Morgan, *Governing Soil Conservation: Thirty Years of the New Decentralization* (1965); H. S. Person, "The Rural Electrification Administration in Perspective." *Agricultural History* 24 (April 1950): 70-89; Wayne D. Rasmussen and Gladys L. Baker, *The Department of Agriculture* (1972); Earle D. Ross, "The United States Department of Agriculture During the Commissionership: A Study in Politics, Administration, and Technology, 1862-1889," *Agricultural History* 20 (July 1946): 129-143; D. Harper Simms, *The Soil Conservation Service* (1970); Maryanna S. Smith, *A List of References for the History of the United States Department of Agriculture* (1947); Harold K. Steen, *The U.S. Forest Service: A History* (1976); and Vivian Wiser and Wayne D. Rasmussen,

"Background for Plenty: A National Center for Agricultural Research," *Maryland Historical Magazine* 61 (December 1966): 283-304.

WAYNE D. RASMUSSEN

DEPARTMENT OF COMMERCE. President Theodore Roosevelt and a number of business and governmental leaders believed early in the present century that the United States lagged behind its industrial competitors in promoting foreign trade. Citing both domestic and foreign problems for American business, Senator Knute Nelson, Republican of Minnesota, beginning in 1901, introduced legislation to establish a Department of Commerce and Industry. Subsequently, Nelson was persuaded by fellow-Senator Marcus Hanna to include Labor with the hope of harmonizing the opposites between the interests of capital and labor. Nelson lamented the fact that all of the U.S. foreign competitors already had such a national governmental agency to assist business. Here the economy was left to itself without leadership so necessary for harmony, unity of action, and effective progress. A national agency would also concentrate in one place all the data-gathering activities now scattered among numerous departments.

Labor was not in complete accord over the development. The American Federation of Labor preferred a separate Labor Department at the outset but went along with the creation and hoped for a rapid separation. The Knights of Labor stood at once in favor of the bill creating the combined entity, even though it, too, desired a separate department in the long run. Unhappily, labor was generally neglected during 1903-1913 within the department. Support among business was widespread, including the National Business League and the National Association of Manufacturers.

Effective July 1, 1903, the Department of Commerce was established with George B. Cortelyou, former Secretary to President Roosevelt, as the first Secretary. Although promoting business and trade emerged later as its chief function, existing services now absorbed by it included: Lighthouse, Coast and Geodetic Survey, Steamboat Inspection, Navigation, Standards, Fisheries, Census, Statistics, Immigration, and the Bureau of Labor.

Two new organizations were created within the department. The Bureau of Corporations was empowered to monitor the American trusts under the Sherman Act and to report its findings to the President. It was transferred in 1915 to the newly formed Federal Trade Commission.* The other new group, the Bureau of Manufactures, did not become functional until 1905, and its first leader, Joseph Hampton Moore, set out immediately to seek the cooperation of business, for example, the National Board of Trade, in a public relations campaign aimed at eventually expanding American trade, especially exports. There soon developed a system of special Commerce agents to examine and improve both domestic and foreign trade conditions. The cotton industry received particular attention.

Throughout these early years, department officials worked diligently but often wondered just what genuine effect, if any, they had on the goal of promoting overseas trade. Congress determined through appropriations the extent of regular activities and research possible, a factor that most interested businessmen apparently could not understand in dealing with the department. Within Commerce and Labor, employees expressed the usual governmental jealousies, in this case over the Bureau of Manufactures getting more attention than other bureaus. Already early in its existence, there ensued arguments with the Department of State,* whose field personnel resented the overseas activities of the commerce agents. Then too, how could the department best strike a balance of monetary promotional support among the largest and smaller American businesses?

Commerce under President Woodrow Wilson had little time for peacetime expansion before American entry into World War I. Leading the newly independent unit was William C. Redfield, former Congressman from New York and a manufacturer. At the outset, Redfield inherited these services: Fisheries, Lighthouse, Census, Coast and Geodetic Survey, Corporations, Steamboat Inspection, Navigation, Standards, and Foreign and Domestic Commerce. The last named began in 1912 and became the focus of departmental commercial energies. Commerce did not yet have its own building; the eight units were scattered all over Washington, D.C. Its total number of employees during 1913-1921 ranged from about nine thousand to fourteen thousand. Important as it was held, the Bureau of Foreign and Domestic Commerce had a budget of only $60,000 during 1913. The parsimonious Congress, as late as 1919-1920, refused expenditures for motion pictures to promote Commerce duties.

Significant innovations early in the Redfield years included the creation of a new force of overseas commercial attachés recruited from Commerce and from the consular service of State. Subsequently, Redfield and his successors encountered a running battle to prevent the corps of commercial agents from being transferred to the Department of State. Domestically, the department opened branch offices in New York, Boston, Atlanta, Chicago, New Orleans, Saint Louis, San Francisco, and Seattle. Though instigated before America's entry into the war, Commerce pushed a drive in 1916 to save waste paper and rags.

Governmental bureaucracy at times irritated Redfield, who scoffed at the existing prejudice against hiring women as special agents for the Bureau of Foreign and Domestic Commerce. Because existing rules did not specifically read that women could be included, his subordinates passed the buck all the way to the Secretary, who quickly allowed the hirings. Internal regulations also included a general ban on paying expenses for professional employees to attend conferences. Redfield hated the uneven existing application of the rules, which granted exceptions to the Bureau of Standards but not to Foreign and Domestic Commerce. The department owned eight ships operated by Fisheries, yet the vessels operated under several different sets of regulations.

Wartime support consisted of numerous heroic and specialized aids as 1,824 personnel entered military service. Sixty vessels assisted the military, fifty of them Lighthouse steamers used most effectively for mine sweeping. One ship assisted the Navy in damaging the German submarine earlier responsible for sinking the *Lusitania*. At home the Bureau of Standards developed optical glass for various instruments, the United States having previously bought this item from Germany. Standards provided the military with a lightweight and durable cotton blanket to replace wool, an improved cotton to replace linen for airplane wings, along with dope or varnish that was less flammable. The Bureau of Standards invented a rather crude beginning of a wireless (radio) direction finder for ships in fog. Fisheries personnel during and after the war promoted the eating of seafood, especially on both coasts, and saved over one hundred thousand fish for use from Mississippi River flood waters (1919). Unhappily, Congress cut all research after the war.

The Republican administrations of Warren G. Harding and Calvin Coolidge left much to be desired in most respects but could boast of a very energetic leader for Commerce in Iowan Herbert Hoover. A professional engineer, Hoover earned widespread popularity in the world at the end of World War I as the U.S. Food Relief administrator. In a decade of shrinking government, Hoover garnered an increase of Commerce appropriations ($860,000 in 1920 to over $5 million in fiscal year 1928), and a quintupling of total personnel. A network of fifty offices spanned the world. Its trade commissioners and attachés submitted periodic analyses complete with information on tariffs, commercial law, and credit ratings of foreign businesses. Hoover employed Dr. Julius Klein, a very active and capable director, to lead Foreign and Domestic Commerce. The unit became a veritable clearinghouse of information and advice for American industry and finance, a buffer for private interests and their foreign counterparts. Klein cheerfully assisted U.S. business leaders on advertising packaging for exporting goods. The department's correspondence with U.S. concerns was kept confidential in order to maintain impartiality. Hoover and Klein could boast of the marked effects on American business and the fact that Commerce officials always gained attractive positions in business after leaving the department.

Historian Joseph Brandes has written at length on the Hoover years in Commerce, correctly describing Hoover's economic philosophy along with its benefits and drawbacks, including its staggering inconsistencies. Hoover scored other world powers for monopolizing the critical natural resources, particularly rubber. But he dreamed of U.S. control. He lauded the fact that Commerce assisted in dispatching billions of dollars of private funds abroad, and yet, through rules and coercion, he picked favorite nations to bless under the aegis of his American individualism. He lashed out at foreign cartels and manipulations of pricing and production but steadfastly accepted U.S. tariff walls against the world. This inconsistent policy has plagued the United States in recent years, especially when Presidents Jimmy Carter and Ronald Reagan imposed their boycotts and economic bans against the Soviets, even though U.S. friends abroad opposed these actions.

The Department of Commerce under Hoover accomplished vast internal reshuffling precluding an entrenched clique. Efficient service to American interests became the keynote. The path to employment at Commerce was successful, practical business experience and technical and professional competence. Hoover personally kept track of all department activities. His vigor incurred the wrath of opponents here and abroad. Fiorello LaGuardia of New York, a liberal Republican, opposed Hoover's unbending stance that America's allies must pay their World War I debts to the United States. John Foster Dulles, a more conservative Republican, disagreed with Hoover's attempts to force European businesses to conform to U.S. domination. Hoover clashed with Winston Churchill (1922), then British colonial secretary, over Churchill's pricing controls on rubber. Generally in Britain, Hoover faced an extremely negative posture for his stand on war debts. The French also greatly disliked Hoover, because he desperately attempted to prevent American investment there. France had not renegotiated her debts. The Dutch and French, however, wondered why Hoover favored another U.S. debtor, Italy. Whenever possible Hoover blocked U.S. loans to the Soviet Union, at the same time confiding to his associates his dream of its potential as a trading source. Commerce denied loans to Czechoslovakian breweries. After all, prohibition reigned in the United States.

Personnel in the State Department complained of Hoover's blindness for economic principles which blocked effective diplomacy in this crucial era. State also emphasized existing duplication in the gathering of business data by its consulates and Commerce officials overseas. It attributed Hoover's vigorous promotion of Commerce to his drive to occupy the White House. Hoover worked diligently to include State, for example, Commerce was ordered to seek the advice of consulars, both here on leave and abroad. He acknowledged that State personnel gathered the best information at numerous remote locations, for example, Seoul, Korea. Although Secretaries Charles E. Hughes and Frank B. Kellogg of State completed numerous amicable sessions with Hoover, the friction among lower ranking employees continually erupted, even in far-flung places such as Paris and Tientsing. The fact that State issued press releases about a European chemical cartel, without initially telling Commerce, irritated Hoover. It was only after the 1929 stock failures that State finally agreed with Hoover's earlier policy to exact promises that portions of private U.S. loans abroad would be returned to the U.S. economy through foreign purchases. By 1930, American businessmen preferred Commerce to State in backing their interests.

Existing laws and department rules proved insufficient for Commerce to prevent numerous loans of a private nature. Hoover could not stem the tide of feverish U.S. speculation, which ruined many investors during the ensuing Great Depression. Commerce only warned.

Hoover disdained such earlier U.S. antics overseas as military intervention and Dollar Diplomacy, preferring a sound economic basis for all monetary considerations. Again, in promoting raw materials, he sought private loans to Latin America and Liberia, and made a futile effort to modify land laws in the Philippines in order to establish large rubber plantations. He opposed all investment in Japanese-held former Manchuria and blocked loans to Brazil (coffee) and to a Franco-German potash cartel.

On the whole, Commerce favored the gigantic surge in U.S. foreign investment as long as it was private and served economically productive ends. Commerce warned Americans if an individual transaction appeared unsound or unduly risky and if a foreign company looked weak or the country's government shaky. By the mid-1920s, foreign securities offered here reached a total of almost $1.4 billion. By 1929, Americans had invested $1.3 billion in branch factories, that is, those abroad wholly or partly under their control. Approximately two hundred U.S. firms possessed about four thousand branches, one-half of them in Canada. Hoover got Commerce officials to frown on the branch factory concept, stressing the adverse competition of foreign tariffs, paying non-American laborers, and taxes going to other countries instead of the United States. Radio Corporation of America, National Cash Register, and Ford in Canada, all faced Commerce restrictions. General Motors in Poland and Ford in Paris faced local riots and customs battles, respectively.

It is small wonder that in the ensuing 1930s a number of Commerce and State officials put far too heavy a stress on American trade as a preventive to the eruption of world chaos by the rising dictators, a bipartisan blind faith of staggering portions. Hoover nurtured this prevailing mood or theory under the previous regime. The depression caused a drastic reversal in fiscal 1931—a fall of 34 percent in U.S. exports and 37 percent in imports, both reflecting a significant drop in prices. With factory output down by 20 percent the following year, U.S. foreign trade stood at its lowest point since pre-1914 years.

During Franklin D. Roosevelt's first year in office, the Bureau of Foreign and Domestic Commerce closed offices in twenty-one of its fifty-three locations. Officials in Washington, D.C., assisted the New Deal programs, mostly the Public Works Administration,* Agricultural Adjustment Administration, and the National Recovery Administration,* and served as the contact point for the Export-Import Bank.* State asked for and received assistance in studying possible new trade sources. Commerce and State collaborated on reciprocal trade agreements with fourteen nations. Moreover, a census of foreign investment in the United States was begun. By 1937, the Patent Office (now in Commerce) received increases in applications, a positive sign of recovery, and Commerce Secretary Harry Hopkins reported the best increase in agricultural exports in seven years (at 20 percent) in 1938. A world study of communications was undertaken in 1936. During these years, Commerce also gained the aviation services of the Bureau of Air Commerce.

Long before Hitler started World War II, officials in Commerce monitored the restrictive trade measures of the Axis forces. By 1940, it estimated that actual war situations curtailed U.S. exports by about 25 percent and imports by 20 percent. At that time, raw cotton was the only commodity showing a marked increase in exports. By fiscal 1941, all of Commerce looked toward war; armaments dominated the trade scene, and the federal government now became the top purchaser of American production. As in the first major war of this century, Commerce made drastic and significant contributions to the war effort during 1941-1945, not only in its trade role for business, but also in its services of a maritime, aviation, and meteorological nature (the Weather Bureau came over from Agriculture in 1940).

After World War II, the process of promoting U.S. trade overseas was drastically different than it had been in 1919. Now all efforts looked toward the rehabilitation of war-torn areas, but this time dominated by government purchases instead of private sources. Export controls were continued. One short corn crop in the United States hampered European recovery that year. As the nation turned against the Russians in the Cold War, so Commerce promoted foreign trade outside the Communist-bloc countries. In 1952, Secretary Charles Sawyer proudly reported State-Commerce collaboration in raising a sunken Lend-Lease cargo, originally destined in wartime for the Soviet Union, and now prevented from coming into Russian possession. At home the same year, the department handled all the publicity in announcing the government seizure of the nation's steel mills.

Operations abroad now were conducted through Commerce's Office of International Trade, later the Bureau of Foreign Commerce, which had turned most of its attention to national defense and the Korean War. An encouraging recent trend saw nearly 100 foreign business leaders visit the United States to obtain advice. For the remaining 1950s, Commerce recommended, among numerous projects, standardized sizes of containers for nineteen items of frozen fruits and vegetables and a new system of sizes for women's apparel, relaxed export restrictions toward the Soviets; renegotiated the General Agreement on Tariffs and Trade; and assisted the Atomic Energy Commission* in the design and construction of a nuclear-powered merchant ship. Serious concern was already expressed over the growing competition facing America from foreign manufactures, just a portion of the unfavorable balance of annual payments which has plagued us ever since.

In the John F. Kennedy Administration's first year, Secretary Luther H. Hodges cited the imbalance despite a boom in U.S. nonmilitary exports for the year to nearly 20 percent of our total exports, although only about 5 percent of manufacturers dealt in exports. Also in 1961, the United States Travel Service (USTS) was established to boost foreign tourism to the United States. Commerce, in conjunction with the overseas branches of the United States Information Agency,* now promoted an ever increasing number of U.S. exhibits and trade fairs, one such mission reaching over one thousand British business contacts for 250 American firms. In 1969, USTS could boast of 1,648,615 foreign visitors to the United States, up by 230.6 percent over its first-year (1961) total. Export bans continued to exist as a tool of diplomacy; Commerce described the adverse effects to Cuba of our denial program there. Racial discrimination caused a ban against Southern Rhodesia.

Cold War hatreds and fears rather than sound economics dictated policy, but the early 1970s witnessed the relaxation of trade barriers against the Soviet Union in addition to the People's Republic of China, and efforts to stimulate U.S. trade with other portions of Eastern Europe. As the major foreign currencies gained markedly on the dollar by 1973, so did foreign tourism in America rise dramatically, to 23 million by 1981. These visitors expended an estimated $14 billion. Too slowly, indeed, Commerce began employing multilingual receptionists at thirteen of America's many gateway airports. Budgets and personnel strengths fluctuated with congressional whim, for example, $2.7 billion and 39,281 employees in 1978.

FOR ADDITIONAL INFORMATION: The reader should begin with Department of Commerce records in the National Archives* (RG 40), Washington, D.C. The Annual Reports, congressional appropriations hearings, and departmental bulletins and other publications are helpful. Unfortunately, no sound comprehensive history of the department exists. Four monographs are quite important. First, Joseph Brandes, *Herbert Hoover and Economic Policy: Department of Commerce Policy, 1921-1928* (1962), is a clear, interpretive analysis of both the department and Hoover's economic ideas which prevailed during that period. Second, Joan Hoff Wilson, in *American Business and Foreign Policy, 1920-1933* (1971), provides numerous cogent accounts of the Department of Commerce's controversial policies and the reactions from American business and other governmental officials. Third, for the Woodrow Wilson years, see William C. Redfield, *With Congress and Cabinet* (1924), an autobiographical variety presented as articles, written by a former Secretary of Commerce. Finally, German scholar Klaus-Georg Wey in his book, *Das U.S. Department of Commerce and Labor und Interessenverbände, 1903-1913* (1976), in German, gives a thorough, if too detailed, story of the department's formulation and early years.

DONALD R. WHITNAH

DEPARTMENT OF DEFENSE. The Department of Defense evolved from what was initially called the National Military Establishment (NME), established by the National Security Act of 1947. This law had its origins in the World War II military experiences of the United States. Between the late eighteenth century and 1941, the War* and Navy* departments operated as separate entities, the former concerned with land forces and the latter with sea forces. World War II demonstrated the necessity of interservice cooperation and unity of command. President Harry S Truman declared that one of the lessons of the war was the clear need for a unified direction of land, sea, and air forces both at home and in foreign countries where our armed forces were stationed.

Other developments suggested the need for revision of the defense structure. Far-reaching technological changes in weapons systems, including the emergence of air power and the atomic bomb, demanded development, production, and deployment decisions based on national security needs rather than the parochial views of individual services. While the costs of these weapons were high, the public after the war demanded more economy in defense spending. Finally, it seemed obvious that the United States would have to play a much more active international role in the future, abandoning the political aloofness that had characterized the nation's foreign policy before 1939. In the long run, this also necessitated a unified national defense structure.

Following House and Senate hearings in 1944 and 1945 on proposals to establish a single department of the armed forces, President Truman in December

1945 recommended the establishment of a Department of National Defense under a Secretary, with three coordinated branches for land, naval, and air forces. By this time, serious disagreements between the Army* and Navy over unification had surfaced. The War Department favored a single department with separate services for army, navy, and air. The Navy Department, led by Secretary James V. Forrestal, opposed this concept and presented a comprehensive alternative proposal for three separate departments (Army, Navy, and Air Force*), a National Security Council,* and several other specialized agencies. Only Truman's insistence on some form of unification eventually softened the Army-Navy dispute.

It was not until July 26, 1947, that the National Security Act became law. This statute was weaker than Truman had wanted, but it was a beginning. The law created the NME headed by the Secretary of Defense, and three executive departments for the Army, Navy, and Air Force. The Secretary of Defense's duties, which he carried out through the Office of the Secretary of Defense (OSD), included the right to exercise general direction, authority, and control over such departments. The law also gave statutory authority to the existing Joint Chiefs of Staff and created the National Security Council, the National Security Resources Board, the Central Intelligence Agency,* the Munitions Board, and the Research and Development Board.

Ironically, even though he had opposed real unification, Secretary of the Navy Forrestal took office in September 1947 as the first Secretary of Defense. He soon found that his powers were insufficient to exercise effective control over the NME and to promote unification, a cause he now espoused. Eventually, Forrestal advocated significant amendments to the National Security Act; his proposals, supported by a report from the Hoover Commission* and specific recommendations by Truman, eventually materialized in modified form in National Security Act amendments signed by the President on August 10, 1949. An executive agency, the Department of Defense, replaced the NME. The three service branches lost their status as *executive* departments and became *military* departments. Each military department was to be headed by a Secretary, but the secretaries lost their membership on the National Security Council. The amendments strengthened the Secretary of Defense's authority, stating that "he shall have direction, authority, and control over the Department of Defense." Other organizational changes included establishment of the offices of Deputy Secretary of Defense and three Assistant Secretaries, creation of the position of chairman of the Joint Chiefs of Staff (JCS), and expansion of the JCS Joint Staff. Before these amendments became effective, Forrestal resigned as Secretary of Defense (March 1949) and died shortly thereafter.

The 1949 amendments represented substantial improvement. But continued interservice rivalry (over such things as roles and missions, control of atomic weapons, and budgets), as well as the Korean conflict beginning in June 1950, demonstrated the need for further strengthening of the Secretary of Defense's power and more effective unification. Both outgoing Secretary of Defense Robert A. Lovett in November 1952 and the Rockefeller Committee on Department of

Defense Organization in April 1953 made strong recommendations for amendment of the National Security Act and other changes in organization and procedure. President Eisenhower soon transmitted Reorganization Plan No. 6 to Congress. Stating as the "three great objectives" in defense organization "a clear and unchallenged civilian responsibility in the Defense Establishment," "effectiveness with economy," and "the best possible military plans," Eisenhower proposed several major changes which became effective with activation of the Reorganization Plan on June 30, 1953. The plan abolished the Munitions Board, the Research and Development Board, and the Defense Supply Management Agency and transferred their functions to the Secretary of Defense. Six additional Assistant Secretaries and a general counsel were authorized. The chairman of the JCS acquired expanded power to select and direct the Joint Staff. Reorganization Plan No. 6 enhanced the powers of the Secretary of Defense, his staff, and the JCS organization. It took the Defense Department further down the road to the kind of unification envisaged by Truman and other supporters of the concept at the end of World War II.

Further experience proved the need for additional reforms in the late 1950s. Scientific and technical advances in the means of warfare, rising costs, and especially the shock caused by the Soviet Union's launching of the first Sputnik in October 1957, led to critical appraisals of Defense organization and functions. Congressional investigations of the U.S. missile program began late in 1957. A January 1958, Rockefeller Brothers Fund Study recommended Defense organizational changes to correct the inefficiency and duplication of effort growing out of interservice rivalry. In his 1958 State of the Union message, Eisenhower described defense reorganization as the most important of the eight priority tasks he identified; subsequently, he proposed legislation, which Congress enacted and he signed on August 6, 1958. The Secretary of Defense received authority to alter the major combat functions of the armed services through transfer, abolition, and consolidation, unless the Congress rejected such actions. He was also given authority to reassign noncombat functions and to reassign procurement, production, and operational control of new weapons systems to a particular service.

The 1958 law was the last major revision of the National Security Act of 1947. Although interservice rivalry still existed, the Secretary of Defense by this time did have the necessary statutory and legal authority to manage his department and the military services in ways generally consistent with the national security needs of the nation. Since 1958, a number of organizational and other changes have been made—for example, a 1977 law established two Under Secretary of Defense positions, for Policy and for Research and Engineering—but the major changes occurred in 1949, 1953, and 1958.

Between 1947 and 1981, fifteen men served as Secretary of Defense. The first, James V. Forrestal (September 1947-March 1949), struggled with the initial organization and management of a department containing military branches which worried about their roles and missions and fought vigorously for their shares of budgets which the President tried to keep controlled and balanced. He also had to preside over a defense structure facing multiple challenges as a result of the emergence of the Cold War between the United States and the Soviet Union. All in all, Forrestal performed well and was a fortunate choice for the formative days of the new department.

Forrestal's successor, Louis A. Johnson (March 1949-September 1950), owed his appointment chiefly to his successful role as President Truman's fund-raiser during the 1948 campaign. His efforts, with Truman's support, to cut the defense budget complicated the still-rampant interservice rivalry and seemed to backfire when the United States found itself poorly prepared when the Korean conflict began in June 1950. This problem, combined with Johnson's personal and policy disputes with Secretary of State Dean G. Acheson, contributed to his dismissal from office. Truman then turned to General George C. Marshall (September 1950-September 1951). Marshall's main task was to manage the military role of the United States in Korea. His next priority was to build up European defenses under the North Atlantic Treaty Organization, founded in 1949. After the rather stormy Johnson period, Marshall restored prestige to the Office of the Secretary of Defense and calmed somewhat the internal differences among the services. Among other important decisions, Marshall supported Truman's dismissal in 1951 of General Douglas MacArthur as commander-in-chief of U.S. and U.N. forces in the Far East.

The fourth Secretary of Defense was Robert A. Lovett (September 1951-January 1953), who previously had been Marshall's Deputy Secretary. A capable and efficient manager, Lovett directed the latter stages of the U.S. military participation in the Korean conflict and contributed importantly to the continuing development of NATO, which during this period moved toward the incorporation into its structure of the Federal Republic of Germany (completed in 1955).

Three men served as Secretary of Defense under President Eisenhower. Charles E. Wilson (January 1953-October 1957), who came to the Pentagon after heading General Motors, ran the Defense Department as he would a large corporation. Wilson keyed defense policy to the Eisenhower Administration's reliance on nuclear weapons as embodied in the "New Look." This approach deemphasized conventional forces and relied on the threat of "massive retaliation" to deter the Soviet Union. Wilson also worked to control the defense budget, which decreased significantly after the end of the Korean War in mid-1953. Although the United States still enjoyed vast nuclear superiority during Wilson's tenure, the Soviet Union embarked on a defense program designed to catch up with the United States and particularly to achieve its own nuclear deterrent capacity. Both countries worked during this period to develop a "triad" of nuclear forces, eventually relying on heavy bombers, land-based intercontinental ballistic missiles, and submarine-launched ballistic missiles. Wilson's two successors were Neil H. McElroy (October 1957-December 1959) and Thomas S. Gates, Jr. (December 1959-January 1961), who had earlier served as Secretary of the Navy and Deputy Secretary of Defense, respectively. McElroy managed well the implementation of the 1958 reorganization law and the accelerated research and development programs, especially for missiles, which followed the SPUTNIK launchings. Gates, who continued the reorganization of the department, set up the Joint Strategic Target Planning Staff, a key agency for coordinating the strategic forces.

Robert S. McNamara (January 1961-February 1968) served both Presidents John F. Kennedy and Lyndon B. Johnson and worked to implement their "flexible response" defense policy. An efficient, hard-headed manager as well as an extremely intelligent thinker, McNamara utilized fully the powers of his office. At the Pentagon he instituted a Planning-Programming-Budgeting System (PPBS) and a Systems Analysis Office, which played a critical role in planning and in other stages of the PPBS process. During his tenure, McNamara not only had to manage the Defense Department's role in such events as the Bay of Pigs invasion (April 1961), the Cuban Missile Crisis (October 1962), and the third Arab-Israeli War (June 1967), but also U.S. participation in the long and controversial Vietnam War. The gradual development in his mind of serious doubts about the Johnson Administration's policy in Vietnam led to his resignation as Secretary of Defense in early 1968. Clark M. Clifford (March 1968-January 1969) was a caretaker whose main duty was to orchestrate the beginnings of U.S. withdrawal from Vietnam.

Melvin R. Laird (January 1969-January 1973) was Secretary of Defense during Richard M. Nixon's first term. A veteran member of the House of Representatives, Laird presided over implementation of the Nixon Administration's policy of "Vietnamization," including the gradual withdrawal of U.S. forces from Vietnam. He supported the SALT I nuclear arms control agreements which the United States and the Soviet Union signed in 1972. Elliot L. Richardson (January-May 1973), who followed Laird, served too short a time to have much impact on the department.

Nixon's final appointee as Secretary of Defense was James R. Schlesinger (July 1973-November 1975), a tough, frank, and intelligent official with prior service as head of the Atomic Energy Commission* and the Central Intelligence Agency. Schlesinger believed that the Soviet Union was catching up with the United States in nuclear capability and that the nation should neglect neither its nuclear nor conventional forces. He gave much thought to nuclear targeting policy, maintaining the McNamara "assured destruction" concept but also favoring a counterforce (military targets) approach. Among the major crises he had to deal with was the fourth Arab-Israeli conflict in October 1973 and the concurrent OPEC oil boycott. His competition with Secretary of State Henry Kissinger and his objections to President Gerald R. Ford's curtailment of the defense budget led to his dismissal in late 1975. The next Secretary of Defense, Donald H. Rumsfeld (November 1975-January 1977), served more as a caretaker than anything else in the remaining months of the Ford Administration.

President Jimmy Carter's Secretary of Defense was Harold Brown (January 1977-January 1981), a physicist with Defense service between 1961 and 1969 as director of research and engineering and Secretary of the Air Force. One of Brown's major tasks was to reverse the pattern of declining defense spending, which had prevailed in the post-Vietnam era. He also had to give considerable thought to the status of the nuclear triad. He supported President Carter's decision to continue using the B-52 rather than adopting the B-1 bomber, and he carried forward planning for multiple-protective shelter deployment of a new ICBM missile, the MX. Brown's public announcement of movement toward a modified counterforce targeting policy in August 1980 (PD 59) caused some controversy in the midst of a presidential campaign in which there was wide debate about defense issues. About the same time, Brown acknowledged that the United States had begun development of a "stealth" technique to make it possible for strategic bombers to avoid radar detection.

Caspar W. Weinberger (January 1981-), the fifteenth Secretary of Defense, took office at the beginning of the administration of President Ronald Reagan. Weinberger was an experienced federal administrator but had no background in defense. His initial task was to decide on how to spend the greatly increased defense funds promised by the Reagan Administration. He also faced important decisions relating to possible production of the B-1 manned bomber and deployment of the MX missile. Other problems early in his tenure were the planned deployment of a new generation of theater nuclear missiles in the NATO region and resumption of the SALT process with the Soviet Union.

From the moment the Defense Department began operations (as the NME) in 1947, it became one of the largest and most important government agencies, with the world as its arena. Given the international situation after World War II, the concomitant necessity to stress national security, and occasional participation in military action (Korea and Vietnam), this status was almost inevitable. Amendments to the National Security Act and other organizational changes after 1947 significantly strengthened the department. The Secretary of Defense, by virtue of his position, has become one of the two most important individuals in the Cabinet, along with the Secretary of State. His influence, of course, depends on his own capabilities and on the wishes of the President he serves. Thus, such secretaries as Forrestal, McNamara, and Schlesinger stand out in the history of the Department of Defense because of their personal attributes and ideas and because of the presidential environments in which they served.

FOR ADDITIONAL INFORMATION: C. W. Borklund, *Men of the Pentagon: From Forrestal to McNamara* (1966), includes informative chapters on the National Security Act and on each of the secretaries from 1947 to 1965. Demetrios Caraley, *The Politics of Military Unification: A Study of Conflict and the Policy Process* (1966), is a study of political conflict over the National Security Act. It provides background on the development and evolution of the unification conflict between 1943 and 1947 and an analysis of influences on congressional behavior during the conflict. Alice C. Cole, Alfred Goldberg, Samuel A. Tucker, and Rudolph A. Winnacker, eds., *The Department of Defense: Documents on Establishment and Organization, 1944-1978* (1979), a comprehensive, indispensable collection, covers the National Security Act of 1947, the 1949, 1953, and

1958 reorganizations, administrative and legislative modifications between 1958 and 1978, and functions of the Armed Services and the JCS. Paul Y. Hammond, *Organizing for Defense: The American Military Establishment in the Twentieth Century* (1961), is a standard study which covers the period from the early twentieth century to 1960. It treats the unification controversy, the National Security Act, and the history of DoD during the Truman and Eisenhower administrations. William W. Kaufmann, *The McNamara Strategy* (1964), an in-depth study of the longest-tenured and perhaps most controversial Secretary, emphasizes McNamara's efforts to redesign both the military and strategic forces of the United States and the decision-making process within the Department of Defense. Douglas Kinnard, *The Secretary of Defense* (1980), considers the office and role of the Secretary of Defense, with separate biographical accounts of Secretaries Forrestal, Wilson, McNamara, Laird, and Schlesinger. Lawrence J. Legere, "Unification of the Armed Forces " (Ph.D. dissertation, Harvard University, 1951, issued in soft cover by the Office of the Chief of Military History, U.S. Army) is a well-documented study which traces Army-Navy relations from the American Revolution to 1939, developments relating to unification during World War II, the movement to unification between 1944 and 1947, and events after unification between 1947 and 1950.

See also John C. Ries, *The Management of Defense: Organization and Control of the U.S. Armed Services* (1964). This comprehensive study of the National Security Act and the 1949, 1953, and 1958 changes stresses the trend toward centralization of control in the Office of the Secretary of Defense. Warren R. Schilling, Paul Y. Hammond, and Glenn H. Snyder, *Strategy, Politics, and Defense Budgets* (1962), includes three essays— on the fiscal year 1950 defense budget, NSC-68, and the Eisenhower "New Look" policy—which contribute to understanding the defense political process. The common theme stresses the importance of the level of the defense budget. Paul R. Schratz, ed., *Evolution of the American Military Establishment Since World War II* (1978), presents a valuable collection of essays focusing on the DoD, the military departments, and the JCS.

ROGER R. TRASK

DEPARTMENT OF EDUCATION. The United States Department of Education was established in 1867 as a free-standing, sub-Cabinet federal agency. One year later, after a bitter debate over a proposal to abolish the department, Congress accepted a compromise plan to reorganize it as an office in the Department of the Interior.* With the inauguration of Ronald Reagan in 1981, it appeared that this minor drama might have been replayed because of the new President's campaign pledge to abolish the recently established Cabinet Department of Education. The threat never materialized.

Throughout a century-long history punctuated with several name changes (from department to office to bureau and to office and department once again), the federal education agency has performed only a partial and limited role in the development and management of federal education policy. The Defense,* Interior, Labor,* and Agriculture* departments, for example, have traditionally received education-related assignments, often with clearer mandates and more acceptable rationales for funding. A commission created by Herbert Hoover in 1930 to study federal involvement in education found to its surprise that every

Cabinet department and several regulatory agencies engaged in educational activities. With policy continuing to emanate from such diverse sources, the result has been duplication of effort, interagency rivalry, and often confusion, but rarely consistent, clear, or persuasive education policy. A single, organizing agency for education has never existed in the federal government.

Proposals for a federal education agency first appeared during the late eighteenth century; however, support for the idea gained momentum only in the 1850s. A common element in the diverse plans was the assertion of a federal responsibility to encourage the growth and improvement of public schools through the nationwide collection and dissemination of data on education. Indeed, such language was used to describe the principal task of the agency proposed in the Department of Education bill introduced in 1866. Modeled after the Department of Agriculture, a sub-Cabinet agency established in 1862, the proposed department received authority to perform service roles only. In addition to gathering and publishing data, it was to conduct studies and otherwise "promote the cause of education." Two research projects were specifically mandated. A study of federal land grants for educational purposes was required in the original act. After approving the first appropriation for the department in 1867, Congress ordered it to complete a study of education in the District of Columbia.

The Department of Education Act described a modest operation: a commissioner aided by three clerks. The appropriation for fiscal year 1868 allowed only $6,000 for expenses beyond salaries ($9,400). Nevertheless, the proposal generated stubborn opposition in a Congress preoccupied with pressing Reconstruction issues. Supporters and opponents alike viewed the department as a federal intrusion on education. Supporters envisioned an activist role in promoting school improvement generally and educational opportunities for Southern black people specifically. Statistical reports and published comparisons of schools' effectiveness in various parts of the country would serve to persuade political leaders and their constituents to improve local schools. The department's opponents feared the agency would not restrict itself to data gathering and dissemination but in time would challenge state control of public schools. Representing both Democrats and a wide spectrum of subgroups within the majority party, from radical to conservative Republicans, they joined a campaign to abolish the department within its first months of operation and allowed only modest increments in funding and personnel when it survived as the Office and later the Bureau of Education. By 1885, its budget of $55,000 supported thirty-eight employees.

The agency continued to grow gradually until the 1950s, with dramatic increases in the size of its appropriations and staff typically occurring during war periods, most notably after World War II. Throughout this time, the Office of Education (as the agency was again named in 1929) gave primary attention to the collection and dissemination of statistics and other information on education and to education research. Critics complained that it was becoming merely a "bureau of information," but on occasion the agency gained authority for projects of a different order. From 1884 to 1931, it provided schools, health services, and other "civilizing influences" for the native population in Alaska. Originally, it administered schools for the white population as well, but that assignment fell to the territorial government early in the twentieth century. Annual funds for the Alaska program equaled those for all other agency activities combined. In 1913, the bureau assumed responsibility for Americanization programs for immigrants, an effort that continued until the end of the decade, and during World War I organized the School Garden Army, a program to increase agricultural production while teaching children rudimentary farming techniques. The school gardens proved to be both economically successful and popular. Other relatively small programs administered by the agency prior to 1950 dealt with vocational education, land-grant colleges, and impact aid to school districts affected by federal operations.

Some of the office's more lasting achievements during the early years occurred as indirect results of formal activities. Others came about as direct consequences of nonlegislated involvements and survival strategies intended to secure a constituency for the agency. The regular collection of school statistics encouraged local and state officials to maintain accurate records and to adopt uniform schedules for reporting school data. It also influenced them to quantify learning outcomes and other measures of schools' effectiveness. The office tacitly supported and through the activities of several commissioners of education directly encouraged strengthening the roles of state and local school superintendents and reducing the number of small, usually rural school districts to realize economies of scale and centralized administrative structures. In an effort to convince Congress initially not to abolish the agency and later to increase its funds, commissioners actively sought support among the nation's school people and allied the office with professional organizations, particularly the National Education Association. In the process, the agency acquired relatively well-organized advocates and became in turn the representative of professional school people in Washington, dulling thereby its appetite for objective, dispassionate research and data gathering on schools' effectiveness. The close identification with its constituency notwithstanding, the office never enjoyed complete latitude to function even as a "bureau of information." Congressmen and senators objected when their states or districts appeared in an unfavorable light in the agency's publications and often succeeded in having offending passages deleted from its reports. Lacking clear authority, adequate funds for even census-taking activities, and firm, consistent support in Congress kept the office vulnerable to criticism and ever alert for friends. It remained a minor and relatively unimportant agency for over seventy-five years.

The office's mission began to enlarge in the 1950s with expansion of the impact aid program and passage of the National Defense Education Act and the Library Services Act. The period of greatest growth, however, occurred a decade later. Of the almost eighty programs within its jurisdiction by 1970, over 40 percent were enacted by the eighty-ninth Congress in 1965 and 1966. Over 80 percent of its programs were authorized in the period following 1957. During these years, its staff doubled and its funds grew to $4 billion, an increase of over 800 percent. By the end of the 1970s, its budget exceeded $12 billion. The character and size of the office's constituency changed accordingly. In addition to local and state public school agencies, it began administering a host of programs to support training, services, research, planning, and construction for a wide array of state and local education-related agencies, nonprofit and profit-making organizations, institutions of higher education, and private elementary and secondary schools. Several programs provided support and services for individuals.

In addition to growing larger, the office's mission also changed qualitatively. The agency augmented statistical reports on education with analyses that compared developments in states and local districts, projected trends, for example, in enrollments, and identified policy issues confronting state and local agencies. The office gained authorization to enforce guidelines prohibiting discrimination against women, racial groups, and handicapped persons in federally supported programs and institutions. With various grants and contracts as incentives, it could also promote directly equal education opportunities. Through the Elementary and Secondary Education Act of 1965 and subsequent reauthorizations, it aided school districts serving low-income populations, strengthened state departments of education, and supported cooperative programs involving public and private schools. Its activities related to school curriculum ranged from subject matter (ethnic studies and experimental social studies courses) to methodology (bilingual education). In all of these efforts, the office did not simply distribute funds, it also required evaluations, compliance with regulations, and accountability procedures. Clearly, it no longer functioned merely as a statistical secretary to the nation's school systems. By the 1970s, its budget and staff exceeded those of several Cabinet departments.

In the decade following 1970, four related types of criticisms were leveled against the Office of Education. First, its organization and procedures were faulted as inadequate for its expanded mission. Included in this complaint were charges that its staff was not large enough or of sufficient quality to manage the myriad programs and that reporting procedures required of aid recipients were inordinately expensive in terms of time and money. Second, the office's preoccupation with program management and pressing current problems in education was viewed as undermining the agency's resolve and capability to invest in basic research and long-term development projects. A third area of criticism saw the office spending too much time and energy attempting to coordinate its activities with other federal agencies assigned overlapping educational missions without the visibility and authority to compete effectively with Cabinet departments for congressional and presidential attention. Finally, some critics complained that it exceeded both constitutional limits on federal involvement in education and the office's original charter. They recommended returning the agency to its earlier assignments to gather and disseminate information and promote research on how to improve schools.

Responses to these criticisms produced a new federal education research agency, a Cabinet-level Department of Education, and finally an effort to abolish the department, all within a ten-year period. The National Institute of Education (NIE) was established in 1972 as a separate agency within the Education Division of the United States Department of Health, Education, and Welfare,* also the administrative home of the Office of Education. Proponents envisioned NIE as developing a research capability for education comparable to that of the National Science Foundation* and the National Institutes of Health, thus correcting one of the office's preceived failures. Through sponsored research, primarily, and selected studies conducted by its own staff, in such areas as effective learning strategies and different modes of school organization and management, NIE was expected to promote improved educational practice and equal educational op-portunities.The agency, however, quickly found itself in trouble with Congress. Attempts to abolish it surfaced within two years. As was the case with the Department of Education in 1867, some congressional opponents took umbrage at NIE's reform-advocacy posture, while others criticized its failure to produce practical results rapidly. There was general dissatisfaction with its senior ad-ministrators. NIE survived and in 1979 was transferred to the new Department of Education.

The National Education Association long supported elevating the federal ed-ucation agency to Cabinet status, but Congress paid little attention to the proposal. Keeping a campaign pledge, Jimmy Carter recommended the creation of a De-partment of Education early in his administration, and after a lengthy debate and numerous compromises, Congress agreed. The new agency was expected to satisfy two persistent criticisms of the Office of Education. By gathering a host of federal education programs under a single administration, the department would eliminate the duplication, rivalry, and confusion that had long character-ized federal involvement in education. Supporters hoped that Cabinet status would attract distinguished leadership and highly competent staff to the agency and give education the authoritative voice it deserved in Washington. Opponents doubted that such results would occur and, more to the point, feared additional federal encroachment on state and local prerogatives in education. They noted, for example, that several major education programs were not transferred to the department. The need for interagency coordination would continue. The Senate approved the department bill by 72 to 21, but the House vote was much closer (210 to 206, with 19 not voting on the House version of the bill; 215 to 201 on the House-Senate Conference Committee report).

Activities transferred from other departments and agencies included most no-tably the overseas schools operated by the Defense Department, but the Education Department consisted principally of programs previously constituting the Edu-cation Division of the Department of Health, Education, and Welfare. Although NIE remained as a separate agency in the new department, the Office of Education lapsed. Program thrusts and major administrative units included elementary and secondary education, civil rights, postsecondary education, special education and rehabilitative services, vocational and adult education, bilingual education,

education research, education for overseas dependents, and nonpublic education. The Intergovernmental Advisory Council of Education was established to monitor and improve relations of federal education programs with state, local, and tribal governments and public and nonpublic educational institutions. The Federal Interagency Committee on Education received responsibility for coordinating procedures and actions of the Education Department with other departments and agencies having education or education-related programs. Most of these administrative and program areas were mandated in the Department of Education Organization Act.

Given the number and importance of the programs not transferred, interagency coordination promised to remain a problem. Head Start, for example, was left in the renamed Department of Health and Human Services,* and the Department of Agriculture retained authority over various school food programs. Eight additional departments and several other agencies, including the Library of Congress, National Endowment for the Arts,* National Endowment for the Humanities,* National Science Foundation,* Smithsonian Institution,* and Veterans Administration,* continued to operate education or education-related programs. The Army,* Navy,* and Air Force* academies and other military training programs remained under the aegis of the Defense Department.

Proponents of the Education Department hoped to see the establishment of an inclusive agency reflecting a broad conception of education. However, decisions on which programs to transfer to the new department rested heavily on political considerations, as special interest groups lobbied to keep particular activities within a familiar administrative structure. Even after compromises that narrowed the department's mission, opposition to creating the agency remained strong. Fears that it would supersede state and local authorities seemed justified when the department issued detailed bilingual-education regulations during its first year. Development of the regulations began five years earlier in response to court decisions and legislation, but that fact did not deter the campaigns to abolish the agency, which confronted it from the start.

Whether such efforts succeed, they are likely to reduce and recast federal involvement in education, particularly in regard to the federal education agency. Although Ronald Reagan has offered few details as to what would replace the department he wants to eliminate, he has received a set of systematic recommendations in "Mandate for Leadership: Policy Management in a Conservative Administration," a report prepared by the Heritage Foundation in anticipation of his election. The lengthy section on the Department of Education argues that "the need to reshape federal policy" is more important than the question of whether to continue or abolish the agency. The report calls for a return to the department's original activities: (1) information gathering and dissemination, (2) consultation and technical assistance, and (3) education research and development. Where possible, program authorities should be consolidated into block grants to local and state agencies, thus eliminating the necessity of a multitude of regulations and reporting requirements. In short, the department should forego coercion, offering instead practical support and services to improve education performance. Such changes, the report concludes, although in many cases requiring prior legislative action, would enable the President to reduce significantly the department's budget and staff.

Debate over the agency's aims and authority thus continues. For over a century, a major issue has been whether a passive or assertive agency best served the nation's interest in education. However, only since the 1950s has it been in a position to test the effectiveness of a more aggressive stance. A more fundamental, but rarely confronted, difficulty has been the absence of any consensus as to what the national interest entailed. Tradition and constitutional silence (the U.S. Constitution does not mention education) are said to forbid federal control of education. Yet, various federal agencies, including the Office of Education, have operated schools. The Department of Education administers overseas schools, arguably one of the nation's largest school systems. Beyond such contradictions remain volatile policy areas: What are the effective means for increasing the nation's human resources? Can the federal government guarantee inclusive opportunities for education?

Although the newest of thirteen Cabinet agencies, the Department of Education began as one of the largest in terms of funds and personnel. Almost half of the personnel were inherited from the Defense Department with the transfer of the overseas schools programs. It administers over 150 programs, the vast majority authorized during the period after 1957. The 1982 fiscal year budget proposed by Jimmy Carter includes $15 billion for the department, an amount previously projected for the Office of Education in the 1979 budget. The 1982 figure will likely be reduced by the Reagan Administration. By what amount, in support of which programs, and managed by what kind of federal agency are questions yet to be resolved.

FOR ADDITIONAL INFORMATION: National Advisory Committee on Education, *Federal Relations to Education* (1931); Donald R. Warren, *To Enforce Education: A History of the Founding Years of the United States Office of Education* (1974); Nicholas Murray Butler, "The Future of the Bureau of Education," *Educational Review* 21 (1901): 526-527; H. Dewey Anderson and Walter Crosby Eells, *Alaska Natives: A Survey of Their Sociological and Educational Status* (1935); Edward G. Hartman, *The Movement to Americanize the Immigrant*, pp. 88-133, also *School Life*, May 1, 1919, p.1; U.S., Congress, House, Committee on Education and Labor, *Study of the United States Office of Education*, 90th Cong., 1st Sess. (1967), House Doc. No. 193. See also Richard W. Lykes, "A History of the Division of Higher Education, U.S. Office of Education (1911-1953)" (Ph.D. dissertation, American University); David B. Tyack, *The One Best System* (1974); U.S. Office of Education, *Administration of Public Laws 81-874 and 81-875* (1977), *The Education of Adolescents* (1976), and *The Condition of Education* (1980). Also helpful are Lee Sproull, Stephen Weiner, and David Wolf, *Organizing an Anarchy: Belief, Bureaucracy, and Politics in the National Bureau of Education* (1978); and Heritage Foundation, "Mandate for Leadership: Policy Management in a Conservative Administration, Education Team Report" (1979).

DONALD WARREN

DEPARTMENT OF ENERGY (DOE). The creation of the Department of Energy in 1977 brought together many of the energy-related functions of the federal government into a single, Cabinet-level organization. Included were programs long administered by the Department of the Interior,* the Federal Power Commission,* and the Atomic Energy Commission* and newer programs from two agencies established in 1974, the Energy Research and Development Administration and the Federal Energy Administration. During its brief existence, the DOE has sought to organize diverse functions inherited from these other agencies into a coherent administrative framework. At the same time, it has been forced to deal with intense political pressures generated by ongoing controversies over energy policy. To understand the history of the DOE, it is thus useful to summarize the histories of the various programs absorbed by it in 1977, to examine how these programs were initially organized within the newly created DOE, and to describe the major changes affecting the department since 1977.

Before the 1970s, the federal government's involvement in energy took place in three primary agencies, the Department of Interior, the Federal Power Commission, and the Atomic Energy Commission. Interior traditionally managed most federal policy affecting the coal and oil industries; the Federal Power Commission regulated natural gas prices; and the Atomic Energy Commission oversaw the development of nuclear power until its abolition in 1974. Each played important roles in the evolution of a particular source of energy, but no mechanism existed for coordinating energy policies as a whole. This long history of industry-specific policies managed by separate agencies established bureaucratic ties and traditions that still affect the DOE.

The Department of Interior traditionally administered numerous federal programs affecting fossil-fuel development and use. Interior's varied responsibilities in the nineteenth century included the surveying of the nation's mineral wealth, including oil, coal, and shale oil, by the United States Geological Survey.* Interior also managed the leasing of the public lands for oil and coal exploration, a function performed within the department by the Bureau of Land Management.* Interior's involvement with minerals and with the public lands made it a logical choice to investigate growing safety problems in mining in the early twentieth century, a task assigned to the newly created Bureau of Mines* in 1910. Expertise developed in the study of mine safety proved transferable to the investigation of production methods in the fossil-fuel industries, and by the 1920s, the Bureau of Mines had established laboratories throughout the nation for the study of the efficient production and use of coal, oil, and synthetic fuels such as shale oil. In the same era, the bureau became the leading government authority for statistics about the oil industry. In addition to these specific functions, Interior also became the center of business-government relations in the petroleum industry, a role that included the administration of the oil code under the National Recovery Act, the housing of the Petroleum Administration for War during World War II, and the organization of the Oil and Gas Division after the war to coordinate oil policies and to serve as the point of contact for the National Petroleum Council, the industry's advisory committee on government policy.

The Federal Power Commission (FPC) took an equally important, if less diverse, role in administering public policy toward oil's sister fuel, natural gas. Although founded in 1920 primarily to regulate electric power, the FPC was given authority to regulate natural gas pipelines by Congress in 1938. Then in 1954, a Supreme Court decision gave the commission responsibility for setting the price of natural gas sold in interstate markets. For several decades before the creation of the DOE, the FPC thus functioned as an independent regulatory agency with a great deal of autonomy. It used its authority to encourage the use of natural gas—at least in the short run while adequate supplies remained—by holding the price of this excellent form of energy below that of other competing fuels.

The Atomic Energy Commission encouraged the use of atomic energy in a variety of ways less direct than price regulation. Created in 1946, it had a mandate to promote and to regulate the use of nuclear energy. The commission's research and development laboratories throughout the nation worked to develop nuclear technologies for both weaponry and peaceful uses. In addition, the commission was responsible for licensing and inspecting nuclear power plants. It also enriched uranium for sale to domestic and foreign customers. In short, it was closely involved in all phases of nuclear energy. The size of the Atomic Energy Commission and the strategic importance of its research assured that its former employees and functions played a prominent role in the efforts to reorganize federal energy agencies in the 1970s.

The energy crises of the 1970s hastened several significant changes in the organization of the federal government's energy-related functions. The replacement of the Atomic Energy Commission with two new agencies, the Energy Research and Development Administration (ERDA) and the Nuclear Regulatory Commission (NRC), in 1974 signaled a shift in attitudes toward nuclear power by separating the responsibility for nuclear development from that of nuclear regulation. ERDA absorbed the Atomic Energy Commission's research and development work, including weapons-development programs as well as research on peaceful uses of atomic energy. In addition, ERDA took over most of the fossil-fuel research programs of the Bureau of Mines, projects dealing with geothermal and solar energy from the National Science Foundation,* and programs to develop alternative automobile systems from the Environmental Protection Agency.* In its brief existence before the creation of the DOE, ERDA had responsibility for most energy-related research programs established before the 1970s as well as numerous new projects to develop alternative energy sources mandated by Congress in response to the energy shortages of the 1970s. ERDA organized these diverse research initiatives by fuel source, grouping programs into one of six categories: fossil energy; nuclear energy; environment and safety; energy conservation; solar, geothermal, and advanced energy systems; and national security (weapons research). The budget and personnel of ERDA reflected the large historical commitment of federal government funds to nuclear research inherited from the Atomic Energy Commission, but the new agency sought to move toward a more balanced research program during its three-year existence. In general, ERDA stressed research on the development and use of energy, leaving programs to study the impact of the use of various forms of energy on safety and health and on overall environmental quality to other agencies that had traditionally performed such research, including the Environmental Protection Agency and the Bureau of Mines. The Nuclear Regulatory Commission* took over the Atomic Energy Commission's traditional responsibility for licensing and inspecting nuclear power plants, thus further focusing ERDA's efforts on the development of energy sources.

Joining ERDA as a focal point of federal government energy policy in the 1970s was the Federal Energy Administration (FEA), which grew to meet the problems caused by the oil shortages of the period. The FEA was created in 1974, and it took over many of the functions of the Federal Energy Office that had been established the year before to coordinate responses to the Arab oil embargo. A primary responsibility of the FEA was the administration of one of the most controversial and difficult energy-related programs of the decade, the regulation and allocation of domestic crude oil. To avoid inequities and severe economic dislocations after the near quadrupling of the price of OPEC oil in the early 1970s, Congress mandated price controls on domestic oil, and the FEA was the lead agency in enforcing these controls. Included was a complex allocation scheme designed to assure all domestic refiners equal access to suddenly less expensive domestic oil. The FEA also administrated programs to encourage the conservation of energy, to promote the use of coal in place of oil and natural gas, and to store large amounts of oil in a "Strategic Petroleum Reserve" designed to provide a buffer against future disruptions of oil supplies. To aid in its performance of these duties and to respond to congressional demands for better information about the rapidly changing energy situation, the FEA also created the National Energy Information Center to collect and analyze information and statistics about energy.

A recurring theme in the energy policy debates which produced the FEA and ERDA was the need to consolidate the federal government's energy functions. Most observers recognized the need for a better administrative arrangement for dealing with energy-related problems. The existing fragmented array of public institutions, each with some limited authority over the numerous programs that had accrued over more than a century of federal government involvement in aspects of the energy industries, was best suited for managing government policies toward individual energy industries. Yet, the need of the 1970s seemed to be the fashioning of an administrative framework capable of coordinating overall "energy" policy to replace the numerous fuel-specific programs that had dominated the government's traditional approach to energy. Such an overview agency also promised to provide an improved framework within which to guide government policy in the relatively new area of managing the end uses of different sources of energy. A final argument for reorganization was more strictly political: the creation of a Department of Energy could be a potent political symbol that something concrete was being done to address the much-discussed shortages of secure supplies of energy in usable forms.

Amid the intense passions engendered by oil shortages in the 1970s, proposals to reorganize energy-related agencies touched many exposed political nerves. President Richard M. Nixon's initiative to create a Department of Energy and Natural Resources around the existing programs of the Department of the Interior set the tone of much of the debate on energy reorganization before being lost in the confusion of the Watergate scandal. During his short stay in office, President Gerald Ford proposed the creation of a department focused specifically on energy-related programs, and the debate on what should and should not be included in the new department continued in the first year of the Jimmy Carter Administration. Under Carter, James Schlesinger, a former head of the Atomic Energy Commission, guided the process of reorganization before being named the first Secretary of Energy. The Carter plan included the unification of the FPC, ERDA, and the FEA into a single agency, but this proposal quite predictably met opposition in Congress, which altered important parts of the DOE's structure in an effort to avoid the concentration of traditionally dispersed powers in the hands of the Secretary of Energy. The resulting compromises, in addition to President Carter's initial choice to create a department devoted to energy rather than to energy and natural resources, shaped the structure and the powers of the Department of Energy when it began operations in October 1977.

The DOE, as finally passed by Congress and approved by the President, absorbed most of the energy functions of the federal government, but several possible conflicts of authority remained unresolved. The most obvious of these is evident on the organization chart of the DOE, which shows a dotted line connecting the Secretary of Energy and the Federal Energy Regulatory Commission (FERC). Most of the traditional powers of the FPC were given to the FERC, which is described in fittingly ambiguous language as "an independent regulatory commission within the DOE." This description reflects the intent of Congress to retain a measure of autonomy for the FERC instead of merging its power over natural gas prices into the Office of the Secretary of Energy as proposed by President Carter. The working relationship between the DOE and the FERC was left vague, with hard questions unanswered about the division of authority on issues involving price regulations. Also excluded from the direct and unequivocal authorities of the DOE were numerous critical functions at the heart of any coherent energy policy: the balancing of trade-offs between the production of energy and environmental quality, which remained primarily in the Environmental Protection Agency; the licensing and inspection of nuclear power plants, which continued as the responsibility of the independent Nuclear Regulatory Commission; the leasing of public lands for mineral exploration, which stayed in the Bureau of Land Management of the Department of Interior with some input by the DOE into the decision-making process; and the administration of the program to increase the gasoline mileage of American automobiles, which remained in large part the responsibility of the Department of Transportation.* Such divisions of authority on important issues reflected the great difficulties of putting together a new department with clear power over a variety of problems already being addressed by numerous government agencies directly and indirectly involved with energy production and use. Although such potential conflicts were perhaps unavoidable in the complex political bargaining required to create the DOE, they will nonetheless present continuing sources of tension for future energy policymakers.

Despite such divided authority on a number of significant issues, the DOE embodied a great deal of power over a variety of other energy-related programs. In completely absorbing ERDA, the DOE took over most federal government research on the production and use of both existing and potential new sources of energy. These programs included a substantial nuclear-weapons development program originally contained in the AEC. The entire FEA, complete with price regulation and allocation programs for crude oil and the Strategic Petroleum Reserve, also came into the DOE. From the Department of Interior came the oversight of the Southeastern Power Administration, the Southwestern Power Administration, the Alaska Power Administration, and the Bonneville Power Administration. Also transferred from the Departmnt of Interior were the programs involving both research and statistical activities formerly performed by oil and coal specialists in the Bureau of Mines. In addition, the DOE absorbed a variety of relatively small, energy-related projects from the Department of Housing and Urban Development,* the Department of Commerce,* and the Interstate Commerce Commission.* Finally, from the Defense Department, the DOE took over the management of the naval oil and shale oil reserves which had been set aside in the early twentieth century to assure an adequate supply of fuel for the armed forces in case of war.

The organizational structure imposed on this agglomeration of programs reflected the difficulty of establishing obvious connections among diverse functions inherited from various organizations. A fundamental decision was to organize the department's programs by stage of development of a technology rather than by fuel. This meant that all projects designed to research, develop, or demonstrate energy technology became the responsibility of the Assistant Secretary of Energy Technology. Programs seeking to develop commercially available energy supplies were placed under the Assistant Secretary of Resource Applications. A separate Assistant Secretary managed all work on conservation and solar applications. Another Assistant Secretary took responsibility for assuring that all DOE programs were consistent with environmental laws, still another for the direction of defense programs. An office of research monitored and coordinated all research being conducted under the various assistant secretaries. All energy-related statistical services, notably the data collection and validation programs of the FEA and the Bureau of Mines, were combined to form the single Energy Information Agency with the goal of consolidating and expanding the energy data available to government decision-makers. Finally, the oil pricing, allotment, and import programs of the FEA became the core of the Economic Regulatory Administration within the DOE.

The organization of research by the stage of development of a technology rather than by fuel type quickly raised problems involving the coordination of research on each energy source. After a study undertaken during the first months in office of the second Secretary of Energy, Charles Duncan, Jr., research programs in the DOE were reorganized with the emphasis on placing all research on each energy source in the same administrative framework. New Assistant Secretaries for Fossil Fuels and Nuclear Energy joined existing Assistant Secretaries for Conservation and Solar Energy, Environment, Defense Programs, and Resource Applications, with the former duties of the Assistant Secretary for Energy Technology distributed primarily between the two new Assistant Secretaries. This reorganization was a partial recognition of the continuing influence within the DOE of the historical pattern of organizing federal energy policies by specific fuel types.

Several much-debated energy programs considered in the late 1970s were significant for what they did not do to the DOE. The first was the creation of an agency independent of the DOE to oversee a large-scale government-backed effort to develop synthetic fuels. This new public corporation seems destined to become the focus of most government research in this potentially important area, thus partially reversing a trend of the last decade toward unifying government research on new energy sources in the DOE. An unsuccessful proposal to push vital energy-related projects more rapidly through the complex environmental regulatory requirements also would have bypassed the authority of the DOE by creating an independent Energy Mobilization Board to oversee and enforce the streamlining of many environmental regulations. The failure of this proposal suggests that the tension between energy development and the safeguarding of environmental quality will be a major concern of the DOE in coming decades.

The Ronald Reagan Administration entered Washington in 1981 amid a great deal of speculation about the abolition or at least the dismantling of the DOE under the guidance of the new Secretary of Energy, James Edwards. The decontrol of crude oil prices, begun under Carter and accelerated under Reagan, should ultimately bring a significant decline in the authority and resources of the Energy Regulatory Agency in the DOE. Phased decontrol of natural gas prices could have the same effect on the FERC. Yet, most of the programs of the DOE will not go away so easily. Nuclear research, including weapons development, remains a hefty portion of the DOE's total budget, and this portion seems immune to cuts from a defense-oriented, pro-nuclear administration. Other important functions such as fossil fuels research, the collection of energy information, ongoing programs on renewable forms of energy, and programs to encourage conservation could be more vulnerable. What seems likely is that some functions of the DOE will be shifted back to the bureaucracies that contained them before 1977, while others will be trimmed or phased out.

Ironically, an agency created in 1977, in part as a political symbol that something was being done to solve pressing energy problems, is being cited less than five years later as an equally potent political symbol in the ongoing crusade against "Big Government." A drastic reduction of the resources and programs of the DOE could thus prove irresistible to politicians in the 1980s. Calls for free markets in the energy industries, however, should not ignore several conclusions from the past. One hundred years of history suggests that this freedom has generally been fostered by government promotion. It also seems clear that such freedom has been constrained in important ways by considerations of safety and health, the need to safeguard the national security, and the desire to cushion the impact of disruptions to the economy that might accompany an effort to shift abruptly from oil and natural gas to new sources of energy. Such concerns traditionally have been the domain of government, and they cannot be expected to disappear with the abolition of the DOE.

FOR ADDITIONAL INFORMATION: Susan Abbasi, "A Brief Summary of the Energy Reorganization Act of 1974," Congressional Research Service (March 15, 1975); and "Summary of the Department of Energy Organization Act," Congressional Research Service (August 15, 1977); Steven Beryer and Paul MacAvoy, *Energy Regulation by the Federal Power Commission* (1974); David Davis, *Energy Politics*, 2d ed. (1978); Robert Engler, *The Brotherhood of Oil* (1977); and *The Politics of Oil* (1961); *Federal Energy Reorganization: Historical Perspective*, 94th Cong., 2d Sess., Committee on Interior and Insular Affairs, U.S. Senate (1976); Craufurd Goodwin, ed., *Energy Policy in Perspective: Today's Problems Yesterday's Solutions* (1981); Richard Hewlett and Oscar Anderson, Jr., *The New World* (1972); Richard Hewlett and Francis Duncan, *Atomic Shield* (1972); and *The Organization of Federal Energy Functions*, a Report from the President to the Congress (January 1977).

JOSEPH A. PRATT

DEPARTMENT OF HEALTH AND HUMAN SERVICES (HHS). The Department of Health and Human Services, created on May 17, 1979, became operational on the following May 4. The former Department of Health, Education, and Welfare (HEW) was abolished, its education functions going into the new Department of Education* and the remainder of its duties being allotted to HHS. In 1980, Education retained approximately 17,000 fulltime employees and a budget of $14 billion; HHS employed about 140,000 persons with a budget of $226 billion.

HHS administer's the Public Health Service;* Food and Drug Administration;* Health Care Financing Administration; Office of Human Development Services; Social Security Administration;* National Institutes of Health; Center for Disease Control; Alcohol, Drug Abuse, and Mental Health Administration; Health Resources Administration; Office of Child Support Enforcement; and Office of Community Services. A number of these functions embraced a long hisory before 1980, especially under HEW (1953-1980), the Federal Security Administration (FSA) during 1939-1953, and earlier. Those functions will be mentioned here if they are not included within the separate articles written on them in *Government Agencies*.

In addition to federal activities in education, the nineteenth-century American efforts included the establishment of St. Elizabeth's Hospital, first, in 1885, as a government hospital for the insane of the Army and Navy. During 1902-1937, it added a department of internal medicine, a rotating medical internship, occupational therapy, and the techniques of social work to assist in the rehabilitation of the patients. In 1940, it was transferred from the Department of the Interior* to the FSA. It received the overflow of other patients from Walter Reed Hospital during World War II, added a chaplain's branch in 1949, and later moved into HEW.

The federal government also sponsored several corporations, which persisted into the present era. Howard University for blacks was established in 1867 and, in 1940, moved into the FSA from Interior. The American Printing House for the Blind was organized as a print shop for blacks in Kentucky (1842), received its first federal grant in 1870, and was transferred from Treasury* to the FSA in 1939. Gallaudet College for the deaf was founded in 1817 at Hartford, Connecticut, and went through a series of name changes and federal-Connecticut appropriations before reassuming its original name in 1894. It moved, in 1940, from Interior to the FSA.

Vocational rehabilitation gained scant attention until World War I, after which sporadic funding by Congress went to veterans, to civilian victims of industrial accidents, and crippled children. Most of the coverage to crippled children before the creation of Social Security (1935) came from the states. Under Social Security benefits also went to the mentally and emotionally handicapped. In 1936, the Office of Vocational Rehabilitation encouraged blind persons to operate vending stands on federal and other properties.

The Office of Education remained in Interior until 1939, when it too was switched into the FSA. Herbert Hoover, while President, sought to appoint undersecretaries of health and education under Interior, but the move failed. Franklin D. Roosevelt succeeded in pulling these activities into the FSA during 1939-1940, while Harry S Truman got the Children's Bureau* into the FSA from the Department of Labor in 1946.

Agitation persisted for additional changes, for example, the famous Hoover Commission* Report of 1949 recommended a cabinet-level Department of Social Security and Education, a United Medical Administration, removal of the FDA to the Department of Agriculture,* and removal of FSA to Labor. Meanwhile, in 1949-1950, President Truman favored creating a Department of Welfare. The American Medical Association (AMA), however, always fearful of so-called socialized medicine, lobbied against every move to enhance federal medical and welfare duties, and the move lost in the Senate by a vote of 60 to 32. Senator John McClellan (Democrat, Arkansas) assisted the AMA in the victory. A number of veterans organizations and public health authorities had favored the proposed law.

Dwight D. Eisenhower won the presidency in 1952 and wasted little time in pressing reorganization legislation that resulted in 1953 in the new Department of HEW. Congress raised scant opposition in the House (291 to 86); only Senator George Smathers (Democrat, Florida) opposed it in the Senate debate. Outside of Congress, numerous educational leaders balked at the inclusion of Education in the new department, fearing a loss of status.

Oveta Culp Hobby was sworn in as the initial HEW Secretary on April 11, 1953. During World War II, she had successfully organized and directed the Women's Army Auxiliary Corps. Only the second woman to hold a Cabinet post (Frances Perkins was the first), this life-long Texas Democrat vigorously attacked the numerous issues at hand. At the same time she fired holdover Democrat Jane Hoey, director of the Bureau of Public Assistance.

HEW always generated a great amount of controversy. Questions were raised on national medical insurance, alleged or real welfare fraud, panic over diseases and vaccines, and on racial issues pertaining to welfare and education. Eisenhower lost his bid for national health reinsurance and vented his anger against the House. In turn, the House chided Hobby for transferring funds within HEW into her own office and for a failure to economize.

In 1955, HEW was given the assignment of distributing the rather scarce, new anti-polio drug, the Salk vaccine. Immediately arguments ensued over distribution priorities, and the liberal Americans for Democratic Action urged Hobby's ouster. She resigned, citing the poor health of her husband as the reason. She was replaced by Treasury Undersecretary Marvin B. Folsom, who earlier had had experience in establishing private social security and unemployment plans. He widened the distribution of Salk vaccine.

Folsom vigorously denied Adlai Stevenson's 1956 presidential campaign allegation that only seven people of HEW worked on bettering the lives of the aged. Accomplishments under Eisenhower had shown definite attention to health and welfare: increases in such programs as social security coverage, old age survivors insurance, rehabilitation of the handicapped for jobs, federal aid to the construction of medical centers, disability benefits, the introduction of tranquilizing drugs at St. Elizabeth's Hospital, consumer protection regarding the use of pesticides, Salk polio vaccine, Asian flu vaccine (1957), and the largest appropriations ever for health research. HEW grants also went to state and local health agencies.

Folsom tendered his resignation in 1957 because of illness but remained until the next year. He was replaced by Dr. Arthur S. Flemming, president of Ohio Wesleyan University, who had held ten federal positions over a period of nineteen years, including World War II agencies, the Hoover Commission (1947-1949), National Security Council* (1953-1957), and the Civil Service Commission* (1939-1948).

Flemming met numerous problems, including the withholding of HEW grants to states not conforming to desegregation guidelines. He invited the views of eleven special-interest groups toward HEW operations and supported the withdrawal of cranberries suspected to be tainted by pesticides containing amino-triazole (November 1959), bringing cries for his ouster by the American Farm Bureau Federation. The beginnings of the Medicare program gave funding to the states, but much reduced from Eisenhower's request, in 1960.

President-elect John F. Kennedy selected Democratic Governor Abraham A. Ribicoff of Connecticut to assume the HEW leadership in 1961.Though he had earlier opposed the creation of HEW, Ribicoff enthusiastically announced plans to curtail welfare cheating through use of the voucher system, pledged aid to sixty thousand Cuban refugees, promoted JFK's war on juvenile delinquency, joined with the Department of Agriculture in having ready civilian defense supplies of food and medicine, and barred the practice in HEW of monitoring telephone calls without first advising the caller of the practice.

Political aspirations for the U.S. Senate led Ribicoff to resign in 1962, whereupon Anthony J. Celebrezze, Italian-born mayor, lawyer, and professional politician of Cleveland, succeeded as Secretary. At about this time government authorities became embroiled in the question of restricting smoking; another controversy erupted over HEW's ban on the use of Krebiozen, an alleged cancer drug, resulting in cancer patients marching in protest to the White House; and Representative Adam Clayton Powell, Democrat of New York, denied the accusations about his European trip involving a $25,000 grant from HEW, flippantly asserting that he did only what other Congressmen did. Junket rules were somewhat tightened. Birth control information and contraceptives were issued by HEW. The Secretary also gained the power to expend $72.5 million to poor college students (1964) and started the AFL-CIO-backed Agency for Elderly the following year.

Celebrezze accepted a federal judgeship in 1965, and President Lyndon B. Johnson appointed as Secretary John W. Gardner, president of the Carnegie Corporation, a psychology Ph.D. from California who had taught for several years, had experience on the Federal Communications Commission,* and had served in the Marine Corps* before joining Carnegie. He inherited the wrath of the National Association for the Advancement of Colored People for HEW's slow pace in school desegregation as well as similar shortcomings in correcting hospital discrimination; President Johnson also reportedly had hoped for more attention to the education portion of HEW. Critics scorned the loose confederation of functions in Gardner's sprawling entity; but Gardner opposed a breakup into separate departments. His internal reorganization emphasized the creation of additional assistant secretaries, strengthening federal ties with state health organizations, an emphasis on birth-control assistance, and the beginnings of regulating auto-exhaust emissions. Meanwhile Gardner transferred to his office all of the civil-rights enforcement duties of his subordinates.

Nevertheless, Gardner encountered additional criticism as 1,000 welfare recipients picketed HEW headquarters in 1967. He resigned early in 1968, and Johnson appointed HEW Undersecretary Wilbur J. Cohen as Acting Secretary. Cohen, of Milwaukee, an FDR employee in Social Security, was a professor of public welfare at the University of Michigan during 1956-1961, and in HEW (1961-1965).

After his election President Richard M. Nixon chose Robert H. Finch, Lieutenant Governor of California, as Secretary. Finch inherited the smoldering problem leading to the phaseout of the famous chemical DDT by Agriculture and HEW in 1971 and a petition of some 2,000 resentful HEW staffers who charged that Nixon lacked dedication to genuine civil-rights enforcement. Widespread outside criticism ensued in 1969 over the disclosure that for years HEW had allegedly utilized a blacklist of scientists who were barred from advisory panels and research funding, supposedly including one Nobel Prize winner. Within HEW numerous employees had strongly disagreed for several years with United States policies in Vietnam and Cambodia, a factor contributing to internal turmoil. At the outset of his tenure, Finch struggled unsuccessfully to gain Senate confirmation of Dr. J. H. Knowles as Assistant Secretary of Health and Scientific Affairs. Nixon finally withdrew the nomination, bowing to the steadfast opposition of the conservative AMA and Senator Everett M. Dirksen (R., Ill.).

Finch escaped the strain in HEW in the summer of 1970 to join the White House staff. President Nixon then summoned as secretary Elliott Richardson, who left his post as Undersecretary of State to head HEW. Meanwhile, Nixon vetoed what he called a too inflationary HEW budget and demanded his own discretionary spending authority at HEW and throughout the executive branch.

The 1970s proved no different than the previous decade as accusations, investigations, and pleas for reorganization continued unabated. Nixon resisted the moves for separate health and education departments. States were ordered in 1971 to conduct spot-checks against Medicaid fraud by doctors. The Senate probed operations of the Division of Biological Standards, and women's organizations sued the National Institutes of Health over discriminatory practices. The ouster of key personnel troubled the scientific community and former HEW employees.

The continued parade of top leadership in and out of HEW persisted with Caspar W. Weinberger succeeding Richardson in 1972. Weinberger had formerly chaired the Federal Trade Commission* and had served in the Office of Management and Budget.*

In 1973, HEW gained Office of Equal Opportunity programs and the Indian and health functions from Labor. Simultaneously, a federal district judge ordered President Nixon to release over $52 million of impounded funds designated for establishing community health centers. Congressmen bemoaned other impoundments, including $1.1 billion intended for health functions. The revelation of a lawsuit in 1973 by eighty survivors of almost six hundred blacks left untreated for syphilis in 1932 in a Tuskegee Institute experiment shocked the nation. Weinberger promised a full range of HEW benefits. Meanwhile, an HEW study conducted by an anthropologist at the University of Pennsylvania linked environment, not racial heredity, to lower IQ scores. Women instigated suits against sexual bias in college sports.

As President Gerald Ford took over after Nixon's resignation, HEW gained a new head in historian F. David Mathews, president of the University of Alabama, a Columbia University Ph.D. and author of books on Southern history and higher education. HEW appointed its own inspector general in the wake of perennial congressional allegations of fraud, involving in particular this time student loans. In the last Nixon years and during Ford's brief tenure, HEW also became involved in questions of caustic detergents, lead poisoning, the regulation of nursing homes, jail reform, drug abuse, and the perennial instances of delayed school integration.

The Jimmy Carter White House years until HEW's demise proved to be no less controversial. His initial Secretary was Joseph A. Califano, Jr., a lawyer and former special assistant to Defense (1961-1965) and to the President during 1965-1969. Califano remained until his removal in 1978, supposedly because he opposed Carter over a new Department of Education, moved relentlessly with his anti-smoking bias, was too favorable toward Carter's arch-rival, Edward Kennedy, and had failed to gain from Congress national health insurance, a check on rising hospital costs, and the overhaul of the welfare system. Califano originally vigorously upheld the controversial quota systems for minorities in job hiring, and ordered a probe of cancer patients who had been exposed to earlier atomic testing.

Welfare and health waste and fraud persisted, one official claiming that 5 percent of the fiscal year budget for 1977 fit that category. In 1978 a federal grand jury indicted fifteen HEW employees, both former and present. HEW, apparently indicating its inability to eliminate waste, sought to reduce the total future slippage to 4 percent in welfare programs. President Carter's proposal for an education department failed in 1978, although most education groups, except for the American Federation of Teachers, favored the bill.

The new HHS began in 1980 with Patricia R. Harris as its first Secretary. A lawyer, she had trial judge experience with the Department of Justice,* was dean of the School of Law at Howard University, and had been Secretary of Housing and Urban Development from 1977 to 1979. Former judge Shirley M. Hufstedler headed Education. A major U.S. Supreme Court decision in 1980 slowed drastically the former HEW practices of underwriting approximately 1,000 abortions per week, rejecting rehearings on Medicaid cases. Carter vetoed a congressional attempt to investigate the effects of dioxin, the chemical used in Agent Orange and in other herbicides.

Critical of and threatening toward HHS operations in his election campaign, President Ronald Reagan preached federalism as the new gospel regarding its functions. Senator Richard S. Schweiker, Republican of Pennsylvania, just retired from two terms in the Senate and five in the House and critical of Medicaid, became Secretary. However, the bureaucracy and Congress, as usual, precluded drastic hatchet attacks on vital services. Moreover, the ever-present controversies emerged. Reagan finally withdrew the nomination of one candidate for an assistant secretaryship who had formerly been employed by an anti-semitic group which considered the Holocaust a myth. In 1982, the Urban League and the Planned Parenthood Federation of America unleashed a scathing attack on HHS's proposal to notify parents of teenage daughters under eighteen years of age within ten days if they obtained birth control devices.

On a more positive note, HHS reorganized certain functions including the establishment in 1981 of the Office of Community Services to administer the community block grants whenever funds existed. Regional offices for HHS now exist in Boston, New York, Philadelphia, Atlanta, Chicago, Dallas, Kansas City, Denver, San Francisco, and Seattle. Its National Institutes of Health continue to concentrate on individual problems, for example, institutes for drug abuse, arthritis, cancer, lung ailments, and dental concerns. The Health Care Financing Administration, created in 1977, focuses on long-term care, including Medicare and Medicaid. The Center for Disease Control, established at Atlanta in 1973, is dedicated both to the prevention and control of disease.

Despite liberal or more conservative trends in congressional appropriations to HHS, its history and that of its predecessors would substantiate the prediction that health and welfare services will continue, if not expand, and the process will produce the usual charges and countercharges of mismanagement. In October 1982, HHS instigated a system of toll-free telephone numbers to encourage citizens to report directly cases of waste or fraud. Perhaps this will prove effective.

FOR ADDITIONAL INFORMATION: A rather detailed evaluation of HEW programs for the early 1970s is available in James G. Abert, ed., *Program Evaluation at HEW: Research Versus Reality*, 3 vols., (1979). Secretary Califano relates his own story of tenure at HEW in Joseph A. Califano, Jr., *Governing America* (1981). Especially revealing is his chapter on the difficulty of gaining welfare reform. A useful account of federal health, education, and welfare activities before HEW was established in 1953 is located in Gordon F. Mixdorf, ''Origins and Development of the Department of Health, Education, and Welfare,'' M.A. thesis, University of Northern Iowa (Cedar Falls), July 1959. Congressional budget hearings and special investigations of HEW-HHS along with the official departmental and subagency files are important for scholarly study. A solid, comprehensive book on HHS and its predecessors is badly needed.

DONALD R. WHITNAH

DEPARTMENT OF HEALTH, EDUCATION, AND WELFARE. See Department of Health and Human Services.

DEPARTMENT OF HOUSING AND URBAN DEVELOPMENT (HUD). President Lyndon B. Johnson signed the law establishing the Department of Housing and Urban Development on September 9, 1965. Speaking to a group of distinguished leaders from Congress, housing organization officials, and city mayors, the President said that, with the new agency, the agency was instituting a rational approach to meeting the problems of modern urban life. The ceremony in the Rose Garden brought to a climax a struggle, stretching back at least a decade, to create a Cabinet office representing the nation's urban interests.

The fundamental argument of proponents of the new Cabinet post centered on the tremendous urbanization that has transformed the face of America in this century. In 1900, about 40 percent of the population lived in urban areas; by 1960, 70 percent of all Americans lived in such areas. By 1960, there were fifty urban places in the United States with a population of more than 250,000 each, as compared to fifteen in 1900. The urban character of American society prompted Dante B. Fascell (Democrat, Florida), author of the bill to establish the new department, to observe on the floor of the House that the new legislation answered the needs of America's major population sector.

Although the real legislative effort to create an agency on urban affairs did not begin until the 1950s, foresighted persons were calling for greater attention to America's cities earlier in the century. For example, in 1912 a man named Philip Kates wrote an article in the magazine *American City* suggesting the establishment of a Department of Municipalities. The department was to be primarily a study group to investigate all aspects of urban living in order to inform local authorities. President Woodrow Wilson read the article and sent a letter indicating that he would like to discuss the proposal with Kates.

Although nothing came from this incident, it did begin a process of arriving at what might be called a "consensus" on the need for an agency concerned with urban problems. The early proposals, like those of Kates, stressed the need for study of urban problems. As urbanization continued, the demand grew for representation of the urban population at the Cabinet table. And finally, with the expansion of federal urban programs arose the desire for a department that could effectively coordinate federal assistance to local communities.

Legislation that emphasized these purposes—study, representation, and co-ordination—was introduced in the Congress in 1954 by Representative J. Arthur Younger (H.R. 1864), but not until 1959 did the establishment of some agency appear likely. The House Committee on Government Operations reported favorably on H.R. 7465, introduced by Representative Dante B. Fascell. This bill proposed the establishment of a Commission on Metropolitan Problems and Urban Development. The committee report stated that the commission would be entrusted with the task of investigating the problems of municipalities and metropolitan expansion, with special reference to the need, in terms of adequate government structures, to establish sound revenue policies as related to state and national revenue policies, and to determine the services such governmental structures should provide. The commission was to recommend federal policies and programs for coping with metropolitan problems.

Congressman Fascell's efforts to establish a commission were not rewarded with success in the Eighty-sixth Congress. The House did not act on H.R. 7465, although the Senate did pass a similar measure. But Fascell's leadership was soon to be influential. The pressure exerted in Congress for some agency on urban problems and the publicity thus created in the nation led to President John F. Kennedy's vigorous support of a Department of Housing and Urban Affairs. In his State of the Union address on January 30, 1961, President Kennedy said, "Our national household is cluttered with unfinished and neglected tasks. Our cities are being engulfed in squalor. . . . We still have 25 million Americans living in substandard homes.'' On the basis of these remarks, the President recommended the establishment of a Department of Housing and Urban Affairs. He felt strongly that an awareness of these problems should be constantly brought to the Cabinet table.

Representative Fascell introduced into the Eighty-seventh Congress H.R. 6433, a bill to bring to reality President Kennedy's proposals. The bill was to create a new department headed by a Cabinet-level Secretary. The Housing and Home Finance Agency was to be the nucleus of the new department. Congressman Fascell's bill incorporated the three major tasks that had come to be agreed on as necessary—study of housing and urban problems, representation of metropolitan areas at the highest government level, and coordination of federal activities.

Fascell's efforts to get the bill passed stimulated lively debate, both for and against. Influential groups such as the U.S. Conference of Mayors and the American Municipal Association supported the measure. But opponents strenuously argued that the creation of such an executive department presupposed a permanent and expanding federal role in urban affairs that would undermine local and state initiatives.

The House Rules Committee refused to grant a rule for floor action on the bill establishing the department. But the supporters of the bill did not give up. Congressman Fascell, who had led the forces for the administration bill, now was given charge of a new tactic: Six days after the Rules Committee action on January 24, 1962, against the bill for a department, President Kennedy submitted to Congress Reorganization Plan No. 1 of 1962, to create a Cabinet-level Department of Urban Affairs and Housing. The plan was submitted under the provisions of the Reorganization Act of 1949, which authorized the President to submit to Congress plans to reorganize government agencies through transfer, abolition, or consolidation of agency functions. The plan was to go into effect within sixty days unless disapproved by a simple majority vote in either House.

Again, opponents were able to thwart the administration. On February 21, 1962, the House adopted a resolution killing the Reorganization Plan by a vote of 264 to 150.

But the struggle to meet the problems of urban living with adequate governmental machinery was not over. President Lyndon B. Johnson in his Housing message of January 23, 1964, stated that the creation of an executive department for housing was long overdue. However, the pressure of other issues before the Congress prevented action on legislation to create the department that year.

In 1965, a new concentrated effort was made. On January 4, the President again urged the creation of a Cabinet-level Department of Housing and Urban Development. Congressman Fascell again laid before his fellow members the undeniable need to have the metropolitan areas represented at the high councils of the nation. He reiterated his views with an eloquent statement in the hearings on the legislation, pointing to the "good management" effects of the legislation as well. He maintained that it would carry out the recommendations of the Hoover

Commission* with respect to empowering the head of an agency with duties and powers commensurate with his department's tasks. He also emphasized the beneficial aspects of governmental coordination, without hindrance to local and state endeavors.

On June 16, 1965, the House passed Fascell's H.R. 6927 by a vote of 217 to 184. The Senate voted for the measure on August 11, 1965, passing it by a vote of 57 to 33.

Public Law 89-174 elevated the Housing and Home Finance Agency to the Department of Housing and Urban Development. Thus, the first step had been taken in bringing urban problems to the full attention of the nation and in providing the necessary organizational machinery to solve them.

HUD's fortunes and misfortunes over the years have been the reflection of politics and personalities. The central personality involved in HUD's birth was Robert C. Weaver. In 1961, he was the administrator of the Housing and Home Finance Agency and the highest ranking Negro in the U.S. government. President Kennedy wanted Weaver to become the first Negro Cabinet member in history. Therefore, the President and the Congress saw the Kennedy Administration's advocacy for a Department of Urban Affairs as a way of bringing Weaver into the Cabinet. In fact, when the Rules Committee blocked the bill, claiming "bad bureaucratic organization," Kennedy told the nation at a press conference that he would have appointed Weaver if the bill had been passed.

Many believe that President Kennedy's effort in 1962 to create the Urban Affairs Department was defeated because of prejudice against a black man. President Lyndon Johnson's successful effort in 1965 was a direct and clear testimony to a change in American attitudes toward black citizens. On the heels of such a civil rights victory, however, President Johnson acted strangely—and cruelly—toward the central symbol of the victory. For months he delayed naming Weaver as the Secretary of HUD, going through a charade of considering hundreds of other names. He may have meant the delay as a means of strengthening Weaver, by appearing to select the "best" man of the long list. Or he may have wanted to make Weaver more indebted to him. Whatever his motive, the result was to cripple HUD at its inception. Weaver should have been appointed immediately, so as to assert his authority over the formerly independent sections of HUD, especially the Public Housing Administration and the Federal Housing Administration. But, instead, doubts about the President's support floated throughout Washington.

To his credit, Weaver, always the statesman, did not complain. He steered the helm at HUD when Congress gave the department a mandate to assume a new role as the leader in the effort to provide a decent home for every American family. In the Housing and Urban Development Acts of 1965 and 1968 and the Model Cities legislation of 1966, HUD was given new programs which went beyond the traditional public housing and FHA insurance approaches—a rent supplement program for low-income families in 1965, a massive inner-city rebuilding program (Model Cities), and a well-funded, interest-subsidy program for both multifamily dwellers and home buyers in 1968. The overarching meaning of the programs was this: they were responsive to the civil rights movement, and they were attempts to redress the grievances of black Americans. They were fitting weapons in Weaver's arsenal.

Richard Nixon called the Model Cities Program one of the worst federal undertakings that he inherited. We now know that, although HUD Secretary George Romney presided over the greatest housing production surge in U.S. history, his own President shut him out of his confidence in 1969 when Romney pleaded for a continuation of the Model Cities Program. It was only a matter of time until Nixon gathered his forces to do what he wanted to do at the beginning—halt all federal involvement in housing programs. Romney, the general of the war against slums, was ordered by his commander-in-chief to surrender. So in January 1973, it fell to Romney—who had achieved unprecedented levels of subsidized housing production—to announce the moratorium on all federal housing programs.

The darkest hours of HUD's history followed for those who had labored for decades to build the foundation of HUD's housing programs. Now Nixon installed a Secretary with instructions to dismantle the still young department—James Lynn. All programs were halted, and a "study" of them was undertaken. When the study was released in September 1973, a disjointed hodgepodge of non-sequiturs and unsupportable opinions were used to justify burying the crucified federal programs. President Nixon went on the radio to declare that the cities' problems had been solved and that only a housing allowance program and a revenue-sharing-type, block-grant program called Community Development would gain his support.

Although Democrats in Congress were able to extract a small housing production program within the new "Section 8" of the legislation from the Nixon Administration in return for passage of the Community Development Program, HUD was able to sabotage any production under Lynn and under President Ford's Secretary, Carla Hills.

The Carter Administration sought to revive housing production without significant increases in expenditures. In truth, Carter housing officials, under Secretary Patricia Roberts Harris, did approach the housing problem with serious intentions to increase housing opportunity. But instead of advancing any new initiatives, the administration decided to try to make the Nixon-Ford program work. And so from zero production, the Carter years saw approximately 100,000 new units built annually for low-income families. But this was still 400,000 to 500,000 units short of the annual number built under George Romney.

As with its predecessors, the Reagan Administration is putting its political stamp on HUD. Budget cutters found a vulnerable target with the Section 8 Program, for Congress was already uneasy with its cost. So, David Stockman's Office of Management and Budget took deep bites, finally leaving only about 50,000 units of newly constructed housing in the budget. Ironically, the duty of imposing this new austerity on HUD has fallen to a black—Samuel Pierce, Jr., the only black man in the Cabinet.

It is somewhat remarkable that since its inception HUD has been used for purposes extraneous to its role as the Department of Housing and Urban Development. It was established in order to elevate a black to the Cabinet. It was invigorated by programs to calm the black protest from the ghetto. It was dismantled by an ideological opponent, as part of Nixon's overall scheme to diminish the federal government. It was half-heartedly revived by President Carter, who wanted credit with his liberal constituency at little cost. And it was gutted by the Reagan Administration intent on reducing government expenditures.

Not one presidential administration has looked on HUD as the focal point for housing opportunity. Each Secretary has served other symbolic purposes—"first black in the Cabinet" (Weaver), "only woman in the Ford Cabinet" (Hills), "first black woman in the Cabinet" (Harris).

No Secretary of HUD has been a homebuilder, a carpenter, or a real estate salesman. The Secretary of Agriculture is usually a successful farmer. The Secretary of Labor is usually a union leader. The Secretary of Commerce is usually a businessman. The Department of Housing and Urban Development represents the housing interests of the nation; perhaps someday someone interested in housing will be its leader.

FOR ADDITIONAL INFORMATION: Tom Forrester Lord, *Decent Housing: A Promise to Keep* (1977), an historical account of federal housing programs since the New Deal; M. Carter McFarland, *Federal Government and Urban Problems: HUD* (1978), an insider's look at HUD from a former official; Blake McKelvey, *The Emergence of Metropolitan America, 1915-1966* (1968), especially pp. 206ff, the best treatment on the impact of urbanization on America; and U.S. Government, *Housing in the Seventies* (October 6, 1973).

TOM FORRESTER LORD

DEPARTMENT OF INTERIOR. Created in 1849 by a coalition of Whigs and public-land state Democrats, the Interior Department became at once the department of the great miscellany. As Congress created bureaus such as Labor and Education in the late nineteenth century, most seemed to have ended up under the Interior Department's jurisdiction. These bureaus were added to other concerns of the department such as public lands; mineral, timber, and water resources; Indian affairs; railroad land grants; war-related pensions; the Patent Office*; and the Census Bureau*; by the dawn of the twentieth century, the department had become a conglomeration of functions.

Soon after its creation, the Secretary's office was divided into three large units called divisions designed to oversee groups of these major responsibilities. They were Lands and Railroads, Indians, and a catch-all Patents and Miscellaneous Division. The titles of the first two divisions reveal their principal concerns. In addition to the management of public lands and their disposal to individuals, state governments, and firms, the Lands and Railroads Division busied itself with administering grants to railroads, canals, and roads under various federal laws and in refereeing the various mineral-land statutes. The General Land Office* reported to the Secretary through this division. Later, the commissioner of railroads and the Geological Survey* came under Lands and Railroads jurisdiction.

The Indian Division supervised the broad range of problems relating to relationships with the various Indian tribes. Through this division the Bureau of Indian Affairs* reported on matters such as education, annuities, and reservation problems. In the event of conflicts, the Indian Division coordinated affairs with the War Department.*

As indicated, the Patents and Miscellaneous Division became the great catch-all for new Interior responsibilities. The Patent Office maintained the files and adjudicated proposals for new inventions. The Census Bureau operated only sporadically as it geared up for the decennial census, and then became inactive. The Pension Office administered the various veteran and dependent pensions authorized by Congress. Concerns such as the Washington, D.C., police department and jail, the Architect of the Capitol, and various federal charitable and educational institutions such as the Columbia Hospital for Women and the government hospital for the insane reported through this division. When responsibility over the territories came to Interior from the State Department* in 1873, it, too, fell under this division. Until the organization of the Justice Department* in 1870, the Patents and Miscellaneous Division took care of many of the administrative affairs of the federal legal arm such as contracting and paying the costs of constructing penitentiaries and paying U.S. marshals.

As a legacy of its role as miscellaneous administrator, the Interior Department continues to supervise a number of U.S. territories. These include Guam and the Virgin Islands which, since 1970, have elected their own governments and have virtually complete control over their internal affairs. American Samoa, the U.N. Mandated Trust Territory of Pacific Islands taken from Japan during World War II, and Puerto Rico also fall under Interior's jurisdiction, but enjoy a form of commonwealth status.

The organization of the Interior Department into three divisions standing between the various bureau chiefs and the Interior Secretary continued until the first decade of the twentieth century. By that time, the division chiefs considered themselves as three super commissioners. Matters referred to the Secretary passed through the chiefs who recommended approval or disapproval of bureau recommendations outlining their own views. This procedure tended to foster inefficiency since it multiplied paper work and wasted time. In fact, by the middle of the first decade of the twentieth century, the department experienced a breakdown in its filing system.

This state of affairs prompted the hiring of an outside consultant and the implementation by James R. Garfield of a number of changes. In 1907, Garfield abolished the three divisions and delegated their responsibilities to the various bureau commissioners. In addition, a new filing system consisting of decimal classifications replaced the old chronological log-in system, which had been in effect before.

Further administrative changes have characterized other twentieth-century administrations. Hubert Work, whose appointment came in 1923 on the heels of the scandal-ridden Secretaryship of Albert B. Fall, became concerned with administrative reorganization. Transferring personnel administration from each of the bureaus, he centralized the appointment procedure in the Secretary's office and through this change as well as the simplification of other administrative practices achieved savings.

Another significant administrative reform took place during the administration of Julius Krug during the Truman years. As the first Interior Secretary who was also a career public administrator, Krug thrived on administrative responsibility. He set up temporary and later permanent field committees in various regions and loosened the control of the various bureaus over their interests in order to promote better interagency cooperation and public consultation. Beyond this, during the winter of 1948-1949, he established a staff to examine all departmental policies and to make recommendations for translating proposals into programs. The principal value of Krug's reforms seems to have been the closer contact promoted between the department and representatives of interest groups.

Krug's successor, Oscar Chapman, built upon the work of his predecessor and, in addition, instituted a number of reforms proposed by the Hoover Commission* on Governmental Reorganization. The major changes included extensive decentralization through delegating most matters to the bureaus and through the development of a staff system to assist the Secretary on major program and policy decisions. Changes in departmental structure since the Truman Administration seem to have built on the reforms inaugurated by Krug and Chapman.

In spite of the miscellaneous character of the duties assigned to the Interior Department, its principal responsibilities in both the nineteenth and twentieth centuries have focused on public lands and on Indian affairs. By the time the Interior Department was created, the accumulation of revenues from the sale of public lands had ceased to be the principal motive of the federal government, and public policy mandated the disposal of public lands to promote social and economic ends. Since the interest groups served by the various pieces of legislation varied, the laws themselves met often contradictory needs, and their administration led to conflicts between and among representatives of interest groups and congressmen. Legislation and administrative practice produced what Paul Gates has called "an Incongruous Land System," since lands disposed of for one purpose were unavailable for other competing individuals and firms.

Increasingly, however, the Interior Department faced two problems which led to a change in emphasis in public land policy and which moved it in the direction characteristic of today. In the first place, laws designed for disposal of land to individual homesteaders in the humid Midwest did not fit well in the region west of the hundredth meridian. In the far West, trees were generally located on land unsuited for agriculture and thus not subject to acquisition under existing laws.

Small-crop agriculture was limited to valleys between mountain ranges in the mountain West and even on the high plains could not be carried on without irrigation. Grazing required large tracts of land for ranches that could not be acquired legally under existing laws except by purchase from railroads and other grantees. At the same time, departmental policy slowed the disposal of land to railroad corporations and thus indirectly retarded the transfer of that land to families and firms.

The second problem was the recognition that resources, once thought to be virtually inexhaustible, were, in fact, finite and in some cases irreplaceable. This recognition led to the development of a conservation movement with essentially two thrusts. The first of these, utilitarian conservation, was led in the nineteenth century by people like John Wesley Powell and William E. Smythe and in the twentieth century by Gifford Pinchot and Theodore Roosevelt. Utilitarian conservationists proposed multiple use of natural resources through sustained-yield management of timber, grazing in line with the productive capacity of range lands, and reclamation projects to husband water resources. The second thrust, that of aesthetic conservation or preservation found its champions in people like George Perkins Marsh, John Muir, and Aldo Leopold, who favored the preservation of nature as a source of strength and enjoyment.

The pressures induced by the need for resource management led to the passage of legislation that altered the role of the Interior Department significantly. Perhaps the most important first step came in the General Revision Act of 1891, which authorized the creation of forest reserves, recognized the need for reclamation, and repealed the Timber Culture and Preemption Acts. Thereafter, the Interior Department began to establish forest reserves, and, after the passage of the Forest Management Act of 1898, it began the sale of mature timber and the leasing of grazing rights on the reserves. This continued until Congress transferred the reserves to the Forest Service* in 1905.

In the twentieth century, the Interior Department has moved increasingly to promote conservation. Attempts to increase the size of homesteads in the arid West and to open public lands to legal acquisition by cattle ranchers, while securing the passage of some laws, proved largely abortive. With the failure to transfer the remaining public lands to the states during the Hoover Administration, Congress sought a new means of administering the national domain. These lands comprised a majority of land in the mountain West and sizable proportions in other states west of the hundredth meridian. In 1935, with the passage of the Taylor Grazing Act, Congress confirmed the right to manage the range lands on a sustained-yield basis. Thereafter, the department created grazing districts and issued permits to ranchers for the use of lands in return for an annual payment based on the number of livestock grazed. Increasingly, management rather than disposal became the principal use of the public lands, a fact that Truman recognized in an Executive Order, in 1946, which consolidated the Grazing Service and the General Land Office in the newly created Bureau of Land Management.* Passage of the Federal Land Policy and Management Act of 1976 further reinforced this tendency by confirming existing policy and declaring the further disposal of the public lands to be contrary to public policy, except as the Secretary of the Interior should find it in the public interest.

The second major concern of the Interior Department has been in the area of Indian affairs. During the nineteenth century, the principal thrust of Indian policy was the removal of Indians to reservations where the process of acculturation was to transform them into something resembling Euro-Americans. Throughout the nineteenth century, the United States pursued this policy through a series of treaties, battles, land acquisitions, and relocations. Treaties and grants by Congress and Interior Department administrative decisions provided for schools, agricultural training, and enforced acculturation. Perhaps the best known statement of this policy was the Dawes Severalty Act of 1887, which authorized the department to divide reservations into individual 160-acre farming tracts and to open the remainder of the land to Euro-American farmers.

The inauguration of the New Deal and the influence of a number of reformers like John Collier led to a reappraisal of this policy. Under Collier's lead and with the approval of Congress in the Wheeler-Howard Act of 1934, the policy of allotment and disposal of Indian lands ended, and tribes were encouraged to form their own organizations and to own lands collectively.

Increasingly, during and after World War II, pressure to end the federal supervision of Indian affairs led to what was called "termination." Under this policy, the states and the Indians themselves were to assume responsibility for their affairs, and the federal government was to end both its subsidies of Indian programs and its interference in the internal affairs of Indian tribes. Implemented among perhaps ten thousand Indians, the policy often proved disastrous as a number of tribes lost land and Indians entered the welfare rolls on their own lands and in cities to which many had been relocated.

Ultimately, in 1958, Interior Secretary Fred Seaton, while defending the idea in general, declared an end to forced termination. In the intervening years, the federal government has vacillated between allowing greater autonomy to Indian tribal governments and exercising control over their affairs. This has led to confrontations and to violence on occasion, but the government's resolve to allow greater self-determination, while maintaining the unique relationship with the Indian people, led to the passage of the Indian Self Determination and Education Assistance Act of 1975.

Nevertheless, in the twentieth century the Interior Department's central concern has increasingly shifted to public lands and resources. New bureaus and laws concerned with resource matters were added to the department. Among them were the Bureau of Reclamation (1903),* the Bureau of Mines (1910),* the National Park Service (1916),* and the United States Fish and Wildlife Service (1939).* Beginning with the Antiquities Act (1906) and continuing with such recent laws as the Wilderness Act of 1964, which established the national wilderness preservation system; the Water Quality and Solid Waste Disposal Act of 1965, which set standards for water quality; and the National Environmental

Policy Act (1970), which established general guidelines for environmental protection, the Interior Department has been drawn increasingly into environmental
protection. All of these measures have involved the Interior Department in an
increasingly central role in regulating the quality of life for Americans.

Internally, the Interior Department recognized the centrality of public resource
management. In 1964, for instance, the department discontinued its annual reports and began instead a series called the Interior Conservation Yearbook. These
volumes highlight the efforts and accomplishments in the management of natural
resources. Thus, from a department of the great miscellany, the Interior Department has evolved into a department of natural resources.

FOR ADDITIONAL INFORMATION: The major sources for the history of the Interior
Department include a number of readily available published items. The serious student
will want to read the *Annual Reports of the Secretaries of the Interior* and the *Conservation
Yearbooks* which succeeded them. Especially useful is the summary of Interior Department
history in No. ll: *America 200: The Legacy of Our Lands* (1976). Perhaps the best source
materials for Interior secretaries through the administration of Stewart Udall will be found
in Eugene P. Trani's *The Secretaries of the Interior, 1849-1969* (1975). The early history
of the department is covered in Norman Olaf Forness's, "The Origins and Early History
of the United States Department of the Interior" (Ph.D. Dissertation, Pennsylvania State
University, 1964); developments in the nineteenth century will be found in Thomas G.
Alexander's *A Clash of Interests: Interior Department and Mountain West, 1863-1896*
(1977). The study of public land policy is best begun with Paul W. Gates and Robert
W. Swenson's *History of Public Land Law Development* (1969), which provides a good
introduction to the conservation movement as well.

THOMAS G. ALEXANDER

DEPARTMENT OF JUSTICE. The Department of Justice was not created
until 1870, but its direct predecessor, the Office of the Attorney General, was
established by the Judiciary Act of 1789. The act provided for the appointment
by the President of a

person, learned in the law, to act as attorney general of the United States, . . . to prosecute
and conduct all suits in the Supreme Court in which the United States shall be concerned,
and to give his advice and opinion upon questions of law when required by the President
of the United States, or when requested by the heads of any of the departments, touching
any matters that may concern their departments.

Edmund Randolph, a friend and lawyer for President Washington, was appointed
as the first Attorney General and served until 1794.

Unlike the duties of the other members of the first Cabinet, the powers and
responsibilities of the Attorney General were vague and for many years the job
was considered as only part-time. Much of the work was providing legal counsel
to members of the executive branch of the new federal government and to
Congress as it wrote legislation. Until William Wirt became Attorney General

in 1817, that practice continued, and the position remained anomalous. Wirt's predecessors had tried important cases in the courts, offered sanguine advice on foreign policies, and participated sporadically in Cabinet meetings, but Wirt discovered no set of records or book of opinions from the previous attorneys general. Wirt set up an opinions and records system, obtained an office and clerk, and limited the number and scope of opinions coming from the Attorney General. Wirt resigned after the election of Andrew Jackson, but having served more than a decade, he established the office as the law department for the executive branch of the federal government.

Between Wirt's tenure and the passage of the bill creating the Department of Justice in 1870, efforts were made to increase the duties, appropriations, and prestige of the Office of the Attorney General in the face of a general hesitance by Congress to establish another full department. Caleb Cushing, who served as Attorney General from 1854 to 1857, acquired functions from the Departments of Interior* and State* which included the commissions of law officers, the accounts of the federal courts, and the processing of pardons and petitions for executive clemency. The acquisition of more functions increased the movement for an official law department, but the bills introduced to that end before the Civil War were never made into law.

The legal and political issues that the attorneys general dealt with during the antebellum period included the national banks, the distribution of public lands, and slavery. In 1819, the national bank issue came before the Supreme Court, and Attorney General Wirt appeared for the United States with the counsel for McCulloch in *McCulloch* v. *Maryland*. The second Attorney General for President Andrew Jackson was Roger Taney, who was on the opposite side of the bank question from his predecessor Wirt. He wrote two opinions for Jackson, stating that the President could fire the recalcitrant Secretary of the Treasury, William Duane, who would not withdraw federal funds from the national bank. In the second (and his last) opinion as Attorney General, Taney stated that the Secretary of the Treasury could in fact put federal funds into depositories other than the Bank of the United States. Taney's successors, Benjamin Butler and John Nelson, continued the fight against the national bank through Jackson's administration.

In the distribution of public lands by the federal government, the role of the attorneys general was as litigant for the government in dealing with the claims of people to land in the Louisiana, Florida, and California territories. Large land frauds were common, and the litigation was difficult for the U.S. attorneys, attorneys general, and solicitors of the Treasury who shared responsibility for defending the government land. Many cases reached the Supreme Court, particularly the huge land claims, and, as the government attorneys used the Mexican archives and fought to adjudicate the settlements fairly, the battles for land increased with the federal government not gaining much popularity from the original claimants, settlers, and land companies. By 1870, most of the California and other claims were settled.

The legal problems about slavery at the federal level were not unimportant, but the attorneys general for the most part attempted to avoid involvement in them. The slave trade, the fate of blacks captured on the high seas, and fugitive slaves in the North were the major slave issues which the attorneys general faced in the antebellum period. No clear policies were followed, and delay and court efforts on behalf of the institution of slavery were the primary legal directions of the federal government. Edward Bates and James Speed were the two Civil War attorneys general, and, though they did not set great policies during the national crisis, they did handle questions of military versus civil rule, disloyal activities, and confiscation of property at sea and on land. The writ of habeas corpus cases were the most important civil cases, and the Supreme Court decided *ex parte Milligan* in favor of the defendant after the end of the war. Reconstruction presented an extremely difficult period for the U.S. attorneys in the South who with the Army attempted to enforce the Reconstruction laws. There were prosecutions to stop the violence against the blacks in the South, but, as the Supreme Court overruled the Civil Rights Acts and prosecution of election frauds became almost impossible, the attorneys general and Department of Justice joined the rapprochement between the North and the South.

The Department of Justice Act, passed in June 1870, created the department beginning in July of that year, with the Attorney General retaining his former duties and the Solicitor General being his principal assistant. The solicitor of the Treasury, as well as the law officers of the State* and Navy* departments and the Bureau of Internal Revenue, were transferred to the new department. In the 1870 act and later legislation, the Department of Justice was authorized to supervise all U.S. attorneys and other law officers of the federal government, to facilitate the business of the courts, to provide for federal prison facilities, to control immigration and administer naturalizations, to advise on paroles, and to investigate federal crimes. These responsibilities and the increasing number of crimes brought under federal responsibility greatly increased the size and amount of work for the Department of Justice throughout its history.

Amos Akerman, a Republican from Georgia and appointee of President Ulysses S. Grant, was the first Attorney General to direct the new department. The new act solidified the politically powerful patronage system in which the Attorney General processed the appointments of federal judges, U.S. attorneys, and marshals. The attorneys general worked with presidents and senators in those appointments, but nonetheless the Attorney General could be a major political figure in an administration. The conflict between administering justice and managing a political system often strained the balance between the two. Akerman issued opinions on payment of interest for the federal railroad construction loans and extension of railroad lines that raised the ire of the railroad companies and caused President Grant's request for his resignation. Late in the next year, 1872, the Credit Mobilier scandal revelations forced the new Attorney General to appoint two "special prosecutors" within the department. That prosecution was unsuccessful, but the merging of party politics and the Department of Justice historically has been a major problem for some presidential administrations—most notably manifested in the resignations under fire of Attorneys General Harry Daugherty and John Mitchell.

The West provided a number of seemingly insurmountable legal problems for the department. The distances were great, prosecutions difficult, and Congress appropriated minimal funds to police the sparsely settled territories. The courts functioned in many places in primitive fashion and surroundings. The fee system for compensating local, federal law officers was an evil that favored many petty legal actions and left many federal attorneys and marshals underpaid. The system was finally abolished in 1897. Protecting the national wealth on federal lands, particularly timber, was an almost impossible task for Department of Justice attorneys. Lumber and railroad interests were politically powerful and locally popular, so that prosecutions for illegal cuttings were seldom successful. Later in the early twentieth century when conservation of natural resources became a more popular issue, the department was somewhat more successful, but political pressures and long legal battles made enforcement of weak conservation laws formidable.

The passage of the Sherman Anti-Trust Act in 1890 produced some of the most publicized prosecutions by the department in the early twentieth century. During the first decade of its existence, the law had minimal effects on the growth of corporations, but after the assassination of President William McKinley, President Theodore Roosevelt and Attorney General Philander C. Knox moved to prosecute five major antitrust cases. The two most important were the *Northern Securities* and *Swift* cases, which the government won by narrow margins. Later victories in civil cases against Standard Oil and American Tobacco were frustrated by the consent decrees agreed to by the attorneys general and the legal machinations by the corporations to establish greater control of industries and markets. Prosecutions and regulation of monopolies after World War I have been sporadic, but the Anti-Trust Division of the department continues to monitor the growth of corporations and sometimes does prosecute effectively to stop mergers.

World War I brought new and onerous tasks to the department, beginning with the prosecutions of neutrality violations. Merchant ships were the most prominent offenders, and they thrust upon the department difficult enforcement questions. The department asked Congress for more specific laws, but war was declared before any new neutrality laws could be passed. New laws against sabotage and sedition were passed during the war. U.S. attorneys oversaw the registration of enemy aliens, assisted in the draft, and instigated the ''slacker'' raids. The department had a bureaucratic fight between its relatively new Bureau of Investigation and the Departments of State and Treasury* over jurisdiction for investigations and prosecutions of internal espionage and sedition. Attorney General Thomas Gregory won most of that battle because of the popularity of the department's American Protective League. The league was a volunteer organization, which began gathering information on neutrality violations. Later, it became part of the department's campaign against pro-German sedition that was minor in scope, and then even later in the Red Scare investigations and prosecutions directed towards leftists and radicals. Attorney General A. Mitchell Palmer's raids on meetings and headquarters of leftist organizations in 1919 and 1920 netted more than two thousand people, and several hundred aliens were deported. The raids were the last of a number of efforts by the department during and after the war that fomented or followed the domestic hysteria against Germans and radicals and that resulted in the abridgement of civil rights for aliens and citizens in the United States.

During the 1920s, prohibition was not a major Department of Justice responsibility, and the department avoided jurisdiction in the prosecution of lynchings. The Teapot Dome scandals during the Harding Administration involved Attorney General Daugherty, who was charged with taking bribes for failing to prosecute violators of prohibition and embezzlers in the Veterans Bureau. The close of the decade saw the creation of the Wickersham Commission to survey crime in the nation and its connections with prohibition. The commission report detailed the extent of crime in the United States but opposed repeal of the Prohibition Amendment.

The administration of Franklin D. Roosevelt reversed the long policy of the federal government seeking injunctive relief against labor organizations during strikes. The Wagner Act, passed in 1935, upheld labor's right to organize and bargain collectively. Homer Cummings, the Attorney General during the New Deal, was the President's legal adviser for much of the New Deal legislation, and he argued several of the cases before the Supreme Court that decided the fate of the New Deal laws.

World War II did not bring with it the anti-German and anti-radical hysteria of the previous world war. Francis Biddle, as Attorney General during the war, opposed in vain the incarceration of Japanese citizens on the West Coast and stopped the Federal Bureau of Investigation's (FBI's) Custodial Detention program. He personally directed the prosecution of eight Nazi saboteurs and successfully argued against their petitions for habeas corpus in the Supreme Court.

The major postwar issues for the Department of Justice were internal security, organized crime, and civil rights. The Cold War stimulated a second Red Scare in the United States, with the Department of Justice working with congressional committees and other executive branch agencies to find subversive activities and prosecute suspected Communists. Alger Hiss, Julius and Ethel Rosenburg, Judith Coplon, Valentine Gubitchev, Rudolf Abel, and others were all arrested and prosecuted under the Smith Act of 1940, the McCarran Act of 1950, or for perjury. Charles Chaplin was denied reentry to the United States, and Robert Oppenheimer lost his security clearance because they were associated at one time with left-wing organizations. As the Communist party in the United States dwindled into insignificance in the 1950s and the perceived internal security threat lessened, the department prosecuted fewer internal security cases each year.

Since the 1930s when prohibition and organized crime were connected and seen as a federal concern, the Department of Justice has directed resources for combatting the activities of organized crime. Certain special efforts have attracted greater attention to the investigations and prosecutions during periods of political pressure and publicity to thwart organized crime. After the Kefauver hearing on the Mafia in the 1950s, Attorney General William Rogers set up a Special Group on Organized Crime to coordinate federal law enforcement agencies in the campaign on organized crime. The group met opposition from J. Edgar Hoover (FBI), who denied the existence of an organized criminal element in the United States, and the bureaucratic reluctance of other agencies to cooperate.

Robert Kennedy, when he became Attorney General in 1961, made the campaign against organized crime his number-one priority. He used special groups of lawyers and investigators in the department and approved extraordinary investigative techniques to break organized crime. The best known campaign was directed against James Hoffa, Teamsters Union president, who was convicted in 1967 of jury tampering. Later, President Richard M. Nixon had two laws passed to give the Department of Justice and other federal agencies more power in combatting crime.

In the school desegregation cases, lynchings, peonage, and other civil rights issues in the 1930s and 1940s, the Department of Justice did little, declaring that most of the issues were not within federal jurisdiction. After *Brown* v. *Board of Education* (1954), the Civil Rights Division of the department was established to enforce federal court integration decrees and the civil rights laws passed, beginning in 1957. During the Dwight D. Eisenhower and John F. Kennedy administrations, the Department of Justice attempted to work with state and local officials to integrate schools and assure the voting rights of blacks in the South. The strategy was to avoid use of federal troops and to make local authorities responsible for keeping the peace, while attempting to have the civil rights laws enforced. The policy broke down a number of times in Little Rock, Oxford, Selma, and other places when lives were threatened and lost, and federalized troops had to be mobilized. By 1965, the FBI and Justice Department lawyers were a major presence in the South. Violence lessened, and blacks in large numbers began to vote and become part of the political process.

The Watergate break-in and ensuing scandals again brought the dilemma between enforcing the law and being a political entity directly to the Department of Justice. Three attorneys general resigned during the crisis for different reasons. John Mitchell and Richard Kleindienst resigned under fire, and Mitchell was convicted of conspiracy, obstruction of justice, and perjury. Kleindienst pleaded guilty to a misdemeanor charge for withholding information. Eliot Richardson resigned as Attorney General because he would not fire Archibald Cox, the Watergate special prosecutor, when ordered to by President Nixon. Since Watergate, attorneys general have tried to depoliticize the Department of Justice, but the dilemma remains.

President Jimmy Carter successfully withstood the opposition of civil rights leaders in selecting Griffin Bell as Attorney General. Bell, a Georgian and Carter friend, was confirmed in 1977 despite the charge that his record as a federal Court of Appeals judge had been unfavorable toward school desegregation. The usual problems continued under Bell, with major attention going each year to questions of anti-trust and school integration, in addition to alleged Federal Bureau of Investigation wiretapping and letter-opening (1977), investigation of Korean businessmen for influence peddling in trade in the United States (1978), food-stamp probes (1979), and cases in 1980 including the reopening of the John F. Kennedy murder investigation.

William French Smith, of Los Angeles, President Ronald Reagan's personal lawyer, succeeded Bell in 1981 as Attorney General. Old issues returned to dot the list of Justice actions, especially pertaining to school desegregation and voting rights. Newer but yet vexing were cases of federal tax fraud against the controversial cult leader the Reverend Sun Myong Moon and his aides in 1982 and abortion cases in Akron the same year. In 1981, the flood of alien refugees arriving in the United States by boat from Cuba and Haiti aroused great concern without satisfactory answers.

FOR ADDITIONAL INFORMATION: The one history of the Department of Justice was published in 1937: Homer Cummings and Carl McFarland, *Federal Justice: Chapters in the History of Justice and the Federal Executive* (1937). A Brookings Institution study of the department was published in 1967: Luther A. Huston, *The Department of Justice* (1967). The most intensive study of a single Attorney General is Victor S. Navasky, *Kennedy Justice* (1971). There are many other memoirs and biographies of other attorneys general.

R. MICHAEL McREYNOLDS

DEPARTMENT OF LABOR. The United States Department of Labor is basically a "people" agency whose function is to see that there is a job for every American who wants work, to ensure that the job provides a safe and healthy work environment, and to assist individuals when they are unemployed or are unable to work. With these goals and concerns, the department has helped develop many social programs, but not without stirring controversy and debate.

The Secretary of Labor is a member of the President's Cabinet and is the President's primary adviser on labor matters. The Under Secretary is his chief deputy, and he is supported by assistant secretaries (in program areas), the solicitor (or general counsel), and the commissioner of labor statistics. Through its major programs, the department helps people find and train for jobs; provides assistance to workers who lose their jobs because of foreign import competition; and administers the Unemployment Insurance program which provides some security to those out of work. It monitors the workplace in an effort to upgrade conditions in health and safety, as well as in the more traditional concerns for wages and hours. It also seeks to assure every worker the opportunity to bargain collectively through responsible unions and to advance free of discrimination on the basis of race, sex, religion, age, national origin, or handicap.

These concerns and activities have made the department part of the various social and economic reform campaigns of this century, from the "Progressive" movement through the New Deal, Fair Deal, New Frontier, War on Poverty, and the "New Federalism." Such activism has often drawn criticism, especially in recent years as the country has grappled with the twin devils of high inflation and high unemployment. Some critics allege costly and inefficient programs, while others charge that some programs actually help fuel inflationary pressures.

Moreover, the agency's personality has been changing. Once primarily advocacy, or educational, or administrative in nature, the department functions more and more as a regulatory agency. As a result, many citizens associate its programs with punitive and burdensome red tape.

The department began its work on March 4, 1913, when President William Howard Taft signed the organic act on his last day in office. The organized labor movement had pressed for its establishment, thereby building in a structural characteristic. As with the Departments of Commerce* and Agriculture,* the Department of Labor is considered a constituent agency serving a specific sector of the public and economy. Its perceived relation to organized labor at any one time has often determined its public and political standing both in Washington and in the country at large.

The department's history stretches back to 1884 and the establishment of the Bureau of Labor in the Department of Interior.* Four years later, in March 1888, Congress elevated the bureau to the status of independent, but not Cabinet-level, Department of Labor. Under the leadership of Commissioner Carroll D. Wright, the bureau department gained a worldwide reputation for providing accurate economic statistics—a role continued by the Bureau of Labor Statistics.

Both the Knights of Labor and the American Federation of Labor (AFL) had called for such an agency, and Wright maintained friendly, if distant, relations with the labor organizations. Yet, the unions came to want more as nascent "Big Labor" and "Big Business" fought for influence in the early years of the century. Preaching the mutuality of interests between employer and employee—and the need to push foreign trade and to secure foreign markets—business interests succeeded in combining the department into an executive-level Department of Commerce and Labor. The AFL, meanwhile, countered with demands for a voice in the President's Cabinet—a card-carrying union leader as Secretary of Labor. Stung by the open-shop campaigns of the National Association of Manufacturers and the Citizens' Industrial Association and court decisions such as Buck's Stove and Danbury Hatters, Samuel Gompers led the campaign which pressed the bill through Congress.

The infant agency contained just four constituent divisions: the renamed Bureau of Labor Statistics, the Bureau of Immigration, the Bureau of Naturalization, and the Children's Bureau.* The Secretary, authorized to mediate and conciliate labor disputes, created a Conciliation Service in his office. The present department exercises considerably more responsibilities through its major program sections: the Bureau of Labor Statistics (lone survivor of the original four), the Women's Bureau,* the Employment and Training Administration, the Employment Standards Administration, the Labor Management Services Administration, and (the two newest) the Occupational Safety and Health Administration* and the Mine Safety and Health Administration.

The first Secretary, William B. Wilson, a former coal miner and official in the United Mine Workers, enunciated the philosophy which most of his successors have followed: encouraging responsible collective bargaining as the best way to secure and maintain industrial peace, while promoting and protecting the welfare of all workers, organized or not.

In his first years, Wilson concentrated on settling industrial disputes and built up his Conciliation Service. World War I brought greatly increased duties, and the Secretary headed the War Labor Administration, which included the National War Labor Board, the War Labor Policies Board, and the United States Employment Service, with responsibility for mobilizing the civilian workforce and mediating industrial peace while also maintaining working standards. Few secretaries since have matched his vigor and influence.

After the Armistice, Congress moved quickly to halt the activities of wartime special agencies and eliminated most of the department's related functions. The Women's Bureau and a skeletal Employment Service comprised the primary survivors among the wartime operations, as programs and funds were slashed in the drive to return to normalcy.

During the 1920s, Herbert Hoover made the Department of Commerce* the center of the government's economic activities, and the Department of Labor turned most of its attention to the problems of immigration and naturalization. Secretary James J. Davis, himself an immigrant, favored restriction and actively campaigned for congressional action. His advocacy of an end to unlimited immigration and his buoyant optimism on the domestic economy certainly reflected the tenor of the times.

Confronted with the depression, however, Davis not surprisingly seemed out of his depth. Under Davis and his successor, William N. Doak, the department finally began to reorganize the United States Employment Service and launched expanded surveys of the unemployment problem. Most of the underfunded and stagnant department's efforts consisted of issuing optimistic forecasts and encouraging employers to maintain the wage level.

Congress did empower the department to use the force of government procurement to upgrade working conditions, arguing that the government should be a good employer and set a proper example. Former Secretary Davis, then a Senator, helped start this program in 1931 by joining the fight for the so-called Davis-Bacon Act, which required government construction contractors to pay the wage prevailing in the locality. Davis-Bacon continues to spark controversy, but it has helped raise wages.

Frances Perkins, Roosevelt's appointee and the first woman Cabinet Secretary, began immediately to energize the department and to provide jobs for the unemployed. Her department advocated, encouraged, and defended many public works programs, one of the first being the Civilian Conservation Corps,* which put some 2 million young men to work between 1933 and 1939. Perkins also succeeded in reviving a modern Employment Service with the Wagner-Peyser Act of 1933.

One of Perkins's most dramatic victories, the Fair Labor Standards Act, also represented a triumph for Roosevelt, who had tried to mandate improved labor standards under the National Recovery Administration.* Finally, in 1938, Congress passed the act which established a national minimum wage of $.25 an hour and a regular work-week of 40 hours and prohibited youth under sixteen years of age from working in most occupations. Since 1938, Congress has raised the wage levels and expanded the coverage, but critics still charge that the minimum wage prices some unskilled workers out of the job market. In recent years, reformers have pressed to establish a subminimum for younger workers as a mechanism for combating high teenage unemployment rates.

Perhaps the Social Security Act of 1935 stands as Perkins's greatest accomplishment. The old Bureau of Labor had publicized such experiments since the 1890s, and Perkins concentrated on insurance against the ravages of unemployment and old age. She served as chairman of Roosevelt's Committee on Economic Security, which developed a proposal, and, then, fought the battles in Congress, erecting the foundations of Social Security and Unemployment Insurance.

One of the victories for organized labor during the period, the Wagner Act of 1935 establishing the National Labor Relations Board* (NLRB), constituted at best a compromise and disappointment for Perkins and the department. An advocate for the department's own Division of Conciliation, Perkins opposed Senator Wagner's proposal because it made the NLRB independent of the department and protected only the rights of labor.

The New Deal surge of reform slowed to a halt in the late 1930s as the country increasingly focused its attention on "preparedness" programs. The department performed valuable services in conciliating labor disputes, protecting labor standards, and providing statistical data and studies. Even so, whereas Perkins played a highly visible role in the reform period, her influence diminished with the onset of "preparedness" and the outbreak of war. Unlike World War I, World War II saw the creation of a number of independent super agencies. Bypassed on major policy issues, the department cooperated with the War Labor Board and the others.

Shortly after Roosevelt's death in 1945, Perkins resigned, and President Harry S Truman appointed Lewis B. Schwellenbach. The former federal Judge and U.S. Senator faced a tumultuous situation as the country tried to demobilize and reconvert to peacetime operations. Battered by the postwar strike wave, Schwellenbach seemed disheartened by passage of the Taft-Hartley Act of 1947, which, for one thing, took the Conciliation Service from the department and established an independent Federal Mediation and Conciliation Service. Schwellenbach died in June 1948 from a respiratory disease. His successor, Maurice Tobin, former mayor of Boston and governor of Massachusetts, campaigned actively during the 1948 elections and rebuilt the department following Truman's surprise victory. After the war, the department had lost the Children's Bureau, along with the Conciliation Service and, temporarily, the United States Employment Service. Then, in 1949, after the report of the Hoover Commission,* the department regained the Employment Service, which formed the Bureau of Employment Security with the newly acquired Unemployment Insurance Service. When the fighting broke out in Korea, Tobin stubbornly fought for and succeeded in preserving for the department a role in manpower mobilization.

After twenty years, the Republicans returned to power in 1952, and Dwight D. Eisenhower appointed Martin P. Durkin as Secretary of Labor. However, Durkin pressed to amend Taft-Hartley, antagonizing the administration before resigning after only some eight months in office. In rather a surprise story, his successor, James P. Mitchell, increased the independent stature and strength of the department, achieving improvements in statistical programs, an increase in the minimum wage, and progress on various manpower issues. The Labor-Management Reporting and Disclosure Act of 1959 gave the department new responsibilities to insure fairness and democratic procedures in union government.

During the 1960s, the department concentrated on manpower, or employment and training programs. When Arthur Goldberg became Secretary, the country faced a severe unemployment situation, especially complicated by technological displacement. With the Area Redevelopment Act of 1961 and the Manpower Development and Training Act of 1962, the John F. Kennedy Administration funnelled money to depressed areas and established projects to provide unemployed workers with the necessary skills and training. Willard Wirtz succeeded Goldberg and helped President Lyndon B. Johnson draft the Economic Opportunity Act of 1964, one of the keystones of the War on Poverty. Wirtz and the department turned their focus more and more toward assisting specific disadvantaged groups with such programs as the Job Corps.

The return of Republicans to power in 1969 resulted in considerable reorganization of several departmental programs because expansion had not also meant efficiency and effectiveness, especially in employment programs. One of the first projects undertaken by Secretary George P. Shultz was reorganization of the Job Corps and other remnants of the War on Poverty. Later combined with President Richard M. Nixon's "New Federalism," this thrust led to the Comprehensive Employment and Training Act of 1973 based on federal-state-local revenue sharing in manpower projects.

The Republicans expanded as well as restructured. In 1970, Secretary James D. Hodgson could proudly point to the Williams-Steiger Act, which established the Occupational Safety and Health Administration in the department. The next year, Congress established the Public Employment Program to fund public service jobs at the state and local level—a countercyclical attack on rising unemployment. Peter J. Brennan, John T. Dunlop, and W. J. Usery followed Hodgson during the tumultuous 1970s, and departmental responsibilities continued to increase. The Trade Act of 1974 established a Trade Adjustment Assistance program for workers who lose jobs because of foreign competition. The Employee Retirement Income Security Act of 1974 seeks to protect the various forms of private pension systems on which workers depend for security in their old age.

For the past four years, the department has again emphasized the employment and training functions. Under Ray Marshall, the department operated extensive Comprehensive Employment and Training Act (CETA) and Public Service Employment programs in an effort to counter historically high unemployment rates. Many affirmative action projects were targeted specifically to benefit women and minority workers through Employment and Training Administration initiatives or Office of Federal Contract Compliance efforts to ensure equal employment opportunity. In 1978, the Mine Safety and Health Administration was transferred from the Department of Interior.

In several respects, the department faces an uncertain future. Many of its job-training programs are criticized as costly and inefficient, and many of its regulatory functions are singled out as punitive and burdensome. Moreover, many of the laws it administers are under challenge. At the same time, for the first time in thirty years, Republicans control the Senate, and, perhaps for the first time ever, the Secretary-designate is an unknown. Thus, the whole operating environment has taken on a new and as yet unclear character.

FOR ADDITIONAL INFORMATION: Jonathan Grossman, *The Department of Labor* (1973), in the Praeger Library of U.S. Government Departments and Agencies; John Lombardi, *Labor's Voice in the Cabinet* (1942); George Martin, *Madam Secretary: Frances Perkins* (1976); and U.S. Department of Labor, *The Anvil and the Plow, A History of the United States Department of Labor* (1963). The Historian's Office has also collected narratives and documents on the department during the Johnson, Nixon-Ford, and Carter administrations.

WILLIAM T. MOYE

DEPARTMENT OF STATE. For most of its history, the United States was represented abroad by two separate entities, the diplomatic and the consular services. Both were born during the American Revolution. Even before declaring independence from Great Britain, the Continental Congress had sent representatives to France and the Netherlands to ascertain the attitudes of those and other governments toward an alliance with the emerging nation. Most famous among these emissaries was Benjamin Franklin, whose earlier experience in London and on the Continent, whose qualities of character and temperament, and whose skill in negotiations all worked to establish him as America's first professional diplomat. The activities of these representatives and others during the war, in obtaining foreign support and negotiating a final settlement, played a large role in securing American victory. Also of great importance was the work of the nation's first consuls, as they purchased military supplies abroad, fitted out American privateers, and disposed of prizes taken on the high seas.

The United States Department of State also traces its origins to the Revolution. In 1781, Congress provided for a Department of Foreign Affairs, with Robert

Livingston as its first Secretary, to handle the correspondence with its overseas representatives. Eight years later, during George Washington's first months in office, it was renamed the Department of State. To handle the department's responsibilities, Thomas Jefferson, the first Secretary of State, employed a staff of two chief clerks, three other clerks, a part-time translator, and two custodians.

The Constitution provided the legal basis for the Foreign Service when it empowered the President to appoint, with the advice and consent of the Senate, "Ambassadors, other public Ministers, and Consuls." No ambassadors were appointed by an American President for over a century, however, partly because appointing lower level ministers or *chargés d' affaires* was more economical and partly because ambassadorial appointments, then characteristic of the European monarchies, were thought to be inappropriate for the world's idealistic new republic. The number of diplomatic posts grew slowly, from two in 1790 to six in 1800 and to only seven by 1820. Therafter the pace accelerated, with posts in fifteen countries by 1830, in twenty-seven by 1850, and in forty-one in 1890 after a century of development. From the beginning, the President also appointed diplomatic secretaries to assist the ministers in carrying out their duties.

The State Department directed the diplomats to send back to Washington accurate information about the host government's policies. To do so they were expected to maintain friendly social relations with members of the host government as well as with other members of the diplomatic corps in the capital. They received modest salaries, not nearly enough to cover the considerable costs of entertaining and socializing required of diplomats; hence, they had to be persons of independent means. Not until the twentieth century could American diplomats live on the salaries they earned; and there are still a few positions in the 1980s, such as ambassador to Great Britain, which require that the incumbent be independently wealthy.

In contrast to the diplomatic branch, the larger consular service grew rapidly from the start. Already in 1790, the young United States maintained ten consular posts (six consulates and four vice-consulates), and ten years later the number had risen to fifty-two, including four consulates-general for the most important cities. By 1820, there were 83 posts, 197 in 1850, and 323 in 1890.

American consuls were instructed, among other things, to receive protests from or against U.S. citizens, give aid to American seamen in distress, perform notarial tasks for their countrymen, settle the estates of American citizens who died abroad without a legal representative, provide bills of health to ships leaving their ports for the United States, issue passports, and verify to Treasury officials invoices of goods being shipped to the United States. Beginning in the mid-nineteenth century, consuls submitted regular reports to Washington about commercial conditions in their districts in order to aid American exporters. With very few exceptions, for the first few decades consular positions were not salaried; their incumbents were remunerated from a portion of the fees they collected, often in addition to their regular trading business.

By 1856, several problems in the diplomatic and consular services had received enough attention to be addressed by important legislation. In that year Congress passed, and President Franklin Pierce signed into law, an act "To Remodel the Diplomatic and Consular Systems of the United States." Salaries of diplomatic officers, long a problem, were raised significantly, although the highest authorized salary for a diplomatic representative ($17,500) would remain the top salary for the next ninety years. It was the consular service, however, which received most of the new law's attention.

For many years, the State Department had received complaints from Americans traveling or doing business abroad that many of its consuls were incompetent and were charging fees that were unequal from post to post, and often unfairly high. From 1830 onward, various secretaries of state, congressmen, and others had recommended compensating the consuls with salaries while prohibiting them from engaging in trade, and also establishing a uniform fee schedule. The 1856 act authorized the President to prescribe the official fees to be charged for various consular services and required the consuls to post these rates at a prominent place in their offices. It also established salaries at the more important posts.

Major problems remained in the foreign service in the latter part of the nineteenth century, notwithstanding the 1856 legislation. In the consular branch, many consuls were still unsalaried, and all consuls could keep any "unofficial" fees they might collect. Both the consular and diplomatic services lacked any system for promotion or a training period for new members. Most damaging was the dominance of the "spoils system" whereby appointments to consulates and diplomatic posts were not based on merit, but were instead used by presidents to reward political supporters. (Ironically, passage of the Civil Service Act of 1883, placing a large number of government positions under the merit system, made the situation worse in the diplomatic and consular services. Those two organizations were not included in the act's coverage, and thus were required to offer refuge to the growing numbers of political appointees who were now denied access to other government jobs.) Consequently, neither branch offered much to persons interested in a career that would survive a turnover in the White House. Although not suffering directly from the spoils system, the Department of State had other problems, notably its isolation from the diplomatic and consular posts, and its failure to provide for geographic specialization.

This unsatisfactory state of affairs was quite understandable, given the nation's traditional disinterest in, and often suspicion of, foreign affairs. It was difficult for the American people to comprehend the function of diplomacy, which Elihu Root once described as keeping the country "out of trouble." After all, to most Americans "trouble" was thousands of miles across the Atlantic in Europe. In 1859, Representative Benjamin Stanton of Ohio doubtless spoke for a good many of his fellow-countrymen when he said that he knew of "no area of the public service that is more emphatically useless than the diplomatic service—none in the world."

Yet, public interest in foreign relations grew slowly during the 1880s and 1890s. The European powers and Japan flexed their imperial muscles, and some influential Americans wished their country to follow suit. In addition, the economic depressions in the United States during the last quarter of the nineteenth century, and especially the wrenching depression of 1893-1897, prompted many Americans to look increasingly toward foreign markets to absorb surpluses of their country's manufactured products. By the end of the decade, the United States had fought and won what Secretary of State John Hay called a "splendid little war" with Spain and found itself in possession of a far-flung overseas empire. In keeping with the spirit of the times, the first American ambassador, former Secretary of State Thomas F. Bayard, was appointed to Britain in 1893, and soon the United States had ambassadors as its representatives at the major capitals of the world.

In this environment, an alliance of State Department bureaucrats, businessmen, civil service reformers, and a few congressmen came together to improve the foreign service and State Department. Their first concern was the consular service, partly because it most needed reform and partly because the tasks of the consuls, especially the supplying of foreign markets information to American businessmen, were more easily understood by the public. Consular improvement was not easy, because a number of vested interests, including congressmen and even presidents, had a stake in the spoils system. But in 1895, President Grover Cleveland issued an Executive Order providing for appointments on a merit basis to certain consular offices. Ten years later President Theodore Roosevelt, working closely with Secretary of State Elihu Root, extended Cleveland's order to include all the major consular offices. One year after, in 1906, in a landmark piece of legislation, Congress reclassified the consular posts, established an inspection system for the consulates, placed the consuls on a salaried basis, and required that all fees be turned in to the Treasury. An accompanying Executive Order by President Roosevelt instituted a system of appointment in the consular service on the basis of examination and promotion for efficiency. Put together by department officials, the examination consisted of written and oral portions, a format which, though modified, has continued to the present day. Later in Secretary Root's administration, State undertook to organize, on an experimental basis, a small Bureau of Far Eastern Affairs, to give close attention to political and economic matters throughout the region and to draft policy papers for the department's top officers. The experiment proved successful, and it paved the way for State's basically geographic organization and orientation.

Under Philander C. Knox, Secretary of State from 1909 to 1913, the bureaucratization of the foreign service and department continued. Following Root's recommendation, State created additional geographic bureaus in 1909: for Western Europe, the Near East, and Latin America. Staffing these bureaus were diplomatic secretaries and consuls brought to Washington from their foreign posts, to provide headquarters with their expertise. Later that same year, President William Howard Taft issued an Executive Order establishing, as Roosevelt's order for the consuls had done four years before, specific regulations governing appointments and promotions in the diplomatic service. The same combination of written and oral examinations was adopted for would-be secretaries of legation or embassy. Building on another innovation of the Root years, State organized a Division of Information, which was responsible for keeping U.S. embassies and legations around the world abreast of current negotiations and other developments. This step helped significantly to overcome much of the isolation between the diplomatic posts and the department, and even among the posts themselves. And, in 1911, Congress passed the first legislation authorizing the purchase of building sites, and the purchase and repair (or construction) of buildings to be used as U.S. embassies.

Because of the interest of businessmen and civil service reformers during the late nineteenth and early twentieth centuries, the foreign service and State Department possessed something they had lacked for many years and would lack again—a powerful domestic constituency. Consequently, most of the reforms occurred in the consular service, whose members were clearly understood by the public to be promoting foreign trade. In contrast, the rather arcane functions of the diplomats have always been more obscure to the public. In 1910, prominent congressmen, for example, Oscar Underwood of Alabama and Champ Clark of Missouri, suggested abolishing the diplomatic service and using that money for the consular service.

When World War I broke out in 1914, one glaring defect of the foreign service was quickly illuminated. Since the 1780s, America's diplomats and consuls had received presidential appointments to specific posts, unlike military personnel, who were appointed to a certain rank and then assigned to one post or another as the needs of the service required. Reformers had long urged such a flexibility for the diplomatic and consular services. When the war forced the closing or shifting of a number of American posts and added to the burdens at others, the State Department's need for the more flexible system became apparent. In 1915, Congress passed legislation establishing the method of appointing diplomats and consuls to grades instead of to posts, and for the first time gave legislative affirmation to the principle of appointment and promotion on the basis of merit, which had previously been a product of various Executive Orders.

The successful bureaucratization of the foreign service was basically completed during the years between World Wars I and II. The most famous piece of foreign service legislation, the Rogers Act of 1924, was written at the State Department, and it was sponsored in Congress by Representative John Jacob Rogers of Massachusetts. With the strong support of businessmen and civil service reformers, it overwhelmingly passed Congress. The Rogers Act amalgamated the diplomatic and consular services into a single entity, the Foreign Service of the United States. The new service contained 633 officers, 511 from the consular service and 122 from the diplomatic. Congress now required for the first time that the President appoint new members to the Foreign Service after an examination and probation period, except for the top posts of ambassador or minister (some 25 to 30 percent of which, in 1980, were still political and not career appointments). The appointees would then be assigned initially to either the diplomatic or consular branch, and their subsequent careers would likely include experience in both branches. Another very important provision was a new salary scale, which for the first time allowed diplomatic secretaries a living wage. No longer was a large portion of the Foreign Service open only to individuals with independent means and therefore only to a certain social class. The legislation also provided for a retirement and disability system, compulsory retirement at age sixty-five, allowances to defray the costs attending diplomatic representation, inspection of diplomatic as well as consular posts, and home leave at government expense.

Although there would continue to be significant Foreign Service legislation, the Rogers Act largely culminated a movement that had its roots in the period before the Civil War, grew very slowly for several decades, and then was revived in the 1890s, to reorganize and modernize the State Department and the Foreign Service, and to place the service on a career basis. The Rogers Act also had an immediate impact on interest in the Foreign Service as a career. Soon after the war, the State Department received only 13 applications for the diplomatic service, while in 1925 it designated 172 applicants to take the first examination under the new system. By a followup measure in 1931, Congress made certain adjustments in the Personnel Board and also established larger salaries for Foreign Service officers.

The years following the Rogers Act witnessed continuing improvements in the government's efforts to make the Foreign Service a career. At first, new officers underwent a training period of several months in the department before overseas assignment, significantly longer than in the prewar consular and diplomatic services. Later, the system was modified to require those successful on the exams to serve a one-year probationary period in a consulate before their course in the Foreign Service School. Appointments as ambassadors and ministers were much more likely to be made from the career service, partly because there was an ever growing body of experienced officers upon which to draw and partly because of the recognition by presidents and secretaries of state that such appointments were beneficial both in themselves and in the improved morale they engendered in the rest of the Foreign Service.

Also in the interwar period, the basic organization of the present-day diplomatic mission took shape. Before the Rogers Act, the diplomatic and consular operations were separately administered and separately housed, even when located in the same city. During the 1930s, they were united into combined offices in the capitals. Consular offices elsewhere in the country were linked to the diplomatic mission through the head of its consular section (usually a consul general), who normally served as the supervisory consular officer for the country. In addition to its consular section, the mission contained a political section headed by a diplomatic secretary, and an economic section under a commercial attaché, a Commerce Department* employee.

The United States emerged from World War II as the world's dominant superpower, into a postwar era that seemed to require additional changes in Foreign

Service organization. The Foreign Service Act of 1946 provided for a new classification of personnel and added the categories of reserve officers (specialized personnel) and staff officers (holding administrative, fiscal, technical, and clerical positions). For the first time since 1856, the salaries of ambassadors and ministers were raised, and new retirement and promotion systems were adopted, including a version of the Navy's "promotion-up or selection out" system. Eight years later, in 1954, the department commissioned and received a report from an ad hoc group headed by Henry M. Wriston, president of Brown University. As a result of the Wriston Report, which echoed similar recommendations by previous investigating bodies, State undertook to bring into the Foreign Service a large number of civil service personnel employed in foreign affairs positions by the department.

Advocates of this step pointed to the greater flexibility inherent in interchangeability of officers between State and the field. Integration was opposed by many Foreign Service officers who thought themselves members of an elite corps and wished to remain so, as well as by many of the civil service employees who had little desire for overseas service. Nevertheless, by the end of the 1950s, due chiefly to the department's vigorous pursuit of "Wristonization," the number of Foreign Service officers (FSOs) had tripled. The Foreign Service Act of 1980, however, reversed Wristonization, after it proved increasingly difficult and unnecessary to require many department-based personnel to serve abroad. Other provisions of the 1980 legislation included the establishment of a new Foreign Service specialist category to replace the reserve and staff categories created in the 1946 act, as well as the creation of a senior Foreign Service officer comparable to the flag officer ranks of the armed forces.

Closely associated with the Foreign Service and State Department are two independent agencies, the United States International Communication Agency (USICA) and the Agency for International Development* (AID). Both had their origins in the expanded work of State during World War II. For a number of years and under several different names, AID operated under the general policy guidance of State in administering the nation's program of foreign aid. USICA, formerly the United States Information Agency* (USIA), was reshaped in 1978 by merging USIA with the department's Bureau of Educational and Cultural Affairs. It is responsible for analyzing public opinion in foreign countries and representing U.S. policies and society to key people in government, education, the media, and the arts.

The legislative landmarks and other organizational developments since World War II have been only partially successful in accommodating the Foreign Service and State Department to their environment. On the eve of the war, the service and department were reasonably well organized to meet the demands which peacetime foreign relations had placed upon them. But the war brought with it a very different international setting and a host of problems. In 1940, a State Department containing 1,128 employees watched over 58 diplomatic and 264 consular posts; by 1980, the number of posts had shrunk to 233 (133 diplomatic and 100 consular), but the department's workforce had mushroomed to 8,433, including approximately 3,200 FSOs.

Although there has been much greater public interest in foreign affairs, World War II also ended an age in which the State Department served as virtually the only U.S. government agency to maintain official relations with foreign countries. Even as the department has grown enormously since the war, its influence has shrunk considerably. As early as the 1950s, some forty-five other agencies had representatives abroad, and that number is at least as great today, as reflected in the organization of an American embassy. At the average embassy fewer than 20 percent of the personnel report to the State Department. The wisdom and necessity of such fragmentation have been widely debated for years, but without question it has had a decidedly negative impact on Foreign Service morale.

At home in Washington, the Defense Department* has become a serious rival to State in matters of policy planning, and, since 1947, State's voice has been only one of several, although a very important one, in the National Security Council.* It remains far from clear how State's traditional role of maintaining official relations relates to the post-World War II world of foreign policymaking within a militarized, "national security" environment. One observer has contended that the important policy issues are decided at the White House, with greater weight given to the opinions of Congress, the Treasury,* the Defense Department, or private business. Accordingly, the State Department does not always prevail in policy selection.

Since the John F. Kennedy Administration, the National Security Council has built a large staff in the White House to contend with State for the ear of the President, and some presidents have relied for advice more upon the National Security Adviser than upon their secretaries of state: Kennedy with McGeorge Bundy, Richard M. Nixon with Henry Kissinger, and Jimmy Carter with Zbigniev Brzezinski. The sight of a President bypassing a Secretary of State and the Foreign Service, and relying on other individuals instead is hardly new; and ever more rapid transportation and communications systems have encouraged presidents to manage their own foreign affairs. Woodrow Wilson relied heavily on Colonel Edward House as an agent and adviser for foreign affairs, and Franklin D. Roosevelt on Harry Hopkins. It is a relationship that is more likely to occur in wartime, during cold wars as well as hot ones. Moreover, particularly since the Kennedy Administration, the White House has often perceived State as a bureaucracy with its own narrow interests. A frustrated President will establish a small, manageable, foreign affairs bureaucracy from the ground up rather than try to gain control over a large one already in place.

Especially important in the matter of relations with the chief executive are the personalities of presidents and their secretaries of state. Both George Marshall and Dean Acheson had good working relationships with Harry Truman, as did John Foster Dulles with Dwight Eisenhower, and Henry Kissinger with Richard Nixon and Gerald Ford. One important difference is that Acheson and Marshall relied a good deal on the career FSOs, while Dulles, and especially Kissinger, did not. During his tenure, Secretary of State Alexander M. Haig, Jr., asserted the predominance of his office in the foreign affairs field, and it seems likely that the National Security Adviser and his staff played a lesser role under Ronald Reagan than under some previous presidents. George P. Shultz, Nixon's Treasury Secretary, succeeded Haig in June 1982. It is clear, however, that no Secretary of State will be able to turn the clock back to the period before World War II and that the older concept of a Foreign Service and State Department having total or near-total responsibility for all official contacts abroad is no longer viable.

In addition to the proliferation of foreign affairs agencies, another source of damage to morale emanated from the attacks of Senator Joseph McCarthy on the department and Foreign Service in the early 1950s. McCarthy was supported by a number of Republicans who were unhappy with the Democrats' foreign policy, and also with the foreign affairs machinery that had carried it out. He made groundless charges that a number of department officers were either Communists or Communist sympathizers; many capable officers, including some of the best China experts, were driven from the service. According to a number of critics, those who remained became too cautious and fearful, with serious consequences in the 1960s when the U.S. government badly needed candid reporting by knowledgeable Asia experts.

Another problem for the service and department in the post-World War II years has been the absence of an important domestic constituency of the kind that supported foreign service legislation early in this century. Other agencies, such as Defense, Commerce, and Agriculture,* all have powerful domestic pressure groups that the Foreign Service now lacks. Critics have urged the department to pay more attention to domestic political realities, as well as to perform more effectively in Washington by working more closely with other government agencies and with private business.

Recent changes in the larger environment have left their marks on the Foreign Service. One development has been the growing incidence of terrorism directed against Americans abroad, of which the Iranian hostage situation was only the most prominent. Another element is the growing desire of the wives of FSOs to pursue careers of their own instead of being viewed by the service administration primarily as ornaments attached to their husbands' careers; until 1972, FSO wives were included in their husbands' annual performance evaluations. The Family Liaison Office, established in 1978, was given legislative sanction by the Foreign Service Act of 1980 in order to help with this problem of careers for spouses, and a related provision of the act provided for retirement and survivor benefits for divorced spouses. Similar to many other areas of American life, the Foreign Service has dealt with "affirmative action," and it has also coped with legal challenges to the "promotion-up or selection-out" procedures established by the 1946 legislation.

The years ahead will be at least as challenging for the Foreign Service and State Department as they have ever been. With the help of the new Foreign Service Act of 1980, the department will continue to attempt to establish in fact as well as in theory its preeminence in the field of foreign affairs and to provide rewarding careers for its employees.

FOR ADDITIONAL INFORMATION: The literature on the Foreign Service and State Department is vast, doubtless exceeding that devoted to any other government agency. The best introduction to their history is William Barnes and John H. Morgan, *The Foreign Service of the United States: Origins, Development and Functions* (1961). Other significant histories include: Warren F. Ilchman, *Professional Diplomacy in the United States, 1779-1939: A Study in Administrative History* (1961); Waldo H. Heinrichs, Jr., "Bureaucracy and Professionalism in the Development of American Career Diplomacy," in John Braeman, et al., eds., *Twentieth-Century American Foreign Policy* (1971), pp. 119-206; Richard Hume Werking, *The Master Architects: Building the U.S. Foreign Service, 1890-1913* (1977); Robert D. Schulzinger, *The Making of the Diplomatic Mind: The Training, Outlook, and Style of U.S. Foreign Service Officers, 1908-1931* (1975); Martin Weil, *A Pretty Good Club: The Founding Fathers of the U.S. Foreign Service* (1978); and U.S. Department of State, Bureau of Public Affairs, *A Short History of the U.S. Department of State, 1781-1981* (1981).

Basic factual information about the present-day service and department may be found in the annual *U.S. Government Manual,* and U.S. Department of State, *Foreign Service Careers* (1980). W. Wendell Blancké, *The Foreign Service of the United States* (1969), is a standard description of the service and department as of the late 1960s, while Richard A. Johnson similarly covers a number of government agencies in *The Administration of U.S. Foreign Policy* (1971). Also important is Jerry Israel, "The Department of State," in Alexander DeConde, ed., *Encyclopedia of American Foreign Policy* (1978), pp. 229-238. Interpretive, and frequently provocative, accounts of recent or current problems include: Smith Simpson, *The Crisis in American Diplomacy* (1980); John F. Campbell, *The Foreign Affairs Fudge Factory* (1971); I.M. Destler, *Presidents, Bureaucrats, and Foreign Policy: The Politics of Organizational Reform* (1972); David H. Davis, "State Department Structure and Foreign Policy Decision Rule," in *Sage International Yearbook of Foreign Policy Studies* 2 (1974), pp. 175-189; John Krizay, "Clientitis, Corpulence and Cloning at State—The Symptomatology of a Sick Department," *Policy Review* 4 (Spring 1978): 39-55; Robert Pringle, "Creeping Irrelevance at Foggy Bottom," *Foreign Policy* (Winter 1977-1978): 128-139; Donald P. Warwick, *A Theory of Public Bureaucracy: Politics, Personality and Organization in the State Department* (1975); and the CBS Reports program, "Embassy," aired on Saturday, January 3, 1981. The Department of State *Newsletter,* published since 1961, and the Department of State *Bulletin,* appearing since 1939, are excellent sources of information, as are the House and Senate hearings on the Foreign Service Act of 1980.

RICHARD HUME WERKING

DEPARTMENT OF THE AIR FORCE. The Department of the Air Force, an agency of the Department of Defense,* was established on September 18, 1947, pursuant to provisions of the National Security Act of the previous July 26. On September 26, 1947, by order of the Secretary of Defense, personnel of the Army Air Forces (AAF) were transferred from the Department of the Army* (formerly the War Department) to the Department of the Air Force and established as the United States Air Force. As this action shows, the Air Force can claim lineal antecedents long predating the 1947 act.

The USAF had its roots in a turn-of-the-century effort at technology assessment. In January 1905, the War Department* took up consideration of an offer it had received from two inventors in Dayton, Ohio, to provide the government with a heavier-than-air flying machine. The fact that many still doubted the claim of Wilbur and Orville Wright to have invented a workable airplane is part of the history of aviation. But the Board of Ordnance and Fortifications, which examined the Wrights' proposal, had other facts to consider as well. Outside the realm of science fiction, the role in warfare of airships, gliders, and airplanes was by no means clear. Only balloons had proven value of any sort. The French revolutionaries had used a balloon at the battle of Fleurus in 1794. In the American Civil War, balloons had seen service, and when the Union Army created the Signal Corps* in 1863, this service had been given the job of procuring and operating them. Only in 1892, however, did the Signal Corps organize a permanent balloon section, and this section's service in the war with Spain in 1898 was undistinguished. In 1898, the Signal Corps contracted with Samuel P. Langley for an airplane, but tests ended with a spectacular dive into the Potomac River on December 8, 1903, nine days before the Wright Brothers flew. The War Department, still smarting from that episode in 1905, turned down the new offer.

But the progress of aviation, the issuance of a patent to the Wrights in 1906, and the interest of President Theodore Roosevelt brought the matter up again. On August 1, 1907, Captain Charles DeF. Chandler became head of the Aeronautical Division of the Signal Corps, newly established to develop all forms of flying. In 1908, the corps ordered a dirigible balloon of the Zeppelin type then in use in Germany and contracted with the Wrights for an airplane. Despite a crash that destroyed the first model, the Wright plane was delivered in 1909. The inventors then began to teach a few enthusiastic young officers to fly.

The progress of American aviation was slow in the early years. Congress voted the first appropriation for military aviation in 1911. The Navy was starting its own program at about the same time. Soon after, the aviators rejected a proposal to separate their service from the Signal Corps. A makeshift squadron had an unlucky time with General John J. Pershing on the Mexican border in 1916. What really proved the importance of military aviation was its role in World War I. There balloons used for artillery spotting and airplanes for reconnaissance over enemy lines made a decisive contribution. Dirigible airships and airplanes proved effective at bombing. Every army sought control of the air, and great battles between the "knights of the air" became the stuff of romance. Yet, at the same time a serious doctrine of air warfare was beginning to emerge. The commanders began to distinguish, for example, between "strategic" air operations, deep in enemy territory, directed at his vital war-making industries and civilian morale, and "tactical" operations against his ground forces.

At the time of America's declaration of war against Germany on April 6, 1917, the Aviation Section was marginal at best. Its 1,200 officers and men had no knowledge of the air war in Europe. Its 250 airplanes and 5 balloons could not have survived long in combat. The nation's aircraft manufacturers had up to that time produced 1,000 planes. Yet, when France asked the United States to provide an air force of 4,500 airplanes and 50,000 men, there was no hesitation. With more enthusiasm than wisdom, Secretary of War Newton D. Baker asked for and received $640 million from Congress for aviation. The result was a fiasco. By the spring of 1918, it was clear that the Signal Corps had failed. The War Department then set up an Air Service of two agencies, one under a civilian to deal with the manufacturers, and one under a military officer to train and organize units. This setup, begun in April and May, was consolidated in August, when President Woodrow Wilson appointed John D. Ryan as aviation "czar" to straighten out the mess.

In the end, the only American achievement in the field of aircraft production was the Liberty engine. Of the 740 U.S. aircraft at the front in France at the time of the Armistice on November 11, 1918, almost all were European-made. Still, the Air Service of General Pershing's American Expeditionary Forces, organized by Major General Mason M. Patrick and Brigadier General William (Billy) Mitchell, had distinguished itself in action against the Germans.

As a result of the important role air power had played in the war, a movement developed during the 1920s and 1930s to create an independent air force. The model for this was Great Britain, which, early in 1918, had combined its Army and Navy air arms into the Royal Air Force (RAF) under an Air Ministry. But the U.S. Army's leaders saw the airplane primarily as a weapon for supporting the infantry and gave the Air Service a status comparable to that of the field artillery or the engineers, responsible for procuring aircraft and training flying units. Local commanders, none of them aviators, ran the air forces assigned to them. A series of boards and commissions studied and restudied the question of air organization, with no result other than the name change to Air Corps in 1926.

Nevertheless, just as in the RAF, the formulation of theories of strategic bombing gave new impetus to the argument for an independent air force. Strategic or long-range bombardment was intended to destroy an enemy nation's industry and war-making potential, and only an independent service would have a free hand to do so. Amid intense controversy, Billy Mitchell came to espouse these views and, in 1925, went to the point of "martyrdom" before a court-martial to publicize his position. But despite what it perceived as "obstruction" from the War Department, much of which was attributable to a shortage of funds, the Air Corps made great strides during the 1930s. A doctrine emerged that stressed precision bombing of industrial targets by heavily armed long-range aircraft. A big step was taken in 1935 with the creation of a combat air force, commanded by an aviator and answering to the chief of staff of the Army. Called the "GHQ Air Force" because it would be under General Headquarters in time of war, this command took combat air units out of the hands of the local commanders in the continental United States. Nonetheless, the GHQ Air Force remained small as compared to air forces in Europe. The Air Corps could only buy a few of the new four-engined B-17 Flying Fortresses, designed for strategic bombing, and, in 1938, there were only thirteen on hand.

World War II was the true age of liberation for American air power. Reports from Europe in 1939 and 1940 proved the dominant role of the airplane in modern war. On June 20, 1941, Major General Henry H. Arnold, then chief of the Air Corps, assumed the title of chief of Army Air Forces and was given command of the Air Force Combat Command, as the GHQ Air Force had been renamed. (Arnold's title was changed to "commanding general, Army Air Forces" in March 1942, when he became co-equal with the commanders of Army Ground Forces and Services of Supply.) The AAF was directly under the orders of the Chief of Staff of the Army, General George C. Marshall. Arnold and Marshall agreed that the AAF would enjoy autonomy within the War Department until the end of the war, when the air arm would become a fully independent service. Soon after the Japanese attack on Pearl Harbor on December 7, 1941, Arnold gained another victory. In staff talks with the Americans, the British always included representatives of the RAF as well as the Army and Navy, so the United States had to include an air representative of its own. Arnold, although technically Marshall's subordinate, became an equal with him on the Joint Chiefs of Staff, the body that served as the focal point of American strategic planning during the war.

In its expansion during World War II, the AAF became the world's most powerful air force. From the Air Corps of 1939, with 20,000 men and 2,400 planes, to the nearly autonomous AAF of 1944, with almost 2.4 million personnel and 80,000 aircraft, was a remarkable expansion. Robert A. Lovett, the Assistant Secretary of War for Air, together with Arnold, presided over an increase greater than that for either the ground Army or the Navy, while at the same time dispatching combat air forces to the battlefronts. Air Force Combat Command was discontinued, and four air forces were created in the continental United States. In the end, twelve more air forces went overseas and served against the Germans and Japanese.

As Arnold's staff saw it, the first priority in the war was to launch a strategic bombing offensive in support of the RAF against Germany. The Eighth Air Force, sent to England in 1942, took on that job. After a slow and often costly effort to bring the necessary strength to bear, joined in 1944 by the Fifteenth Air Force stationed in Italy, the Eighth finally began to get results. By the end of the war, the German economy had been pounded to rubble. Meanwhile, tactical air forces supported the ground forces in the Mediterranean and European theaters, where the enemy found Allied air supremacy a constant frustration. In the war against Japan, Douglas MacArthur made his advance along New Guinea by leap-frogging his air forces forward, using amphibious forces to open up new bases. The AAF also assisted Admiral Chester Nimitz's carriers in their island-hopping across the Central Pacific and supported Allied forces in Burma and China. Arnold directly controlled the Twentieth Air Force, equipped with the new long-range B-29 Superfortresses used for bombing Japan's home islands, first from China and then from the Marianas. Devastated by fire-raids, Japan was so weakened by August of 1945 that Arnold believed neither the atomic bomb nor the planned invasion would be necessary. The fact that AAF B-29s dropped the atomic bombs on Hiroshima and Nagasaki, nevertheless, demonstrated what air power could do in the future. The U.S. Strategic Bombing Survey provided ammunition for the leaders of the AAF in the postwar debates over armed forces unification and national strategy.

After World War II, independence for the Air Force was virtually inevitable. The War Department favored unification of the Army and Navy, with co-equal land, air, and sea services under a single head. The Navy opposed this plan and forced adoption of a compromise in the National Security Act of 1947. This law created the Department of the Air Force and gave a Secretary of Defense limited authority over the services. By the time the law went into effect in September, the Air Force was beginning to rebuild after the postwar demobilization. Its leaders had defined a goal of establishing 70 combat groups with 400,000 men and 8,000 planes. Stringent postwar budgets delayed the program in spite of concern at the growing threat from the Soviet Union. As the United States came to rely upon a strategy of deterrence, the Air Force gave highest priority to its long-range atomic bombing force, using air refueling to lengthen its reach. Acrimonious disputes with the Navy resulted, focusing on the roles of the services in modern warfare, until the large budget increases after 1950.

In 1946, the AAF had created three major combat commands in the United States: the Strategic Air Command (SAC), the Tactical Air Command (TAC), and the Air Defense Command (ADC). The Strategic Air Command now became the centerpiece of Air Force planning. Yet, surprisingly, the first important intervention of the Air Force in the Cold War was by the Military Air Transport Service (MATS) during the Berlin Airlift of 1948-1949. Still, SAC's role remained predominant, especially during the service of Curtis E. LeMay as its commander (1948-1957). Rising to a level of peacetime readiness unprecedented in American history, SAC was not dethroned even during the fighting in Korea (1950-1953). Tactical forces were built up to take part in the fighting in support of the United Nations forces, and SAC even sent B-29 bombers. The American air forces achieved control of the air and poured bombs onto the Communist supply lines. But the increased budget for the Air Force also went to build up tactical forces in Europe and for a worldwide strategic striking force. After the Soviets detonated an atomic bomb in 1949, a new emphasis on air defense brought the ADC into the picture, but the TAC remained slighted throughout the 1950s, even with the development of tactical nuclear weapons.

The 1950s also witnessed the centralization of the Department of Defense. In 1949, the Secretary of Defense gained greater authority over the services, and the service secretaries ceased to be members of the National Security Council. By 1958, this process had reached the point that, not only the commands overseas, but even SAC and ADC were under the overall control of the Joint Chiefs of Staff. Nevertheless, the Chief of Staff of the Air Force held great influence as a member of the Joint Chiefs, and the Air Force kept the direct responsibility to "organize, train, and equip" combat air forces.

Under the influence of such farsighted officials as Trevor Gardner (at one time Assistant Secretary of the Air Force for Research and Development) and Major General Bernard A. Schriever, who founded what was to become the Space and Missile Systems Organization, the Air Force developed ballistic missiles during the 1950s. SAC began to supplement its great armada of bombers with missiles in 1959. By the end of the 1960s, over a thousand intercontinental missiles were in place, while the long-range bomber force had been cut back. The Air Force thus had two elements of the "Triad" of strategic weapons (bombers and land-based missiles), while the Navy had the third (submarine-launched missiles). Also in the 1960s, as a result of Secretary of Defense Robert S. McNamara's emphasis on "flexible response" in the strategy of deterrence, the TAC enjoyed something of a revival. Thus, even before large-scale intervention in Southeast Asia, the Air Force's conventional capabilities were increasing.

As part of the American effort to assist the government of South Vietnam in counterinsurgency operations during the early 1960s, the Air Force sent advisers to the Vietnamese Air Force. During 1964 and 1965 the commitment was increased, and combat units went into action. In South Vietnam, tactical forces, with the assistance of B-52s from SAC, supported U.S. and Vietnamese ground forces. Tactical forces in Vietnam and Thailand took part in strikes at crucial targets in North Vietnam and along supply trails in southern Laos. There were also strikes in support of the counterinsurgency operations of the Laotian government. Operations over Cambodia were in support of the war in South Vietnam. SAC provided tanker aircraft for refueling. Yet this, the first war fought under the 1958 reorganization act, was fought without a single Air Force agency controlling all air operations in Southeast Asia. Most operations were controlled by the theater commanders.

As the war went on into the climactic bombings of 1972, the Air Force struggled to remain ready in other areas. SAC had to divert much of its bomber and tanker forces to Southeast Asia, and tactical forces in Europe were affected as well. With the end of the fighting, contending with stringent budgets, the Air Force turned to the job of upgrading the strategic deterrent force and maintaining readiness in Europe. In the meantime, the strategy of deterrence had evolved to the doctrine of mutually assured destruction, enshrined in the strategic arms limitation agreement with the Soviet Union in 1972. The declining emphasis on defensive forces affected the Aerospace Defense Command, as ADC had been renamed. The following table gives 1980 Command data.

Because of the highly technical nature of Air Force equipment, the demand for skilled personnel has always been high. Although the combat crew, consisting of the pilot and other flying personnel (or, today, the missile launch crew), is the mainstay, the bulk of the Air Force's people are occupied with the upkeep of equipment and bases. During the period of the postwar draft (1948 to 1973), the Air Force was able to attract volunteers, emphasizing programs to win recruits

Organizing, Training, and Equipping
Air Force Major Commands, 1980

COMMAND	HEADQUARTERS	REPORTS TO
Strategic Air Command	Offutt AFB, Nebraska	Joint Chiefs of Staff
Tactical Air Command	Langley AFB, Virginia	Headquarters, USAF
Military Airlift Command	Scott AFB, Illinois	Joint Chiefs of Staff
Air Training Command	Randolph AFB, Texas	Headquarters, USAF
Air Force Logistics Command	Wright-Patterson AFB, Ohio	Headquarters, USAF
Air Force Systems Command	Andrews AFB, Maryland	Headquarters, USAF
Air Force Communications Command	Scott AFB, Illinois	Headquarters, USAF
Electronic Security Command	San Antonio, Texas	Headquarters, USAF
United States Air Forces in Europe	Ramstein Air Base, Germany	European Command
Pacific Air Forces	Hickam AFB, Hawaii	Pacific Command
Alaskan Air Command	Elmendorf AFB, Alaska	Alaskan Command

NOTE: The Air Defense Command (later renamed Aerospace Defense Command) was discontinued in 1979. The Aerospace Defense Center, in Colorado Springs, Colorado, preserves some of its functions.

and keep people who could be trained in a variety of skills. The Air Force Academy* (founded in 1955) and higher service schools at the Air University, Maxwell Air Force Base (AFB), Alabama, developed the leadership cadres of the service. In the age of the all-volunteer force, the Air Force's biggest problem has been keeping pilots, but other skills are also hard to retain. The Air National Guard and Air Force Reserve have kept up forces of remarkably high quality.

Before World War II, the Air Corps excluded blacks. During the war, the AAF maintained segregation in accordance with War Department policy. Some of the AAF's leaders were willing to recognize the inefficiencies inherent in segregation, and President Harry S Truman's order of 1948 integrating the armed forces won relatively quick compliance from the Air Force. Integration seemed to be going well until a series of disturbances, notably at Travis Air Force Base in 1971. Following these episodes, the Air Force moved to identify and remove sources of tension. Still, in 1979 hardly 4 percent of the officers were black.

Historically, the Army and the Air Force have relied upon private industry for the manufacture of airplanes. Procurement and contracting policies have evolved with the twin goals of obtaining the most modern equipment available and preserving a strong industrial base for the future. Stimulated by Arnold, the Air Force has continued to invest heavily in research and development. The results appear in such modern aircraft as the F-15 fighter, while the missile force is to be modernized with the M-X. Likewise, as the coining of the term *aerospace* in 1959 indicates, the Air Force is interested in the exploration of space and the development of systems to operate in space.

In 1980, the Air Force had a strength of nearly 560,000 military personnel, nearly 10 percent of whom were women. Officers numbered 98,000. The department employed approximately 240,000 civilians in the United States and overseas. To this could be added 240,000 personnel in the Air National Guard and Air Force Reserve. There were nearly nine thousand active aircraft in all components, plus over one thousand strategic missiles. Major installations totaled 134 (27 overseas). The department's budget for fiscal 1981 was expected to come to $23 billion. The Air Force's principal goals were to develop the M-X missile system, deploy cruise missiles for launch from strategic bombers or from mobile ground launchers in Europe, acquire a new long-range cargo plane, and improve the readiness of tactical forces. A good deal of emphasis also went into the Air Force's work with the National Aeronautics and Space Administration* and the space shuttle program. Essential to any achievement would be a raise in pay to stanch the outflow of skilled people. Through progress, the Air Force could continue to fulfill its role in the nation's strategy of deterrence.

Air Force Leaders

Chief, Bureau of Aircraft Production
   John D. Ryan   May 21, 1918-August 27, 1918
Director of Air Service
   John D. Ryan   August 27, 1918-December 23, 1918
Assistant Secretary of War for Air
   F. Trubee Davison   1926-1932
   Robert A. Lovett   April 10, 1941-January 31, 1946
   W. Stuart Symington   January 31, 1946-September 18, 1947
Secretary of the Air Force
   W. Stuart Symington   September 18, 1947
   Thomas K. Finletter   April 24, 1950
   Harold E. Talbott   February 4, 1953
   Donald A. Quarles   August 15, 1955
   James H. Douglas   May 1, 1957
   Dudley C. Sharp   December 11, 1959
   Eugene M. Zuckert   January 24, 1961
   Harold Brown   October 1, 1965
   Robert C. Seamans, Jr.   February 15, 1969
   John L. McLucas   July 19, 1973
   Thomas C. Reed   January 2, 1976
   John C. Stetson   April 26, 1977
   Hans Mark   July 26, 1979
   Verne Orr   February 9, 1981
Director of Military Aeronautics
   Major General William L. Kenly   May 20, 1918

Director (later Chief) of Air Service
    Major General Charles T. Menoher   December 23, 1918
    Major General Mason M. Patrick   October 5, 1921
Chief of Air Corps
    Major General Mason M. Patrick   July 2, 1926
    Major General James E. Fechet   December 13, 1927
    Major General Benjamin D. Foulois   December 19, 1931
    Major General Oscar Westover   December 22, 1935
    Major General Henry H. Arnold   September 29, 1938
Chief (later Commanding General),
Army Air Forces
    Major General (later General)
      Henry H. Arnold   June 20, 1941
    General Carl A. Spaatz   February 10, 1946
Chief of Staff of the Air Force
    General Carl A. Spaatz   September 26, 1947
    General Hoyt S. Vandenberg   April 30, 1948
    General Nathan F. Twining*   June 30, 1953
    General Thomas D. White   July 1, 1957
    General Curtis E. LeMay   June 30, 1961
    General John P. McConnell   February 1, 1965
    General John D. Ryan   August 1, 1969
    General George S. Brown*   August 1, 1973
    General David C. Jones*   July 1, 1974
    General Lew Allen, Jr.   July 1, 1978

*Later became chairman of the Joint Chiefs of Staff.

FOR ADDITIONAL INFORMATION: Carl Berger, et al., *The United States Air Force in Southeast Asia, 1961-1973: An Illustrated Account* (1977); Wesley F. Craven and James L. Cate, eds., *The Army Air Forces in World War II* (1948-1954), 7 vols.; R. Frank Futrell, et al., *Aces and Aerial Victories, 1965-1973* (1977), *The United States Air Force in Korea, 1950-1953* (1961), and *Ideas, Concepts, Doctrine: A History of Basic Thinking in the USAF, 1907-1964* (1971); Alfred Goldberg, ed., *A History of the United States Air Force, 1907-1957* (1957); Alan L. Gropman, *The Air Force Integrates, 1945-1964* (1978); James J. Hudson, *Hostile Skies: A Combat History of the American Air Service* (World War I) (1968); Alfred F. Hurley, *Billy Mitchell: Crusader for Air Power*, revised ed. (1975); Marcelle S. Knaack, *Encyclopedia of US Air Force Aircraft and Missile Systems: Post-World War II Fighters* (1978); Mauer, ed., *Air Force Combat Units in World War II* (1960), and *Combat Squadrons of the Air Force, World War II* (1969); Alan M. Osur, *Blacks in the Army Air Forces During World War II* (1977); Gordon Swanborough and Peter M. Bowers, *United States Military Aircraft Since 1908* (1971); U.S. Strategic Bombing Survey, 1945-1947, over 300 vols. Summary reports are: Strategic Bombing Survey, European War, No. 1, *Summary Report*, and Strategic Bombing Survey, Pacific War, No. 1, *Summary Report*.

The most useful periodical on the Air Force is *Air Force Magazine*, published monthly by the Air Force Association. Each May the issue contains the Air Force Almanac, a collection of general and statistical information.

WALTON S. MOODY

DEPARTMENT OF THE ARMY. The evolution of the United States Army and its executive agency, the Department of the Army (War Department to 1947), is rooted in strong traditions dating from the colonial era. They include civilian supremacy over the military; public distrust of large professional armies; dependence in major wars primarily on citizen-soldiers hastily raised and, upon the cessation of hostilities, quickly demobilized; preference of volunteer forces for distant missions and of militia for nearby defenses; emphasis on strategy of annihilation rather than of attrition and on tactics of offense instead of defense; and an individualistic style of soldiering that reflected the self-reliance and optimism of a dynamic society moving inexorably toward independence and democracy. Serving as militia or volunteers, many colonists gained military experience alongside British regulars in the imperial clashes over North America, 1689-1763, especially the French and Indian War, which proved invaluable in molding a national army during the American Revolution.

In June 1775, two months after the Revolutionary War began in Massachusetts, the Second Continental Congress established the Continental Army and appointed George Washington as commander-in-chief. The next year Congress created a five-man Board of War and Ordnance, which it abolished in 1781 in favor of a single Secretary of War (General Benjamin Lincoln). Upon the attainment of national independence two years later, Congress reduced the Army to less than seven hundred troops. Its peacetime functions during the Confederation period consisted mainly of garrisoning the posts of West Point and Fort Pitt and deterring Indian attacks on the frontier.

Under the Constitution ratified in 1789, Congress was empowered to declare war, raise and support an army and a navy, and call forth the militia to defend against invasions, execute laws, and put down insurrections. The President became commander-in-chief of the armed services, with the Secretary of War henceforth responsible to him rather than to Congress. In August 1789, Congress established the Department of War, and President Washington retained General Henry Knox as Secretary of War (held by him since 1785). Until the Navy Department* was created in 1798, the War Department served as the executive agency over both ground and sea defenses. It also had responsibility over Indian affairs and bounty lands until those functions were transferred, in 1849, to the Department of the Interior.* The actual strength of the Army in 1789 was about 800 soldiers; it was gradually increased to 3,300 by 1796, mainly because of demands to fight Indians. The Militia Act of 1792 preserved the concept of a citizen-soldiery but, in leaving compliance and support to the states, failed to produce the "well organized Militia" that Washington had recommended.

During the first half of the nineteenth century, patterns were set for the Army's future, such as utilizing a dual system of regulars and citizen-soldiers, proportioning force strength according to the pressures of war (expansion during hostilities and contraction in peacetime), and developing a War Department bureaucracy whose activities were poorly coordinated with the needs of field commands. The Army's staff organization was based on the current British system, while American tactical doctrine after 1815 was influenced more by Napoleon's campaigns than by technological innovations, for example, rifled field artillery and long-range infantry rifles. The Secretary of War oversaw a growing staff that included bureaus headed by the adjutant general, inspector general, quartermaster general, commissary general, and branch chiefs of Infantry, Artillery, Ordnance, and Engineers. While the Army's general performance in the War of 1812 was less than laudable, three decades later it showed remarkable improvements in training, organization, and command in the Mexican War. This progress was due, in part, to advances in War Deparment administration when John C. Calhoun (1817-1825) and Jefferson Davis (1853-1857) served as Secretary of War and, in part, to the maturation of the United States Military Academy* (founded in 1803), which was instrumental in producing a professionally competent and dedicated officer corps. In the West, meanwhile, the Army contributed significantly to exploration, mapping, and engineering, along with defending frontiersmen against belligerent Indians.

From a strength of 16,200 officers and men in 1860, the Army grew during the Civil War to a zenith of nearly 1.1 million troops in 1865. The conflict's enormous casualty toll was attributable, in large measure, to belated adjustment of tactics to new long-range weapons and to the efforts, largely futile, of commanders on both sides to fight decisive Napoleonic battles. The raising, training, and support of the ground forces of 1861-1865 evolved in makeshift fashion; too often officer selections were politically influenced, while conscription was inequitable and ineffectual. During the Civil War and the later Reconstruction, the War Department's leadership and policies were sometimes linked with Radical Republican politics.

In the former Confederate states, 1865-1877, the Army played an important, if unpopular, role in a variety of functions from maintaining law and order to supervising elections, educational reforms, and land redistribution. In addition, during the years 1865-1890 the Army was engaged in ten major campaigns and over one thousand separate engagements against Indians in the West. Army units were also employed in the East to suppress several incidents of labor violence. Yet, the Army's strength from the 1870s to the 1890s was usually less than twenty-five thousand troops.

Although some military historians have pictured the late nineteenth century as an ebb tide in the Army's development, with promotions slow, appropriations meager, and garrisons isolated, it was also a time of intellectual ferment in the officer corps. When Generals William T. Sherman and Philip H. Sheridan served successively as commanding general of the Army, 1869-1888, their power over administration and logistics was severely limited by the entrenched bureau chiefs, particularly the adjutant general. But they and a considerable body of enterprising officers were bent on bringing the Army to the professional level of the major European armies. With the founding of the School of Application for Infantry and Cavalry (later to become the Command and General Staff College) at Fort Leavenworth in 1881 and the subsequent beginning of other branch schools and of several service journals, officer education was vitalized, and the call for reforms grew. General Emory Upton became one of the most influential, intelligent spokesmen advocating a professional system modeled after that of the highly successful Prussian Army.

In the Spanish-American War of 1898 and the Philippine Insurrection of 1899-1902, the Army's top-level control was characterized by gross inefficiency and mismanagement. Secretary of War Elihu Root spearheaded the enactment of four reforms in 1903 that were of far-reaching consequence. First, the office of chief of staff was created to provide a military head, who, under the Secretary of War, would command and control all personnel and organizations of the Army, including the War Department bureaus. Second, the General Staff was set up under the chief of staff to prepare plans and directives on military policies and programs, some of which formerly had been regarded by the bureaus as their special provinces. Thus, for the first time the Army obtained authorization for a centralized command and an effective, peacetime planning body, but the bureaus would continue to fight the curtailment of their authority. Third, the Militia Act of 1903 provided for the Organized Militia, commonly called the National Guard since the 1880s, to be trained and equipped more effectively and uniformly. Militia training would now be supported by federal funds, with Army regulars providing instruction and joint exercises. While federal control over militia personnel was still closely restricted, the measure ultimately led to marked improvement in National Guard training. Fourth, the Army War College was founded to provide education in strategy and high command, while much of the rest of the Army's school system was modernized and expanded.

American Army medical and engineer personnel scored some remarkable achievements in Central America, 1900-1914: in Cuba and Panama, malaria and yellow fever were virtually eliminated as epidemic threats, and the Panama Canal was completed. The favorable impact of these feats on Latin Americans was offset when President Wilson ordered the Army to intervene twice in Mexico, with expeditions to Veracruz in 1914 and Chihuahua in 1916. The Chihuahua mission at least proved useful in identifying assets and liabilities in command and field organization preparatory to entering World War I. The National Defense Act of 1916 provided the basic framework for structuring, mobilizing, and strengthening the ground forces soon to be deployed to France, to be organized in three components: the Regular Army, the National Guard, and the National Army (conscripts).

With America's entry into World War I, the War Department General Staff was expanded from 19 to nearly 1,100 officers, while about 3.7 million troops served in the Army in 1917-1918. Nearly 70 percent of the soldiers were drafted under the Selective Service Act enacted in May 1917. About 2 million men served in General John J. Pershing's American Expeditionary Force in France, divided into three armies and forty-three divisions. The American input into Allied strategy was negligible, but at the tactical dimension the size, firepower, and offensive-mindedness of the American forces helped to swing the momentum against the German Army on the Western Front. Pershing patterned his staff organization after the French system, with five basic sections: administration (G-1), intelligence (G-2), operations (G-3), supply (G-4), and training (G-5). After the war, his staff plan would be adopted with some modifications by the War Department General Staff. Following the Armistice in 1918, some U.S. Army units were retained on duty in the Rhine Occupation, but the bulk of the "doughboys" were hastily demobilized. By early 1920, the Army had only 214,000 officers and men. War Department expenditures, likewise, fell sharply: from over $9 billion in 1919 to $357 million in 1923.

Based on War Department studies of lessons learned in World War I, the National Defense Act of 1920 was an enlightened measure that authorized a reasonably adequate peacetime organization and strength for the Regular Army, the National Guard, and the Organized Reserves. But retrenchment in federal spending was a favorite aim of Congress in the 1920s, and funds to implement the 1920 act were inadequately provided. After the onset of the Great Depression, the War Department was hard put to get minimal funding for even the Army's most basic needs. By 1932, the United States Army's strength was down to 135,000 officers and men, or less than half the total authorized by the act of 1920; it ranked seventeenth in size among the world's armies. Progress was limited largely to activities that were relatively inexpensive, such as promoting the Reserve Officers Training Corps and Citizen Military Training Camps, drafting economic and manpower mobilization plans, and developing strategies for hypothetical war scenarios. Beginning in 1933, Army personnel were detached to oversee a New Deal work-relief program, the Civilian Conservation Corps.* While the General Staff's War Plans Division was occupied in important, if economical, strategic studies, fundamental Regular Army needs like training, pay, and force strength were crippled by the budgetary stringency, firepower depended on obsolete World War I stocks, and developments in armored and air warfare lagged far behind European efforts.

In the late 1930s the Army Air Corps (called the Army Air Service to 1925 and the Army Air Forces in 1941) began to receive funds for expansion, but both American air and ground forces were still weak when World War II began in 1939. Although belated efforts were undertaken to attain partial mobilization prior to the Pearl Harbor attack, the Army had to share much of the American industrial output of military materiel in 1940-1941 with the Allied powers already engaged against the Axis forces. Thanks, in part, to the enactment of the nation's first peacetime draft, the Selective Service and Training Act of September 1940, the aggregate strength of the Army and Army Air Forces had grown to 1.6 million soldiers and airmen by late 1941.

Under the strong leadership of Secretary of War Henry L. Stimson and General George C. Marshall, the chief of staff, the Army and Army Air Forces were expanded during World War II to a peak strength in 1945 of 8.3 million personnel, including eighty-nine divisions and fifteen area air forces. Marshall, together with General Henry H. Arnold, commanding general of the Army Air Forces, served on the wartime U.S. Joint Chiefs of Staff and the Anglo-American Combined Chiefs of Staff. In an important reorganization of the War Department in February 1942, the Operations Division was created from the nucleus of the old War Plans Division and developed into Marshall's command post. The three major commands under Marshall in the reorganization became the Army Ground Forces, which was involved mainly in training the ground combat arms; the Army Service Forces, which included the administrative, logistical, and technical services; and the Army Air Forces, which gained virtual autonomy in matters unique to air training, personnel, and supply. Among the special wartime programs under the War Department the Manhattan Project on atomic bomb development was one of the most important and costliest. World War II introduced the American Army to its first large-scale experience of global coalition warfare, and, unlike the situation in World War I, its input into combined operations was significant, if not dominant, compared to Allied contributions. By the end of the conflict, the Army was the most powerful in the world (smaller in size than the Soviet Army, but superior in firepower, mobility, and logistics), while the American Army Air Forces by 1945 had no close rival in total missions, sorties, and strength in aircraft and personnel. Meanwhile, the War Department had gained the dubious distinction of becoming the largest of all the federal bureaucracies. Its many offices in the Pentagon and elsewhere in Washington now included a considerable force of civilian experts—a practice that would grow in the postwar period as the Army came to depend on civilian professionals in such fields as science, technology, and management.

As in the wake of previous wars, American public pressure forced a rapid demobilization after Japan's surrender. By mid-1946, the Army was reduced to 1.9 million troops, and by 1948 to 554,000. Army expenditures fell from $50 billion in 1945 to less than $8 billion three years later. Nevertheless, the Army faced unprecedented responsibilities abroad in maintaining numerous posts in Allied countries and in administering occupations in Japan, Austria, and West Germany. In addition, with the beginning of the Cold War, American Army leaders were committed to trying to keep their forces prepared to contain Communist incursions into the borderlands of the Soviet Union. Growing U.S. collective-security arrangements, especially with the NATO Treaty of 1949, and numerous military advisory assistance missions to defense-weak small nations put enormous pressures on the Army's already inadequate forces.

The National Security Act of 1947 was intended to produce unification of the armed services and integration of national security policymaking. It was a landmark measure in the military's institutional history, but its implementation fell short of achieving the main objectives. Among its provisions, the act created the National Military Establishment made up of the Office of the Secretary of Defense and the Departments of the Army, Navy, and Air Force* (new). Amendments to the act in 1949 established the Department of Defense,* strengthened the authority of the Secretary of Defense, and removed the Secretary of the Army and the other two service departments' secretaries from Cabinet-level status. The Army Organization Act of 1950 set forth in a single comprehensive statute the revised administrative structure for the Department of the Army that was necessitated by the acts of 1947 and 1949. The line of command of the Army now ran from the President through the Secretary of Defense and hence to the Secretary of the Army and his principal military adviser, the chief of staff. The measure also authorized changes dictated by World War II experiences, for instance, elevating Armor as a separate branch and reorganizing the system of area commands.

The Korean War, 1950-1953, was reminiscent of World War II in ground forces' tactics, weapons, and equipment. The American Army became the dominant member of the United Nations coalition and bore the principal logistical burden of the ground war. The United Nations Command was headed successively by U.S. generals—Douglas MacArthur, Matthew B. Ridgway, and Mark W. Clark—and the American Far East Command headquarters in Tokyo served as the nucleus of the U.N. military staff organization. Nearly all U.N. field units and operations were under the control of the U.S. Eighth Army headquarters. At its zenith, the American Army's commitment in the Korean conflict numbered about 275,000 soldiers. The war led to an overall buildup of U.S. Army strength to 1.7 million troops by 1953. Whereas in 1950 NATO's military capacity was nil, the Korean action's implied threat of an outbreak of general war produced by 1953 a National Atlantic Treaty Organization (NATO) ground force of fifty divisions, besides considerable naval and air elements. The U.S. Army's NATO role was sizable from then onward.

Under the Dwight D. Eisenhower Administration, 1953-1961, emphasis in defense planning was placed on strategic nuclear weapons and air-naval delivery systems to the neglect of conventional means of ground warfare. For the Army, the result was another decline in strength, to 858,000 troops by 1961. The Defense Reorganization Act of 1958 augmented the authority of the Joint Chiefs and the Secretary of Defense, while the status of the three service departments in the administrative chain declined further. Trying to stay abreast of technological changes that were altering strategy and tactics, the Army became involved in developing a host of devices ranging from surface-to-air missiles and atomic artillery to helicopters and armored personnel carriers. In 1956, it changed from the triangular to the pentomic divisional organization, the latter comprising five relatively self-sufficient battle groups equipped with the latest weapons systems (including tactical nuclear) and airmobile transportation to provide maximum firepower, rapid movement, and adaptability on a potential limited-nuclear battlefield.

The American Army's involvement in the Vietnam War grew from a small body of advisers to the South Vietnamese Army in 1961-1962 to full-scale combat participation in 1965, with 543,000 American soldiers in Vietnam by 1968. In the meantime, the overall strength of the U.S. Army had grown to 1.4 million. Trained primarily for conventional warfare, the American forces had to adjust to tactics of counterinsurgency. The war was a painful lesson in the need to keep the Army prepared for flexible responses; its other lessons are still being heatedly debated. With the U.S. withdrawal from the war in 1973, Army strength was cut to 785,000 troops before the end of the year—the lowest it had been since the eve of the Korean conflict.

Under the aggressive leadership of Secretary of Defense Robert S. McNamara, 1961-1968, the Defense Department,* including its three military departments, underwent managerial reforms aimed at producing cost effectiveness through planning-programming-budgeting systems and at instilling rationality in the bureaucratic structure through techniques of centralized control and modern management similar to those used in large corporations. For the Department of the Army, McNamara's reforms spelled the elimination of the offices of five chiefs of technical services who, like the traditionalist bureau chiefs of old, had opposed centralized regulation of their spheres. The trend through the 1970s was toward further rationalizing of the Army's administration along functional lines. The major field commands that emerged in the 1970s were the Training and Doctrine Command, the Forces Command, and the Materiel Development and Readiness Command, with the last-named incorporating many of the functions of the former technical services. A significant tactical organizational change occurred with the introduction of the ROAD (Reorganization Objective Army Division) plan that discarded the pentomic concept in favor of tailoring divisions to fulfill specific combat missions.

With the end of the draft in 1973, the Army moved into a new era of dependence on all-volunteer forces. Since then, it has become involved in the nation's most massive experiments in the equal opportunity employment of minorities and women. Among its unheralded nonmilitary contributions, the Army continues to pioneer in some fields of medicine, and its Corps of Engineers* still bears the responsibility for vast inland waterways projects, such as dams, levees, river dredging, and locks. Among the Army's most vexatious problems in the 1970s were the quantity and quality of recruits, the decline in ROTC enrollments, the steady loss of skilled noncommissioned officers, and the old problem of inadequate funding in peacetime. The Army's leaders have continued to try new management and command arrangements that show promise of improving organizational effectiveness and combat readiness, as in the host of administrative changes launched in 1972-1974. Fresh thinking has been apparent in the development of tactical doctrine, best evidenced in the adoption in 1976 of Field Manual 100-5, *Operations*. In its concepts of how to win against superior odds on hypothetical future battlefields, FM 100-5 has provoked more debate in the officer corps than any and all previous field manuals in the Army's history. Indeed, the controversy is indicative of a spirit of frank reappraisal and of open-mindedness toward change among Army professionals during the period of flux in organization and tactics that continues into the 1980s.

FOR ADDITIONAL INFORMATION: The official Army records are in the National Archives* and National Records Center in Washington, while many personal papers of Army individuals are deposited in the U.S. Army Military History Institute at Carlisle

Barracks, Pennsylvania. The best secondary study on Army administrative history is James E. Hewes, Jr., *From Root to McNamara: Army Organization and Administration, 1900-1963* (1975). No work of comparable quality and depth exists yet for the earlier or later periods. For a survey of the Army's institutional development, see Russell F. Weigley, *History of the United States Army* (1967). The best current reference is *The Department of the Army Manual* (1979).

D. CLAYTON JAMES

DEPARTMENT OF THE NAVY. Throughout the colonial period, navies played a historic role in determining the fate of European empires in North America. The prominence of naval affairs in the New World also became evident during the War of American Independence when the British fleet undertook extensive operations in the Western Atlantic and the Continental Congress and many states established maritime forces. In the campaign at Yorktown in 1781, a French squadron assured the defeat of General Cornwallis by isolating his army from outside support, a development that precipitated the British decision to abandon the American conflict. Despite these early naval successes, however, the Continental and state navies were disestablished soon after the war.

Interest in an American fleet was revived in the early 1790s when Congress authorized the War Department* to construct six frigates following the seizure of American merchant ships by the Barbary pirates of North Africa. British and French attacks on U.S. shipping added further urgency to naval rearmament. Although diplomatic settlements soon were reached with the Barbary Powers and Great Britain, the French resumed depredations on the American carrying trade in 1797, resulting in an undeclared naval war between the United States and France. During the Quasi War, Congress established the Navy Department (April 30, 1798) and Benjamin Stoddert became its first Secretary. By the conclusion of the conflict with France in 1801, the foundations were laid for the United States Navy. In addition to operating approximately thirty sizable ships, the service was developing several navy yards and other shore establishments to support this fleet.

The incoming administration of Thomas Jefferson called for reduced military expenditures and a defensive naval policy. However, assaults by the North African state of Tripoli on American merchantmen caused the Barbary War of 1801-1805 and led to the deployment of a U.S. naval squadron to the Mediterranean. Seven years after the American victory over Tripoli, the United States and Great Britain engaged in the War of 1812. This conflict featured a far-flung American campaign against British shipping and a number of dramatic actions demonstrating that in single-ship engagements the nation's new navy could meet the mighty Royal Navy on equal terms. Although the relatively small American fleet did not prevent the British from concentrating forces for assaults on Washington, Baltimore, and New Orleans, the naval balance was more equal on inland waters. At Lake Erie in 1813, a decisive victory by Oliver Hazard Perry assured America's reconquest of the Northwest. In the next year, Thomas Macdonough blocked an invasion of the United States by defeating a British squadron on Lake Champlain.

Near the end of the War of 1812, the more systematic participation of naval officers in the administration of the department was assured by the creation of a Board of Naval Commissioners. Congress established this body, consisting of three senior captains, in 1815, to assist the Secretary of the Navy. Among other duties, it oversaw the construction and outfitting of ships, improved supply and fiscal procedures, and offered advice on long-range shipbuilding programs. In 1842, the board was replaced by several material bureaus, each of which eventually was headed by a naval officer reporting directly to the Secretary. These organizations built and repaired warships, maintained shore facilities, offered medical and supply services, and provided a continuing opportunity for career officers to share in the management of the Navy. Nevertheless, the absence of a central group of officers capable of giving general advice on fleet operations, strategy, and policy was a basic problem in naval organization. This was especially the case since many secretaries of the Navy had little familiarity with naval affairs and served for relatively short terms.

At various times between 1815 and 1861, the Navy maintained squadrons in the Mediterranean, Caribbean, South Atlantic, Pacific, Far East, and off the African coast. These commands were particularly important in protecting American overseas commerce. Several special operations, such as the United States Exploring Expedition under Charles Wilkes in 1838-1842 and Matthew C. Perry's mission to Japan in 1853-1854, were landmarks in American history because of their contributions to scientific knowledge and the promotion of American trade. During the Mexican War of 1846-1848, U.S. naval forces blockaded the coast of Mexico, participated in the conquest of California, and launched an amphibious operation at Veracruz that placed the Army in a position to advance against Mexico City.

The Civil War saw a remarkable increase in the Navy from less than 50 to approximately 700 active ships. To assist Secretary Gideon Welles in administering this complex organization, Congress authorized an Assistant Secretary of the Navy. That position was filled by Gustavus V. Fox, a former naval officer with an intimate knowledge of the service. Welles, Fox, and senior officers instituted a naval blockade of the South that became increasingly effective. At the same time, the Navy and Army cooperated in a series of decisive campaigns on the Western rivers. The Navy also undertook assaults against New Orleans, Mobile Bay, and other seaports, and provided logistical support for Union armies.

A rapid decline of the Navy in the first fifteen years after the Civil War reflected postwar demobilization, the diminished importance of the American merchant marine, and the nation's waning interest in foreign affairs. In the 1880s, however, modern steel cruisers began to be built for the traditional mission of protecting American commerce and attacking enemy shipping. In the 1890s, the United States started to develop a battleship force designed to defeat a hostile fleet. The famous writings of Alfred Thayer Mahan gave impetus to this new strategy, which aimed to secure control of sea areas vital for the defense of the United States or the projection of American power overseas.

The Navy built in the last two decades of the nineteenth century demonstrated its value in the Spanish-American War by achieving victories at Manila Bay and Santiago, Cuba. During the war, a temporary Strategy Board of naval officers advised the Secretary of the Navy on the employment of the fleet. The General Board of the Navy, established in 1900, was to some extent an outgrowth of that body. The new advisory board suggested shipbuilding programs, prepared war plans, and recommended general policy. Yet, the General Board's lack of executive authority troubled many naval officers who believed that career officers should have greater influence. These naval reformers sought a general-staff system, giving uniformed professionals immediate control over fleet operations, strategic planning, and the preparation of the fleet for war. Their ambitions were only partially satisfied by the establishment of a chief of Naval Operations in 1915, since that officer initially received detailed supervision from the Secretary of the Navy. The Secretary also continued to exercise direct control over the technical bureaus first established in 1842.

When America entered World War I, the nation was undertaking a long-range, capital shipbuilding program designed to create a navy equal to the strongest in the world. The most pressing need in 1917, however, was for destroyers and other small anti-submarine ships to protect the movement of an army to France. This requirement delayed the construction of battleships that were the backbone of early twentieth-century fleets. During most of the interwar years, the expansion of an American battle force was constrained by other factors, including international arms limitation treaties and limited defense budgets. Nevertheless, there were significant qualitative improvements. One of these was the building of a strong force of aircraft carriers (numbering seven by December 1941) that rivaled the battleship as the Navy's major offensive weapon. Plans to secure advance Pacific bases in a possible war with Japan resulted in enhanced amphibious capabilities. Long-ranged submarines, also designed for a potential conflict with Japan, represented another significant advance.

In World War II, Ernest J. King emerged as one of the strongest leaders in the Navy's history. In addition to serving as chief of Naval Operations and overall fleet commander, King received specific authority to coordinate and direct the technical bureaus. The admiral also was the Navy's representative on the newly created Joint Chiefs of Staff, which formulated American grand strategy. Since the Secretary of the Navy exercised only general control over King, these institutional arrangements indicated the realization of the long-sought general staff system.

One of King's achievements was to assure that major attention was given to the Pacific theater, despite the agreement among Anglo-American officials to assign first priority to the defeat of Germany. During the summer of 1942, following the U.S. triumph at the Battle of Midway, King obtained approval for a limited offensive at Guadalcanal in the South Pacific. In 1943, the Joint

Chiefs of Staff authorized a two-pronged advance through the Central and South-west Pacific areas. By 1945, both thrusts reached the Western Pacific and forces were poised to assault Japan. The United States Navy further contributed to victory in the greatest naval war in the nation's history by undertaking a ruinous submarine campaign against the merchant shipping serving the island kingdom of Japan and by employing its carrier aircraft in the aerial bombardment of the enemy's home islands.

In the Atlantic, the United States worked closely with the Royal Navy in a war that demanded the mass movement of troops and supplies across oceanic shipping lanes. The highly successful German submarine attack on Allied merchantmen finally was defeated in the spring of 1943. The combined British and American fleets also launched a series of amphibious operations that directly confronted the enemy ashore. These began at North Africa in 1942, extended to Sicily and Italy the following year, and culminated in the invasion of France during 1944.

The United States Navy, which emerged from World War II with more than twenty-eight hundred combatant and auxiliary ships, was by far the most powerful maritime force in the world. Demobilization, the absence of potential enemy fleets, and the widespread belief that nuclear weapons made surface navies obsolete, resulted in a sharp reduction of naval strength during the first five years of the postwar era. Starting in 1950, the service shared in the general American rearmament prompted by the Cold War with the Soviet Union and the Korean Conflict. By the 1960s, the service operated a powerful, modern fleet built largely around aircraft carriers. Many of these forces were assigned to the Sixth and Seventh Fleets operating continuously in the Mediterranean and Far East in support of U.S. foreign policy. A further achievement was the construction of a large force of submarines capable of firing long-range nuclear missiles that began to go to sea in 1960. These units became an essential part of the nation's nuclear deterrent.

Throughout the postwar era, the chiefs of Naval Operations continued to exercise the great influence achieved during World War II by Admiral King. In 1966, this senior naval officer also was given outright control over the technical bureaus that now were known as systems commands. Nevertheless, the authority of the Navy as a whole increasingly was submerged in the complex, unified defense structure created after 1947. Indicative of this trend was the loss of the Secretary of the Navy's Cabinet status in 1949. In 1958, the chief of Naval Operations gave up his operational control over naval forces. After that date, most naval and military units were assigned to unified commands reporting directly to the Joint Chiefs of Staff, in which the chief of Naval Operations was but one member.

The United States Navy demonstrated its continued utility during the Korean Conflict, the Cuban Missile Crisis of 1962, and many other Cold War confrontations. From 1964 to 1973, the service was committed to the prolonged, controversial, and ultimately unsuccessful attempt to maintain an independent, pro-

Western state of South Vietnam. In addition to deploying ships and small craft to the rivers and coastal waters of that country, the Navy's carriers participated in the extended air campaign against North Vietnam.

During the closing years of the Vietnam War and throughout the 1970s, the financial drain of Southeast Asian operations and the waning support by Americans for military preparedness slowed naval construction and modernization. It also became necessary to decommission many aging ships built during World War II, with the result that, by 1979, the Navy operated fewer than five hundred active fleet and auxiliary ships, the smallest number since before World War II. During this decline, the service became responsible for maintaining forces in the Indian Ocean, in addition to its commitments in the Mediterranean and Far East. More ominously, the Soviet Union was rapidly developing a powerful navy that posed a grave danger to the American fleet, which had been without a serious rival for almost thirty years. As the 1980s began, these factors led to renewed efforts to expand and update American naval capabilities. Many of the issues raised at that time were reminiscent of the discussions 190 years earlier when the foundations were laid for the United States Navy.

FOR ADDITIONAL INFORMATION: The primary repository for U.S. Naval Records is the National Archives,* but naval files and private paper collections also are held by many other organizations. A summary of these materials appears in Dean C. Allard, Martha L. Crawley, and Mary W. Edmison, eds., *U.S. Naval History Sources in the United States* (1979). Recent, critical bibliographies discussing the voluminous published literature on the Navy are included in Robin Higham, ed., *A Guide to the Sources of United States Military History* (1975). The essays in that volume will be updated in future supplements.

DEAN C. ALLARD

DEPARTMENT OF THE TREASURY. Although the Treasury Department can trace its origin to the appointment by the First Continental Congress of a standing committee to superintend the Treasury, the Department of the Treasury, under the Constitution, was created by an act of September 1, 1789 (1 Stat. 65). This act provided for a Secretary of the Treasury as head of the department, a comptroller, an auditor, a treasurer, a register, and an Assistant to the Secretary. The position of Assistant to the Secretary was abolished on May 8, 1792, but was reestablished on March 3, 1849.

The duties of the Secretary were to prepare and implement plans for the management and improvement of the revenue; to devise forms for keeping accounts and making returns; to grant under certain established limitations all warrants for monies issued from the Treasury; to execute such services relating to the sale of public lands as was required of him; to report to either branch of Congress on all matters referred to him by those bodies or that pertain to his office; and to perform all services relating to the public finances as directed.

Alexander Hamilton, the first Secretary of the Treasury, assumed office on September 11, 1789. The adoption by Congress of policies Hamilton recommended in his reports on the public credit, on the establishment of a national bank and of a mint, and on manufactures not only secured the success of the newly created federal government, but also laid the basic structure of the department, much of which is still evident today. The assumption of responsibility for the payment of the foreign and domestic debts incurred by the government under the Continental Congress and of the state debts laid the basis of our national debt policy. Thus, the federal government continues to issue federal loans backed by interest-paying securities, stocks, and bonds, subscribed to by the public, banks, and corporations to maintain our public credit.

Between 1776 and 1817, subscriptions to loans were handled in the states through loan offices under the direction of commissioners of loans. By an act of March 3, 1817, the loan offices were abolished, and their records and duties were transferred to the Second Bank of the United States, chartered on April 10, 1816. Upon the expiration of the charter of the Second Bank, April 20, 1836, the loan records and functions were transferred to the register of the Treasury. In 1868, a Division of Loans was created in the Secretary's Office, and in 1876 this division was combined with the Division of Currency (also created in 1868) to form the Division of Loans and Currency. After 1894, the Register's Office retained only those functions relating to the issuance of securities. In 1919, a commissioner of the public debt was given supervision of the Public Debt Service that became the Bureau of Public Debt* in 1940. The Office of the Register became the Division of Retired Securities within the bureau in 1956, and the position of register, established in 1781, was abolished.

Hamilton's second report to Congress provided a plan for a central bank. Chartered for twenty years by an act of February 25, 1791, the Bank of the United States received monies collected from customs duties, from excise taxes on whiskey and tobacco products, and from the sale of public lands. The United States Customs Service* became a part of the Treasury Department when the department was established. The threat of war with France necessitated the collection of more revenue, and so, in 1798, laws were passed that permitted the levying of taxes on many additional products such as carriages, window panes, jewelry, watches, and deeds and other legal papers. The War of 1812 saw similar taxes levied. After the restoration of peace, revenue from impost duties was sufficient to pay the federal government's expenses, and so, the position of commissioner of the revenue was abolished and all laws levying internal taxes were repealed in 1817.

The Civil War saw the recreation of the Internal Revenue Service* under the commissioner of revenue. Excise taxes were collected on a variety of products including incomes. In 1866, the commissioner was given responsibility to terminate the direct tax commissions created to collect direct taxes in the states in rebellion. Gradually, all wartime taxes levied in all the states were abolished until, by 1883, only taxes on liquor and tobacco products remained. An act of August 2, 1886, levied a tax on oleomargarine and established the Analytical and Chemical Division within the service to test adulterated food products and tax them to regulate and limit their sale to the public. With the passage of the Pure Food and Drug Act of 1906, this division and its functions were transferred to the Department of Agriculture.* An abortive income tax law of 1894 was declared unconstitutional. The adoption of the Seventeenth Amendment in 1913 rendered constitutional the collection of income taxes, the greatest single source of federal revenue today. By Treasury Order No. 221, June 6, 1972, the Internal Revenue Service was divided, and a separate Bureau of Alcohol, Tobacco, and Firearms was established.

Between the expiration of the charter of the Second Bank of the United States and 1846, the federal government's receipts were placed in selected state banks designated by the administration's political opponents as "Pet Banks." The first attempt to establish an Independent Treasury System failed when an act of August 13, 1841, repealed the act of July 4, 1840, creating such a system. A second attempt succeeded with the passage of the Independent Treasury Act of August 6, 1846, amended March 3, 1857, and August 5, 1861. Subtreasuries, headed by assistant treasurers and under the general supervision of the treasurer of the United States, were established in Philadelphia, New York, New Orleans, Boston, Charleston, Saint Louis, Baltimore, Cincinnati, Chicago, and San Francisco. The establishment of the National Banking System in 1863 and the use of national banks as designated depositories tended to lessen the effectiveness of the system. The adoption of the Federal Reserve System* in 1913 and the authorization of Federal Reserve banks as depositories for federal funds and as fiscal agents for the government proved the subtreasuries to be less efficient than the Federal Reserve banks, and so the system was abolished on May 20, 1920. On June 30, 1940, the Office of the Treasurer of the United States was made part of the Fiscal Service in the Secretary's Office.

Hamilton's third report recommended the creation of a mint. The Mint of the United States was established at Philadelphia on April 2, 1792, to supply coinage and to assay the value of foreign coins that circulated freely in the early days of the new government. Nominally an independent agency, from 1835 to 1873 the Treasury supervised the coinage operation. On February 12, 1873, the Bureau of the Mint was created in the Treasury Department, and the director of the Mint became head of the bureau and of the other mints and assay offices that had been established. In 1838, mints had been established at Charlotte, North Carolina, Dahlonega, Georgia, and New Orleans, Louisiana. Following the discovery of gold in California, a mint was opened at San Francisco. Mints were authorized at Denver and Carson City in 1862 and 1863, respectively, but no coinage was minted at Carson City until 1879. In 1893, the Carson City Mint was closed.

The mints at Philadelphia and Denver struck medals authorized by Congress in recognition of distinguished service to the government. These medals are part of a series commemorating presidential inaugurals, the service of secretaries of the Treasury, and directors of the Mint; there are also Indian Peace Medals, Life Saving Medals, Military Medals, Medals for Scientific Achievement, and medals commemorating historic buildings. The Philadelphia and Denver mints sell copies of many of these medals. At the present time, mints are operated at Philadelphia, Denver, and San Francisco, and Assay Offices at the Gold Depository at Fort Knox, Kentucky, and at the Silver Depository at West Point, New York. The bureau supervises the production of coins for distribution to Federal Reserve banks, which in turn distribute them to commercial banks. It also collects data on a worldwide scale relative to gold and silver supplies.

Before the Civil War, government obligations were paid in specie, that is, hard money. The pressing need for money during the war saw the suspension of specie payments and the creation of two new Treasury agencies, the Office of the Comptroller of the Currency and the Bureau of Engraving and Printing.* The National Banking Act of June 3, 1863, provided a national currency secured by United States bonds and for the chartering and examination of national banks by the comptroller of the currency. The comptroller also supervised the issuance and redemption of national bank notes that circulated as national currency through 1935.

The Bureau of Engraving and Printing originated in an act of July 11, 1862, that empowered the Secretary of the Treasury to have notes or any part thereof engraved and printed at the department in Washington and to purchase machinery and materials and employ personnel needed for that purpose. From August 27, 1862, the Treasury seal and the signatures of the register and the treasurer were overprinted on one-and two-dollar notes provided by private bank note companies. Gradually, the whole printing process was taken over by the bureau, which printed internal revenue, customs, postage, and savings stamps, U.S. currency, public debt securities, and Federal Reserve notes. The only U.S. currency printed by the bureau since 1972 are Federal Reserve notes.

The need to curb counterfeiting of paper currency led to the establishment of the United States Secret Service.* Following the assassination of President McKinley, the protection of the President became a duty of the Secret Service. This activity was formalized in 1906. Today, protection is accorded to the President and members of his family, to the Vice-President and his family, to candidates for presidential office, ex-presidents, their wives or widows, to visiting heads of states, and to other persons designated by the President.

The Civil War occasioned the establishment of several temporary agencies administered by the Treasury Department. An act of July 13, 1861, provided for the administration and regulation of trade in areas of the South where the Union military forces had regained control. Between 1862 and 1864, nine special agencies had been established, supervised by the commissioner of customs until July 30, 1864, when the supervising special agent for the First Special Agency was designated general agent. These agencies kept account of captured and abandoned lands and property, issued trade permits, and were responsible for the employment of freed slaves and their welfare until the creation in the War Department of the Bureau of Refugees, Freedmen, and Abandoned Lands.*

Closely allied to the work of the special agents was that of the Southern Claims

Commission that adjudicated Civil War claims. The settlement of these claims led to the creation, in the Office of the Secretary of the Treasury, of the Division of Captured and Abandoned Property. This division evolved into the Division of Captured Property Claims and Lands that eventually became the Miscellaneous Division. The Miscellaneous Division was abolished in 1906.

The act creating the Treasury Department provided systems for receiving and disbursing public monies and for maintaining accounts of their receipt and expenditure. Originally, the accounting function and recording of warrants issued by the Secretary were assigned to the register; and the custodian of public funds was the treasurer of the United States. An act of July 31, 1894, established a Division of Bookkeeping and Warrants that had evolved in the Secretary's Office from the Division of Warrants, Estimates, and Appropriations (1875) and the Division of Warrants (1868). The new division took over functions and records relating to the receipt and expenditure of public funds from the Division of Receipts and Expenditures of the Register's Office. In 1920, the Division of Bookkeeping and Warrants was placed under the supervision of the commissioner of accounts and deposits. In 1921, certain functions of the Division of Public Moneys (established in the Secretary's Office in 1877) and relating to covering revenues and repayments into the Treasury, the issue of duplicate checks and warrants, certification of outstanding liabilities for payment, and special accounts of the Secretary were transferred to it. In 1933, a presidential Executive Order centralized in the Treasury's Division of Disbursements disbursing operations formerly performed by various departments and agencies.

Presidential Reorganization Plan No. 3, dated April 2, 1940, effective June 30, 1940, by joint resolution of Congress dated June 4, 1940, created the Fiscal Service of the Treasury Department composed of the Bureau of Accounts, the Bureau of Public Debt, and the Office of the Treasurer of the United States. The Bureau of Accounts was formed by combining the Office of the Commissioner of Accounts and Deposits and the Division of Disbursements. On February 1, 1974, Treasury Order No. 229 transferred the position of the treasurer of the United States to the Office of the Secretary of the Treasury and merged the operations of the Bureau of Accounts and the Office of the Treasurer into the Bureau of Government Financial Operations. The latter disburses payment for most government agencies, settles claims involving loss or forgery of Treasury checks, manages the government's central accounting and reporting systems and the government's cash resources, and overseas disposal of wornout currency and the investing of government trust funds.

The founding act of September 2, 1789, created one auditor and one comptroller. In 1792, an accountant for the War Department* was appointed to assist with the auditing of military accounts. In 1817, a reorganization in the department provided for a second comptroller and for four additional auditors. The first auditor audited Treasury accounts, the second auditor audited quartermaster, Indian, and other military accounts, the third auditor, military accounts, the fourth auditor, Navy accounts, and the fifth auditor, State Department,* and other accounts. In 1846, a sixth auditor was established to audit Post Office accounts, and in 1849 the commissioner of customs was created to audit customs accounts. In 1894, the functions of the second comptroller and the commissioner of customs were restored to the first comptroller now designated the comptroller of the Treasury.

The Budget and Accounting Act of June 20, 1921, effected a major reorganization in the Treasury. It established the General Accounting Office* under the comptroller general as a congressional agency. To this office were assigned the duties of the Treasury auditors and the comptroller of the Treasury, together with those functions which the Division of Bookkeeping and Warrants had acquired from the Office of the Register. The General Accounting Office performs an independent audit of all government receipts and expenditures and the use of appropriated government funds, settles fiscal accounts of accountable officers, and settles claims against the government.

The Office of the Chief Clerk was created by an act of April 20, 1818. At the same time, an Office of the Superintendent of the Treasury Building was established. These offices were combined by an act of March 3, 1853, and remained under the chief clerk until May 1937, when a separate Office of the Superintendent of Treasury Buildings was created.

During the nineteenth and part of the twentieth centuries, the chief clerk was the chief executive officer of the department, responsible for the superintendence of all Treasury buildings throughout the nation, supervision of Treasury clerks, distribution of mail, custody of records of the Secretary's Office, expenditure of appropriations for government exhibits at International Expositions, custody of the Treasury seal, and preparation of certified copies of documents. He was secretary of the Board of Awards of the General Supply Committee that became Treasury Procurement and later the Federal Supply Service. The Office of the Chief Clerk continued until October 1, 1947, when it became part of the Office of Administrative Services. When the Division of Office Services was established in 1948, the position of chief clerk was abolished.

Except for the Secret Service and the Federal Law Enforcement Training Center the only current nonfiscal agency of the Treasury Department is the U.S. Savings Bond Division, created on March 19, 1941, to plan the sale of Series E, F, and G bonds and Savings Stamps. Treasury Order No. 50, dated June 25, 1943, created the War Finance Division to coordinate and integrate volunteer bond selling throughout the country. By Treasury Order No. 62, effective January 1, 1946, the Savings Bond Division was created and continues through payroll savings and bond-a-month programs to promote the sale of Series E and H bonds to broaden the base of ownership of the public debt and reduce the rate of inflation.

Many nonfiscal functions once performed by the department have been transferred to other departments. The General Land Office was transferred to the Department of the Interior* in 1849; the Office of the Solicitor of the Treasury to the Department of Justice* in 1870; and the documentation of vessels, the

Steamboat Inspection Service, National Bureau of Standards,* Coast and Geodetic Survey,* Bureau of Statistics, Lighthouse Board, Bureau of Navigation, and the Immigration and Naturalization Service* to the Department of Commerce and Labor. The United States Coast Guard,* formed by combining the Revenue Cutter Service and the Life-saving Service in 1915 and to which the Lighthouse Service was transferred in 1939, became part of the Department of Transportation* in 1966. The Bureau of Prohibition was transferred to the Department of Justice in 1930. The Public Buildings Service, successor to the Office of the Supervising Architect (which had been transferred to the Department of the Interior in 1939), and the Federal Supply Service (formerly Treasury Procurement) were combined in 1949 with the National Archives and Records Service* and the defunct War Assets Administration to form the General Services Administration.* In 1968, the Bureau of Narcotics was transferred to the Department of Health, Education and Welfare, now the Department of Health and Human Services.*

The Treasury Department of today is headed by the Secretary, who is assisted by the Deputy Secretary, the Under Secretary for Monetary Affairs, and the Under Secretary. The Deputy Secretary assists the Secretary and acts for him in his absence. The Under Secretary for Monetary Affairs assists the Secretary and Deputy in all domestic and international financial and economic affairs. He is assisted by the Assistant Secretary for International Affairs and the Fiscal Assistant Secretary. The Fiscal Assistant Secretary oversees the Fiscal Service comprised of the Bureau of Government Financial Operations and the Bureau of the Public Debt.

The Under Secretary advises and assists the Secretary and the Deputy Secretary in formulating and executing policies relating to presidential protection, foreign assets control, departmental administration management, coin and currency manufacture, sale and retention of savings bonds, legislative liaison, law enforcement, including alcohol, tobacco, and firearms regulations, Treasury financing operations, and revenue sharing. He is assisted by the Assistant Secretary for Enforcement and Operations, who oversees the administration of the United States Customs Service, the Bureau of the Mint, the Bureau of Engraving and Printing,* Bureau of Alcohol, Tobacco, and Firearms, the Secret Service, the Federal Law Enforcement Program, and the Office of Foreign Assets Control. The last-named administers regulations that implement freezing controls on trade and financial transactions with certain foreign countries, namely, Korea, Vietnam, Cambodia, and Cuba and their nationals. Under a general license contained in an amendment to Foreign Assets Control Regulations, transactions with the People's Republic of China, with certain exceptions, are now permitted.

The Under Secretary is also assisted by the Assistant Secretary for Administration who directs the work of the offices of Administrative Programs, Budget and Program Analysis, Audit, Computer Science, Management and Organization, Personnel, and Equal Opportunity Program; and by the treasurer, who oversees the U.S. Savings Bond Division. Assistant Secretaries for Tax Policy,

Economic Policy, Domestic Finance, Legislative Affairs, and Public Affairs also advise and assist the Secretary. They report directly to him as do the comptroller of the currency, the commissioner of internal revenue, and the general counsel.

FOR ADDITIONAL INFORMATION: *Annual Report of the Secretary of the Treasury on the State of the Finances, Fiscal Year 1979* (1980). Earlier reports are available. For a listing of them for the period 1789-1909, see *Checklist of U. S. Public Documents, 1789-1909* (1911). *Guide to the National Archives of the United States* (1974), 152-181, contains a brief administrative history of the Department of the Treasury and descriptions of records of the Office of the Secretary and of various department bureaus that are in the National Archives.* Another useful source is Jesse P. Watson, Kenneth Munden and Henry P. Beers, *Guide to Federal Archives Relating to the Civil War* (1962).

See also *The Bureau of the Mint, Its History, Activities, and Organization* (1926), Institute for Government Research Service Monographs of the United States Government, No. 37. Other monographs published by the Institute for Government Research on Treasury Department agencies exist for the United States Customs Service and for the Office of the Comptroller of the Currency. Herman E. Krooss, ed., *Documentary History of Banking and Currency in the United States* 4 vols. (c. 1969), according to the Preface, "is the most comprehensive documentary history of American money and banking ever published." Carmelita S. Ryan and Hope K. Holdcamper, comps., *Preliminary Inventory of the General Records of the Department of the Treasury, 1789-1965* (Record Group 56) (1977) describes a series of records of the Office of the Secretary of the Treasury and its various divisions that are in the National Archives. Robert Mayo, *The Treasury Department and Its Various Fiscal Bureaus* . . . 2 vols. (1847) may also be consulted.

HOPE K. HOLDCAMPER

DEPARTMENT OF TRANSPORTATION. Created in 1966, the United States Department of Transportation constitutes the third largest agency within the executive branch of the federal government. The Department of Transportation represents an amalgamation of numerous transportational promotion activities that were separately administered by numerous federal agencies prior to 1966. Even though there were seventeen legislative proposals to create a Department of Transportation before 1966, each of these failed because they attempted, one way or another, to modify the existing structure of economic regulation of transportation.

The primary purpose of the department is to assure the coordinated, effective administration of the transportation programs of the federal government into developed national transportation policies and programs conducive to the provision of safe, fast, efficient, and convenient transportation at the lowest cost consistent therewith. The department became operative in April 1967 and essentially consisted of elements transferred from eight other major departments and agencies.

The dominant managerial theme of the department is that operating programs are administered primarily by the various modally aligned administrations. Therein lies one of the principal strengths of the organizational structure of the United States Department of Transportation. This structure contributes to eliminating or diminishing historical deficiencies traditionally affiliated with federal promotion of transportation.

Essentially, the agency was created, first, to deal with and solve numerous historical deficiencies associated with the federal government's transportation promotional activities. These included the lack of a uniform investment policy, which, in effect, resulted in duplication of facilities and a general suboptimization of the transportation activity by the executive branch. Second, the agency was created in order to correct the historical deficiency of a lack of long-range planning. Previous planning was conducted along modal lines with no overall consideration of aggregate transportation needs. Third, a total lack of program coordination between the various administering agencies created a situation wherein highways were being constructed without any reference to the concurrent location of airports and railroad abandonments.

Policy was highly fragmented before the Department of Transportation was created, even though these activities emanated primarily from the Department of Commerce* under the Secretary of Commerce for Transportation. No maximum effort was directed towards administering the safety laws relating to automobiles, airplanes, boats, and other transportation.

The United States Department of Transportation maintains a unique organizational structure among executive agencies within government inasmuch as it is patterned along a holding-company approach. In the past, transportation promotion was conducted along modal lines (promotion of railroads, highways, air and water carriers) with no overall emphasis upon developing an integrated transportation system. This dispersed organizational structure, of course, and resulted in suboptimization of the overall transportation function.

The present Department of Transportation consists of a Secretary of Transportation, and, at the Assistant Secretary level, the modes of transportation are functionally aligned by topics. For example, these include the Assistant Secretary for Policy and International Affairs, Assistant Secretary for Budget and Programs, Assistant Secretary for Governmental and Public Affairs, and Assistant Secretary for Administration in addition to a general counsel. These assistant secretaries coordinate all of the activities of the Department of Transportation on an intermodal basis, thereby assuring the elimination of past historical deficiencies affiliated with the federal government's transportation promotion program.

In order effectively to promote each mode of transportation, modal administrations were created with each modal administrator being appointed by the President with confirmation by the Senate. Presently, there are eight modal administrations that administer the day-to-day promotional activities of transportation: the United States Coast Guard,* Federal Aviation Administration,* Federal Highway Administration,* Federal Railroad Administration, National Highway Traffic Safety Administration, Urban Mass Transportation Administration, Saint Lawrence Seaway Development Corporation, and Research and Special Programs Administration.

The United States Coast Guard maintains a system of rescue vessels, aircraft, and communication facilities primarily to enforce its basic function and activities. These programs are divided on the basis of maritime law enforcement, commercial vessel safety, Great Lakes pilotage, marine environmental protection, port safety and security, aid to navigation, bridge administration, ice operations, deep water ports, boating safety, Coast Guard Auxiliary, marine science activities, military readiness, reserve training, and Marine Safety Council.

The Federal Aviation Administration is charged primarily with regulating air commerce to foster aviation safety, in addition to promoting civil aviation and a national system of airports as well as managing the navigable air space in this country. The principal functions and activities of the Federal Aviation Administration involve safety regulation, registration and recordation of aircraft and pilots, research and development, air navigation facilities, civil aviation abroad, airport planning and development programs, and other programs allocated under the defense material system regarding priorities for allocation of civil aircraft and civil aviation operations.

The Federal Highway Administration is responsible for coordinating highways with other modes of transportation and is concerned basically with the total operational activities involved under the highway system, with primary emphasis directed toward improvement of the highway-oriented aspects of highway safety dealing with motor vehicles. The principal functions and activities of the Federal Highway Administration entail administering the Federal Aid Highway program, managing the highway safety programs dealing with hazardous materials and construction activities, and all programs dealing with highway construction, regional highway development, the Alaska Highway Program, research and development, and training.

The Federal Railroad Administration is principally responsible for managing and enforcing federal laws relating to safety on railroads, in addition to exercising jurisdiction over all areas of rail safety under the comprehensive Rail Safety Act of 1970, which embraced track maintenance and inspection standards dealing with equipment and tracks. Other activities involve research and development, maintaining the transportation test center, policy and program development, federal assistance to railroads, the Northeast Corridor Project, the minority business resource center, and operating the Alaskan Railroad.

The National Highway Traffic Safety Administration was established (by 84 Stat. 1739) in 1970 to administer the Highway Safety Act. This legislation provided for programs relating to the safety of performance in motor vehicles and driving equipment, in addition to vehicle drivers and pedestrians under an original National Traffic Motor Vehicle Act of 1966 and subsequently amended in addition to the Motor Vehicle Information Cost Saving Act. The principal functions of the administration involve rule-making and enforcement programs focusing upon motor vehicle safety, automotive fuel economy, and research and development programs designed to collect scientific and technical information relating to motor vehicle safety.

The Urban Mass Transportation Administration was originally created under the authority of the Urban Mass Transit Act of 1964, and subsequently transferred to the Department of Transportation as a result of Section 3 of the President's Reorganization Plan No. 2 of 1968. The administration is charged with developing improved mass transportation, facilitating equipment techniques and methods, in addition to encouraging planning systems and financing such systems. The principal programs entail research development and demonstration, university research and training grants, managerial training grants, discretionary capital assistance grants and loans, advanced land acquisition loans, formal operating capital assistance, and technical studies grant.

The Saint Lawrence Seaway Development Corporation was established by an act of Congress on May 13, 1954, and subsequently transferred to the Department of Transportation by the original Department of Transportation Act. The corporation is entirely government owned and is responsible for developing, maintaining, and operating the Saint Lawrence Seaway between Montreal and Lake Erie within the territorial limits of the United States. The Seaway Corporation in essence charges tolls in accordance with established rates for using the seaway in addition to promoting its active use.

The Research and Special Programs Administration was formally established on September 23, 1977, and consists of activities previously assigned to the Office of the Secretary. The administration serves as the research and technical development arm of the department as well as conducts special programs. To achieve these objectives, the following functions are administered: Materials Transportation Bureau, safety regulations dealing with all forms of transportation, and maintaining the transportation system center and the Transportation Program Bureau which are responsible for security engineering, emergency transportation facilitation, and university research.

Before the Department of Transportation was created in 1966, the federal government administered hundreds of disoriented, fragmented transportation promotional programs which prevented the government from maximizing its promotional activities in transportation. In order to develop a manageable program structure, the Department of Transportation, utilizing its planning program and budgeting systems, divided aggregate programs into four components. These involve intercity transportation, intracity transportation, safety, and national interest. By utilizing PPBS in restructuring the overall organizational program administration, the department was able to compartmentalize and identify all parts of interrelating programs and subsequently to maximize their promotional activities. This program structure represents one of the major contributions by the United States Department of Transportation in correcting past historical promotional deficiencies affiliated with the government transportation effort.

The goals and objectives of the Department of Transportation were enumerated in the legislation that created the department in 1966. These goals focus upon economic efficiency in transportation, maximizing safety in all forms of transportation, environmental considerations, and supporting other national interests programs. Under this congressional mandate, the Department of Transportation has moved forward in contributing to the development of a national transportation policy, has been active in injecting competition into the transportation industries, and, in general, has opposed the economic regulation of transportation.

In summary, the Department of Transportation represents a viable consumer group within the executive branch of the government and as such has moved forcefully to correct historical deficiencies affiliated with past government promotional activities. The department has been extremely active as an advocate of transportation, and as such has changed its traditional role from one of protecting the public interest to representing the public interest in initial transportation decisions.

FOR ADDITIONAL INFORMATION: See Grant M. Davis, "Modifications in the Identifying Characteristics of Several Transportation Activities," *Transportation Journal* 10, No. 3 (Summer 1970):5-15; *The Department of Transportation* (1970), Chapter 1, and "Policy Challenges and Objectives of the Department of Transportation—A Comment," *The Quarterly Review of Economics and Business* 10, No. 2 (Spring 1970):76-79. See also Grant M. Davis, "Significant Changes Derived from Establishing the Department of Transportation—An Evaluation," *The Nebraska Journal of Economics and Business* 9, No. 3 (Summer 1970):53-68; "The Necessity for Uniform Investment Standards in Federal Transportation Investment Decisions," *Alabama Business* 41, No. 9 (May 15, 1971):1-5; and "Proposed Federal Changes in Interstate Highway Route Selection and Design," *Alabama Business* 39, No. 9 (May 15, 1969):1-3.

For an in-depth analysis of the National Highway Traffic Safety Administration, see Grant M. Davis, "The Department of Transportation: A Study on Organizational Futility—A Later View," *Public Utility Fortnightly* 87, No. 11 (May 27, 1971):29-33. For a detailed analysis of why the Urban Mass Transit Administration was originally excluded from the Department of Transportation, consult U.S. Congress, House, Subcommittee of the Committee on Government Operations, *Creating a Department of Transportation, Hearings Before the Subcommittee of the Committee on Government Operations*, House of Representatives, on HR13200, 89th Cong., 2d Sess. (1966). See also Department of Transportation, *United States Department of Transportation: Its Organization and Function* (1967), and Grant M. Davis, "Are Transportation Companies and One Regulatory Agency Requisite for Physical Distribution Management?" *Traffic Quarterly* 25, No. 3 (July 1971):419-428.

GRANT M. DAVIS

DRUG ADMINISTRATION. See Food and Drug Administration.

E

ECONOMIC ADVISERS COUNCIL. See Council of Economic Advisers.

EDUCATION DEPARTMENT. See Department of Education.

ENERGY DEPARTMENT. See Department of Energy.

ENGINEERS CORPS. See United States Army Corps of Engineers.

ENGRAVING AND PRINTING BUREAU. See Bureau of Engraving and Printing.

ENVIRONMENTAL PROTECTION AGENCY (EPA). The Environmental Protection Agency was created in 1970 by a Reorganization Plan that consolidated several existing agencies. Under Reorganization Plan No. 3 of 1970, the Environmental Protection Agency, which began operations on December 2, 1970, brought together nearly 6,000 employees from fifteen government programs located in three departments (Health, Education, and Welfare [Health and Human Services*], Agriculture,* and Interior*). Many of these employees were scattered throughout the United States in laboratories and regional offices. The two biggest organizational components were the Federal Water Quality Administration (FWQA) with 2,700 employees from the Department of Interior and the National Air Pollution Control Administration (NAPCA) with 1,150 employees from the Department of Health, Education, and Welfare (HEW). The smaller organizational units were as follows: from HEW—the Bureau of Water Hygiene, the Bureau of Solid Waste Management, the Office of Pesticides, and the Bureau of Radiological Health; from Agriculture—Pesticide Regulation; and from Interior—the Pesticides, Wildlife, and Fish Office.

In his 1970 Message Relative to the Reorganization, President Richard M. Nixon called for a system of comprehensive waste management to be achieved by centralized administration. William Ruckelshaus, the first administrator, tried to carry out Nixon's plan by developing a "functional" organization for the agency. He called for amalgamating EPA's programs into functional administrative offices, such as planning and management, standards and compliance, and research and monitoring. Only one administrative office, the Office of Planning and Management, today adheres strictly to this scheme. Other offices, such as Research and Development and Enforcement, roughly correspond to it, but are divided into units that carry out different parts of diverse statutes. Air pollution specialists, for example, pursue different activities than water pollution specialists and have little contact with them.

A major reason for the failure to complete the functional plan was legislative—there was no statutory basis for comprehensive management. The air and water pollution programs have different legal foundations. In addition, these acts were not the only pieces of legislation EPA had to administer. Its responsibilities in the solid waste and pesticides areas were expanded by Congress in 1970, when it received new solid waste authority, and in 1972, when it received new pesticide authority. Congress also created entirely new programs. In 1972, it passed a noise bill, in 1974 a drinking water act, and in 1976 a toxic substances control act. In addition, EPA has major research responsibilities. Of its nearly $2.5 billion budget in 1972, the second biggest appropriation was for research, which received nearly $0.7 billion.

The agency's behavior can be understood in terms of three factors: (1) the roles of the White House and Congress; (2) the situation and tasks of bureaucrats; and (3) the influence of lawyers and the courts. These factors affect environmental progress and pollution control costs, and have led to proposals for regulatory reform.

The White House and Congress have different criteria for assessing EPA performance. The White House has a broad policy orientation and seeks social welfare and efficiency (the extent to which the agency contributes to the net social welfare of society as a result of its activities), while Congress has a narrower program orientation and seeks organizational and production effectiveness (goal achievement in a stipulated time period). These different criteria are reflected in the situation and tasks of bureaucrats.

The bureaucrats who serve EPA have different perspectives depending on the positions they occupy and the tasks they perform. They can be divided into three groups: (1) those with a policy perspective; (2) those with a program perspective; and (3) those with a research perspective.

Those with a policy perspective defend the agency against charges that its actions are contributing to unemployment, inflation, and energy dependence. They are accountable to the national policy concerns that are of importance to the White House, such as the conflict between environmental objectives and other national priorities. They reflect White House thinking within the agency and provide the evidence and arguments EPA needs to justify its decisions. They do economic determinations, and, after the oil embargo, energy-related studies. They are found mostly in the Office of Planning and Management, not among the numerous accountants and management-systems analysts that this office employs, but in a few specialized jobs in deputy assistant administrator offices, such as the Office of Policy and Evaluation.

The program perspective is held by most of EPA's bureaucrats who have no reason to be concerned about broad policy issues, as their tasks are to carry out specific statutory requirements. The great bulk of EPA's bureaucrats are program managers and operators, tied to specific laws, functions, and appropriations, and taking their cues from Congress. They reflect the fragmented nature of the legislative branch, which passes separate pollution control statutes and amends them according to different principles.

EPA's research scientists enjoy the luxury of an "ivory tower." There is a time-perspective difference between bureaucrats with program and policy perspectives and bureaucrats who function as research scientists. Research scientists are more discipline-oriented. They see their task as expanding the state of the art and making contributions to the environmental sciences that will have a long-term impact. Those with a program or policy perspective, on the other hand, have a need for immediately relevant information. They require detailed answers to specific questions and are not seeking ultimate answers to long-term problems.

William Ruckelshaus, EPA's first administrator, was a former Justice Department* official accustomed to managing attorneys. He brought many young and ambitious lawyers to the agency and gave them responsibility for enforcement. The earlier pollution control agencies had almost no lawyers on their staffs. Composed almost entirely of research scientists, they had the reputation of being able to "study a problem to death," rather than of solving a problem quickly. Ruckelshaus stressed EPA's enforcement duties as opposed to its research responsibilities.

At first these lawyers were on the offensive. They brought criminal actions against major corporations. However, court cases took a long time to complete and often did not result in compliance. As time passed, EPA's attorneys increasingly found themselves on the defensive. Permits issued were contested, and industry brought many lawsuits.

The courts limited the bureaucracy's discretionary behavior. They restricted EPA's freedom by deciding issues on a case-by-case basis, interpreting the law using different principles at different moments.

EPA made some progress in cleaning the air and water, but it did not make the rapid and dramatic advance that Congress envisioned. In 1975, only 70 percent of the nation's 247 air quality regions met primary health standards. Nearly 20 percent of the industrial sources of air pollution had not complied with state implementation plan requirements. The noncomplying sources were major emitters, in particular utilities and steel mills, that contributed most to the total emission problem. New-car pollution, although it had been reduced substantially, did not meet the original 90 percent reduction requirement, and, in 1977, nearly 10 percent of the nation's water pollutors had not installed the required technology.

Evaluations of the costs of making this progress and its impact on the economy are uneven in quality. A few of these studies will be noted. The Council on Environmental Quality estimates that pollution control cost each person living in the United States $47 in 1974 and $187 in 1977. Costs will continue to rise to 2.5 percent of gross, medium-family income before they start to decline in the mid-1980s. Robert Dorfman estimates that wealthy people pay more for pollution control than poor people. At the same time, Dorfman argues that wealthy people generally have been willing to spend more for pollution control than poor people. Around twenty thousand employees have lost their jobs because of plant closings, and the additional inflation attributable to pollution control is between 0.3 and 0.5 percent. Costs for pollution control escalate greatly as the required amount of pollution reduction increases.

Cost studies, however, are not useful unless they are compared with benefit studies, but measuring benefits generally is difficult. The most sensitive problem is how to express in monetary terms the value of human life and health. The other problem of great concern is how to express in monetary terms the value of recreation and aesthetic pleasure. In spite of these difficulties, Lave and Seskin concluded in a 1977 study that the benefits of controlling industrial smoke-stack emissions outweighed the costs, while the costs of controlling automobile emissions outweighed the benefits.

The available studies suggest that EPA's impact on environmental quality and the nation's economy has been somewhere between what the White House wanted and Congress was seeking. Although some progress has been made in cleaning the environment, neither congressional goals for rapid program achievement nor White House goals for minimizing the negative impact on the economy have been achieved entirely.

In 1977, Congress substantially revised earlier air and water pollution control statutes. The new pollution control amendments modified, eliminated, and changed deadlines in the 1970 and 1972 pollution control laws. They also required that EPA explicitly take into account factors such as technology innovation, economic impact, and employment impact.

Many analysts maintain that environmental regulations have not been cost-effective: that is, they abate pollution at higher than necessary costs to society. State agencies, for example, treat uniformly major steel industry processes in spite of the widely varying marginal cleanup costs. EPA has responded to this concern through a variety of "controlled-trading" measures, including offsets, the bubble concept, and "banking." Offsets allow a source that adds new emissions to find equivalent reductions from existing sources to compensate for the new emissions. Under the bubble concept, regulators replace stack-by-stack controls with a single limit that applies to a whole plant or region. The total pollution is the same, but by operating under an imaginary bubble, there is greater flexibility to define a cost-effective mix of pollution controls to meet a standard. Emissions-reduction banking takes place when a firm controls its emissions more than necessary in a nonattainment area. Additional-levels control can be quantified and then credited to the firm, and firms can either hold these emissions for growth or trade them to other firms for profit.

Other mechanisms for achieving cost-effective pollution abatement that show promise include effluent charges and marketable permits and pollution control cooperatives. With regard to effluent charges and marketable permits, economists generally consider effluent charges to be the optimal method for reducing pollution. The underlying logic—the "pollutor pays principle"—is simple and compelling. The government determines the damage caused by different concentrations of pollution, and pollutors pay for the damage. Instead of charges based on a difficult-to-determine damage function, the economist J. H. Dales has proposed establishing market-in-pollution rights. The government sets an upper limit to the amount of pollution that the environment of a particular region can absorb. It then issues pollution rights, or licenses, based on this limit, and puts them up for sale, requiring anyone that discharges in the area to hold these rights. The rights command a positive price and a continuous market develops in response to competition among buyers and sellers.

While less frequently mentioned in the literature than effluent charges or marketable permits, cooperatives are an extension of the bubble notion to multi-plant and multi-firm settings. Successful cooperatives have been set up by German companies which discharge pollutants into the Ruhr River. Under a cooperative scheme, area-wide, pollution control guides set by the government remain the same, but firms belonging to the cooperative act in concert, thereby having the flexibility to allocate pollution control burdens among members in such a way as to reduce total costs.

The EPA encountered a major furor in the winter of 1982-1983 over the potential ill effects of dioxin wastes in Missouri, causing the government to offer fair-market purchase of residents' homes in Times Beach. Long suspected as a concern, the problem was accentuated by devastating floods. Congressional investigations ensued and, in March, Director Anne Gorsuch Burford resigned. She was succeeded by the first director, William D. Ruckelshaus.

FOR ADDITIONAL INFORMATION: "William D. Ruckelshaus and the Environmental Protection Agency," in Joseph L. Bower and Charles J. Christenson, eds., *Public Management: Text and Cases* (1978); "Message of the President Relative to Reorganization Plans Nos. 3 and 4 of 1970" (July 9, 1970), found in *Environmental Quality: The First Annual Report of the Council on Environmental Quality* (1970); Alain Enthoven, "A Functional Organization and Financial Plan for the Environmental Protection Administration" (memo dated October 5, 1970); William Ahern, Jr., *Organizing for Pollution Control: The Beginnings of the Environmental Protection Agency, 1970-1971* (1973); and Alfred A. Marcus, "The EPA," in James Q. Wilson, ed., *The Politics of Regulation* (1980).

Also helpful would be Alfred A. Marcus, *Promise and Performance: Choosing and Implementing an Environmental Policy* (1980). The statistics on EPA's progress in achieving congressional objectives can be found in Council on Environmental Quality, *Environmental Quality: The Sixth Annual Report* (1975). See also Lester Lave and Eugene Seskin, *The Costs and Benefits of Air Pollution Control* (1977). Their findings can be contrasted with an earlier National Academy of Sciences study which concluded that the cost to achieve motor vehicle standards would be between $5 billion and $11 billion, while the benefits would be between $3.6 billion and $14.3 billion. National Academy of Sciences, *Air Quality and Automobile Emission Control, the Cost and Benefits of Automobile Emission Control—A Report by the Coordinating Committee on Air Quality Studies*, Vol. 4, prepared for the Committee on Public Works, U.S. Senate, pursuant to S. Res. 135, approved August 3, 1973 (1974).

ALFRED A. MARCUS

EQUAL EMPLOYMENT OPPORTUNITY COMMISSION (EEOC). The passage of Title VII of the Civil Rights Act of 1964 proscribed discrimination in employment on the basis of race, color, religion, sex, and national origin. As Title VII stipulated, the Equal Employment Opportunity Commission was established one year later (July 2, 1965) as the agency to enforce the act.

The commission has broad jurisdiction. It was authorized to enforce the act with respect to the employment and employment-related activities of most employers, employment agencies, labor organizations, and joint labor-management committees. The act did not apply to state and local governments or educational institutions in 1964; however, as a result of the passage of the Equal Employment Opportunity Act of 1972, Title VII was made applicable to those organizations. In general, Title VII as amended bans discrimination in employment by all but a very few of the nation's employers and certain other organizations involved with employment.

Although the jurisdiction of the commission is broad, the Congress severely limited the means by which the agency was to enforce the act. These means were restricted to the informal methods of conference, conciliation, and persuasion. As mentioned earlier, Title VII was amended in 1972; this amendment also granted the commission the authority to bring suit when it found itself unable to enforce the act through the informal means. The authority to bring individual suits was effective upon passage of the amendment on March 24, 1972; however, the authority to bring pattern and practice suits did not become effective until two years later. Prior to the 1972 amendment, the commission was limited to referring unconciliated charges to the Department of Justice.* The original act designated the Department of Justice as the agency that would enforce Title VII through court action.

The commission is a bipartisan body of five commissioners appointed for five-year terms by the President with the advice and consent of the U.S. Senate. The President appoints one member as chairperson and another as vice-chairperson. The chairperson serves as the administrative officer of the commission and appoints all staff other than the general counsel, who is also appointed by the President, and the regional attorneys, who are appointed jointly by the chairperson and the general counsel.

As of 1975, the administrative staff of the commission consisted of approximately 2,300 employees, and the commission budget was in excess of $54 million. Some of the staff are assigned to the Washington Headquarters offices, while others work out of regional and district offices.

The commission is significant because of the climate in which it was authorized and established and because it has used its limited authority to reduce discrimination in employment in a comprehensive way. Prior to the passage of Title VII, the Congress had not authorized the establishment of any agency to eliminate discrimination in employment. Moreover, as mentioned earlier, the Congress defined broadly the commission responsibility. Not only has the commission been successful in getting the courts to uphold most of its policies outlawing overt and individual acts of employment discrimination, which more than likely were the primary concerns of Congress when it passed the act; the commission has also been successful in getting the courts to outlaw many subtle and systemic forms of employment discrimination.

The commission was authorized and established during a time of intense protest. During the late 1950s and the early 1960s, black America and its supporters were very actively attempting to topple the system of racial segregation and discrimination. The protests of this period became known as the civil rights movement. The movement was characterized by mass nonviolent demonstrations that were staged throughout the Southern and border states. These demonstrations included freedom rides, sit-ins, boycotts, and other direct action tactics designed to force local authorities and white bigots to demonstrate to the rest of America the injustices of the system of segregation and the inhuman way of life that developed from this system. Frequently, these demonstrations brought out some of the worst instincts of local authorities and other white citizens. They attacked the demonstrators with clubs, dogs, and waterhoses in an attempt to intimidate the protesters. This violent response of the local authorities to the nonviolent protests of black Americans caused much of white America to express moral outrage. The events of the civil rights movement were well reported by the media, especially television. The television showing of these events may have caused a majority of white Americans to express to Congress their support for the aims of the civil rights movement through opinion polls and communications. The movement of the collective conscience of white America to action provided the impetus for Congress to pass Title VII and other pieces of civil rights legislation during the mid-1960s.

The establishment of the commission has resulted in widespread banning of various forms of discrimination against members of other groups. In addition to reducing discrimination in employment against black Americans, the commission has also helped reduce discrimination against women and members of other racial minority groups, as well as persons of certain national origins and religious backgrounds.

Perhaps the commission has experienced its greatest success in reducing employment discrimination in a widespread manner through the issuing of its employment guidelines. The guidelines are essentially statements or interpretations of the way the commission will rule if it is presented with charges covered by the guidelines.

The commission began issuing employment guidelines within its first six months of operation. Since promulgating the *Guidelines on Discrimination Because of Sex*, the commission has continued to issue and update these guidelines; they are now the most complete and comprehensive set of guidelines of any of the government agencies dealing with employment discrimination. In addition to the *Guidelines on Discrimination Because of Sex* (37 FR 6836, April 5, 1972), the other guidelines include the *Guidelines on Discrimination Because of Religion* (32 FR 10298, July 13, 1967), the *Guidelines on Discrimination Because of National Origin* (39 FR 10123, March 18, 1974), and the *Guidelines on Employee Selection Procedures* (35 FR 12333, August 1, 1970). The sex discrimination and the employee-selection guidelines are very detailed and have had a tremendous impact on employment practices.

The sex discrimination guidelines state that it is a violation of Title VII to advertise or classify jobs as "male" or "female" unless sex is a bona fide occupational qualification. This bona fide occupational qualification (bfoq) is interpreted very narrowly in the guidelines. Furthermore, the guidelines indicate that it is a violation of the act to maintain separate lines of progression and seniority based on sex. The guidelines also indicate that pregnancy should be treated as any other temporary disability and that sex discrimination in fringe benefits is prohibited.

The employee selection guidelines require employers to scrutinize very closely all steps of their selection processes. Basically, the guidelines require the employer to show that there is significant positive correlation between a particular requirement and job performance and to validate any selection procedure that disqualifies a disproportionate number of minority or women applicants.

Although these guidelines do not have the force of law, the courts have frequently relied upon them in upholding charges of discrimination. Because *Griggs* v. *Duke Power Company* (401 U.S. 424, 1971) was the first time that the U.S. Supreme Court had occasion to dispose of a discrimination matter under Title VII and to pass judgment on the employee selection guidelines, its response was very significant. The basic issue in *Griggs* v. *Duke Power Company* was whether under Title VII an employer lawfully can require a high school education or a passing score on a general intelligence test as a condition of employment or transfer when neither standard is shown to be significantly related to job performance and both standards disqualify a higher percentage of black than white applicants. The United States Supreme Court ruled unanimously in favor of Griggs. Moreover, in commenting on the employee selection guidelines, the Court supported the EEOC.

In contrast to the praise which the commission generally has received about its guidelines, it has been criticized heavily for its inability to process the charges of discrimination in a timely way. The development of a backlog of charges might have been inevitable in that the commission enforcement options initially were severely limited. Until 1972, its only options were to encourage the filing of complaints and/or to gather data about employment practices. The commission emphasized the complaint mechanism and within its first year of operation received more charges than it could handle. At the end of this first year, the backlog was approximately 6,000 charges; it rose to more than 15,000 charges in 1969, 98,000 in 1974, and 130,000 in 1977.

The backlog and its continuing expansion occurred for two basic reasons. First, as mentioned earlier, the development of the backlog was probably inevitable in light of the fact that the commission's authority was limited initially to receiving complaints and/or gathering data. Second, the United States Commission on Civil Rights* reported that in 1965 the EEOC was budgeted to deal with 2,000 charges but actually received almost 9,000 charges. The number of new charges was approximately 12,000 in 1969, 23,000 in 1971, 49,000 in 1973, and 71,000 in 1975.

Generally, the commission conciliation record has received the same kind of critical review as has its record in processing of charges. It has been cited frequently as being less than adequate. For instance, in its 1975 report, the United States Commission on Civil Rights noted that between July 1, 1972, and March 31, 1973, the EEOC had obtained only 533 conciliation agreements out of 2,107 attempts, a rate of 25 percent. Later, in its 1977 report, the United States Commission on Civil Rights indicated that those figures were 2,618 agreements out of 8,279 attempts, a slight increase to 31.5 percent.

Although the commission's overall conciliation record has not been impressive, it has obtained a number of agreements that require respondents to provide relief to large numbers of minority and/or female employees and to take affirmative action to overcome the present effects of past discrimination. The most famous of these agreements are the American Telephone and Telegraph Company (AT&T) Consent Decree and the Steel Industry Settlements.

In early 1973, AT&T and its operating companies entered a landmark agreement with the commission, Department of Labor,* and the Department of Justice. The agreement was landmark because it involved the nation's largest employer and the size of the backpay settlement.

The basic elements of the agreement were the backpay and affirmative action provisions. The initial size of the backpay component was approximately $39 million; however, supplemental agreements increased this figure by more than $19 million. In addition, AT&T agreed to distribute a total of $23 million among its women employees who were allegedly victims of wage discrimination as prohibited by the Equal Pay Act. The affirmative action provision required AT&T to set goals and timetables by job groups so as to increase the utilization of women and minority persons in all levels of the company.

A little more than a year later, the Steel Industry Settlement was reached. The commission, Labor, and Justice reached agreement with nine major steel companies and the United Steelworkers of America in April 1974. At that time, these companies were producing more than 70 percent of the nation's steel.

Similarly to the AT&T agreement, this one also contained the backpay and affirmative action provisions. Again, the backpay provision was significant in that the agreement provided that more than $30 million be distributed to 40,000 minority and women employees. The affirmative action provision included numerical goals for several job groups. It also contained a seniority provision, which provided that promotion, demotion, layoff, and recall be determined on a plant-wide rather than a departmental basis.

The enforcement of Title VII through litigation is the ultimate tool available to the commission. While the EEOC did not gain this authority until 1972, in 1971 the Civil Rights Commission noted that the "EEOC must bear part of the blame for the Justice Department's failure to bring more 707 (pattern and practice) actions. The Commission recommended a relatively small number of cases to the Attorney General for suit; 35 in fiscal year 1967, 26 in fiscal year 1968 and 26 in fiscal 1969" (*The Federal Civil Rights Enforcement Effort—1977*, p. 225).

It was widely thought that the commission's litigation record would improve after the authority to sue was granted. However, as reported by the Civil Rights Commission in 1975, of the 1,319 unconciliated cases referred to the litigation centers after this authority was granted, only 81 suits were filed and another 124 were approved for suit.

It appears that the difference in standards of evidence between the commission and the Department of Justice is in part the explanation for the poor litigation record. During most of its existence, the commission has used a probable-cause standard, which focuses its review on whether the matter could be conciliated, and less weight has been given to the question of whether the case could be made in court. Moreover, as the Commission on Civil Rights notes, "previously EEOC had no uniform standard for what constituted reasonable cause. In some instances complainants had to supply little or no evidence in support of their allegations before the burden was shifted to the respondent to prove that they were untrue" (*The Federal Civil Rights Enforcement Effort—1977*, p. 225).

While employment discrimination remains a major problem in the United States, the commission must be credited with several notable achievements. First, overt employment discrimination has been essentially eliminated. Second, the commission has helped move the focus of inquiry into employment discrimination matters from a mere review of intent or motive to a consideration of effect and outcome. Third, although the legal line of demarcation between permissible affirmative action and "reverse discrimination" has not been completely drawn, the commission has experienced some success in getting employers to take steps to undo the historical underrepresentation of racial minority groups and women in many occupational groups. It is now well established and commonly understood that mere passive nondiscrimination will not insulate an employer from enforcement action by the commission.

FOR ADDITIONAL INFORMATION: Joan Abramson, *Old Boys, New Women* (1979); Stokely Carmichael and Charles V. Hamilton, *Black Power: The Politics of Liberation* (1967); Kenneth B. Clark, "The Civil Rights Movement: Momentum and Organization,"

Journal of the American Academy of Arts and Sciences 95 (Winter 1966): 239-267; Harold C. Fleming, "The Federal Executive and Civil Rights: 1961-65," *Journal of the American Academy of Arts and Sciences* 94 (Fall 1965): 921-948; James C. Harvey, *Black Civil Rights During the Johnson Administration* (1973); Louis E. Lomax, *The Negro Revolt* (1962); and Jerome C. Skolnick, *The Politics of Protest* (1969).

Helpful on legal interpretations and developments are Robert Belton, "Title VII of the Civil Rights Act of 1964: A Decade of Private Enforcement and Judicial Developments," *St. Louis University Law Journal* 20 (1976): 225-307; Herbert Hill, *Black Labor and the American Legal System* (1977), and "New Judicial Perception of Employment Discrimination—Litigation under Title VII of the Civil Rights Acts of 1964," *University of Colorado Law Review* 43 (May 1971): 243-268; James E. Jones, Jr., "The Development of the Law Under Title VII Since 1965: Implications of the New Law," *Rutgers Law Review* 30 (Fall 1976): 1-61; *Kaiser Aluminum and Chemical Corp. v. Weber*, 99 S.Ct. 2721 (1979); Lawrence A. Katz, "Investigation and Conciliation of Employment Discrimination Charges Under Title VII: Employers' Rights in an Adversary Process," *Hasting Law Journal* 28 (March 1977): 877-929; Cornelius J. Peck, "The EEOC: Developments in the Administrative Process 1965-1975," *Washington Law Review* 51 (1976): 831-865; Barbara J. Schlei and Paul Grossman, *Employment Discrimination Law* (1976); and Michael I. Sovern, *Legal Restraints on Racial Discrimination in Employment* (1966).

On affirmative action and equal employment policies and administration, see Alfred W. Blumrosen, "The Newport News Agreement—One Brief Shining Moment in the Enforcement of Equal Employment Opportunity," in John H. McCord, ed., *With All Deliberate Speed: Civil Rights Theory and Reality* (1969); Joe R. Feagin and Clairece B. Feagin, *Discrimination American Style: Institutional Racism and Sexism* (1978); Nathan Glazer, *Affirmative Discrimination* (1975); Barry R. Gross, *Discrimination in Reverse: Is Turnabout Fair Play?* (1978), and *Reverse Discrimination* (1977); Ray Marshall, Charles B. Knapp, Malcolm H. Liggett, and Robert W. Glover, *Employment Discrimination Law: The Impact of Legal and Administrative Remedies* (1978); Herbert R. Northrup and John A. Larson, *The Impact of the AT&T—EEO Consent Decree* (1979); and Robert M. O'Neal, *Discriminating Against Discrimination* (1975). See also the numerous publications of the U.S. Commission on Civil Rights and the annual reports of the EEOC.

MACARTHUR DARBY

EXPORT-IMPORT BANK OF THE UNITED STATES (EXIMBANK). The initial Export-Import Bank of Washington was established on February 2, 1934, by presidential Executive Order under authority of the National Industrial Recovery Act (NIRA). The Second Export-Import Bank was similarly created one month later on March 9. Both were organized as banking corporations under the laws of the District of Columbia, and both were declared necessary, without geographical limitation, to aid in financing and to facilitate exports and imports between the United States and other nations or agencies. This remains the bank's statutory purpose today.

The first of the two banks was actually intended as a trade-oriented offshoot of U.S. recognition of the Soviet Union in 1933. Loans were never made to the Soviet Union in this era, however, because its pre-Revolution debts had not been settled.

In a single transaction, the Second Bank carried out the sole stated purpose for its creation—the financing of Cuban silver purchases for coinage, with minting in the United States. In July 1934, however, the Second Bank announced the extension of its operations from the U.S.-Cuban market to all countries other than the Soviet Union.

The two-part rationale given for the bank's operations in this earliest period was much the same as that given today: (1) the failure of private sector financial institutions to meet the particular financing needs of export trade; and (2) the competitive distortions created by export financing programs subsidized by foreign governments.

In June 1936, the Second Bank was liquidated, and its assets and liabilities were transferred to the previously dormant original bank, which then began its worldwide operations. The bank's executive branch origin was reflected in an eleven-member board consisting of representatives from the Reconstruction Finance Corporation* (RFC) and four executive departments (State,* Treasury,* Agriculture,* and Commerce*).

During this pre-war period, the bank provided both trade-oriented and developmental loans under conditions of relatively little controversy regarding the validity of its economic role. The major problem in the 1930s was the availability, rather than the cost, of capital for the specific purpose of export financing.

At the close of 1938, the bank's total stated capitalization was $46 million, $1 million of which was common stock held by the secretaries of State and Commerce and $45 million preferred stock held by the RFC. Following initial losses through 1935, the bank by the end of 1938 had generated retained income sufficient to pay all accrued dividends on the RFC-held preferred stock. During 1938 and 1939, the bank's prevailing interest rate was 4 percent as compared with yields on (then partially tax exempt) government bonds of around 2.5 percent and corporate bonds yields, depending on quality, from 3.77 to 4.19 percent.

In 1940, under conditions of war in Europe, Congress doubled Eximbank's lending authority from $100 to $200 million in loans outstanding at any one time. This was in response to a variety of urgent needs in Europe itself. Later in the same year, in order to bolster the production of resources, stabilize the economies, and promote the marketing of products in the Western Hemisphere, an additional $500 million was authorized as a revolving fund for loans to war-impacted South and Central American governments and banks.

As a reflection of its dominant wartime mission and its free-floating nonstatutory organizational status, Eximbank in 1942 and 1943 was placed successively under the Secretary of Commerce, the Office of Economic Warfare, and the foreign economic administrator.

At the close of World War II, Congress took stock of the structure and authority of the bank in relation to what was widely seen as the unavoidable need for increased foreign economic assistance. The compelling need was capital for reconstruction. The Bretton Woods Agreement had provided for the creation of the World Bank (International Bank of Reconstruction and Development). An indefinite hiatus was projected, however, before its operations could begin. To fill the gap, the administration envisioned the use of Eximbank at levels of lending authority far in excess of its current limits.

One immediate need was to vest the bank with a statutory status more commensurate with its proposed role as a principal instrument for implementing the nation's postwar foreign economic policy. That aim was achieved in the Export-Import Bank Act of 1945 (Title 12 U.S.C. Sec. 635), under which the bank was established as a permanent statutory agency of the United States. Although much amended, that act provides the basic framework for the bank's current operations.

Throughout the postwar period to mid-1954, Eximbank continued to function mainly as an instrument for implementing foreign aid and national defense policies. The main criterion for both reconstruction and development loans was their potential utility for increasing the productive capacity of the recipient country as a means of improving its ability to earn dollars and other hard currencies through exports.

In 1954, the bank was accurately described in Senate hearings as a financing institution that had been a responsive instrument in government programs to assist foreign governments, but that had done relatively little export trade financing directly for the U.S. manufacturer. Despite these dominant aid goals, at the close of this initial postwar period in 1953-1954, Eximbank's lending rates, consistent with policies and practices throughout the period, generally exceeded its own and the government's cost of money and were above, or at comparable levels with, the more analogous commercial interest rates.

A 1953 reorganization plan proposed by President Dwight D. Eisenhower sought replacement of the bank's five-member board by a managing director. Far from being responsive to newly emergent foreign trade competition, the plan and its rationale were explicitly predicated on the continued operation of the bank as an instrument for implementing executive branch foreign aid and national defense policies. Following a strong reaction by the exporting constituency directed against the plan, by mid-1954 the President and congressional leadership had reached a legislative compromise. Its essence was to recognize the legitimacy of greater constituency influence on the operations of an expanded and more trade-oriented bank, while keeping it on a tighter presidential leash through the replacement of existing, fixed board terms by appointments at the pleasure of the President.

During the balance of the Eisenhower Administration, the extension of long-term aid-type loans continued as the bank's main work. But the transition toward a predominant trade purpose was already under way. In early 1961, an important confluence of public and private exporting objectives was embodied in President John F. Kennedy's Special Message to the Congress on Gold and the Balance of Payments Deficit. The emphasis was now on maximizing a favorable trade balance to remedy a net balance-of-payments deficit resulting from such nontrade factors as overseas military expenditures, foreign business investment, and government economic assistance programs. While the shortfall of $1.5 billion was characterized as ''manageable,'' the message declared that the deficit should now come to an end. Among other means, President Kennedy directed the president of the Export-Import Bank to prepare and submit to the Secretary of the Treasury, as chairman of the National Advisory Council on International Monetary and Financial Problems, a new program under the Export-Import Bank to place U.S. exporters on a basis of full equality with their competitors in other countries.

The bank began its implementation with the conviction that the United States already surpassed its competitors in the long-term, project-lending area as well as in the direct assistance in medium-term credits. The problem it saw was to improve its participation regarding the short- and medium-term projects. The resulting 1961 legislation included the expansion of its guarantee and insurance authority to $1 billion outstanding at any one time, covering political and credit risks, as distinguished from marine and casualty risks that were left for private sector coverage. The principle of charging only 25 percent of outstanding guarantees and insurance against the bank's total program authority was also established.

Another noteworthy development in the period was the establishment, through the appropriations process, of annual limitations on the bank's program authority, comprised of new loans, guarantees, and insurance commitments. (Before 1961, annual appropriations were used to set limits only on administrative expenses.) Reflecting the bank's primary postwar role, in 1961 its appropriations (as they still are today) were handled as a part of the ''foreign assistance'' budget function rather than as part of any trade-related function. Prior to the imposition of this added annual limit on the bank's program authority, the sole statutory limits on the volume of its activities consisted of ceilings (1) on total obligational authority outstanding at any one time (loans, guarantees, and insurance) and (2) on debt owed to Treasury at any one time.

In 1968, the bank's name was changed to the Export-Import Bank of the United States. In addition, at the close of the Lyndon B. Johnson Administration in the context of the Vietnam War, the act was amended to place in the Export-Import Bank Act itself the first major, foreign-policy-based limitations on the bank's operations. In general, these put varied restrictions on the bank's financial support for any exports to Communist or enemy countries, or of defense articles and services to less developed countries. The same 1968 legislation also required the bank, in connection with any loans, to consider the possibility of unfavorable reaction within the U.S. economy.

Other legislation in 1968, however, increased the bank's trade promotion capability by authorizing it to utilize up to $500 million in program authority at any one time (with guarantees and insurance again reckoned at 25 percent) in support of transactions offering sufficient likelihood of repayment to justify the bank's support. Thus, these transactions were not required to meet the existing and more stringent statutory standard requiring ''reasonable assurance of repayment.'' By the conclusion of the Johnson Administration, the bank was on the brink of its modern era, in which programs were increasingly responsive to the growth of subsidized, competitive export financing by the major industrial nations of Western Europe and Japan.

An important characteristic of the bank's operations in the modern era since 1969 has been the promotional activism and program expansion of the Richard Nixon and Jimmy Carter administrations followed by subsequent declines in its financial condition. These occurred in the context of growing negative spreads between borrowing and subsidized lending rates. This general trend was reversed temporarily during the Gerald Ford Administration for reasons of general economic policy and financial pressure. Since 1981, the Ronald Reagan Administration has been sparring with Congress over executive branch initiatives to reduce the bank's program authorizations and budget deficits.

The overall impact of these program and financial trends is summarized in the following tabular comparisons between fiscal 1969 and 1981 (taken from Bank Annual Reports and U.S. Government Budget Appendices).

Export-Import Bank Operations:
Fiscal 1969 and 1981

PROGRAM ACTIVITIES (millions)

Authorizations	1969	1981
Regular Loans	$1,110	$5,079
Discount Loans	185	352
Total Loans	1,295	5,431
Guarantees	397	1,506
Insurance	825	5,910
Total Authorizations	$2,517	$12,847

FINANCIAL RESULTS (millions)

	1969	1981
Net Income	$104	$12
Dividends to Treasury on Capital Stock	50	0
Addition to Retained Income Reserve	54	12

During this period, trends in the bank's annual earnings (as calculated under its particular accounting standards) lagged by one or two years the periods of greatest program expansion and concessional financing. This reflects the delays between initial loan authorizations, or commitments, and actual drawdowns, as well as increasing disparities between lending rates and borrowing costs during much of the period. Thus, in the period 1969 to 1981 earnings peaks of $148 and $159 million were realized in 1972 and 1979. The Office of Management and Budget* (OMB) estimates in early 1982 for fiscal 1983 and 1984 were for net operating losses of $117 and $216 million.

This projected deterioration in earnings results entirely from the bank's loan programs. Thus, in fiscal 1981 the bank's total net income of $12 million reflected $29 million in operating income from guarantee and insurance programs offset by a $17 million loss from loan programs.

In fiscal 1980, the last full fiscal year of the Carter Administration, the bank made direct loans of $4.045 billion at a weighted, average interest rate of 8.35 percent. In the same period its weighted, average borrowing rate on $3.704 billion from the Federal Financing Bank was 11.2 percent. The inevitable negative impact on net income from these inverse rate relationships is offset to a degree by modest increases in concessional interest rate levels that track general upward movements in interest rates. Higher lending rates, as applied to the bank's virtually costless equity financed loans, generate higher profits.

At the close of fiscal 1981, the bank's total equity was $3.2 billion consisting of $1 billion in capital stock held by the U.S. Treasury and approximately $2.2 billion of retained income. The bank is obliged by law to pay dividends on its capital stock following reasonable adjustment for any losses. From the $50 million (or 5 percent) paid annually from 1969 to 1974, the dividend declined to $20 million in 1975-1976, followed by an increase to $35 million in 1977-1979, after which it was eliminated in 1980 and 1981. Given the projected decline in its retained income reserve as against expanded risk exposure and reserve requirements, the early resumption of dividends is not likely. More significant to the financial impact of the bank's operations on the U.S. government, however, is its "costless" use of retained income as against the opportunity costs of such use to the Treasury. These costs are not reflected in the bank's annual net income statements.

For many years the absence, or relatively modest level, of interest subsidies (whether measured against prevailing commercial rates or the bank's borrowing costs, based in turn on the government's cost of money) has generated only minimal controversy.

More recently, in the context of increasing interest subsidies and projected deficit operations, the Reagan Administration has been especially critical of the bank's role. Its views were concisely summarized in the following statement from the OMB's FY 1982 Budget Revisions, which declared that the

policy of using the Export-Import Bank as a vehicle for meeting foreign export subsidy programs has not been justified by documented offsetting gains in economic efficiency. The Export-Import Bank has grown so rapidly in the past few years, and its lending policies have become so generalized, that the Bank's credit facilities have become widely regarded as virtual entitlement programs. That private businesses should be "entitled" to special taxpayer subsidies is a concept firmly rejected by this administration.

The basic welfare assumption by which bank programs have been justified is found in the statutory declaration that the "expansion of exports" contributes "to the promotion and maintenance of high levels of employment and real income and to the increased development of the productive resources of the United States." Although the assumption, as stated, is undifferentiated as to the type of product or service export worthy of support, other sections of the act establish an array of both priorities and countervailing considerations that have been expanded and refined, principally through the following major legislative enactments from 1971 to 1978: Export Expansion Finance Act of 1971 (85 Stat. 345); Export-Import Bank Act Amendments of 1974 (88 Stat. 2333); an Act (of 1977) to extend and amend the Export-Import Bank Act of 1945 (91 Stat. 1210); and Export-Import Bank Act Amendments of 1978 (92 Stat. 3641, 3724).

At the core of these implementing provisions is the 1971 directive that the bank provide financial support "competitive with the government-supported rates, terms, and other conditions" available to exporters of other major exporting countries. In 1978, this 1971 directive was left intact, but augmented by a separate authorization to provide financial support which, in the board's opinion, is "competitive with those provided by the government-supported, export-credit instrumentalities of other nations." (92 Stat. 3641, 3724).

During the Nixon and Carter administrations, the bank moved vigorously to respond in kind to foreign, government-supported, export-financing subsidies. Such responses find widespread support among economists when limited to neutralizing the nonmarket distortions imposed on international trade by competitive, below-cost and below-market interest subsidies. Even under this "second best" theory, however, such support is not universal. Objections are made on the grounds of basic allocational inefficiencies arising from the subsidized diversion of capital from potentially more productive uses. Such objections are intensified to the extent that the bank is perceived to go beyond the neutralization of nonmarket subsidy distortions to the voluntary offsetting of market-based impediments to exports such as disadvantages of price, quality, reliability, or location. The general issue is whether Eximbank financing should operate as a surrogate in support of industrial policy for other subsidies which Congress has not chosen to provide more directly.

The Bank's total program of financial support, as indicated above, consists of loans, guarantees, and insurance. The largest loan category, and the most significant in respect to competitive financing and financial impact, is the *direct credits*, or *regular loans* category. (For authorizations in fiscal 1981, see the prior table.) For the most part, these are extended for periods usually falling in a range from six to fifteen years. They tend to cover heavier capital goods. In recent years, a large portion of such loans have supported commercial aircraft and nuclear power plant exports.

These direct credit transactions commonly include commercial bank loan participation for the short-term maturities less than five years. These commercial bank loans are made at variable interest rates related to the prime rate (commonly

1 percent or more over prime). The respective Eximbank and commercial bank interest rates combine to provide a blended effective interest rate on the total financing, which often covers 80 to 90 percent of the export value. A major feature of Eximbank loans is their fixed interest rate over the entire term. Another important source of private sector, cooperative financing is the Private Export Funding Corporation (PEFCO), owned by U.S. commercial banks and other corporations. PEFCO provides long-term, fixed-interest loans supported by bank guarantees at rates closer to commercial levels.

The bank's *discount loan* program was established to encourage commercial bank, medium-term lending (up to five years) at fixed rates through the availability of Eximbank loan "bailouts" in periods of capital shortages or rising interest rates. Eximbank's lending rate on discount loans has been generally pegged at around a 1-percent discount from the commercial bank's loan rate, subject to a minimum related to the federal discount rate.

The bank's guarantees are divided into the major categories of *financial guarantees* and *commercial bank guarantees*. Financial guarantees are largely provided in support of commercial bank loans made in participation with Eximbank direct credits. Commercial bank guarantees provide guarantees for commercial bank medium-term loans in which Eximbank does not participate as lender.

Eximbank's insurance program provides credit insurance against commercial and political risks. A major bank insurance role is that of a reinsurer of insurance risks assumed by the Foreign Credit Insurance Association (FCIA), a private consortium of cooperating export insurers organized in 1961.

Eximbank's future will be greatly influenced by the movement of interest rates and the success or failure of international negotiations in eliminating or lessening the intensity of government-supported, export-financing subsidies. Should agreements be reached by Organization for Economic Cooperation and Development (OECD) countries to strengthen the existing, but inadequate, arrangements, the principal (and many would say the only) rationale for *concessional* financing by Eximbank could be removed or reduced accordingly. In the unlikely event of the termination of concessional financing, the bank might continue to serve a useful role in overcoming deficiencies in domestic, export-financing markets relating to length of loan terms, risk assumption, and possible need for long-term fixed interest rates.

The bank today continues under the direct management of a five-voting-member board of directors appointed by the President to serve at his pleasure. The bank's president and first vice-president, who are similarly appointed from among board members, serve *ex officio* as board chairman and vice-chairman. Under President Carter, the Secretary of Commerce and the U.S. trade representative were designated as nonvoting board members. The bank's policies are subject to the "coordination" authority of the National Advisory Council on International Monetary and Financial Policies, comprised of the secretaries of the Treasury (chairman), State, and Commerce, the Federal Reserve Board* chairman, the Eximbank chairman and, for limited purposes, the director of the International Development Cooperation Agency.

FOR ADDITIONAL INFORMATION: Useful reading should be pursued in the following books and monographs: F. Adams, *Economic Diplomacy: The Export-Import Bank, 1934-1939* (1976); H. Arey, *History of Operations and Policies of Export-Import Bank of the United States* (1953); W. Glick and J. Duff, *Export-Import Bank of the United States*, unpublished and undated forty-three-page monograph, circa 1979-1980. (At the time the monograph was completed, the authors were general counsel and deputy general counsel of Eximbank, respectively); J. Hillman, *The Export-Import Bank at Work: Promotional Financing in the Public Sector* (1982); G. Holliday, *History of the Export-Import Bank of the United States* (1975); and H. Piquet, *The Export-Import Bank of the United States* (1970).

In addition, there are a number of pertinent articles, government agency reports and documents, and congressional publications on Eximbank.

JORDAN JAY HILLMAN

_F_

FAIR EMPLOYMENT COMMITTEE. See Committee on Fair Employment Practices.

FARM SECURITY ADMINISTRATION (FSA). During the depression, farm poverty, especially that of the tenant class, received much attention, owing partly to the activities of the Southern Tenant Farmers Union. The Federal Emergency Relief Administration and Department of the Interior* took a few steps to assist families, but the main effort began with the Resettlement Administration (RA) established in 1935. Rexford G. Tugwell was head of the RA, which administered a program of land utilization, resettlement, and rehabilitation for tenants and sharecroppers. But Tugwell was a controversial figure and brought much criticism to the RA. He resigned in January 1937. Nonetheless, the Roosevelt Administration remained sympathetic to the plight of the rural poor. In early 1937, the President's Special Committee on Farm Tenancy recommended federal action against rural poverty through a program of landownership, rehabilitation, and use of cooperatives. In July 1937, Congress passed the Bankhead-Jones Act, which authorized low-interest loans to tenants, farm laborers, and small landowners for the purchase of farms. By mid-1937, the conviction grew that the tenant class should receive more assistance than had previously been available. Accordingly, Secretary of Agriculture Henry A. Wallace established the Farm Security Administration, giving it control over the programs of the RA and the new farm ownership program provided by the Bankhead-Jones Act. Will W. Alexander, head of the RA after Tugwell left, became the first administrator. One historian correctly reported that the new agency was nothing but an RA with congressional home loan program attached.

From its inception the FSA had considerable autonomy. It had inherited the programs of the RA created by Executive Order. Both agencies had been created by liberal ideologists in the New Deal who wanted to assist the class of rural poor portrayed in Erskine Caldwell's *Tobacco Road* and John Steinbeck's *Grapes of Wrath*. Whereas the Agricultural Adjustment Administration and other agencies in the United States Department of Agriculture *(USDA) dealt exclusively with prices, marketing, and other aspects that affected only landowners, the FSA was created to deal with those people receiving little or no benefits. In this respect, the RA and FSA were the first federal agencies designed to focus directly on the chronic rural poor. By the same token, the FSA had no constituency to draw upon, nor did it have congressional authorization beyond the loan program provided by the Bankhead-Jones Act. The FSA then became the heir to a large number of rural welfare programs which had no support from established agricultural organizations, private or public. So, although the FSA enjoyed much independence, despite its presence in the USDA, it was highly vulnerable to external pressure.

The heart of the FSA was the Rural Rehabilitation Program, a series of assistance programs designed to encourage farm families to become self-sustaining and economically sound. Rehabilitation loans, for example, were given to small landowners to increase their productivity through purchases of equipment, fertilizer, livestock, and land. FSA officials hoped that, with this limited financial assistance, families could improve their operations enough to reach profitability. These loans were governed more by welfare objectives than by conventional banking principles and were consciously intended to serve higher risk client families, thus increasing the government's gamble. In 1937, the loans averaged $240 per family; by 1940, the average was $600 per family. By 1946 when the FSA ended, a total of 893,000 families had received a rehabilitation loan. Despite the uncertainty of repayment by the clients, the collection record was good: the collection rate in 1943, for example, was 93.5 percent.

Another feature of the Rural Rehabilitation Program involved grants with no demand for repayment. Grants were given to families usually for small emergencies such as natural disasters. Averaging about $20 per family, the grants were meant to be temporary and used in special circumstances. Some people resented the free cash assistance given to FSA clients, looking upon them as rewards to unworthy people for sin and sloth.

Many farmers were burdened by debt and could not afford improvements for recovery. To help them adjust their cost of operations with income, the FSA had a Farm Debt Adjustment Program. Farm debts had, of course, mounted during the depression, causing hardship for creditors as well as the farmers. Some relief had been extended to debt-burdened farmers beginning in 1933, and the Resettlement Administration took over the program, spending approximately $1.6 million per year during its operations. The FSA brought the debtor and creditor together and worked out an arrangement that encouraged the farmer to meet his obligations. In some cases, the loans were extended or refinanced at a smaller rate of interest, or creditors agreed not to demand interest for a specified period of time. For the most part, this aspect of the FSA was supervisory, that is, FSA employees provided guidance for farm families. By the end of 1943, the FSA reported some 187,272 cases of debt adjustment. The overall cost to the government of the farm debt adjustment program was in the order of $12 to

$15 million. Ideologically, the FSA officials thought that their guidance for families with debts was another step toward rehabilitation.

In its effort to put farm families on a sound economic footing, the FSA promoted a variety of informal group services. The President's Committee on Farm Tenancy had recommended the idea of cooperative activities. Without clear authorization, the FSA assisted small, local cooperative enterprises already in existence, and it encouraged the creation of new ones. Generally, these "cooperatives" worked together to purchase equipment and livestock. Over $8 million had been loaned to such enterprises by 1942, most of it to groups in the South and Middle West. The FSA also promoted more formal cooperative undertakings. In the Midwest, about 177 cooperative grain elevators went into operation with FSA backing and supervision. In the South, cooperative arrangements were made for families to lease cotton plantations. Similar arrangements were made in Western states for grazing areas, but the cooperative leases were concentrated in Arkansas and Louisiana.

One type of group activity engendered much political opposition to the FSA: cooperative farming operations that were part of the Resettlement Program. These associations organized according to the laws governing their behavior in the respective states and proceeded to elect directors and board members. The participants in the association worked as employees and received wages. During the year, the member lived in a house with a garden plot furnished by the association. Land for the farm was usually leased for five to ten years. To finance the cooperative, the FSA loaned funds at 3 percent interest. Altogether, about fifty-two land-leasing associations were created, mostly in the South. Many of these ventures proved to be unprofitable, and opposition was stiff. In 1943, Congress refused to grant further appropriations for their operation and ordered those in existence to be discontinued.

Within the FSA there was a conviction that tenant families deserved a chance to own their own farm, that ownership was one of the best means toward full rehabilitation. The Bankhead-Jones Act had specifically provided funding for that purpose, and the FSA had a farm ownership and enlargement program. As described by Murray Benedict, this legislation authorized loans up to 100 percent of the value of the farm. Interest was set at 3 percent, with payments amortized at forty years. Popular with Congress, this feature of the FSA was given substantial appropriations over the years (see table).

Tenant Purchase Loans

Year	Appropriation
1938	25,000,000
1939	50,000,000
1940	50,000,000
1941	50,000,000
1942	50,000,000
1943	30,000,000

Year	Appropriation
1944	24,000,000
1945	13,000,000

Source: Murray Benedict, *Can We Solve the Farm Problem?* (New York, 1955), p. 198.

Tenants responded enthusiastically to the opportunity; in the early years, applications far outnumbered the funding, enabling the FSA to accept only the most qualified tenants. This action, though successful, only reached, of course, a handful of the total number of tenants in the United States, and for that reason, government-financed loans were not the answer to the surplus of manpower in agriculture. Nonetheless, ideologists have looked upon the Tenant Purchase Program as a successful example of large-scale government assistance of the rural poor.

Like the Resettlement Administration, the FSA engendered opposition, especially after the United States entered World War II. The resettlement projects were the principal cause of the agency's unpopularity, although they accounted for a small proportion of FSA's expenditures, about 10 percent. The FSA inherited these projects from the RA and did not emphasize them, although the leasing associations, disliked by large landowners and business interests, were started by the FSA. Altogether, about 15,000 families received assistance via the Resettlement Program, compared with 950,000 in the Rehabilitation Program. A total of 164 resettlement projects, consisting of 14,000 homes, were in the Resettlement Program. The FSA purchased land and subdivided it among clients. Small houses and plots of land were given to the participants who had an option to purchase the farm on a forty-year, amortized loan.

Within its resettlement division, the FSA operated a migrant labor program. Migrant labor had caught the public eye owing to the migration of people out of the Dust Bowl, and a sense of urgency existed among some administration officials that assistance be given to migrants. The agency constructed camps along the main routes of the migrants which included both domestic and Mexican labor. Most of the housing consisted of shelters with facilities for cooking, washing, and sanitation. The shelters were located in California, Texas, Arizona, Florida, Idaho, Michigan, Missouri, Oregon, Washington, Arkansas, and Colorado. Employers stiffly opposed these camps on the grounds that they interfered with farming operations, and in 1943 Congress transferred the program to the War Food Administration. By the time of its transfer, the FSA had built 95 camps capable of housing 75,000 persons.

Probably the most unusual part of the FSA was its medical care program. As officials in the RA coped with the difficulties of assisting rural families, they realized that poor health was a contributing factor to the poor's economic woes. By the 1930s, it had become clear that rural inhabitants had a higher rate of disease and physical defects. When the FSA inherited the RA, it put the medical program into the rehabilitation division. Medical cooperatives were established to which participating families made a prepayment fee ranging from $15 to $45 per year. The arrangement provided a modest level of medical service at less-than-standard rates of compensation to the doctors. In 1942, the program had 787 medical cooperatives and 221 dental cooperatives in 41 states. Local physicians proved to be quite cooperative. As the doctor shortage worsened during World War II, however, local physicians were not as cooperative, and the program tapered off until Congress discontinued the FSA in 1946.

In 1941, the House of Representatives began an investigation into the FSA that would prove unequaled in bitterness. By mid-1943, the agency was badly weakened, and by the end of 1946 it had ceased existing. In summary, opponents such as the American Farm Bureau Federation disliked the FSA's general goal of making tenants and migrant laborers independent. Indeed, the FSA had been created to assist the rural poor to reduce or end their dependence in the tenant-landlord relationship. Landlords in the South and West complained that the resettlement projects and migrant camps violated traditional landholding patterns in the United States, that the FSA projects represented collectivism and encouraged radicalism. Organized medicine expressed some dissatisfaction with the medical cooperatives; operators of grain elevators worried about cooperative elevators.

Some complaints came from the clients. They resented the paternalistic nature of the agency, insisting that the supervision commensurate with the loans interfered with their private lives. In one case, a family spent the FSA loan on children's clothes instead of seed as directed by the agency. When FSA officers complained, the family thought it was entitled to the money and could use the funds for anything. Scholars have mentioned, too, that some top-level FSA administrators had no background in agriculture. Probably the most serious drawback was the role thrust upon the agency from the beginning: it had inherited the suspicion of Tugwell's Resettlement Administration, and it had taken over several homestead and relief programs dating to the Federal Emergency Relief Administration (FERA) in 1933. These programs were stop-gap measures taken when pressure for rural relief was greater than during World War II. Having no constituency to draw upon, the FSA was almost helpless against its attackers. Furthermore, opponents emphasized that the FSA encouraged small farms too inefficient for survival when the trend was toward larger farms.

Beginning in 1941, Congress steadily trimmed appropriations for the FSA and even discontinued or transferred some programs. By 1943, the agency was struggling for survival. In 1946, Congress created the Farmers Home Administration and gave it responsibility for those programs of the FSA that Congress had not already ended. Outstanding loan obligations incurred by tenant families through the FSA were to be liquidated as soon as possible. And the Secretary of Agriculture was prevented from making further loans to any corporations or cooperatives for any collective farming operations. Thus, the first real experiment in helping the rural poor ended. It has received mixed reviews, generally being praised by liberal ideologists but criticized by conservatives.

In retrospect, the FSA was a symbol of America's agricultural ills in the twentieth century. It symbolized the pathos of the rural poor, bringing attention to the long decline of agriculture in the United States and the painful transition of those people caught in the change. In this respect, the FSA was admired for its work, being regarded as a sincere attempt by the federal government to alleviate the suffering of the downtrodden. Yet, the FSA symbolized the difficulty of coping with the web of social, economic, and political forces responsible for rural poverty. To some extent, the FSA refused to acknowledge the surplus of agricultural manpower, thereby opening itself to critics. As is often the case with socioeconomic programs, the FSA demonstrated the tough and cruel barriers blocking any effort to bring relief and assistance to the most deserving.

FOR ADDITIONAL INFORMATION: Several secondary works deal exclusively or at some length with the Farm Security Administration. The most thorough is Sidney Baldwin's *Politics and Poverty: The Rise and Decline of the Farm Security Administration* (1968), which is primarily an administrative history. The FSA is a major part of the discussion in Grant McConnell, *The Decline of Agrarian Democracy* (1969). McConnell interprets the end of the FSA as an example of the rise of special interests in agriculture. Useful information is available in Murray R. Benedict, *Can We Solve the Farm Problem?* (1955); the FSA is included as part of a general history of farm policy. The origins of the FSA are presented in Donald H. Grubbs, *Cry from the Cotton: The Southern Tenant Farmers' Union and the New Deal* (1971). One study, Paul Conkin, *Tomorrow a New World: The New Deal Community Program* (1959), includes the FSA in the New Deal's resettlement program. A valuable source of technical information and a picture of political opposition to the FSA is *Farm Security Administration Hearings*, Select Committee of the House Committee on Agriculture to Investigate the Activities of the Farm Security Administration, 78th Cong., 1st Sess., H. Resolution 119, May 11 to 28, 1943.

D. CLAYTON BROWN

FEDERAL AVIATION ADMINISTRATION (FAA). Since 1926, the Aeronautics Branch in the Department of Commerce* and its successors have overseen the development and regulation of commercial aviation, promoting airmail, passenger, and cargo services. The original thrust stressed the licensing of all flight personnel, the establishment of safety rules, and Civil Air Regulations for the crews, aircraft manufacturers, airport operators, and other ground employees. Moreover, the branch certified the airworthiness of each aircraft and mandated periodic subsequent inspections of the craft and personnel. These chores initially proved to be rather vexing because seasoned, private aviators looked with utter disdain at the notion of showing their skills to federal inspectors, who, in turn, sometimes displayed their own arrogance of power. A number of years elapsed before these federal regulators finally caught several unwilling pilots.

A fortunate combination of widespread congressional backing, enthusiasm from Herbert Hoover, both as Commerce Secretary and as President, and excellent administrative leadership within the branch combined to bless the initial years of regulation. William P. MacCracken, Jr., World War I pilot and lawyer, who was in the thick of the congressional battle to enact the Air Commerce Act of 1926, as Assistant Secretary of Commerce, started the agency with a budget of $550,000 and 423 personnel. Clarence M. Young, also a World War I pilot and lawyer, became MacCracken's top assistant as director of aeronautics.

Promotional and developmental activities predominated for these leaders as the nation witnessed the first establishment of regular air service and the expansion of airways in addition to the existing transcontinental route. During this time in which the airmail sacks yet held priority over passengers on the small aircraft in service, various fairs, races, and demonstrations proved highly significant in catching the public eye for aviation. Charles Lindbergh's epoch-making solo, trans-Atlantic flight in 1927 was only one of many instances of the Aeronautics Branch lending him assistance; he always reciprocated by helping pilots, manufacturers, and the federal officials in testing and improving facilities, aircraft, and actual flying techniques.

Technological advancements boosted aviation; for example, the already existing beacon light along the airways was augmented by the radio-range beacon, two-way radio communication from ground to air, and the radio-marker beacon, all within the first decade. Teletype remission of weather data from the Weather Bureau* proved invaluable, but radio transmission revolutionized the process despite the persistence of static in foul weather. So-called blind landings could now be attempted, at least up to the very final approach for the airliner; this was the beginning of instrument flying. Air traffic control evolved only slowly, now adapting a system of lights—effective only in clear weather—to replace the original hand signals on the ground, and then in 1931 developing a projector "gun" light, its red and green lights visible in clear weather for several miles in the air. Earlier, the airlines had worked out a uniform system adopted by the branch (renamed bureau) in 1936, at various airports. It was based on pilot reports to the airport from several check points before landing and with radio communications between the airport and plane.

At the onset, in 1927, the Aeronautics Branch was assigned the task of investigating accidents; the Accident Board began carrying out the function in 1928. Harassed by insurance companies and litigants as well as Congress, board officials eventually assumed the practice of determining and announcing the official, probable cause of each mishap. Grounding of aircraft, still a controversial practice inviting lawsuits in the 1980s, was practiced by Young in 1931. Young grounded thirty-six planes of the same type in which Knute Rockne, Notre Dame football coach, was killed after a wing ripped off the airplane.

The inauguration of the New Deal under Franklin D. Roosevelt in 1933 brought a change of leadership with the appointment of South Dakotan Eugene L. Vidal, an Army Air Corps veteran and West Pointer, and a man experienced with airline operations. In 1934, the agency's name was changed to the Bureau of Air Commerce to replace the Aeronautics Branch. Vidal encountered internal strife and outside criticism, which forced his ouster in 1937; he was succeeded by

Fred Fagg, Jr., who stayed in the job just one year before resuming his duties as Commerce School Dean at Northwestern University.

At this time, a wild scramble ensued in and out of Congress over the status of the bureau. Basically, three plans existed: to give it independent status, to place it under the Post Office,* or to turn it over to the Interstate Commerce Commission.* Completely forgotten in the contest was the axiom that correct regulation emanates from the right personnel and not the location of the regulating entity. The same factor has eluded government reorganization schemes down to the present. The resulting Civil Aeronautics Act of 1938 offered a wide departure by removing for the time being control of aviation from the Department of Commerce. The new Civil Aeronautics Authority was run by a five-person body, which assumed economic regulation—a brand-new function—of commercial aviation. A Civil Aeronautics administrator directed the chores previously conducted by the bureau while the Air Safety Board, operating outside the above structure, now would perform the sole function of accident investigation. The total operation of the three bodies now entailed appropriations of $14,351,480 with over four thousand employees. The final dreary reorganization to ensue for a number of years came in 1940 when Roosevelt's Executive Order placed the economic regulation and accident investigation under the new Civil Aeronautics Board* (CAB) and renamed the remainder the Civil Aeronautics Administration (CAA), returning it to Commerce.

Meanwhile, rather significant technological improvements appeared to match the advent of the workhorse DC-3 passenger liner, namely, the perfecting of an instrument landing system (ILS), which was first tested in 1929 but not ready for installation at six major airports until 1941; and the heralded simultaneous radio ranges (1938), which allowed voice radio communication and range signals at the same time.

No account of aviation before World War II would be complete without relating the tensions, rivalries, and frustrations both within and among the CAA, the Airline Pilots Association, the aircraft manufacturers and operators, as well as the private pilots, and the military. The CAA leadership time and time again received complaints about military pilots violating Civil Air Regulations and causing near-misses, if not crashes, on the airways and around airports. Pilots, unnerved over the large number of crashes attributed to pilot error, rebelled by attacking instances of incorrect or misleading information given by CAA controllers, faulty radio ranges, and other malfunctioning CAA equipment. The Trans World Airways crash of 1935 killing Senator Bronson Cutting of New Mexico soured the politicians toward the federal authorities and the rivalries and deficiencies, alleged or otherwise, inside Commerce and the Bureau of Air Commerce. Debated even before the attack on Pearl Harbor was the feasibility of militarizing the CAA because of its critical functions relating to national defense. Fortunately, even after December 1941, the Roosevelt White House retained the civilian status of this important agency.

After the reorganization of 1938, CAA-Air Line Pilots Association (ALPA) relations apparently improved. One administrative innovation within the CAA in 1938 pointed toward modernization with the establishment of regional offices. Another cheerful note was struck when U.S. commercial aviation went from March 26, 1939, to August 31, 1940, without a fatal accident. The accident record of the 1926-1941 era was like that of 1941-1981, as to probable cause, for example, drunken private pilots, flying without a license, flying without instrument training in bad weather, air controller mistakes, faulty airplane or CAA instruments, midair collisions, and, in general, failure to abide by flight rules as pilot error continued to lead all categories of cause.

Long before America entered World War II, the CAA began to contribute to the eventual war effort. Notable among these undertakings was the instigation of the Civilian Pilot Training Program in 1939. Ridiculed at the outset by certain military critics, the CAA program, which evolved later into the War Training Service (WTS), provided a pool of 75,000 trained pilots before the U.S. war entry with only 21 fatalities. After June 7, 1942, the WTS trained an additional 300,000 pilots in its two-year existence.

After the Japanese attacked Pearl Harbor, the CAA launched a valiant effort to assist the military at home and all over the world, helping build airports, testing engines and new fighter and bomber planes, providing and servicing radio ranges and numerous other examples of equipment along critical airways to Europe, Africa, and the Pacific area. Under fire at Guadalcanal, the Aleutians, and elsewhere, individual CAA experts served as civilians and were denied the benefits of the wartime life insurance accorded military and Pan American Airways personnel. Dozens of CAA engineers took part in the invasion of North Africa (1942) and other activities in the European theater of operations. The CAB served as an active CAA partner in many of the wartime activities, assigning a pool of commercial airliners for military transport use, advising and planning for the new Civil Air Patrol, and setting and enforcing all travel priorities by air. The War Department* aided the CAA, for example, placing very-high-frequency radio ranges with voice communications at 100 key airports, all of which were later used for civilian traffic, and perfected an improved homing range. The CAA also provided air traffic control duties in numerous overseas locations. Civilian interests suffered at home; the CAA simply did not have the time and personnel. For example, installation of more ILS systems was delayed by over two years. Moreover, throughout the war, the CAA waged a continuing battle attempting, often unsuccessfully, to gain draft exemptions for its personnel. One of the foremost CAA leaders of this era was C. I. Stanton, a civil engineer and graduate of Tufts College, a flier in World War I, who later tested planes for the Post Office* before joining the old Aeronautics Branch as one of its first engine and airplane inspectors. After heading the engineering and later the airways divisions, Stanton served as acting CAA administrator during 1942-1944. He then returned to his position as second in command when Theodore Wright became administrator. Wright, in Navy flying during World War I, later worked for Curtiss Airplane and Motor Company and then joined the wartime Office of

Price Administration.* After Wright resigned early in 1948, leadership of the CAA shifted rapidly to and fro until 1959.

Postwar conversion brought numerous headaches as well as widespread opportunities for the CAA to improve its regulation and promotion of civil aviation. Faster and larger four-engine aircraft, the DC-6 and Lockheed Constellation, would eventually replace the fleet of slower and smaller craft. Expansion of the ILS system, reinstigation of mandatory flight recorders on planes, introduction of radar at selected airports, and the slope-line approach system all greatly enhanced air travel. President Harry S Truman, long a staunch aviation supporter, established several commissions and boards during his tenure in an effort to improve technology and service. Airport spacing and location became a major bone of contention in several instances, notably in the Washington, D.C.-Baltimore area, Dallas-Fort Worth, Kansas City, Minneapolis-Saint Paul, Chicago, and New York. Feuds arose over noise around airports, admittedly caused sometimes by the complete lack of zoning by local officials years earlier. These officials had wanted to prevent housing from developing near many airports which had originally located away from the city. Overseas, the CAA again issued the call to provide support—this time as air traffic controllers in Berlin during the crucial airlift of 1948-1949.

Meanwhile, the CAA encountered problems with the airlines over no-shows and overbooking of flights, the poor safety performance of nonscheduled operators, excessive flight times for crews, and bugs overlooked in the DC-6 and Constellation—overflow gas vents leading to in-flight fires and subsequent fatal crashes. As usual, the CAA attempted to balance the interests of public safety and the demands for profits within the aviation industry. Out of necessity, it allowed the aviation industry to perform a number of aircraft, component parts, and flight-crew inspections while spot checking these activities. By 1958, the Fokker F-27 (turboprop) and the British Britannia jet had been certified, while the Lockheed Electra (turboprop) and the jets—DC-8, Boeing 707, and Convair 880—all neared final approval. Indeed, by 1958, the CAA activities had grown tremendously to appropriations of $406,100,000, and 25,805 personnel.

Once again the battle over reorganization surfaced, and Congress, effective in 1959, created an independent organization away from Commerce known as the Federal Aviation Agency to replace the old CAA. Ironically, the new jets also began their service in 1959, and President Dwight D. Eisenhower secured a most controversial appointment, General E. R. Quesada, to head the FAA. A career military person, Quesada possessed vast aviation experience, including most recently the chairmanship of the Airways Modernization Board. Ike's personal pilot on D-Day, Quesada held aviation safety uppermost in his mind but in two stormy years incurred the wrath of fellow employees, pilots, the CAB, the aviation industry, and a number of politicians for his showmanship and his by-the-numbers approach in getting tough with all concerned. Unhappily, a series of crashes marred the era. Quesada refused to ground the Electra following several accidents—here the pilots backed him—and stole the show from the CAB in New York following the collision in 1960 of a United Air Lines DC-8 and TWA Constellation (136 people died). Quesada's successor, Najeeb E. Halaby, got along much better with everyone. An appointee of John F. Kennedy, he was a pilot-lawyer, financial consultant, and experienced industry and government-aviation expert.

The past two decades have brought widespread progress in the jet age of commercial aviation, in addition to burgeoning acceptance of private or general aviation. Many of the problems encountered pointed to solution by the CAB and eventually by the National Transportation Safety Board* (NTSB) in the case of accident causes. Here, too, the FAA continued to investigate a number of minor crashes and assisted the NTSB with numerous major cases.

No sooner had the jet transports begun scheduled operations than the FAA assumed the obligation to promote the development of the supersonic transport, the SST, to rival the Anglo-French building of the famous, fuel-guzzling Concorde. Fortunately, Congress scuttled the project in 1971 following a running battle with environmentalists and years of technical problems. Truly, the issues of noise, pollution, and congestion pertaining to all facets of American aviation had been neglected too long by the FAA and the aviation industry. The public vented its spleen against the SST dream.

Meanwhile, another reorganization fracas loomed; President Lyndon Johnson pushed the issue as his pet in 1965. The result in 1966 saw the establishment of the new Department of Transportation* (DOT), despite the opposition of both FAA and CAB leadership. Johnson masterminded the plan through Congress, which renamed the FAA the Federal Aviation Administration and placed it under the new DOT, and removed the accident investigation powers from the CAB by creating the NTSB, also in the DOT. The NTSB would cover all types of transportation accidents. So far as aviation is concerned, the creation of yet another Cabinet department brought little benefit. One expert who opposed Johnson's plan was FAA Administrator William F. McKee (1965-1968), who formerly served the National Aeronautics and Space Administration*(NASA) and the Air Force* as a four-star general.

In the last twelve years, the FAA has contended with all the problems already cited in addition to new dilemmas. For example, airplane hijacking became more frequent and led to more stringent airport surveillance. Midair and even ground collisions of aircraft encouraged the efforts to require proper warning devices. Swans, ducks, lightning, and bombs caused other accidents. Civil rights protections were claimed by surviving pilots who were now reluctant to reveal their actions prior to accidents. Leading journalists accused the FAA of giving higher priority to general aviation than to commercial flights with their large numbers of passengers aboard. Both operations were mixed at busy airports. In fact, beginning in 1978, the FAA joined the DOT and CAB in promoting the economic deregulation of aviation. This was a very definite boon to smaller operators, among them the commuters who crowded out the established airlines in numerous medium-sized cities and yet often charged high fares and scored a vastly inferior safety record. A major cleavage persisted between the NTSB and FAA, because the NTSB recommended a number of safety measures and stiffer flight rules which the FAA did not impose on the industry. In August 1981, the air traffic controllers' strike ended in their dismissal and the breaking of the union. These and other problems remain to confront us in the 1980s.

FOR ADDITIONAL INFORMATION: For primary sources, the researcher should examine the FAA files, Record Group 237, and the older materials from predecessor agencies in the National Archives,* particularly Record Group 40, Department of Commerce. The presidential libraries hold valuable records. One comprehensive scholarly account, Donald R. Whitnah, *Safer Skyways: Federal Control of Aviation, 1926-1966* (1966), covers developments and controversies for both the FAA and predecessors and primarily the accident chores of the CAB for this period. The FAA sponsored a four-book series on its history. Nick A. Komons, *Bonfires to Beacons: Federal Civil Aviation Policy Under the Air Commerce Act, 1926-1938* (1978), is especially sound on the cutthroat aviation competition without regulation before 1938 and the political infighting. John R.M. Wilson, *Turbulence Aloft: The Civil Aeronautics Administration Amid Wars and Rumors of Wars, 1938-1953* (1979), stresses the airport programs and research developments. Stuart I. Rochester, *Takeoff at Mid-Century: Federal Civil Aviation Policy in the Eisenhower Years, 1953-1961* (1976), describes in detail the feuding between the CAA and Commerce and the battles of General Quesada as administrator. Richard J. Kent, *Safe, Separated, and Soaring: A History of Federal Civil Aviation Policy, 1961-1972* (1980), concentrates on the Halaby-McKee administrations, the scrapping of the SST program, the rise of the DOT, and unsuccessful attempts to place the FAA under the military. The reader should also consult the various aviation journals which nearly always reflect the biases of their individual constituents, for example, pilots, owners, general aviation, or the military.

DONALD R. WHITNAH

FEDERAL BUREAU OF INVESTIGATION (FBI). The Attorney General of the United States has been a Cabinet appointee since the 1790s. At that time, his responsibilities were to advise the President on the constitutionality of legislation passed by the Congress and to represent the government in cases argued before the Supreme Court. Only after 1870, with the passage of legislation creating a Department of Justice,* did the Attorney General administer a federal department. Even then, no investigative division was established to further this new department's authorized prosecutive responsibilities, although, in 1871, the Congress did approve a discretionary fund of $50,000 to be used for prosecutive purposes. To meet the department's investigative needs, until 1908 the Attorney General relied either on federal marshals or temporarily hired private detectives and Secret Service* agents. Attorney General Charles Bonaparte's apparently belated decision to create an investigative division, the Bureau of Investigation (BI) but renamed the Federal Bureau of Investigation (FBI) in 1935, was the indirect consequence of two congressional restrictive actions.

In 1893, Congress enacted legislation banning the department from hiring Pinkerton agents on a contractual basis for specific investigations. Congress shortly therafter approved riders to appropriation legislation—first, in 1907, specifying that the Secret Service could use appropriated funds only to investigate violations of federal pay and bounty laws and counterfeiting, and to protect the President; and, second, in 1908, prohibiting the expenditure of Department of Justice funds to hire Secret Service agents. The Secret Service's role in developing information leading to the indictment for land fraud of two Oregon congressmen provoked these budgetary restrictions. Adopting a states rights position, congressional proponents of these restrictions also likened the Secret Service's actions to Czarist Russia and charged that the Department of Justice's ability to target congressmen for criminal prosecution threatened the independence of the legislative branch.

President Theodore Roosevelt denounced these budgetary restrictions as of benefit only to the criminal classes and believed that the government should be given ample means to prosecute criminals if found in the legislative branch. Then, on July 26, 1908, following the adjournment of Congress and relying on a "miscellaneous expense" fund, Attorney General Bonaparte hired nine former Secret Service agents on a permanent basis under the direction of Chief Examiner Stanley W. Finch.

Bonaparte's unilateral decision contravened the spirit of congressional policy of 1907-1908 and was vulnerable because it was dependent on continued congressional funding. Appearing before a House subcommittee in 1909, the outgoing Attorney General defended his action as necessary to meet the department's prosecutive responsibilities. Opposing legislation to specify this new investigative division's authority, Bonaparte assured congressmen that personal and political activities would not be investigated. The new division's responsibilities would be confined to investigating violations of interstate commerce and antitrust laws. Furthermore, to preclude future abuses, Bonaparte affirmed, Congress could rely on the Attorney General's close supervision. Nonetheless, in 1909, when approving appropriations for the Department of Justice, Congress limited the Attorney General's use of funds to frauds and crimes and the like against the United States.

This intent to delimit the Bureau of Investigation's role and to rely on the Attorney General's direct supervision for accountability did not long determine BI investigative policy. In 1910, Congress enacted legislation, the Mann Act, making it a federal crime to transport women across state lines for illicit purposes. That same year, Congress broadly authorized the use of funds for additional investigations determined by the Attorney General.

The 1910 appropriation authorization has been the closest approximation of an FBI legislative charter. Thereafter, the FBI's formal investigative responsibilities expanded piecemeal and indirectly as new legislation was enacted redefining federal responsibilities. First, in 1932-1934, Congress made it a crime to transport kidnapped persons across state lines, to use the mails for extortion, and to rob national banks and from interstate commerce. In 1938-1940, Congress required individuals to register as agents of a foreign power, proscribed revolutionary speech and association, and barred Communists and Fascists from holding a civil service appointment. During the Cold War years, moreover, Congress required FBI investigations as a condition for sensitive appointments (the Atomic Energy Act of 1946, for example) or to enforce the registration and preventive detention provisions of the Internal Security Act of 1950 and the Communist Control Act of 1954.

Cumulatively, these and other legislative measures contributed to the growth in size and prestige of the once fledgling and distrusted investigative division. The FBI's most dramatic growth, however, resulted less from legislation proscribing new criminal activities than from its conduct of "intelligence" investigations, that is, investigations whose purpose was to amass noncriminal information about the activities of targeted individuals and organizations. This shift in investigative purpose was the consequence of bureau and administration officials' concerns about suspected "subversive" threats to American society.

In some cases, such "intelligence" investigations were predicated on specific (if often secret) presidential directives and highlighted a recently redefined conception of "inherent" presidential powers. These FBI investigations were not directed exclusively at foreign powers and their agents. Since 1940, the FBI has acted as the intelligence arm of the White House, providing timely and personal information about the incumbent President's domestic critics (including the sending of a special FBI squad to the Democratic National Convention of 1964 to monitor the activities of civil rights activists). In some cases, such investigations were conducted solely on the authorization of the FBI director and highlighted an arrogant disdain for legal prohibitions. During the World War II and Cold War years, FBI officials knowingly authorized "clearly illegal" activities (such as break-ins to obtain membership or subscription lists of targeted organizations); created separate filing procedures to avert public or court discovery of FBI agents' resort to illegal investigative methods; covertly leaked derogatory personal and political information to "friendly" reporters, congressmen, and congressional committees for the purpose of shaping public opinion; in a series of now infamous programs (the so-called COINTELPROs of 1956-1971) sought to "expose, disrupt, misdirect, or otherwise neutralize" specified targeted organizations and their leaders; and covertly cooperated with private interest groups (such as the American Legion, the U.S. Chamber of Commerce, the Chicago-based Legion of Justice, and the California-based Secret Army Organization) to keep radical activists under surveillance.

The FBI's surveillance of domestic dissent evolved fitfully and, more recently, covertly. Its origins dated from the World War I period when the BI investigated first individuals for failing to register under the Conscription Act of 1917, then violators of the Espionage Act of 1917, and finally (with the end of the war) alien residents who might be deportable under the provisions of the Immigration Act of 1918. Morever, during 1913-1923, while appropriations for the Bureau of Investigation increased from $415,452 to $2,166,197, the number of criminal convictions actually declined from 11,474 to 11,205. These statistics indirectly highlight the shift in BI investigations from criminal law violations. Instead, the

BI amassed dossiers on 70,000 individuals (including Jane Addams, Fiorello LaGuardia, and Senator Robert LaFollette), filed and indexed 625 newspapers and periodicals, collaborated with Immigration Bureau* officials in the deportation raids of January 1920 (the so-called Palmer raids), in 1919 and 1922 investigated and provided information to private employers on the labor organization and strategies of striking steel and railroad workers, in 1922 cooperated with local officials in Bridgman, Michigan, to indict under state criminal syndicalist laws individuals attending a Communist convention, and investigated those congressmen active in the Teapot Dome investigation of 1923 (including the use of wiretaps, opening the mail, and breaking into their offices).

By 1924, these dramatized abuses of power created a major political scandal. Responding in May 1924, the newly appointed Attorney General, Harlan Fiske Stone, issued a series of Executive Orders and appointed a new BI director, the then assistant director J. Edgar Hoover, to professionalize the bureau and preclude the recurrence of these abusive practices. Stone dissolved the bureau's antiradical General Intelligence Division, forbade wiretapping, and prohibited investigations of political activities. The Attorney General ordered the FBI not to meddle with individuals' politics or opinions, rather to watch for the breaking of the laws.

The newly appointed acting director (who became director on a permanent basis in December 1924) formally agreed to comply with this ban against political investigations. (Whether Hoover did or did not is unclear. Recently released FBI files on the American Civil Liberties Union (ACLU), for example, confirm that the BI continued to investigate the ACLU after May 1924.) More important to the public image of the bureau was the fact that Hoover moved quickly to terminate personal corruption, political favoritism, and incompetence. Bureau appointments and promotions were to be based strictly on merit, preference was to be given to university graduates holding law or accounting degrees, and the BI director was to be responsible only to the Attorney General. In addition, Hoover modernized the bureau's crime-fighting techniques and resources. In 1924, he established an Identification Division to amass fingerprint files on a national basis which were made available to local and state police; in 1932, he established a Crime Laboratory to insure the use and development of the latest technology; and in 1967 he established a National Crime Information Center, a computerized collection of information relating to crime. At the same time, the FBI director promoted a more favorable image of the bureau by extensive speaking and writing and by helping Hollywood movie producers, as well as a radio and later a television series, propagandize the FBI's achievements.

The FBI director was not content to refurbish the bureau's image and to modernize FBI crime-detection capabilities. Politically conservative, Hoover remained committed to circumscribing what he deemed a potentially serious "subversive" threat to American society. This obsession, in effect, skewered FBI investigative priorities. Thus, between 1940 and April 1978, almost 30,000 of the 37,000 FBI informers were used in "security" investigations, and 35,000 of the 58,000 linear feet of files in the new FBI building in Washington were devoted to "security" investigations.

In part, these so-called security investigations were predicated on the counter-subversive legislation of the 1938-1940 and Cold War years. The vast majority of FBI "intelligence" investigations, however, was not based on these statutes. Having convinced President Franklin Roosevelt, in August 1936, to authorize FBI investigations of the relationship between Communist and Fascist activities in the United States and foreign powers, FBI Director Hoover stretched this oral and limited authorization to focus on the domestic front. Then, having failed in September 1939 to convince President Roosevelt to issue an expansive directive specifying the FBI's responsibility to investigate "subversive activities," Hoover misrepresented Roosevelt's more limited directive in 1950, and again in 1953, to obtain such an authorization first from President Harry Truman and then from President Dwight Eisenhower. Not satisfied with President Roosevelt's limited wiretapping authorization of May 1940, the FBI director drafted a letter, which Attorney General Tom Clark sent, in July 1946, under his own signature to President Truman, misrepresenting Roosevelt's authorization of FBI wiretapping during "national defense" investigations as having included "subversive activities." Furthermore, when Attorney General Francis Biddle, in July 1943, ordered Hoover to terminate investigating and listing individuals for preventive detention (a program Hoover initiated in 1939), the FBI director, in effect, ignored Biddle's order by simply renaming the program. Securing Attorney General Tom Clark's later approval for this program (although Hoover had not then advised Clark that the FBI had such an ongoing program in violation of Biddle's order), FBI officials in 1950-1952 convinced the Department of Justice to base the standards for investigating and listing individuals for preventive detention on the secretly initiated program, which Clark had authorized in August 1948, and not those mandated by the Internal Security Act of 1950. Consistent with this degree of independence—the operational reality of the relationship between the Department of Justice and the FBI—in 1956, and then again in 1961, 1964, 1967, and 1968, Hoover unilaterally authorized a series of programs to harass and discredit certain targeted organizations and their leaders. Under these programs, FBI agents resorted to illegal and questionable tactics (including attempts to break up marriages and deny individuals private employment).

The radical expansion of the FBI's role was the byproduct of the Cold War obsession over "national security." FBI Director Hoover's ability to preclude public knowledge of the scope and nature of the bureau's illegal and politically motivated investigations was important to this expansion. At various times between 1940 and 1949, the FBI director devised a series of separate filing procedures to insure that the FBI's most questionable practices could not be discovered: the "Do Not File" procedure for "clearly illegal" break-ins; the "June mail" procedure for "sources illegal in nature"; the "administrative pages" procedure for "facts and information which are considered of a nature not expedient to disseminate or would cause embarrassment to the Bureau, if distributed"; and having specially sensitive documents stored in a "separate file room," such as copies of letters illegally obtained through the FBI's and the CIA's mail-opening programs.

The changed political climate resulting from the Watergate Affair of 1972-1973, and the impeachment hearings of 1974 involving President Richard Nixon, led in 1975 to the first intensive congressional investigation of the federal intelligence agencies. As a consequence of this investigation, and the resultant disclosure of the extent of the FBI's past abuses of power, leading congressmen and public opinion leaders demanded the enactment of an FBI legislative charter and tighter congressional and executive oversight over the bureau. Formally introduced in 1979-1980, an FBI charter has not yet been enacted. In March 1976, however, Attorney General Edward Levi issued a series of guidelines to govern future FBI investigations and to preclude the recurrence of the more dramatic abuses. In response to these guidelines and to the priorities set by the newly appointed FBI director, William Webster (the Omnibus Crime Control and Safe Streets Act of 1968 required Senate confirmation of the FBI director), by 1978 the focus of FBI investigations shifted from "domestic security" to organized and white collar crime.

FOR ADDITIONAL INFORMATION: Because FBI files have been totally classified until recently, there have been few scholarly studies of the bureau's history. The Freedom of Information Act of 1966 (as amended in 1974) and the release of FBI documents through congressional hearings of 1975-1978 have now permitted scholarly research. Nonetheless, most FBI files still remain closed, and, thus, recently published scholarly monographs are hardly comprehensive. The best studies are Athan Theoharis, *Spying on Americans: Political Surveillance from Hoover to the Huston Plan* (1978); Frank Donner, *The Age of Surveillance: The Aims and Methods of America's Political Intelligence System* (1980); Robert Goldstein, *Political Repression in Modern America: From 1870 to the Present* (1978); and John Elliff, *The Reform of FBI Intelligence Operations* (1979).

Earlier published studies on the FBI are based on public source information, interviews with FBI officials, privileged access to selected FBI documents, or the memoirs of former FBI agents. They tend to be highly opinionated, either praising or condemning the FBI and/or FBI Director Hoover. The critical studies include Pat Watters and Stephen Gillers, eds., *Investigating the FBI* (1973); Sanford Ungar, *FBI* (1975); Fred Cook, *The FBI Nobody Knows* (1964); and Max Lowenthal, *The Federal Bureau of Investigation* (1950). The sympathetic include Don Whitehead, *The FBI Story* (1959); Ralph deToledano, *J. Edgar Hoover: The Man in His Time* (1973); Harry and Bonero Overstreet, *The FBI in Our Open Society* (1969); and Richard Wright, ed., *Whose FBI?* (1974). Of the books written by former FBI officials, William Turner, *Hoover's FBI: The Men and the Myth* (1971) and William Sullivan, *The Bureau: My Thirty Years in Hoover's FBI* (1979), are critical, while W. Mark Felt, *The FBI Pyramid from the Inside* (1979) is sympathetic.

ATHAN THEOHARIS

FEDERAL COMMUNICATIONS COMMISSION (FCC). The Federal Communications Commission, an independent regulatory agency of the federal government, regulates a wide range of communications activity in the nation. The FCC regulates both wire communications and wireless, or much of the spectrum of electromagnetic radio waves which includes television and other forms of communication. This means that the agency is empowered to regulate interstate telephone and telegraph rates and services as well as most of the realm of commercial and noncommercial broadcasting.

In the major area of broadcasting, the FCC regulates activites as diverse as (1) the licensing of television and radio stations, (2) the assignment of frequencies and rules in broadcasting, including those for police band, (3) certain aspects of cable television (CATV) systems, (4) satellite communications, (5) international short-wave communication, (6) two-way radio and "ham" operations, and (7) citizens' band frequencies, or "CB" operations.

In one sense, the origin of the FCC occurred at the birth of independent, federal regulation in the public interest with the establishment of the Interstate Commerce Commission* (ICC) in 1887. In a more logical sense, however, the origin of the FCC dates from 1912 when the Radio Communications Act was passed. This act required radio transmitting stations to obtain licenses from the United States Department of Commerce and Labor.* All later licensing of broadcasting stations was derived from that act. Under the act, licensing became a routine matter of registration, a trend which some of its critics claim the FCC is continuing.

During the 1920s, as radio grew at a phenomenal rate, listening to it often became a frustrating experience. Many stations ignored the air-time restrictions placed upon them by the Commerce Secretary. For example, the renowned evangelist Aimee Semple McPherson operated her Los Angeles radio station at whatever frequency and power the Lord told her to use. Chaos reigned over the airwaves, and, as a result, the 1920s saw the extraordinary occurrence of an entire industry calling upon the federal government for more regulation. The government responded with the Radio Act of 1927, which established the Federal Radio Commission (FRC), the direct progenitor of the FCC.

In 1934, following the recommendation of his Interdepartmental Committee, President Franklin Roosevelt proposed legislation to Congress, which merged the functions of the FRC with the telephone and telegraph regulation of the ICC and the Postmaster General. Congress passed the subsequent Federal Communications Act with little debate, and the seven-member Federal Communications Commission was created.

Having been assigned to regulate telephone communications, the FCC soon discovered that it lacked sufficient data on the industry. In 1935, the FCC launched a massive fact-finding investigation, which was finally completed in 1939. The resulting study, *Investigation of the Telephone Industry in the United States*, was a monumental work of 8,441 pages of testimony and 2,140 exhibits which remained, for decades, a benchmark for any serious scholarship on the telephone industry. The study uncovered no large scandals other than expense-account padding, but it did reveal that long-distance rates were unfairly high. Since the FCC lacked direct regulatory authority over much of the Bell system, it worked closely with various state commissions to persuade the appropriate Bell companies to lower their long-distance rates by a large margin.

As far as regulation of the telegraph industry was concerned, the FCC was faced with the problem of regulating an industry in decline. In the 1930s the FCC wisely realized that fostering competition in this branch of communication was not needed and recommended that Congress allow the merger of the Postal Telegraph and Western Union, a merger that was eventually granted during World War II. Since the 1950s, the FCC has granted several increases in telegraph rates as well as allowing many offices to close and hours of service to be reduced.

It is in the area of broadcasting regulation, however, that the FCC performs its primary responsibility and produces the greatest impact and interest. Broadcast regulation is what makes the FCC function distinct from all other forms of industry or utility regulation. In the normal regulatory process, such as for a utility, the government concentrates on control of entry, services, and rates. In broadcasting, entry is severely limited, services are examined casually, and rates, primarily in the form of advertising fees, are not regulated at all but are controlled by competition, in the form of broadcast ratings.

The 1934 act, which created the FCC, also created conflicting mandates for the agency. On the one hand, Section 309 stated the implied threat that a station's license may be revoked if the commission deemed that "public interest, convenience, or necessity" had not been served by a particular broadcaster. On the other hand, however, Section 326 forbade the FCC the power of any censorship except for cases of "obscene, indecent, or profane language." Obviously, to determine if a vaguely defined public interest has been served, the FCC must examine the programming content of the airwaves, but, in doing so, the agency has run head-on into the First Amendment guarantees of the Constitution against government interference in freedom of the press.

Another section of the original act, 315, has evolved into the so-called Fairness Doctrine. The Fairness Doctrine is closely related to Section 309 and mandates that broadcasters air, on occasion, issues of public importance, however controversial. The second part of Section 315 demands that broadcasters grant equal airtime to political candidates when differing viewpoints are aired. The Fairness Doctrine has also proven to be a thorny issue to an FCC caught between broadcast regulation and the First Amendment. In 1959, Congress exempted news broadcasts from the "equal time" provisions of Section 315. Critics have charged that the Fairness Doctrine has produced a result counter to the original intent of the act by discouraging diversity and debate. Many believe that the Fairness Doctrine has made broadcasters timid, and this avoidance of controversy has helped cause blandness and mediocrity in both editorial and entertainment programming.

The 1930s saw a listless and generally ineffectual performance by the FCC, perhaps best shown by its decisions regarding the introduction of FM, or frequency modulation, radio. In 1939, James Lawrence Fly became chairman of the agency, and the FCC entered possibly its most ambitious regulatory period.

After studying the nature of the major networks and being given its mandate to foster competition, in 1941, the FCC ordered the National Broadcasting Company (NBC) to divest itself of one of its networks. In 1943, the United States Supreme Court upheld the FCC ruling, and NBC then sold its "blue" network, which eventually became the American Broadcasting Company (ABC). In the same decision, the Supreme Court gave broad power to the FCC to regulate individual licensees.

In 1946, the FCC issued *Public Service Responsibility of Broadcast Licensees*, which became known as the *Blue Book* (due to its cover color). This was a landmark report in the history of the commission because it marked the first entry of the agency into the regulation of programming content. The *Blue Book* contained an investigation of programming practices and compared station promises of programming with actual schedules, the result being a severe imbalance. The *Blue Book* frightened the industry with the threat of massive regulation of programming content, but the threat soon evaporated for reasons that might bear further historical examination. Very quickly, the FCC returned to routine licensee renewal due, in part, to a decline in the quality of personnel and a lack of adequate funding for regulation.

For the FCC, the period from the late 1940s until the 1960s marked the nadir of the agency. Historian Gabriel Kolko has developed an intriguing theory that regulatory agencies eventually become "captured" by the industries they were set up initially to regulate. This has certainly occured to the FCC to some degree. In 1947, FCC Chairman Charles R. Denny, Jr., resigned to become an NBC vice-president. This move followed several decisions by the commission favorable to Radio Corporation of America (RCA), the parent company of NBC. In reviewing the history of the FCC, however, it appears that the independence of the agency has been threatened, not so much by the broadcasting industry, but rather by the executive and legislative branches of the federal government. For example, in the late 1940s and early 1950s, Federal Bureau of Investigation* Director J. Edgar Hoover and some FCC members who were protegés of U.S. Senator Joseph McCarthy of Wisconsin exerted pressure on the agency to deny licensee renewal based on unfounded allegations of "communism" and for purely political reasons. Later, the actions of the administrations of Presidents Lyndon B. Johnson and Richard M. Nixon contained other instances of political pressure being brought to bear on the FCC in a manner more threatening to its independence than anything done by the official industry lobby, the National Association of Broadcasters (NAB). In retrospect, the Kolko thesis is interesting and bears further investigation by social scientists, but for the FCC, it seems inapplicable.

In the late 1950s and early 1960s, the commission was heavily criticized for its inability to anticipate and correct the abuses demonstrated by the television quiz-show scandals and "payola" on radio. At that time, the FCC maintained that its regulatory authority could not resolve the scandals. Congress responded with legislation making such practices illegal. In 1960, the FCC again entered the field of programming regulation by requiring that the local broadcaster determine "the public interest," not the FCC. This was the "ascertainment" requirement, which was expanded in the late 1960s to require that broadcasters seek out and determine their communities' "needs, problems, and issues" rather than programming preferences in order to demonstrate that the broadcaster has met the "public interest" requirement of Section 315.

In 1961, the FCC got a new chairman in Newton N. Minow, who stunned the NAB in a speech, which called the bulk of TV programming "a vast wasteland." Despite his famous statement, Minow could do little to elevate programming. His tenure at the FCC, however, did mark a strengthening of the position of noncommercial, or educational, television.

In 1970, the commission instituted the Prime Time Access Rule (PTAR), which attempted to reduce the dominance of the TV networks by giving an additional half-hour of prime time to local broadcasters. Much of the decision was born out of the mandated "localism" of FCC regulation, or the agency's belief that local stations can best determine what is needed for their audience. The PTAR is another example of the intent of an FCC decision gone astray. The agency attempted to open up more local programming for the evening hours, but most broadcasters, now deprived of a half-hour of network programming, opted for reruns of older programs and syndicated game shows rather than the less profitable local programming.

The future for the FCC appears fraught with problems. The agency may be overwhelmed by the sheer magnitude of the revolutionary new developments in communications forecast for the next several decades. Home videotaping systems, CATV, and other subscription formats will obliterate the notion of prime-time viewing and listening for the American audience as well as, perhaps, the power of the networks. Copyright law will have to be transformed radically, and more advanced satellite technology may make the entire planet's communications available to all people. The FCC will have to face these changes in the world it regulates with increased technical expertise, greater legal acumen, and a heightened anticipation. Considering its history, the agency's capacity to meet the challenges of the future is uncertain.

FOR ADDITIONAL INFORMATION: See Kent Anderson, *Television Fraud: The History and Implications of the Quiz Show Scandals* (1978); William Peck Banning, *Commercial Broadcasting Pioneer, the WEAF Experiment: 1922-1926* (1946); and Erik Barnouw, *A Tower in Babel: A History of Broadcasting in the United States*, Vol. 1—to 1933 (1966), *The Golden Web: A History of Broadcasting in the United States*, Vol. 2—1933 to 1953 (1968), and *The Image Empire: A History of Broadcasting in the United States*, Vol. 3—from 1950 (1970). The three volumes by Barnouw are a monumental achievement and an absolute "must" for serious students of broadcasting and the FCC.

See also Barnouw, *Tube of Plenty: The Evolution of American Television* (1975), a lively and excellent history of television. Of less value for the FCC are James Baughman, "Warriors in the Wasteland: The Federal Communications Commission and American Television, 1958-1967" (Ph.D. Dissertation, Columbia University, 1981), eagerly awaited by serious scholars and a fine example for the direction of FCC research; David L.

Bazelon, "The First Amendment and the 'New Media'—New Directions in Regulating Telecommunications," *Federal Communications Law Journal* 31, No. 2 (1979), an excellent article; Merle Fainsod, Lincoln Gordon, and Joseph Palamountain, Jr., *Government and the American Economy* (1959), a classic work and a good general beginning for any governmental agency; Henry Goldberg and Michael Couzens, " 'Peculiar Characteristics': An Analysis of the First Amendment Implications of Broadcast Regulation," *Federal Communications Law Journal* 31, No. 1 (1979), a superb article on the subject, with a good review of FCC regulation; Vincent Mosco, "Reforming Regulation: The FCC and Innovations in the Broadcasting Market" (1976), a very handy pamphlet with an excellent chronology of FCC history; Roger Noll, Merton Peck, and John McGowan, *Economic Aspects of Television Regulation* (1973), an advanced study and not a good place to begin; Craig and Peter Norback, *TV Guide Almanac* (1980), an encyclopedia of TV data; John Pennybacker and Waldo Braden, *Broadcasting and the Public Interest* (1969), a fair collection of articles, many of which are now out of date; and Dwight L. Teeter, Jr., review of *The Fairness Doctrine and the Media*, by Steven Simmons, in *Federal Communications Law Journal* 32, No. 1 (1980).

KENT ANDERSON

FEDERAL ENERGY REGULATORY COMMISSION. See Department of Energy.

FEDERAL HIGHWAY ADMINISTRATION. For more than three-quarters of a century, the Federal Highway Administration has served as the principal agency for the federal government's interest in highway development. During that period, federal road administrators have attempted to secure revenues in order to fund construction by the states of a unified system of highways serving an ever increasing population of automobiles, trucks, and buses. Yet, the construction of roads funded by the federal government proceeded according to two sets of criteria. On the one hand, federal highway engineers entertained their own definition of good highway construction standards and were generally successful in implementing them. But on such vitally important questions as how much to spend and where to spend it first, federal engineers functioned as one among many competitors in the political arena. Thus, in addition to engineering considerations, economic, political, and social factors shaped the operations of the Federal Highway Administration.

The rapid increase in motor vehicles underpinned the demand for good roads. Increases in automobile, truck, and bus registrations took place at a phenomenal pace. In 1905, Americans registered nearly 79,000 motor vehicles; by 1910, with 468,500 registrations, America was already the leading automotive culture in the world. The 1920s was the first decade of mass auto buying, and by 1929, the total of all registrations had jumped to more than 26 million. Even during the dreary years of the depression, Americans purchased new vehicles, by 1940 boosting combined auto, truck, and bus registrations to 32.4 million. For the thirty years following World War II, a population enjoying substantial gains in income demanded more autos, buses, and trucks, and by 1975 total registrations had risen to 133 million.

The problem facing federal and state engineers was to build the roads these motorists were demanding. During the entire period of federal funding of state road construction, which began in 1912 and continues up to the present day, the facts of traffic increases and the demand for additional mileage mobilized officials to seek greater expenditures. The key idea was to serve motorists.

The consensus ended there. Because tax revenues were never sufficient to construct roads everywhere and at once, those affected industries such as trucking and others in each state, city, and region sought funds at the expense of competitors. As one illustration, farm operators routinely sought to increase rural mileage by stripping funds from the more costly intercity routes. In this climate, where a gain to one represented a loss to the next, roads were never adequately designed, and new mileage was always insufficient. In brief fashion, such were the economic and political realities that confronted the directors of the federal road-building agency.

The modern period of federal highway building began in 1893 with the founding of the Office of Road Inquiry. It constructed demonstration roads and disseminated information about building standards and the benefits of improved highways. The Post Office Appropriation Act of 1912 provided for the first substantial commitment of federal funds to road construction. The Federal Aid Highway Act of 1916 increased the funding level, designated the state governments as the recipients, and insisted that each state organize a highway department in order to qualify. By 1917, every state had created a road agency. The Federal Highway Act of 1921 authorized an enormous increase in aid for road building, and also mandated the Bureau of Public Roads (the successor to the Office of Road Inquiry) to designate 7 percent of mileage as the U.S. highway system. In effect, the federal government created a constituency for its Bureau of Public Roads and forced cooperation between them in the development of a national highway system.

Beginning after 1921, bureau chief and highway engineer Thomas H. MacDonald undertook the task of bringing order to the nation's road network and traffic systems. In particular, he sought the creation and adoption of national standards as the key to the development of a uniform system of national roads. Up to the early 1920s, each state promulgated its own rules for designating routes and for highway design and the grading of materials. State officials expended federal funds for the construction of roads of different height, width, subsurface capacity, and ability to handle drainage and freezing. As a result, roads deteriorated rapidly and were often dangerous, and motorists could not travel conveniently. By creating liaison groups between bureau and state highway engineers as well as between the bureau and trade groups such as the Asphalt Institute, MacDonald managed within a few years to secure concurrence as to minimum standards for pavement and road design. So effective was his method of coordinating the bureau with state engineers and industry groups that, by 1925,

MacDonald was able to join with state highway engineers in designating a national system of routes. East-west roads, they had decided, received an even number, and those running north and south an odd one.

Within a few years, then, MacDonald had created the institutional network, through which bureau engineers operated in the design and construction of roads. On one hand, MacDonald cooperated with trade and engineering groups with a view toward implementing a highway engineer's vision of good road programming, design, and standards. On the other, he and his subordinates understood the importance of serving a widening constituency for federal road funding.

During the 1930s, leaders of several groups interested themselves in road construction. President Franklin D. Roosevelt perceived road building as another tool for putting men back to work. City planners and a few downtown business executives argued for the fixing of route coordinates in terms of preserving the central business district and upgrading urban civilization. In 1933, truck operators had organized into a national trade association, and in their view roads were to be built to serve commerce. In a time of scarcity, these plans were mutually exclusive. Eventually, MacDonald favored each of these notions, but he always kept the engineering ideal, the truck operators, and the presidents of the United States front and center. His success rested upon the active support of the engineers and trade groups, which had been so carefully cultivated in earlier years, and no doubt upon their conviction that the bureau served them faithfully.

Certain it is that the federal government spent millions on road construction during the 1930s in order to create jobs. Yet, construction contractors complained of jobs given to local governments, and truckers and engineers objected to the construction of routes that failed to serve traffic. As long as the national emphasis was upon jobs, bureau officials never protested. By 1939, however, the bureau supplied the data sought by members of Congress who were attempting to block a proposed superhighway system aimed at job creation. In addition, MacDonald and one of his key aides, Herbert S. Fairbank, authored *Toll Roads and Free Roads*, a model of engineering logic applied to highways. This publication demonstrated the futility of constructing toll roads (to which truck operators objected as double taxation) and argued that a system of new, express highways connecting cities and running to their cores would eliminate traffic congestion as well as urban deterioration.

The exigencies of war limited federal road spending to streets and highways deemed essential to national defense. Bureau officials turned their attention to a campaign among highway engineers and members of Congress to secure permission to contruct the Interstate Highway System, the network MacDonald and Fairbank had sketched in 1939. This network, they promised, would provide excellent roadway for the increasing numbers of trucks and autos, as well as an inexpensive method of slum clearance and urban revitalization. Two birds with one stone became a favorite aphorism in engineering circles. The Interstate, if it ever came into being, would be constructed according to design principles long-favored by bureau engineers such as the transitional curve and perhaps even contain the limited-access feature. In 1944, Congress authorized construction of the Interstate system by the state highway departments, but refused to appropriate funds for its construction.

Between 1945 and 1956, competition for road funds and conflicting visions of appropriate highway service blocked substantial construction of the Interstate system. Bureau officials continued to plan for the Interstate—by 1947, they had designated the interurban routes, and in 1955, the urban corridors were approved—but they and their allies in the state road departments found it increasingly difficult to serve each of the competing interests. As one illustration, in 1947, MacDonald had sought to unite Interstate system construction with urban renewal and public housing. President Harry S Truman insisted for reasons of expedience in Congress on keeping them separate. In another case, MacDonald and state highway engineers prepared federal legislation promising a large increase in funding for every category of roads. In this scheme, proponents of each federal network would eventually enjoy additional mileage, and highway engineers could also construct the Interstate system. Truck operators objected on the basis of taxes, and President Truman on the grounds of his own efforts to limit federal spending to combat the growing inflationary danger. Underlying these issues was the fact that the Interstate promised to become immensely expensive, thus eventually limiting outlays for other roads, especially in sparsely settled areas.

By the early 1950s, the Interstate system became the focus for substantial divisions between the bureau and state engineers as well as among leaders in the highway-related industries. By 1953, so intense were differences that congressmen spoke occasionally of abolishing the bureau, or of reducing it to a fact-gathering agency. In 1954, the head of the association of state road engineers wrote members that continuation of disputes threatened the solidity of the association as well as the federal aid road program.

In 1954, President Dwight D. Eisenhower proposed his own "grand plan" for a national road program and appointed General Lucius D. Clay to fashion its details. Bureau engineer Francis C. Turner served as secretary to Clay's committee, once again providing the bureau with a vital place in writing legislation. Thereafter, the new commissioner of the bureau, Francis V. DuPont, resigned his post in order to lobby directly for approval by Congress of the Clay committee's plan.

Clay, Turner, DuPont, and President Eisenhower proved no luckier or more skillful in writing legislation acceptable to highway-minded men. Farm-road advocates wanted increased funding for local mileage, not for the costly Interstate system. Long-distance truck operators liked the prospect of concentrating federal attention on the Interstate but objected to hefty tax increases. Not until 1956, when Congressmen Hale Boggs and George H. Fallon wrote legislation promising more mileage for all and only a small increase in taxes on gasoline and diesel fuels, could the bureau finance rapid construction of the Interstate system. In the areas of funding levels, tax rates, and allocation formulas, the bureau had proved as ineffective and confused as everyone else. Because these matters were social, economic, and political in nature and thus not intimately related to the esoteric knowledge of highway engineers, the bureau was no better prepared than its competitors to raise before Congress a superior set of criteria lodged in cherished engineering principle and time-honored professional practice.

The 1956 Act also contained engineering and professional standards routinely sought by bureau and state engineers. In 1956, design standards such as the limited-access feature engendered little controversy. Creation of the Highway Trust Fund was equally agreeable to members of Congress. Several states had constructed trust arrangements by dedicating their gasoline tax revenues to road building, and the Highway Trust Fund performed the identical service for federal automotive and gasoline levies. The fact that motorists would finance highway construction and that the federal government would return Interstate system funds to the states on the basis of a ninety-ten sharing arrangement also served to obviate further construction of toll roads. For years, bureau and state highway engineers had routinely celebrated the advantages of focused construction, limited access, and no additional tollway mileage. The act of 1956 federalized those ideas.

After 1957, the bureau completed most of its mandated goals as a part of a new and enlarged agency, the Federal Highway Administration. As before, federal engineers funded the construction of new mileage, reviewed plans, certified construction standards, directed research activities, and, in particular, fostered the substantial completion of the Interstate system. By the late 1960s, most sections of the Interstate were completed, and it became the nation's principal traffic carrier, just as its proponents had promised.

As long as the trust fund provided sufficient revenues and as long as the highway administration's control of standards remained unchallenged, officials were able to deal successfully with peripheral issues. In 1967, Congress included the Federal Highway Administration in the new Department of Transportation.* Afterward, administrators added phrases such as modal complementarity to their publications. When issues such as energy and women's participation in the labor force reached the national agenda, federal highway officials served on the appropriate panels and funded the appropriate research.

Federal highway officials often failed to coordinate and channel those who challenged engineering standards, professional judgments, and control of the trust fund. Leaders of new constituencies in highway politics such as academic economists, urban officials, and community leaders argued that the limited-access feature disrupted urban neighborhoods. In San Francisco, local groups intervened in the planning process and actually blocked construction of the Embarcadero Freeway. Dedication of gasoline tax revenues to highway building, according to critics, created a road network that "siphoned off . . . traffic" from public carriers, and in 1973 Congress permitted the diversion of trust funds for the construction of urban mass-transit facilities. Whether in 1955 and 1956 or again during the 1960s and 1970s, only rarely could federal highway administrators cope successfully with those not immersed in the routines and rituals of highway-engineering logic and federal road-construction practices.

Beginning in 1912, the Office of Road Inquiry and its successors funded the building and fixed the standards for the key routes in the national highway system. Measured against its original goal of coordinating the construction of an integrated road network, the Federal Highway Administration was immensely successful. Evaluated against the notion that the critical measures of an organization's vitality are survival and growth, the highway administration functioned as a model of bureaucratic adaptation to the chilling winds of political and economic change. But if the highway administration is judged by its ability to manipulate the principal, nonengineering actors in the turbulent environment of the post-World War II years, then its record is undistinguished. The development and dissemination of engineering standards served as the key to its successes and its failures. Federal highway administrators never understood the degree to which social, political, and economic factors had conditioned the national acceptance of the professional standards they liked so much.

FOR ADDITIONAL INFORMATION: Warren J. Belasco, *Americans on the Road: From Autocamp to Motel, 1910-1945* (1979); John S. Bragdon Papers, The Dwight D. Eisenhower Library, Abilene, Kansas; John C. Burnham, "The Gasoline Tax and the Automobile Revolution," *Mississippi Valley Historical Review: A Journal of American History* 98 (December 1961): 435-469; James J. Flink, *The Car Culture* (1975); Mark S. Foster, *From Streetcar to Superhighway: American City Planners and Urban Transportation, 1900-1940* (1981); Helen Leavitt, *Superhighway-Superhoax* (1970); and John B. Rae, *The Road and the Car in American Life* (1971); Mark H. Rose, *Interstate: Express Highway Politics, 1941-1956* (1979); Bruce E. Seely, "Highway Engineers as Policy Makers, 1893-1944" (Ph.D dissertation, University of Delaware, 1982); George M. Smerk, *Urban Transportation: The Federal Role* (1966); U.S. Department of Agriculture, Bureau of Public Roads, *Toll Roads and Free Roads*, House Document No. 272, 76th Cong., 1st Sess., (1939); and U.S. Department of Transportation, Federal Highway Administration, *America's Highways, 1776-1976: A History of the Federal-Aid Program* (1976).

MARK H. ROSE

FEDERAL MARITIME COMMISSION (FMC). The Federal Maritime Commission derives its authority primarily from the Shipping Act of 1916, as amended, and traces its ancestry back to the Shipping Board created by that act. It is an independent agency responsible for regulating the international water-borne commerce of the United States and for policing the trade between the mainland and noncontiguous territories and states.

The FMC is concerned principally with enforcing the provisions of the Shipping Act of 1916 which deal with joint actions of carriers in the same trade, nondiscriminatory freight rates, and unreasonable competition. It consists of five members appointed by the President (by and with the advice and consent of the Senate), one of these five being designated by the President as chairman. The commissioners are assisted by a staff, the most prominent of whom are the administrative law judges.

In order to understand the functions of the commission, some aspects of its procedures will be outlined in the following paragraphs.

Two or more steamship operators decide to form a "conference," that is, an association of carriers in the same trade established for the purpose of stabilizing competition and setting mutually acceptable freight rates and passenger fares. This kind of joint action is contrary to the stipulations of the Sherman Anti-trust law, but the Shipping Act of 1916 granted exemption from these restrictions on condition that all joint actions be regulated by the Shipping Board or whatever agency the Congress might designate for this purpose.

The associated carriers draw up a formal agreement, stating the objectives and bases for common action, and submit this document to the commission for approval. Pursuant to the mandate contained in Section 15 of the Shipping Act of 1916, as amended, the commission examines the proposed agreement and assigns an administrative law judge to conduct appropriate public hearings and to offer a "recommended decision" to the commission. This decision may be accepted in whole or in part, or may be rejected in its entirety. It may be rewritten to any extent the commission desires. Final action on the agreement must be taken by vote of all five members of the commission. The carriers are not permitted to operate under the agreement until the commission grants approval; the law provides heavy fines for such premature activity.

Once approval is granted, the conference is set up, a chairman is employed to administer its operations, and the public is informed. As a basic requirement of the law, the conference must furnish the commission with copies of minutes of all meetings, freight and passenger tariffs, changes in those tariffs, and any documents that the conference may offer to the public. Freight rates cannot be increased without prior notice, but reductions may be effected immediately after filing.

As a means of stabilizing competition, the conference seeks to bind shippers to it by obtaining pledges that they will patronize conference member lines exclusively. The inducement to make this commitment is that a lower freight rate will be charged. This "dual rate system" is permitted under the law, so long as it is not discriminatory nor used selectively to destroy nonconference competitors. The conference must approve the terms of the "exclusive patronage contract" before it can be offered to the public.

Shippers who are aggrieved by practices of conferences or independent carriers for any reason may file protests with the commission, which will investigate the matter and, if it is found to have substance, will assign an administrative law judge to conduct an appropriate hearing. In some instances, the proceedings have extended over a period of a year or longer.

Another form of joint action, not necessarily related to the conferences, is an arrangement by which carriers in the same trade put all freight earnings into a common fund, or "pool," and divide the earnings in accordance with the agreed percentages. For instance, three carriers which normally transport 45, 30, and 25 percent, respectively, of the tonnage moving on that trade route will form a pool and, regardless of the actual tonnage lifted by individual carriers, will divide the total revenue according to those percentages. Approval of pooling agreements requires action of the commission and almost invariably involves protracted hearings and long intra-commission debate before the final vote is taken.

The Shipping Act of 1916, as amended, requires that steamship conferences be open to all carriers engaged in the foreign commerce of the United States. These "open" conferences are deemed beneficial to the public because they prevent the formation of monopolies. Critics of the open conferences assert that this provision has brought about serious overtonnaging of major trade routes, with disastrous freight-rate "wars" between the carriers, as well as instability of both rates and service, to the ultimate detriment of the shipping public.

The alternative is the "closed" conference, which admits new members only on the affirmative vote of the carriers that are already part of the association. While proponents of this type of conference admit that it resembles the illegal trust, or monopoly, they intend that shippers form councils, also to be regulated by the commission, which will be empowered to negotiate with the conference to obtain reasonable concessions and fair rates. To permit closed conferences in United States trade requires an amendment to the Shipping Act of 1916, which has not been accomplished despite several efforts in the Congress.

The FMC is a regulatory and supervisory agency concerned with the water-borne commerce of the United States. It is the only agency in the world that attempts to regulate both its own national-flag shipping and those carriers of other countries that participate in the foreign trade of the United States. This regulatory effort has brought about major disputes with maritime states, and the commission's demands that documents housed in foreign jurisdictions be produced in response to requirements of the commission have been the cause of intergovernmental exchanges marked by some bitterness. England, in retaliation, passed laws that prohibit its citizens from complying with orders to make available documents maintained in, and pursuant to the laws of, England. This type of dispute has arisen sufficiently often for critics to urge that the law be changed to avoid these confrontations. No action, beyond reducing its insistence upon production of documents, has been taken to date by either the commission or Congress.

Historically, the FMC was created as part of a reorganization plan submitted to the Congress by President John F. Kennedy in 1961. Up to that time, the functions of the commission had been assigned to the Federal Maritime Board, an agency of the Department of Commerce.* The chairman of that board also was the Maritime administrator and in that capacity was responsible for the operation of the shipping subsidy system set up by the Merchant Marine Act, 1936, as amended. The incompatibility of the two areas of responsibility had resulted in many problems, in part rooted in the demands placed upon the interests and time of the chairman/administrator by the two divisions of his office.

To present the story in chronological fashion, it is necessary to go back to 1912. A committee of the Congress, under the chairmanship of Representative

Joshua W. Alexander of Missouri, conducted extensive hearings over a two-year period and, in 1914, submitted its report. This document served as the basis for the Shipping Act of 1916, which authorized the conference system and also approved the continuation of the ocean-mail contracts program, which had been used intermittently since 1845 to subsidize ship operations under the United States flag. The agency established to administer this law was the United States Shipping Board. By the time the law was effective, the United States was involved in World War I, and, therefore, it was not until about 1920 that any attention was directed to the regulatory aspects of the law. It is interesting to note that from 1916 to 1960, only 127 proceedings were docketed dealing with rates and practices of steamship lines engaged in the foreign commerce of the United States. The Shipping Board considered only two cases involving exclusive patronage contracts, one in 1922 and one in 1933. Of the 127 proceedings, only one-half produced any kind of regulatory order from the agency. In 1958, the Supreme Court decided, in *Federal Maritime Board* v. *Isbrandtsen* (356 U.S. 481), that the dual-rate contract was unjustly discriminatory and hence illegal. This precipitated congressional action to strengthen, for the first time since enactment of the 1916 law, the regulatory program.

The ineffectiveness of the Shipping Board and the decline of the United States Merchant Marine attracted the attention of President Franklin D. Roosevelt, who prompted congressional effort to enact the Merchant Marine Act, 1936. This abolished the Shipping Board and transferred all its functions to the newly created United States Maritime Commission, composed of five men appointed by and reporting directly to the President. The promotion of the Merchant Marine was of critical importance at that time, and the regulatory functions were sidetracked. With the outbreak of World War II in Europe, in September 1939, and continuing until 1946, the commission's energies were directed toward building ships.

In 1950, President Harry S Truman proposed (as part of Reorganization Plan No. 21) to separate the regulatory and promotion functions but did not go so far as to recommend that two distinct agencies be created. The result was the creation of the Maritime Administration and the Federal Maritime Board, both placed in the Department of Commerce and headed by a presidential appointee who held the titles of Maritime administrator and chairman of the Federal Maritime Board. The new arrangement became effective on May 23, 1950. The board was the regulatory agency, and the administration was the ship construction and subsidy-administering organization.

There was no compatibility between these two functions. The administrator had to delegate much of the subsidy activity to his deputy in order to find the time to perform as chairman of the Maritime Board. Unfortunately for the enforcement of the law, the members of the board differed seriously in their attitudes, and their quarreling resulted in an almost complete stoppage of regulatory activity. This brought about the Kennedy proposal of 1961. For the first time, there was appreciation of the fact that administration of the ship subsidy program was so different from regulation of ocean-going foreign commerce that two organizations should be set up without any relationship to each other. The Federal Maritime Commission, which was charged with the regulatory duties, was made an independent office reporting directly to the President, while the Maritime Administration remained in the Department of Commerce until 1981, when it was shifted to the Department of Transportation.*

Since 1961, the Federal Maritime Commission has been active in a number of cases. The exclusive patronage contract, as previously noted, was revised. Cargo and revenue-sharing pools were studied intensively, especially in the trades between the United States and Argentina and the United States and Japan. The deliberations on these pools were protracted and marked by gross differences among members of the commission. To give the commission the necessary background for reaching decisions, trade-route analyses were initiated. Typical of these efforts were the *North Atlantic Trade Study* (April 1979) and the *South American Trade Study* (February 1980). The problems which resulted in freight-rate wars were examined, as was the disparity of freight rates on routes to and from the United States.

Examination of the record since 1961 justifies the conclusion that the creation of an independent, quasi-judicial body charged solely with the regulation of the nation's ocean-borne commerce has been in the best interests of the United States. The problem of trying to impose the attitudes reflected by long-standing antitrust legislation in the United States upon the carriers of foreign nations in which cartels are part of the economic system has been a major irritant for the commission. Another area of friction is the continuing conflict between the advocates of open conferences, a requirement of the 1916 act, and proponents of the closed-conference system. Finally, it is a reasonable judgment that the Federal Maritime Commission has been able to accomplish more as an independent regulatory agency than was possible under the systems in vogue until 1961.

FOR ADDITIONAL INFORMATION: Samuel A. Lawrence, *United States Merchant Shipping Policies and Politics* (1966), is an excellent source of information on the origins and difficulties surrounding the regulation of transoceanic commerce. Daniel Marx, Jr., *International Shipping Cartels: A Study of Industrial Self-Regulation by Shipping Conferences* (1953), provides a carefully researched background concerning the origins, rise, and operations of steamship conferences. For day-to-day coverage of the proceedings of the Federal Maritime Commission, the columns of the New York *Journal of Commerce* provide the most detailed reports readily available.

LANE C. KENDALL

FEDERAL POWER COMMISSION (FPC). Created by an act approved on June 10, 1920 (41 Statutes at Large 1063), the Federal Power Commission was an independent administrative agency initially composed of the secretaries of War, Interior, and Agriculture. Its purpose was to exercise general administrative control over all water-power sites and kindred establishments located on the navigable waters, on the public lands, and on the reservations of the United

States. To achieve this purpose, the commission was required to cooperate with both the states and the federal government in preparing reports based on the investigation of water resources. The commission was further authorized to issue licenses and permits for the construction and utilization of dams, power houses, transmission lines, reservoirs, water conduits, and related projects. It also regulated under specified conditions the financial operations of water-power industries, including service rates. In addition, the commission was charged with the responsibility of making physical valuations of the properties of power enterprises, of determining the extent of their services, and of regulating the operation of power projects.

By 1920 water power, owing to improved technology, was being increasingly utilized in industry. In 1921, the United States Geological Survey* estimated the potential water-power resources of the United States at 53,905,000 horsepower, of which less than 10 million horsepower, including 1,430,000 horsepower developed on public lands and navigable streams, was being generated into electricity. It was also estimated that there was sufficient water power available in the United States to do the work of 500 million tons of coal annually, and through transmission lines the energy derived from water power could be utilized thousands of miles away from its source for seemingly unlimited uses in all phases of industry, at home, and on the farm. In all aspects of human endeavor, widespread use of electric power helped to ease physical burdens and promote a rising standard of living. Power permits granted by the FPC to corporate applicants seeking to develop these vast energy resources furthered the Progressive concern for conservation through federal regulation of a basic natural resource in the public interest.

The Federal Water Power Act organized the three secretaries into a single administrative agency, provided them with subordinates (an army engineer and an executive secretary), and consolidated their several, largely administrative, legal powers. At their first meeting on July 1, 1920, O. C. Merrill, chief engineer of the Forest Service*, was appointed executive secretary, and President Woodrow Wilson was asked to detail an officer from the Corps of Engineers* to serve as engineer. Since the act provided no personnel for the commission other than the two already mentioned, it was necessary to borrow personnel of the three departments to conduct its various activities organized into divisions: Accounting, Engineering, Legal, Licensing, Operation, Regulatory, and Statistical. Several state legislatures, following the establishment of the FPC, responded by creating similar commissions to cooperate with the new agency in an endeavor to coordinate or harmonize conflicting claims of state and federal governments to control the leasing of water-power sites.

Difficulties or weaknesses quickly appeared because the commission was unable to secure a qualified staff of experts to assist in determining rates, measuring excess profits, and projecting the recapture price to be paid at the end of fifty years for privately constructed facilities. Licenses were usually granted for fifty years with annual fees paid by the licensee to the government. At the end of this period, a license could be renewed with the original company, be granted to a new company, or the plant could be taken over by the U.S. government. The licensee also agreed to keep the plant in good condition, to follow a pre-scribed accounting system, and to accept the rate, service, and security regulation of the commission where no state had jurisdiction or where states found them-selves unable to agree on such regulations.

To perform many of these functions, valuation engineers were needed and none were included among the employees of the War,* Interior,* or Agriculture* Departments. A busy executive secretary with a borrowed office force directed an important agency dispensing valuable power sites with a minimum scrutiny of contractual details. In addition, in the 1920s many conservationists and power people were critical of O. C. Merrill and the commission for discouraging public ownership and operation, despite a provision in the law granting preference to public corporations.

Recognizing some of these difficulties, President Herbert Hoover in his first message to Congress on December 3, 1929, called for "the creation of a real Federal Power Commission, with teeth." Congress responded with a measure approved on June 23, 1930, transferring to a new Federal Power Commission the authorities of the interdepartmental committee. The three-secretary FPC was replaced by one consisting of five full-time members and provided with funds for a full-time staff. The reorganization became effective on December 22, 1930, after the Senate approved the appointment of George Otis Smith, chief of the United States Geological Survey, as chairman and four other commissioners. Through 1934, however, the commission had taken no significant action over rates, services, and securities, despite the fact that some of the power transmitted by licensees went into interstate commerce and was subject to state regulation only when it was finally resold to local consumers. Until 1935, the federal government had taken no adequate steps to control interstate transmission. Over a small portion of this energy, that produced by licensees of the FPC, the commission had sufficient authority, but this authority had never been exercised. For the bulk of the interstate transmission of electric power, no regulatory agency existed.

Title II of the Public Utility Act of 1935 amended the Federal Water Power Act of 1920, renaming it the Federal Power Act. It added to the authority of the FPC the supervision of all electric energy transmitted in interstate commerce regardless of whether it derived from water or from fuel sources. Interstate transmission was declared to be "affected with a public interest" and subject to public regulation as a supplement to that exercised by state commissions. The only exceptions to this mandate were power generated at Tennessee Valley Authority* and Bureau of Reclamation* projects, as well as power from projects in national parks or national monument areas. Power produced at Army Engineers projects and marketed through agencies of the Interior Department was subject to regulation. Federal agencies, however, were not subject to licensing by the FPC, needing instead the authorization of Congress to construct hydro projects.

But, beginning in 1938, the commission was required to investigate the power potential of all authorized federal multi-purpose projects.

With this legislation the FPC gained broad regulatory authority over public utilities under its jurisdiction: over their rates, securities, accounting systems, selling or leasing property, and service. In addition, the commission was authorized to assist state commissions by furnishing them such information and reports as would be of assistance in state regulation of public utilities. Finally, the FPC established regions to promote the coordination of equipment involving the generation and sale of electricity. Regional offices were established in New York, Atlanta, Chicago, Denver, and San Francisco. Power pooling was encouraged and promoted within and between these five regional districts. In time of war or other national emergency, it would become mandatory. But in either peace or war, the economies attained through such coordination proved to be substantial.

To assist the commission in conducting its many functions, it was also authorized to provide for the compilation and publication of essential information pertaining to both publicly and privately owned utilities of every kind involved with light and power. The FPC quickly became a clearinghouse of information regarding all phases of the electric industry. This function became possibly the most constructive aspect of the commission's work. A National Power Survey provided for the first time an engineering study of the power resources and requirements of the entire country. Electric-rate surveys set forth in understandable terms the rates charged consumers in every state and helped establish for the first time a sound factual basis for an understanding of the problems of the electric light and power industry. Moreover, their publication aroused widespread public interest and led to adjustments when rates were shown to be out of line with those charged in similarly situated communities.

Under the terms of the National Gas Act, approved on June 21, 1938, the FPC was charged with exercising regulatory powers over natural gas companies (comparable to those it already exercised over electric utilities) engaged in interstate commerce. Moreover, authorization by the commission became necessary either to export or import natural gas to or from the United States. As the President and Congress became increasingly concerned about safeguarding and insuring adequate energy supplies in the event of a war emergency, the responsibilities imposed upon the FPC, chiefly through Executive Orders and presidential directives, increased.

During the war years, the commission through its rate regulation played a role in seeking to keep down the cost of living and effectuate the purposes of the stabilization program. Its monthly surveys of the rapidly changing power situation throughout the nation based on information from all the principal utility systems and from the manufacturers of electric generators proved invaluable in resolving wartime energy demands. To coordinate its activities with those of the War Production Board,* the FPC agreed on April 24, 1942, to work with the board in meeting wartime power problems and in administering the wartime natural gas program. Its problems during the war period were manifold: helping to meet sudden and sharp increases in the demand for electricity, coping with shortages of electric energy as well as facilities for generating energy, and encouraging power pooling for the interstate transmission of electric energy.

The FPC came to public attention in the immediate postwar period when the Senate on October 12, 1949, rejected the renomination of Leland Olds for a third, five-year term despite a strong endorsement from the President. On the other hand, the President on April 15, 1950, vetoed a bill, introduced by Senator Robert S. Kerr of Oklahoma, limiting the authority of the FPC in regulating sales of natural gas to interstate pipeline companies. These actions, and the fact that the FPC in July 1950 decided that the Phillips Petroleum Company was not a "natural gas company" within the meaning of the Natural Gas Act and, therefore, not subject to commission jurisdiction, indicated not only a shift away from the more liberal or public power outlook of the New Deal years, but also a shift in emphasis in the work of the commission from electrical energy to natural gas.

Increasingly after 1950, FPC rulings focused on natural gas, and by the 1970s, the agency was being charged with an anti-consumer bias because of prices and rates it approved in order to assure an adequate and reliable supply of natural gas. By the mid-1970s, natural gas accounted for more than 31 percent of the nation's energy supplies. Earlier, in 1961, President John F. Kennedy noted this dramatic shift when he observed that some four thousand rate increases by independent natural gas producers and pipelines were pending before an inundated FPC. He urged the addition of two members to the commission, but Congress chose not to heed his request. What was apparent to President Kennedy in 1961 became increasingly evident in the following decades: namely, that the Natural Gas Act of 1938, which gave the FPC the authority to regulate this industry as a supplement to its work in electrical energy, now dominated the work of the commission as the United States coped with an energy crisis surrounding the use of fossil fuels. By April 1976, filings with the FPC totaled 15,315.

The techniques and knowledge needed to handle problems in the fields of natural gas and electric power are different. An understanding of one does not provide a background for dealing with the other. Confusion and delay more and more characterized gas regulation, while problems surrounding the future of hydroelectric generation also called for reappraisal and further attention. Meanwhile, the inadequacy of consumer protection in cases where rate increases were requested became a matter of increasing concern, as an energy shortage and mounting inflation impacted upon the American people in the 1970s. In addition, safety became a factor, leading the FPC to investigate and report, for example, on the November 1965 Northeast Power Blackout and to examine pipeline failures because of the highly flammable and explosive nature of natural gas.

As energy needs increased, so too did the need for the FPC to prepare nationwide surveys. But expansion on the basis of orderly and planned growth

became increasingly difficult in the 1970s because of energy shortfalls and inflation. Natural gas producers continually argued that the best way to achieve
this goal was through deregulation, and their arguments gained increasing support. In February 1977, President Jimmy Carter signed an Emergency Natural
Gas Act directing the chairman of the FPC to take the lead in initiating action
for the orderly transfer of natural gas to the eastern part of the nation, the area
most severely affected by the shortage. In the following month, he proposed the
abolition of the commission and the incorporation of its responsibilities into a
new Department of Energy* which was established in October 1977. Thereafter,
the Federal Energy Regulatory Commission, an independent agency within the
Department of Energy, exercised the authority and discharged the responsibility
previously conferred upon the FPC.

Established in 1920 to provide an orderly means for the development of the
nation's hydroelectric resources by licensing and regulating specific uses of these
waters, the FPC in the course of its fifty-seven-year history was given additional
responsibilities, including the regulation of electric rates and services for wholesale transactions, and the regulation of natural gas pipelines and producers, all
operating in interstate commerce. By 1977, as an energy crisis compounded by
inflation and environmental concerns became acute, the work of the FPC was
merged into the new Department of Energy, thereby providing the means of
better coordinating electric power and natural gas regulations with an overall
national energy program.

FOR ADDITIONAL INFORMATION: There is no history of the FPC. Background material
and information about its early years can be found in James G. Kerwin, *Federal Water
Power Legislation* (1926) and Milton Conover, *The Federal Power Commission* (1923).
Its varied responsibilities were annually noted in *Congressional Directories* from 1921
through 1950, and the sets of *Presidential Papers* from Herbert Hoover through Jimmy
Carter contain basic general information about the commission's changing role. Its Annual
Reports present the specific details.

                                                                    RICHARD LOWITT

FEDERAL RESERVE BOARD. The Federal Reserve Board is the governing
body of the Federal Reserve System. The board, through the system, is assigned
the oversight of the financial sector, the implementation of monetary policy, and
the task of carrying out the government's financial affairs. The system is intended
to be independent of political considerations. The long terms granted to the
members of the Board of Governors were intended to insulate the board from
political pressures, and the system does not depend on congressional appropriations for its operating budget.

There is, however, a great difference between the system created by the Federal
Reserve Act in 1913 and the system as it exists today. Enormous changes have
taken place in organization, philosophy, and policy. Two events played an
important role in the system's evolution. The first was the economic upheaval
of 1929-1930 and the subsequent depression. This economic cataclysm and the

wave of bank failures that accompanied it caused a reevaluation of the roles of the system and the board. The second event was World War II. The enormous government debt created by the war wrought a permanent change in the financial system. The large government debt created the opportunity and, some argue, the necessity for active monetary policy on the part of the Federal Reserve. The emphasis, after 1946, of fiscal policy on growth and full employment has also affected the role played by the Federal Reserve System in the nation's economic policy.

At times, individuals were important, too. Various members of the board have had a profound impact on its policy and stature, and the power and development of the board have been influenced by other strong personalities within the system.

The history of the Board of Governors of the Federal Reserve System is, above all, a history of change. Some of those present at its creation would not recognize it now and would lament the changes that have come to pass. Others would view the alterations in its structure and powers as necessary and desirable. Even today the debate over the proper role of the Federal Reserve continues, with no clear winner.

The Federal Reserve Board was intended to be little more than the coordinator of the activities of the Federal Reserve banks created by the act, which President Woodrow Wilson signed in December 1913. The individual banks, finally twelve in number, reflected a compromise between complete centralization of financial control through a true central bank and the complete decentralization of the financial sector that existed before 1913. The powers granted to the board also show this compromise. The wording of the act gives few definite powers to the board vis-à-vis the Federal Reserve banks, while at the same time conferring heavy responsibilities for financial stability on the system.

The original intention of the Federal Reserve Act was for the Federal Reserve System to play a passive role, providing an "elastic" currency by discounting eligible securities of member banks when they were presented at the Federal Reserve banks. In this setting, the variable to be controlled was the rate of discount, set by each bank, subject to the board's approval. The board's legal power to force changes in a particular bank's rate of discount was never clear during the first two decades of the system's operation, and the board did not achieve clear control over the discount rate until 1935.

The original board was made up of seven members: the Secretary of the Treasury,* the comptroller of the currency, and five members appointed by the President with Senate approval. In 1922, an additional appointive member was added because some members of Congress felt the board failed to represent adequately agricultural interests. This issue had plagued the board (and the act) from its legislative inception. The Secretary of the Treasury served as chairman. This proved to be an important structural arrangement, since the war broke out soon after the system's creation, and handling the Treasury's* financing needs became the principal occupation of the Federal Reserve.

The period of preoccupation with wartime finance lasted well into the 1920s.

The board, dominated by the Treasury, often found itself in a subordinate position. Throughout the 1920s, the New York Federal Reserve Bank exercised enormous influence, particularly during the time that Benjamin Strong was president of the New York Bank. One original member of the board, Paul M. Warburg, would probably have been important during the early years, since he was a major force in the development of the Federal Reserve Act. But Warburg, who had been born in Germany, felt compelled for political reasons to resign his position at the outbreak of war, and the board lost the one person who might have emerged to challenge Benjamin Strong as the dominant spokesman on monetary matters. The board was, however, ably served by several competent members, particularly C. S. Hamlin and A. C. Miller, original members who served into the 1930s.

Throughout the 1913-1933 period, the influence of the board was limited. Often the appointive members found themselves caught between the desire of the Treasury for low interest rates to facilitate bond issues and the New York Bank, which desired higher rates to limit expansion or speculation.

From an organizational standpoint, the Federal Reserve System of the 1920s had a long way to go before it became a true central bank. Likewise, the board was some distance from becoming a locus of control over the nation's monetary policy. The economic collapse of the early 1930s set in motion powerful forces that would completely reshape the system and lodge power over monetary policy in the board. The collapse exposed two weaknesses in the Federal Reserve Act. First, it showed the error of the simplistic monetary and banking theory imbedded in the act as well as the error of the policies that sprang from the theory. Second, the collapse demonstrated the need for more centralized control over monetary policy.

The Banking Act of 1935 centralized power in the renamed Board of Governors of the Federal Reserve System. The Secretary of the Treasury and the comptroller of the currency were removed from the board, which was now composed of seven appointive members. The new board was given power over open-market operations through a formalization of the Federal Open Market Committee, which restructured that group and placed the board in the majority. Before 1935, the Open Market Committee had been made up of one member from each district. The new legislation created a committee made up of the seven appointed members of the Board of Governors plus five representatives of the banks. The latter positions rotated among the twelve districts, though later the representative of the New York Bank was made a permanent member because the committee's policies were carried out through the New York Bank. The new board was also given more power over the rate of discount, but the discount rate was rapidly eclipsed by open-market operations as a policy tool.

A change of no less importance was the appointment of Mariner Eccles as first chairman of the Board of Governors. Eccles was a banker (from Utah) and a strong supporter of President Franklin D. Roosevelt. His arguments regarding the proper government policy during the depression anticipated the theory put forward by John Maynard Keynes in the *General Theory*. Eccles was to serve for more than twelve years as chairman of the board and, along with William McChesney Martin and Arthur F. Burns, was one of three strong chairmen who were powerful forces in monetary policy between 1935 and the present.

Though problems had changed and the points in contention were different, the board continued to find it difficult to escape dominance by the Treasury in monetary matters. The two waged continual skirmishes over points minor and major through the 1930s and 1940s. Eccles saw that the end of the war would bring a potentially inflationary situation similar to that which had existed at the end of World War I and continually fought to minimize it. He argued for financing the war through taxes rather than bond issues and tried to find a middle ground on which the Federal Reserve could maintain its independence. This was not to be, however. The war was financed principally by huge bond issues, and the Federal Reserve did what was necessary to support the government's financing needs.

The end of the war brought renewed pressure from the Treasury for low rates to ease debt servicing. The board resisted this pressure as far as possible throughout the late 1940s because of the board's fear of inflation. Finally, in 1951, the Treasury and the board signed an accord which, after thirty-eight years, set the board free to follow a monetary policy separate from the financing needs of the Treasury Department.

With the Treasury-Federal Reserve Accord of 1951, the Federal Reserve was released from the historical strictures placed on it which had made the Treasury's desires regarding interest rates paramount in policy decisions. This did not mean, however, that the Federal Reserve was to be free to implement whatever policy seemed to the board to be correct. More and more after 1951, the Federal Reserve Board's monetary policy was integrated into the larger economic policy set by the President. Recent research shows very clearly that, since 1951, presidents have received from the board the policy decisions that they desired on almost every occasion. On the other hand, the chairmen of the Board of Governors, at least from 1951 through 1978, were strong-willed and influential in policy decisions.

Martin and Burns together created a system under which the chairman clearly became the dominant figure on the board. They also oversaw a system whose main preoccupation has been to limit the inflationary aspects of the rest of government policy. Particularly since the middle 1960s, the board, while at times following expansionary policy, has seen as its main task stabilizing the value of the dollar, both at home and abroad.

The board has, therefore, acted generally as a force for conservatism since 1951, but even so, activism has not been without its problems. The board's activist monetary policy has been criticized on two different counts by two widely differing groups. On one side are those who argue that the conservatism of the board has stifled economic growth because policy has caused interest rates to be too high. The other major criticism is directed at the policy of activism itself, the argument being that the board's monetary policy has fostered increased instability, the reverse of its intention.

The board's conservatism in policy has resulted mainly from its attempts to balance the expansionary, and hence possibly inflationary, effects of the government's fiscal policy. The board's activism has developed from a real belief that changes in monetary policy can have predictable effects on the economy. Often, however, the board's policies are overambitious, such as its attempts to hit target figures for both interest rates and growth in the money stock, targets that were sometimes inconsistent.

At the same time, there has been increased pressure, notably from Congress, to end the Federal Reserve Board's "independence." What some congressmen no doubt have in mind is to end its independence from Congress. These tendencies have manifested themselves in demands that the chairman appear before Congress and explain the board's intentions regarding policy. While the intentions of the founders of the Federal Reserve System were clearly to create in the board a sort of "Supreme Court of Finance," which would keep the financial system in working order without political interference, the issue of independence seems increasingly to be viewed as a legitimate one to raise. After all, in one way or another, the system has never been completely independent of the Executive. In 1980, the appointment of a chairman with strong credentials appeared to move the system back in the direction of independent action, but the independence of the board remains a political and philosophical issue.

The 1980s brought with them changes in the environment and structure of the U.S. financial system. These changes will interact to complicate the board's activities if it continues to follow an activist policy. Notices of Withdrawal (NOW accounts) allow savings and loan companies to take on some aspects of commercial banks, at least on the liabilities side. The demise of regulation Q, the board's regulation of the maximum interest payment on time deposits, will allow commercial banks to compete more effectively with thrift institutions in attracting funds. The complex and numerous definitions of the money supply now used by the board reflect the difficulty in coming to grips with changes in the financial system. The sophistication of financial institutions and the varied means available to them to offset undesired effects of the board's policy decisions make monetary policy, at least of an activist sort, more difficult.

It is not unlikely that after nearly seven decades of operation the board, now in charge of the Federal Reserve System, could finally come to a policy that is consistent with the intentions of the system's creators. Those intentions, simply stated, were that the system would accommodate the needs of business. For most of the first forty years, the system and the board were trapped into providing support for the Treasury's policies. Over the next three decades, the board, now in ascendance, developed the framework and the theory for a monetary policy that was aimed at controlling the level of economic activity rather than accommodating it. Acting mainly as a counterweight to fiscal policy, the success of monetary policy has been questionable. The board and other monetary authorities have learned a great deal. There are those who argue that what the board should have learned was that "monetary policy," in the activist sense of that term, is not practical and can even be dangerous.

The board's increased emphasis on hitting monetary growth targets indicates some agreement with this view. Setting, and then attempting to hit, monetary growth targets will not put the board in the position of passively accommodating business, but such a policy does imply less activism on the part of the board. It would be ironic if the seventy-year struggle of the Federal Reserve Board, now the Board of Governors of the Federal Reserve System, to achieve dominance and freedom of action led the board full circle to a position more consistent with the intentions of the system's founders.

FOR ADDITIONAL INFORMATION: Benjamin H. Beckhart, *The Discount Policy of the Federal Reserve System* (1924); Board of Governors of the Federal Reserve System, *Federal Reserve: Purposes and Functions* (1978); Lester V. Chandler, *Benjamin Strong, Central Banker* (1958); Marriner Eccles, *Beckoning Frontiers* (1951); Federal Reserve System, *Annual Reports*; Carter Glass, *Adventure in Constructive Finance* (1927); E. A. Goldenweiser, *Federal Reserve System in Operation* (1925); Dudley Luckett and Glenn Potts, "Monetary Policy and Partisan Politics," *Journal of Money, Credit and Banking* (August 1980); Sherman Maisel, *Managing the Dollar* (1973); Paul M. Warburg, *The Federal Reserve System* (1930); Robert Craig West, *Banking Reform and the Federal Reserve, 1863-1923* (1977); Elmus Wicker, *Federal Reserve Monetary Policy 1917-1933* (1966); Henry Parker Willis, *The Federal Reserve* (1923); and Elmer Wood, *Monetary Control* (1965).

ROBERT CRAIG WEST

FEDERAL TRADE COMMISSION (FTC). The passage of the Federal Trade Commission Act in September 1914 was viewed by many political observers as the solution of a decades–old controversy over methods of regulating business. The dispute had centered on the question of whether business could be regulated more effectively by stringent legislation to bolster the Sherman Antitrust Act, or by an administrative commission imbued with broad powers. Originating chiefly within the ranks of Progressive reformers, the controversy quickly spread to the business community and to the two major political parties. It became a prominent issue in the bitterly fought presidential campaign of 1912. Now, in 1914, the issue was seemingly resolved when Congress created the Federal Trade Commission.

President Woodrow Wilson initially had conceived of the FTC as a fact–finding body that would provide explicit guidance to businessmen on how to avoid those unfair methods of competition and deceptive practices that would undermine the economic system, but Congress added legislative and adjudicatory authority to the commission with Section 5 of the FTC Act. Under the law, the FTC was vested with unprecedented powers to investigate, publicize, and prohibit all "unfair methods of competition." This accorded with the reformers' ideal of strict regulation and vigorous antitrust activity.

Broad consensus on the importance of the FTC Act did not mean universal approval of its provisions. The public was sharply divided on the wisdom and potential benefit of the law, and, in contrast to the united support offered by Progressives, the FTC received a divided reaction from the business world. Many businessmen had hoped that the law would produce genuine cooperation between business and government, but others viewed the new agency as a threat to free enterprise.

From the start, the FTC adopted a case–by–case approach to application of the trade laws, done in the expectation that it would clarify the laws, and, under threat of litigation, those engaged in illegal action would stop. However, in its first decade of activity, the FTC proved a disappointment to many of its original supporters. During 1915-1928, for example, 14,193 charges of unfair competition were lodged with the commission. Of these, the great majority were summarily dismissed; and 3,081 out of the 4,830 filed for investigation were dismissed after further inquiry. The commission's effectiveness was greatly hampered by the courts, which denied the FTC the right to define the specific meaning of "unfair methods of competition," and by large business interests which denied the commission access to their records. Many conservative congressmen also condemned the agency's investigative methods and findings, beginning with its vigorous probe of the meat-packing industry in 1919, and subjected it to repeated political attack.

The FTC, then, made little progress in stopping unfair competition except in instances that would have been outlawed by the courts if the FTC Act had never been passed. These cases had only a minor effect in preventing the growth of industrial concentration in the 1920s.

The year 1925 was a critical turning point in the early history of the FTC. As a result of a change in its membership and leadership from a Progressive to a conservative majority during the administration of President Calvin Coolidge, it experienced a drastic transformation of its basic purposes and practices, thereby becoming the subject of serious concern, reevaluation, and controversy among government officials, politicians, consumers, and businessmen. This controversy, occasioned by the appointment of William E. Humphrey as chairman, in February 1925, culminated in a remarkable reversal in the roles of the agency's former allies and enemies. Businessmen overnight became staunch defenders of the commission, as it completely reoriented its activities to conform to the prevailing pattern of "normalcy," whereas Progressives united in attacking it and even in demanding its abolition.

The controversial change in the personnel of the FTC foreshadowed a still more significant transformation of its rules of policy and procedure. Under Humphrey's guiding influence, investigations were confined strictly to those cases that included definite allegations of unfair practices harmful to the public interest. The commission further decided to resolve most of its cases through stipulation rather than through the costlier, more time-consuming process of formal action. Defendants also were given the opportunity to present their arguments informally, and without publicity, in a preliminary hearing before a board of review. Finally, in 1926, Humphrey established the trade practice conference division within the FTC to encourage industrial self-regulation.

These procedural changes marked a sharp departure from the Wilsonian ideal of strict regulation to a more trusting, more cooperative attitude toward business. The Progressives, fearful that the commission might now do more harm than good, attempted unsuccessfully to persuade Congress either to restrict its activities or to abolish it altogether. It was not until the election of Franklin D. Roosevelt and the advent of the New Deal that Humphrey was forced to resign as chairman after a bitter fight. But, during the National Recovery Administration* (NRA) period of 1933-1935, antitrust went into an eclipse, and so did the FTC. Roosevelt allowed the commission to sink into a swamp of political cronyism, making it a fiefdom of the "Tennessee Gang" led by Memphis political boss Ed Crump and Senator Kenneth M. McKellar, chairman of the appropriations subcommittee with jurisdiction over regulatory agencies.

After the Supreme Court declared the NRA unconstitutional in 1935, the Roosevelt Administration renewed antitrust activity and revitalized the FTC. Congress, in 1936, passed the Robinson-Patman Act as an amendment to the Clayton Act of 1914. It was designed to counter price concessions to large buyers, especially chain stores like A&P; enforcement was vested in the FTC. The commission's appropriations also were increased, and its forays into consumer protection gained favor. Prohibition of deceptive advertising was becoming the most generally approved of FTC functions by the courts. FTC economists also played an active role in the investigations of the Temporary National Economic Committee (TNEC), which Congress had set up in 1938, at the request of the President, to study the concentration of economic power and its "detrimental consequences." The FTC's earlier studies served as the foundation for the TNEC's final reports on the basing point problem, the natural gas industry, and the relative efficiency of large, medium, and small businesses.

Toward the close of the 1930s, Congress again enlarged the FTC's jurisdiction in response to a series of adverse court decisions. In 1938, it passed the Wheeler-Lea Act, which reflected a growing preoccupation with unfair and fraudulent trade practices in contrast to the earlier emphasis on antitrust. In 1939, it followed up with the Wool Products Labeling Act, which authorized, for the first time, the FTC to draw up substantive rules governing practices in a particular industry. Congress further indicated its approval of this specialized form of regulation in the 1950s by adding the Fur Products Labeling Act, the Flammable Fabrics Act, and the Textile Fiber Products Identification Act. Congress then increased the forcefulness of FTC cease-and-desist orders by legislation, in 1950, that each day of continuing violation of a final order should be deemed a separate violation. The anti-merger section of the Clayton Act was strengthened when Congress passed the Cellar-Kefauver Act (1950), which prohibited mergers through purchases of assets rather than of stock. The agency's jurisdiction over interstate commerce also was enhanced in the 1950s by a series of court decisions that brought many local activities within the scope of the commission.

Following World War II, the FTC continued its involvement in consumer protection but tended to deemphasize a prosecutorial approach to antitrust. Both Earl W. Kintner, President Dwight D. Eisenhower's chairman, and his successor, Paul Rand Dixon, chairman of the commission during the Kennedy-Johnson administrations, attempted to pursue a middle course by combining industry guidance with voluntary procedures, and reserving litigation for the few. Dixon, especially, placed improvement of FTC-business relations high on his list of priorities, as he tried to make the FTC the servant of the legitimate business community as well as the consumer. But Dixon's policies seemed to be out of step with the mood of the nation. President Kennedy's words and actions before his assassination had encouraged a great release of critical energy throughout American society. A new literature of protest examined hitherto sacrosanct corners of American life, freely assailing such national idols as television, the cigarette, the pesticide, billboards, the funeral parlor, the automobile, and the brand-name drug. The outpouring of social criticism quickly engulfed the FTC.

Criticism of the FTC, in fact, had been an integral part of the agency's history since Gerard C. Henderson, in 1924, first evaluated its contributions to the development of substantive law and procedure. Henderson had noted then that the commission's record was one of failure in cases involving tieing clauses and contracts for exclusive dealing. In cases involving trade discounts, its judgments had been overruled by the courts, and, in cases involving price cutting, it had made little effort to grapple with the difficult questions of law and accounting involved. Henderson's criticism of the FTC for concentrating on trivia, failing to set priorities, and professional incompetence became a recurrent theme in the agency's history.

The major criticism of the FTC has been that it has been out of step with the mood of the nation. In 1949, a Hoover Commission* task force found the agency's record "disappointing." Conceding that it had been hampered by insufficient funds, hostile court decisions, and mediocre appointments, it nonetheless concluded that the commission had become bogged down in bureaucratic red tape, had failed to probe into new areas of anticompetitive practices, and had fallen far short of achieving its statutory objectives. Two reports submitted by Tennessee Congressman Estes Kefauver of the House Small Business Committee, in 1949 and 1951, came to essentially similar conclusions. In 1960, former FTC Commissioner James M. Landis, serving as chairman of the Twentieth Century Fund's Committee on Cartels and Monopoly, referred to the "utter bankruptcy of the F.T.C." The deterioration had gone "beyond redemption," and Landis recommended that President-elect Kennedy wipe it out completely and start afresh.

As the consumer movement rode the crest of its wave, the FTC was derided as "the Little Old Lady of Pennsylvania Avenue." In January 1969, consumer advocate Ralph Nader's investigators issued a 185-page report that demanded the resignation of Chairman Dixon and a sweeping overhaul of the commission's practices, policies, and staff. The report asserted that Dixon had neglected his responsibilities to consumers, had favored big business, and had led the FTC into a quagmire of "political and regional cronyism." The agency, it observed, was marked by incompetence and discrimination against employment of Ivy League lawyers and blacks, and was preoccupied with trivial cases. In its conclusion, the report presented twenty-six recommendations for change, many of which were quite specific.

In spotlighting FTC deficiencies, the Nader report encouraged a majority of the commissioners to admit that the agency had been torn by internal disagreements over policies and practices. Late in 1969, Senator Edward M. Kennedy, chairman of the Subcommittee on Administrative Practice and Procedure, undertook a full-scale inquiry into the FTC. The results were revealing. Commissioner A. Everette McIntyre admitted that there had been no agreement on the public policies the agency should pursue. The issues in dispute were whether the agency should pursue industry-wide regulation rather than the conventional case-by-case approach; whether the wording of commission orders against price discrimination had really constituted an infringement upon price competition; whether the FTC should enter into consent settlements involving conglomerate mergers; whether it should move into the controversial area of racial discrimination in housing; and how much latitude should be permitted in discriminatory advertising and promotional allowances under the Robinson-Patman Act. Commissioner Philip Elman, a Kennedy appointee since 1961, criticized the commission's excessive secrecy and reluctance to support the findings of its own examiners. He believed that the FTC should not have devoted its limited resources to hard-core antitrust cases but to those susceptible to administrative expertise.

A number of the commissioners also conceded that the FTC had not been functioning effectively because of poor administrative practices which they later attempted to rectify with only partial success. Commissioners Elman, Mary Gardiner Jones, and James Nicholson argued with Chairman Dixon that the commissioners as a corporate body, rather than the chairman, had the authority to hire and fire high-ranking personnel and to exercise administrative oversight. The embattled Dixon resisted this internal revolt and lay the blame for the FTC's shortcomings squarely on the shoulders of Congress for not having funded it adequately. In his defense, Dixon pointed to the agency's attack on the tobacco industry, its crackdown on auto-tire advertising, its questioning of coffee-industry pricing policies, its enhancement of consumer protection, a number of antitrust rulings, and truth-in-lending and packaging laws which, he declared, had further broadened the work of the commission.

Dixon's defense did little to assuage critics of the FTC and of regulatory agencies in general. In May 1969, President Richard M. Nixon asked the American Bar Association (ABA) to conduct a thorough investigation of the FTC. Its sixteen-member study group, headed by future FTC Chairman Miles W. Kirkpatrick, supported the major findings of the Nader report. In September 1969, in unusually blunt language, the ABA group summarized the agency's "failure on many counts." Singled out for special criticism were professional incompetence, gross mismanagement of resources, heavy reliance on public complaints rather than taking the initiative in consumer fraud, and undue reliance on voluntary proceedings. The ABA report recommended that the commission reorient its strategy toward the detection and eradication of consumer frauds and concentrate on vulnerable groups (that is, the poor, the elderly, the uneducated). Revitalization depended heavily on the appointment of a new chairman, the report emphasized.

Nixon moved swiftly to implement the major recommendations of the ABA report, incorporating them into his program of ''consumerism in the America of the 1970s.'' He appointed a new chairman, Casper W. Weinberger, to head the FTC and asked Congress for legislation to enable the commission to proceed more vigorously against consumer abuses. Weinberger centralized control of caseload decisions in the chairman and top-bureau personnel, rid the FTC of deadwood, strengthened the field offices, and sought regulation of automobile standards and manufacturers' warranties.

After six months in office, President Nixon named Weinberger to direct the Office of Management and Budget,* which caused some concern that reform and revitalization would fail. These fears did not materialize as Nixon then appointed Kirkpatrick chairman. Kirkpatrick continued his predecessor's emphasis on consumer protection by allowing, for the first time, consumer groups to intervene in agency proceedings on behalf of the public. It was during the tenure of Kirkpatrick and his successor, Lewis Engman, that the FTC instituted proceedings against the oil (Exxon), breakfast foods (Kellogg's cereals), and document-copying (Xerox) industries.

In 1975, Congress passed a bill sending new waves of energy through the commission, again dramatically increasing its power. Called the Magnuson-Moss Act, the law enabled the FTC to set industry-wide standards of behavior. No longer did the FTC have to take on one company at a time; now it had the authority to make rules that affected broad, economic interest groups. The commission strategies now centered on those areas of the economy most affected by inflation. Between 1975 and 1979, the commission instituted twenty proceedings under the law to regulate the practices of businesses as diverse as mobile homes, companies that made over-the-counter drugs, funeral parlors, children's advertising on television, used car sales, and makers of hearing aids.

Recharged by new leadership and new laws, the FTC had thrust itself into the forefront of regulation. In so doing, it also embarked on a different approach to antitrust enforcement. In 1978, the commission allocated 59 percent of its antitrust budget to so-called structural cases that were aimed at attacking fundamental market imperfections that facilitated anticompetitive behavior among the dominant firms in an industry. Simultaneously, it deemphasized Robinson-Patman actions, that is, cases whose impact was usually to maintain small, inefficient businesses at the expense of competition. In contrast to 173 Robinson-Patman investigations initiated in 1967, the FTC approved only 6 cases in 1976.

This new stratagem, it was hoped, would yield substantial economic benefits to the consumer, particularly in the form of lower prices.

Despite this shift in emphasis, the FTC continued to encounter difficulties in prosecuting the big structural cases. For the mechanism whereby cases were selected for prosecution too often simply exacerbated bureaucratic differences. The commission's caseload, from 1970 onward, was determined by the five commissioners in consultation with the Bureau of Competition (the lawyers' unit) and the Bureau of Economics (the economists' unit). In practice, disagreements arising from competing ideologies, professional norms, and personal goals divided the economists and the lawyers. The economic staff, largely from the Chicago school, had a deep belief in the unfettered market as the solution to social and economic problems. In contrast, the lawyers had fewer qualms about government intervention and even less confidence in industry self-regulation. Moreover, since most economists hoped to return to academe, they were not inclined to advocate any kind of radical approach to economic concentration that might jeopardize their job prospects. Hence, in the opinion of the Bureau of Competition, they were all too willing to veto antitrust prosecutions. Most lawyers, on the other hand, viewed prosecutions as stepping-stones to a lucrative career with a private law firm. They were eager to try cases. Frustrated by the veto authority of the economists, the FTC, between 1972 and 1975, suffered a turnover of 89 percent of its most promising young lawyers after two years of service.

The instability of the legal staff made it extremely difficult for the FTC to prosecute successfully structural cases and called into question those critics of the 1960s who had assumed (incorrectly) that the consumer movement would spawn enough talented young lawyers in the years ahead to work in this field. Nader-like critics neglected to consider the possibility that the public concern of the late 1960s would peter out, or that the staff attorney might be concerned not so much with the social or economic benefits of structural litigation as he would be with his own career.

As the economy faltered toward the close of the 1970s and the nation's political mood became more subdued, the FTC encountered the strongest attack on its powers since its creation. Conservative critics charged that the commission had gone overboard on consumerism, that rulings by the FTC's unelected commissioners pervaded the entire spectrum of American business life, having the same impact as laws passed by Congress. That argument was increasingly persuasive because some members of Congress felt that the federal regulatory bureaucracy had slipped beyond the control of the legislative branch and talked about using a legislative veto against the agency. Their reservations were echoed by business groups which complained that FTC regulations were adding needlessly to manufacturers' and consumers' costs. The commission's supporters countered that the FTC was getting into trouble because it was doing its job too well and was being made a whipping boy for any group encumbered by federal regulation.

The controversy came to a head in the fall of 1979 when the House appropriations subcommittee, unhappy with consumer-activist Chairman Michael Pertschuk, urged the full committee and the House to slash the FTC's budget and halt the agency's investigations of the petroleum and car-manufacturing industries. This signaled a departure from the equable relationship between Congress and the FTC. It was caused by Pertschuk publicly endorsing the idea that the FTC should pursue antitrust actions against large institutions which exercised undue social and political influence as well as market power, a notion that corporate interests and many legislators viewed with alarm.

Efforts to forge a compromise between a consumer-oriented FTC, Congress, and the new conservative administration of Republican President Ronald Reagan proved unavailing. The Reagan Administration had campaigned on the pledge to ''get government off the backs of the people'' and was committed to deregulation throughout the federal bureaucracy. In February 1980, the President's budget director proposed that Congress cut $23 million from FTC funding and eliminate its antitrust activities within three years. Shortly thereafter, the deputy of the commission's consumer protection bureau and his assistant were transferred to other positions. Reagan's own choice to head the FTC, James C. Miller III, an economist and long time critic of federal regulation, left little doubt at his confirmation hearing that there would be a major change of course at the FTC; it would institute fewer antitrust cases and intervene less frequently in consumer and business affairs.

In conclusion, then, among federal administrative agencies, the FTC historically was potentially one of the most powerful because of the broad discretion conferred upon it by its 1914 enabling legislation, supplemented by numerous amendments over the course of more than half a century. At the same time, it was also a little-understood body, although frequently in the spotlight and an object of controversy because of the conflicting demands made on its time and resources by Congress, the business community, and consumers.

FOR ADDITIONAL INFORMATION: The FTC's activities may be followed in the *Annual Report of the Federal Trade Commission* (1914-), supplemented by Stephanie W. Kanwit's *Federal Trade Commission* (1980), a volume in the Regulatory Manual Series that explains both the powers of the agency and the numerous acts it administers. The FTC also was the subject of a twenty-five-and fifty-year symposium. See S. Chesterfield Oppenheim, ed., ''The Federal Trade Commission Silver Anniversary Issue,'' *The George Washington Law Review* 8 (1940); and Milton Handler, ed., ''The Fiftieth Anniversary of the Federal Trade Commission,'' *Columbia Law Review* 64 (1964). The first general survey of the FTC emphasizing its contribution to administrative law is Gerard C. Henderson's *The Federal Trade Commission* (1924); more up-to-date is the sympathetic but not uncritical account by Susan Wagner, *The Federal Trade Commission* (1971). The Progressive origins of the FTC are well covered in G. Cullom Davis, ''The Transformation of the Federal Trade Commission, 1914-1929,'' *Mississippi Valley Historical Review* 49 (December 1962): 437-455; Alan Stone, *Economic Regulation in the Public Interest: The Federal Trade Commission in Theory and Practice* (1977); and Thomas C. Blaisdell, Jr., *The Federal Trade Commission* (1932). The commission's difficulties in litigating structural cases in the 1970s are clearly discussed in the excellent work of Robert A. Katzmann, *Regulatory Bureaucracy: The Federal Trade Commission and Antitrust Policy* (1980).

There is no shortage of material critical of the FTC. Beginning with the Nader report, Edward Cox, et al., *The Consumer and the Federal Trade Commission* (1969); the most significant are: U.S. Congress, House, Committee on Interstate and Foreign Commerce, Subcommittee on Oversight and Investigations, *Hearings on Regulatory Reform*, 94th Cong., 2d Sess. (1976); *Report of the American Bar Association Commission to Study the Federal Trade Commission* (1969); Commission on Organization of the Executive Branch of the Government, *Task Force Report on Regulatory Commissions* 125 (1949); U.S. Congress, Senate, Committee on the Judiciary, *Report on Regulatory Agencies to the President-Elect*, 86th Cong., 2d Sess. (1960).

PHILIP J. FUNIGIELLO

FISH AND WILDLIFE SERVICE. See United States Fish and Wildlife Service.

FOOD AND DRUG ADMINISTRATION (FDA). In 1927, the Congress, in an appropriations bill, created the Food, Drug, and Insecticide Administration to enforce the Food and Drugs Act of 1906 and other protective laws. The 1906 statute had given enforcement authority to the Bureau of Chemistry of the Department of Agriculture,* which had maintained its previous research functions. As costs of regulation mounted, money for research grew tight. The Secretary of Agriculture hoped that appropriations for each function might increase if administratively separated. The Congress accepted the Secretary's suggestion. Three years later, Congress abbreviated the name to Food and Drug Administration.

Congress had banned the importation of adulterated drugs in 1848 but did not become exercised about a pure food issue until 1886. Then a spirited debate raged between farm interests, championing butter, and spokesmen for that new, allegedly counterfeit, product, oleomargarine. A tax was placed on margarine, which was not removed until 1950. In the meantime, in 1879, the first broad bill was introduced into the Congress aimed at protecting an increasingly urbanized American public from the growing problem of adulteration in the processed foods upon which their diet was ever more dependent.

With a wide range of interest groups concerned, getting congressional agreement to specific provisions of a broad bill took more than a quarter-century. The more reputable wing of food processors favored a law, plagued by competition from adulterators who could sell at cut-rate prices. Unable to bring order from chaos by actions in the private sector, the threatened businessmen turned—through the medium of their trade associations—to the national government for help in maintaining marketplace stability. A national law might also serve as a model to bring harmony among divergent state laws. As one jam-maker complained, they all had to manufacture differently for each state.

Farm groups, also imperiled competitively, favored a law, as did state agricultural chemists whose exposures of adulteration alarmed both farmers and the broader public. Professional groups, like the physicians leading the revitalized American Medical Association, wanted a law to control hazards in patent medicines. The General Federation of Women's Clubs took up the pure food crusade. So, too, with the new century, did muckraking journalists.

Harvey W. Wiley served as the prime mover in forging this disparate group into a coalition. Physician and chemist, state chemist of Indiana, Wiley had gone to Washington in 1883 as chief chemist in the Department of Agriculture. His continuing study of foods revealed the extent of adulteration, which for some years he deemed a fraud, but not one posing harm to health. His so-called Poison Squad experiments in the first years of the new century, in which young governmental employees ate fare containing chemical preservatives, changed Wiley's mind about danger. By this time, his coalition had gained considerable strength, led in the Congress by men elected from the agrarian West. Twice broad bills passed the House, only to be bottled up in the Senate by parliamentary maneuver. Proprietary medicine manufacturers, whiskey rectifiers, and processors dependent on preservatives appeared to be the most potent behind-the-scenes forces thwarting action.

Public alarm at the unhygienic conditions in Chicago's meat-packing plants, revealed in Upton Sinclair's novel, *The Jungle*, and confirmed by governmental investigation, finally pushed both a meat-inspection law and the Food and Drugs Act through the Congress. President Theodore Roosevelt, at last aroused, lent Wiley and his allies crucial assistance.

The law forbade adulteration and misbranding of foods and drugs in interstate commerce. Except for ensuring cleanliness, the law did not explicitly ban ingredients. Requiring some ingredient listing, it left things to the prudence of consumers. Much voluntary improvement to conform to the law's provisions followed its enactment. Wiley's Bureau of Chemistry cleaned up unprocessed foods, especially milk, eggs, poultry, oysters, and wheat, and acted against the most frequently adulterated botanical drugs. Such regulation mainline business appreciated. But business did not want a crusading enforcement of the law, which was exactly what Wiley had in mind. He aroused strong protests when he sought to bar the preservative sodium benzoate from catsup, to ban saccharin from canned corn, and to eliminate sulphur dioxide in the drying of fruit. Complaints from both farmers and processors disturbed both the Secretary of Agriculture and President Roosevelt, who set up review committees to curtail Wiley's independence. Frustrated, in 1912 he angrily resigned.

With the flamboyant chemist's departure, the regulation of food and drugs and the enforcing agency virtually disappeared from the headlines and from significant public awareness for half a century. Walter Campbell, whom Wiley had chosen as his chief inspector, emerged as the dominant figure in enforcement policy, his concepts prevailing through more than the next five decades. Under Wiley's successors, Campbell put regulation on an unpublicized but more systematized, workaday basis, creating a project system with priorities that concentrated resources on major abuses. For example, Campbell intensified a campaign Wiley had launched against hazardous patent medicines, a campaign curtailed in 1911 by a Supreme Court decision declaring that the law's ban on false and misleading labeling did not apply to therapeutic claims. Congress plugged the loophole partially in 1912, barring therapeutic promises that were "false and fraudulent." Campbell moved against the most egregious quackery. Modest appropriations from the Congress plus the pro-business climate of the 1920s led Campbell, who himself became director in 1927, to stress voluntary enforcement with mainline businesses, cooperating with trade associations to educate food and drug processors into improving their technology. This stance brought criticism from spokesmen for consumers, as in Arthur Kallet and F. J. Schlink's *100,000,000 Guinea Pigs*, published in 1933.

The year 1933 also brought the New Deal and, in the new climate, produced an effort by Campbell and his aides to secure a new law that would remedy weaknesses they had long recognized in the 1906 statute. After a five-year legislative course, involving compromises to satisfy powerful interests, the Federal Food, Drug, and Cosmetic Act of 1938 became law. The push for the law received significant support from another President Roosevelt only in the final stages, and again required a shocking threat to the public health to ensure success. FDA's most faithful ally during the legislative struggle proved to be a coalition of women's organizations. The catastrophe in this case involved sulfanilamide, a wonder drug from Europe, which produced many marvelous recoveries—including that of Franklin D. Roosevelt's son—from hitherto fatal infections. The trouble lay not in the drug itself but in the solvent, the poisonous diethylene glycol, employed without toxicity testing in a liquid dosage form of sulfanilamide marketed by a small manufacturer. The solvent killed more than a hundred people before the drug could be tracked down and confiscated.

The 1938 act—which remains the nation's basic governing statute—considerably expanded consumer protection. It increased the minimal penalties of the 1906 law and added to the law's seizure and criminal sanctions the power of injunction. Foods harmful to health could be better controlled, and labeling could be made more informative. The FDA was empowered to establish food standards that had the effect of law, parallel to the 1906 act's declaring official the drug standards contained in private reference volumes, the *United States Pharmacopoeia*, and the *National Formulary*. Cosmetics and therapeutic devices came under control for the first time. FDA was authorized to make factory inspections. The government need no longer prove fraudulent intent on the part of the maker or false therapeutic claims in proprietary medicine labeling. False labeling was defined so as to extend beyond erroneous positive statements, to encompass failure to provide adequate warnings. A section of the new law directly prompted by the "Elixir Sulfanilamide" disaster required a manufacturer to convince FDA of a new drug's safety before it could be marketed.

FDA shouldered its expanded mandate just as it accepted added drug-testing burdens made necessary in a nation at war. The agency aimed the new law's provisions at curbing the most dangerous abuses involving foods, proprietary drugs, health devices, and cosmetics. Yet, problems proliferated faster than FDA could come to grips with all of them satisfactorily. Proud of the value given the public in return for the modest appropriations granted the agency, Campbell and his successor, Paul B. Dunbar (1944-1951), did not aggressively seek expanded funds. Sometimes, indeed, regulatory actions offended powerful members of Congress with unfortunate results. In 1953, while Charles W. Crawford (1951-1954), another of the up-from-the-ranks dynasty, served as commissioner, the chairman of the House Appropriations Committee, angered at an advisory opinion given to one of his constituents by FDA, cut the agency's budget by about 10 percent. FDA had termed illegal the selling of small beet balls, carved from big beets, because consumers might mistake them for tender baby beets. In 1955, FDA had fewer personnel than it had had in 1941.

The technological revolution, which made necessary the 1906 law, had never ceased expanding, and a new and more vigorous phase began concurrently with the campaign for the 1938 law. Sulfanilamide, the bellwether of a chemotherapeutic revolution, had been responsible for that law's "new drug" provision, which provided a crucial entry barrier to the marketplace, guarded by FDA, which hundreds of new therapeutic agents following sulfanilamide had to confront. Great benefits were bestowed upon humankind by the new drugs, but experience was to reveal that the law's barrier was insufficient to protect the public health. Simultaneously, a chemogastric revolution burgeoned. The old lead and arsenic insecticides were replaced by a new generation of chlorinated carbon and organic phosphorus pesticides, and potent herbicides also came into use. In food processing, the simple preservatives that worried Wiley were succeeded by a vast and complex array of additives that moved from chemical laboratories into food production lines. These changes permitted agriculture to become much more productive and preserved processed food from bacterial contamination, as well as enhancing its palatability. But the chemogastric revolution also posed grave problems, the perplexing and threatening nature of which only gradually emerged.

FDA's plight in the 1950s worried Crawford and his successor in the agency's dynasty of leadership, George P. Larrick (1954-1965). They asked their superiors in the Department of Health, Education and Welfare* (HEW) for help in seeking public support to strengthen the agency. (FDA had left Agriculture in 1940 when the Federal Security Agency was created and had gone on to HEW in 1953.) Mainline business also feared turmoil in the marketplace, which a too weak FDA might permit. The Republican administration appointed a Citizens' Advisory Committee in 1955, which recommended that FDA shift its emphasis from punitive enforcement to voluntary compliance, striving to educate manufacturers into more knowledgeable and better law-abiding behavior. The committee also suggested an enhancement of FDA's in-house scientific capability and urged Congress to begin a progressive increase in appropriations to FDA. A second citizens' committee in 1961 made similar recommendations.

Congress responded by steadily adding to FDA's budget, a fifty-fold increase between 1955 and 1979, when the sum exceeded $300 million. But Congress also kept expanding the agency's tasks. In 1951-1952, a select committee of the House, chaired by James J. Delaney, held extensive hearings at which a host of witnesses gave their judgments on how to handle problems arising from chemicals in food and cosmetics. From these and later hearings came in due course three major laws: the Pesticide Chemicals Act (1954), the Food Additives Amendment (1958), and the Color Additives Amendment (1960). This legislation followed the 1938 act's "new drug" clause precedent, and subsequent measures requiring batch testing by FDA of insulin and antibiotics before their release, toward a system of preventive law. Proof of safety prior to marketing became the rule. The 1958 law exempted food additives which were "generally recognized as safe" by appropriate authorities. But Congressman Delaney included in this law a clause, which has since borne his name prohibiting any use of a food additive that is found to cause cancer in man or experimental animal.

An extension of the preventive principle became the key feature of the Kefauver-Harris Drug Amendments of 1962. Beginning in late 1959, Senator Estes Kefauver conducted hearings at which academic scientists presented their sober second thoughts about the floodtide of miracle drugs. Overuse and inappropriate use of the powerful agents accelerated statistics of therapeutic misadventure. Manufacturers were accused of promoting drugs to physicians with more enthusiasm than candor. FDA was criticized for inadequacy in policing the drug marketplace. A new catastrophe, which mainly might-have-been in the United States, again moved the Congress to action on a law. Thalidomide, a sedative drug widely distributed in Europe, turned out, when used in pregnancy, to possess terrible teratogenic potential. A physician at FDA prevented all but preliminary distribution in the United States; nonetheless, public opinion became alarmed. The 1962 law expanded the purpose of premarket testing beyond safety to include the requirement that efficacy for conditions listed in labeling of drugs must also be proven by adequate and well-controlled trials. The law also increased FDA's authority to set standards for good manufacturing practices and gave the agency control over pharmaceutical promotion, henceforth required to tell the bad news as well as the good.

Kefauver was a master at creating publicity. The headlines from his hearings ended the obscurity in which food and drug regulators had largely rested since Wiley's departure from office. Since Kefauver, other members of the Senate and House have continued to keep FDA affairs under a glaring spotlight. Journalists found food and drug hazards alluring copy. These hazards took their place within a broad spectrum of environmental dangers. In the year of the Kefauver law, Rachel Carson published *Silent Spring*. In 1966, the first book came from Ralph Nader's pen, marking the start of a harder-hitting, more intransigent consumerism.

The year 1966 also marked the end of FDA's dynastic system of leadership. When Commissioner Larrick retired, the HEW Secretary brought in an outsider, James L. Goddard, a physician who had directed the Public Health Service's* Communicable Disease Center, to speed and toughen up enforcement of the Kefauver law's provisions. This change inevitably politicized the commissionership, which hitherto had been immune to party shifts in the White House. Since 1966, commissioners have held office for shorter terms. These changes, several internal reorganizations, the expanding size of the agency, and the complexity of its regulatory problems put stress upon decision-making. FDA's traditional status of virtual independence from superior departmental authority somewhat declined.

Nonetheless, while the flavor of decisions about problems might differ to a degree depending upon the party in power, at base the problems with which FDA wrestled were apolitical. A large portion of the agenda involved an effort to assess risk or to balance risk against benefit, especially with respect to drugs and food additives. Such tasks became incredibly time-consuming and complex, their conclusions not always clear-cut. Indeed, as FDA spokesmen asserted, the methodology available, despite great advances in which FDA scientists played important innovative roles, might not yet be sufficiently sophisticatd to provide the public policy answers which society required. Sanford A. Miller, director of FDA's bureau of foods, noted in 1979 that in its debates over the safety of food the scientific community was using nineteenth-century testing methods to interpret data predicated on twentieth-century understanding of life processes.

By the 1970s, besides applying the Kefauver efficacy provision to the admission of new drugs, FDA had retroactively assessed for efficacy drugs admitted between 1938 and 1962. A debate raged about whether a falling off of new drug entities entering the marketplace resulted from undue caution in FDA's reviewing process. FDA began a restudy of the safety and efficacy of all over-the-counter medicines. Also launched was a restudy of food additives. Some FDA decisions, like the banning of cyclamates and of saccharin, provoked considerable reaction. So great was business pressure with respect to saccharin that, in 1977, the Congress stayed FDA's regulatory hand. Congress also yielded to lobbying from health food advocates in passing Vitamin Amendments in 1976 that eliminated much of FDA's authority to control vitamins, minerals, and other food supplements. Curtailing FDA's power marked a new congressional posture.

At the same time, the Congress continued to expand FDA's responsibilities. Especially significant were the transfer in 1972 to FDA from the National Institute of Health of control over serums, vaccines, and other biological products, and the enactment of a law in 1976 applying the preventive principle to medical devices. During the late 1970s, a law that would completely restructure the nation's drug regulation received much attention from business, from FDA, and from the Congress. Increasing awareness of subtle risks seemed to demand a new law defining anew the scope of FDA's mission. As Commissioner Donald Kennedy (1977-1979) frequently insisted, the people's representatives in the Congress, not an administrative agency, should bear the obligation of deciding what risks citizens should involuntarily assume.

The range of FDA's workaday concerns—the content of food labeling, nitrites in bacon, aflatoxins in milk, the status of red food dyes, the contamination of crabs, patient package inserts for prescription drugs, the growth-promoter DES in animal foods, the labeling of blood for transfusions, safety standards for mercury vapor lamps, the unorthodox cancer treatment laetrile, to cite a few examples—extends far beyond compact summary. The agency's priorities may be suggested by the allocation of funds in FDA's 1979 budget (in percentages): food safety, 28; human drugs, 23; program management, 13; medical devices, 11; biologics, 7; radiological health, 7; animal drugs and feeds, 6; National Center for Toxicological Research, 5; food economics, 1; and cosmetics, 1.

FOR ADDITIONAL INFORMATION: FDA records for the earlier period form Record Group 88 under the custody of the National Archives* and are housed in the Washington National Records Center; some later records, still under FDA jurisdiction, may be made available to historical scholars through FDA's Office of Legislative Affairs, Rockville, Maryland. Bureau of Chemistry and FDA Annual Reports provide a useful entry to FDA's history. The Food Law Institute reprinted *Administrative Reports, 1907-1949* (1951), and W. F. Janssen compiled *Annual Reports, 1950-1974* (1976). An index to Janssen's volume has been prepared by Edward Shoemaker. The Food Law Institute also has compiled a series, *Federal Food, Drug, and Cosmetic Act*, containing mainly court decisions stemming from the law. A basic list of secondary material could include J. H. Young, " 'This Greasy Counterfeit': Butter Versus Oleomargarine in the United States Congress, 1886," *Bulletin of the History of Medicine* 53 (1979); Young, *The Toadstool Millionaires: A Social History of Patent Medicines in America Before Federal Regulation* (1961); O. E. Anderson, Jr., *The Health of a Nation: Harvey W. Wiley and the Fight for Pure Food* (1958); Anderson, Young, and Janssen, "The Government and the Consumer: Evolution of Food and Drug Laws," *Journal of Public Law* 13 (1964); Young, "The Science and Morals of Metabolism: Catsup and Benzoate of Soda," *Journal of the History of Medicine* 23 (1968); Young, "Botulism and the Ripe Olive Scare of 1919-1920," *Bulletin of the History of Medicine* 50 (1976); Young, *The Medical Messiahs: A Social History of Health Quackery in Twentieth-Century America* (1967); Young, *American Self-Dosage Medicines* (1974); Paul Talalay, ed., *Drugs in Our Society* (1964); H. F. Dowling, *Medicines for Man* (1970); Milton Silverman and P. R. Lee, *Pills, Profits, and Politics* (1974); Peter Temin, *Taking Your Medicine: Drug Regulation in the United States* (1980); R. D. Lamb, *American Chamber of Horrors* (1936); J. B. Blake, ed., *Safeguarding the Public: Historical Aspects of Medicinal Drug Control* (1970); C. O. Jackson, *Food and Drug Legislation in the New Deal* (1970); Richard Harris, *The Real Voice* (1964); R. E. McFadyen, "Thalidomide in America," *Clio Medica* 11 (1976); McFadyen, "The FDA's Regulation and Control of Antibiotics in the 1950s," *Bulletin of the History of Medicine* 53 (1979); J. S. Turner, *The Chemical Feast* (1970); P. J. Quirk, "Food and Drug Administration," in J. Q. Wilson, ed., *The Politics of Regulation* (1980); W. F. Janssen, "The U.S. Food and Drug Law: How It Came; How it Works," *Food, Drug, Cosmetic Law Journal* 35 (1980); R. E. Miles, Jr., *The Department of H.E.W.* (1974); S. A. Miller, "The New Metaphysics," (1979 speech); the files of *Food, Drug, Cosmetic Law Journal* and *FDA Consumer*.

JAMES HARVEY YOUNG

FOREST SERVICE. The Forest Service evolved from interest in the preservation, management, and proper development and use of federal forest lands. Interest in forest preservation became increasingly evident during the third quarter of the nineteenth century. More appeals were made for some kind of public action to halt widespread destruction of American forests. In 1864, George P. Marsh, an American diplomat and extensive traveler, in a provocative book,

Man and Nature, declared: "It is certain that a desolation like that which has overwhelmed many once beautiful and fertile regions of Europe, awaits an important part of the territory of the United States, unless prompt measures are taken to check the action of destructive causes already in operation." A few years later there began a tree planting movement, from which in 1872 emerged the popular "Arbor Day" idea. Meanwhile, the federal government in 1873 enacted the Timber Culture Law, which aimed to encourage forestation by requiring the planting and successful growing of a certain number of trees as the consideration of a deed to a quarter-section of the public domain. In the same year, a committee of the American Association for the Advancement of Science asked Congress to appoint a commissioner to conduct forest investigations. Congress responded in 1876 by appropriating $2,000 for a study of forest conditions in the United States by an official to be appointed by the commissioner of agriculture. Dr. Franklin B. Hough, superintendent of the U.S. Census of 1870, was appointed to conduct the forest study. In this modest way, federal forest work began.

In a series of reports, Hough pointed out the detrimental effects of forest destruction and found support of his ideas by the American Forestry Association, which in the 1870s began to advocate greater government action to preserve forests. Hough's reports and increased public concern for the forests led to the creation in 1881 of a Division of Forestry in the Department of Agriculture,* which was authorized to study forest conditions and disseminate forest information on a continuing basis. The stature and influence of the division increased with the appointment in 1886 as its chief Bernhard E. Fernow, a leader of the American Forestry Association, who had been trained in forestry in his native Germany. Under his direction, the division initiated limited assistance in timber testing, tree measurement, and identification of tree specimens, and offered occasional informational service to state and private forest owners. Studies of Hough and Fernow and the views of a growing number of public-spirited Americans indicated that public forests represented a great but vulnerable national asset that should be protected from reckless use. Accordingly, Congress in 1891 was influenced to authorize the President to withdraw portions of the public domain and designate them as "forest reserves." With this authority during the next six years, Presidents Benjamin Harrison and Grover Cleveland set aside some 39 million acres of reserves.

Although much of the stimulus for creating the reserves had come from the Division of Forestry, headed by a trained forester (Fernow), this unit was not placed in charge of the reserves. Instead, they were placed under the control of the General Land Office of the Department of the Interior,* which employed no trained foresters (except Filibert Roth in 1901 and 1902) and had no effective plans for protecting and managing the reserves. This ironical situation was strongly criticized by Gifford Pinchot, who became head of the Division of Forestry in 1898. America's first native professional forester, Pinchot, with the support of President Theodore Roosevelt, strove to influence Congress to change this situation. He was successful in 1905, when legislation was enacted authorizing the transfer of control of the reserves to his unit, which had grown considerably since 1881 and had been renamed the Bureau of Forestry in 1901. Soon after the transfer, the bureau was designated "Forest Service," and two years later the reserves were renamed "national forests." The new agency decentralized administration of field work by establishing district offices with authority to handle forest work within their respective areas.

The newly created Forest Service launched a varied program of forestry on some 63 million acres of national forests in fifteen states and territories. This program came during one of the great crusades of the twentieth century, a movement for the conservation of forests and other natural resources led by Pinchot and enthusiastically supported by Theodore Roosevelt. Meanwhile, the Forest Service adopted the principle that the best use of the forests should be to provide the greatest good for the greatest number over the long run. This concept was the forerunner of the multiple-use and sustained-yield principles which were to become more firmly established during later years of Forest Service administration. In accordance with the concept, the agency developed a timber-management program which provided for the sale of mature timber wherever there was demand for it and silvicultural considerations permitted its cutting. Accompanying the concern for prevention of destructive cutting, there was a systematic effort to protect the national forests against the menace of forest fires.

At the same time, under a new policy of range management, the Forest Service prohibited unrestricted use of national forests for grazing-range livestock and established a system of controlled use that gave priority to those users longest established on the ranges and most dependent on their grazing resources. Pinchot contended that timber and range management policies should stress conservative and regulated use, and this emphasis became a key element in federal forest policy. There also emerged in the Pinchot era a program of forest research, which included varied studies in silviculture and forest economics. The Forest Service in 1908 began the establishment of forest experiment stations which were to become important centers for the solution of forest and related range problems in various regions of the United States. To these research efforts was added in 1910 the Forest Products Laboratory at Madison, Wisconsin, which has become the world's outstanding institution for the scientific study of wood and its uses.

Many individuals and groups in the Western states opposed the extension of the national forest system under Forest Service administration. They contended that national forests tended to restrict mining and agriculture, since they caused large areas of the public domain to be withdrawn from settlement and unregulated use. They also maintained that national forest timber sales promoted competition with private lumbering and that the forests obstructed the building of plants for generating cheaper power and light for industrial and domestic purposes and caused large portions of land to be withdrawn from state taxation. Moreover, they held that fees for forest uses imposed burdens on the development of natural resources.

This criticism of the national forest system influenced Congress in 1907 to prohibit any further additions to national forests in Oregon, Washington, Idaho, Montana, Colorado, and Wyoming, without the consent of Congress. Other states were later added to this prohibition. Critics of the national forest system also won another concession in 1908, when Congress stipulated that states in which national forests are located should receive 25 percent of the receipts from the forest uses for allocation to schools and roads in counties where the forests were situated.

Pinchot's conflict with the Secretary of the Interior, Richard Ballinger, over the management of public lands in Alaska and his dismissal from the Forest Service, in 1910, by President William Howard Taft were highly publicized events that did not adversely affect the general growth of the Forest Service and its work. This growth was importantly stimulated by the Weeks Act of 1911, which authorized the purchase for national forests of private lands considered necessary to the protection of the flow of navigable streams. Such lands were mainly east of the Great Plains, where there was left little of the public domain. This law also established a program of federal-state cooperation in fire protection. The Clarke-McNary Act of 1924 expanded the Weeks Act by authorizing the purchase of lands needed for the production of timber and agreements with the states for the protection of state-owned and private lands against fire. This act was also significant in that it represented a compromise in a controversy after World War I between persons favoring federal regulation of forest operations on private lands and persons opposing such regulation. William B. Greeley, then chief of the Forest Service, favored federal-state cooperation in forest protection and management rather than federal regulation, and was the chief architect of the program established by the Clarke-McNary Act. The program continues today as a cornerstone in federal-state cooperative forestry.

Also in 1924 there began an extensive wilderness and primitive area system of the Forest Service with the setting aside of a 1-million acre tract in the Gila National Forest in New Mexico. Many other tracts of land were added to the system in later years. Under the McSweeney-McNary Act of 1928, the Forest Service launched a comprehensive program of forest research, which led to the establishment of more federal forest and range experiment stations to conduct studies in timber, range, wildlife, and watershed management; and in fire control and forest economics. The act also authorized a nationwide survey of forest resources, which has become an important continuing activity of the Forest Service.

The role of the service expanded during the New Deal era, especially as the principal technical cooperating agency with the Civilian Conservation Corps* (CCC). During the operation of the CCC program (1933-1942), the Forest Service planned and supervised the work of more than a million young men engaged in tree planting; collecting tree seeds and seedlings; fighting forest fires and tree pests; and improving forest recreational facilities. Meanwhile, in the Prairie States Forestry Project (1935-1942), the service cooperated with farmers in the Dakotas, Nebraska, Kansas, Oklahoma, and northern Texas in planting strips of trees to lessen drought conditions, protect crops and livestock, reduce dust storms, and provide useful employment. Also during the 1930s, unsuccessful efforts were made by Secretary of the Interior Harold Ickes to have the Forest Service transferred to his department, which was proposed to be renamed the Department of Conservation.

During World War II, the Forest Service was called upon for many special jobs, such as surveys of war requirements and supplies of forest products, production of guayule and other rubber-bearing plants, a large-scale logging project in Alaska for the production of urgently needed aircraft spruce, manning of lookout stations as part of the U.S. Army aircraft warning system, surveys of forest product resources in Latin America, and war-related studies at the Forest Products Laboratory. Also during the war years Earle H. Clapp and Lyle F. Watts, heads of the Forest Service, promoted the idea of federal regulation of private timber cutting to protect the nation's timber resources against abuse. Their efforts failed to obtain federal regulatory legislation, but they helped to stimulate enactment of regulatory measures in Oregon, Maryland, Massachusetts, Minnesota, California, and Washington. The Cooperative Forest Fire Prevention Campaign, organized early during the war, produced in 1945 the Forest Service's famous Smokey Bear symbol, which became one of the best known advertising symbols in the United States.

After the war, the agency's activities continued to expand. Under the Cooperative Forest Management Act of 1950, it strengthened its cooperative programs to give direct technical assistance to private forest owners and processors of forest products. The Forest Service began to play a greater role in international forestry affairs. In 1957, it launched a five-year program to improve and expand recreational facilities in national forests. The passage of the Multiple Use-Sustained Yield Act in 1960 gave legislative sanction to a long-standing Forest Service policy of administering national forest resources for multiple use and sustained yield of their several products and services. Similarly, the Wilderness Act of 1964 provided endorsement of early agency policy for creating wilderness and primitive areas. With the increase of environmental concern during the 1970s, the agency was forced to assess more carefully the impact of timber clearcutting and environmental effects of all of its operations. The Forest and Rangeland Renewable Resources Planning Act of 1974, a landmark legislative measure, has stimulated Forest Service planning activity by requiring the agency to make periodic analyses of present and anticipated uses, demands for, and supply of renewable forest and range resources. The act represented the first congressional recognition that management of natural resources can be fully efficient probably only when planning and funding are done on a long-range, not year-to-year, basis.

The organizational structure of the Forest Service has not changed greatly over the years. The agency has a central authority in Washington, D.C., that operates through a decentralized organization and inspection system to ensure application of uniform principles in the field. It has three major program areas: national forest administration, state and private forestry, and research. The field activities of the first two program areas are supervised by ten regional offices, and those of the third area are conducted through eight forest and range experiment stations, the Forest Products Laboratory, and the Institute of Tropical Forestry. The agency manages 154 national forests and 19 national grasslands, comprising 188 million acres in 41 states and Puerto Rico.

FOR ADDITIONAL INFORMATION: The most useful single publication concerning the history of the Forest Service is Harold K. Steen, *The U. S. Forest Service: A History* (1976). Many details concerning the agency's history are presented by Frank E. Smith, ed., *Conservation in the United States: A Documentary History*, 5 vols. (1971). Varied aspects of Forest Service history are found in Henry Clepper, *Professional Forestry in the United States* (1971); Samuel T. Dana, *Forest and Range Policy* (1956); Samuel P. Hayes, *Conservation and the Gospel of Efficiency: The Progressive Conservation Movement, 1890-1920* (1959); and Harold T. Pinkett, *Gifford Pinchot: Private and Public Forester* (1970).

HAROLD T. PINKETT

FREEDMEN'S BUREAU. See Bureau of Refugees, Freedmen, and Abandoned Lands.

_G_

GENERAL ACCOUNTING OFFICE (GAO). The General Accounting Office was established in law by Title III of the Budget and Accounting Act of 1921. It was then regarded as a counterpart on behalf of Congress to the Bureau of the Budget* and budgeting process, enhancing the President's authority over the executive branch, which the act also provided for, and which drew more public attention and controversy.

Functionally, the GAO is the lineal descendant in organization and statutory authority of parts of the Treasury,* the offices of the comptroller and of the six auditors, which the 1921 act detached and consolidated under a new name and a new chief, "independent of the executive departments." The old offices had worked in obscurity, with relative autonomy, and a low-paid clerical staff, some 1,700 in number, employed in checking the legality and procedural regularity of government payments, voucher by voucher, in the course of settling the accounts of disbursing officers, by whom nearly all government payments were made, from advances entrusted to them. The comptroller was empowered to interpret any applicable statutes, and the balances he certified were "final and conclusive on the executive branch"—language repeated verbatim in the 1921 act. The new comptroller general (CG) was empowered in addition to investigate "all matters relating to the receipt, disbursement and application of public funds," and in reports to Congress to "make recommendations looking to greater economy or efficiency in public expenditures" (Sec. 312). Furthermore, he was directed to "prescribe the forms, systems, and procedures for. . .accounting in the several departments and establishments" (Sec. 309).

The 1921 act gave the comptroller general and an assistant comptroller general fixed terms (except for mandatory retirement at age seventy) of fifteen years, longer than that of any other federal (nonjudicial) officer. Their appointments required Senate confirmation, and they were made virtually irremovable; a joint resolution after notice and hearing is stipulated. (An awkwardness in the original statute emerged when the first assistant comptroller general, who "shall perform such duties as may be assigned to him by the Comptroller General, and during the absence or incapacity of the Comptroller General, or during a vacancy in that office, shall act as Comptroller General,'' retired for age in 1930. Consequently, comptrollers general inherited a statutory and irremovable assistant not of their choice. A 1969 amendment substituted an office of deputy comptroller general with a term coterminous with that of the comptroller general.) The powers of the comptroller general were to "be exercised without direction from any other officer" (Sec. 304), and he was vested with nearly complete authority to arrange and rearrange the internal organization of his agency. His salary was fixed at $10,000, the same then as that of a member of Congress.

The GAO Act of 1980, anticipating the expiration of the incumbent comptroller general's term in March 1981, and taking note of an existing vacancy in the deputy comptroller general's office, attempted to provide congressional guidance to the President in making future nominations. Whenever a vacancy in either office occurs, a commission is automatically constituted, consisting of the leadership of both parties in both chambers, to give the President a list of at least three names to consider. He can disregard them at his peril. For a vacancy in the deputy position, the comptroller general is a member of the commission.

The GAO in its first sixty years underwent three metamorphoses that transformed it practically beyond recognition. In the process, it not only moved from its original base in the Treasury* to independence of the executive departments; in 1945, it became "a part of the legislative branch," in the purposeful words of a seeming aside in the Reorganization Act of that year exempting the GAO from its scope. But for many years its appropriations were carried in the Independent Offices Appropriation Acts, its budget estimates were reviewed in the Budget Bureau, and its pay scales and personnel procedures were under the jurisdiction of the Civil Service Commission.* Not until the GAO Personnel Act of 1980 gave the agency its own system, separate but equal, in parallel with the Civil Service Reform Act of 1978, was the last of these administrative ties to the executive branch broken. But the President still appoints the comptroller general.

The transformation embraced goals, methods, and staffing, indeed, the very concept of accountability—to whom, for what, when, and by what means—on which the existence of the agency rested. Some statutory amendments in the post-World War II years—the Government Corporation Control Act of 1945, the Legislative Reorganization Acts of 1946 and 1970, the Budget and Accounting Procedures Act of 1950, the Congressional Budget and Impoundment Control Act of 1974, in particular—facilitated these changes. But the driving forces were the responses of the successive comptrollers general to great changes in conditions and in their perceptions of their jobs. The evolution of the GAO is a remarkable example of the impact of strong personalities on the organizations they head, given independence, undivided responsibility, and freedom of action in recruiting and managing the disposition of their resources.

Four comptrollers general spanned the sixty-year period 1921-1981, except for an interregnum 1936-1940. Each made his mark, and three sharply differentiated phases can be distinguished. The first of them, J. Raymond McCarl, a patronage appointee of Warren Harding's, rewarded for the successful Republican congressional campaigns in 1918, kept his inherited staff doing more vigorously what was accustomed and congenial for them. This consisted in checking the legality and procedural regularity of government payments, voucher by voucher, as already noted. Payments disapproved were disallowed in these accounts. McCarl also issued advance decisions giving restrictive interpretations to the statutes governing outlays. This was the meaning of accountability in the first GAO. It disclaimed responsibility for the wisdom or effectiveness of expenditures, or concern for the operating consequences of GAO decisions.

This course brought McCarl into frequent and abrasive confrontations with executive agencies—some politically potent, like the Veterans Bureau; others were government corporations, notably the Tennessee Valley Authority,* that claimed exemption from his jurisdiction. In 1937, as part of his larger executive reorganization proposals, President Franklin D. Roosevelt attempted to take the GAO apart, returning the voucher-checking to the Treasury and setting up a new Office of Auditor General, limited to post-audit reviews and reports to Congress—the Brownlow Committee's recommendation. This effort failed by a narrow margin in Congress in 1938, and the interregnum ensued.

The second GAO started with the appointment of Lindsay Warren in 1940, who accepted reluctantly at FDR's urgent request and on condition that attacks on the GAO cease. A popular congressman from North Carolina, Warren was devoted to making the GAO an "agent of Congress." But he recognized that the centralized voucher-checking system was overrun by the volume of transactions. World War II greatly aggravated this situation and made it plain that the auditing, whatever it was, must be decentralized to the locations of the major workloads—to Europe, to the Far East, or wherever. Taking his cue from the mandate in the Government Corporation Control Act of 1945 to perform "comprehensive audits," along commercial lines, on the transactions of these huge corporate agencies, he commenced hiring accountants on a large scale and therefore altered permanently the nature and caliber of the staff. Warren's successor, Joseph Campbell, appointed in 1954 by President Dwight D. Eisenhower (without consulting the congressional leadership), was the first accountant, a CPA who had been connected with one of the leading firms, to fill the position. Under his regime, the GAO was shaped increasingly on the model of a large accounting firm, concerned with the validity of financial statements.

The third GAO was largely the work of Elmer B. Staats, whom President Lyndon B. Johnson appointed in 1966. Staats was a Budget Bureau veteran, a public administrator by training, intimately familiar with the details of federal operations over the previous two decades. He brought a budgeter's concern for evaluating and maximizing the effectiveness of federal programs in attaining the ends for which they were established. He greatly diversified the professional qualifications of the staff to improve its capabilities to this end. He turned over to the Treasury and other agencies the voucher-checking business. He worked to improve the systems of internal financial controls in the departments, and he revived an interagency cooperative endeavor with the Treasury and the Budget Bureau (later, the Office of Management and Budget*), known as the Joint Financial Management Improvement Program, first undertaken in 1950. Above all, he concentrated on making the GAO useful to Congress.

One way of doing so is to assign GAO professionals directly, on request, to the staffs of committees or subcommittees, for limited periods on a reimbursable basis. In fiscal 1980, about ninety people were so assigned, to supply needed expertise. Another way is to furnish expert witnesses or written reports or legal opinions at committee hearings, relevant to pending legislation. In 1980, GAO witnesses appeared on 178 occasions, and 169 reports on bills were supplied.

GAO's principal method, however, is to make audits of programs, covering any agencies involved, rather than of agencies as such, and then submit "evaluative reports"—the "blue cover reports"—with recommendations based on the findings, addressed to Congress as a whole, to relevant committees, to individual members, or to the executive agencies concerned. These may be undertaken in response to requests, or the GAO may initiate them itself. In 1980, projects under way totaled 1,262, and 935 reports were issued, 714 to congressional addressees and 221 to executive agencies. About half are self-generated in the GAO.

To accomplish its work, the GAO employed approximately 5,200 people in 1980 and had a budget of about $200 million. About half the professionals were located in fifteen regional offices and in four overseas offices in Bangkok, Honolulu, Frankfurt, and Panama City. The internal organization of the GAO rests on a dozen divisions, most of them program areas such as Community and Economic Development, Energy and Minerals, Federal Personnel and Compensation, Financial and General Management, Procurement and Systems Acquisitions, and Human Resources.

Apart from these mainstream activities, the GAO continues some inherited functions. It settles claims against the United States that cannot be handled elsewhere: 6,805 claims in 1980 for $443 million. It pursues debt claims on behalf of the United States: 16,314 in 1980, and $4.7 million collected. It entertains and adjudges protests by unsuccessful bidders on government contracts. It maintains a nationwide "hot line" and special unit to receive and investigate citizen allegations of fraud and waste.

The GAO is perennially asked how much money it saves the government. In 1980 its Annual Report provided an answer. It identified an estimated savings of $3.7 billion attributable to its work. Too many intangibles enter into such calculations, however, to regard specific amounts with confidence.

In conclusion, a number of general observations are in order. First, the GAO is an institution unique to the American constitutional system. In addition to its post-auditing and reporting, it has controlling powers (to disallow expenditures and prescribe accounting systems, for example) that in any other major government are vested in the executive. This was controversial for two decades, and since then has been accepted.

Second, it is ironic that the agency's main goals have swung around 180 degrees from the first to the third GAO—from efforts to control individual expenditures to broad evaluative reports to Congress on programs. On its own volition, the GAO has made itself into the kind of agency that Roosevelt's rejected reorganization proposal, based on the Brownlow Committee report, would have made it. This means a profound change in the concept of accountability, from procedural regularity to substantive outcomes.

Third, evaluative reports are inherently subjective and often rest at bottom, whatever objective evidence or measures are offered, on essentially moral premises. Consequently, the standards of accountability the GAO is to apply are often at issue, both with the agency audited and with the congressional recipients of the report. GAO standards must be acceptable to Congress if GAO's stature is to be kept.

Fourth, it is a mark of GAO's reputation for integrity, competence, and prudence that Congress has drafted it for various odd jobs—membership on the Chrysler Loan Guarantee Board, for instance.

Fifth, access to books, records, and witnesses is fundamental to an auditor's work. The motives for denying or delaying it are manifold and manifest. The GAO Act of 1980 strengthened previous legislation by invoking the aid of the courts to enforce subpoenas from the comptroller general as against government contractors and government officials to secure disclosures of evidence.

Sixth, now that the distinctions between public and private actions and property are so blurred, and so much of the government's work is accomplished through grants and contracts, the comptroller general has perplexing choices in deciding how far, with his limited resources, to pursue the federal dollar beyond the initial payees to ultimate recipients.

Seventh, the fullest possible publicity for its reports is usually the surest method of obtaining action on GAO recommendations. It is also a sure way of discouraging future cooperation and access on the part of an agency put in the spotlight. This is a perennial dilemma for the GAO.

FOR ADDITIONAL INFORMATION: The leading work is Frederick C. Mosher, *The GAO: the Quest for Accountability in American Government* (1979). Along with a companion volume, Erasmus Kloman, ed., *Cases in Accountability* (1979), it was sponsored jointly by the comptroller general and the National Academy of Public Administration. It is authoritative, comprehensive, and especially good in tracing the historical evolution of goals and methods. It contains a bibliographical note and a selected bibliography. Joseph Pois, *Watchdog on the Potomac: A Study of the Comptroller General of the United States* (1979), was also prepared with GAO cooperation, but not sponsorship. It is informative but difficult to use. Roger L. Sperry, Timothy D. Desmond, Kathi F. McGraw, and Barbara Schmitt, *GAO 1966-1981: An Administrative History* (1981) is a thorough and discerning review of the regime of Comptroller General Staats. Richard E. Brown, *The GAO: Untapped Source of Congressional Power* (1970), deals chiefly with the GAO-TVA controversy. For many years, the only book on the GAO was Harvey C. Mansfield,

The Comptroller General: A Study in the Law and Practice of Fiscal Administration (1939); it is confined to the first GAO period. Apart from a few law review articles, other sources are almost entirely in government documents, hearings, and reports.

HARVEY C. MANSFIELD, SR.

GENERAL LAND OFFICE. See Bureau of Land Management.

GENERAL SERVICES ADMINISTRATION (GSA). The federal government's housekeeping agency, the General Services Administration, carries out the routine but crucial functions that allow other agencies to concentrate their energies on the foreign and domestic policies that attract public attention. GSA is a service organization whose customers are primarily other government agencies. It manages public property, having responsibility for most nonmilitary goods and services within the executive branch. Its scope encompasses government supplies, buildings and records, and, in recent years, data processing, transportation, and communications functions.

Although Congress did not create GSA until 1949, many of the activities it administers go back to the early days of the U.S. government. However, public building, supply, and records management were not placed under unified, centralized direction. Although Congress and the executive branch had been moving in that direction for some years, the breakthrough toward a centralized system came in 1949 with the report of the First Hoover Commission (Commission on Organization of the Executive Branch of the Government*). This bipartisan body was chaired by Herbert Hoover and was composed of eleven other members appointed by the President, speaker of the House, and president pro tempore of the Senate. The Hoover Commission divided its work into more than twenty fields, with a task force of experts in each area. Its task force on federal supply activities concluded that the problem of supply had been treated too casually by the U.S. government, that no large private corporation could survive with the waste and extravagance condoned in the public sector. The federal government was the nation's largest single consumer of supplies and equipment, having at least 147,000 employees involved in supply activities. The task force on records management found 340,000 employees involved in its area, with paper increasing at a rate that threatened to swamp the government.

Based on these reports, the Hoover Commission stated flatly that the three major internal activities of the federal government—supply, records management, and operation and management of public buildings—suffered from lack of central direction. Since these activities related to all agencies, authority should be vested in the President. Therefore, it recommended that Congress place responsibility for the three activities in an office of general services under a director appointed by the President.

In February 1949, the Federal Works Agency (FWA) director, with President Harry S Truman's approval, drafted property management legislation. The bill made the FWA the central agency for property management, but it excluded both records management and major units of government, including the military, from its provisions. However, the bill was drafted before the Hoover Commission reported. By mid-1949, the public had begun to call for rapid action on the Hoover Commission proposals. The administration and Congress were under pressure to respond positively, and this legislation provided the first major opportunity for it to do so. Powerful Republican Representative Clarence Brown (Ohio), author of the act creating the Hoover Commission, appeared before the House committee handling the administration bill and recommended that it be redrafted to embody the commission recommendations. This no doubt showed the Democratic majority that it could get support for a stronger bill than it had earlier thought possible.

The Senate and House Committees on Expenditures in the Executive Departments rewrote the bill to conform generally to the Hoover Commission recommendations. It passed the House and Senate easily after very short debate. After conference committee action, which resolved differences quickly, the House and Senate passed the measure on June 28 and 29, respectively, and Truman signed it on June 30, 1949.

The Federal Property and Administrative Services Act of 1949 created the General Services Administration, an independent agency headed by an administrator appointed by the President with the advice and consent of the Senate. This law transferred to the GSA administrator the activities of a variety of units including the functions of the Bureau of Federal Supply and Office of Contract Settlement, both previously in the Department of Treasury,* the functions of the Federal Works Agency (including, most importantly, the Public Buildings Administration), the functions of the National Archives* Establishment, and the functions of the War Assets Administration.

The act's policy statement declared that it was the intent of Congress to provide for an economical and efficient system of procurement and supply of personal property and nonpersonal services, utilization of available property, disposal of surplus property, and records management. To achieve this, the act granted the administrator broad power over property management. It gave him authority to prescribe policies and methods of procurement and supply of personal property and nonpersonal services, to procure and supply personal property for use by other executive agencies, and to operate or arrange for operation of warehouses and supply centers. He could prescribe policies and methods to promote utilization of excess property by executive agencies and could supervise and direct disposal of surplus property. The act gave him additional powers to carry out the congressional policy directives. However, Congress wrote several exemptions into the law, including one for the National Military Establishment in the interests of national security.

The GSA had a dual role: as a service agency for the executive branch, and as an advisory agency for assisting in establishing standards by which other agencies could manage their supplies, records, and space. Truman immediately pushed GSA to begin this work. On July 1, 1949, he wrote all agency heads implementing the new act and directed them to give special emphasis to improving the efficiency of their operation. He notified them that the GSA administrator was now responsible for setting standards by which other agencies would carry out these activities.

On July 1, 1949, Truman appointed Jess Larson as the first GSA administrator, and the Senate confirmed him on July 6. Even before the act passed, Larson had asked the directors of all the units scheduled for consolidation to begin planning with him for the transition. Several national-level units were set up, including the National Archives and Records Service, Federal Supply Service, and Public Buildings Service. In 1950, Larson also designated ten regional offices. This was the foundation from which the modern GSA evolved.

A housekeeper's path is often strewn with pitfalls, and GSA was no exception. After it had been in operation about seven years, the Second Hoover Commission* submitted a series of reports, several of which evaluated GSA's operations. Behind the scenes, many people connected with the commission were extremely critical of the agency but toned down this criticism in the public reports. Still, it found that the GSA lacked aggressive drive to attain fully all the responsibilities that had been envisioned for it. It was not carrying out a full-scale, government-wide program in paper work management. It had failed to bring the military under its policy direction in areas where Congress had given it such authority. Many agencies were not complying with its real property regulations. There were many other such criticisms. Part of the problem was that the GSA had responsibility for functions that touched all other executive branch agencies. This created constant conflict, requiring continuous negotiation over major and countless minor matters. Even with presidential and congressional mandates, the obstacles were tremendous.

More disturbing were persistent charges of mismanagement and corruption. After only seven years of GSA operations, a *Fortune* magazine reporter referred to GSA as "Washington's most durable mess." Its second administrator, Edmund F. Mansure, resigned in 1956 in connection with a congressional investigation into GSA contract procedures and awards. Periodic charges of dishonesty continued over the years, with allegations in the late 1970s that the corrupt activities of GSA employees amounted to millions of dollars each year. Some critics charged that it was plagued by being a dumping ground for second-rate political appointees. Probably some corruption was inevitable because of large amounts of supplies, property, and contracts involved in GSA's operations. If Congress tightened controls enough to eliminate such problems, then the agency would bog down in red tape.

Another continuing controversy stemmed from concern that the 1949 act placed the National Archives, a cultural agency, in a service organization. The National Archives had been created in 1934 as an independent agency. Congress provided it with a huge new building and with wide authority over executive branch records, and it quickly built an excellent staff. However, in June 1948, when

Wayne C. Grover became archivist, he found that the organization faced serious problems, especially lack of funds and space. Therefore, when the Hoover Commission started to work, Grover decided that it provided an opportunity to deal with these problems. He called on the Hoover Commission to set up a task force on records management. He thought that the Commission would strengthen the National Archives case for new programs and funding.

However, Grover lost control of the situation. The Hoover Commission appointed as chairman of the task force Emmett Leahy, director of the private National Records Management Council. Leahy was a hard-driving, confident individual, who wrote the entire task-force report himself, although the other members approved its recommendations. Rather than formulating reasoned alternatives, the task force presented its report as an action document designed to stampede the Hoover Commission into supporting its recommendations. The task force recommended that Congress create a federal records administration, including the National Archives, and enact a federal records management bill.

Leahy emphasized the service aspect of National Archives activities, which the agency itself had also stressed to win bigger budgets. Therefore, when the Hoover Commission recommended creation of a general service agency it also recommended that the National Archives be a part of it. Grover and other archivists opposed the recommendations, but the drive for reorganization was too strong and swift for effective opposition.

The loss of independence of the National Archives has caused concern since 1949. It seemed incongruous to many to place a cultural agency in a housekeeping service. Many archivists believed that the GSA leaders had little understanding of archival needs. The National Archives also was cut off from direct access to the President and Congress.

The Federal Property and Administrative Services Act of 1949 has been amended many times, and GSA had also been altered by reorganization acts and Executive Orders. It has been given expanded jurisdiction over space, supplies, records management, and new authority in transportation, communications, and data processing.

The 35,000-employee agency is organized into six services. The Federal Supply Service purchases annually about $3.5 billion worth of goods and services from pencils to civilian aircraft, for virtually all civilian agencies. It also sets standards of quality and performance for other agencies. It maintains a nationwide system of supply depots and self-service stores. The Public Buildings Service, the nation's largest landlord, employs over eighteen thousand people and builds or leases offices, warehouses, and other space. It manages about 284 million square feet in about ten thousand federally owned or leased buildings. The National Archives and Records Service designs and effects systems of records management, holds recent records for less frequent use, and decides what materials shall remain as part of the nation's permanent holdings. It performs additional activities, such as publishing the *Federal Register* and the *United States Statutes at Large*.

The Federal Property Resources Services deals with utilization and disposition of government-owned real property, personal property, acquisition and management of the stockpile of critical and strategic materials, and the sale of excess stockpile material. The Transportation and Public Utilities Service administers the government-wide transportation management program, operates the 88,000-vehicle interagency motor pool, and purchases utility services for federal use. The Automated Data and Telecommunications Service is responsible for managing data processing for all federal agencies and for procurement, leasing, and maintenance of government computers. It also leases a national system of communications lines for use by civilian agencies, including telephone, teletype, and data and facsimile traffic.

Other GSA activities include operating Federal Information Centers to answer questions about government, Business Service Centers to deal with questions from enterprises doing business with government, and Consumer Information Centers to provide information about government publications for consumers. It increasingly tries to respond to environmental and energy concerns and quality of life activities, such as including money for fine arts in its buildings.

Except when it does something wrong, GSA usually is part of the background of the government structure, supplanted in the public eye by those agencies that carry out more dramatic activities. However, by assuming so many routine but necessary duties, it frees these agencies to focus their resources more completely on their substantive functions.

FOR ADDITIONAL INFORMATION: Many government records were used in preparation of this sketch, including committee hearings and reports, *Congressional Record, United States Statutes at Large*, GSA Annual Reports, and other GSA publications. Additional sources include: Wayne C. Grover, "Recent Developments in Federal Archival Activities," *The American Archivist* 14 (January 1951):3-12; Oliver W. Holmes, "The National Archives at a Turn in the Road," *The American Archivist* 12 (October 1949):339-354; Michael J. Luciano, "A Study of the Origin and Development of the General Services Administration as Related to Its Present Operational Role, Direction, and Influence" (Ph.D. dissertation, New York University, 1968); and Donald R. McCoy, *The National Archives: America's Ministry of Documents, 1934-1968* (1978).

WILLIAM E. PEMBERTON

GEOLOGICAL SURVEY. See United States Geological Survey.

_H_

HEALTH, EDUCATION, AND WELFARE DEPARTMENT. See Department of Health and Human Services.

HIGHWAY ADMINISTRATION. See Federal Highway Administration.

HOOVER COMMISSIONS. COMMISSIONS ON THE ORGANIZATION OF THE EXECUTIVE BRANCH OF THE GOVERNMENT, 1947-1949, 1953-1955. Reorganization of the executive branch of government has taken place continually from the earliest days of the Republic. It became an important reform goal after the Civil War, when the executive branch began to expand and fragment as it attempted to cope with the new domestic and foreign problems of a rapidly industrializing society. Early reorganization studies and investigations yielded few results, but by 1947 the depression and World War II had created a government whose size dwarfed the earlier structure. This development produced fears in some quarters that amounted almost to hysteria. Many people had a confused and ill-defined desire for "normalcy" in matters relating to bureaucracy, often supporting public programs but opposing the bureaucratic structure they entailed.

When the Republican Eightieth Congress met in 1947, its leaders quickly focused on means to attack the waste and extravagance they believed existed in the executive branch. Powerful Republican House member Clarence Brown (Ohio), realizing that past reform investigations had been ineffective, had been considering new ways to approach the problem. He decided that a body capable both of undertaking an expert investigation and of attracting general public support for its recommendations promised hope of success.

In January 1947, Brown introduced a bill, co-sponsored by Senator Henry Cabot Lodge (Republican, Massachusetts), to create a Commission on Organization of the Executive Branch of the Government. The bill provided for a bipartisan, twelve-member commission, with four members each to be appointed by the President, the president pro tempore of the Senate, and the speaker of the House. The commission would not report until after the 1948 election. The proposal's declaration of policy gave the commission almost unlimited authority to make recommendations on virtually every aspect of government service, including abolishing activities that were not necessary to the efficient conduct of government and defining and limiting executive functions, services, and activities. It passed both houses of Congress without opposition.

The commission began to take shape on July 7, 1947, when President Pro Tempore Arthur Vandenberg (Republican, Michigan), appointed Senators George Aiken (Republican, Vermont) and John L. McClellan (Democrat, Arkansas), Political Scientist James K. Pollock, and businessman Joseph P. Kennedy. Speaker of the House Joe Martin (Republican, Massachusetts), named Congressmen Brown and Carter Manasco (Democrat, Alabama), Herbert Hoover, and Washington lawyer James Rowe. On July 17, President Harry S Truman announced his appointments: Secretary of Defense James Forrestal, Civil Service Commissioner Arthur Flemming, Ohio industrialist George Mead, and Dean Acheson, appointed Secretary of State while on the commission.

After his fellow commissioners elected Hoover chairman, he quickly established dominance over the commission, partly because of his prestige as an ex-President, but mainly because of the time and energy he devoted to the work. Hoover controlled appointments, agenda, and information flow. Most of the staff were his friends and admirers, who tended to be responsive to him rather than to the commission generally. Especially during the first year, Hoover kept the other commissioners isolated from the twenty-four task forces, set up in various fields and staffed by several hundred experts to provide studies for the basis of later commission action. When colleagues objected, the usually mild and genial Hoover showed his tough and stubborn side. Asked how the commission settled disputes, James Pollock answered that Hoover sometimes simply rode roughshod over the persons or problem involved.

Another major source of Hoover's control stemmed from his leadership of the conservative individuals who dominated the commission. The commission's sponsors intended it to be the "grand overture" of a Republican era, and they hoped to eliminate many governmental activities undertaken during the New Deal. Brown, a Robert Taft campaign manager, passed word to Hoover that he deliberately planned for the body to report after the 1948 election in order to carry out the "complete housecleaning" that he anticipated after a Republican victory. Speaker Joe Martin intended the Hoover Commission to spearhead an all-out war on "conniving, scheming" federal agencies that were attempting to subvert the American form of government. McGeorge Bundy, who considered taking a position with the group, reported that the members of the Hoover Commission were basically functioning as anti-New Dealers. The Senate Republican Conference described the commission as preparing a major operation on the expensive, sprawling bureaucracy that was the legacy of the New Deal.

However, when the commission reported in 1949, observers noted that it generally stayed out of policy matters. On November 11, 1948, a few days after the presidential election, Hoover told reporters that it was not the commission's job to determine whether a government activity should exist, but only how to make it work better. A major reason for this switch stemmed from Truman's victory. It became obvious to Hoover and his supporters that without Truman's support nothing could be accomplished. Other factors also moderated the commission's report. Truman and Hoover had developed a close relationship, and they found it easy to cooperate. The administration, especially the Bureau of the Budget,* had intertwined with the commission, supplying information and even personnel. In addition, a "liberal" bloc composed of Rowe, Pollock, and Acheson, backed by the Bureau of the Budget and various administration officials, including Truman himself, fought the conservatives step by step.

The final reports were of generally high quality. They kept the focus on the President and his need to have authority to manage the executive branch, with increased staff services to help him carry out this burden. Political scientist Peri Arnold viewed the Hoover Commission as taking the "critical, final step" toward bipartisan acceptance of the modern strong presidency. It recommended restructuring the departments to reduce overlapping and to clarify lines of command. It proposed granting the Cabinet secretaries authority to manage and organize all the units within their domains. It recommended rebuilding weak agencies like the Labor Department* and strengthening the Department of State* and the National Military Establishment to prepare them for new responsibilities in the Cold War world.

After the Hoover Commission reported, the Truman Administration responded positively. Its reorganization program, backed now by Hoover and Truman, also received great public acclaim and support. Capitalizing on this support, Truman submitted many administrative reform bills, as well as forty reorganization plans, most of them based on Hoover Commission reports. Congress renewed Truman's reorganization authority in the Reorganization Act of 1949, carried military unification a step further by creating the Department of Defense,* and restructured the Department of State to equip it better to deal with the complexities of the modern world.

Following the administration's lead, Congress also created the General Services Administration* to unify government housekeeping functions, rebuilt the decimated Department of Labor, and accepted many reorganization plans that transferred management authority from subordinates to the departmental secretaries and that placed executive functions in the hands of regulatory commission chairmen. These undramatic but important plans gave agency heads continuing authority to deal with changing problems. Truman also furthered the consolidation of housing, transportation, and social agencies, preparing the way for the later creation of the Departments of Housing and Urban Development,* Transportation,* and Health, Education, and Welfare.*

When Dwight Eisenhower was elected President in November 1952, conservative congressional leaders saw a chance to gain what Truman's election in 1948 cost them. At a January 12, 1953, meeting with his future Cabinet, Eisenhower told the group that Brown and Senator Homer Ferguson (Republican, Michigan) wanted to create another commission of the Hoover type. Eisenhower, who had already set up the President's Advisory Committee on Government Organization, composed of people very close to him, tried to talk them out of it by contending that Congress should not wait for a report before taking action to reorganize the executive branch. However, Brown and Ferguson were like two "newborn children" and would not be put off. The group decided that presidential adviser Sherman Adams and others would talk to congressional leaders Martin and Robert Taft to halt any reorganization effort until they could go about doing their own job.

The administration failed to control the congressional conservatives, and Ferguson and Brown introduced their bills. They announced that the new commission would help conserve the American way of life. In addition to repeating the mandate from the 1947 bill, the new act declared the policy of Congress to be that of promoting economy and efficiency by eliminating nonessential services, functions, and activities competitive with private enterprise. After the act passed in July 1953, Eisenhower appointed Attorney General Herbert Brownell and director of the Office of Defense Mobilization Arthur Flemming, former New Deal official James Farley, and Herbert Hoover. Vice-President Richard Nixon named Senators Homer Ferguson and John L. McClellan (Democrat, Arkansas), Cornell University Dean of Engineering Solomon C. Hollister, and Southern Methodist University Dean of Law Robert G. Storey. Speaker Martin added Representatives Brown and Chet Holifield (Democrat, California), Joseph Kennedy, and Sidney A. Mitchell, who had served as executive director of the First Commission. When Ferguson resigned in 1955, Senator Styles Bridges (Republican, New Hampshire) replaced him and served for a brief time.

The new commission was considerably more conservative than the first one. Men of more conservative bent controlled its task forces, with fewer scholars and even more dominance by businessmen than before. A number of commissioners had also served on the First Hoover Commission, but none of the dissenting liberal bloc was retained. Chet Holifield was the one isolated liberal, although the outspoken Californian was far from being intimidated. Rather than focusing on broad problems of management and organization in the tradition of the First Hoover Commission, the new body, in search of economies, directed much of its attention to surveying government operations and methods, especially in the Department of Defense. It also devoted much more of its attention to policy rather than organizational matters. The recommendations often were complicated and detailed, and not of great interest to the public.

In most cases, the commission was more conservative than the middle-of-the-road Eisenhower Administration. The commission's water resource recommendations would have drastically restricted public power development. The commission failed to understand the role of foreign aid in modern foreign policy. It also devoted a great amount of its effort to uncovering and recommending the elimination of government competition with private enterprise. Perhaps its most revolutionary proposals were its legal services and procedures recommendations which would have judicialized the regulatory system by, among other things, allowing appeals to the federal courts at every stage of the administrative process.

Ironically, Hoover found it easier to work with Democrat Truman than Republican Eisenhower. In 1952, Hoover had supported Taft for the Republican nomination, but then had backed Eisenhower in the fall campaign and had offered to aid the new President in any way he could. But, admitted Sherman Adams, the work between Hoover and Eisenhower on commission matters "never really jelled." Eisenhower did urge his Cabinet to avoid adverse public reaction to the commission recommendations and to take rapid action on those that were acceptable. He noted that to do so would alleviate public apprehension that the administration would not act on the recommendations. Eisenhower also appointed Chicago businessman Meyer Kestnbaum as his special assistant on Hoover Commission matters. Kestnbaum encouraged implementation of the proposals but found executive branch and congressional resistance strong. He told Adams that the commission could indeed be said to be progressing too slowly. Yet, many of the commission recommendations were simply not acceptable to the administration. For example, at a Cabinet meeting on March 9, 1956, President Eisenhower supported Secretary Wilson's belief that the recommendations lacked feasibility because the commission failed to weigh all the necessary factors.

Hoover's relations with the administration were continually frustrating to him. In April 1955, one of his aides notified an administration official that the report had hit "dead center" at the White House. Hoover discussed the matter with Sherman Adams but could not gain access to the President himself. Hoover, unappreciative of the difficulty Kestnbaum faced, accused the special assistant of turning himself into a "third commission." An aide reported that Hoover was profoundly disappointed.

Nonetheless, some important Second Hoover Commission recommendations were carried out. The commission contributed to further defense unification and to modernized budgeting; it eliminated many examples of unnecessary government competition with private business; and the federal career service was improved by executive action. Additional recommendations helped improve the environment for federal research, as well as the handling of government paperwork, and led to the establishment of a National Medical Library.

The two commissions conducted the most extensive survey of U.S. government in the nation's history. Despite the limitations imposed by the goals of their conservative congressional creators, the two bodies made many recommendations whose implementation helped bring order and increased effectiveness to a government structure that was suffering from real problems stemming from its rapid expansion and new responsibilities. The commission reflected a particular merging of need, political currents, and available personalities that is not likely to be repeated.

FOR ADDITIONAL INFORMATION: The most important sources for this article were relevant papers in the Hoover, Truman, and Eisenhower Presidential Libraries and in the National Archives,* followed by many other manuscript collections in archives across the country and about sixty oral history interviews with people connected with the Hoover Commissions.

Other sources are Peri E. Arnold, "The First Hoover Commission and the Managerial Presidency," *The Journal of Politics* 38 (February 1976): 46-70; Herbert Emmerich, *Federal Organization and Administrative Management* (1971); and William E. Pemberton, *Bureaucratic Politics: Executive Reorganization During the Truman Administration* (1979).

WILLIAM E. PEMBERTON

HOUSING DEPARTMENT. See Department of Housing and Urban Development.

HUMANITIES ENDOWMENT. See National Endowment for the Humanities.

I

IMMIGRATION AND NATURALIZATION SERVICE (INS). Although immigration has been the very source of American existence, it took almost a century for any kind of systematic regulation of immigration to develop. The creation of a federal bureaucracy to enforce immigration laws came only after immigration restriction had begun. Not until 1882, the year of the Chinese Exclusion Act, did Congress attempt to supervise general immigration. The immigration act of that year placed the Treasury Secretary in charge but authorized a dual system of administration under which the Secretary was to enter into contracts with state commissions or boards to run it. All was to be financed by a fifty-cent head tax on each seaborne immigrant: those who walked across from Canada or Mexico were exempt. The only persons not admissible were Chinese, contract laborers, prostitutes, and nonpolitical criminals under sentence or whose sentence was remitted on condition of their emigration.

Nine years later, with immigration growing and a consciousness of the closing of the frontier increasing, Congress, after two separate investigations, set up what became the Immigration and Naturalization Service. The 1891 act added new and significant categories to the excluded list: idiots, the insane, paupers or persons likely to become public charges, those with a "loathsome" or dangerous contagious disease, felons, and persons convicted of anything involving moral turpitude. Contract labor, the great bugaboo, was defined more precisely and stringently than before, but to little avail. To enforce these restrictions Congress created a new office, the superintendent of immigration, and placed his bureau in the Treasury Department.* He received a salary of $4,000 (Cabinet officers got $8,000) and was authorized twenty-seven subordinates, including one inspector for each of twenty-four inspection stations. Medical examinations were to be made either by surgeons of the Marine Hospital Service or by private surgeons under contract. From the very beginning, with some notable exceptions, those in the immigration service, from top to bottom, have seen it as their mission to protect America from possible harmful effects of immigrants and immigration.

Once in place, the new bureau grew quickly and for good reasons. Not only did immigration increase greatly, but also increasingly nativistic Congresses also made immigration laws harsher and more complex. In 1895, the bureau head's title became commissioner general of immigration. In 1903, the bureau was moved to the new Department of Commerce and Labor* (when that split, in 1913, the bureau went to Labor*), and the law added new categories to the list of excluded: epileptics, persons who had been insane within five years or experienced two "attacks" of insanity, professional beggars, and, in the wake of McKinley's assassination, anarchists or persons who believed in or advocated the overthrow by force and violence of the U.S. government. Immigration officials, previously instructed to admit political "criminals," from 1903 on would be increasingly concerned with the political ideas of immigrants. By the end of fiscal 1906, the bureau had more than twelve hundred employees. Despite this phenomenal growth, Commissioner Frank P. Sargent insisted that the bureau needed more staff. Recommendations during his tenure (1902-1908) were congruent with the aims of the restrictionist movement. He recommended still more classes for exclusion: moral perverts, those with serious physical disabilities, and those prospective immigrants who were over sixty or under seventeen traveling alone, unless they had relatives in America able to provide for them. Sargent was convinced that a literacy test ought to be added and that both U.S. land borders were inadequately guarded. He began an almost unbroken tradition of commissioners who claimed that illegal immigration from Mexico was constantly increasing.

In 1906, Congress regularized naturalization procedures, which were scandalously erratic, by establishing a Naturalization Service and placing it in the bureau, which now became the Bureau of Immigration and Naturalization. While naturalization ceremonies still took place in federal courts, the paper work and investigation were centralized.

In terms of restriction, the statutes and the bureau had only a minimal effect on immigration. During 1892-1907, more than 9.3 million immigrants were recorded as entering the United States. Those refused admission during the whole period numbered just over 85,000 or about 0.009 percent. Of these, 54,000, (63 percent) were kept out because they were too poor (paupers or persons likely to become public charges); 14,000 (16 percent) because they were found to be contract laborers or illegally assisted immigrants; and 14,000 (15 percent) because of "loathsome" or contagious diseases. Of the rest, 839 were found mentally defective, 752 were said to be convicts, 676 were Chinese, 189 alleged prostitutes, 60 without passports, 19 said to be polygamists, 10 pimps, and a grand total of 3 anarchists. During these years, and beyond, the volume of immigration was such that head taxes more than paid for the cost of the service. Between 1894 and 1913, the head tax, which went up to $4, brought in more than $37 million, more than $5 million above outgo.

Ironically, the years of World War I saw both a drop in the number of immigrants—from just over a million a year in the five years before the war to a low of 110,000 in fiscal 1918—and a heightening of restrictionist sentiment and legislation as wartime nationalism and postwar xenophobia began to define Americanism as the antithesis of the foreign. In 1917, a literacy test was passed over Wilson's veto, but it had little effect as a retardant. Restrictionists, in the Immigration Service and out, watched with dismay as postwar immigration increased to almost 150,000 in 1919, over 400,000 in 1920, and just over 800,000 in 1921, still only four-fifths of the prewar highs. As early as 1910, Commissioner General Daniel J. Keefe had argued for ethnic restriction because many of those who had entered recently belonged to races differing radically from the Teutonic and Celtic stocks, thereby posing a real problem of assimilation. By 1921, Congress, and probably the country, were ready to put their ethnic prejudices into the statute book. First, the so-called per centum quota act of 1921 and then the 1924 Immigration Act, which set up the National Origins Quota System, not only drastically reduced the total number of European immigrants—357,000 annually under the 1921 act, 164,000 under the 1924—but also established national quotas based, eventually, on the presumed percentage of the 1890 population which each group represented. Thus, Italy, which had sent more than 200,000 the year before quotas were instituted, was cut to a maximum of 42,000 under the 1921 act and fewer than 4,000 under the 1924.

Before the quota acts, the bureau had to handle and screen large numbers of immigrants; much of that screening was now done abroad by the consular service through visas, and the concerns of the bureau turned to more rigid enforcement of existing laws and to deportation. As the volume of immigration shrank, relatively and absolutely, so did the alien segment of the population. By 1930, only about 12 percent of the population was foreign-born and more than half of those had become citizens. In fiscal 1933, essentially the last year of the Hoover Administration, the bureau achieved a kind of nativist dream: it deported and excluded more aliens than it admitted as immigrants: 25,392 as opposed to 23,068. In addition, another 10,000 left the country voluntarily. This was due, of course, more to the rigors of the depression than to the terms of the immigration laws or the zeal of this bureau.

Franklin D. Roosevelt, whose administration changed so much of the government and the nation, brought no new deal to the immigration bureaucracy, although he did change its name to the Immigration and Naturalization Service. It is true that his Secretary of Labor, Frances Perkins, who inherited a service of 3,600 persons, did eliminate a good deal of corruption and the notorious "Section 24 squad" of the bureau which, in pursuit of radicals, real and imagined, often violated even the most rudimentary forms of due process. But most of the personnel stayed on. Perkins herself noted that none of them were miracles of liberalism. INS reports continued to show a distinct nativist bias. When the refugee crisis set off by the spread of Nazism began, the main concern of the INS was to check, with particular care, the travel documents of aliens whose departure from their home countries had been practically in the nature of an expulsion and whose likelihood of becoming public charges if admitted to the

United States had to be considered dispassionately, in spite of the tragic circumstances surrounding their plight.

The coming of war in Europe precipitated major changes in the INS. In 1940, in the midst of chimerical fears about alien "fifth columnists," it was transferred to the Department of Justice.* The passage of the Alien Registration Act of that year, advertised as a temporary national security measure but still on the books, required the fingerprinting and annual registration of all aliens over fourteen. Because of the war, the INS felt that "greater vigilance" was required to keep out "dangerous aliens" and that investigation of applicants for naturalization had to be made more strict lest enemy aliens become American citizens. In addition, the INS was made responsible for the internment, parole, deportation, and repatriation of enemy aliens, although the selection of internees was left to other agencies. More than 10,000 enemy aliens, about half of them Japanese, were interned at facilities like the internment camp at Crystal City, Texas.

In the immediate postwar era, the most significant immigration laws were the several statutes that admitted over 400,000 displaced persons between mid-1948 and mid-1952. The INS bureaucracy clearly resisted that legislation and its implementation, and reconciled themselves to the idea that, although the National Origins Plan was "temporarily thrown off balance" by the refugee influx, its "broad objectives," the preservation of the original racial composition of the United States, could, over time, be maintained.

The passage of the Internal Security Act of 1950 and the Immigration Act of 1952, each authored, in part, by Senator Patrick A. McCarran (Democrat, Nevada), changed the major orientation of the INS. In 1952, Harry Truman's appointee, Argyle R. Mackey, reported that the investigative activities of the service were of "prime importance" so that it could proceed with the expulsion of aliens and the denaturalization of persons illegally naturalized who were or had been connected with the worldwide Communist movement. Despite this sound and fury and the fact that the next administration gave subversive hunting "top priority," very few alien subversives were deported and even fewer citizen subversives denaturalized. In 1954, the peak year, only 61 of over 26,000 deportations were for subversion. Between 1951 and 1965, when 2,480 persons were denaturalized, only 31 were for subversion.

Along with its drives against subversives, the INS continued to be concerned over the increasing illegal entry of Mexicans into the United States. This problem, which has spread to illegal aliens generally, has become the major INS concern. On several occasions in the recent past, the service has mounted well-publicized "anti-wetback" drives and, more than once, claimed victory. In 1955, for example, Dwight Eisenhower's appointee, Joseph M. Swing, declared that the problem had been solved. The fact of the matter, of course, is that the border has not been secured and that, as a 1977 General Accounting Office* study reported, the enforcement efforts of a number of agencies have failed to stem the flow of drugs and people.

The passage of the reformed immigration act of 1965, the spread of relatively cheap air transportation, and a vast market for semi-skilled laborers willing to work long hours close to, at, or even below the minimum wage have created an almost unmanageable crisis in illegal aliens, or as they are sometimes called, undocumented persons. In 1965, the United States admitted through legal procedures 2.6 million aliens, of whom 323,000 were immigrants. This number grew steadily until, in 1978, it had reached a level of 9.9 million admissions, of whom just over 600,000 were immigrants. The notion that any conceivable bureaucratic apparatus can, in a free country, regulate that number of aliens is absurd. In addition, an obstinate refusal to jail or even fine employers of illegal aliens makes enforcement a farce. In recent years, more than a million illegal aliens have been apprehended and sent home annually, many of them to return. As long as there are significant wage differentials between the United States and its closest southern neighbors and an unregulated labor market in the United States, one can expect the problems of illegals to continue.

In addition, special strains have been placed on the INS by three recent streams of refugees: first, from Southeast Asia, where the United States had a moral obligation; second, from Cuba, where this country had an ideological obligation; and, most recently, from Haiti and Central America, where the government has seen little or no obligation toward the refugees. Only those in the third group have experienced substantial difficulties in achieving refugee status.

Most authorities now agree that the present system is all but bankrupt. David Crosland, acting commissioner, was understating the case when he testified, in March 1980, that we were in a position from which we could not easily extricate ourselves. A fruitless reorganization proposal emanated from the Carter Administration, and the Reagan Administration proposed, in 1981, a sweeping plan, which included a much discussed "amnesty," a concept that the INS bureaucracy has long resisted.

As of March 1982, no plan had been accepted by Congress. On February 22, 1982, a California corporation lawyer, Alan Nelson, was sworn in as Commissioner, the first permanent head since September of 1979.

FOR ADDITIONAL INFORMATION: For hostility, see Terrence V. Powderly, *The Path I Trod* (1940), pp. 408-414, and Hart H. North, "Chinese Highbinder Societies in California," *California Historical Society Quarterly* 23 (1944): 335-347 and "Chinese and Japanese Immigration to the Pacific Coast," ibid. (1949): 343-350. For friendliness, see Fiorello La Guardia, *The Making of an Insurgent* (1948). For early administrative detail, see Darrell Smith and H. Guy Herring, *The Bureau of Immigration* (1924).

See also *History of the Immigration and Naturalization Service*, Committee on the Judiciary, U.S. Senate, 96th Cong., 2d Sess. (1980), pp. 12-14 (Committee Print). Useful too, are the Annual Reports of the INS, Labor, and Justice* Departments. Other citations include George Martin, *Madam Secretary* (1976), and for a description of the general program, see Jerre Mangione, *An Ethnic at Large* (1978). For Crystal City, see N. D. Collaer, "The Crystal City Internment Camp," *INS Monthly Review* (December 1947). This internment of selected enemy aliens should not be confused with the quite different program of mass incarceration of Japanese American citizens and aliens under the auspices of the U.S. Army and the War Relocation Authority. See, too, Helen F. Eckerson and

Gertrude D. Krichefsky, "A Quarter Century of Quota Restriction," *INS Monthly Review* (January 1950): 4.

ROGER DANIELS

INDIAN AFFAIRS BUREAU. See Bureau of Indian Affairs.

INFORMATION AGENCY. See United States Information Agency.

INTERIOR DEPARTMENT. See Department of Interior.

INTERNAL REVENUE SERVICE (IRS). The Internal Revenue Service is responsible for the determination, assessment and collection of all internal revenue and miscellaneous taxes, and for the enforcement of internal revenue laws. It is the largest bureau within the Treasury Department.* Headed by a commissioner, who is appointed by the President, with the advice and consent of the Senate, the bureau was created during the Civil War in the Revenue Act of July 1, 1862, which also established the outlines of the present internal revenue system. The Internal Revenue Service was known as the Bureau of Internal Revenue until 1952 when the present name was adopted.

Until the Civil War, there was no system of internal taxation and no permanent administrative agency for the collection of internal taxes. But internal taxes were levied by Congress and collected by the Treasury Department during two earlier periods: 1791-1802 and 1813-1817. The administrative system ultimately established as a permanent part of the federal government is based largely upon the experience of these early efforts.

The difficulties of financing the War for Independence and the reluctance of the states under the Articles of Confederation to contribute to the operation of the central government convinced the delegates to the Constitutional Convention that the powers to tax were crucial to the stability of the new government. Article I, Section 8, provided those powers. The Revenue Act of March 3, 1791, was the first in which internal taxes were used for the support of the government. This was a broad act, which provided taxing authority as well as the establishment of a collecting agency under the supervision of the Assistant to the Secretary of the Treasury. The country was divided into fourteen districts consistent with the boundaries of the states. Revenues were collected by supervisors appointed in each district. The act imposed a tax on distilled spirits and carriages. Taxes on retail dealers in distilled spirits, refined sugar, snuff, snuff mills, property sold at auction, bonds, and legal instruments were soon added. A Revenue Act of 1792 placed collection in an officer of the Treasury who was denominated the commissioner of the revenue whose compensation was fixed at $1,900 annually. Trench Coxe of Pennsylvania, who held several other offices simultaneously, was the first commissioner.

Receipts from internal revenue were meager compared with those received from customs duties, but the revenue acts evoked stronger political opposition.

In 1794, a "whiskey rebellion" broke out in western Pennsylvania where farmers objected in principle to the "obnoxious levey" on distilled spirits.

In the Revenue Act of 1798, a direct tax on real property was levied for the first time. It also established the administrative machinery for the valuation of lands and dwellings, and the enumeration of slaves. Each state was divided into divisions consisting of several counties, and a commissioner was provided for each division. The commissioners in a particular state divided the state into assessment districts, appointed assessors, and made regulations.

The outlines of the present system of internal revenue collection were well defined when Thomas Jefferson took office. He abolished the "infernal" excise system and the offices then held by 400 revenue officials. No further internal taxes were levied until 1813.

The heavy costs of the War of 1812 again made it necessary to supplement the financing of governmental affairs through internal taxation. The Revenue Act of July 24, 1813, levied taxes on refined sugar, carriages, distillers, and sales at auction. During the next two years, taxes on retail liquor dealers, retailers of foreign merchandise, bank notes, legal instruments, distilled spirits, manufactured articles, household furniture, watches, gold, silver, plated ware, and jewelry were added. The act of 1813 also recreated the administrative machinery for the collection of these new taxes and revived the Office of the Commissioner of the Revenue.

The nation recovered rapidly from the financial pressures of this brief war, and, despite strong recommendations by the Secretary of the Treasury in 1815 that a permanent internal revenue system be established, Congress again abolished all internal taxes as well as the offices of collection.

Financing the Civil War necessitated a fiscal revolution. Although it was not until 1900 that internal revenue receipts equaled the amounts collected by customs, the requirements of federal financing produced a new class of taxes. The first Civil War Revenue Act of August 5, 1861, levied a direct tax of $20 million apportioned among the states. It also authorized the nation's first income tax.

The Revenue Act of July 1, 1862, taxed so many new items that a definite administrative system for their collection became essential. Instead of reviving the old machinery, Congress created the Office of the Commissioner of Internal Revenue under the Secretary of the Treasury. The act authorized the division of the country into 185 collection districts and the presidential appointment of an assessor and a collector for each district. The act of 1862 gave the commissioner the right to enforce tax laws through seizure and prosecution.

The principal tax officials were assessors and assistant assessors. Assessors were paid by the day, whereas collectors were paid commissions on the money they collected which was to cover their own compensation as well as that of the deputies they appointed. Collectors also appointed inspectors who were the chief enforcement officers of the period. Their activities were largely confined to the enforcement of taxes on liquor. The act provided no money for payment of the inspectors who were compensated by fees paid by the manufacturers whose goods they inspected. This was by far the weakest link in the system and led to many abuses.

The first commissioner of internal revenue was George S. Boutwell of Massachusetts. He and a handful of clerks divided the states into collection districts, assisted in recommendations for appointment of assessors and collectors, prepared the forms, books, and instructions needed for records and returns, and contracted for printing of the revenue stamps.

As the war continued, new taxes such as those on inheritance were passed. The position of deputy commissioner was created. Most citizens felt it was their patriotic duty to pay taxes during the war, but areas far removed from the battlefield became increasingly resentful of the inequities of the system.

The Revenue Act of March 3, 1865, authorized the appointment of a United States Revenue Commission to study the whole problem of taxation, including the present and past methods of collection. The report of this commission, which was chaired by David A. Wells, was particularly critical of the amount of patronage exercised in the appointment and promotion of the bureau personnel. It proposed a variety of changes in appointment and payment, and urged that each leading source of revenue be recognized as a separate division of the bureau.

Congress responded with new legislation in 1866, which authorized the appointment of two additional deputy commissioners, a solicitor, seven heads of divisions, clerks, messengers, and laborers for the national office. But reforms in the patronage system were postponed.

After the Civil War, Congress progressively reduced taxes. The system of rate progression in the income tax was abandoned in 1867, the inheritance tax was repealed in 1879, and the income tax in 1872. A reorganization in 1872 eliminated assessors and assistant assessors, and centralized responsibility in the Office of the Commissioner.

From the end of the Civil War until 1875, the Bureau of Internal Revenue was plagued by whiskey fraud. Taxes on distilled liquors were so high that a premium was placed on fraud and evasion. A conspiracy involving the corruption of government officials was exposed. A congressional investigation in 1874 recommended a significant reduction in the liquor tax and the elimination of collections by contract. Revenues increased and corruption declined. However, violations of tax laws, particularly those on alcohol, made enforcement a dangerous occupation. Between 1876 and 1880, twenty-six agents were killed and fifty-seven wounded in the conduct of their duties.

By the end of the century new and in some cases unrelated functions were assigned to Internal Revenue. An 1886 act sought by the dairy industry imposed a tax on oleomargarine to prevent oleo from competing with butter. The same act established the Analytical and Chemical Division. First used to check samples for violations of the oleomargarine law, it was later used to test adulterated food products and alcohol samples. The Pure Food and Drug Act in 1906 transferred this unit to the Department of Agriculture.*

Drug regulation began with the passage in 1890 of a tax on opium manufactured in the United States. When this tax proved insufficient, Congress passed the Harrison Act in 1914, which gave the commissioner the power to regulate the domestic manufacture of this and other narcotics. Despite the protests of Commissioner John W. Mason in 1892 that responsibility for regulatory enforcement lay more correctly in other departments, the bureau administered legislation determining and collecting a tax on sugar and white phosphorous matches, issued residence certificates to Chinese laborers, and taxed industries employing child labor. Despite later invalidation of some of these taxes by the courts, regulatory taxes have remained a function of Internal Revenue.

From 1868 to 1913, nearly 90 percent of all revenue derived from taxes on distilled spirits, tobacco, and fermented liquors. However, political debate over the necessity of an income tax continued. The Wilson Tariff Act of 1894 included a wide array of excise regulations, but its most important section restored the progressive income tax. Subsequent legislation provided funds for collection and established an Income Tax Division. A year later, the law was declared unconstitutional in the controversial decision *Pollack* v. *Farmers' Loan and Trust Company*.

In 1909, increasing government expenditures and renewed political pressures led to the enactment of a tax of 1 percent on the net income of corporations in excess of $5,000. A Corporation Tax Division was organized. William Howard Taft's strong support of an income tax led to the passage and ratification of the Sixteenth Amendment in February 1913. Congress enacted a new income tax law drafted by then-Representative Cordell Hull, which imposed a 1 percent tax on net personal incomes over $3,000, with a surtax of up to 6 percent on incomes over $500,000. The same act repealed the corporation tax of 1909 and levied a new tax on net incomes of corporations.

The Sixteenth Amendment inaugurated an era of bureau expansion. The Personal Income Tax Division was established and bureau staff enlarged dramatically. One of the most significant sections of the 1913 income tax statute provided for collection at the source. This method of withholding was repealed in 1916 but became a permanent feature of tax law with the passage of the Social Security Act of 1935. Commissioner William H. Osborn of North Carolina had only a few weeks to draft all the necessary forms and regulations, and to train collectors before the new taxes were to be paid. Despite congressional criticism of the Overman Act of 1913, which authorized the appointment of bonded deputy collectors without regard to Civil Service rules, Osborn's "shock unit" of clerks successfully educated the public as to the requirements of the income tax. Revenue for the fiscal year 1914 showed an increase of $40 million.

Financing the major wars of the twentieth century required higher tax rates which elicited ever increasing tax revenues. The sheer magnitude of the tax to be collected overwhelmed bureau administration and necessitated a reorganization first in 1918 and again in 1952.

The War Revenue Act of 1917 was a sweeping measure. It dealt with income, excess profits, beverages, tobacco, manufacturers, public utilities and insurance, excises, stamp taxes, and estate taxes. The law also reorganized the bureau. New divisions, such as the Child Labor Tax Division, the Sales Tax Unit, and Miscellaneous Unit were created. New auditing and accounting procedures as well as machines to duplicate records were introduced.

Commissioner Daniel C. Roper noted in his Annual Report that 1918 marked the beginning of a new era of internal revenue taxation. The revenue act of that year was the first to codify all existing tax laws. The U.S. Tax Code was revised in 1939 and 1952. The 1918 act also established the Intelligence Division headed by former Postal Inspector Elmer L. Irey. Irey's unit became famous in American law enforcement when his special agents sent many notorious gangsters and racketeers to prison in the course of prohibition law enforcement. By 1920, Roper's decentralized management strategy had established the practice of field auditing.

Although the 1918 reorganization brought increased efficiency, the continuing proliferation of responsibility created new internal tensions. During the 1920s, the national office of the bureau was housed in a dozen different buildings scattered over a wide area of metropolitan Washington. Communication problems alone created administrative inefficiency and serious slowdowns.

Congress became sufficiently exercised about the inefficiency of the Corporate Audit Division to begin an investigation of bureau practices in 1924. The Report of the Senate Committee headed by James Couzens of Michigan, issued in 1926, indicted the bureau for the unlimited discretionary power exercised by the heads of the divisions whose rulings and restrictions were neither reviewable by the taxpayer nor questionable by subordinates. Such attacks on bureau practice, along with the well-publicized difficulties of equitably enforcing prohibition laws and the growing conflicts between political and civilly appointed staff, laid the groundwork for the large-scale overhauling of the agency at the end of World War II.

World War II, with its shift of emphasis from a narrow-base income tax affecting 8 million taxpayers to a broad-based mass tax involving more than 60 million, placed intolerable burdens on the organizational structure of the bureau. New methods of collection and enforcement had to be devised. Individual tax returns were received twice as fast as they could be handled. Investigation of corporate and profits tax fell two years behind. Fraud and evasion were rampant. Compounding the problem was the unreformed patronage system headed by sixty-four politically appointed collectors whose power and invulnerability outraged the civil service staff.

In 1945, Secretary of the Treasury John W. Snyder launched a concerted program to overhaul, streamline, and modernize the whole tax collection system. Officially labeled the Management Improvement Program, the effort was aided by a Hoover Commission* study and by a House Ways and Means Subcommittee investigation begun in 1951. The initial result was a housecleaning in early 1952 by Commissioner John B. Dunlap in which 103 employees were dismissed on charges ranging from inefficiency to misconduct and the acceptance of bribes.

The massive restructuring of the bureau began in March 1952 with the imposition of Reorganization Plan No. 1, which created four basic changes. Functional organization changed from type of tax structure to one with like functions grouped together under one management official. Field programs were integrated under the line management control of district directors. Regional offices were established to provide direct field supervision. The civil service career system was strengthened throughout the bureau. All patronage appointments were abolished.

Subsequent reorganizations, mild by comparison to that of 1952, have continued the trend toward decentralization. There are presently 7 regional directors, 58 district directors, and 10 regional service centers utilizing a total staff of 86,000. A major change in tax administration came with the introduction of modern electronic equipment. The Automatic Data Processing system was inaugurated in 1962 when the national computer center in Martinsburg, West Virginia, was opened. This system revolutionized the collection and audit process by maintaining a masterfile of every taxpayer's account. In 1966, the Data Center in Detroit, Michigan, completed the technical revolution of bureau procedures.

There has always been controversy surrounding Internal Revenue practices. In recent years, the most controversial administrative issues have centered on the collection of alcohol, tobacco, and firearms taxes, the determination of legitimate travel and entertainment expenses, and the overenforcement practices of revenue agents.

The Volstead Prohibition Enforcement Act of 1919 assigned enforcement of the Eighteenth Amendment to Internal Revenue. The Prohibition Unit was created to enforce the penal and regulatory features of the act. In 1925, this unit made over seventy-seven thousand arrests. In 1927, prohibition enforcement was transferred to the Federal Prohibition Bureau within the Justice Department.*

After ratification of the Twenty-first Amendment in 1933, collection and enforcement of taxes on alcohol and tobacco were placed in the newly formed Alcohol Tax Unit and Excise Tax Unit, respectively. The 1952 reorganization created the Alcohol and Tobacco Tax Division, which also administered the National Firearms Act of 1941. As a result of the Omnibus Crime Control and Safe Streets Act of 1968 and the Gun Control Act of the same year, the unit was reorganized to include all these tax and enforcement areas. Subjected to a steady barrage of criticism, the division was transferred out of the Internal Revenue Service in 1972, and a separate Bureau of Alcohol, Tobacco, and Firearms was established in the Treasury Department. The budget reorganization imposed by the Reagan Administration in 1981 eliminated the bureau and its functions.

The corporate merger movement of the 1950s and new tax laws beneficial to business brought new administrative headaches. Revenue agents spent increasingly more time attempting to determine legitimate corporate and individual travel and entertainment expenses, hobby losses, dividend and interest payments, and transactions between domestic companies and foreign affiliates. Equitable and uniform enforcement was impossible, and taxpayer abuses were encouraged by controversial rulings and loopholes in the law.

Commissioner Mortimer M. Caplin attempted to change the image of Internal Revenue in 1961 with his "New Directions" program, which emphasized better service to the taxpayer, more reasonable enforcement policies, and elimination of personnel abuses. Caplin's policy resulted in fewer corporate audits which subsequent congressional inquiry criticized. New auditing procedures and new schedules requiring major recordkeeping changes were adopted, but the travel and entertainment expense problem remains unresolved and controversial.

By the late 1960s, private citizens as well as Congress became concerned about the awesome investigative powers wielded by IRS. Public outcry at agent abuses reached new heights. *Reader's Digest* articles in 1967 exposed investigative practices that "bullied, degraded and crushed countless citizens while unaccountably favoring others" (John Barron, "Tyranny in the Internal Revenue Service," *Reader's Digest*, August 1967, p. 42). While bureau spokesmen deny any such official policies as agent quotas and production goals, criticism of overenforcement practices and violations of privacy persists.

The Economic Recovery Tax Act of 1981 promises to impose new administrative burdens. The bureau is once again in the center of political debate, and its enforcement of this controversial legislation will be closely watched. Taxation and internal revenue collection and enforcement remain inherently a political matter.

FOR ADDITIONAL INFORMATION: Records of the Internal Revenue Service are in Record Group 58 in the National Archives.* Forrest R. Holdcamper, comp., *The Preliminary Inventory of the Records of the Internal Revenue Service* (1967) is the principal guide. Closely related records are those of the Treasury Department, U.S. General Accounting Office, and the Department of Justice. Both the *Annual Report of the Commissioner of Internal Revenue* and the *Annual Report of the Secretary of the Treasury* are important primary sources. *The Internal Revenue Record and Customs Journal*, which flourished from 1864 to 1897, is a storehouse of tax information for the period.

Reports of the various congressional inquiries into the Internal Revenue Service are available in appropriate committee documents. George S. Boutwell, *A Manual of the Direct and Excise Tax System of the United States* (1863), provides a basic understanding of the establishment of the tax collection system.

There is no objective, scholarly history of the IRS, and one is badly needed. The best secondary analyses are Lawrence F. Schmeckebier and Francis X.A. Eble, *The Bureau of Internal Revenue*, Institute for Government Research, Service Monographs of the United States Government, No. 25 (1923); John C. Chommie, *The Internal Revenue Service* (1970); and Joseph P. Crockett, *The Federal Tax System of the United States* (1955). Lillian Doris, ed., *The American Way in Taxation: Internal Revenue 1862-1963* (1963), is the official centennial history of the agency. Herbert Ronald Ferleger's doctoral dissertation *David A. Wells and the American Revenue System 1865-1870* (1942, reprint 1972), is an important analysis of the first congressional investigation of the bureau. Also uncritical but essential for understanding compliance division functions is Singleton B. Wolfe, "Tax Compliance—History of Significant Internal Revenue Service Developments" *Georgia Journal of Accounting* (Spring 1981):14-41.

Hints as to the inner workings of the agency can only be pieced together. Informative sources include Elmer L. Irey, *The Tax Dodgers*, as told to William J. Slocum (1948) and more sensationally in *Reader's Digest* (August 1967-September 1968): 91-93.

The important relationship between IRS and Congress is explored by Archie Parnell, *Congress and the IRS: Improving the Relationship* (1980). A suspect but interesting exposé of IRS practices can be found in Jeff A. Schnepper, *Inside IRS: How Internal Revenue Works (You Over)* (1978).

LINDA J. LEAR

INTERNATIONAL TRADE COMMISSION. See United States International Trade Commission.

INTERSTATE COMMERCE COMMISSION (ICC). On February 4, 1887, President Grover Cleveland signed the Interstate Commerce Act into law. Based on the commerce power of the Constitution (Article I, Section 8), it stated that all charges by common carriers crossing state lines must be "reasonable and just" and that discrimination in rates or service was unlawful. Rebates, draw-backs, long-haul/short-haul differentiations, and pools were prohibited. A commission of five members, appointed by the President and approved by the Senate for six-year terms, was to keep track of carriers and enforce the act through the U.S. circuit courts.

The precedent was the state commissions used in New England for more than half a century to supervise banks and insurance companies and those later created to oversee the railroads. In the 1870s, commissions came into increasing use and were operating in one form or another in twenty-five states, most strongly in the Midwest. State regulation was not effective, and Texas Congressman John H. Reagan and Illinois Senator Shelby M. Cullom led the push for a national law. When the U.S. Supreme Court ruled in the 1886 Wabash case (*Wabash, St. Louis and Pacific Ry. Co.* v. *Illinois*, 118 U.S. 557) that only the national government could regulate commerce that crossed state lines, the Congress felt impelled to act. The next year the Interstate Commerce Act became law.

The railroads were the nation's largest business and the prime means of travel and shipment of goods. Between 1860 and 1900, railroad mileage grew from 30,000 to 194,000 miles, making possible a national market and the American industrial revolution. The resulting railroad system had many problems. In the West, construction in advance of settlement made earnings slow to come. In some areas, there were too many lines for profitable operation, and in others there was monopoly control. Hasty construction, stock watering, market manipulation, kickbacks (rebates and drawbacks), and other forms of unequal treatment made the railroads a national problem. Farmers had long complained about the railroads, but the primary pressure to pass the Interstate Commerce Act came from Midwestern and Southern merchants and shippers. While the level of rates was important to farmers and consumers, equal treatment with their competitors was more important to shippers and merchants. In the public mind, controlling the railroads was one of the nation's most crucial problems.

The same element that objected to railroad misbehavior and monopoly was also suspicious of giving that power to the government. Since regulating the railroads combined setting standards (a legislative function), measuring behavior and compliance, and seeking punishment (executive and judicial functions), the proposed solution was an independent regulatory body. It was to be freed from the "politics" of presidential or congressional control by nonremovable, fixed-term appointments, and its rulings were subject to court review and enforcement.

In the twentieth century, after the Interstate Commerce Commission was strengthened by the Hepburn Act of 1906, the independent regulatory commission became the dominant American means of direct control of business activity. Over time, the Federal Reserve Board* (1913), Federal Trade Commission* (1914), Federal Power Commission* (1930), Tennessee Valley Authority* (1933), Securities Exchange Commission* (1934), Federal Communications Commission* (1934), National Labor Relations Board* (1935), Federal Maritime Commission* (1936), Civil Aeronautics Board* (1938), Consumer Products Safety Commission (1972), and Nuclear Regulatory Commission* (1975) were created on the model of the Interstate Commerce Commission. Other monetary, fiscal, and regulatory controls, particularly since the New Deal of the 1930s, have been under executive authority and do not operate as independent regulatory commissions.

During the unhappy first twenty years, it would have been difficult to predict that the ICC would become such a model. The meaning of "just and reasonable rates" was undefined, and the commission had to create its own procedures and path. Under its able but cautious first chairman, Thomas M. Cooley, a former law professor and jurist, the commission adopted what became its enduring path. It did not attempt to set general policies but waited for complaints, which it decided on a case-by-case basis, building precedents. Despite this restrained approach, the railroads treated it as an enemy. As the historian of commissions, Robert Cushman, has summed it up, the railroads "fought, harassed, obstructed, and delayed at every possible point" (Robert Cushman, *Independent Regulatory Commissions* [1941], pp. 65-66).

In appealing commission decisions, the railroads counted on being upheld by the extremely property-conscious federal courts. Instead of limiting themselves to points of law, the courts retried cases and usually ruled for the railroads, sustaining long-haul/short-haul discriminations, and negating the right of the ICC to set rates to replace rates it found unreasonable. Until Congress passed the 1893 Compulsory Testimony law, the Supreme Court denied the commission the power to require witnesses to give information (*Kentucky & Indiana Bridge Co.* v. *L&N Ry. Co.*, 37 Fed 567 [1889], *ICC* v. *Alabama Midland Ry. Co.*, 168 U.S. 144 [1897], *ICC* v. *Cincinnati, N.O. & Texas Pacific Ry. Co.*, 167 U.S. 497 [1897], and *Counselman* v. *Hitchcock*, 142 U.S. 547 [1892]).

By 1900, the commission was a failure, but forces for change were at work. Rates were rising, and the consolidation of the roads into the enormous Vanderbilt, Morgan, Harriman, Pennsylvania, and Gould-system empires caused increasing popular and political protest. This concern found expression through a group of magazine journalists, known as muckrakers, and in congressional and presidential politics. The reform-minded President, Theodore Roosevelt, took the lead. The railroads were happy to have the Elkins Act of 1903 attempt to free them from paying kickbacks (rebates) to large shippers such as John D. Rockefeller's Standard Oil Company, but this and an Expediting Act to speed cases through the courts were not enough.

The enactment of the Hepburn of 1906 was, at least in the hands of the historians, the great adventure story of the independent regulatory commissions. With Midwestern Progressives such as Senators Jonathan Dolliver of Iowa and Wisconsin's Robert M. La Follette seeking even stronger regulation, the struggle was fought out in the U.S. Senate between the forces of President Roosevelt and those of the conservative Republican Senator Nelson W. Aldrich. The resulting law brought express, sleeping car, and other railroad activities under the commission, which was given power to prescribe railroad recordkeeping and accounting practices. The commission could now replace unreasonable rates with rates of its own, and penalties were strengthened. The broad court review, which the conservatives had counted on to negate these powers, was rejected by the U.S. Supreme Court, which refused to act as a court of first instance and rehear the facts of cases on appeal (*ICC* v. *Ill. Central RR Co.*, 215 U.S. 452 [1910]).

The Mann-Elkins Act of 1910 strengthened protection against long-haul/short/haul discrimination, gave the commission power over proposed rates, shifted the burden of proving the reasonableness of rate increases to the railroads, and extended jurisdiction to interstate communication systems. A special Commerce Court, dear to the heart of President William Howard Taft, was to speed appeals on commission rulings, but it became so hostile to the commission that Congress abolished it in 1913. The Panama Canal Act of 1912 limited railroad control over competing water transportation. The Valuation Act of 1913 set the commission on a twenty-year task to realize Senator La Follette's goal of determining the value of railroad property for rate-setting purposes. Under the Erdman Act of 1898 and the 1913 Newlands Act, the ICC chairman could be called upon as a mediator in railroad labor controversies. In 1917, the commission was enlarged to nine members and permitted to operate three-member panels. Altogether, the ICC had emerged with sufficient strength to regulate railroad rates and service and to be the model for future regulatory agencies.

In actuality, it had neither the power nor the foresight to meet the needs of the railroads and the nation. The instrument created was prepared to ensure the reasonable, nondiscriminatory treatment of goods and passengers, which had been the basic demand of the Populist and Progressive Eras. It was not ready, and it did not guide the maintenance of an effective, financially sound national railroad system. As the historians Albro Martin, *Enterprise Denied: Origins of the Decline of American Railroads, 1897-1917* (1971) and Ari and Olive Hoogenboom, *A History of the ICC: From Panacea to Palliative* (1976) point out, the ICC failed to permit the railroads sufficient rate increases to draw investment and keep up the system. Net earnings remained unhealthily low and the operating ratio (the proportion of revenue that went into operating expenses) increasingly high.

During World War I, Woodrow Wilson's administration went around the newly expanded commission to solve a breakdown of freight car availability, by assuming federal control of the nation's railroads on December 28, 1917. After the war, Congress rejected the labor-backed Plumb Plan for permanent nationalization. Instead, it passed the Esch-Cummins Transportation Act of 1920, returning the railroads to private ownership and ICC regulation. The commission's power was extended to minimum rates and the general supervision of railroad financial policies. Pooling was legalized and a 5.5 percent-profit standard set, with a recapture clause by which excess revenues would be shared with weaker railroads. On March 1, 1920, the railroads went back into private hands.

In returning the railroads, Congress enlarged the ICC to eleven members and expanded its now traditional role of regulating rates and service. In a major shift, the commission was also asked to guide the development of a healthy national system by planning consolidation of the railroads into a limited number of large, financially sound lines. The commission did not accomplish this goal. During the business-dominated 1920s, it took a passive role. A loophole in the 1920 act denied the commission control over noncarrier companies, and whatever consolidation there was came as the result of titanic holding-company battles. It took a decade for the commission unenthusiastically to produce a plan, which died during the depression. In the meantime, the commission submissively approved security issues proposed by the noncarrier holding companies which, exempt otherwise from regulation, struggled with each other to acquire new railroad properties. The historians Ari and Olive Hoogenboom fault the commission for not reducing bonded debt and establishing a proper cost-of-service measure for railroad rates.

The impact of the depression was devastating. Adding to loss of traffic to the trucking industry, the depression decreased freight volume by almost one-half. Nearly three-quarters of the railroad mileage was not meeting fixed costs. The governmental response was the Emergency Railroad Transportation Act of 1933, the facilitation of debt restructuring by an amendment to the 1898 Bankruptcy Act, and funds from the Reconstruction Finance Corporation.* Noncarrier holding companies were brought under commission regulation. The shifting of indebtedness from bonds to stocks helped abate the payment problem but made railroad investment even less attractive. The able commission chairman, Joseph Eastman, was appointed to the new Office of Temporary Coordinator of Transportation, charged with creating a more efficient national railroad system. However, during the adversity of the depression, the railroads were no more willing to cooperate than they had been during the prosperity of the 1920s, and the politicians and the public did not push them to do so. Although neither the American railroad system nor the regulatory role of the ICC was basically changed during the depression years, the scope of commission responsiblity was substantially broadened. The Motor Carrier Act of 1935 and the 1940 Transportation Act extended its supervision to commercial trucking and inland and coastal water carriers. The ICC now regulated all forms of interstate commerical traffic except the airlines.

The railroads prospered during World War II. Motor use was restricted, and the two-ocean war prevented the Atlantic Coast freight car jams which had brought governmental takeover during World War I. Even so, the railroads emerged from the war with even greater problems. Automobiles, buses, trucks, planes, pipelines, and barges all ate into railroad business. Passenger traffic was a money-losing proposition, but not until 1958 was the ICC given supervision of discontinuance. Although a 1945 ruling ended the freight classification system, which the South had long claimed was discriminatory, the ICC could do little for the suffering railroads, which claimed that they in turn were being badly disadvantaged by governmental expenditure on highways and airports.

In 1970, the newly consolidated Penn Central system failed and was soon followed into bankruptcy by the six major Northeastern railroads and the Midwest's Rock Island. This was a national economic disaster. Although the railroads, generally unwillingly, transported less than 10 percent of interurban passenger travel, they were still the best heavy freight carrier and basic to the nation's industrial heartland.

In the face of crisis, no one thought of turning to the ICC to cope with the problems and future of the railroads. Even with the replacement in 1970 of rotating chairmen with long-term presidential appointments, the ICC did not itself assert leadership. The commission continued its regulatory role on a case-by-case basis, slowed even more by the 1946 Administrative Procedures Act, and continually charged with being a "barnacle-encrusted bureaucracy," closely identified with the carriers and headed by undistinguished political appointees. As during both world wars, the government created new agencies to deal with the larger transportation problems. The 1966 Department of Transportation* (DOT) took over most of the planning function, which resulted in the National Railroad Passenger Corporation* (AMTRAK), Consolidated Facilities (CONFAC), and Consolidated Railroads* (CONRAIL) which sought to maintain national passenger and Northeastern track and freight systems.

The 1960s and 1970s had produced a major expansion of regulatory activity, particularly characterized by concern for safety, consumerism, and the quality of life. By the 1980s, the troubled state of the economy produced a reversal. Trucking regulation, instituted during the 1930s to prevent cut-throat competition, had become a highly complex and economically costly protection for franchised companies. Not only were the profit-starved railroads suffering from lack of maintenance capital and tied to money-losing lines, but they were also enjoined against meaningful competition in those services in which they enjoyed an advantage over highway and water carriers. The Motor Carrier and Rail Acts of 1980 gave greater freedom to both industries to adjust routes and rates and opened up entrance into the interstate trucking business. Although the estimates of shipper and consumer savings ran into billions and mergers among profitable railroad lines moved the industry toward more unified systems, the immense capital needs of the railroads remained unmet.

As the father of national regulation, the Interstate Commerce Commission, approached its hundredth birthday, the key slogan was "deregulation." However, as the Republican planners of the 1980s struggled with problems of inflation, stagnation, and capital investment, the ICC occupied a somewhat diminished but general business-as-usual role, not important enough to be strengthened but still useful enough not to be replaced.

FOR ADDITIONAL INFORMATION: The *Annual Reports* of the Interstate Commerce Commission; David Chalmers, *Neither Socialism Nor Monopoly: Theodore Roosevelt and the Decision to Regulate the Railroads* (1976); Robert E. Cushman, *Independent Regulatory Commissions* (1941); *The Economic Regulation of Business and Industry*, Vols. I-II, Bernard Schwartz, ed. (1973); Ari and Olive Hoogenboom, *A History of the ICC: From Panacea to Palliative* (1976); and I. L. Sharfman, *The Interstate Commerce Commission: A Study in Administrative Law and Procedure*, 5 vols. (1931-1937).

DAVID CHALMERS

J

JOB CORPS. The Job Corps, created by the Economic Opportunity Act of 1964, was a centerpiece of Lyndon Johnson's War on Poverty. Designed as a residential program offering vocational training and basic education to disadvantaged youths, the first Job Corps center opened in 1965. Unlike much of the War on Poverty, the Job Corps has managed to survive the intervening years and is today widely recognized as an effective program. Before reviewing the development of the Job Corps, however, it is helpful to glance back a few decades to the Civilian Conservation Corps* (CCC) (1933-1942), which was the grandfather of Job Corps, Neighborhood Youth Corps, Youth Conservation Corps, and other modern youth-employment efforts sponsored by the federal government. The CCC was a tremendously successful conservation-oriented youth-employment organization, and was one of the most popular of the New Deal social programs. The public, the press, and the Congress were extremely supportive of the CCC, and this popularity left a legacy. The CCC idea has remained alive in the policymaking process, and the Job Corps was created in CCC's very long shadow.

Senator Hubert Humphrey proposed legislation in 1958, which led eventually to the Job Corps program. Humphrey proposed a youth conservation corps patterned after the CCC of the 1930s. This idea was taken to the American people in a 1959 article entitled "Plan to Save Trees, Land, and Boys." Although there was great public support, the White House opposed Humphrey's initiative. The bill barely passed in the Senate (1959), and a companion bill in the House received no action.

There was a specific promise of a youth conservation corps in the Democratic platform of 1960. However, as legislation was introduced in 1961, it became clear that President John F. Kennedy was weakly committed to the idea, offering a very limited "pilot" formula designed to hold down expenditures. Over White House opposition, the Senate Labor Committee approved a watered-down Humphrey plan rather than Kennedy's proposal. The House Committee on Education and Labor, on the other hand, more nearly supported the President's requests. Neither bill reached a vote on the floor.

During 1962 and 1963, discussion of various versions of a youth-employment program continued. Debate was intensified by James Conant's report, *Social Dynamite*, which identified an explosive unemployed and out-of-school urban youth population. Support expressed for a youth conservation corps before congressional committees was remarkable —almost no one was opposed. A Gallup poll in 1961 reported that 80 percent of the American people thought it was a good idea to revive the CCC; 59 percent thought it should be required for young men unemployed and not in school. In 1963, President Kennedy also proposed a National Service Corps. None of these initiatives, however, resulted in new programs during the Kennedy Administration.

When Lyndon Johnson became President, congressional bottlenecks to social legislation began to dissolve. Job Corps and the Neighborhood Youth Corps were created as the youth-employment initiatives of the War on Poverty. The Office of Economic Opportunity (OEO) was given overall program authority. The Job Corps was designed to improve employment prospects for sixteen-to twenty-one-year-old males and females. Program objectives were mixed. In the early days of Job Corps, both work experience and job training were emphasized. The original Job Corps concept also emphasized removing disadvantaged youth from poverty environments.

The conservation lobby pushed through a provision that 40 percent of Job Corps enrollees be located in Civilian Conservation Centers doing conservation work. Management of the Conservation Centers was given to the National Park Service* and the Forest Service.* It was not coincidental that these centers resembled the camps of the old CCC, carried the same initials, and involved the same major conservation agencies. Unlike the old CCC, however, the original Job Corps Conservation Centers were not very successful. Enrollees from urban backgrounds who were a large majority of Job Corps participants did not always see the relevance of conservation work to future employment opportunities. The first Job Corps Conservation Centers had a multitude of problems, and dropout rates were high. Eventually, after continuing difficulties, the emphasis on conservation work was replaced by more specific job training.

Urban Job Corps Centers, oriented more toward job training from the beginning, also had problems. Most centers were administered by contract with large companies such as IBM and General Electric. Early evaluations were not complimentary. Objectives appeared to be unclear. Confusion and a crisis-like atmosphere characterized these first attempts at training disadvantaged youth, and the entire program withstood a barrage of negative publicity.

This inauspicious early performance and a growing realization that the nation could not simultaneously afford guns for Vietnam and butter at home led to a scaling down of original projections for program size. The Job Corps was to have 100,000 enrollees by the end of the second year, but Congress decided to cap the program at 45,000 enrollees. President Richard M. Nixon further reduced the size of the program and, to deemphasize the Job Corps' visibility, shifted program authority from OEO to the Department of Labor.* As a result of these changes, the Job Corps endured some very lean years during the 1970s. Program size remained at about twenty thousand throughout the decade. In fiscal 1978, there were twenty-eight Conservation Centers in operation, and thirty-six other centers were administered by business firms, nonprofit organizations, state and local government agencies, and labor unions.

During this period of austerity, objectives within the Job Corps program were sharpened. The urgent need for remedial education, specific job training, and connections to jobs became more clearly defined and operationalized. One of the important lessons learned from Job Corps experience—one that may be particularly relevant to future institutional training programs—is that Job Corps performance improved rather than deteriorated when many of the frills were slashed. Training and education were narrowed to specific job requirements. The key seemed to be the ability to gain access to jobs rather than efforts to alter the enrollees' attitudes and values. It has also been helpful to establish specific links to employers and unions and to provide adequate placement services. Cooperative arrangements between the Job Corps and some labor unions have been one of the most effective approaches to youth employment in the past forty years. Under these arrangements, Job Corps training is shaped to fit union jobs, and enrollees enter the union as apprentices with a foot in the door toward a promising career. As of 1978, cooperating unions included the Brotherhood of Railway, Airline and Steamship Clerks, AFL/CIO; Stewards Training and Recreation, Inc., of the Marine Cooks and Steward's Union, AFL/CIO; International Brotherhood of Painters and Allied Trades; International Union of Operating Engineers; and others. In addition, the Job Corps has a well-developed and organized network of community volunteers who assist in placing enrollees as they leave the program.

With these changes in the Job Corps, combined with more careful screening of applicants, retention of enrollees has improved and improvement in enrollee placement upon leaving the program has been dramatic. According to government statistics, the Job Corps placement rate for fiscal years 1977, 1978, and 1979 was about 93 percent. This figure includes enrollees placed in employment, military service, school, or further job training. It is all the more remarkable that this placement rate has been achieved with a disadvantaged population, 85 percent of whom had not completed high school and 50 percent of whom were reading at below seventh-grade level when they entered the program.

Following congressional recognition of the program's effectiveness, appropriations were approved in 1978 to double the size of the Job Corps, and this expansion has been gradually taking place. By the end of fiscal year 1979, there were ninety-five Job Corps Centers. Recent innovations include the Advanced Career Training (ACT) program, which allows corps members to attend college or receive other advanced training, and a program for refugee Indochinese youth, which emphasizes language skills along with job training. These and other innovations offer a great deal of promise in meeting the job-training needs of disadvantaged youth. It seems unlikely, however, that the program will continue to expand and innovate in the years immediately ahead. As of this writing, President Ronald Reagan is proposing a 15-percent cut in Job Corps expenditures. In light of the Job Corps record, this is one of the more short-sighted proposals of the new administration.

Because of the size and thoroughness of the current Job Corps research effort, a great deal is known about program outcomes. Among other things, former Job Corps enrollees make more money; are less likely to be unemployed; are less dependent on welfare assistance and other public transfers; are less often arrested on criminal charges; are more likely to receive a high school diploma; and are more likely to attend college than a comparable group of youngsters who have not enrolled in the Job Corps. These positive impacts, translated into economic terms, represent an excess of program benefits over costs. The findings from a comprehensive evaluation of the social benefits and costs of the Job Corps suggest that public investment in the corps is economically efficient. The benchmark estimate is that the value of benefits in fiscal year 1977 exceeded costs by almost $2,300 per corps member, or by approximately 45 percent of costs. Furthermore, the program is found to be economically efficient under a wide range of alternative assumptions and estimates. Because over forty thousand youths enrolled in the Job Corps during fiscal year 1977, the benchmark estimate of the net social benefit for the entire program is approximately $90 million for that year.

Probably the most intriguing research issue related to the Jobs Corps is its transformation from a program with severe problems to a program which today has a reputation of effective service. No other federal program in the employment and job-training field has made so dramatic a turnabout. The turnabout occurred over an extended period of time, nearly a decade, and in the context of widespread public criticism, unhelpful presidents, and restricted resources. From this crucible the Job Corps emerged sound and successful. Perhaps the Job Corps became strong as a result of its trials. On the other hand, it is possible that the Job Corps, if given more consistent support, could have made much more substantial progress in training and placing disadvantaged young people in jobs. At some point, and with sufficient perspective, it will be useful to examine this question. It will also be useful to ask why the Job Corps "works," while so many other targeted jobs programs remain in a pillory exposed to possible scorn. How has the Job Corps, which serves only impoverished and unemployed youth, outdistanced the "welfare" image? If this question can be answered and knowledge applied more generally, the Job Corps may make contributions far beyond its direct impact. Learning how a program for poor people defeats the stigma of "welfare" would be an extremely valuable lesson.

FOR ADDITIONAL INFORMATION: The most complete source on the background and early years of the Job Corps is Christopher Weeks, *Job Corps: Dollars and Dropouts* (1967). For a first-hand view and critique of the early Job Corps Centers, see Harold Lewack, "Requiem for a Dream: The Job Corps on Trial," in Ira Goldenberg, ed., *The*

Helping Professions in the World of Action (1973). Helpful in looking at the period from 1968 to 1972 is Dave O'Neill, *The Federal Government and Manpower: A Critical Look at the MDTA—Institutional and Job Corps Programs* (1973). See also Louis Harris and Associates, *A Survey of Ex-Job Corpsmen* (1969). The most recent, thorough review, which analyzes the major changes and eventual success of the Job Corps, is Sar Levitan and Benjamin Johnston, *The Job Corps: A Social Experiment That Works* (1975).

The best sources for data and evaluation of the Job Corps on an annual basis are the *Employment and Training Report of the President*, and U.S. Department of Labor, *Job Corps in Brief* (U.S. Department of Labor, both published annually).

Currently, the Job Corps is fortunate to be the target of one of the most comprehensive research efforts ever focused on a single social program. This research effort, which incorporates a longitudinal design following a sample of enrollees and a control group, has resulted in the following reports: U.S. Department of Labor, *Assessments of the Job Corps Performances and Impacts*, 2 vols. (1979); U.S. Department of Labor, *The Non-economic Impacts of the Job Corps* (1978); and Mathematica Policy Research, Inc., *Evaluation of the Economic Impact of the Job Corps Program: Second Follow-up Report* (1980). A large number of reports documenting specific topics are also available from Mathematica.

MICHAEL W. SHERRADEN

JUSTICE DEPARTMENT. See Department of Justice.

L

LABOR DEPARTMENT. See Department of Labor.

LABOR RELATIONS BOARD. See National Labor Relations Board.

LAND OFFICE. See Bureau of Land Management.

M

MANAGEMENT AND BUDGET OFFICE. See Office of Management and Budget.

MARINE CORPS. See United States Marine Corps.

MARITIME COMMISSION. See Federal Maritime Commission.

MILITARY ACADEMY. See United States Military Academy.

MINES BUREAU. See Bureau of Mines.

N

NATIONAL AERONAUTICS AND SPACE ADMINISTRATION (NASA).

The National Aeronautics and Space Administration originated as part of the United States response to Sputnik, the first man-made satellite of earth, launched by the Soviet Union on October 4, 1957. Sputnik touched off a national debate, pitting congressional Democrats and other preparedness advocates against a Republican administration confident of American military and technological superiority. As the debate proceeded in the closing months of 1957, it became clear that our military preparations for space activity, which had been under way on a modest scale for some years, would have to be augmented by a new and larger program. But what should the national space program be, and where should it be lodged?

President Dwight D. Eisenhower answered both questions in April 1958 when he sent Congress a bill providing for a civilian space program run by a National Aeronautics and Space Agency, to be formed around the nucleus of the National Advisory Committee for Aeronautics (NACA). The NACA was the principal aeronautical research institution of the United States, created by Congress in 1915 to engage in the scientific study of the problems of flight, with a view to their practical solution. It served thereafter as a source of fundamental aeronautical research for the military services and the aircraft manufacturing industry. Over the years, the committee itself grew from twelve to seventeen members, while the staff expanded from a single clerk in 1915 to some eight thousand employees in 1958, distributed at a Washington headquarters and three major and three minor laboratories across the country. Langley Laboratory in Hampton, Virginia, was founded in 1917 as the committee's research arm. After 1940, it spawned the other NACA laboratories: Ames Laboratory in Sunnyvale, California, and Lewis Flight Propulsion Laboratory in Cleveland, Ohio, during the buildup for World War II; the High Speed Flight Station at Edwards Air Force Base, California, and the Pilotless Aircraft Research Station at Wallops Island, Virginia, to conduct flight research with supersonic aircraft and missiles; and, finally, Plum Brook Station on Lake Erie near Sandusky, Ohio, the nuclear propulsion subsidiary of Lewis Laboratory. These expanded facilities and staff and the diverse research program they encompassed raised the NACA budget from a modest $5,000 in 1915 to a considerable $77 million in the year of Sputnik.

The legislation transforming the NACA into NASA also laid out the new agency's responsibilities and authority. In general, NASA was to conduct the civilian space program of the United States, cooperate with the military services to prevent duplication, and cooperate with other nations in joint space activities. As functions were actually distributed in practice by executive decision during the summer and fall of 1958, NASA became the principal operating agency for manned space flight, space science, and launch-vehicle development, and provided research and development services for space-flight technology and aeronautics, in addition to weather, communications, and nonmilitary earth-sensing satellites. As an operating agency, NASA has developed and conducted its own programs, as in the Apollo missions to the moon and the Viking mission to Mars. As a service agency, it has developed new technologies and hardware and then turned them over to operating agencies like the Weather Service* and the National Oceanographic and Atmospheric Administration, providing in most instances the necessary launch and tracking services.

From the original NACA nucleus, NASA quickly expanded its staff and facilities by transfer from other government agencies. The Vanguard research team of the Naval Research Laboratory came to NASA in 1958, bringing along the U.S. program to launch a scientific satellite in the International Geophysical Year, 1957-1958. The contract under which the Jet Propulsion Laboratory of the California Institute of Technology conducted rocket research for the Army was transferred to NASA, adding an anomolous new research center to the civil service laboratories inherited from the NACA. Completing the transfer of personnel and facilities, Wernher von Braun and his Development Operations Division of the Army Ballistic Missile Agency at the Redstone Arsenal in Huntsville, Alabama, joined NASA in 1960 and soon became the nucleus of the Marshall Space Flight Center.

At the same time that people and facilities from military programs were augmenting the NACA nucleus of the new space agency, paper transfers of military programs were under way as well. For example, the Air Force transferred to NASA control of two lunar probes and several engine-development projects. Plans for unmanned exploration of the moon and passive satellite communication followed from the Army. To house the agency's rapidly expanding programs and staff, NASA began construction of its first new field center, the Goddard Space Flight Center in Greenbelt, Maryland, just outside Washington, D.C.

As dramatic as this growth was in the last years of the Eisenhower Administration, it was to be dwarfed by the scale of activity undertaken in the John F. Kennedy years. Early in his administration, after the embarrassments of the Bay of Pigs invasion and the Russian launching of the first man into space, Kennedy called for a national commitment to land an American on the moon and return him safely to earth in the decade of the 1960s. Congress quickly endorsed the proposal and appropriated the first of the $25 billion that would fund the mission. Within a year, two more field installations were operating and beginning to grow. The Manned Spacecraft Center in Houston, Texas, later renamed the Lyndon B. Johnson Space Center, was formally established on November 1, 1961. In March 1962, Marshall Space Flight Center's Launch Operations Directorate at Cape Canaveral, Florida, became the independent Launch Operations Center, nucleus of the John F. Kennedy Space Center, from which all Apollo launches would be made.

Apollo dominated the U.S. civilian space program in the 1960s. While NASA insisted on pursuing a broad range of space activities that included significant advances in weather and communications satellites and space science researches, like the Mariner flybys of Venus and Mars, all seemed to live in Apollo's shadow. The moon mission captured the lion's share of the NASA budget, public attention, and agency concerns. When Apollo flourished, as it did after the first Saturn launch-vehicle test shots or in the wake of the two-man Gemini flights that proved the feasibility of rendezvous in space and long-duration space flight, NASA prospered with it. When Apollo faltered, as it did in the tragic fire that killed three astronauts at Cape Kennedy in 1967, NASA suffered not only public recrimination but internal stress and upheaval as well. When the program mission was achieved by Apollo 11, in July 1969, NASA secured for itself an institutional reputation for managerial competence and technological virtuosity that time and circumstance have hardly tarnished.

Manned space flight in the first half of the 1970s seemed somewhat anticlimactic. The remaining Apollo missions, 12 through 17, were exciting in their own right, but only Apollo 13 matched the high drama of the first landing: an explosion in the service module on the way to the moon turned that perilous mission into a fight for survival, in which the versatility and redundancy of the spacecraft and the resourcefulness of the earth-based engineers controlling the mission provided the narrow margin of safety. Skylab provided a different kind of spectacle in 1973 and 1974, a series of experimental flights in an orbital space station fashioned from a Saturn upper-stage rocket. The Apollo-Soyuz Test Project linked American and Soviet space vehicles in earth orbit for an as-yet unexploited demonstration of the feasibility of joint operations and rescue.

Even before the first Apollo astronaut landed on the moon, public and congressional sentiment cooled toward the project and, in fact, toward the expense of manned space flight in general. The domestic protest and upheaval of the 1960s, the spiraling costs of the War on Poverty and the war in Vietnam, and the growing awareness that the United States had won the space race long before the first landing on the moon, all contributed to an increasing skepticism about the wisdom of grandiose space projects. The first moon landing dispelled for a while this mild disenchantment, but it did not long deflect Congress from a more critical approach to the post-Apollo space program. From its peak of $5.25 billion in 1965, the NASA budget declined steadily in real dollars for fifteen years. Personnel strength similarly declined from a 1967 high of almost 37,000 to less than two-thirds that number in 1980.

In the 1970s, emphasis in the civilian space program turned from manned space flight to space science and earth applications. Surely the most spectacular scientific mission of the decade was the dual Viking mission to Mars, which put two landers on the red planet to send back to earth not only close-up pictures but also information from on-board equipment designed to search for signs of life. Viking found no life, but it returned data about our nearest planetary neighbor that will keep scientists busy for years. Other space science probes sent back similarly dramatic data, like the Mariner pictures of Mercury and the breathtaking Voyager pictures of Jupiter and Saturn and their rings and moons in 1979 and 1980. Less spectacular but nonetheless productive scientific missions throughout the decade have swamped the scientific community with data and demonstrated Congress's continuing willingness to support a fairly constant level of space science research.

While manned space flight declined in the 1970s and space science continued more or less steadily, earth applications within NASA rose dramatically. Landsat, the earth-resources technology satellite, grew from an untested, experimental program of the late 1960s to a demonstrated system of wide-ranging capabilities, from crop forecasting to pollution monitoring. As the decade ended, NASA prepared to turn over operation of Landsat to the National Oceanographic and Atmospheric Administration, as it had earlier turned over operation of communications satellites to Comsat and weather satellites to the Weather Service. In other fields, for example, space-flight technology and aeronautics, NASA continued to provide the research and development services that have made it one of the leading technological agencies in the federal government. Through its technology transfer program, NASA made a concerted effort to ensure the widest practical dissemination and exploitation of the hardware and techniques developed for flight in the atmosphere and space.

NASA's reputation for managerial excellence, established largely in the Apollo era, derives less from revolutionary innovations in management techniques than from imaginative and diligent application of traditional methods and the availability of adequate funding. The agency has employed reorganization as a management technique and has adapted to its own needs such other management strategies as the Program Evaluation and Review Technique, Planned Programming and Budgeting, and management by exception (the concentration of top-level attention on problem areas). NASA is organized hierarchically, with broad general programs managed from headquarters and the implementing projects within those program areas managed at the field centers which enjoy considerable autonomy in executing their responsibilities. Approximately 90 percent of NASA's work is performed under contract, requiring a staff of scientists and engineers with sufficient training and expertise to evaluate and supervise contract performance.

After more than twenty years of experience, NASA continues to live with some unanswered questions. NASA is an R & D (research and development) agency. Within, or in addition to, that role, what emphasis should be assigned to operating more or less developed systems? To providing service to other agencies? How will the expanding military space program, whose budget exceeded NASA's for the first time in 1979, influence the civilian program? Will the United States, with its unparalleled launch and tracking facilities, continue to dominate joint space projects among Western nations, or will expanding programs in Japan and Europe challenge American leadership? Perhaps most importantly, will the space shuttle routinize space flight and open up near-earth space to less expensive exploitation and commercial and industrial applications?

The space shuttle, or more properly the Space Transportation System, was originated in the late 1960s as a plan to replace the expensive, expendable launch vehicles of the early space age with a more economical and versatile vehicle that would be launched piggyback aboard a vertical-trajectory rocket and fly back to earth aerodynamically to be landed, refurbished, and launched again. Budget constraints forced NASA to accept a more modest shuttle than at first envisioned, and the resulting development program has been beset by delays and cost overruns greatly at odds with NASA's Apollo reputation. With many civilian and military programs already committed to use of the shuttle, NASA awaited the first launch in 1981 with great expectations that the coming decade would witness renewed enthusiasm for space and a richer, more diversified exploitation of its potentials. Success followed into 1983.

FOR ADDITIONAL INFORMATION: A brief overview of NASA and its predecessor agency is provided in Frank W. Anderson, Jr., *Orders of Magnitude: A History of NACA and NASA, 1915-1976* (1976). See also Richard Hirsch and Joseph John Trento, *The National Aeronautics and Space Administration* (1973). The NACA is treated in detail in George W. Gray, *Frontiers of Flight: The Story of NACA Research* (1948); and Alex Roland, *A History of the National Advisory Committee for Aeronautics, 1915-1958* (in press). On the creation of NASA, see Enid Curtis Bok Schoette, "The Establishment of NASA," in Sanford A. Lakoff, ed., *Knowledge and Power: Essays on Science and Government* (1966), pp. 162-270; Alison Griffith, *The National Aeronautics and Space Act: A Study of the Development of Public Policy* (1969); and James R. Killian, Jr., *Sputnik, Scientists, and Eisenhower: A Memoir of the First Special Assistant to the President for Science and Technology* (1977).

The early years of NASA are described in Robert L. Rosholt, *An Administrative History of NASA, 1958-1963* (1966). See also Constance McL. Green and Milton Lomask, *Vanguard: A History* (1970). On Goddard, see Alfred Rosenthal, *Venture into Space: Early Years of Goddard Space Flight Center* (1968). The Kennedy initiative is thoroughly examined in John M. Logsdon, *The Decision to Go to the Moon: Project Apollo and the National Interest* (1976). On the Kennedy Space Center, see Charles D. Benson and William Barnaby Faherty, *Moonport: A History of Apollo Launch Facilities and Operations* (1978).

Manned space flight through the first moon landing is covered in Loyd S. Swenson, Jr., James M. Grimwood, and Charles C. Alexander, *This New Ocean: A History of Project Mercury* (1966); Barton C. Hacker and James M. Grimwood, *On the Shoulders of Titans: A History of Project Gemini* (1977); and Courtney C. Brooks, James M. Grimwood, and Loyd S. Swenson, Jr., *Chariots for Apollo: A History of Manned Lunar Spacecraft* (1979). On the Apollo launch vehicle, see Roger E. Bilstein, *Stages to Saturn: A Technological History of the Apollo/Saturn Launch Vehicle* (1981). An excellent overview of the Apollo program is provided in John Noble Wilford, *We Reach the Moon* (1969). A more impressionistic account is Norman Mailer, *Of a Fire on the Moon* (1970). Henry S.F. Cooper describes the Apollo 13 mission in *13: The Flight That Failed* (1973). On Skylab and ASTP, see W. David Compton and Charles D. Benson, *A History of Skylab* (in press); and Edward Clinton Ezell and Linda Neuman Ezell, *The Partnership: A History of the Apollo-Soyuz Test Project* (1978).

Statistical data on the space program appear in Jane Van Nimmen and Leonard C. Bruno with Robert L. Rosholt, *NASA Historical Data Book, 1958-1968,* Vol. 1: *NASA Resources* (1976); and in *The Aeronautics and Space Report of the President* (annually since 1959). The Viking mission is described in Edward Clinton Ezell and Linda Neuman Ezell, *On Mars: Exploration of the Red Planet* (in press). On space science in general, see Homer E. Newell, *Beyond the Atmosphere: Early Years of Space Science* (1981). See Frederick I. Ordway III, Carsbie C. Adams, and Mitchell R. Sharpe, *Dividends from Space* (1971).

Management of NASA is treated extensively in W. Henry Lambright, *Governing Science and Technology* (1976), and is the exclusive focus of Arnold Levine, *Managing NASA in the Apollo Era* (in press). See also James E. Webb, *Space Age Management: The Large-Scale Approach* (1969).

ALEX ROLAND

NATIONAL ARCHIVES AND RECORDS SERVICE (NARS). The official origins of the National Archives and Records Service lay in the creation of a building. After decades of agitation to keep the federal government's archives safe, Congress in 1926 appropriated funds for the building's construction in Washington. Ground was broken for the structure in 1931, and the cornerstone was laid in 1933. It was not until 1934 that serious attention was given to the organization that should occupy the attractive new building. Then, on June 19, the National Archives Act was signed into law. The new agency was to be headed by an archivist of the United States, who was to be responsible to Congress and the President. The archivist was empowered to arrange for the transfer of the government's enduringly valuable records to the National Archives Building and to provide for their preservation and use for research purposes.

In October 1934, President Franklin D. Roosevelt appointed as archivist a veteran historical administrator, Robert D.W. Connor of the University of North Carolina. Professor Connor not only had to superintend the outfitting of the Archives Building and recruit a staff, but he also had to decide precisely what the new agency would do and how it would be organized. He quickly took matters in hand. Successfully, the archivist rallied the President, various federal agencies, and key members of Congress in support of making the National Archives a comprehensive archival agency. Connor's chief objectives were to broaden research access to federal archives, to preserve them effectively, and to make the new agency a force in determining the government's records policies.

In order to do this, he was effective in obtaining funds to outfit, expand, and staff the large and complicated National Archives Building. Moreover, Connor by 1935 had provided an organizational framework for his agency, and he was immensely successful in recruiting able professional employees.

The professional staff were pioneers, for they had the need, the resources, and the enthusiasm to approach archival problems on a scale larger than ever before tackled anywhere. They surveyed federal records in thousands of locations in Washington and the field, which was essential in developing appraisal standards to decide which records should be preserved. Moreover, the staff used and even developed a variety of methods to enhance preservation, including new cleaning and repair techniques, temperature and humidity controls, fire safety methods, and microreproduction. By the end of 1935, records began to arrive in the Archives Building. By the middle of 1941, the National Archives had acquired custody—often after difficult negotiations—of 302,114 cubic feet of archives, in addition to large collections of maps, films, sound recordings, and still pictures. This accumulation made the Archives the nation's largest center for historical research; and already the agency was processing tens of thousands of research requests by mail, telephone, and in person, mostly from government agencies.

The National Archives early assumed other functions. In 1935, it became the home for the Federal Register, which published the government's administrative regulations. The Archives was highly significant in establishing an American archival profession, by participating in the formation of the Society of American Archivists, by pioneering archival instruction, and by publishing technical literature. The agency acquired a new dimension, in 1939, when Congress authorized the establishment of the Franklin D. Roosevelt Library to house the President's papers. In 1939 and 1940, Congress gave the National Archives authority to speed the disposal of useless federal records. In 1941, the agency established the record group as its basic unit for the work of arrangement and description, and it accelerated its program of preparing finding aids.

When Connor retired in 1941, he was succeeded by one of his assistants, another veteran historical administrator, Solon J. Buck. Dr. Buck carried on Connor's innovative ways, though not as smoothly. It fell to Buck to try to protect the National Archives from being cut back as a result of wartime exigencies and postwar economy drives. This he tried to do by making the agency increasingly useful to the government, though at the cost of allowing with little protest a Saturnalia of security classification that would impede research access. Under Buck's austerely efficient direction, the staff plunged into providing leadership in records management in order to save valuable space, equipment, and staff time in federal agencies; giving war-related research and technical assistance; participating in the protection of cultural resources at home and in war areas; and almost doubling its research service load. The Archives found itself, however, in the position of doing more with less, as its staff was cut by one-third between 1942 and 1945.

After the war, the National Archives endeavored to make up for lost time on a number of fronts. One result of this effort was the production of a variety of guides to the agency's holdings, most notably the comprehensive *Guide to the Records in the National Archives* (1948) and *The Federal Records of World War II* (1950, 1951). There was the acceleration of the file microcopy program, which allowed purchasers to work on a considerable body of archival materials in their offices or homes. The accessioning of records of enduring value continued at a rapid pace, as the holdings of the Archives grew by 1948 to 855,925 cubic feet along with vast amounts of films, recordings, maps, and photographs. The organization made some progress in catching up on its backlog in preparing materials for use and in spurring records management in federal agencies. Successful initiatives were made in preparing the *Code of Federal Regulations* (1949); fostering international cooperation among archivists through the formation of what would become the International Council of Archivists; and stepping up the agency's program of exhibits in the capital and across the country.

The impressive spectrum of the postwar accomplishments of the National Archives came despite serious problems. The agency was bursting at the seams with records that it could not satisfactorily process for use or, where necessary, rehabilitate. Not only was it a question of having accessioned too much too quickly, but the Archives was adversely affected by the government's postwar economy drives which kept it from recapturing the large number of staff positions it had lost during the war. Indeed, the Archives even lost more staff authorizations. Archivist Buck's reorganization and economy efforts helped in coping with the dire fiscal situation, but they also fomented serious discontent among his staff, which undermined his authority and led to his resignation in 1948.

Buck was succeeded by his chief assistant, Wayne C. Grover, a trained archivist who had been a pioneer in the records-management profession. During his first year, Dr. Grover was able to secure some increases both in funding and staff for the National Archives. His agency's resources were too slender, however, to deal with the archival tasks at hand, much less to supply effective leadership in managing the government's records which were threatening to swamp federal operations. Moreover, the autonomy of the Archives was jeopardized by the work of the Hoover Commission* in reorganizing the federal government. Grover tried to turn the reorganization movement to advantage by working for the establishment of an independent federal records agency, the dominant force in which would be the National Archives. The upshot of the fencing over the issues involved was the placement of the Archives in the new General Services Administration* (GSA) in 1949. The National Archives had lost its battle to preserve its autonomy within the executive branch, but in the process it had made the government more conscious of the need to manage its records properly.

The National Archives, although now under GSA, had in effect become the government's records organization. With encouragement from GSA, the agency, soon renamed the National Archives and Records Service (NARS), moved rapidly to advance federal records management. NARS, making full use of its new records-management operations and gaining new authority under the Federal

Records Act of 1950, was able soon to enhance and systematize the control and disposition of records within executive agencies. It also established an empire of records centers to provide more economical, efficient, and effective storage and processing of records. By 1953, it was estimated that NARS's records-management efforts had saved the government some $34 million; more important, by 1954, the agency had curbed the trend toward an out-of-proportion accumulation of federal records. By 1955, NARS as a result of the work of the Second Hoover Commission, had acquired more power to carry out its records-management program. Consequently, the agency's records-management forces were able to enlarge their training programs with excellent results in achieving better controls on the creation of records and the use of equipment, personnel, and space. The effect of this work, much of it pioneering, went well beyond federal service as many state, local, and foreign governments and private organizations sought to learn and apply what NARS was doing. NARS's Office of Records Management and its later twin, the Office of Records Centers, because of resistance in some quarters, internal difficulties, and insufficient funds, did not achieve all they wanted. There is no doubt, however, that over the years they contributed significantly to improvements in the creation, use, and disposition of federal records. They also facilitated the flow of records of enduring value to their archival counterpart, the Office of the National Archives.

While Grover had been successful in gaining control of the government's records-management program for NARS, he had not made his archivists happy with the arrangement. The staff of the Office of the National Archives felt that they were constantly undercut in funding and influence by the larger records-management group. Whether or not this was true, the archivists indeed had too little funding to meet all of their obligations. Nevertheless, the Office of the National Archives, during Grover's long incumbency, did make progress in dealing with accessioning, rearrangement, and, to a lesser extent, preservation. The archivists kept up with their heavy load of work with researchers. And they produced a large number of publications, including training materials, guides to the archives, facsimiles, edited documents, and professional articles. They were able to accomplish this largely because of the greater emphasis on training to equip them for their tasks. The archivists also had their moments of glory, especially the transfer, in 1952, of the Declaration of Independence, the Constitution, and related older records from the Library of Congress to the National Archives Building.

Grover's years at the helm of NARS included further expansion of the work of the Federal Register, which among other things had taken on the publication of the *Statutes at Large*. In 1950, the National Historical Publications Commission, which had been inoperative for years, was resurrected; it soon became a vital force in encouraging with grants-in-aid and advisory services the publication of scholarly editions of significant historical documents. When President Harry S Truman indicated that he wanted an institution similar to the thriving Roosevelt Library to house his papers and memorabilia, the question arose as to how to systematize such operations. This led Congress in 1955 to pass the Presidential Libraries Act, which provided for the private construction of such facilities, but their subsequent administration and maintenance by the federal government. Under this act, by the late 1970s, libraries had been built for Presidents Hoover, Truman, Eisenhower, Kennedy, Lyndon Johnson, and Ford. Along with the Roosevelt Library, they were encompassed in the presidential library system, which NARS administered for purposes of research and education. A related development in 1957 was the authorization of the Federal Register to publish the documentary series entitled "The Public Papers of the Presidents of the United States."

By 1966, the organization of the National Archives and Records Service reflected its main functions and was largely set for the next fourteen years. The agency was divided under the archivist and a deputy archivist into offices of the National Archives, Records Management, Records Centers, Federal Register, and Presidential Libraries, with the National Historical Publications Commission (NHPC) operating theoretically separate with the Archivist as its chairman. An Office of Educational Programs was added later.

NARS had prospered in many respects under GSA. Yet, by the mid-60s, it suffered from several nagging problems. Functionally, space was the worst of these problems, but the construction of the Washington National Records Center in 1967 temporarily relieved that. Administratively, the most serious situation was the plight of an agency with cultural functions located in the General Services Administration, which as one Congressman said, is "the custodian of washrooms, store-rooms, and work-rooms." Too often, GSA and the Bureau of the Budget* expected NARS to meet administrative "targets" and "missions" that did not well apply to an agency that could neither control nor predict the amounts of service required by its research clients. In addition, NARS was too often slighted on its archival funding, and its leadership feared that some future administrator of General Services might for political reasons interfere in the operations of the presidential libraries.

Therefore, when Grover retired in 1965, he proposed the reestablishment of NARS as an independent federal agency. He gained widespread support from archivists and historians, and his so-called Independence Movement became a matter of serious concern for the new archivist, Robert H. Bahmer, GSA, and the Bureau of the Budget. The upshot was that, although NARS remained in GSA, it was substantially upgraded in funds and personnel. The archival and presidential library functions particularly benefited from this change, but, in addition, among other things, clients of NARS had a chance to voice their concerns formally through a new National Archives Advisory Council; *Prologue,* the agency's own scholarly journal, was begun; and archival branches were established in many records centers to facilitate research in the regions. What it all meant was that, when James B. Rhoads, another veteran archivist, succeeded Dr. Bahmer upon his retirement in 1968, the agitation for an independent archival agency had been weakened and NARS was on a better and broader footing.

That did not mean there were not serious problems remaining for NARS or even worse ones to be met down the road. Shortage of space would again become a problem, as would the protection of the agency's always growing holdings from theft and fire. Most threatening were disagreements between GSA and NARS and political interference from GSA, for example, in connection with the disposition of President Richard M. Nixon's official papers. This gave new momentum to the Independence Movement from 1975 to the present. Moreover, problems with the preservation of materials (particularly films), staff morale and space concerns, and a new spate of administrative disagreements led to the retirement of Dr. Rhoads in 1979 as well as intense and well-publicized skirmishes between GSA and the custodians and users of archival materials. With the appointment as archivist in 1980 of Dr. Robert M. Warner of the University of Michigan, an uneasy truce came into effect. He revised operations into offices of Records and Information Management and Public Programs and Exhibits, as well as new offices of Program Development and Program Support. In 1982, GSA assumed greater authority in regional federal records operations.

Despite the problems of NARS, there were many accomplishments during the 1970s and 1980s. The agency showed mounting interest in relaxing restrictions on access to archives. Useful in this respect were the Freedom of Information Act of 1966, as amended in 1974, and the Presidential Records Act of 1978, which declared official presidential records to be the government's property. NARS contributed substantially to reducing restrictions on federal records by assisting in the drafting of appropriate Executive Orders by Presidents Nixon (1972) and Jimmy Carter (1978). The agency accelerated its work with sound recordings and motion picture and television films and with exhibits and public education. In 1975, NHPC was reorganized as the National Historical Publications and Records Commission in order to assist other archival, manuscript, and historical operations in conducting a variety of germane projects. NARS also made progress in handling records produced by computers in federal agencies, and it developed computer programs to control better the materials in its custody. Thus, NARS continued to be in its services the world's most broad-ranging archival institution, even though funding problems under Presidents Carter and especially Ronald Reagan impaired its development.

FOR ADDITIONAL INFORMATION: For detailed histories of NARS, see H. G. Jones, *The Records of a Nation, Their Management, Preservation, and Use* (1969), and Donald R. McCoy, *The National Archives: America's Ministry of Documents* (1978). Also of interest are Milton O. Gustafson, "The Empty Shrine: The Transfer of the Declaration of Independence and the Constitution to the National Archives," *American Archivist* (July 1976); Oliver W. Holmes, "Toward an International Archives Program and Council, 1945-1950," *American Archivist* (July 1976); and Donald R. McCoy, "The Beginnings of the Franklin D. Roosevelt Library," *Prologue: The Journal of the National Archives* (Fall 1975).

DONALD R. McCOY

NATIONAL BUREAU OF STANDARDS (NBS). Science can be defined as a branch of knowledge or study dealing with a body of facts or truths systematically arranged and showing the operation of general laws. Such "facts" or "truths" are usually postulated theoretically and verified by experimental measurements. Indeed, following his discovery of x-radiation, Professor Röntgen was asked, "What did you think?" Röntgen snapped, "I did not think; I measured!"

Measurement, an act or process of ascertaining the extent, dimensions, or quantity of something, especially by comparison with some widely accepted accurate standard, is the foundation for scientific verification. In addition, a uniform measurement system is crucial for equity in all forms of commercial endeavor.

Thus, measurement as a basis for scientific and commercial growth was uppermost in the minds of the founders of the National Bureau of Standards. Indeed, in the latter part of the nineteenth century, representatives of science and industry concluded that only federal legislation could establish the necessary measurement criteria or standards that would have national and international validity. Other industrial nations had long since recognized this need and had established national standards laboratories such as the National Physical Laboratory in the United Kingdom. The United States had nothing comparable but was rapidly growing in commerce and industry—exports had exceeded imports for the first time in 1899. Thus, growing needs in measurement as a foundation for science and industrial technology, coupled with a sense of national pride, exemplified by Theodore Roosevelt, contributed to the momentum leading to the creation of the National Bureau of Standards in 1901.

In 1900, Roosevelt spoke out in favor of all things that would benefit the American laborer and manufacturer. One of those "things" was the creation of a federal standardization bureau to provide better measurements and more uniformity, precision, and control in laboratory, factory, and at the consumer level. Such a federal bureau had been the subject of discussions for nearly twenty years prior to introduction of the legislation that led to its foundation.

The prime movers responsible for the legislation were Lyman J. Gage, Secretary of the Treasury, and Samuel W. Stratton, a professor of physics at the University of Chicago. Gage invited Stratton to Washington and, in late 1899, appointed the thirty-eight-year-old professor "Inspector of Standards." Stratton set to work drafting what was to become the basis for the Organic Act of the National Bureau of Standards. Stratton obtained the support of many influential organizations including the National Academy of Sciences and the American Chemical Society. Furthermore, individual scientists, representatives of industry, and other federal agencies strongly endorsed the draft bill.

The draft bill ran into the customary trials and tribulations in its passage through both houses of Congress; the Senate reduced proposed salaries and eliminated eight of twenty-one positions. But finally on March 3, 1901, the bill was enacted into law as Public Law 56-177. As enumerated in this Organic Act, NBS has six major functions: (1) comparison of the standards used in scientific investigations, engineering, manufacturing, commerce, and educational institutions with the standards adopted or recognized by the government; (2) construction when necessary of standards, their multiples and subdivisions; (3) testing and calibration of standards-measuring apparatus; (4) solution of problems that arise in connection with standards; (5) determination of physical constants, and (6) properties of materials when such data are of great importance to scientific or manufacturing interests and are not to be obtained of sufficient accuracy elsewhere.

NBS has no regulatory or enforcement powers; enforcement is left to the individual states. But responsibility for development of standards, test methods, instruments, and determination of properties of materials makes the scope of NBS research in the physical sciences essentially unlimited. Since NBS can investigate any problem relating to standards, NBS competence must keep pace with new developments in science and technology.

Samuel Wesley Stratton was appointed first director, and he served for twenty-one years. In certain ways, Stratton and NBS brought to fruition the dreams of America's first great physicist, Joseph Henry. As first secretary of the Smithsonian Institution,* Henry had envisioned a scientific research institute dedicated to the diffusion of knowledge. But Congress never allowed the Smithsonian to develop fully into a national research center; rather, the functions leading to a great national museum were encouraged. In retrospect, the need for a national laboratory dedicated to the physical sciences was not perceived until about 1900, by which time the Smithsonian had long since become heavily involved with natural history. Indeed, the Arts and Industries portion of the Smithsonian had fallen almost out of existence by that time.

Hence, within the federal establishment, Stratton and the staff of the fledgling NBS had a clear field for developing programs responsive to the needs of science and industry as they existed in the early part of this century. In fact, NBS found its responsibilities increasing at a rate faster than the bureau could grow, and, in less than fifteen years, NBS was forced to reinterpret its own functions.

In 1902, Stratton decided that NBS must establish a strong program in basic research and maintain that program at a high level in order to provide the pool of knowledge needed to assure appropriate standards and test methods for industry and technology. Stratton believed that all engineering enterprise could be improved by scientific research and study. That goal was—and is—the best single statement of NBS's reason for being.

A key requirement for any scientific and technical research is an objective means of review by accepted authorities. To this end, the NBS Organic Act calls for a Visiting Committee of prominent persons of science and industry to review the work of the bureau and to make recommendations concerning current and proposed programs. From Stratton's time to the present day, the Visiting Committee has been an integral part of NBS and a major factor in helping to identify new ventures.

Among the first Visiting Committee recommendations was that NBS embark immediately on a major program of electrical research since electricity was seen to be the "prime mover of the future." By 1900, the electrical industry accounted for a $200 million investment in the United States. But lack of recognized standards caused the industry to be involved in frequent and expensive litigation. Thus, continued growth of the industry was seen to be threatened.

Stratton engaged Dr. Edward B. Rosa to head the bureau's electrical research efforts. Immediate efforts were begun in order to arrive at an internationally accepted standard of electromotive force, that is, voltage. Discrepancies of about 0.1 percent existed between U.S. and European standards. New determinations of the absolute values of the fundamental electrical quantities, the ampere, ohm, and volt, were undertaken.

At the Saint Louis World's Fair, the NBS electrical exhibit was awarded a grand prize for its display dealing with calibration of electrical instruments. The bureau also set up luminous script signs in glass tubing; the neon gas in the tubes was lit to a reddish glow by electrical discharge. Commercial application of neon signs did not occur until 1930, however.

By 1908, nearly 70 percent of all bureau testing was for other federal agencies. These tests involved primarily performance standards for the procurement of goods by other agencies. For example, light bulbs, of which the government purchased over 1 million per year, were found to be defective 75 percent of the time. By 1909, Stratton feared that such routine testing would relegate NBS to "job shop" status. By turning the testing into more generic research on the properties of the materials such as steel, cement, brick, or others, better performance specifications could be drawn up.

With the bureau serving this need, voluntary standards organizations such as the American Society for Testing and Materials could proceed to devise performance specifications and tests to verify these specifications. Hence, the "job shop" specter never fully materialized. Today, NBS still investigates basic properties and cooperates closely with voluntary standards groups.

In addition, NBS prepares and distributes standard reference materials (SRMs) through which industry—or any other party—can calibrate its own testing and/ or production capabilities. This program began in 1905 when a group of irons of certified composition was prepared with the aid of the American Foundrymen's Association. Again, NBS competence in basic and applied research is applied to development of the SRM; the routine testing is left to the client. At present, there are hundreds of SRMs ranging from steels to samples for measuring atmospheric pollution. By 1909, the NBS administration recognized that the bureau's most valuable resource was its staff. Hence, NBS began the first major federal program to provide continuing education for its young people. Since then, hundreds of the staff have earned advanced degrees under the auspices of this program. More than anything else, the advanced degree programs have aided in retaining top-quality, young researchers at NBS.

The bureau was to have need of trained metrologists; outcry against public service monopolies such as electric light and gas companies resulted in regulation of these giant trusts. Equitable regulation always requires an objective measurement foundation. Hence, both regulator and regulatee viewed NBS as an appropriate agency for developing the technical basis of regulation. This aspect of NBS activity began in 1907 with the development of new and consistent standards for electric and gas lamps. As part of this effort, NBS suggested the sale of gas based upon its heating value rather than on a volume basis. Since NBS was in no way concerned with the financial regulation and since the utilities needed public confidence, the companies agreed to consider the proposal. Some ten years passed before it was adopted, however. NBS work to provide the technical basis for regulation continues today; examples include SRMs developed to calibrate pollution control devices and research concerning hazardous waste disposal.

In fact, safety regulation led NBS into the fields of metallurgy and failure analysis and prevention. Railroad accidents, averaging 4,000 per year between 1907 and 1912, prompted the bureau to become involved on behalf of the Interstate Commerce Commission.* Uniform manufacturing processes and special compositions and physical characteristics were suggested as remedies, but final results took more than fifteen years to produce.

Similarly, corrosion was identified as a major source of pipe and cable failures. Thus, NBS established research on the basic processes of corrosion in 1909. Since then, NBS work has been in the forefront in understanding and preventing losses from corrosion. Still, in 1978, in response to a Senate directive to estimate the economic effect of metallic corrosion in the United States, a team of bureau scientists suggested that these costs ranged from $50 billion to $90 billion annually.

By 1920, the bureau had become something of a clearinghouse for industry and the states by assembling facts in laboratory and/or field studies and reducing them to standard practices. For example, as a service to the states, complete sets of primary weights and measures standards were provided, while tests for other agencies included structural materials, tires, ink, paints, and other "everyday" items used throughout the economy. In 1915, NBS published a 149-page guide, "Measurements for the Household," which became—at forty-five cents each— a best-seller, some 33,000 copies being sold by 1917. NBS continued its work in the consumer area until 1981 when its Center for Consumer Product Technology was subsumed into other bureau activities.

Dr. Stratton attempted to codify the myriad activities of NBS in 1915. His views of the standardization activities of NBS included the following, as paraphrased by R. C. Cochrane: *Standards of measurement*: their custody, construction, and comparison, with methods of comparison presently available ranging from those capable of measuring the thousandth part of a milligram to the large testing machines capable of measuring a load of thousands of tons. *Standard values of constants*: requiring accurate and authenticated determinations of the many fixed relations between physical quantities, ranging from the relation between heat and mechanical energy required in designing steam engines and boilers, to the amount of heat required to turn liquid ammonia into vapor or to melt a pound of ice, as in the refrigeration industry. *Standards of quality*: confined almost exclusively to government purchases, involved the physical and chemical investigation of materials to prepare methods of measurement and uniform specifications for their composition or manufacture. *Standards of performance*: whether of an engine, boiler, or pump, an electric generator or motor, a weighing device, or a telescope, involved the use of standards of measurement, standard values of constants, and standards of quality, and sought to arrive at specifications based on correct scientific and mechanical principles. *Standards of practice*: ordinances relating to the regulation of public utilities, and to the establishment of building and safety codes. The almost wholly pragmatic cast of these functions could not be missed, nor their overwhelming reference to government testing and government investigations.

World War I activities at NBS emphasized the practical bent that these statements suggested. The staff rose from 517 in 1917 to 1,117 by the end of 1918. The bureau participated in virtually the entire range of wartime problems. Some of the research undertaken included optical glass, submarine detection devices, aircraft construction standards, and camouflage uses.

World War I briefly raised the hope that the metric system might be adopted in the United States. Stratton had failed, in repeated efforts, to get Congress to adopt the metric system, and he had concluded that a major educational effort was necessary in order to persuade the public and, hence, the Congress, to the appropriateness of a metric America. His opportunity arose when, in early 1918, the War Department* announced that the metric system would be adopted for all material for use in France. Accordingly, general instruction in the metric system was to be provided. NBS took the lead; thousands of pamphlets, charts, and a soldier's manual were prepared and distributed. Stratton believed that the metric system might well be adopted after the war; it was not. Dozens of metric bills have failed; the United States is still not officially on the metric system.

The end of the war also brought other problems for NBS. Only nine days after the armistice, the Secretary of Commerce, to whom the director of NBS reports (NBS has been a part of the Department of Commerce* since 1903), asked Stratton what activities could be curtailed and how many persons could be dismissed via reduction-in-force (RIF).

In order to prevent such an occurrence, NBS turned toward transfers of funds from other agencies to carry out measurement-based research in aid of the mission of the funding agency. Such transfers were legalized under wartime legislation. Thus began the bureau's so-called other agency research. Today, approximately 40 percent of total NBS funding arises from this source. Stratton seems to have opposed this means of obtaining funds, but he bowed to the realities posed by congressional desire to reduce sharply postwar spending.

The bureau and industry had built closer relations during the war. Both were beginning to realize how scientific approaches to problems could contribute to industrial technology and efficiency. For its part, industry began to recognize that basic research could lead to product development and diversification. The golden age of business was about to begin; the professional managers hired by large firms were concerned with efficiency, public image, and increased profits. Thus, the industrial laboratory, including basic research, gradually came into being. Naturally, the trained personnel at the bureau were made offers at stipends that were often double government wages. Coupled with postwar congressional desires for cutbacks, NBS found itself in dire straits.

To combat this threat, the bureau turned to the trade associations with which it cooperated. NBS proposed that, where specific research on problems of importance to the entire industry was required, such research be carried out by qualified personnel sent to the bureau. These research associates would be paid by their sponsoring industry, would work cooperatively with NBS staff, and would publish their results under the bureau's aegis. This program had attracted sixty-one associates by 1925; the program is still a major NBS activity. The present director recently announced plans to enlarge the number of associates currently at the bureau.

During 1921-1928, staff and appropriations changed but little, increasing from 850 to 889 and $2,209,000 to $2,540,000, respectively. But the Secretary of Commerce, Herbert Hoover, assigned new areas of interest to the bureau, including building technology and standard methods research, the latter aimed at reducing waste in industry.

In 1923, Stratton left the bureau to become president of MIT; he was succeeded by George Kimball Burgess, then senior division chief within NBS. At about this time, the Bureau of the Budget, forerunner of the present Office of Management and Budget,* was created. No longer could the NBS director deal directly with the Congress on needs. Bureaucrats within the Budget Bureau had what amounted to a final say on resources for all programs; negotiation with Congress was forbidden to the director. In addition, as other agency funds flowed into the bureau, the director lost freedom since such work was ultimately in aid of the mission of the funding agency. All directors since Stratton have labored under these constraints.

NBS work on standardization reduced the costs of items procured by the federal government by large amounts; for example, the price of light bulbs went down from $1.30 to $0.16. Hence, ironically, one of the first acts of the Bureau of the Budget was to create the Federal Specifications Board to take advantage of the savings offered by application of the bureau's research. Simultaneously, it cut the NBS budget.

In the 1920s, NBS increased its research devoted to industrial output. Chemical processes were investigated using German patents, use of waste fibers to make paper products was investigated, and colors were standardized in aid of many industries (textiles, paints, and even crayons). NBS even developed the first engine diagnostic machine—a device that automatically measured and recorded eighteen values of the performance of the engine and the vehicle itself in operation. Radio standards were also needed at this time; thus began NBS work in the electromagnetic spectrum. Harry Diamond developed the first visual-type radiobeacon system.

In 1932, Dr. Burgess died at his desk; he was succeeded by Lyman J. Briggs. In addition, the NBS budget was drastically reduced as part of federal response to the depression. President Franklin D. Roosevelt created a Science Advisory Board which became concerned with a redefinition of bureau functions. However, the board failed to make recommendations acceptable to Roosevelt or to the bureau. Still, with a certain prescience, this board was concerned with the social objectives of science, consumer problems, and certain special programs. Since 1967, the Congress has assigned many special programs to NBS dealing with most of the items the board discussed in the 1930s.

In any case, the 1930-1938 period was largely a holding period in the history of NBS. In 1938, a new high-voltage laboratory was approved; it was completed in late 1940. The building technology group aided the Roosevelt program in low-cost construction. Considerable work on refining fundamental standards was also carried out.

At the end of the 1930s, NBS, which had isolated heavy water following a suggestion by Harold Urey, was asked to participate in what later became known as the Manhattan Project. NBS served as the central control laboratory for determining the purity of uranium and other products. Bureau scientists participated in developing chemical-analysis methods for the nuclear program. The proximity fuze group was also called into service in this area. The nonrotating proximity fuze was developed at NBS and was used on over 2 million bombs, rockets, and mortars as well as on nuclear weapons. Other wartime research centered on substitutes for critical materials such as rubber, certain metals, and optical glass. At the war's end, Dr. Briggs retired; he was succeeded by Edward U. Condon.

Condon wished to enlarge the NBS staff and budget; he proposed a fivefold increase in appropriations in 1947—which was not forthcoming. Still, Condon redirected NBS efforts in the industrial research area and began efforts in nuclear technology and in other areas of research. The bureau began to shift away from its industrial support role to a more basic research-oriented role. But still, NBS was able to conceive and construct what was known as SEAC (Standards Eastern Automatic Computer). This was the fastest general-purpose digital computer then in existence. Dedicated on June 20, 1950, it operated 4,000 hours in its first nine months without a single malfunction. This device remained in service until 1964; it can fairly be called the forerunner of the modern computer.

Nuclear research dealt with "tracer" technology, that is, the tracking of nuclear isotopes in biology, medicine, and chemistry. Carbon dating was also investigated.

Another new research area added by NBS was plastics and high polymers. NBS is presently a world leader on the theory of high polymers.

Condon left NBS in 1951 and was succeeded by Dr. Alan V. Astin. The new director was caught up in what is still known at NBS as the ADX-2 disaster. NBS tests for the U.S. Navy suggested that a battery additive, ADX-2, was not effective in prolonging battery life or improving battery performance. The producers of ADX-2 created serious problems for NBS via the political process. The new director was temporarily relieved of his duties. But, in the end, independent evaluations confirmed that NBS test results were correct and that ADX-2 was without merit. Since that time, NBS test results have never been successfully challenged.

Dr. Astin moved NBS strongly into basic research areas and away from industrial research. In the 1950s and up until about 1967, this policy was strongly supported by the public and the Congress, especially after the advent of Sputnik. By the late 1960s, however, Congress was concerned that the swing away from the more practical aspects of standardization and industrially oriented research had gone too far. To remedy this situation, Congress assigned additional specific duties to NBS via the legislative process. Since 1967, there have been about twenty such new assignments-all meant to direct NBS research into applied areas of national concern, for example, solar energy, mine safety, recycling, earthquake prediction, and others. Unfortunately, NBS never received appropriations for most of these additional assignments. Thus, resources were reprogrammed from more traditional bureau activities into the new areas. By the late 1970s, the Visiting Committee warned that, as a result of this reprogramming, bureau competences had been badly eroded. Heeding these warnings, Congress approved a five-year program for rebuilding competences at a level of $2 million per year beginning in 1978. In addition, certain legislatively mandated programs were given their own direct appropriations, for example, recycled materials and standard reference data.

Astin perhaps will be best remembered as the director who convinced Congress to allow NBS to move from its overcrowded-but beautiful-site on upper Connecticut Avenue in Washington, D.C., to Gaithersburg, Maryland, some twenty miles to the northwest. There, 640 acres were developed as a permanent home for the bureau. In addition, during the early 1950s, NBS had built its Boulder, Colorado, radio and cryogenic laboratories.

During the Astin years, the Department of Commerce reduced the director's prerogatives further by creating the post of Assistant Secretary for Science and Technology. From 1963 until 1981, there were some who wondered openly who was in charge of NBS-the director or the Assistant Secretary. The Reagan Administration has ended this state of affairs by abolishing the role of Assistant Secretary. Once, again, the NBS director reports directly to the Secretary of Commerce.

The bureau grew under Astin as never before or since; upon his departure, approximately 3,000 positions existed at NBS. Lewis V. Branscomb was appointed to succeed Astin as director. Branscomb had been a protegé of Astin's and was first chief of the Joint Institute for Laboratory Astrophysics, a joint venture of NBS and the University of Colorado. Branscomb left the bureau to join IBM and was followed as director by Richard Roberts. Roberts, after a short period, was succeeded by the present director, Ernest Ambler.

Ambler reorganized NBS in the winter of 1977-1978. Today, the bureau consists of a National Engineering Laboratory, a National Measurement Laboratory, an Institute for Computer Sciences and Technology, and support personnel. In real terms, the bureau's budget has remained virtually constant since 1967, as has the staff. But in 1981, in keeping with President Reagan's vow to reduce federal activities, NBS was instructed to reduce its staff by about 10 percent. Over 200 employees were removed from duty by September 1981. Direct appropriations for fiscal 1982 were expected to be slightly over $100 million.

At present, the Congress is considering revisions in the Organic Act; hearings were held in June 1981, and changes were endorsed by several witnesses. Once again, NBS is in a period of transition. A significant trend is the bureau's return to industrial cooperation as one means of going forward into the future. Other clear directions are difficult to ascertain. Such hard times have hit NBS before; the bureau has always emerged from these difficulties better able to continue to contribute to the nation's scientific and technical requirements.

FOR ADDITIONAL INFORMATION: Rexmond C. Cochrane, *Measures for Progress*, (1966), is an excellent history of NBS. *Hearings...on S. 2615, 1978*, and *Hearings before the Subcommittee on Science, Research and Technology, Committee on Science and Technology, June 16 and 17, 1981*, provide some material for the last two decades. The National Engineering Laboratory and National Measurement Laboratory at NBS produce informative Annual Reports.

MARILYN SARA COHEN

NATIONAL CAPITAL PLANNING COMMISSION. The National Capital Planning Commission administers the federal concern with the national capital city that has existed for nearly two centuries. Article 1, Section 8, of the Constitution specifies that Congress shall have power "to exercise exclusive legislation in all cases whatsoever, over such district (not exceeding ten miles square) as may, by cession of particular states, and the acceptance of Congress, become the seat of government of the United States'. . . ." The Residence Act of July 12, 1790, implemented the constitutional provision and authorized President George Washington to determine the precise boundaries of the federal district. But earlier, between 1783 and 1790, Congress had developed the concept of a federal "district." It also deliberately advanced toward the idea of a distinctive site for the capital city, rejecting thereby the idea of locating the capital at Philadelphia or some other existing city.

President Washington took a keen interest in the development of the city that was ultimately to bear his name. He contributed to its location on the Potomac, a short distance upstream from his Mount Vernon plantation; he specified its exact location and boundaries; and he appointed its first planner, Pierre Charles L'Enfant, and its first surveyor Andrew Ellicott, both of whom possessed unequaled qualifications. In a short period between his arrival at the site of the future city on March 9, 1791, and June 22, L'Enfant had arrived at the fundamentals of his city plan, locating its major buildings and system of streets and avenues, parks, and drainage canals, and presented these ideas to Washington for the President's approval. Slightly revised, this plan was used on August 19 as the basis for the sale of lots in the city. Differences with the presidential commissioners appointed to supervise the creation of the city caused L'Enfant to be discharged by Washington, but his plan, with slight changes, was incorporated in Ellicott's plan dated July 16, 1790. The dramatic evolution of a work of civic art, then and since widely admired and maintained, has attracted major historical attention, but much remains to be learned, and a biography of L'Enfant is still needed.

The capital city developed more slowly than had been expected, constrained by the limited resources of the new republic, but when the Civil War had affirmed the hegemony of the federal government and doubts about the relocation of the capital city had been laid to rest, the Army Corps of Engineers* took up the task of completing what had been planned. By the end of the century, the city had expanded to fill L'Enfant's design, and modern transportation and bridges had encouraged suburban development. With the challenge of a new century before it, the opportunity was grasped by Senator James McMillan of Michigan, and the Senate Park Commission, more commonly named for its initiator, was established in 1901. Its members were architects Daniel Burnham of Chicago, Charles F. McKim of New York, and the young landscape architect Frederick Law Olmsted, Jr. While strongly reaffirming the basic outlines of the L'Enfant plan, the McMillan Commission plan corrected the accumulated discrepancies of a century, and boldly looked ahead with the vision acquired from the urban parks movement of the period and the more spectacular evidence of the Chicago World's Fair of 1893.

Not for a quarter of a century, however, would the means to effectuate these ideas be found. In 1924, Congress created the National Capital Park Commission (43 Stat. 462; Public Law 202, June 6, 1924) but soon enlarged this concept to form the National Capital Park and Planning Commission (44 Stat. 374; April 30, 1926). These actions need to be viewed in recognition of the parallel creation of the Commission of Fine Arts, active from 1910, with whom was associated the powerful and influential figure, Charles Moore. Moore believed that planning could be accomplished mainly by the cooperation of constructing agencies, and he viewed the Commission of Fine Arts as the guardian of the 1902 McMillan Commission plan. While the lines of responsibility appeared over a period of years and are still difficult to determine on some occasions, the Commission of Fine Arts has concentrated on its aesthetic interests, and the planning function has been more fully defined with its historical evolution. The role of the Corps of Engineers has also been a fundamental factor in shaping the work of the Planning Commission.

Two figures dominated the early history of the planning commission, Olmsted and Frederic Delano. When asked about the initial planning program of 1926, the first director, Charles W. Eliot II, said, "Olmsted dictated it and I wrote it down." Given this origin, the strong emphasis on parks and other physical features of the city in the early years of the commission may be explained, although most contemporary city plans similarly reflected the ideals of the "city beautiful" movement and the efforts to adjust cities to the impact of the motor vehicle. Delano's credentials were those of a civic leader, with planning background in Chicago and New York. While much was later made of his kinship to President Franklin D. Roosevelt, his nephew, little of specific value to the planning commission's program appeared to result from this. Not only did the planning commission emerge on the losing end of such battles as the location of the Pentagon, but also its administrative fortunes declined during the 1930s and 1940s.

As an independent government agency, the planning commission, nevertheless, had a large component of ex-officio members. The influence of operating agencies was further strengthened by the de facto powers exercised by professionals and technicians who served on a "coordinating committee." Here planning proposals were given staff review, and the compromises were worked out that were later presented to the commission and usually adopted. An independent voice for the planning commission came later and against the interests of such line agencies as the Army engineers, the National Park Service,* public works, and building officials.

Over the years, more public representatives were added to the commission membership. The National Capital Planning Act of 1952 (66 Stat. 781, July 19, 1952) gave the commission new vigor as well as a streamlined name. It recognized that the city had overspilled its original "ten mile square" by creating a regional planning body. It added locally representative as well as public members. The act further strengthened the planning powers of the agency and gave it review powers over all federal and District of Columbia projects in the region (the District of Columbia and four suburban counties). With a larger and stronger staff, the commission moved forward in directions defined in its 1961 *Policies Plan for the Year 2000*. This expansive document was strongly reflective of the surge of metropolitan growth and a reawakening to the importance of mass transportation as a structuring element for the urban region.

Hesitant steps toward a greater measure of "home rule" for the District of Columbia, voteless since the end of the territorial form of government in 1874 whence three presidential appointees constituted a commission form of government, took form on December 24, 1973, when Congress enacted the District of Columbia Self-Government and Governmental Reorganization Act (87 Stat. 774).

The planning commission then assumed the role of central planning agency for the federal government in the national capital region, and a separate municipal planning office was created in the new District government. It prepares and adopts local elements of the Comprehensive Plan which the commission then reviews for impact on the federal interest. The commission continues to prepare and adopt federal elements of the Comprehensive Plan and to review federal and District of Columbia projects. While the experience is not uncommon in cities, a decade passed without seeing the Comprehensive Plan.

A further dilution of planning functions came with the transfer to the Metropolitan Washington Council of Governments—a conference of local governments—of the commission's regional planning work, which has reconsidered but not changed the 1961 Policies Plan.

The proliferation of agencies has not been accompanied by any marked increase in planning activity or powers. Neither powerful and significant programs of urban mass transportation (Washington's Metro system), massive federal building activity (suburban office building centers and the Pennsylvania Avenue redevelopment program), nor a reawakening to the symbolic, architectural, cultural, and touristic functions of the capital city have been adequately reflected in this field. The lack of planning has perhaps accurately reflected the failure to advance Washington's self-government program beyond the mayor-commissioner formula, the decline of presidential interest in the capital city since the Kennedy-Johnson administrations, or the absence of any coordinated congressional policy to implement the joint congressional resolution of 1960, which originated with the Congressional Joint Committee on Washington Metropolitan Problems. The responses have not materialized to such momentous events and challenges as the 1968 civil disturbances, the aborted expressway system, massive housing shortages in rehabilitation and redevelopment, plans for Georgetown, Capitol Hill, and other historic districts. Pennsylvania Avenue projects and the Metro system are weak and uncoordinated; planning powers are divided by jurisdiction, administration, and function; and the effort to build participatory support at the neighborhood level has failed to give planning new vigor or to strengthen the activity itself.

FOR ADDITIONAL INFORMATION: The history of Washington as a planned national capital city and the establishment and evolution of the federal planning activity have been well documented in three separate but related studies. Most comprehensive is Frederick Gutheim, *Worthy of the Nation: The History of Planning for the National Capital* (1977). A more specialized legislative and administrative history (with a biographical register of commission members and principal staff) is Frederick Gutheim, *Planning Washington 1924-1976, An Era of Planning for the National Capital and Environs* (1976). More succinct and with illustrations drawn from a continuing exhibition at the Smithsonian Institution is Frederick Gutheim, *The Federal City: Plans and Realities* (1976), accompanied by documentation from the exhibition by Wilcomb E. Washburn. While all have appropriate bibliographies and citations, the most comprehensive is *Worthy of the Nation*. Little exists beyond the level of administrative-report documents on the municipal planning activity since 1974.

FREDERICK GUTHEIM

NATIONAL ENDOWMENT FOR THE ARTS (NEA). The birthdate of the National Endowment for the Arts is September 29, 1965, the day President Lyndon B. Johnson signed the act creating the National Foundation on the Arts and Humanities (Public Law 209—Eighty-ninth Congress). However, there was a long gestation period preceding this birthdate that included efforts by Presidents Harry S Truman, Dwight D. Eisenhower, and John F. Kennedy to create an Advisory Commission on the Arts. President Kennedy went so far as to announce that he was appointing a Federal Advisory Council by Executive Order, but the tragedy of his assassination intervened. To go further back into the courtship of this idea, there were many times in our country's brief history that the federal government contracted with artists for specific items such as memorials, building designs, and the government museums of Washington. President George Washington hired Pierre L'Enfant to create a grand design for the new capital city, and it was an ominous sign that L'Enfant was fired after eighteen months because of political jealousies. He was never paid for his work, and most of his design was discarded, only to be reinstigated by Andrew Ellicott, his successor.

The most important liaison between the federal government and the arts world occurred within the Works Progress Administration.* A small program, accounting for only 3 percent of total funding, was assigned to writers, playwrights, authors, musicians, dancers, and actors. It was the first time the federal government showed the willingness to concede that the artists of America are working people and deserved assistance in those difficult days.

The first years of the Arts Endowment were full of big ideas and little money. Roger L. Stevens, noted Broadway theater producer, real estate giant, and fundraiser for the Democratic party, was chosen by President Johnson as the first chairman. It would have been difficult to find a better leader for those crucial early days. Congress showed little interest in providing funds and many congressmen, particularly H. R. Gross and William Scherle, were actively hostile.

The appropriations for the first years were as shown in the table.

	1966	1967	1968	1969
Program Funds	$2,500,000	$4,000,000	$4,500,000	$3,700,000
State Arts Councils (bloc)		2,000,000	2,000,000	1,700,000
Treasury Funds[a]	34,308	1,965,692	674,291	2,356,875
Total Programming	2,534,308	7,965,692	7,174,291	7,756,875
Administration[b]	727,000	1,019,500	1,200,000	1,400,000

[a]Treasury funds are special funds requiring a 3-1 match.
[b]Administration funds are for the National Fundation for Arts and Humanities and include the National Endowment for the Humanities.

The National Council on the Arts was enlarged to twenty-six from its original twenty-four members. Members were appointed by the President for six-year terms. The council included arts leaders, such as John Steinbeck, Leonard Bernstein, Marion Anderson, Helen Hayes, Isaac Stern, Gregory Peck, Charlton Heston, Rene D'Haroncourt, Lawrence Halprin, and Harper Lee. The emphasis during the early years was on the appointment of artists, but during the Richard Nixon Administration members of arts-organization boards and arts patrons began to be included and eventually they predominated.

The grants of the first few years could best be described as "pilot-project grants" as it would be difficult to find a policy position that could have led to future development. The needs of the artists and struggling arts organizations took first priority. The heaviest emphasis was in the support of theaters; the most noticeable deficiency lay in major support of orchestras. This appeared unusual because the orchestras were the best organized of any arts organizations. A determining factor may have been the hostility of the American Symphony Orchestra League to the formation of the Arts Endowment and covert opposition to the appropriations in the early years.

The council awarded a major grant ($500,000) to establish new laboratory theaters and much needed assistance ($350,000) to the American Ballet Theatre. Choreographers, composers, writers, "promising graduates," and other individual artists received grants. The American Film Institute was created with matching funds from the major film companies, but this move never materialized.

It could be argued that such wide ambiguity proved important during the formative years as the council and the Arts Endowment needed political experience before committing to programs of support. Actually, the appropriations were so meager that major arts organizations, many of which had budgets larger than the Arts Endowment, considered the possible results too small to justify serious effort.

The critics within Congress were relentless because they enjoyed demonstrating their vigilance to the taxpayer as well as a philosophical stance that they felt appealed to their constituents. Congressman Gross delighted in referring to Chairman Stevens as "the high poohbah of the Arts" and claiming that governmental support would lead to subsidization of belly dancers. Congressman Scherle's position intensified after he was embarrassed on the floor of Congress by Congressman Frank Thompson (Democrat, New Jersey) for not knowing correct facts. Through a painstaking search, Scherle found an Arts Endowment grant that fit his needs—a one-word poem by Aram Saroyan that was used in an anthology to demonstrate concrete styles of poetry. The poem had been printed by the University of Chicago Press, and the standard fee of $500 was paid for use of the poem. It appeared—one word in the middle of a blank page—lighght. Scherle calculated the cost per letter to the "hard working American taxpayer" and preached about the endowment's extravagance at every opportunity. The results were devastating to the NEA budget, which was reduced from an already rock-bottom figure. Most congressmen recognized the political technique of using one small, individual grant as being representative of an entire program, but not enough of them felt sufficiently interested to fight it. Many of their younger staff members were apologetic about the actions and became a positive resource in future years. Some congressmen even expressed an opinion that they had found a poem they could memorize.

Nixon's election spelled the end of Stevens's chairmanship, and he was asked to clear his desk and depart in March 1969. Douglas MacAgy, deputy director, was named acting chairman while the search for a new chairman took place.

It was an awkward period as MacAgy, a Canadian, who was quickly converted to U.S. citizenship, possessed little power and was treated badly by the administration, Congress, and the arts world. Each week a new prospective chairman emerged, and in April the word became so convincing that Morton May of Saint Louis would be the new chairman that his choice as deputy, John Macfadyen, helped chair a meeting of the National Council on the Arts. May's candidacy was dropped when he made known his wishes to be a part-time chairman while maintaining involvement with his department stores.

Nancy Hanks gained eventual nomination and confirmation by the Senate on October 2, 1969. Thus began the second era of the Arts Endowment, the developmental phase. Hanks was attractive, young, and one of the finest natural politicians to reach Washington in years.

Her winning ways were demonstrated immediately at a meeting of the leading symphony-orchestra chairmen and managers held in Lincoln Center. In the middle of her soft, friendly, and positive speech that urged the seeking of cooperation between the orchestras and the Arts Endowment, she was rudely interrupted by the chairman of the Baltimore Symphony, who stood up and began telling his colleagues that they should not listen to her, that they had the clout to reach Congress without meddling with this small agency, and that they were "backing the wrong horse." Hanks broke in with her warm smile belying the steely quality of her voice. "Did you know that I was named for a race horse? But what we need are some jumpers to get over the problems we face."

She won the support of the orchestras. The museums also readily backed the endowment's push for larger appropriations. The results were reflected immediately with funds doubling time and again.

	1970	1971	1972	1973	1974
Program Funds	$4,250	$8,465	$20,750	$27,825	$46,025
State Arts Agencies	2,000	4,125	5,500	6,875	8,025
Treasury	2,000	2,500	3,500	3,500	6,500
Total Programming	8,250	15,090	29,750	38,200	60,775
Administration	1,610	2,660	3,460	5,314	6,500

The appropriation increases were accomplished with little help from the sister Endowment for the Humanities.* Its chairman, Barnaby Keeney, was not pleased to be riding on Nancy Hanks's efforts. The two endowments, never close, grew farther and farther apart.

The Hanks era (1969-1977) showed enormous growth in all phases. Development of new programs provided support for orchestras, museums, theaters, and dance companies. Touring programs became operational, particularly in the dance, and the enormous surge of dance popularity owed much to the Arts Endowment efforts under the leadership of two excellent program directors, June Arey and Don Anderson.

New programs appeared each year, for example, City Spirit, City Edges, Expansion Arts, Opera and Musical Theatre, Special Projects (changed to Inter-Arts), Folk Arts, Design Arts, all with many variations and directions within all programs.

A program of Challenge Grants was created to provide fund-raising incentives to large-budget organizations with its 3-1 matching provisions. It was highly successful and soon became a line item within the budget. The Artists in Schools program was borrowed from successful programs run by a few state arts councils and was enlarged to involve all of the states.

State Arts Agencies were also growing at a healthy pace. In 1968, they were organized into an association for mutual support that led to Congress allotting 20 percent of all NEA program funds to the states. Three-fourths of this allotment must be made as a bloc grant and the remainder used for programs supporting the states' program.

One of the many triumphs of the Nancy Hanks years was the positive stand of the chairman and Michael Straight, her deputy chairman, on congressional censorship. No U.S. government program (or states') will ever be free from publicity-seeking legislators and administration critics, but the Hanks-Straight manner of dealing with this problem in a sensible, straightforward manner proved highly successful. Their insistence that grants be made for artistic excellence and their efforts to find that excellence by the use of outstanding artists in the country as advisory panelists did much to quiet the critics.

The greatest success of Nancy Hanks and Michael Straight lay in the unification of the arts world in support of the Arts Endowment. This feat appeared remarkable as the arts organizations are notorious for self-protection in their daily scramble for existence. This unification may have had some self-serving goals, but the endowment leadership held it together during the years of fast-growing budgets.

In 1977, Jimmy Carter was sworn in as President, and Hanks's days as chairman were numbered. After the long hiatus following Stevens's dismissal in 1969, Congress amended the chairman's four-year tenure to continue until a new chairman could be sworn in. This became a moot point as Hanks resigned on her anniversary date. Straight assumed the acting chairmanship for the month-long interim period.

Hanks was certainly the right person to be chairman (she preferred that term to chairperson) during the developmental period of the Arts Endowment. Her personal charm was the Arts Endowment's primary asset during her first NEA years. Her management style was very personal. Her immediate staff worked her long, prodigious schedule with intense loyalty and affection. As the Arts Endowment staff grew, it became more difficult to maintain the personal relationship. Staff competition and jealousies began to surface. An unfortunate choice of an administrative director added to the problem by cutting off access to the chairman by key people and constituents.

This tension carried over into the month-long transition period. When Straight expressed concern about the politicization of the search for the new chairman, his remarks were given national press coverage and created an antagonism with the new chairman that was never resolved. It was truly a disappointing end to the Arts Endowment careers of Hanks and Straight who gave so much and so well.

Livingston Biddle took over the chairmanship in November 1977. He prepared for the job as he had been a primary force as legislative assistant to Senator Claiborne Pell (Democrat, Rhode Island) in writing the original legislation that created the Arts Endowment. He served as the first deputy chairman to Stevens (1965-1977) and returned to the endowment as a special legislative liaison with Hanks.

In an effort to reorganize the Arts Endowment's administration, Biddle established three deputy directors (programming, governmental cooperation, and administration). On paper the new system made sense, but in practice it created open season on turf protection, and the "Washington survivors" squeezed out one of the three within a year. Another ruling that limited the tenure of program directors to five years was awkwardly implemented. The departing directors and many of their friends throughout the country were unhappy and hurt. In fact, some directors used the technicality of switching programs to justify staying on, while others who had been involved with policymaking were declared immune to the ruling.

Problems that emerge with any government agency after the first decade began to plague the Arts Endowment. As its appropriations became respectable, the large organizations, other government agencies, and a wide variety of service organizations began to pressure for additional money. Council members pushed for their own interests. Minority groups demanded better representation. Women's groups expressed dissatisfaction. The unions involved with the arts wanted to diminish the state arts participation to enhance their own members, and the state agencies requested a larger share of decision-making.

The 1980 election created a whole new set of problems. President Ronald Reagan's initial budget message called for a massive cut—the first in over a decade. There was confusion about the percentage of cut as endowment supporters measured the Reagan-David Stockman budget of $88 million against the Carter-approved request for $175 million. Others measured it against the previous year's budget of $158.5 million. In either case, it was a disastrous reduction and stood far in excess of cuts to other agencies. It seemed that the old question of whether the arts and the humanities deserved assistance from the government had been resurrected. The budget question will not be resolved for fiscal year 1982 until the year is, in a practical sense, over, as the appropriations of the Arts and the Humanities are insignificant to the combatants in the struggle for control of the U.S. budget.

On November 13, 1981, Frank Hodsoll was sworn in as the fourth chairman of the National Council and the National Endowment for the Arts. He faced different problems than his predecessors with anticipation of lower budgets and increased needs of arts organizations. Early appraisals indicate that he will be equal to the task.

On September 29, 1981, the National Endowment for the Arts was sixteen years old. During its short existence, it exerted an enormous influence on the development of the arts in the United States. Beyond the financial assistance to the arts organizations and the artists, it has produced a focus to the country for the arts world. It participated and provided leadership in the development of a network of state arts agencies and, more recently, community arts agencies, which are also devoted to the growth and support of artists and arts organizations. However, there is no doubt that the Arts Endowment should be constantly monitored by outsiders. The budget should meet the requirements being made of other agencies—which means trimming, not emasculation.

Whatever the future of the National Endowment for the Arts, it has already been demonstrated that government support for the arts in the United States has worked.

FOR ADDITIONAL INFORMATION: See the *Annual Reports National Endowment for the Arts, 1980*, and other years. Also helpful are Lois Craig, et al., Staff of Federal Architecture Project, *The Federal Presence* (1978); Fraser Barron, *Government and the Arts* (1981); and Michael Straight, *Twigs for an Eagles Nest* (1979).

CLARK MITZE

NATIONAL ENDOWMENT FOR THE HUMANITIES (NEH). The National Endowment for the Humanities, an independent agency, was established by Congress in 1965. The legislation creating NEH also established the National Endowment for the Arts* (NEA), but the two agencies are distinct.

The road leading to the creation of the two endowments was arduous. Federal support for cultural activities materialized during the 1930s when the New Deal's Works Progress Administration* (WPA) included efforts to assist unemployed artists, writers, musicians, and actors. These cultural projects were scuttled in 1943 when Congress dismantled the WPA. Yet, a precedent had been set, and after World War II arts advocates called for renewed federal subsidization without the work-relief aspect.

It was not until the 1960s that the fate of federal support for the arts became linked with a growing concern about the status of the humanities in the United States. Following the Russians' orbiting of Sputnik in 1957, humanities faculties at colleges and universities saw unprecedented opportunities available for their colleagues in the sciences. They took note of the rapidly growing budgets of the National Science Foundation* (NSF) and the National Aeronautics and Space Administration* (NASA) and began to argue that their efforts also merited recognition. Advocates of the humanities achieved some measure of success when the National Defense Educational Act of 1958, though largely directed at the support of scientific and technical education, did earmark governmental funds for foreign-language training. But after the John F. Kennedy Administration's decision to put an American on the moon, the truly massive increases for publicly financed scientific and technological endeavors only underscored the paucity of support for the humanities.

In 1964, various noted academic bodies, having formed a Commission of the Humanities, called for the creation of a humanities foundation. Meanwhile, those pushing for a national arts foundation had not yet been successful. President Kennedy, despite his highly publicized bringing of artists and intellectuals to the White House, did not give arts legislation high priority. This disappointed congressional Democrats who were arts advocates, the chief of whom was Claiborne Pell, the freshman Senator from Rhode Island. As chairman of a special Senate subcommittee on the arts, Pell urged in vain that the administration assume more vigorous action.

In September 1964, President Lyndon B. Johnson endorsed the Humanities Commission's call for a foundation, and numerous bills were quickly introduced in Congress. This momentum provided arts advocates with a unique opportunity. Led by Pell, they joined with humanities proponents and introduced a bill calling for the creation of a foundation with co-equal endowments. Early in 1965, Pell chaired joint hearings on the proposed legislation, and on September 25, President Johnson signed into law the National Foundation on the Arts and Humanities (NFAH) Act. As Pell later put it, "we in the arts were riding in piggy-back on the humanities."

The NFAH Act detailed the structure of each endowment. The term "humanities," it said, included the study of "language, both modern and classic; linguistics; literature; history; jurisprudence; philosophy; archaeology; the history, criticism, theory, and practice of the arts; and those aspects of the social sciences which have humanistic content and employ humanistic methods." The act also reflected basic assumptions of the Great Society, that "a high civilization, democracy, and world leadership" made it necessary for the United States not to restrict its efforts to science and technology. The encouragement of the arts and the humanities was, therefore, an appropriate matter of concern to the federal government.

The NFAH act contained a number of mechanisms to guard against governmental domination. Each endowment was to have a twenty-six-member National Council of private citizens whose task was to direct policy. Though presidential appointees, council members were to serve for six-year terms. Heading the councils and the agencies were the two endowments' chairmen, who were also presidential appointees but had guaranteed terms of four years. The legislation also authorized the endowments to utilize consultants from outside the government to review and make recommendations with regard to applications for funds, and both NEH and NEA immediately came to rely upon "peer review" for the great bulk of their grant-making decisions. To encourage and stimulate private support, the act allowed for specified Treasury Department* funds to match, on a one-to-one basis, each dollar that a fundable project could generate from outside sources. Finally, the legislation creating the endowments was to expire after three years, and their continuation and funding levels would depend upon periodic congressional reauthorizations. For the first chairman of NEH, President Johnson named Barnaby Keeney, who assumed his duties in July 1966.

The early years of NEH were characterized by modest budgets and relatively low visibility. The agency's initial appropriation was $2.5 million for 1965, which increased to only about $6 million by 1969. NEH established basic operating divisions: Fellowships, to make awards to individual scholars; Research, to fund collaborative efforts; and Education, to support humanities projects involving curricula. These divisions began making grants in 1967, and in 1969 a Public Programs Division was created with the dual aim of bringing the humanities to nonacademic adult audiences and encouraging, to quote new language added to NEH's reauthorization in 1968, "the study and application of the humanities to the human environment."

These few words reflected a serious debate taking place within NEH and the humanities community in general. Were the humanities a series of academic disciplines practiced by specialized scholars and largely confined to institutions of higher education, or were they something more—a way of approaching issues that had practical value and interest for people outside academia? In the late 1960s, with urban and antiwar unrest stimulating discussions about the "relevance" of education, the National Council on the Humanities had heated exchanges between members with opposing views. Under Keeney, the endowment took the position that, along with the obligation to strengthen traditional scholarship and teaching, it had the responsibility to explore new avenues through which the humanities could be of service to society. This position rankled many academic traditionalists, but with NEH's small budget, the controversy remained muted.

Both endowments grew rapidly during the Richard Nixon Administration. From a budget of about $10 million in 1970, by 1975 NEH's budget increased to almost $80 million. Much of the increase was earmarked for the agency's Public Programs Division, which in addition to supporting media and museum projects, began to organize and fund humanities committees in each state modeled after the state arts councils which the NEA had successfully utilized for several years. In NEH's 1970 reauthorizing legislation, Congress added that the disciplines of the humanities should be studied and applied "with particular attention to the relevance of the humanities to the current conditions of national life." On numerous occasions, Senator Pell made it known that the endowment's increased appropriations required it to support more than cloistered scholarship.

In November 1971, President Nixon nominated Ronald Berman, a professor of English at the University of California at San Diego, to be the NEH's new chairman. Although Berman's academic credentials were solid, much of the impetus for his appointment came from conservative intellectuals who admired Berman's 1968 book, *America in the Sixties*, in which the Shakespeare scholar had characterized the decade's political and cultural developments as naive, faddish, and intellectually sterile. The Senate approved Berman's appointment without serious opposition.

Although Berman modified some NEH programs to emphasize a more traditional view as to what the humanities constituted, the endowment's dramatic budgetary growth enabled it to increase its support of both academic and public-oriented activities. The number of fellowships awarded to scholars rose, while the state humanities committees were formed to fund public forums that brought together academic humanists and nonacademics to explore such issues as energy, the environment, and America's ethnic diversity. By 1975, every state had a humanities committee, which joined with the NEH in Washington to sponsor an American Issues Forum designed to bring reflections on the meaning of the nation's bicentennial to every nook and cranny of the country. The endowment also supported ambitious research projects that involved preparing definitive editions of the works of American authors and the collected papers of prominent historical figures. It also funded elaborate public television projects, such as "The Adams Chronicles," which brought humanities programming to millions. Beginning in 1972 with Lionel Trilling, NEH annually selected a distinguished humanist to offer a highly publicized and prestigious Jefferson Lecture in the Humanities.

These expanded activities brought NEH considerably more attention but also more vigorous criticism. Fiscal conservatives in Congress took note of the appropriations increases and preached woe. Senator William Proxmire of Wisconsin, for one, hung several of his "Golden Fleece" awards for government boondoggles on NEH-supported projects, and these resulted in a barrage of unfavorable publicity. But this type of opposition had always existed just beneath the surface and did not affect overall congressional and White House support for the endowment. More significant was the criticism directed against NEH by segments of the humanities community itself, which held that too many endowment grants went to already-established institutions and individuals, and that others, especially those outside the Northeast, were being underserved. Proponents of this view did not question the legitimacy of federal support for the humanities, but they attacked the NEH as "elitist."

The elitism issue became entangled with the question of Berman's reappointment as NEH chairman. In 1975, President Gerald Ford, whose administration largely maintained the policies of its predecessor toward both endowments, nominated Berman to another four-year term. Congress at the time was considering amending NEH's reauthorizing legislation by making the recently formed state humanities committees into autonomous state agencies on the order of arts councils. The sponsor of this amendment was none other than Senator Pell. Berman actively opposed Pell's amendment, claiming that placing the state committees under the authority of the governors would politicize them and lead to a decline in the quality of their activities. An infuriated Pell responded by refusing to bring Berman's renomination to a Senate vote. The impasse lingered on through 1976 with Berman remaining on as NEH chairman even though he lacked the necessary confirmation.

The episode brought the "elitism versus populism" issue further into the open. Pell claimed that Berman wanted to centralize NEH control in Washington, and Pell was quoted as saying that the state humanities committees should, if they desired, have the option of offering small grants to "mom and pop store operators" to study great books. Both conservatives and liberals from the intellectual and academic communities lambasted Pell for this position, but the Senator remained adamant. In acrimonious public hearings, Pell charged that, under Berman's leadership NEH, once the more vigorous of the two endowments, had become the "pale shadow" of NEA. Pell agreed with those who accused NEH of being elitist. Despite the Congress's adoption, with NEH's concurrence, of compromise legislation that gave more autonomy to the state humanities committees, the Senate failed to reconfirm Berman, and he resigned in January 1977.

The 1976 legislation also established a challenge-grant program to assist humanities institutions to improve their general financial stability by using federal monies, one dollar for every three dollars of outside money. The intention was to generate increased private support to be used for basic operating expenses rather than for the specific projects funded by NEH's program divisions. The program, highly popular and successful, in 1977 and 1978, brought from donors approximately $100 million in challenge grants.

As the Jimmy Carter Administration searched for a new chairman, the elitism charge continued to haunt NEH. Minority and women's organizations made it known that they considered the existing NEH funding patterns unsatisfactory. Spokespersons for small colleges also expressed displeasure, as did those for labor groups. Critics turned their attention to NEH's peer-review system, maintaining that it was unnecessarily secretive and too dependent upon a closed network of established scholars. In a March 1977 speech, President Carter personally criticized NEH for its "elitist image" and indicated that the search for a new chairman would take into account prospective candidates' commitment to extend humanities opportunities. Privately, the President seemed perturbed by the amount of press attention and White House staff time being devoted to the appointment. Finally, in August, Carter nominated his Assistant Secretary of State for Educational and Cultural Affairs, Joseph Duffey, a former theology professor at Hartford Seminary and Yale, whose activities in Democratic politics had included managing the Carter presidential campaign in the District of Columbia. Some academics complained that Duffey's appointment was too "political," and on several occasions the nominee offered reassurances that his efforts to broaden NEH's activities would be undertaken without abandoning traditional notions of scholarship and excellence. He was easily confirmed by the Senate and began his appointment in October.

On the whole, Duffey did not basically alter the nature of the NEH's activities. He did insist that more women and minority humanists be included on endowment peer-review panels, which also began to reflect a greater degree of institutional variety than had been the case in the past. Likewise, he increased the number of women and minorities on the endowment's senior professional staff. To the consternation of some and the relief of others, however, the endowment found that this did not dramatically change the distribution of awards, particularly in NEH's fellowship programs which had become the favorite target of those who believed the endowment to be elitist. The continued, albeit more moderate, increases in NEH's budgets did enable some new programs to be developed which could be targeted to specific audiences. In 1977, the state humanities committees were placed under a separate Division of State Programs, and in 1979, a Division of Special Programs was created to encourage humanities projects involving nontraditional audiences.

In the spring of 1978, the Rockefeller Foundation sponsored a new commission to reassess the status of the humanities. This Commission on the Humanities was frankly concerned that the "elitism versus populism" debate had greatly oversimplified perceptions about the humanities and the role of the endowment. In a widely publicized report issued in September 1980, the commission affirmed the importance of the humanities and emphasized that the most pressing single need was to upgrade the quality of humanities education in primary and secondary schools. While there was some criticism of NEH for failing adequately to address this problem, the Humanities Commission's overall finding gave the endowment high marks.

The Heritage Foundation, a research institute with a conservative orientation, undertook its own study with the specific purpose of making policy recommendations should a new administration be elected in 1980. Its report criticized both endowments for their recent tendencies "to emphasize politically inspired social policies at the expense of the arts and humanities." The Heritage Foundation emphasized that "excellence" in the humanities should be NEH's foremost concern, and it made a number of specific recommendations ranging from doing away with special efforts to having minorities represented on NEH review panels to eliminating the Division of Special Programs. Following the election of Ronald Reagan to the presidency, the Heritage Foundation's report became a working paper of Reagan's arts and humanities transition team, and it was widely expected to be indicative of the new administration's policies toward the endowments.

President Reagan's intention to reduce federal spending significantly soon overshadowed the debate over NEH's alleged politicalization. After first proposing that both endowments be abolished, the President's budget director, David Stockman, announced that the administration was recommending cutting the existing appropriations ($170 million for NEH) for each by 50 percent. The Reagan Administration claimed that the endowments' growth was eroding private support for the arts and humanities. This was immediately disputed not only by arts and humanities advocates but also by corporate spokesmen who insisted that the private sector could not pick up the slack. There was, in fact, little evidence to support the administration's position; indeed, statistically it could be demonstrated that endowment funds had generated private support. Not even the Heritage Foundation had claimed that the road to excellence in the humanities lay in a 50-percent budget cut for NEH.

By the spring of 1981, in the face of outcries against the proposed cuts, President Reagan created a special Task Force to consider how private support for the arts and humanities could be increased and to evaluate the overall management and structure of the two endowments. In October the Task Force issued its findings. To the surprise of many who had initially viewed it as a first step toward the abolition of NEH and NEA, the Reagan Task Force concluded that the endowments should remain as originally conceived. It also flatly denied that federal money drives out private money. It predicted that by significantly reducing taxpayer incentive to make deductible contributions, the tax cuts would actually decrease private support for the arts and humanities at the same time that federal funding was being drastically reduced.

Over the years, NEH, unlike many federal agencies created during the halcyon days of the Great Society, has survived and even prospered. It has enjoyed an unusual degree of bipartisan support and has weathered several searching independent evaluations by individuals and groups of various persuasions. The ultimate actions of the Reagan Administration will, of course, greatly affect its future. But it could not be claimed in 1981, as it had been said in 1964, that humanists were the "forgotten people" of America's educational system.

FOR ADDITIONAL INFORMATION: There is no detailed history of NEH, but a forthcoming study by Stephen Miller will eventually fill this void. Michael S. Mooney, *The Ministry of Culture: Connections Among Art, Money and Politics* is a shrill, heavy-handed examination that finds both endowments guilty of conspiring to define and control American cultural life.

The serious student of NEH must turn to scattered legislative and agency documents. Among the more significant of these are *Hearings on Bills to Establish a National Foundation on the Arts and Humanities*, Special Subcommittee on Arts and Humanities of the Senate Committee on Labor and Public Welfare (1965); *National Foundation on the Arts and Humanities Act of 1965* (Public Law 209, 89th Cong., September 29, 1965), along with subsequent amendments; *Annual Reports of the National Endowment for the Humanities* (1965-); and NEH's *Announcements of Programs* (1967-).

For the Berman-Pell controversy, see *Nomination Hearings on Ronald S. Berman . . . to be Chairman of the National Endowment for the Humanities*, (Senate Committee on Labor and Public Welfare, 1976).

There are several key commission and foundation reports. *Report of the Commission on the Humanities* (1964) led directly to the creation of NEH. The Rockefeller Foundation study is *The Humanities in American Life: Report of the Commission on the Humanities* (1980). The Heritage Foundation study is Michael S. Joyce, "The National Endowments for the Humanities and the Arts," in Charles S. Heatherly, ed., *Mandate for Leadership: Policy Management in a Conservative Administration* (1981). On President Reagan's Task Force, see *Report to the President* (1981).

MORTON SOSNA

NATIONAL LABOR RELATIONS BOARD (NLRB). Administrative agencies, such as the National Labor Relations Board, have become vital and pervasive forces in our society. The NLRB is among the most important administrative agencies, not only because of its widespread effect on administrative law, but also because of its major role in making and implementing national labor policy.

The NLRB is an independent agency created by the National Labor Relations Act of 1935 (Wagner Act) as amended by the acts of 1947 (Taft-Hartley Act), 1959 (Landrum-Griffin Act), and 1974 (extending NLRB jurisdiction to privately operated health care institutions). The NLRB has two main functions under the act: to conduct secret-ballot representation elections among employees in appropriate bargaining units to determine whether or not they chose to be represented by a particular union; and to prevent and remedy certain unlawful, unfair labor practices by employers or unions.

Beginning in 1947, the NLRB became the only "two-headed" federal agency consisting of a five-member board responsible for adjudication and the conduct of elections and an Office of General Counsel with final authority to investigate charges of unfair labor practices, to issue and prosecute complaints before the board, and to represent the board in judicial proceedings. There are also thirty-three regional offices under the general supervision of the General Counsel.

The Wagner Act NLRB had two immediate predecessors: the National Labor Board (NLB), which existed from August 1933 to June 1934, and the old National Labor Relations Board (old NLRB), which functioned from June 1934 to July 1935. President Franklin Roosevelt created both of these boards by Executive Order as part of the New Deal's economic recovery program during the depression. These precedessor boards were intended to prevent major industrial strikes that would seriously impede the recovery program.

No decision-making authority was conferred on these boards. They sought the amicable settlement of industrial conflict through mediation, nonlegalistic informal discussions, and voluntary cooperation. The tripartite NLB, chaired by Senator Robert Wagner, and the old NLRB, chaired by Lloyd Garrison and subsequently by Francis Biddle, soon recognized the incompatibility of their two goals: strike settlements based on formulas mutually acceptable to employers and unions and the interpretation of Section 7(a) of the National Industrial Recovery Act, which set forth principles of law, namely, that employees had the lawful right to organize and bargain collectively through representatives of their own choosing free from interference or coercion from their employers.

Noncompliance with NLB and old NLRB efforts increased, particularly in the open-shop steel and automobile industries, conclusively demonstrating the weakness inherent in the boards' total dependence upon the voluntary cooperation of employers and unions, the force of public sentiment, and the influence and prestige of its members. Under the pressure of these circumstances, both the NLB and the old NLRB moved reluctantly and cautiously into the role as quasi-judicial bodies formulating principles rather than fashioning compromises. The old NLRB, in particular, decided that it could not act as both mediator and judge.

The old NLRB and NLB through these "decisions" pioneered in the creation and development of a common law of labor relations. These first efforts toward a clear statement of a national labor policy irritated Roosevelt, who was not prepared to support a specific public policy favoring collective bargaining as defined by the old NLRB and NLB. Such a policy conflicted with his empirical approach to economic recovery, which required that he be sensitive to the incidence of power and ready to compromise—particularly to obtain and retain the cooperation of powerful employers.

As a consequence of this attempt to formulate a national labor policy, the NLB and the old NLRB were frequently thrust into a series of turbulent and dramatic conflicts with employers and unions, President Roosevelt, Congress, the National Recovery Administration,* the Department of Labor,* the National Association of Manufacturers, the Liberty League, the press, and the Department of Justice* and the federal judiciary, including the Supreme Court of the United States.

In the course of these struggles, what began in 1933 as a tripartite NLB created to settle strikes through mediation eventually became a quasi-judicial body of neutrals deciding cases by setting forth principles of law, conducting formal hearings, issuing rules and regulations, and requiring legalistic uniformity in procedure. The experiences of these predecessor boards made it clear that the unenforceable common law they created had to be made into an enforceable statutory authority. The opportunity to obtain passage of such legislation (the Wagner Act) was created when, in the spring of 1935, the Supreme Court in the Schechter Poultry Corporation case struck down as unconstitutional the cornerstone of the New Deal's national recovery legislation.

All of the major provisions of the Wagner Act were legislative embodiments of the practical experiences of the pre-Wagner Act labor boards: majority rule and exclusive representation; the specification of employer unfair labor practices, including the right of employees to organize and the obligation of employers to bargain with the representatives of their employees; and the creation of a quasi-judicial administrative agency to enforce rights, not to mediate disputes. This agency, the National Labor Relations Board, was made independent of the Labor Department or any other branch of government, was composed of three impartial rather than partisan representatives, was free to seek enforcement of its own orders through the courts without obtaining the approval of the Department of Justice or other governmental bodies, was endowed with wide-ranging administrative discretion concerning its remedy powers and its identification of new forms of unfair labor practices and bargaining unit determinations, as well as with power to subpoena witnesses and documents—all subject to only limited judicial review of its fact-finding expertise and no direct review of its representation-election orders or bargaining-unit determinations.

The Wagner Act, which remains today the basic foundation of the national labor policy, culminated a transformation whereby American labor policy would be developed by law and litigation through legislative enactment, the growth of a body of NLRB case precedent, and the application of administrative law.

The Wagner Act remained essentially inoperative, however, from September 1935 to April 1937, while the NLRB formulated a litigation strategy designed to withstand the inevitable Supreme Court test. That litigation strategy included the centralization of administrative authority in the Washington office, the establishment of an Economics Division (to gather economic material for use as evidence in particular cases and to make general studies of labor relations problems to guide the board in its formulation of policy), the use of and cooperation with the LaFollette Civil Liberties Committee investigation to publicize employer violations of the law, and the careful selection of test cases.

In a major reversal of precedent, the Supreme Court ruled on April 12, 1937, that the Wagner Act and the NLRB were constitutional. The NLRB's litigation efforts made a vital contribution not only to the ratification of the Wagner Act labor policy but also to the creation of a radically changed role for the federal government in labor relations. In fact, the NLRB's efforts had historical significance well beyond labor relations, since the Supreme Court's Wagner Act decisions eliminated long-standing restraints on the exercise of national power by establishing precedents for submitting to federal regulation affairs that had never before been considered the business of the federal government.

After constitutionality, the NLRB, chaired by J. Warren Madden, chose to make a record of vigorous enforcement of the act unmatched in the history of administrative agencies. The board's vigorous and literal enforcement of the Wagner Act did not go unchallenged. For four years after the Supreme Court's Wagner Act decisions, the board was under continual attack by anti-New Deal congressmen in the House and Senate, by powerful employers, by the press, and, most importantly, by the American Federation of Labor (AFL).

The AFL, after the split in the labor movement in 1936 and the creation of the Congress of Industrial Organizations (CIO), publicly condemned the board for even handling CIO cases, for voiding AFL contracts on grounds that the companies had illegally assisted the AFL unions, and for its allegedly pro-CIO bias. The unchecked and often overt ideological involvements of certain key NLRB personnel also weakened the NLRB from within and increased its vulnerability to charges of pro-CIO bias and left-wing domination.

The NLRB was in the main invulnerable to political attack, however, until the Democrats suffered a sound trouncing in the 1938 congressional elections and the AFL entered into an alliance with powerful anti-NLRB employer interest groups and with Virginia arch-conservative Congressman Howard Smith, who in 1939 succeeded in establishing a Special House Committee to Investigate the NLRB (the Smith Committee).

The Smith Committee investigation of the Madden Board was a watershed in the history of the NLRB and American labor policy, even though the committee's proposed legislation was subsequently killed by the Senate Labor Committee. Smith's hostile investigation of the NLRB created a public distrust of the board that lasted over the years. The final consequences of that investigation were only delayed by World War II when the War Labor Board became the dominant influence on national labor policy. The AFL-business-conservative-Southern-Democrat alliance during the first half of the twelve years between the Wagner and Taft-Hartley acts has had a lasting effect on labor history and labor law.

In sum, Smith's investigation succeeded, at first without legislative changes, in bringing about fundamental changes in the NLRB's administrative setup, its doctrines, its personnel, and its overall mode of operation. By 1946, for the first time since the Wagner Act was passed, the opponents of the act and the NLRB had sufficient congressional and public support to change legislatively the nation's labor policy with the passage of the Taft-Hartley Act in 1947. (The Hartley Bill was written in Congressman Smith's office using Smith's 1940 bill as a model, and the Taft-Hartley Act eventually included most of the more severe provisions of the Hartley Bill.)

The Taft-Hartley Act added, among other provisions, six union unfair labor practices, a free speech for employers section, an expansion of board membership from three to five, an independent Office of General Counsel, and a proviso officially prohibiting the NLRB from engaging in "economic analysis." Despite a serious and publicly embarrassing conflict between the board and the NLRB's first independent General Counsel which lasted until that General Counsel was forced to resign in 1950, relations between the board and General Counsel have been generally cooperative.

Just as there was insufficient evidence in 1947 to justify the bifurcation of the NLRB's prosecutory and adjudicative functions, the NLRB's Division of Economic Research was eliminated for all kinds of reasons that had nothing to do with the merits and importance of its work: political pressures and maneuverings, jealousy and empire building between and among lawyers and economists inside the board, opposition to leftist ideologies, a personal attack on the chief economist, and a mighty hostility to the administrative process. It is an historical anachronism that the NLRB remains today the only administrative agency forbidden to seek pertinent economic and industrial relations data on its own.

This seldom-noted prohibition strikes at the fundamental purpose of the NLRB as an expert administrative agency. The more the board is forced to rely on unverified behavioral assumptions, untested suppositions, and abstract legal principles to make labor law on a case-by-case basis, the stronger the demand that the board substantiate its decisions with evidence concerning the realities of industrial relations. This congressional prohibition also prevents the NLRB from conducting its own studies of how its administration of the law is working in practice. It is dismaying to realize that the NLRB's basic reinstatement remedy, for example, after forty-seven years, has not been subjected to comprehensive empirical investigation to assess its effectiveness. An empirical research and analysis unit at the NLRB would also contribute to more knowledgeable judgments and policy choices and would give more meaning and factual content to evaluations of legislative and administrative actions as well as to the formulation of legislative policy. Such a unit would reduce, although not eliminate, the possibility that ignorance, emotion, prejudice, or the political horsetrading of self-interest groups would determine the content of labor policy.

The NLRB is most vulnerable politically since it must decide disputes involving controversial and emotional issues affecting economically powerful and politically influential groups. The NLRB has definitely been a whipping boy without rival. After passage of the Taft-Hartley Act, the NLRB, which in its early years had attracted idealists dedicated to social and economic justice for the workingman and woman, lost the zeal characteristic of new agencies and became a more bureaucratic "mature" organization.

In the 1950s, Dwight Eisenhower, first Republican President in twenty years, used his appointment power to create a solid Republican majority on the board for the first time in its history. When this "Eisenhower Board" reversed many board precedents to favor management, the labor movement charged that the NLRB had a pro-employer bias. In this context, in 1959, the Landrum-Griffin Act was passed regulating internal union affairs and amending the Taft-Hartley Act.

In the 1960s, the Kennedy-Johnson or "New Frontier" NLRB returned the NLRB to a more liberal course, causing management to label the NLRB "pro-labor." The NLRB, therefore, remained subject to the vicissitudes of political change and at the center of labor-management controversy to the present day.

The NLRB, although technically an independent administrative agency, is in many ways a creature of Congress and the executive. At the same time, the board's performance of its judicial duties is supposed to be independent of congressional or executive influence or control. The ideal result is a delicate balance of judicial independence and congressional and executive dependence— a delicate balance that has never reached an equilibrium from the Wagner Act to the present time.

FOR ADDITIONAL INFORMATION: Several useful and informative studies of the NLRB and national labor policy are available in book form. Harry Millis and Emily Clark Brown, *From the Wagner Act to Taft-Hartley* (1950), traces the development of a national labor policy by concentrating on the doctrines evolved by the NLRB. Irving Bernstein, *The New Deal Collective Bargaining Policy* (1950), is an analysis of the legislative history of the Wagner Act. For other related works, see R. Alton Lee, *Truman and Taft-Hartley* (1966) and Louis Silverberg, ed., *The Wagner Act: After Ten Years* (1945). Another excellent source of information on NLRB activities is the NLRB's *Annual Reports*, 1935-1982.

Two recent studies reverse the usual line of labor relations inquiry and, instead of concentrating on legislative histories and legal doctrines, focus on the NLRB itself as the primary object of investigation: James A. Gross, *The Making of the NLRB: A Study in Economics, Politics and the Law* (1974) and James A. Gross, *The Reshaping of the NLRB: National Labor Policy in Transition* (1981).

JAMES A. GROSS

NATIONAL OCEANIC AND ATMOSPHERIC ADMINISTRATION. See National Ocean Survey; National Weather Service.

NATIONAL OCEAN SURVEY (NOS). The history of the National Ocean Survey, which began in 1807 as the Survey of the Coast, is closely intertwined with the history of the American scientific community. Those who colonized North America faced a hostile and untamed environment whose climate was significantly harsher than Europe's. They were drawn to the practical sciences that could furnish tools for understanding (perhaps modifying) the world around them. Among the questions they faced, none proved more important than those involving the sea. For between the United States and the source of its goods, both material and spiritual, lay the North Atlantic Ocean. Thus, the techniques for bringing ships safely across the ocean and into harbor gave those who worked in the exact sciences their opportunity.

As the key sector of the American economy in the early Federal period and a vital sector thereafter, the ocean shipping industry was the economic base on which to develop scientific institutions. In 1807, at the height of prosperity for the American sailing fleet, Thomas Jefferson (of all presidents the most scientifically oriented) founded what is now the National Ocean Survey as the federal government's first scientific agency. In modern terms, the role of the new survey was to provide research and development services to the shipping industry.

Thirteen people (among them James Madison) put forward plans for the Survey of the Coast in response to Jefferson's request. Jefferson chose the plan presented by Ferdinand Rudolph Hassler, a recent immigrant from Switzerland with impeccable credentials as a geodesist. With his European conception of the deference owed by society to a man of learning, Hassler set about his task as director of the survey with little regard for the political problems he might face. He began without suitable instruments or trained assistants under the eye of a Congress committed to keeping the national government as small as possible and unable to see any difference between the scientifically based surveys of professional geodesists and those of practical people without scientific training.

Hassler's first step was to go to England for instruments. There he was stranded by the War of 1812. Not until 1816 did he make it into the field to establish his first baseline. He completed only two seasons' work around New York Harbor when the Congress took the survey from the civil government and gave it to the Navy.*

Although the result was a setback for Hassler and his Coast Survey, the Congress followed its priorities. Maintaining an adequate defense force in peacetime is always a problem, and never is it more difficult than just after a war. The United States Navy emerged from the War of 1812 with an officer corps much larger than it needed to man its ships. The small shore establishment could employ only a handful of the trained officers. Their hope for further cruises, and with them the chance for promotion, depended on finding new tasks to take them to sea. They also had financial incentives, for the nineteenth-century Navy provided only half-pay for officers who were not on duty afloat or ashore. Assigning the Survey of the Coast to the Navy was a way to keep its officers employed, at the expense of Hassler's plans for a survey second to none. But the Navy was not able to publish accurate charts of the coast.

Finally, in 1832, the civilian Survey of the Coast was restored under Hassler's leadership. One of his tasks in the interim was standardizing the weights and measures of the U.S. customs houses; it remained a survey responsibility until the twentieth century.

Totally unskilled in politics, Hassler continued to have his troubles with the Congress until his death in 1843. For two years, from 1834 to 1836, his civilian survey was part of the Navy Department, rather than the Treasury Department* where it began in 1807 (and stayed until the Department of Commerce and Labor was formed in 1903). When it returned to Treasury, the organization had a new name: the Coast Survey.

Hassler divided his task into three parts: geodesy, topography, and hydrography. Since the first was key to the rest, he spared no effort to make it as exact as possible. The initial baselines that he and his colleagues laid out are still part of the nation's network of primary triangulation. Hassler's rigorous techniques gave the Coast Survey's efforts a scientific accuracy that contemporary surveys of the interior did not reach. A congressional investigation in 1843 vindicated Hassler's high standards, giving the Coast Survey a charter that lasted without major change for a century.

On Hassler's death in 1843, the superintendency passed to Alexander Dallas Bache after intensive lobbying led by Joseph Henry, professor at Princeton and the leading American physicist of his day. Member of a prominent Philadelphia family, great-grandson of Benjamin Franklin, and grandson and namesake of Alexander Dallas (Madison's Secretary of the Treasury), Bache had the political connections and skills that Hassler lacked. He could count on the support of his fellow students at West Point,* where he graduated first in the class that included Jefferson Davis of Mississippi. Bache's scientific qualifications were no less impressive. He had served the University of Pennsylvania as professor (of what we now call physics) and the city of Philadelphia as superintendent of schools. Well known in European scientific circles from his extensive travels, he had established at Girard College in Philadelphia the first magnetic observatory in the United States.

Bache took over a Coast Survey that had tried to meet the threat of a Navy takeover by staffing its ships with Navy men. He expanded its activity considerably. Determined to make his agency the center of science within the federal government, Bache built bridges to the scientists in colleges and institutes with joint projects for the precise determination of longitudes and for collecting the myriad creatures of the sea. He placated the Congress by doubling the number of field parties and by coaxing testimonials from shipping and insurance companies. Bache kept the Coast Survey a permanent part of the federal government by riding the wave of seaborne commerce.

From 1815 to 1860, the American Merchant Marine quadrupled; yet, it could not keep up with the headlong expansion of maritime trade. The law gave American vessels a monopoly of domestic cargoes, but they could handle only about 70 percent of foreign ones. More than shipowners and their insurers had a stake in this expansion of commerce. The entire American economy became tied to an expanding international market, centered on the Atlantic Ocean, in whose dramatic growth falling freight rates played a vital part. In ocean shipping, Bache found a burgeoning industry to harness to the cause of science.

The Coast Survey attracted powerful support by furnishing what we now call research and development services to maritime commerce, the sector of the economy on which a developing country depended to keep it in touch with civilization. By serving the practical needs of the shipping industry, Bache earned the wherewithal to pursue science's higher goal: broadening human knowledge of the natural world. He outflanked ignorance and parsimony by hiring for ostensibly practical work only those with training in basic science and provided them with the opportunity to make fundamental contributions. These contributions could bring renown in the European-dominated halls of science. The practical work performed at the same time insured the continued support of the American commercial community and its representatives in the Congress.

Bache's program for American science had its opponents, however. Until the South seceded in 1861, there was continuing pressure to turn charting over to the Navy. The Navy also laid claim, during Bache's tenure as superintendent of the Coast Survey, to other areas of science of interest to him, especially astronomy. Disputes between Bache and his rival, the equally energetic naval officer Matthew Fontaine Maury, lasted for almost two decades, until Maury went south in 1861.

By the time of Bache's death in 1867, the Coast Survey was the dominant scientific institution in the United States. The continuing expansion of America's seacoast had brought permanence to an agency that was supposed to complete its task and disappear. Bache began operations along the Gulf of Mexico after the annexation of Texas, which increased the coastline by 8 percent. Shortly after Oregon and California joined the Union, the Gold Rush brought incredible numbers of ships to San Francisco. Bache rushed men out to chart the West Coast, including George Davidson, who was later put in charge of the Coast Survey's work there.

The expansion of the Coast Survey under Bache brought many innovations. Steam replaced sail. To help mariners use their compasses, Bache and his colleagues measured the earth's magnetic field and developed theories of its behavior. He himself measured a seven-mile baseline in North Carolina to a hitherto-undreamed of accuracy of one inch. Automatic gauges recorded the rise and fall of the tide. The telegraph lines spreading across the country made it possible to determine longitude with great accuracy; these longitudinal determinations brought Benjamin Peirce, professor of astronomy and mathematics at Harvard, on to the Coast Survey payroll.

Bache and his friends were leaders of the American Association for the Advancement of Science. They founded the Nautical Almanac Office. Though part of the Navy, it was located in Cambridge, Massachusetts, to keep it away from the Naval Observatory under Maury. During the Civil War, Bache's Coast Survey expanded rapidly, helping the Union Navy blockade the South and publishing maps of the battle zones. Bache and his friends got the Congress to set up the National Academy of Sciences to offer advice to the government. When Bache suffered a stroke in 1864, Julius E. Hilgard took over the running of the survey.

After Bache's death in 1867, the superintendency of the Coast Survey passed to Peirce, one of Bache's closest allies.

Under Peirce the Coast Survey resumed primary triangulation, halted during the war, and began to join the East and West coasts by a network of stations across the country. The purchase of Alaska in 1867 once more expanded the American coastline. The survey rushed a chart into print to assist the Senate debate on the treaty of acquisition and began surveying in Alaskan waters.

Until after the Civil War, coast pilots—the volumes of sailing directions used by navigators—were the product of a private publisher. The Coast Survey printed sailing directions on its earliest charts. Not until 1858, however, when a pamphlet on the Pacific Coast appeared, were the directions gathered into a printed volume. Only after the government bought the copyright of Blunt's *American Coast Pilot* did the Coast Survey put out an official volume, the *United States Coast Pilot*, which first appeared in 1874.

Peirce's successor was Carlile P. Patterson, a former Navy captain who had spent part of his career in the survey. In 1878, the Congress asked the National Academy of Sciences for a plan for the government's map and chartmaking. The General Land Office* of the Interior Department* had charge of the cadastral (boundary) surveying of the public lands, which it carried out in a slipshod manner. After 1867, four separate groups, known as the Territorial Surveys, fanned out to explore and map the West. By 1874, they were running into each other, and the Congress felt it might be time to consolidate them. As it asked the academy for a report, the Congress renamed the Coast Survey the Coast and Geodetic Survey to recognize its responsibility to triangulation.

The academy's report recommended a further change—that the survey be renamed the Coast and Interior Survey and transferred from Treasury to Interior with responsibility for all surveying. This increased responsibility would bring the Coast Survey's high standards to cadastral mapping. But the General Land Office's surveyors general had too much political power. All the Congress did in 1879 was to consolidate the Territorial Surveys into the United States Geological Survey.*

As the Coast Survey dominated American science before the Civil War, so did the Geological Survey for the rest of the century. With Congress's refusal to give the Coast and Geodetic Survey any additional responsibility, the task of making topographic maps of the interior fell by default to the Geological Survey, whose maps continued the high standards begun by the Coast Survey. The Geological Survey used the Coast and Geodetic Survey's triangulation, and the Coast and Geodetic Survey continued to map the topography along the coasts. Cadastral mapping remained, unreformed, in the General Land Office.

When the Congress investigated the government's scientific agencies in 1884-1885, the pressure was greatest on the Coast and Geodetic Survey. Hilgard, old and ill, was forced to resign. His place was taken by the chief clerk of the Bureau of Internal Revenue, a friend of President Grover Cleveland, who was brought in to tighten up the survey's accounting. Not until the physicist Thomas

C. Mendenhall became superintendent in 1889 did the Coast and Geodetic Survey return to its tradition of having a scientist as its leader.

Although no longer paramount in the halls of government science, the Coast and Geodetic Survey continued its notable contributions. Peirce brought with him from Cambridge the mathematician William Ferrel, who developed his pioneering meteorological theories to be useful to sailors and built the first tide-predicting machine in the United States, forerunner of large-scale computing machinery. Mendenhall extended the observations of the earth's gravity that the survey had begun in 1872 under Benjamin Peirce's son Charles. He called together representatives of all the government agencies concerned with maps and their features. From their occasional meetings grew the Board of Geographic Names, a federal activity (now shared between the Geological Survey for domestic names and the Defense Mapping Agency for foreign ones) that assures that place names in American publications are uniform.

In the 1870s, Lieutenant Commander Charles D. Sigsbee developed a deep-sea sounding machine that made possible the first chart (of the Gulf of Mexico) on which the detailed bottom topography extended into deep water. In 1876, Lieutenant John E. Pillsbury, another naval officer with the survey, invented a meter to measure ocean currents. From 1884 to 1890, he anchored the survey steamer *Blake* in the Gulf Stream, one of the swiftest ocean currents, to make a classic series of measurements of its velocity. N. H. Heck constructed a wire drag in 1904 that made it possible to find submerged pinnacles not revealed by soundings.

In the 1890s, parties crossed the United States to complete the world's longest arc of primary triangulation and to measure the force of gravity with the portable gravimeter developed by Mendenhall. From their results J. F. Hayford calculated a new datum or base for mapping that tied all reference points together. William Bowie persuaded Canada and Mexico to adopt it. As the North American Datum, it remains the basis of the maps of all three countries. Hayford extended his efforts to the world, developing in 1909 a reference ellipsoid, or mathematical model of the earth's surface, that was accepted internationally in 1924. Hayford and Bowie used the gravity data to try to prove that the earth's crust was in isostatic equilibrium. If isostasy held, any one vertical column of the crust would weigh the same as any other, implying that mountains are made of lighter material than lowlands.

When war with Spain began in 1898, the naval officers and men who had manned Coast Survey ships departed. Civilians replaced them until 1917, when an independent uniformed service was established. The growth of the uniformed staff members, with their need for shore duty between cruises and for expertise when at sea, led in time to their domination of the agency. After 1929, the superintendent was a commissioned officer of the rank of rear admiral.

Continuing improvement of its traditional tasks marked the survey's history in the twentieth century. The copperplate engraving introduced by Bache gave way in 1905 to photolithography, first from stone and then (from 1915) from aluminum plates. In 1910, Rollin A. Harris and E. G. Fischer built a mechanical tide predictor (in modern terms, a special-purpose analog computer) to replace an earlier one built by meteorologist William Ferrel. Steel and then invar tapes made more precise the measurement of baselines. There were new and improved instruments to use in running a line of levels across the country and a number of lines from north to south. The laying of telegraph cables across the oceans permitted international longitudes to be determined by telegraph. Begun under Hilgard in 1872, telegraphic determination of international longitudes gained momentum after 1900. The San Francisco earthquake of 1906 sent the geodesists back to the field to measure the shifts in the earth's crust, which were monitored continuously thereafter.

The electronic age came to charting with the introduction in the 1920s of the fathometer, which measured water depth with a pulse of sound. Underwater sound was also used to measure horizontal distances. Since sonic measurements were continuous, contour lines replaced individual soundings to show the depth of water on the survey's charts. With World War II, a series of electronic positioning systems came into use to control offshore surveys. Improvements were continually made in tide and current meters. First, they could record their data automatically; now they telemeter it to central locations.

Aviation came to the Coast and Geodetic Survey in 1926, when it became responsible for aeronautical charts. At the same time, aerial photographs from high altitudes became available. Their use to display terrain stereographically led to a revolutionary new way to make maps: photogrammetry. Multi-lens precision cameras and optically sophisticated plotting machines made it possible to map terrain hitherto inaccessible on the ground. After World War II, photogrammetry virtually replaced traditional plane-table mapping. The war also revolutionized geomagnetic observations. Sensitive magnetometers carried in aircraft to detect enemy submarines were modified to measure the earth's magnetic field.

The Congress in 1925 put the Coast and Geodetic Survey in charge of the government's work in seismology. The survey helped develop a network of stations worldwide that determined where an earthquake had occurred. After a seismic sea wave in 1946 killed many people in Hawaii, the survey organized a warning system. In 1971, the survey lost geomagnetism and seismology to the Geological Survey.

This loss was only one of the upheavals that in recent decades have transformed the federal government's oldest scientific agency. The Coast and Geodetic Survey had been in the Commerce Department* since 1913 when the department was founded by splitting the Department of Commerce and Labor. In 1965, the Commerce Department formed the Environmental Science Services Administration (ESSA) by merging the Survey and the Weather Bureau.* Their research, data, and satellite components became independent within the larger agency. Before this reorganization was complete, the Congress responded to the Stratton Report on Marine Sciences by creating the National Oceanic and Atmospheric

Administration (NOAA). The largest of Commerce's bureaus, NOAA was formed by joining to ESSA the Bureau of Commercial Fisheries and giving the new agency the mapping duties of the U.S. Lake Survey, which had been part of the Army Corps of Engineers.*

One of NOAA's components is the National Ocean Survey, a new title for what used to be the Coast and Geodetic Survey. NOS remains responsible for the government's charts, both marine and aeronautical. One of its components, the National Geodetic Survey, continues to measure the earth with the increasing precision that modern instruments make possible. The commissioned officer corps now belongs to all of NOAA, not just NOS. Its members thus have greater scope for their talents, since NOAA added the Fisheries' fleet to the surveying fleet of the Coast and Geodetic Survey. As the American people make more use of the coastal zone and the Outer Continental Shelf, the National Ocean Survey continues to provide the information that they need to manage these resources wisely.

FOR ADDITIONAL INFORMATION: Research on the Coast Survey and its predecessors begins in the NOAA Library in Rockville, Maryland. The official correspondence of the Coast and Geodetic Survey in the National Archives* is exceptionally complete for the nineteenth century. Secondary accounts are Roy Popkin, *The Environmental Sciences Services Administration* (1967); A. Joseph Wraight and Elliott B. Roberts, *The Coast and Geodetic Survey 1807-1957* (1957); and Rear Admiral Allen L. Powell, *National Ocean Survey—The Government's First Technical Agency* (1976).

HAROLD L. BURSTYN

NATIONAL PARK SERVICE. When President Woodrow Wilson signed the act creating the National Park Service in late August 1916, there were already in existence seventeen national parks and twenty-two national monuments, military battlefields, and cemeteries administered by the Interior Department,* the Forest Service* in the Department of Agriculture,* or the Army.* The parks included Yellowstone, the first national park, created in 1872, and by 1916, such additional important ones as Yosemite, Glacier, and Grand Canyon.

These national parks had been brought into existence haphazardly. The initial suggestions for their being came from such diverse interests as railroads which would profit from subsequent tourist travel, land speculators, nature lovers, and politicians trying to please their constituents. Not until passage of the Antiquities Act in 1906 was there a federal statute providing for the segregation of public lands for the purposes of historic value, anthropological interest, or—as application evolved—of scenic value. However, the resultant national monuments, though erected under provisions of this single statute, were administered by whichever government bureau had jurisdiction over the land in which the monument originally existed.

The period 1890-1916 was one of active conservationist endeavor, led by President Theodore Roosevelt. Consulting with him was Gifford Pinchot, a forester who advocated multiple use of forests and looked with disdain upon the advocates of national parks as protective enclaves for the scenic wonders contained therein. Taking a firm stand to protect America's scenic wilderness was J. Horace McFarland, president of the American Civic Association. Supporting one side or the other were such diverse interests as the Army Engineers,* utility companies, lumber, mining, and grazing groups, the General Federation of Women's Clubs, the Boone and Crocket Club, and hunting and fishing organizations. In this period, the Pinchot utilitarians won most of the battles. Their power so permeated the concerned government agencies that the national parks and monuments languished. Little more than inefficient, uncoordinated caretaking was done, and no overall policy was formulated for their administration.

Although a number of bills advocating a bureau of national parks (which would include national monuments) were submitted after 1900, none of them made significant headway in Congress. The reason was simple: the parks and monuments lacked a constituency. Without voting, outspoken, persuasive advocates, legislation aiding the parks was sure to remain in limbo. All of this changed when a wealthy Californian, Stephen Tynge Mather, came to Washington to work as a special aide to Secretary of the Interior Franklin K. Lane. Mather, a handsome outdoorsman with a flair for public relations, and his young fellow Californian, Horace M. Albright, set out to recruit a constituency for the national parks. They succeeded admirably, enticing wealthy men with political power into becoming active participants in the park movement. National parks began to be advertised; as protectors of an American heritage, they entered the American psyche and have remained there ever since. Mather's first great achievement was the passage of the bill creating the National Park Service in the Department of the Interior.

For nearly a generation, until, roughly, the coming of World War II, the National Park Service thrived and grew, operating with greater esprit, more imaginativeness and originality, more willingness on the part of its personnel to experiment, make spot decisions, and mold policies, than the usual government agency. It was a bureau whose employees knew most fellow career men on a first-name basis, in which the work was demanding and men strove to achieve for the good of the service. Mather's and Albright's ideals and dreams for the service, and for the nation, challenged all park personnel from maintenance men to superintendents.

Since it was not yet under civil service, Mather found incompetent political appointees running many parks. He discharged such men and replaced them with competent administrators. Sometimes he recruited them from business. An outstanding example was Edmund B. Rogers, who was superintendent of Yellowstone from 1936 to 1956. Rogers was an executive of the Denver Tramway Company but became interested in park matters and left his lucrative business practice to serve the National Park Service. Gradually, as the 1920s progressed, the quality of personnel improved. In 1925, the park rangers were brought under civil service and were joined in 1931 by park superintendents and monument custodians.

Mather and Albright used politics, persuasion, and pressure to rid the reservations of the Army, and especially the Army Engineers. (They had been in some parks since the 1880s, the Engineers with road-building duties and the Cavalry and Infantry policing the reservations.) Automobiles were allowed into parks where they previously had been prohibited. A chaotic concessions situation was brought under at least a modicum of control when Mather adopted a near-monopoly policy, often allowing just one concessionaire (or, in Park Service parlance, concession*er*) to run the visitor services of food, lodging, public transportation, and retail purchases at any given park or monument. Problems with the concessioners continued, however. Those entrepreneurs, geared to an upper middle-class clientele that arrived by railroad, were unprepared for the automobile tourist. Pressure had to be exerted upon the companies to get them to construct adequate facilities. To this day, the Park Service does not handle the concessions problem satisfactorily.

The administrators of the new Park Service also demonstrated their political acumen by successfully fighting off moves by outside interests threatening the inviolability of the reservations. Yellowstone, for example, was menaced immediately following World War I by Idaho interests, backed by veterans' organizations. They proposed segregating the ''Cascade Corner'' of the park—the southwestern corner—placing it outside of Yellowstone's boundaries, and contructing therein an irrigation dam and lake. As this raid was being checked, Montana interests in the Yellowstone Valley suggested damming up the Yellowstone Lake at the outlet for irrigation purposes. Again, the dedication and political sagacity of Park Service management warded off the raid, even though Montana's powerful Senator Thomas Walsh favored the plan.

Mather and Albright also worked toward instilling in the public mind a concept of the national parks as a national resource to be guarded constantly. They felt that the best insurance for park inviolability was a loyal, growing portion of the electorate, and that each visitation added a new supporter. A publicist, Robert Sterling Yard, added to the publicity drive. ''See America First'' became a catch-phrase embodying Park Service policy toward the public. The results were successful—and ultimately, perhaps, too much so. Even without publicity, the popularization of the automobile insured a rapidly rising visitation.

Still other problems loomed early in Park Service history, and many of them remain to this day. For example, most parks and monuments when acquired have embraced some private property. It has always been Park Service policy to acquire such parcels of real estate whenever possible. Often, however, it is valuable property, and the proprietors are both wealthy and stubborn. So the task continues.

Policy had to be established setting up criteria for the acquisition of new reservations. During the 1920s, the Park Service took an extremely narrow view of what consitutes acceptable Park terrain; in retrospect, this was a mistake. Some of the areas rejected in the 1920s would be considered acceptable by present criteria, but they are no longer available. The conflict over the Grand Tetons lasted for decades and left bruised feelings on both sides.

Beset with problems but with vigorous administrators to meet them, the Park Service rapidly became an entrenched government bureau. Its budget, personnel, and parks and monuments under its jurisdiction increased through the 1920s. Then came the Great Depression. Park concessioners lost money, and in the first years of the economic collapse visitation declined drastically. However, with the coming of the New Deal, the Park Service grew rapidly as its personnel were entrusted with administering the activities of the Civilian Conservation Corps* (CCC) in all work done in federal, state, and municipal parklands. Between 1933 and 1940, the Park Service received nearly $300 million from various New Deal agencies. At its peak employment, more than 7,000 people worked for the service. Four regional offices were established to better coordinate its activities; today there are nine. Arno Cammerer, one of the service's best directors, guided the bureau during these years (1933-1940).

It was also in the depression decade of the 1930s that the Park Service's mission was expanded. Whereas it was initially to oversee national parks and monuments, in a few years the bureau was entrusted with many more obligations, for the New Deal years witnessed a blossoming of official concern over preserving historic sites as well as scenic ones. Such legislation as the Historic Sites Act in 1935 and the Park, Parkway, and Recreation Study Act in 1936, mandated tasks to the Park Service that demanded highly educated, strongly motivated personnel carrying out field and office work, giving planning assistance to state and local units manifesting an interest in park development. Meanwhile, new acreages joined the park and monument galaxy. Perhaps most notable of these additions were the Blue Ridge Parkway (1936), the Cape Hatteras National Seashore (1937), and Lake Mead (1936), formed by Boulder Dam. Each of these marked a new type of reservation: a national parkway, a national seashore, and a national recreation area.

These were exciting times in the Park Service. Morale was high, and assignments were challenging. Director Cammerer provided inspired, hard-driving leadership. Many of those who joined the service at this time, often by way of an affiliation with the CCC, continued with the Park Service for many more years. Conrad Wirth, a future director, was one of those who came to the bureau by way of the CCC.

Then came World War II. Park Service personnel were drastically reduced, and visitation to parks and monuments again declined drastically. Service headquarters were moved to Chicago so that more war-oriented government operations could use its Washington office space. This transfer may or may not have been a portent of a loss of power and prestige in Washington. It is significant, however, that during this period many of the first wave of Park Service administrators, idealists and men of dedication, some of whom had entered during Mather years, reached retirement age. Decent, trained personnel moved to their positions, but they were people of a more typically bureaucratic orientation. Some of them were far more concerned with their own careers than with the good of the service: they were people with less dedication and a less realistic view of the Park Service's situation within political, bureaucratic Washington.

The service was unprepared for the incredible flood of visitors who flowed into the parks and monuments following the war. It is equally true that the service failed—and there were many reasons and some of the blame did not lie with the bureau—in gaining a successful hearing before Congress. Year after year, the service muddled through with less money and fewer personnel while problems intensified. Finally, Conrad Wirth, who became director in 1951, succeeded in launching a "catch-up" program. Known as Mission 66, his plan proposed a ten-year crash program culminating in 1966, the fiftieth anniversary of the Park Service. By that time the plan was to upgrade the National Park system to a point at which it could adequately meet the increasing demands upon the nation's parks and monuments. Director Wirth obtained President Dwight D. Eisenhower's backing; Congress supported the plan with necessary funds, and by 1966 great progress had been made.

Meanwhile, Congress burdened the National Park Service, in its capacity as protector of the nation's historic and natural heritage, with still more duties. Among many pieces of legislation were the Water Conservation Act and the Wilderness Act (1964), the Historic Preservation Act (1966), and the Wild and Scenic Rivers Act (1968). The legislation invariably imposed new obligations upon an already overburdened bureau. As the years went on, a pattern began to emerge resulting in constant growth of the service. A new form of pork-barrel legislation appeared. Besides the usual civic improvements, projects such as new post offices, dams, and highways, Congress now began creating new reservations—urban parks, parkways, seashores, lakeshores, historic houses, and so on—all of which it entrusted to the National Park Service.

Today the service is trying to bear up under the strain of these multitudinous obligations, for, indeed, the park ranger today wears many hats. The service administers thirty-six national parks plus historic parks, national monuments, military parks, memorial parks, battlefields, cemeteries, seashores, lakeshores, parkways, riverways, recreation areas, the capital parks and White House, and assorted reservations for a grand total of 26,281,496.4 acres in more than three hundred separate units. It employs nearly ten thousand men and women and operates on a budget in excess of $300 million. To cope better with its problems, the service has established a training center at Harper's Ferry and the Horace Albright Training Center at the Grand Canyon, and it maintains a Service Center in Denver.

Problems besetting the Park Service today are enormous. Reluctant as its people are to admit it, politics loom large in its destiny. The annual budget, assignments foisted upon it by Congress, the politics of land acquisition, activating new parks and monuments, fixing concessioner policy, defending park lands from raiders seeking the right to construct dams, cut timber, graze cattle and sheep, or mine, all place the service on the firing line of the big controversies of our time. The service has suffered from the instability of national politics since a presidential assassination in 1963, and this has been reflected in occasional lapses in fulfillment of its obligations.

Its personnel are generally dedicated and have a potential esprit de corps similar to the traditional high morale of the military. The personnel of both are often transferred from one assignment to another, both are stationed at some kind of a reservation, and most wear a uniform. Yet, in so large a bureau there are enervating quarrels over policy. Philosophically, the purists who strive for a continuing wilderness quarrel with the realists who know that the ideal can but rarely be maintained amidst a population of 226 million. Some programs are adequately administered, while others go virtually ignored. Some tasks, such as administering urban parks with wilderness-trained superintendents, have not yet been mastered. The concessioner problem still begs for a satisfactory solution. Continuing conflicts with other bureaus such as the Forest Service, the Bureau of Reclamation,* and the Army Engineers demand the constant diligence of Park Service officials.

From Stephen Mather's first year (1916) and a budget not to exceed $19,500, the National Park Service has grown into a massive, sometimes stultifying and incompetent, bureaucracy with many tasks. But the intelligence, dedication, and plain decency of most of its staff bear promise of better years ahead.

FOR ADDITIONAL INFORMATION: William C. Everhart, *The National Park Service* (1972); Samuel P. Hays, *Conservation and the Gospel of Efficiency* (1959; 1979); John Ise, *Our National Park Policy: A Critical History* (1961); Alfred Runte, *National Parks: The American Experience* (1979); Robert Shankland, *Steve Mather of the National Parks*, 3d ed. (1970); Donald Swain, *Wilderness Defender: Horace M. Albright and Conservation* (1970); and Conrad L. Wirth, *Parks, Politics, and the People* (1980).

RICHARD A. BARTLETT

NATIONAL RAILROAD PASSENGER CORPORATION (AMTRAK). Amtrak, the popular name for the National Railroad Passenger Corporation, took over the operation of most intercity railroad passenger services on May 1, 1971. It is a federally chartered and supported corporation.

After World War II, American railroads fully expected to continue to play a major role in long-distance passenger transportation. The new streamliners they had pioneered just before the war were popular. Highway travel was slow on two-lane roads that went through the center of every little town. Airlines could not move the masses in DC-3 aircraft, which had a payload seating capacity of twenty-one. In contrast, the railroads in wartime had given a dazzling demonstration of the train's ability to move thousands of people at high speeds through congested areas. When the war was over, railroads spent millions of dollars to reequip their long-distance trains with diesel locomotives and streamlined cars, some with domes on top so travelers could better view the scenery. In those days, the track was good, and these trains often went 80 miles per hour or more. And for a time, into the late 1950s, railroad stations and trains were crowded and bustled with excitement.

In the 1950s, however, rival modes of transportation were on the threshold of major technological breakthroughs. Jet aircraft were introduced commercially in the United States in 1959. These aircraft had a much greater payload capacity than their predecessor and could shuttle more people back and forth in less time with less labor than the train. They became the preferred mode of travel for the businessmen who had traditionally filled the railroads' sleeping cars night after night. Once business travel was gone, railroads were left with a huge passenger-carrying physical plant that was used fully only at holiday times and in inclement weather. The toll roads opened across the Northeast in the late 1950s, and coach travel on parallel railroads dropped precipitously. The New York Central Railroad, for example, claimed it dropped 40 percent within six months of the opening of the New York State Thruway. The passage of the Federal-Aid Highway Act in 1956 promised that government-sponsored "interstate" highways would eventually parallel every major passenger-train route.

Highways and airlines were receiving many direct and indirect subsidies from various levels of government, while the passenger train was still operating under the traditional rules of profit-and-loss. Special interests lobbied for the subsidies to the rival modes, many of them companies that supplied air and automotive equipment and stood to make a lot of money if the government underwrote the cost of basic facilities. General Motors, Firestone, and Standard Oil of California, for example, were convinced of a criminal conspiracy to replace metropolitan rail services with buses, and some thought this was only the most obvious case of what was going on throughout the country. Train travel remained popular in other parts of the world. Of those countries that had developed railroad systems, only in the United States did the system die. It has been suggested that it did not die but was murdered.

Other factors discouraged railroaders about the future of the passenger train in the late 1950s. Passenger trains were regulated by state authorities which, under the influence of local special interests, had required railroads to run many local services that were no longer used. Whatever profits the streamliners earned—and these were probably not great—were more than wiped out by the huge losses of these "plug" runs. Likewise, once the shopping and theater crowd deserted trains for automobiles, commuter rail services required a physical plant that was in use only on weekdays during the morning and evening rush hours, and, as such, lost money in amounts that private enterprise could not bear. Finally, by the late 1950s, the technology of railroad freight transportation was beginning to change in a way that made freight and passenger operations incompatible on the same track, a trend that would continue with increasing intensity into the Amtrak age. Diesel locomotives permitted the operation of long, long freight trains that could not easily get out of the way of short, fast passenger trains. In addition, heavier freight cars, weighing up to seventy-five tons apiece when loaded, ruined finely manicured high-speed passenger track. It cost a lot less to maintain track at 50-mile per hour freight-train standards than at 90-mile per hour passenger-train standards.

By the end of the 1950s, railroads had already begun to divide into pro- and anti-passenger camps. The "pros" were mostly the western roads and those serving the New York-Florida route, where demand for train travel remained strong and where railroads had a relatively small proportion of their total investment in passenger services. Even if trains lost money—so long as it was not Niagaras of money—they were thought to be worthwhile to show the company's flag and to keep its name before the public. But in the East, where passenger traffic was historically the heaviest, where railroads had invested in hundreds of cars, huge stations, and multiple-track high-speed rights-of-way, passenger losses were becoming a burden that could not be written off as advertising.

The Transportation Act of 1958 transferred jurisdiction over passenger-train discontinuances from state authorities to the Interstate Commerce Commission* (ICC) in the hope that, removed from local pressure, the money-losing locals could be abandoned once and for all. But almost immediately, the Lehigh Valley Railroad asked to discontinue all service, and the Milwaukee Road asked to discontinue a popular train between Chicago and Seattle, which indicated that the problems ran deeper than merely the local runs. Case-by-case, through the 1960s, the railroads came before the ICC to discontinue one famous train after another. Until about 1967, at least a skeleton service connected principal cities. Northern New England became the first whole region to lose all service after the Boston & Maine and Maine Central Railroads dropped most passenger services. After that, gaps began to open up elsewhere.

Three crises were overtaking the passenger services. The first was a long-term "inevitable" kind of crisis that everyone saw coming. The streamlined passenger cars that had been bought mostly between 1946 and 1954 were going to wear out eventually. Only a few cars had been bought by only a few railroads after 1954, and virtually none at all in the 1960s. Railroad leaders, even when they could justify a degree of loss from passenger-train operations, could not justify capital expenditures for new cars. By the late 1960s, many trains were already getting raggedy. Mechanical breakdowns were frequent, and the cost of maintenance uneconomic. Eventually, trains would have to be discontinued even on roads that were pro-passenger.

A second crisis was the realization that some railroads were simply not making enough money from freight operations to underwrite any passenger service at all. The crisis came in 1965 on the New Haven Railroad, which petitioned to discontinue all of its 273 daily interstate passenger trains. The railroad was bankrupt and its track in such a state of disrepair that even the safety of its high-speed trains between New York and Boston was in doubt. The *New Haven Discontinuance Case* made it clear that solutions were beyond the capability of private enterprise to solve and that Congress could no longer muddle through.

A third crisis struck like a thunderbolt in 1967 with the announcement by the Post Office Department* that it would no longer carry mail on passenger trains and would instead transfer most of it to airplanes or trucks. Mail had been a constant source of revenue to passenger trains and had often made their losses endurable. Some railroad leaders were bitter, feeling they had been encouraged to invest in mail-carrying facilities, even in recent years, and then had the business arbitrarily taken away. After the announcement by the Post Office Department, the Santa Fe Railroad, for example, which had consistently run one of the nation's finest passenger services, announced that it had no choice but to make drastic curtailments.

Early in 1970, with service already gone on many once-famous routes and shabby in the extreme on many others, the Penn Central Railroad, the now-bankrupt combination of the old New York Central, Pennsylvania, and New Haven Railroads and the largest carrier of long-distance passengers, petitioned to discontinue all passenger service west of Harrisburg and Buffalo. This would end all service on the symbolic New York-Chicago route. The *Penn Central Discontinuance Case* made it clear to Congress that if any rail passenger service were to be preserved, government was going to have to support it somehow.

The solution finally adopted created a federally chartered, for-profit corporation, the National Railroad Passenger Corporation, originally nicknamed "Railpax" and later "Amtrack." Railroads could join Amtrak by paying the equivalent of their 1969 passenger service losses in cash to the company and by contributing their passenger-train equipment. This was a kind of ransom for being freed of the obligation to run intercity passenger trains. Railroads that did not join would have to operate all the passenger trains they were then operating until at least 1975. Three railroads did not join: the Rock Island because it could not afford to, and the Southern and Denver & Rio Grande Western because they did not want to. Railroads that did join would be prohibited from operating intercity passenger trains, at least any in competition with Amtrak. Railroads that joined could receive Amtrak common stock or take a tax write-off. Only three railroads, the Milwaukee Road, the Burlington Northern, and the Penn Central, elected to take stock. Eight members of Amtrak's fifteen-person board of directors would be nominated by the President with the advice and consent of the Senate. Three would be named by the common stockholders (the railroads) and four by preferred stockholders (nonrailroad investors). The preferred stock was never sold, and the board was later restructured to put consumer representatives in place of preferred-stock representatives.

With a rather skinny congressional appropriation of $340 million in loans, loan guarantees, and subsidies, and with the money and equipment received from the railroads, Amtrak was to design and operate a national system of passenger service and to contract with the railroads to operate it over their tracks. Outside of the Boston-Washington corridor, this system would be only a skeleton of the once vast network. Indeed, only about half of the trains still operating would be continued under Amtrak. If states wanted additional service, Amtrak would operate it for them provided they would pay a portion of the cost. In Amtrak's first decade, New York, Michigan, Illinois, and California took extensive advantage of this provision. Amtrak was prohibited from operating any commuter service.

Amtrak inherited a mess from most of the railroads. Most of their passenger cars were in an advanced state of disintegration. Even those that were relatively intact were built to different specifications by different railroads and were not easy to integrate into a single fleet. Amtrak selected the best cars from those that the railroads offered it, but as long as they operated, into the late 1970s, they required constant maintenance, especially in their heating and air conditioning systems, and were plagued with breakdowns. As a result, operating costs were outrageous. Trains were late, and travelers who had been led to believe a new day in rail travel was going to dawn overnight felt let down. To make matters worse, trains operated over different railroads, each with their own traditions and procedures, with crews that were employed by, and owed their allegiance to, the railroads, not Amtrak. There were all kinds of complaints and frustrations in Amtrak's first years. Given the situation, some thought it was amazing the system functioned at all.

While some of the railroads over which Amtrak operated tried to cooperate as best they could, relations with some others were initially poor. There was ongoing debate over what constituted proper compensation for the use of the tracks, or what costs should be charged to passenger operations, a debate the railroads had never settled for themselves when they operated the trains. Penn Central, the largest operator of Amtrak trains, was especially persistent in demanding more money. Others thought Amtrak's cost-plus contracts gave the railroads no incentive to minimize costs and that Amtrak was being taken. No railroad, now that it was presumably out of the passenger business forever, had any incentive to maintain tracks to high-speed passenger standards. It was unlikely that passenger travel could ever be revived if trains were limited to 50 miles per hour. Some railroads treated Amtrak like a nuisance they would like to be rid of. It was believed that some railroads may have privately lobbied against Amtrak, or at least against any expansion of Amtrak operations on their lines. Two lines, the Missouri Pacific and the Southern Pacific, so harassed Amtrak operations that Amtrak was forced to take them to court.

Amtrak could not protect itself from politics either. Some of it was petty as, for example, when it joined with the Kellogg Company in a joint promotion of train travel and a popular sugared cereal, and was scored by consumer groups for promoting tooth decay among children. More serious was the fact that no administration through the 1970s gave it wholehearted support, and some tried to kill it. It was widely believed, for example, that the Nixon Administration saw Amtrak initially as no more than a graceful way of burying the passenger train once and for all, and supported its renewal in 1973, over the objections of its own Department of Transportation,* only because of the national panic about the future of automobiles following the Arab oil embargo. Congressmen wailed at Amtrak's deficits, but when it came to specific cuts, they fought to keep a train in their district. Indeed, just hours before Amtrak was to start, two powerful congressmen threatened to torpedo the whole plan unless trains were added through their districts in Montana and West Virginia. While Amtrak funding always passed, there was usually bickering up to the last minute, and the company lurched from one funding crisis to another, not knowing what trains it must operate, what staff it could afford to hire, and unable to undertake any long-range planning. The result was frustration and a feeling that this was no way to run a business.

Despite all these problems, ridership on Amtrak's trains increased steadily from 16.6 million passengers in calendar year 1972 to 21.2 million in fiscal year 1980. When Conrail* was created to take over the operation of six bankrupt Northeastern railroads in 1976, Amtrak charged with the operation of the Northeast Corridor, the route of the former Pennsylvania and New Haven Railroads between Washington and Boston. Amtrak was mandated to make this into a 120-mile per hour railroad, and arrangements were made to transfer ownership to Amtrak. In 1975, Amtrak was finally able to proceed with the purchase of a fleet of new passenger cars. Orders were placed for new coach, sleeper, and dining cars and new diesel and electric locomotives. Delivery on this equipment began in 1977 and was nearly complete by 1981. In addition, Amtrak was able to install a new computerized reservations system.

There was constant debate over whether Amtrak's continued subsidies were justified. Some argued that the train was economic only in medium-distance corridors of high-traffic density. Others thought the long-distance trains were also important to serve, for example, sightseers as an adjunct to the tourist industry (many of whom were foreign tourists who earned the country important foreign exchange) or residents of local towns who used the train between intermediate points. Many of these local stops had lost air service. Indeed, several airlines helped Amtrak set up its original reservations system, apparently in the hope that it might reduce their need to serve local points. Greyhound Corporation attacked Amtrak as unfair competition, seldom mentioning its own use of the public highways, though by the end of the 1970s, along with other bus lines, it had signed interline agreements with Amtrak to coordinate service and ticket sales. Unfortunately, not a great deal of progress had been made in the true integration of the different modes of travel.

Some insisted that the only regular users of Amtrak were "buffs" who rode trains for emotional reasons, not as a practical way to get to a destination. As such, they said, Amtrak constituted a rather handsome subsidy to a generally well-off segment of the population. Others noted a high proportion of young people on the trains, which signified that Amtrak had introduced rail travel to a generation that had never known it in its original heyday. As gasoline prices and air fares soared at the end of the 1970s, train travel became increasingly attractive to a broad constituency.

A principal justification for continued subsidy was the assertion that trains were fuel-efficient. There were different interpretations of statistics on this point, depending on what one was trying to prove. Basically, if a train carried a trainload of people—200 or more—it was efficient; if it carried only a busload, it was not. There was a widespread feeling that unless Amtrak could renegotiate some of its labor contracts, economical train service was doomed. The problem was low productivity, the result of having to pay crews according to an old railroad practice based on mileage, when 150 miles constituted a day's work, rather than by hours actually worked.

Toward the end of the decade, as inflation continued unabated and as the need for a balanced federal budget came to be seen in the popular mind as a panacea for its control, the Carter Administration and then the Reagan Administration proposed major curtailments of Amtrak service. The Carter Plan was, for the most part, beaten back by Congress in 1979, although several trains that were notorious losers, including one between New York and Kansas City, and one between Chicago and Miami, were dropped. But the Reagan Administration, which took office in January 1981, felt it had a mandate for major budget cuts and Amtrak was an obvious target. The proposed curtailments would render useless most of the new long-distance cars and the computer reservations system that was just going into service. Amtrak's tenth anniversary was celebrated amidst concern that service would be abolished just as it was getting to be good.

FOR ADDITIONAL INFORMATION: A collection of documents from the National Railroad Passenger Corporation and the Department of Transportation and Congress regarding Amtrak is available at the Interstate Commerce Commission Library in Washington. Also useful are articles in *Trains, Passenger Train Journal,* and the *Newsletter* of the National Association of Railroad Passengers.

RICHARD SAUNDERS

NATIONAL RECOVERY ADMINISTRATION (NRA). The National Recovery Administration was a federal agency created by the National Industrial Recovery Act (NIRA) of June 13, 1933, to promote industrial recovery from the Great Depression of the 1930s. The agency operated, amid much initial acclaim and hope for its success, as well as much subsequent criticism, until May 1935, when the Supreme Court declared it unconstitutional. The NRA, headed by a presidentially appointed administrator, was empowered to supervise the drafting, approval, and enforcement of rules, called codes, drawn up by the various industries. Two types of rules were envisioned: those defining labor standards and those limiting competition among the firms of the industry. The codes were exempt from antitrust laws and, therefore, could contain provisions fostering cartel-like arrangements. Section 7(a) of the law asserted the obligation of employers to recognize workers' rights to organize and engage in collective bargaining. Title II of the NIRA set up the Public Works Administration* with an appropriation of $3 billion to stimulate employment through federal construction projects. A two-year lifetime clause provided for the automatic expiration of the NRA's powers unless renewed.

The NIRA was the last of the major proposals Franklin D. Roosevelt made during the One Hundred Days, the dramatic period following his inaugural in March 1933, during which Congress quickly passed a series of measures designed to reverse the depression and promote economic reform. The NRA became the centerpiece of the New Deal recovery effort during 1933 and 1934, but it was not on Roosevelt's agenda at the outset of the Hundred Days. The recovery act was, rather, the result of demands made upon Roosevelt by several different and somewhat conflicting, influential political groups, motivated by self-interest or ideology. Seeking to be responsive, yet to avoid what he deemed the harmful implications of certain recovery proposals, Roosevelt fashioned a compromise proposal, which, he believed, might restore industrial prosperity.

Among the influences that formed the NIRA must be included the urgings of a group of Senate liberals led by Robert Wagner of New York, which pressed Roosevelt for massive public works spending; the popularity in Congress of the AFL-sponsored Thirty-Hour bill (known as the Black Bill, after Senator Hugo Black), which would mandate a sharply and inflexibly foreshortened work-week; the arguments of Secretary of Labor Frances Perkins, who was an enthusiastic champion of federal labor-standards legislation; the persistent, influential lobbying efforts of business organizations, such as the Chamber of Commerce of the United States and the National Association of Manufacturers, which insisted that liberalization of the antitrust laws was the answer to the recovery problem; and, finally, the allure of what might be termed the "start-up" conception of recovery, the notion that concentrated, concerted reemployment efforts among the nation's employers could restart the economy. This last-named conception had attained great currency and popularity over the preceding year. Partisans of the various "start-up" plans had seized every opportunity to present their ideas to Roosevelt, and he clearly had been intrigued but remained uncertain of their practicability.

Among these influences the business lobbyists were the best organized and most effective. They had been seeking antitrust relaxation for years. Now they made every effort to convince Roosevelt and his advisers that antitrust revision permitting limitation of competition could stem the downward spiral of the economy by preventing further erosion of prices, wages, and purchasing power.

Wishing to satisfy the proponents of all these conflicting demands and yet to avoid the excesses he felt the Black bill and the Wagner spending proposals contained, Roosevelt encouraged his advisers to draft a compromise recovery bill. During May, several such proposals emerged, with the supporters of the different recovery viewpoints endeavoring to control the outcome. Late in that month, these draft measures were put together in a compromise bill, which became the NIRA. The central feature of the measure, the codes, held out the prospect of improved labor standards, and the measure also offered concessions to the spenders, as Title II provided for moderate public works appropriations. However, the spokesmen for business clearly had won a favored position. The antitrust laws would be suspended, and the industries would have the initiative in drafting the codes.

The political figures in the administration and in Congress who were in a position to influence the development of NRA policy represented several schools of thought. Some of FDR's close advisers, such as Raymond Moley, sympathized with the business viewpoint, felt competition was outmoded, and hoped the NRA would become the basis of a new, cooperative, business-government relation in which business would be freed of antitrust restrictions. More orthodox advisers hoped that the main impact of the codes would be improvement of labor standards and the prevention of unfair competition. At the other extreme, some New Dealers, notably Rexford Tugwell, another member of the Brain Trust which had helped Roosevelt plan his campaign the previous year, hoped that the NRA would evolve into a mechanism for central planning of the economy with a major role for government direction.

Roosevelt himself seems to have regarded the NRA primarily as a recovery measure, as a "start-up" plan, thinking in terms of generating purchasing power through higher wages and additional employment through the provisions of the codes. Therefore, an administrator capable of swiftly creating the code system was needed. Roosevelt believed he had the right appointee in Hugh Johnson, a former Army general and more recently an aide to Bernard Baruch, who was one of the era's leading Wall Street speculators and an influential Democrat. The business community however, fearful that Section 7(a) would compel management to recognize unions and skeptical that the government actually would allow price-stabilizing arrangements in the codes, delayed for weeks the submission of proposals. Wishing to secure codes through voluntary cooperation rather than coercion, Johnson was at pains to reassure businessmen that Section 7(a) would not be interpreted to upset existing labor arrangements, including company unions, and that the codes could contain provisions influencing prices.

Johnson's pronouncements did speed up code submission by industry but, intent upon making a major impact upon the economy immediately, he easily persuaded Roosevelt to let him initiate a nationwide campaign to convince employers to raise wages and reemploy workers on a major scale, and at once. Imitating propaganda tactics used during World War I to manipulate public opinion, Johnson opened his campaign on August 1, 1933, to secure every employer's signature for the President's Reemployment Agreement (PRA). The symbol of compliance was the Blue Eagle certificate, which a cooperating employer could display and without which, presumably, in the aroused state of public feeling Johnson was stimulating, he would be without customers.

In a whirlwind of public pronouncements and appearances, amid predictions of imminent reemployment of millions of workers and an end to the depression, Johnson pressed the PRA campaign during August while negotiating with most of the major industries over the terms of their codes. By the early fall, it had become clear that the hopes of quick recovery through the PRA would not be fulfilled, and a somewhat disillusioned public now began to take stock of the edifice of codes Johnson had been building.

By late October, most of the codes had been drawn up. A review of their contents readily demonstrates that the business viewpoint dominated during the drafting. Nearly all the codes contained provisions designed to limit competition within the industry. Few codes mandated outright price agreements, but a very high proportion contained prohibitions against selling below cost, provisions that could be used, in practice, to restrict sales below a commonly agreed-upon "cost" of production. Another widely adapted price-stabilizing provision was the open-price arrangement which made it difficult for a seller to change, for competitive maneuvering, his publicly posted prices. Most codes carefully regulated the terms and conditions of making sales, thus making the enforcement of price-control provisions feasible. Finally, many codes provided for the regulation of the rate of production, sometimes by banning additions to new production machinery and plant. Policing was provided for by establishing a code authority to enforce each code.

Scarcely had codification of industry been substantially completed, however, than Johnson and his policies became immersed in controversy. The history of the NRA after the fall of 1933 consists mainly of a contest between Johnson and his business-oriented policies, on one hand, and critics, both within and outside the NRA, on the other.

Criticism emanated from several sources within the NRA, but especially from two divisions, the Consumers Advisory Board (CAB) and the Research and Planning Division. These divisions were not, like the other layers of the agency, staffed and directed by figures from the business world. The NRA's CAB, headed by the public-spirited and independent Mary Rumsey, began to assert itself volubly, attacking the codes from the consumerist viewpoint. The Research Division, staffed by economists who had believed from the outset that the codes should have been designed to raise the plane of competition, not to smother it, found a voice when Leon Henderson became the division's head in February 1934.

Outside the NRA, the most persistent criticism of Johnson's policies came from old-line Progressives who had opposed the NIRA when it passed Congress and now asserted that their objections had been vindicated. When Congress reconvened in January 1934, senators such as Gerald P. Nye of North Dakota and William E. Borah of Idaho opened an attack, which would end only with the demise of the NRA.

Criticism took several forms. The Senate Progressives were especially sensitive to charges by the smaller businessmen in certain industries that codes favored the larger firms and thus were fostering monopoly. The NRA's CAB and Research Division concentrated upon exposing the implications, for consumers and for economic recovery, of the price raising and stabilizing practices the codes had enshrined.

Johnson attempted to blunt criticism by staging public hearings during January and February 1934 at which critics could ventilate their ideas. But the strategy backfired as the press and public opinion, disappointed by the failure of Johnson's promises of the previous summer, listened carefully to the flood of acrimonious debate. Seeking to forestall a congressional investigation, Johnson agreed with Roosevelt's plan for an independent National Recovery Review Board (NRRB). The appointment of the widely respected Clarence Darrow, the famous criminal lawyer, to head the NRRB proved a serious mistake. The Darrow Board report, issued in several installments, was a damning indictment. The result more of Darrow's ideological presuppositions than of provable argumentation, the Darrow report was widely reported. Its conclusion that the codes were injuring small business and gouging consumers was played up extensively by the Hearst newspapers, among others.

Under siege, Johnson, through the first six months of 1934, desperately sought to recapture public confidence. In early March at a meeting of code authority representatives, Johnson pleaded for an agreement by businessmen to increase wages and reduce the working hours of employees, but this effort to rehash the policies of the previous summer was coldly received by the businessmen, who were preoccupied with maintaining the code price provisions. In May, Johnson tried to reestablish the NRA's credibility by reorganizing the Policy Board, the unit responsible for setting basic policies, and appointing as its head a respected economist, Leverett S. Lyon of the Brookings Institution. The new Policy Board, now freed of business domination, formulated a new departure in Office Memorandum 228, declaring code revision to eliminate noncompetitive price policies as an immediate goal. Johnson balked and, in response to pressures from businessmen, declared the memo was intended only for codes still to be drafted.

Despite the growing dissatisfaction with the codes, Johnson was unwilling to push through reforms abolishing cartel practices for two reasons. First, he sympathized with the business viewpoint. Second, he believed that the labor benefits in the codes would not survive if businessmen were deprived of their price and profit benefits. Even though improvement in wage and hour benefits under NRA had been very modest, at best, they could be and were convincingly portrayed by Roosevelt and his associates as positive accomplishments of the New Deal. The President, therefore, felt caught in a dilemma and, despite Johnson's inability to devise a code-revision strategy to quell criticism, was reluctant to demand his resignation. In August, however, Johnson was forced out and replaced by a five-man board. This directorate for NRA was split between competition-restoring ideas and the businessmen's viewpoint, and failed to solve the policy deadlock. Very little significant revision of the codes ensued during the remaining months of the agency's life.

As the expiration date for the NIRA approached, rival plans for renewal were debated. The administration hoped to secure a revised law continuing the wage- and hour-elements of codes, but curbing somewhat their anticompetitive elements. In a decision read by Chief Justice Charles Evans Hughes on May 27, 1935, ending the case of *Schechter Poultry Co.* v. *U.S.*, however, the Supreme Court found the law unconstitutional, chiefly upon the ground that the code-making process was an improper delegation of legislative authority to the executive branch. The codes forthwith became unenforceable, and the NRA was soon reduced to a skeleton review force. By this time, the agency had lost public support even among many of the business groups, such as the Chamber of Commerce, which had lobbied so hard to create it. Although many businessmen continued to want to escape the antitrust laws, they now felt that the NRA approach to that objective was too risky, involving, as it did, an ever-present threat of governmental interference with code arrangements and even with labor relations.

The judgment of most economists, in the 1930s and since, has been that NRA policies did not promote and probably actually retarded recovery. The real wages of workers in codified industries improved only very modestly, although, it should be added, in certain industries, long-standing abuses such as child labor were eliminated. Moreover, the price-raising effect of the codes would have exerted a negative pressure upon consumption and production.

Moreover, despite the Schechter decision, many industries used their codes as the basis for continuing cartel arrangements in the absence, until 1937 at least, of any substantial administration effort to enforce the antitrust laws. If benefits to labor were modest under the code provisions, aid given to unionization by Section 7(a) was equally disappointing to union leaders. Initially, 7(a) did boost the enthusiasm of labor organizers and workers, and it did create an atmosphere in which employers were more amenable to recognizing and bargaining with independent unions. However, the great majority of employers endeavored to sanitize their industry against 7(a) or to contain its influence by forming company unions. Johnson was always averse to disturbing the existing balance of labor relations. During 1933, the NRA agency, the National Labor Board (NLB), which was responsible for enforcing 7(a), did seriously attempt to persuade employers to honor the law. But when the NLB's policies seemed to be stimulating disturbances in the auto industry, the President himself stepped in and determined that unions were not entitled to the status of sole bargaining agent. Companies could insist upon the rule of plural representation, a rule that undercuts a union's strength when the employer recognizes it as a bargaining agent. Roosevelt's decision, together with the fact that the NLB's enforcement powers were weak, determined that unionism received little effective help from the government during 1934 and early 1935.

On the whole, Roosevelt intended the NRA as a mechanism for achieving recovery and improving labor conditions through a partnership with business, without disturbing the economic structure or the relative strength of business and organized labor. He probably viewed the cartelistic codes more as a necessary evil than as the initiation of a new epoch for business-government relations in which the government role would be to underwrite business planning of production and prices in replacement of marketplace guidance of the economy.

FOR ADDITIONAL INFORMATION: The roots of the NRA are traced in Robert F. Himmelberg's *The Origins of the National Recovery Administration: Business, Government, and the Trade Association Issue, 1921-1933* (1976). Chapters 1 through 6 of Ellis Hawley's *The New Deal and the Problem of Monopoly* (1966) make up the standard modern account of NRA policies. Bernard Bellush's *The Failure of the NRA* (1975) covers the same ground but also gives detailed attention to the NRA's labor policies. The agency's voluminous records are held by the National Archives* as Record Group

9. They are described in *Preliminary Inventories, Records of the National Recovery Administration*, No. 44, National Archives (1952).

ROBERT F. HIMMELBERG

NATIONAL SCIENCE FOUNDATION (NSF). The National Science Foundation, an independent federal agency, was established by act of Congress in 1950 after a long debate. Five years before, Vannevar Bush, director of the wartime Office of Scientific Research and Development,* had recommended the creation of an agency to develop a national policy for science and to support basic scientific research and education. A reply to President Franklin D. Roosevelt's request to suggest a means of applying wartime lessons to peacetime uses, Bush's report, *Science—The Endless Frontier*, was also a conservative response to a proposal by Senator Harley M. Kilgore of West Virginia for a National Science Foundation of similar purposes but more responsible to political authority.

The five-year debate over federal support of research and education revolved around several issues: ownership of patents; geographic and institutional distribution of funds; eligibility of the social sciences; basic research versus applied; and, especially, control of the agency. The 1950 act compromised or sidestepped most of these issues. Thus, NSF was to avoid "undue concentration" of its funds, and while the social sciences were not mentioned, the act's term *other sciences* allowed their inclusion in NSF's program along with mathematical, physical, biological, medical, and engineering sciences.

The most important compromise concerned control and direction of the NSF. Economic and political conservatives, backers of the Bush proposal, feared political domination of research and wanted to vest control in an independent board which would appoint a director responsible to it. In 1947, President Harry S Truman vetoed a bill providing such an arrangement. The act he later signed created an unusual federal organization—a policymaking National Science Board of twenty-four members and a full-time foundation director, all to be appointed by the President and confirmed by the Senate. Although the director was subject to removal by the President, his six-year statutory term, like that of board members, showed a desire to insulate the agency from politics.

The first director, Alan T. Waterman (1951-1963), took care not only to keep NSF out of politics, but also to avoid the enmity of other federal science agencies. Resisting the Bureau of the Budget's* efforts to enlist NSF's help in evaluating federal science programs, Waterman and the board defined the foundation's policy role as one of compiling and publishing reliable information on scientific research and manpower, advocating greater support for basic research, and improving government-university relations. Under his guidance, NSF guarded the freedom of academic scientists and the integrity of their institutions against government interference. The foundation's stand in the mid-1950s against the denial of support for unclassified research, on the basis of unsubstantiated charges of an individual's disloyalty, challenged and helped bring to an end a practice that might have spread throughout a security-conscious federal establishment.

Until 1968, NSF's charter restricted its support to basic research—research "performed without thought of practical ends," in the words of the Bush report. Nearly all of the early research grants were for "little science" projects, awarded to colleges, universities, and other nonprofit institutions for research by individual investigators, often with the help of junior colleagues and graduate students. NSF research programs—generally organized by discipline (chemistry, physics, and so on) in the mathematical, physical, and engineering sciences, and by function (regulatory, systematic, and so forth) in the biological and medical sciences—judged the quality of unsolicited proposals and the ability of the investigators with the aid of mail reviewers and assembled panels. Competition for NSF's limited funds was keen as the peer review system sifted out the most meritorious proposals.

Emphasis on quality similarly characterized NSF's first educational program—fellowships for graduate students and postdoctoral scientists. Free to choose where they wished to study, NSF graduate fellows tended to concentrate in a rather small number of graduate schools, causing criticism from "have-not" universities. Later programs of "cooperative" fellowships and traineeships offset most of the criticism and increased the supply of scientists and engineers by spreading NSF support of graduate education among a much larger number of institutions during the 1960s. Although NSF was authorized to award undergraduate scholarships as well as graduate fellowships, it chose not to, reasoning that scholarships should not be restricted to science and engineering. The foundation has, however, operated a variety of other programs to improve science and engineering instruction in undergraduate colleges.

Beginning in the mid-1950s, Congress, by making substantial appropriations for teachers' institutes, required the NSF to emphasize science education in high schools. Institutes, programs, and other kinds of support for precollege science education, elementary as well as secondary, grew greatly as a result of public anxiety following the launching of Sputnik by the USSR in October 1957. The foundation had already begun to sponsor the development of new curricula in physics, biology, chemistry, and mathematics, and these up-to-date courses were widely adopted. While they provided a sound base for advanced training for scientific careers, some of the new courses came under attack in the 1970s as too difficult for most students. Not for its rigor but because it seemed threatening to conservatives' values, an elementary social science course—*Man: A Course of Study* (MACOS)—met especially harsh criticism.

NSF support for the social sciences had to overcome strong opposition, much of it from the board and staff. By the end of its first decade, NSF had gradually extended coverage to most social science disciplines for projects that were characterized by "objectivity, verifiability, and generality." Amendments of the foundation's charter in 1968 at length included the social sciences among those the agency was directed to support.

Besides making many thousands of grants for individual projects in college and university laboratories, NSF has since the late 1950s increasingly sponsored "big science" enterprises. National centers for radio and optical astronomy and for atmospheric research require facilities and instruments so costly that only the federal government can build and equip them and pay for their continuing operation. Since NSF's charter prohibits the agency from directly operating research laboratories, the national centers are normally managed under contract by associations of universities having special competence in the centers' fields of science, but the facilities are open to all qualified investigators.

NSF sponsorship of other large-scale activities, some international in scope, also began in the 1950s and grew greatly in the next two decades. The foundation managed to ease Cold War restrictions on exchanges of scientists and scientific information, to place science attachés in several American embassies, and to develop cooperative bilateral programs with a number of countries. The designation of NSF as the funding agent and government coordinator of U.S. participation in the International Geophysical Year (IGY) of 1957-1958—a highly successful scientific undertaking in which sixty-seven nations joined—gave the agency a strong push into international cooperation and into such other large ventures as global atmospheric and oceanographic research and worldwide ecological studies. NSF's main interests during the IGY focused on Antarctica, and by the close of the year arrangements had been made for a continuing research program there. In 1959, the United States and the eleven other nations engaged in IGY Antarctic operations signed a treaty reserving the continent for peaceful and scientific purposes.

The large projects were made possible by substantial growth in the foundation's budget. The first big boost in appropriations—to $40 million—was for fiscal year 1957. Congress held to the same figure the following year, but then Sputnik sparked a series of increases—to $134 million in fiscal 1959 and to nearly $500 million by fiscal 1968. A sharp drop the next year in part reflected congressional dissatisfaction with the escalating costs of the Mohole project—an ambitious attempt to gain knowledge of the earth by drilling through its mantle from an ocean platform. (Congress ended the Mohole effort, but a continuing program of deep-sea drilling has been notably successful in yielding knowledge of such geologic phenomena as plate tectonics, including what is popularly called continental drift.) NSF's appropriations passed the half-billion mark in fiscal 1971 and generally continued to rise thereafter, although inflation largely offset the increases. By 1980, NSF's budget reached the billion-dollar level and about 90 percent of its money supported research and related activities; only about 8 percent supported science education, although two decades before over 40 percent had gone for educational programs.

Despite the growth of national and international research programs, NSF's chief concern continued to be academic science. In addition to its support of individual project research, during the 1960s the foundation operated several broader programs of institutional grants. Matching facility grants helped universities build or renovate graduate research laboratories. Formula grants—computed from the amount of an institution's federal research support—gave the officials of nearly a thousand colleges and universities a flexible means of balancing and strengthening their science programs. University science development awards, intended to double the number of centers of excellence in graduate research and instruction, provided grants of several million dollars each to thirty-one institutions, and departmental development awards went to many more. College science improvement grants helped raise the quality of science instruction in undergraduate institutions. These institutional programs—some of which inspired other agencies to establish counterparts—were designed not only to strengthen science in colleges and universities in all parts of the country, but also to bolster institutional autonomy by shifting decision-making from the capital to the campus. Institutional programs met disfavor with the Nixon Administration, however, and notwithstanding congressional support for their continuance, they were generally eliminated in the early 1970s.

By that time, NSF was moving in a new and somewhat controversial direction, largely owing to amendments of its charter in 1968. The amendments instituted several important changes in the agency's management and operations: the foundation's annual appropriation must first receive congressional authorization; five new presidential appointees—a deputy director and four assistant directors—were added to the staff; the board was required to submit an Annual Report on science policy issues; and—stimulating the new direction—NSF was permitted to sponsor applied research.

Coinciding with rising popular interest in environmental protection and socially relevant public programs, NSF's entry into applied research revived arguments about the purpose of the agency, arguments that were reminiscent of the debate preceding the 1950 act. During his directorship, Waterman had warned repeatedly that "applied research drives out basic." His successor, Leland J. Haworth (1963-1969), believing that social benefits would be gained by occasional linkage, worked closely with Congress for the amendment permitting basic researchers to pursue ideas promising practical utility into the applied area. The third director, William D. McElroy (1969-1972), welcomed the permission to back applied projects as a way to increase the NSF budget for the support of good science, whether pure or applied. Like them, their successors—H. Guyford Stever (1972-1976), Richard C. Atkinson (1977-1980), and John B. Slaughter (1980-   )—have all proclaimed support of basic research as NSF's dominant mission. Applied research has won an important lesser role in the foundation's program, but the meshing of applied and basic research—deciding which applied fields NSF should enter and fitting applied science into the agency's structure—has not been easy.

The foundation has always considered improvement of the means of disseminating scientific information to be one of its main duties. The National Defense Education Act of 1958 extended this function by directing NSF to establish a Science Information Service and an advisory Science Information Council, though the council was terminated by legislation in 1975. Long concerned with such problems as the development of systems of documentation research, information storage and retrieval, and mechanical translation, NSF in recent years has especially emphasized basic and applied research aimed at increasing understanding of the properties and structure of information and the designing of information systems.

Besides supporting the advancement of information science, NSF has from its inception been an important producer of information about funds and personnel for science and technology in government, industry, and universities and other nonprofit institutions. The foundation's series of publications on scientific and technical resources—generally the most comprehensive and reliable available for such data—are widely used by students of governmental, economic, and academic change and by policy planners.

Although NSF has avoided the dangers of attempting to evaluate and coordinate federal science activities, its periodic data on research and development and its policy analysts have furnished essential tools for others who attempt to formulate science policy. The foundation was relieved of some of its unwanted policy responsibilities by the appointment of the first presidential science adviser in 1957 and by the establishment of the Office of Science and Technology in 1962, but the NSF director again had policy duties thrust upon him when President Richard M. Nixon liquidated the White House science advisory apparatus in 1973. The science adviser's office was restored by legislation three years later but not his former advisory committee. The new Office of Science and Technology Policy has called on NSF for help in preparing required reports and on other matters. The course of presidential science advice and NSF's possible supporting role under the Reagan Administration are not clear.

NSF faced some uncertainties as the Reagan Administration began. The Reagan budget for fiscal year 1982 would eliminate the agency's science education programs and "sheltered" programs for women and minorities, greatly reduce support for social science research, and drop new initiatives proposed by President Jimmy Carter, such as renovation and new instrumentation for graduate science laboratories. Besides likely programmatic changes resulting from the Reagan budget, an impending internal reorganization promised to give enhanced status for engineering research and to spread responsibility for support of applied research among programs that were formerly exclusively basic.

Over three decades, NSF's administrative practices have lost much of their original simplicity owing to demands for tighter controls on the use of federal funds. Even so, the foundation is widely regarded as less bureaucratic than its sister agencies and as especially concerned for the health of the universities. It continues to uphold standards of quality in the face of egalitarian pressures and to defend the value of fundamental research, which is often attacked as wasteful of taxpayers' money. During its thirty-two-year history, the foundation has established a solid position as the only general-purpose federal science agency and the government's flagship for basic research.

FOR ADDITIONAL INFORMATION: The fullest published information on the foundation's activities may be found in the agency's Annual Reports, issued every year since fiscal 1952. Since fiscal year 1964, the Annual Reports have appeared in two volumes, the first volume narrative and descriptive, and the second listing all grants and contracts made during the year.

Two general books on NSF are Milton Lomask, *A Minor Miracle: An Informal History of the National Science Foundation* (1976), a readable popular history; and Dorothy Schaffter, *The National Science Foundation* (1969), a volume in the Praeger Library of U.S. Government Departments and Agencies.

Articles describing and appraising NSF's work generally include Lee Anna Embrey, "The Lengthened Shadow: The National Science Foundation," *The Graduate Journal* 5, No. 2 (Winter 1963): 301-318; Alan T. Waterman, "National Science Foundation: A Ten-Year Résumé," *Science* 131 (May 6, 1960): 1341-1354; and Dael Wolfle, "National Science Foundation: The First Six Years," *Science* 126 (August 23, 1957): 335-343.

Articles dealing with the origins of NSF are J. Merton England, "Dr. Bush Writes a Report: 'Science—The Endless Frontier,' " *Science* 191 (January 9, 1976): 41-47; Daniel J. Kevles, "Scientists, the Military, and the Control of Postwar Defense Research: The Case of the Research Board for National Security, 1944-46," *Technology and Culture* 16, No. 1 (January 1975): 20-47; Kevles, "The National Science Foundation and the Debate over Postwar Research Policy, 1942-1945," *Isis* 68 (March 1977): 5-26; and Robert F. Maddox, "The Politics of World War II Science: Senator Harley M. Kilgore and the Legislative Origins of the National Science Foundation," *West Virginia History* 41, No. 1 (Fall 1979): 20-39. Vannevar Bush's *Science—The Endless Frontier* (1945) has been twice reprinted by NSF: in 1960 with an introduction by Alan T. Waterman, and in 1980 with an introduction by Richard C. Atkinson.

Writings on particular NSF programs are too voluminous to list, but one book at least deserves mention: Hillier Krieghbaum and Hugh Rawson, *An Investment in Knowledge* (1969), a detailed account of the foundation's summer institutes programs for high school teachers, 1954-1965.

The writer of this short essay has written a history of NSF covering the years 1945-1957, but it is still unpublished.

J. MERTON ENGLAND

NATIONAL SECURITY COUNCIL (NSC).

The National Security Council is unique among U.S. governmental agencies. Aside from the President's Cabinet, it is the highest level, executive branch advisory and coordinating body on national security affairs. Unlike the Cabinet, it is based upon statutory authority. It is a principal instrument in both the formulation and implementation of foreign policy. Nonetheless, it has no power other than to advise the President. Indeed, apart from the President, it does not exist. It is the President in Council.

The NSC had its origins in the experience of World War II. President Franklin D. Roosevelt had largely administered the war through the Joint Chiefs of Staff (JCS), which was an ad hoc and de facto body, without statutory basis; through personal advisers such as James F. Byrnes and Harry Hopkins; and in collaboration with Winston Churchill. Congress was concerned that the ad hoc advisory system of the Roosevelt era should, with President Harry S Truman, be replaced by more formal structures. Thus, for example, in 1946, the Council of Economic Advisers* was created by statute.

As early as 1944, both War Department* Secretary Henry L. Stimson and Navy Secretary James L. Forrestal had perceived the need for a high-level, national security policy-planning body, which should extend beyond the armed services. Largely through Stimson's efforts that year, the State-War-Navy Coordinating Committee (SWNCC) had been formed. Stimson, who had served from 1929 to 1933 as President Herbert Hoover's Secretary of State, appreciated, as did few other Americans in the early 1940s, the vital relationship between diplomatic, military, and political affairs.

The wartime experience had also shown the need for unification of the armed forces. However, the Navy Department* resisted congressional, presidential, and War Department initiatives. In 1945, Forrestal turned to his friend, Ferdinand Eberstadt, to counter these proposals. In what came to be called "Forrestal's revenge," Eberstadt proposed the creation of the National Security Council; he also proposed a Central Intelligence Agency* (CIA) under the NSC.

In the ensuing two years, the NSC was the least contentious portion of the proposed national security legislation. Only President Truman, who viewed with suspicion any possible limitation on presidential prerogatives, viewed the NSC proposal with some reserve. Reluctantly, the Navy came to accept an independent Department of the Air Force,* while successfully resisting the military departments giving up autonomy to a National Military Establishment (Department of Defense*). In November 1946, the Republicans had gained control of the Congress. As enacted by the Eightieth Congress and signed into law on July 26, 1947, the National Security Act included the creation of the NSC, to advise the President with respect to the integration of domestic, foreign, and military policies, relating to the national security. Although "domestic" policies were recognized as vital to national security, the only executive department heads designated as members were State, Defense, Army, Navy, and Air Force. The President could, however, "from time to time" name other executive department heads to sit on the NSC.

While the National Security Act did create the CIA, the Director of Central Intelligence* (DCI) was not designated as an NSC member. The CIA, which was an outgrowth of the wartime Office of Strategic Services and of the National Intelligence Authority that had succeeded it at the war's end, was designated to serve in an advisory capacity to the NSC.

Since the NSC is an advisory body, its organization and use have undergone change, according to the concepts of each President. Although President Truman attended the first session, he viewed the NSC with continuing reserve. He believed that only the President made policy, and he looked at any creation of the Eightieth Congress with special suspicion, as seeking to circumvent his authority. Reflecting his opinion, he named the Secretary of State to chair subsequent NSC sessions. Saint Louis insurance executive, Rear Admiral Sidney W. Souers, ably served as the first executive secretary of the NSC, 1947-1950, followed by James S. Lay, Jr., from 1950 to 1953.

The first review of NSC operations came in January 1949 from the Hoover Commission* (Commission on Organization of the Executive Branch of Government). The commission found the NSC lacking in developing comprehensive national strategy plans. It recommended strengthening the position of the Secretary of Defense and reducing the roles of the Army, Navy, and Air Force service secretaries. Its recommendations were reflected in the August 1949 amendment, which dropped these service secretaries from membership on the NSC, making the Secretary of Defense the principal spokesman of the armed services and recognizing the JCS as the principal military advisers to the President. The 1949 amendment added the Vice-President to membership on the NSC.

With the outbreak of the Korean War in 1950, Truman began presiding on a regular basis. He did so in sixty-two of the seventy-one meetings between June 1950 and January 1953. Furthermore, with the advent of the Korean War, the JCS began attending NSC meetings. Nonetheless, the NSC under Truman remained of subordinate use. The doctrine of limited war, which he espoused, was largely that of his Secretary of State, Dean Acheson. Moreover, the most important strategic planning document, NSC 68, which was produced on the eve of the Korean War, was not the work of the NSC or its senior staff but rather that of a joint State-Defense study group. At no time under Truman was the NSC a decisive policy instrument.

It remained for President Dwight D. Eisenhower to bring to fulfillment the promise of the NSC as the principal instrument in both the formulation and implementation of national security policy. He institutionalized the NSC and gave it clear lines of responsibility and authority. He created the position of special assistant for National Security Affairs, replacing the executive secretary, and he related the succeeding incumbents in that position, Robert Cutler and Gordon Gray, to his staff secretary, General Andrew Goodpaster. The special assistant coordinated the NSC studies, and the staff secretary, its implementation. Moreover, Eisenhower greatly expanded the staff to its largest number of permanent positions (seventy-six) in the entire history of the NSC. Emphasizing the vital importance of the council, he convened its sessions weekly throughout the eight years of his presidency and, except during his illness, personally presided. On a regular basis he included in the meetings not only the statutory members plus the Secretary of the Treasury, the chairman of the JCS, and the DCI, but also many second and third-level members of the executive departments. He established two major NSC adjuncts: the Planning Board and the Operations Coordinating Board. Moreover, he established the Board of Consultants on Foreign Intelligence Activities, later redesignated as the President's Foreign Intelligence Advisory Board (PFIAB).

Although critics of the Eisenhower NSC admit there was a high volume of work, they level charges of mediocrity, lack of innovation and of achieving consensus at the cost of imprecision and vague generalities. Such charges have scant basis. Indeed, one of the 1960 critics, then Associate Professor Henry Kissinger, testified twenty years later as to the error of his charges and the precision and vigor of Eisenhower's leadership. A part of the quality of Eisenhower's leadership was that everyone, including the Secretary of State and the special assistant for National Security Affairs, clearly understood who was in charge.

Meeting with President-elect John F. Kennedy, Eisenhower emphasized the special importance of the NSC. However, the young President, presumably on the advice of Professor Richard E. Neustadt, proceeded to dismantle the NSC apparatus. As a result, there was scant long-range planning. Emphasis was on current operations and crisis management, with ad hoc groups. For example, Kennedy utilized what he termed the Executive Committee (ExCom) in the October 1962 Cuban Missile Crisis.

The Kennedy downgrading and deinstitutionalizing of the NSC was accompanied by the politicizing of the position of the special assistant for National Security Affairs. It would never have occurred to Eisenhower's aides to make public pronouncements. However, beginning with McGeorge Bundy (1961-1966); Walt Rostow (1966-1969); and Henry Kissinger (1969-1975), incumbents were increasingly public advocates of particular policies and came to dominate the Secretary of State as administration spokesmen. Rostow's title was simply special assistant to the President.

President Lyndon B. Johnson essentially continued Kennedy's ad hoc system, but, by contrast, he relied heavily on his Secretaries of State and Defense, Dean Rusk and Robert McNamara, respectively. Policy leadership was left to the State Department, and there was little or no long-range planning as the nation drifted in the quagmire of the protracted Vietnam conflict. Thus, by 1969, the NSC was practically nonexistent as a policy instrument.

President-elect Richard Nixon and Henry Kissinger, his designated assistant to the President for National Security Affairs, went to the dying President Eisenhower for counsel on national security organization. The result was a revitalizing of the NSC, much in the Eisenhower image. This complemented Nixon's own views to transform the Kennedy-Johnson focus on current operations and crisis management to longer range planning, for which the NSC had been designed. Nixon and Kissinger, however, unlike Eisenhower, declined to involve the large numbers of subordinates in decision-making options, and limited NSC sessions to the statutory membership plus the chairman of the JCS and, for intelligence matters, the DCI.

Nixon had elevated Kissinger's title first to assistant to the President for National Security Affairs and subsequently to assistant to the President. The Kissinger dominance of the NSC, chairing the key committees, however, led to one-man rule and by September 1973 to Secretary of State William Rogers's resignation and Kissinger being named as his successor. This was followed for the balance of the Nixon Administration by the unprecedented instance of the

Secretary of State also serving at the White House as the President's security assistant.

President Gerald Ford ended Kissinger's wearing of two hats by naming Kissinger's assistant at the White House, Lieutenant General Brent Scowcroft, as the assistant to the President for National Security Affairs (1975-1977). Scowcroft's professional training and concept of the position as low-key stood in contrast to the political activist roles of all of his predecessors, from Bundy through Kissinger. But, one might inquire, how else could one occupy the position with the irrepressible Kissinger shuttling back and forth between the Oval Office and Foggy Bottom? To Ford's and Scowcroft's credit, Scowcroft proved to be his own man and earned an independent position of respect. No longer did one person chair a multitude of committees. President Ford reaffirmed the NSC's overall control of policy as related to foreign intelligence and created the Intelligence Oversight Board with three civilians as members to review the legality and propriety of the intelligence community's operations.

President Jimmy Carter vowed to restore a sense of collegiality among the executive departments and to reduce the NSC's presumed dominance over State and Defense. He did reduce from six to two the NSC committees (Special Coordinating Committee (SCC) and Policy Review Committee (PRC), but this change was largely cosmetic. Actually, he ultimately elevated rather than downgraded the assistant for National Security Affairs, making Dr. Zbigniew Brzezinski (1977-1981) the first incumbent with Cabinet rank. Brzezinski presided in the White House Situation Room over the SCC, including the Vice-President, the chairman of the JCS, and the DCI, in such sensitive areas as intelligence, arms control, and crisis management. The relationship between Brzezinski and Secretary of State Cyrus Vance became reminiscent of that between Kissinger and Rogers. In both instances, the Secretary of State eventually resigned. President Carter discontinued the President's Foreign Intelligence Advisory Board.

The Ronald Reagan Administration has committed itself to a fundamental restructuring of the National Security Council and its staff. According to the Eisenhower concept, in which President Reagan concurs, the NSC should serve not as the decision-making, but rather as the decision-facilitating, instrument of Cabinet government. By the Eisenhower and Reagan conceptions, the NSC staff serves as the secretariat of the NSC, coordinating policy formulation among the agencies represented in the NSC and ensuring that decisions taken by the President are effectively implemented. The goal is to provide the President with the means to make the most vital decisions as related to national security, including defense programs, budget, force structures, and resource allocations—in brief, to create and implement national strategy. Furthermore, to strengthen the NSC's institutional aspects, Reagan restored the President's Foreign Intelligence Advisory Board.

This return to an institutional role, as compared to a policy-advocacy, political role is, of course, easier said than done. A necessary part of this effort has been the subordination of the position of the assistant to the President for National

Security Affairs. Cabinet rank has been eliminated. President Reagan has placed management responsibility for the NSC staff in the counselor to the President (with Cabinet rank). The counselor, Edwin Meese III, and the initial assistant, Richard V. Allen, perceived of the NSC staff much as Cutler, Gray, and Goodpaster did in the Eisenhower years: as a catalyst of interagency activity, initiating or accelerating interagency coordination of national security issues, but not as an independent policy agency and not as the instrument for exercising direct White House control of the interagency process.

Even with these assurances, however, in the first months of the Reagan Administration the Secretary of State, Alexander Haig, went to great lengths to assert his own dominant position, not only at State but also in the White House Situation Room. For clarification, a directive from President Reagan has placed the Vice-President in charge of crisis management. In retrospect, it may be observed that a part of Secretary Haig's dilemma was his recollection of his former service with assistant to the President Kissinger, who, from the White House vantage point, dominated the senior executive department. According to Brzezinski, the control wielded by McGeorge Bundy, or Henry Kissinger, or himself was not due to any special personal talents, but was largely derivative of the Presidents' (Kennedy, Nixon, and Carter) involvement.

The Congress has found little comfort in such a view and in the last year of the Carter Administration conducted hearings on the role and accountability of the assistant for National Security Affairs. This much is certain: NSC is indispensable; the assistant is not. Such a perception augurs well and is fundamental for future institutional planning.

FOR ADDITIONAL INFORMATION: The basic document establishing the NSC is found in U.S. Congress, House, *National Security Act of 1947, as Amended through September 30, 1973*, Committee on Armed Services (1973). The most comprehensive source concerning the genesis and development of the NSC through 1960 is contained in a collection of hearings, studies, reports, and recommendations compiled by Senator Henry M. Jackson and published as U.S. Congress, Senate, Committee on Government Operations, Subcommittee on National Policy Machinery, *Organizing for National Security*, 3 vols., 86th and 87th Cong. (1961). Other sources include a number of articles and books: Dillon Anderson, "The President and National Security," *Atlantic Monthly* (January 1966); Demetrios Caraley, *The Politics of Military Unification* (1966); and Keith C. Clark and Laurence S. Legere, eds., *The President and the Management of National Security*, Report for the Institute for Defense Analyses (1966).

See also I. M. Destler, "National Security Advice to U.S. Presidents: Some Lessons from Thirty Years," *World Politics* (January 1977); "National Security Management: What Presidents Have Wrought," *Political Science Quarterly* (Winter 1980-1981); and *Presidents, Bureaucrats and Foreign Policy: The Politics of Organization* (1972). Helpful too are Stanley L. Falk and Theodore W. Bauer, *The National Security Structure* (1972); Paul Y. Hammond, "The National Security Council as a Device for Interdepartmental Coordination: An Interpretation and Appraisal," *American Political Science Review* (December 1960); R. Gordon Hoxie, *Command Decision and the Presidency* (1977); "The Not So Imperial Presidency: A Modest Proposal," *Presidential Studies Quarterly* (Spring

1980); Hoxie, ed., *The Presidency of the 1970's* (1973); and Hoxie, ed., *The White House: Organization and Operations* (1971).

R. GORDON HOXIE

NATIONAL TRANSPORTATION SAFETY BOARD (NTSB). On April 1, 1967, accidents involving air, water, highways, railroads, pipelines, and hazardous materials became the responsibility of the National Transportation Safety Board within the Department of Transportation* (DOT). As a result, the Civil Aeronautics Board* (CAB) and Interstate Commerce Commission* relinquished their accident-investigation duties. In reality throughout the subsequent years, the NTSB relied heavily on the Coast Guard,* Federal Highway Administration,* and Federal Railroad Administration (FRA) to carry on the primary field work pertaining to mishaps in their spheres. Moreover, the NTSB allowed the Federal Aviation Administration* (FAA) to investigate all nonfatal accidents within the area of general aviation, usually a total annually exceeding 1,300 incidents.

The familiar probable cause, long associated with the CAB, culminated the investigation but was augmented in 1969 by the introduction of a strictly factual preliminary report. In 1970, the NTSB cogently summarized transportation safety's ten worst enemies: (1) alcohol, leading to as many as 25,000 lives lost (about 50 percent of the total) annually on the highways and as high as 10 percent in pleasure flying and other forms of general aviation; (2) ineffective packaging of motorists and pilots—poor crashworthiness; (3) youth highway fatalities—over seventeen thousand for the ages seventeen to twenty-four, or twice this age group's share of the deaths; (4) approach and landing aviation accidents—including visual illusions in poor weather, often in fog, for example, the Marshall University football team at Huntington, West Virginia; (5) "induced" pilot error—instruments difficult to locate hurriedly or many other shortcomings of design, weather-related problems, a special study alleging various of these factors in one-half of air carrier and over three-fourths of general aviation accidents; (6) recreational boating—over 1,300 deaths each year; (7) highway traffic mix—small versus large vehicle collisions; (8) rail-highway grade crossings—about fourteen hundred fatalities per year; (9) highway pedestrians—almost ten thousand killed in 1969, approximately one-fifth of all highway deaths; and (10) hazardous materials—an increasingly dangerous menace with relatively few effective regulations.

The probable cause challenged the safety officials of the NTSB, which spread its teams of investigators over eleven field offices. Major disasters resulted in one of the five politically appointed board members joining the team at the accident site. In one recent year, the NTSB issued the probable cause of 5,408 aviation accidents and visited 896 air-accident scenes, 14 of which involved major airlines. The NTSB staff totals approximately 250 persons. The NTSB also investigates a number of railroad disasters; the FRA handles the remainder in that category. Aviation teams are joined by personnel from the FAA, and these experts divide the scrutiny among factors of structures, systems, power plants, operations, air traffic control, weather, flight data and cockpit voice recorders, human factors, and appropriate miscellaneous data. Not all sites are easily accessible. For example, in 1973, in took five days to reach a World Airways cargo-accident site at the 3,500-foot level in Alaska.

Weather proved to be a factor in at least 36.6 percent of the general aviation crashes during 1974 and has continued to emerge in the study of numerous air-carrier mishaps. Two of the most sensational accidents involving weather apparently related to a similar cause, the ingestion of water and ice in massive amounts into the engines during severe thunderstorms. One accident involved a Southern Airways DC-9 (1977) in the Atlanta area, and the other an Air Wisconsin commuter flight (1980) in Nebraska. Both accidents raised the question of why the pilots were allowed to fly into the severe weather. Allegedly, radar attenuation falsely minimized the intensity of the storm to the Air Wisconsin crew. In neither case did air traffic control inform the pilots of the storm's intensity. For years, the NTSB warned pilots not to proceed into severe storms and urged the FAA to instigate a formal ruling to that effect. Moreover, FAA air traffic controllers apparently did not as routine duty relay a weather report of moderate to severe icing (SIGMET) to the crew of a Bristol Britannia, which crashed on take-off at Logan, in Boston (1980).

Weather seldom leads to midair collisions or to near misses. The NTSB report issued in 1969, stated that most fatalities resulting from such collisions occurred in general aviation, at or near uncontrolled airports, below 5,000 feet, under Visual Flight Rules, and on a weekend in the months of July-August. The final approach, it said, posed the greatest threat. Six days after this study was released, a twin-jet commercial airliner and light plane collided (1969) at Indianapolis killing eighty-three people. On September 25, 1978, a Pacific Southern Airways (PSA) Boeing 727 and private Cessna 172 collided over San Diego; the board blamed the lack of the Terminal Radar Service Area at Lindbergh Field and the PSA pilots for not reporting their loss of visual separation from the smaller craft. Ironically, the worst aviation disaster on record had occurred a year earlier at Tenerife, Spanish Canaries, in which a ground collision of Pan American and KLM jumbo jets killed 580 people and padded the year's total of 654 dead, an all-time record. Even so, the fatal accident rate for air carriers that year stood at only 0.002 per million miles flown.

The NTSB's most extensive investigation ever followed the crash of an American Airlines DC-10 on May 25, 1979, on take-off at Chicago's O'Hare Field. The left engine and pylon tore away, traveled over the wing, and fell to the ground. Within two days the board caused the inspection of all DC-10 pylon attach points, and several days later advised the FAA to warn the airlines not to raise or lower a pylon with the engine still attached. This had been a common maintenance process using a forklift, which apparently had caused fatal cracks. The probable cause was issued with unusual dispatch before the year's end.

A flurry of accidents occurred in 1969. Five of nine accidents took place on approach, four of them in thirteen days, with two involving the same airline, the same type of aircraft, and the same airport, Allegheny's CV 580s at Bradford, Pennsylvania.

These and many other accidents led the NTSB to issue a large number of recommendations, mostly to the FAA, aimed at preventing the occurrence of similar incidents. The board's advice created a dilemma at the FAA, which often encountered major opposition from aircraft owners, pilots, and manufacturers who complained about undue regulations or prohibitive costs for the implementation.

Another of the numerous difficulties involving the tragedy-ridden DC-l0—a faulty cargo door mechanism—arose in July 1972 in a flight over Windsor, Canada. No fatalities resulted from that mishap. The NTSB warned the FAA of the problem, but in 1974 near Paris, France, a Turkish DC-10 with the same type of cargo door crashed on take-off, with the loss of 346 people. Only following this second incident was the closed-loop door mechanism required.

A continually vexing problem involved in crash survival concerns the inability to evacuate the aircraft. Occasionally a remedy will come to light when the passengers and crew survive. For example, in the crash of a Texas International DC-9 in 1976, all eighty-six people aboard were evacuated, despite the flight attendants' inability to open the rear door. Smoke had prevented the attendants from locating the tail-cone exit; after this crash, emergency lights were installed on these planes. In another incident, a near-miss, the crew had misunderstood the air controllers' instructions, whereupon the NTSB obtained a rule requiring that the pilot repeat such data.

Disconcerting human error can occur. A UAL DC-8 allegedly ran out of gas at Portland, Oregon (1978), and a Western DC-10 landed on the wrong runway (one blocked for repairs) at Mexico City (1979).

As already mentioned, air traffic controllers do not automatically receive severe weather data for dispatch to pilots. The controllers' inadequate and unclear information was partially the blame for Trans World Airlines' crash into Mount Weather on the way to Dulles Airport on December 1, 1974. All ninety-two people aboard died. A Beech Travel Air crash occurred in Nevada (1979) when a controller's faulty directions led the pilot into a mountain. Thereafter, NTSB required that an emergency obstruction video map be made available to the controllers.

In 1979, a National Airlines 727 sank off Florida; fifty-eight survived and three drowned. However, the seat cushions of fourteen people failed to float. The FAA disagreed as to the need of floating seats, claiming that life jackets were sufficient. Similarly, the NTSB failed to convince the FAA that general aviation planes should be required to carry flight recorders.

The time lapse between an NTSB recommendation and enactment by the FAA has long plagued aviation. For example, in 1969, the NTSB began calling for the development of a ground proximity warning system to warn pilots on descent for landings. This recommendation was prompted again by an incident in 1971 involving a Southern Airways DC-9 at Gulfport, Mississippi. In fact, the NTSB believed that this equipment might have prevented over one-half dozen such accidents, beginning with the plunge of a United Air Lines 727 into Lake Michigan near Chicago in 1965. Instead, the FAA stressed the need of better cockpit discipline and reliance on existing instruments. Finally, after a fatal crash in 1977, the FAA took favorable action on the request. In 1973, a flight attendant was pinned to the ceiling and seriously injured by a galley lift aboard a DC-10 operated by National Airlines. The board warned all operators about correcting procedures with the lifts. In autumn 1981, a flight attendant lost her life in a galley-lift accident on a World Airways DC-10 one hour west of London. A Delta DC-9 crashed in 1972, at Fort Worth, killing four persons after entering the vortex of the DC-10 ahead of it. As a result, the aircraft separations (landings and take-offs) in terminal areas were extended. Despite these earlier setbacks, the major U.S. commercial airlines compiled a new record of no fatalities from October 31, 1979, until January 13, 1982, when an Air Florida Boeing 737 crashed at National Airport.

In October 1978, Congress, in a bipartisan move, adopted legislation moving toward the so-called deregulation of aviation. A major boon to the small commuter lines, this very debatable innovation soon focused NTSB attention upon the serious defects inherent in certain of these commuter enterprises. In 1978, the accident rate for commuter lines was more than six times higher than that of the U.S. air carriers, and seven and one-half times higher in the case of fatal accidents. Adjusted to the number of departures, the death rates for 1975-1979 were five times higher for commuters than for the local service carriers. The probable cause in several accidents during 1979 failed to inspire confidence in these commuter operations: (1) a badly deteriorated rubber air-hose line led to the feathering of one propeller on take-off and a plunge into Santa Monica Bay; (2) an unsecured baggage door opened, was hit by the propeller, and the Beech Model 70 crashed, killing all eight aboard at Gulfport, Mississippi; and (3) a DeHavilland Heron, which was more than 1,000 pounds overweight, with the weight badly distributed, met disaster at Saint Croix, Virgin Islands. The operator, PRINAIR, had a history of loading problems over seven years, and the board alleged that FAA surveillance of it was inadequate. The FAA cited the line for repeated earlier violations.

Commuter misconduct accounted for fourteen fatal crashes and sixty-three deaths in 1979. As a result, the NTSB urged the FAA to force commuters to comply with all the safeguards demanded of the major carriers. Meanwhile, the board called for a most unusual "en banc" hearing on commuters' problems for early 1980. But the carnage persisted into 1980, with a Piper PA-31 operated by COMAIR crashing at Cincinnati and killing eight persons. The pilot's records, obviously falsified, stated 205 hours of multiple-engine training instead of 93; only 1.5 hours of it checked out in that type of craft.

The board issued a devastating exposé of a Downeast Airlines' DHC-6 crash in 1979 at Rockland, Maine, in which seventeen people died. The board found undue stress on the chief pilot; two weeks before the crash he had suffered exhaustion, chest pains, and breathing problems. The company president forced the pilots to complete instrument approaches below FAA minimum conditions at Rockland. The board contended that the FAA had not taken action when informed earlier of these shoddy practices.

The board urged the FAA to apply the sixty-year pilot limit to the commuters, but the FAA begged off pending a study by the National Institutes of Health. In 1980, the NTSB scrutiny covered 35 percent of all commuter passenger enplanements and forty-five commuter lines. The 3,900 man-hours spent on the study delayed six aircraft accident reports. Late in March, Chairman James B. King informed a Senate hearing that the FAA promised to conduct a vigorous enforcement program for the commuters which was designed to weed out the "bad apples." Unfortunately, the public had already paid a horrible toll for this brand of service which some proponents boasted would carry 10 percent of all air passengers by 1990.

The NTSB status within the DOT caused a major argument by 1972 among the five members who voted 4-1 in favor of recommending independence. Only Chairman John H. Reed expressed satisfaction with the current arrangement. Meddling and intimidation from the Richard Nixon White House were apparent. The impasse extended to hearings before the Senate Commerce Committee and elsewhere in Congress. Public Law 93-633, the Independent Safety Board Act, removed the board from the DOT and granted independence, effective April 1, 1975.

Board members possessed a variety of backgrounds, including politics, law, journalism, engineering, the military, and aviation. Senate confirmation was usually pro forma. However, in 1974, one member, Isabelle Burgess, lost her reappointment bid in the Senate because of alleged conflict-of-interest charges. She was castigated for allegedly accepting free railroad passes and retaining stock in Allegheny Airlines at the time both companies underwent investigation by the board. She reportedly logged 30 percent absences from board meetings and turned in unusually high expense accounts, twice as high as those of Chairman Reed. A Nixon appointee, she was a former state Senator from Arizona.

Continuity of board membership remained elusive. A major exception, Francis H. McAdams, brought long-term experience from the CAB to the board upon its inception. A lawyer by training and experienced with aviation matters as counsel for Capitol and United Air Lines, McAdams was a Navy pilot in World War II, later a trial lawyer for the CAB, and finally, as a Democrat, served to date on the NTSB. Queried by senators during the reappointment hearing in 1978, McAdams insisted that several times he had dissented from majority findings on probable cause, stressing always the need to answer why the pilot made the error, and not just explaining what happened. He noted an increase in board credibility and integrity since the break from DOT. He bemoaned the fact that the NTSB encountered roadblocks in the name of invasion of privacy when it sought to account for the pilot's pre-accident personal life. Six months before the midair collision at San Diego, McAdams admitted the dangers inherent in the mix of traffic among private, military, and commercial aircraft at high-density airports. He easily gained reappointment.

Another leader on the five-person board in recent years has been James B. King, who for eight years was a special assistant to Senator Edward M. Kennedy of Massachusetts, followed by ten months of similar duty for President Jimmy Carter. He was also a teacher and newsman, and among his interests were the problems relating to hazardous wastes, especially tank-car disasters. Another board member, Elwood Driver, was a command pilot with the Air Force for twenty years, and concentrated on safety engineering in both aviation and highway safety. Patricia A. Goldman, a free-lance writer, stressed economic concerns; she had experience in urban, manpower, and poverty programs. Finally, Rear Admiral George H. Patrick Bursley (retired), a lawyer, had vast experience in maritime and international law, spending a large part of his career with the Coast Guard.*

As mentioned earlier, the NTSB has relied heavily on the other agencies with regard to accidents involving the highways, water, pipelines, and hazardous wastes. But the board has not hesitated to issue remedial directives in all these areas. It has announced no official recommendations about airbags for automobiles but has consistently supported stringent helmet laws for motorcycles.

In the initial year of its existence, the board charged that railroad management and labor could not or would not arrest the worsening railroad picture. Faulty track or maintenance caused 60 percent of all rail accidents. DOT was requested to force railroads into hiring more rail inspectors because undetected broken rails caused numerous accidents. High carbon content in a railroad car wheel led to a derailment (1979) in which 27,000 gallons of liquid propane gas exploded later while being transferred into tank trucks; fifteen people died. Amazingly, chlorine, a deadly gas, and radioactive materials remained uncontrolled. Of the 10,220 railroad accidents in 1977, hazardous materials were found in 808 instances, and 14,805 persons had to be evacuated.

In 1972, an Illinois Central commuter train in Chicago overshot a station, backed up, and was rammed by another train, killing forty-five people. As a result, the board called for a block system that would prevent backing into another block. A man, caught in the door of a Long Island commuter train, met death in 1975 when dragged onto the third rail. The NTSB demanded a foolproof system preventing the trains from advancing until all doorways had been cleared. Human error led to another Illinois Central Gulf accident near Chicago, in 1979, as a passenger train traveling at 65 miles per hour was shunted by hand switch onto a siding and into a standing freight train.

While the Coast Guard ruled on most of the marine accidents, the board expressed consternation regarding selected highway accidents. For example, it found a separation on school bus floors which contained no riveting, and it attempted to overcome this grave manufacturing shortcoming.

In the 1980s, board members anticipated a continuation of the crusade and mandate to make all phases of transportation safer, to promote various safety measures, and, finally, to attempt better followup techniques in persuading other agencies to enact their many recommendations.

FOR ADDITIONAL INFORMATION: Primary sources on this relatively new agency are practically impossible to locate. Annual Reports, official probable cause announcements, and congressional hearings are useful. Aviation and business journals reflect the broad range of official interest in accidents—from the Air Line Pilots Association, the airlines, general aviation owners and operators, to the manufacturers. *Aviation Week and Space Technology, Flying,* and *Business Week* are several examples of these journals. Pre-1967 civil aviation accidents are surveyed in Donald R. Whitnah, *Safer Skyways: Federal Control of Aviation, 1926-1966* (1966-1967).

DONALD R. WHITNAH

NATIONAL WEATHER SERVICE. By the midnineteenth century, the technology of meteorology had advanced sufficiently to combine with the recent perfection of telegraphy to provide the basis for organizing a nationwide collection of data for a weather service. Keen interest in the winds, storms, and precipitation ever since ancient times led to such instruments as the weather vane, rain gauges, the barometer, various thermometers, later thermographs and barographs, the psychrometer, and the hygrometer. Moreover, kites and balloons were used to record upper-air data, while manned balloons proved that man could carry instruments aloft. A general science of storm progression had also evolved by this time, featuring the usual west-to-east movement, the definition of low- or high-pressure centers and their progress, and the rather intensive study of cloud heights with a kite and sextant to determine the intensity of both clear and foul weather phenomena. Dramatic temperature differences at varying altitudes intrigued the scientists, as did the effects of weather on health and the climatic changes following land clearance in an area. Already in the 1840s, synoptic weather charts provided the means to plot the interesting data and to analyze storms, but not particularly to forecast these phenomena. Sunspots, the condensation of moisture, the convective theory of atmospheric circulation, and the explanation of tornadoes, hailstones, and hurricanes all gained considerable preliminary attention in these years.

Collecting weather records was hardly a new practice in Europe or America by 1870. Gathering spontaneous observations of the phenomena and providing one center or forecaster with the means to determine the future effects of the massive data were revolutionary. Thomas Jefferson and Henry Thoreau compiled earlier records, while collection networks had been known on a state or regional basis by the surgeon general during the War of 1812, later the General Land Office,* the U.S. Patent Office,* and the states of New York, Massachusetts, Pennsylvania, and South Carolina. The most competent network of 150 stations reporting simultaneously was run by Joseph Henry for the Smithsonian Institution.* Helpful maps daily charted the temperature and precipitation data for

Americans from the Smithsonian during 1849-1861. Naturally, with these data available, the next step involved the forecasting of weather, the unofficial efforts then ranging from average to poor.

At the end of the Civil War, Professor Henry urged Congress to create a weather service. He was joined by another astute scientist, Cleveland Abbe of the Cincinnati Observatory, who also hoped to instigate regular forecasting. Western Union had cooperated with the Smithsonian network and now promised similar cooperation for another national endeavor. A third prominent scientist, Increase A. Lapham of Wisconsin, had gathered weather data since 1827, long urged a national service, and in 1869 promised to organize the data collection for the new service in the Great Lakes region. Now the scientists sought the necessary political support to launch the national enterprise. Foremost of the politicos was Congressman H. E. Paine of Wisconsin, who worked closely with Lapham. There ensued numerous discussions about the best location within the federal structure for the new agency. Abbe deplored the possibility of Army personnel taking the meteorological observations, but Signal Service Chief Colonel A. J. Meyer retorted that his group had the telegraph facilities, the discipline, and the know-how to fill the bill. By February 9, 1870, President Ulysses S. Grant had signed the bill creating the weather service within the United States Army Signal Corps.* The press showed little interest in this achievement, which had been guided through the Senate via a joint resolution to match Paine's intent in the House.

Hardly prepared for the new venture except for the telegraph, the Army Signal Service hastened to acquire the services of meteorologists Lapham and Abbe. Lapham issued the initial storm warnings for the Great Lakes on November 8, while Abbe began the popular twenty-four-hour forecast from Washington, D.C., on February 19, 1871. Reports west of the Mississippi remained scarce, except for Omaha, Cheyenne, and San Francisco, within the next few months. Regular stations were increased from 24 in the first autumn to 55 within the next year and to a total of 178 by 1890. Optimal spacing was sought at 100 miles.

Immediately, the frustrations of faulty predictions dampened the experts' hopes for foolproof accuracy. Along came unpredicted killer freezes or heavy precipitation, or worst of all, an untimely hurricane along the southern or eastern coasts or an inland tornado. Abbe expressed pleasure at 85-percent accuracy, but Congress sometimes responded with reduced appropriations to register its dismay. Nevertheless, the meteorologists and military personnel remained undaunted in establishing additional facets of service, including river-flood warnings (1873). They also were able to trace hurricanes in the same decade, leading to a more elaborate forecasting system in the 1890s, and they stimulated efforts to collect data and provide extra predictions to agriculture during each growing season. Fruit-growing regions continued to gain the most attention. To augment research and to provide special reporting locations, the Signal Service and its successors enlisted the services of thousands of voluntary cooperative observers throughout the nation, 2,000 by 1892.

From the outset, Abbe and his colleagues set out to facilitate climatological research both in the United States and abroad. Early examples featured the exchange of observational information with European nations, which was especially geared to the study of Atlantic Ocean storms, and initial efforts were made to learn more about cold waves through intensive studies of the Arctic area. Manned balloon ascensions constituted another form of experimentation at this time. The *Monthly Weather Review* was established in 1873 and soon became the service's leading means of disseminating all types of research data.

Despite these auspicious beginnings in providing splendid public service and conducting pertinent research, bitter rivalries ensued between the civilian and military personnel. As a result, in 1891 the weather service was transferred to the Department of Agriculture,* where it was designated the U.S. Weather Bureau. The previous ten years had witnessed an increasing uproar against the Signal Service, which suffered through a major embezzlement by its disbursing officer and congressional retrenchment which at times drastically curtailed services and collection of data even in such large centers as New York City. In the Army, considerable misgivings existed in the other branches about the status of the Signal Service. A joint congressional committee was appointed in 1884 to investigate the Signal Service which was now under the command of General W. B. Hazen. Reporting two years later, the committee recommended placing the weather service under civilian designation. During the next four years, the battle to achieve civilian status coincided with the move to create a new Department of Agriculture. General A. W. Greely, who became director of the Signal Service upon Hazen's death in 1887, did not oppose the change. The first civilian chief was Mark W. Harrington, a scientist at the University of Michigan.

Primary alterations included the decentralization of forecasting in 1894 to district forecast centers, with local bureau employees given freedom to amend the general forecasts to adhere to changing local conditions. The public was now alerted to dangerous conditions through, among other means, whistles, flag systems, electric searchlights, fire alarms, bombs and rockets, and warnings by telephone. Research efforts continued; in 1891 attention turned to rainmaking and to hiring new scientists, for example, Charles Francis Marvin, who conducted kite experiments in the 1890s and later became chief of the bureau. Unfortunately, another political feud, this one between Harrington and Agriculture Secretary J. Sterling Morton, erupted, resulting in Harrington's dismissal in 1895. Morton relentlessly attacked all opposition and stooped so low as to reduce Abbe's salary during this struggle.

The energetic Willis Luther Moore of Pennsylvania, a career scientist in the service since 1876, became the next leader and vowed to expand public services and research. By the late 1890s, forecasts covered the next thirty-six hours and were issued twice daily. No exact maximum or minimum temperatures were indicated—just "warmer," "colder," or other descriptions. The network of cooperative observers was more than doubled under Moore by 1912. Bureau authorities considered verification of a forecast if the stated prediction was followed by the actual change of six degrees of temperature in summer or ten degrees in winter. Poor records led Moore to revoke the forecasting duties of several colleagues. Intrigued by the problems of long-range forecasting, in 1901 the bureau issued three-day forecasts for the Atlantic Ocean and in 1908 began experimental weekly forecasts which became official and permanent two years later. Meanwhile, the special services entailed increased emphasis on river-flood and hurricane warnings as well as severe inland storms, despite the bureau's unwillingness to use the word "tornado" in forecasts until the 1960s.

The rapid expansion of data to the public was facilitated during 1870-1913 by other communication improvements besides the telegraph, namely, the telephone, Atlantic cable, rural-free-delivery, electricity, public kiosks with displays, and the further increase in newspaper dissemination of weather information. The new aeronauts, such as Wilbur and Orville Wright and Octave Chanute, repeatedly contacted Weather Bureau personnel for applicable data. Within the bureau, Professor Frank H. Bigelow conducted pioneer research in solar radiation. Likewise, these federal scientists turned their attention to work on evaporation. Furthermore, improving the basic instruments caught the attention of Professor Marvin, who helped produce better recording precipitation gauges, a kite meteorograph, a theodolite for the direction and velocity of clouds, an electrical-resistant thermometer for measuring solar radiation, and another instrument for earthquake measurement.

But once again scandal and political upheaval interrupted progress. Trouble began in fiscal year 1903 over alleged duplication of services within the Department of Agriculture in compiling weekly climate and crop bulletins. A year later, Moore started diverting funds into a new research center at Mount Weather, Virginia, including appropriations which Congress had really intended for other new stations throughout the nation. By 1909, it appeared that Moore had weathered the storm of congressional inquiry about the alleged mountain resort, but, internal strife eventually proved to be embarrassing as disgruntled employees gave interviews to eager muckraking reporters who quickly presented more serious accusations about Chief Moore. According to the testimony presented to Secretary of Agriculture James Wilson, Moore administered the bureau in a most dictatorial fashion. Moreover, the bureau missed badly on the inaugural forecast for President William Howard Taft (1909), calling for "clear and colder" only to witness a snowstorm. Wilson continued merely to tolerate Moore. What finally caused Moore's downfall was his drive to be appointed Secretary of Agriculture by incoming President Woodrow Wilson. In this campaign, he utilized the services of countless bureau field employees who engaged in partisan political activities to gain him the Cabinet position. Wilson fired Moore in March and as his successor appointed another renowned scientist, Professor Marvin, who led the service until 1934.

Under Marvin, the Weather Bureau finally gained the administrative stability necessary to concentrate on scientific innovation and expansion of services during the 1913-1941 period. Meteorologists on assignment and weather advice were extended to the U.S. military services during World War I. At home the hurricane warning system was expanded dramatically from the earlier fifteen-hour daily coverage. Ship-to-shore observational reports, improved by 1935 with perfection of the two-way radio, provided by far the one most essential improvement in tracking and predicting the advancement of these devastating storms. Sadly, public apathy led to ignored warnings, and 500 deaths occurred from a Labor Day 1935 hurricane on the Florida Keys. Next, the bureau instigated additional upper-air balloon observations, the sounding balloons, to obtain better data between altitudes of 50,000 and 100,000 feet. Another vexing problem confronted the bureau in modernizing its river-flood service. For example, during 1924-1937, damaging floods occurred in all but 15 of 168 months, and the average yearly fatalities reached 90; property damage stood at over $102 million annually. Droughts in 1930-1931 and 1934-1936, coupled with Great Depression appropriations cuts, hampered improvements in the service. Floods of unparalleled intensity during 1936-1937 led to decentralization of the river-flood program, cooperation with the Army Engineers* in establishing a hydrometeorological research section in the bureau, volumetric type forecasting, and increased attention to snow melt and evaporation statistics. Agricultural interests also benefited with widespread attention given to fruit growers; when below-freezing temperatures were predicted, orchard heating became a common practice in the 1920s. The Pacific Coast had been well blanketed with fruit-frost warnings by this time; now, similar warning networks were established in Florida and other smaller fruit regions where a combination of federal, state, and private funds brought success.

One of the most popular innovations of the era came with the establishment of the new fire weather service in cooperation with the United States Forest Service.* Keeping track of the fuel-moisture content of sticks, dropping firefighters by airplane, and maintaining hundreds of lookouts and observations stations, coupled with the tremendous impetus of the improved two-way radio, elevated this service to untold efficiency by the 1930s. In the realm of regular forecasting, the Weather Bureau finally expanded the general forecasts in 1939 to four times daily, while extended forecasts were modified the next year to inaugurate the highly successful five-day forecast to supplant the earlier weekly variety.

By far the most spectacular innovation was the bureau's assistance to the development of aviation. From the outset, forecasters, more than pilots, often realized the danger of the weather elements to flights and the necessity of providing the best possible data. The majority of early American aviation was carried on by the military, which augmented the bureau's reporting network with its own appropriations for seeking upper-air data, including additional kite and pilot-balloon stations. Flight-forecast centers were first established at bureau city offices in Chicago, Washington, and San Francisco. Prime impetus for the service was to assist the air mail and other military flights. However, from the teens on, much attention was paid to the popular special flights, cross-country and trans-Atlantic, both military and civilian, bureau assistance to Charles Lindbergh in 1927 was just one of numerous examples.

In technology, it was obvious that the radio had to be improved to enable aviation to establish regular commercial passenger service; this dream became a reality by the mid-1930s with two-way transmission—pilot to ground. Meanwhile, by 1930 the teletype, used to distribute data among ground stations facilitated the use of forecasts, as did the speedy transmission of page-type weather maps. Bureau aviation forecasting gained significantly from the Air Commerce Act of 1926 and subsequent appropriations for the federal regulation and support of civil aviation. Twenty-four-hour service could now be inaugurated at bureau airways stations for the pilots; there were fifty such stations by 1930. The Department of Commerce* was designated to control civil aviation through its new agency, the Aeronautics Branch, which was soon renamed the Bureau of Air Commerce and is today called the Federal Aviation Administration.* As a result of this close tie between aviation and the Weather Bureau, the bureau was transferred to the Department of Commerce in 1940. It remains there to this day. In 1965 it was under the new Environmental Science Services Administration, and in 1970 under the new National Oceanographic and Atmospheric Administration. In 1970, its title became the National Weather Service.

Augmenting not only aviation forecasting but also the other special activities and regular forecasts in the 1930s was the adoption of refined and improved meteorological techniques known as air-mass analysis. Moreover, the radiosonde mode of collecting simultaneously the upper-air data of temperature, pressure, and humidity proved to be another major breakthrough to meteorology, aviation, and the bureau. By 1937, the radiosonde replaced airplane observations of the upper air.

Marvin stepped down as chief in 1934 before many of the improvements had been realized. His successor, Willis Gregg, served until his death in 1938. Gregg had served the bureau for many years as a meteorologist. Francis W. Reicheld-erfer, a commander in the Navy's meteorological program, was named chief in December 1938 and proceeded to serve the longest tenure as its leader until retiring in 1963. He came to his appointment with extensive Navy experience and cooperation with the Weather Bureau in aviation forecasting and research.

When the Japanese attacked Pearl Harbor in 1941, the Weather Bureau was, of course, called upon to assist the war effort. Over seven hundred junior-level bureau personnel entered the armed forces, and over 900 women were employed to fill these jobs and other expanded duties. Bureau officials helped to train military meteorologists for both the United States and numerous allied or friendly countries.

After the war, the bureau participated in many cooperative scientific ventures in the polar regions. The Coast Guard initially supplied the vessels for an ocean weather service which Chief Moore had earlier envisioned. The bureau sponsored the rebuilding of weather units in war-devastated nations. Furthermore, in 1951 Chief Reichelderfer became the first president of the World Meteorological Organization, a well-deserved tribute to the role of the Weather Bureau as the world's leading service. Even the Cold War paranoia failed to curtail the bureau's advances. The gigantic strides made in space technology were beneficial to all types of climatological and forecasting services. Significant in this area was U.S. cooperation with the USSR during the International Geophysical Year (1957-1958). At home, bureau officials realized further support and cooperation, with the establishment in 1958 of the National Aeronautics and Space Administration.*

The Weather Service's accomplishments since 1945 also included the establishment of state climatological offices, tremendous strides in tracking storms and gaining research information from radar and satellite weather photos, daily revision of five-day forecasts, addition of the thirty-day outlook, inclusion of percentage chances in the forecasting of precipitation, and airplane observations of hurricanes. One special advance was the increased accuracy of forecasts involving the possibility or actual existence of the deadly tornado, with official alerts issued in the former case and warnings given after spotting a tornado. Research on weather modification and air pollution continues.

FOR ADDITIONAL INFORMATION: For research material on the service and its predecessors, the holdings in the National Oceanic and Atmospheric Administration (NOAA) Library are helpful. Numerous bulletins and reports, the *Monthly Weather Review*, and countless other in-house papers and research findings are essential. Official correspondence in the National Archives* traces the service's history. The secondary literature includes the scholarly work of Donald R. Whitnah, *A History of the United States Weather Bureau* (1961, 1965), and Roy Popkin, *The Environmental Science Services Administration* (1967).

DONALD R. WHITNAH

NATIONAL YOUTH ADMINISTRATION (NYA). Mrs. Eleanor Roosevelt had moments of real terror in May 1934, when she thought the United States might be losing a whole generation. There was good reason for her fear, nor was she the only American publicly expressing such sentiments. The question of unemployed and unemployable young people was a crucial concern to many in the depression United States. Accurate statistics on unemployment levels during the 1930s are difficult to obtain, and those for youth have a far greater margin for error than for adults, most of whom, having already worked, were more readily traceable. All the surveys that do exist, however, point to the conclusion that between 20 and 30 percent of Americans sixteen to twenty-four years of age who were in the labor market were totally unemployed. Youth were among the cruelest casualties of economic collapse. Denied work, they were denied the chance to live normally, to grow in independence and maturity, in short, to become adults. The United States was in danger of producing a whole generation of misfits, lacking confidence in themselves and their country, unskilled and untrained, utterly incapable of becoming the productive adults upon whom social and economic recovery would depend.

The New Deal administration moved swiftly to combat the problem. Within weeks of Roosevelt's inauguration, the Civilian Conservation Corps* (CCC) was in full operation, with thousands of young men engaged in a myriad of conservation tasks. But the CCC, impressive as it was, was no permanent answer to the problems of young people in depression America. It catered only to the most desperate cases. For most young people, moving halfway across the continent in order to work in the woods was simply not possible for many reasons, the most compelling of which, of course, was that 50 percent of deprived young people were female and the CCC was for males only. Hence, there was a clear need for a much more wide-ranging youth program, one based on the home community and one that would impart skills of permanent value. The National Youth Administration was an attempt to meet this need.

The NYA had its origins in a number of disparate programs developed during 1934 and the first months of 1935. One was a Federal Emergency Relief Administration (FERA) plan for enabling college students to continue their education, another FERA scheme aided transient young people, and a third stimulated vocational training. When, in 1935, the President decided to substitute work relief for direct grants, and the Works Progress Administration* (WPA) was created, a decision was also made to expand, develop, and coordinate such schemes. After a fairly intensive period of preparation and lobbying in which Mrs. Roosevelt played a central role, on June 26, 1935, the President, by Executive Order, created the NYA as part of the new work-relief scheme.

There were two main divisions in the new project. One was student work, which was really an extension of the program initiated earlier. College and high school students, mainly from relief families, were to be given grants in return for work, to enable them to complete their education. No attempt was made to provide full scholarships; the grants were entirely supplementary ones—$15 to $30 monthly for college students, $6 monthly for high school enrollees—intended to bridge the gap between the student's own resources and what he needed to stay in school. The intent was twofold—to encourage those young people with skills and talents to develop these fully, and to hold them out of the job market as long as possible.

The second of the new agency's tasks, and the more difficult one, was to do something for those young people who had already left school and who had not found work. The NYA was charged with providing them with relief, but it was also intended that they be given specific job training, which would be of permanent value. Consequently, programs had to be developed which were relevant both to the individual and to the community in which he or she was living.

To head the new agency, Roosevelt selected the deputy-director of the WPA, Aubrey Williams, one of the men most closely connected with its planning. A

Southerner, a former social worker, and a committed liberal, the outspoken Williams was already closely identified with the left wing of the New Deal, and it was inevitable that the NYA should take on some of the political coloration of its leader. He was to hold the job in addition to his WPA duties and was to be assisted by an advisory council of prominent citizens.

Williams had no desire to run a tightly centralized agency. He believed the NYA would succeed only if local project supervisors were given the widest possible latitude in developing community-oriented work schemes. Consequently, he conceived of the NYA national office as doing little more than setting the broadest policy guidelines, leaving state and local officials to fill in the details. He also insisted that an advisory council of local citizens be set up in each area where there was an NYA project, to assist the local director, in an endeavor to institutionalize community participation in the work.

There were few difficulties in getting the student work program off the ground. By early 1937, more than 440,000 young people were receiving assistance, and the monthly number rarely dropped under 300,000, until student work ended in 1943. By then, more than 2 million young people had been helped by it. At peak enrollment in 1938-1939, just under 26,000 high schools and 1,700 colleges were receiving NYA funds. The educational institutions virtually ran the scheme themselves. It was the responsibility of the college president or school principal to see that the money was equitably distributed, that NYA regulations governing its use were complied with, and that the students performed some task around the campus in return. Many of these tasks were routine janitorial or clerical jobs, but some students showed a high degree of resourcefulness and a sense of social service. NYA students at one Midwestern university, for example, served as teachers' aides in a home service for crippled children. High school students in the Utah town of Payson built a telescope for use in school science courses. Indeed, the variety of activities carried out under NYA auspices was profoundly impressive. The student aid scheme was immensely popular. It worked smoothly from its inception, and the degree of decentralization was such that the NYA's function in it was little more than processing applications, distributing funds, and, through local officers, making sure that no gross financial abuses, of which there were suprisingly few, occurred.

Somewhat more difficult to get going was the program for out-of-school youth. One important reason for this difficulty was Williams's inability to give NYA the time it deserved. He continued in his WPA job as well as heading the NYA until December 1938, and it was the youth agency which suffered, especially in the first few months. No important policy decisions were made, state directors received little direction, and no money was allocated. Not until a deputy director took over detailed planning did the program even begin to work, and even then it fell far below expectations. In an effort to spread funds as widely as possible and to create community goodwill, projects involving high-labor, low-capital outlay content were preferred. By the beginning of 1936, youths all over the nation could be seen developing parks and other recreation areas, cleaning up public buildings, repairing school property, and performing similar tasks. Such an approach, while no doubt beneficial to the community, scarcely gave the enrollees the vital training they needed if they were to find jobs once their year or so in the NYA was over.

Fortunately, this approach had been abandoned by 1937. In its place was an insistence that only projects involving a substantial degree of training were to be adopted. Wage scales had been regularized (enrollees were paid $14 to $24 monthly, depending on the region and the hours of work), and the work projects were much more solid and positive. For example, in New Haven, Virginia, a small village of 700 people, NYA enrollees built a community center including an auditorium, a library, a gymnasium, and study rooms, thus gaining experience in a wide variety of construction tasks. The emphasis on acquiring skills had been firmly established.

By the end of 1936, the NYA had started to develop its own placement offices. These offices grew slowly, and nowhere near all the enrollees who wanted jobs could get them, but at least some attempt was made to help them find work. Then, by 1937, those who ran the agency realized that not all the needy young people lived in cities and that the type of urban group project, to which enrollees came from home each morning, simply did not suit rural environments. So they began organizing hundreds of resident centers in order to accommodate boys and girls from rural counties. At first, these centers tended to be agriculturally oriented, but before long a more varied training program was developed. For example, at the Conway, Arkansas, resident center, NYA boys worked on the city power plant, in the heating plant of the local college, and in carpentry, cabinet-making, sheet metal, and auto mechanics shops. As with the main program, the aim of these centers was to give the enrollees the widest possible variety of work experience. Rates of pay varied from between $18 and $30 monthly, with the board taking between $13 and $25 of this amount.

One further development should be mentioned. Williams was committed to the cause of racial justice in America and attempted to use his agency to further this end. Black Americans were enrolled as far as possible according to need and not in strict proportion to their relationship to the total population, as was the case with some other New Deal agencies. A fund was created to aid Negro college students, over and above the amount blacks happened to receive from NYA general revenues. In 1936, a special Negro Division was created within the national office, headed by Mary McLeod Bethune, a prominent black educator, and Williams insisted that similar divisions, staffed by blacks, be formed at the state level. Not everyone was happy with this kind of pressure, but blacks certainly regarded the NYA as one of the agencies from which they could always expect fair treatment.

When Williams took over the NYA full-time in 1939, it was a well-established, thriving agency, full of ideas, solidly democratic in organization, and decentralized in operation. He wanted to keep it this way, but he also wanted to change its focus slightly. Realizing that the growing war threat could lead to a rise in defense production, he decided that the NYA should concentrate on training youth for defense industry work, providing them with basic machine-shop techniques and then turning them over to individual plants for specific instruction. Overcoming agency objections to this idea and with the fullest cooperation from the President, the Secretary of War, and other national defense officers, Williams quietly began to put it into practice. By mid-1940, when FDR finally announced the development of a general defense program, the NYA was already halfway to becoming a defense-oriented agency. Throughout 1941, its nondefense functions were progressively shed until by 1942 it was involved solely in the war effort. The NYA introduced enrollees to machines, gave them basic shop training, and then poured them into the nation's industrial plants. It combed the country looking for young people to train, looked after their health, transported them to areas of labor shortage, found them jobs, and acclimatized them before letting them go. It was particularly concerned to bring black and female enrollees into the industrial mainstream. The enthusiastic testimony of thousands of businessmen from all over the nation is compelling evidence of its importance to the general defense effort.

Nevertheless, the agency was abolished in 1943, despite its acknowledged successes. It had always had its critics, partly because of Williams's supposed radicalism, partly because of his insistence that blacks be treated fairly within it, but probably most importantly, because a powerful conservative lobby was ranged implacably against it. This was the National Educational Association (NEA), the corporate voice of the nation's educational administrators. The NEA had always seen the NYA as the thin end of the wedge of federal involvement in education, and, especially after 1940, when it moved explicitly into the industrial training area, the NEA waged a bitter campaign against the NYA, accusing it of inefficiency, of duplicating the functions of the vocational schools, and of attempting to subvert the locally controlled public school systems. Moreover, the NEA had powerful congressional allies, especially within the Joint Committee for the Reduction of Non-Essential Federal Expenditures, a body set up in late 1941 and charged with recommending the elimination of all federal agencies not considered vital to the war effort. The Joint Committee duly investigated the NYA, and, in May 1943, recommended its termination. Williams and his congressional supporters fought desperately to save the agency, but to no avail. In a climate somewhat distorted by a massive NEA publicity campaign against the youth agency, Congress concurred with its Joint Committee's recommendation, and the NYA ceased to exist as of June 30, 1943.

The National Youth Administration was never as popular as its sister youth agency, the Civilian Conservation Corps, even though it was clearly much wider in scope, touched many more people—over 5 million young Americans were aided by it in one way or another—and in human terms was a much more valuable creation. Moreover, it was less expensive. It cost the government more than $1,000 annually to keep an enrollee in a CCC camp but only $628 to keep one at an NYA resident center. However, because most NYA people were not in residence but lived at home, the average individual cost per work year was only $341, which was remarkably cheap considering the value of the work done and the training given. But it was the CCC that was considered the glamor agency, partly because of the President's close personal identification with it but also because of its image. The spectacle of young men working together in the woods had a romantic appeal about it which the urbanized, variegated NYA was unable to match. Nevertheless, despite the impressive record left by the CCC in the field of conservation, the National Youth Administration was by far the more important agency. The NYA enabled millions of young Americans to complete an education, which would have otherwise been denied them, gave millions more vocational training of lasting value, was a vital contributor to the nation's defense effort, allowed minority groups to participate in its benefits according to need and not simply by population ratio, and provided community amenities of permanent value. Of all the myriad New Deal agencies, the NYA stands almost alone as an example of what can be accomplished when enlightened, committed people, if only for a short time, can get a grip on the public purse strings.

FOR ADDITIONAL INFORMATION: In addition to the official records of NYA in Washington, D.C., the reader would find helpful Paul B. Jacobson, "Youth at Work," *Bulletin of the National Association of Secondary School Principals* 25 (May 1941); James R. Kearney, *Anna Eleanor Roosevelt: The Evolution of a Reformer* (1968); Joseph P. Lash, *Eleanor and Franklin* (1971); Ernest K. Lindley and Betty Lindley, *A New Deal for Youth: The Story of the National Youth Administration* (1938); National Youth Administration, *Final Report of the National Youth Administration, Fiscal Years 1936-1943* (1944); and George P. Rawick, "The New Deal and Youth: The Civilian Conservation Corps, the National Youth Administration, the American Youth Congress" (Ph.D. dissertation, University of Wisconsin, 1957).

JOHN SALMOND

NATURALIZATION SERVICE. See Immigration and Naturalization Service.

NAVAL ACADEMY. See United States Naval Academy.

NAVY. See Department of the Navy.

NUCLEAR REGULATORY COMMISSION (NRC). The Nuclear Regulatory Commission, created by the Energy Reorganization Act of 1974, licenses and regulates most privately owned nuclear activities in the United States. The agency's history, however, dates from its predecessor agency, the Atomic Energy Commission, which was established by the Atomic Energy Act of 1946 and given a government monopoly in the development and utilization of nuclear energy. In 1954, Congress passed a revised Atomic Energy Act that allowed private commercial participation in many areas of nuclear technology. While charging the commission with responsibility for promoting the new industry, the 1954 act also recognized the public health and safety (as well as national security) implications of the production and use of nuclear materials and the generation of nuclear energy. Accordingly, the act vested broad regulatory powers in the commission.

In early 1955, the commission embarked on its dual functions of promotion and regulation of atomic energy. The agency's Power Demonstration Reactor Program was a keystone of its promotional activities. Although several promising nuclear-reactor designs to produce heat for electrical generation were being developed, it was by no means clear in the mid-1950s which ones would become the mainstays of the industry. Throughout the Demonstration Program, from 1955 to 1963, the commission offered funding to private companies for conducting research and development, waived charges for the loan of government-owned nuclear materials, and provided free research in government laboratories for certain mutually agreed-upon projects. The commission justified these federally provided incentives on the basis that private industry took on the economic risks of its proposed projects. By the end of the program, the light water reactor (boiling water and pressurized water designs) had emerged as the favored power generator of the nuclear industry.

Most American industries have been federally regulated only after they have been fully developed. In contrast, because of the recognized dangers in nuclear technology, the commission regulated this new industry before it came into general use. In fact, commission regulation progressed uniquely side-by-side with the promotional program. Regulation meant establishing standards by which the safety of plants was judged, commission review of designs and operating plans against those standards, and inspection of the construction and operation to ensure that all conditions were met. Each utility that planned to construct a power reactor had to apply to the commission for a construction permit; once the reactor was constructed, the utility needed a license to operate the reactor. During reactor operation, the utility had to comply with relevant commission regulations. Thus, the complete life cycle of the reactor was subject to commission oversight.

The commission initially organized a regulatory division reporting to the general manager, who was the overall operations officer for the agency. The division assembled its own staff of experts to evaluate applications for licenses and to develop safety criteria. Regulations were promulgated covering procedures for obtaining construction permits and operating licenses, the licensing of fuel materials for the reactors, the licensing of nuclear plant operators, standards for radiation protection, and rules of practice for licensing proceedings. But developing standards to judge whether reactors met the statutory requirement for "adequate" protection of the public health and safety proved to be a complex and time-consuming task. Design standards and siting criteria which were drafted early in the program were not always satisfactory simply because there were so many unanswered questions about the evolving technology and so little relevant operating experience. The commission's regulatory staff often had to rely on the development staff and, through informal cooperation, on license applicants for much of the basic data needed for safety evaluations. This soon led to charges about the compatibility of regulatory and promotional functions within the same agency.

The first serious doubts about the validity of the agency's regulatory process occurred in 1956 when the commission, in a three-to-one vote, authorized a construction permit to a utility consortium, the Power Reactor Development Company, to build a 100-megawatt (electric) fast breeder reactor at Lagoona Beach, Michigan, near Detroit. The commission did so despite a report by the agency's prestigious Advisory Committee on Reactor Safeguards that questioned whether the consortium could provide adequate information assuring safe operation prior to issuance of an operating license. The Safeguards Committee report's contents, held in confidence by the commission, were given by the dissenting commissioner, Thomas Murray, to the agency's congressional oversight committee, the Joint Committee on Atomic Energy. The doubts raised in the report led three AFL-CIO unions to initiate the first legal action in a reactor-licensing proceeding. The unions charged that the Atomic Energy Commission had violated its own regulations in issuing the contruction permit. After a protracted hearing and court appeals, the U.S. Supreme Court in 1961 ruled that the commission had followed correct procedures, thus validating the construction permit.

More important, however, because of the controversy raised by the case, the Joint Committee and the commission studied the regulatory framework. As a result, there were many changes in the commission's regulatory practices. A 1957 amendment to the law required public hearings on construction permits for power reactors and publication of key safety-related documents. Subsequent studies by the commission and the Joint Committee brought about several internal changes that, by 1963, separated organizationally the agency's regulatory functions from the operational and developmental programs. In 1961, the director of regulation for the first time reported directly to the commission rather than to the general manager. In 1963, the regulatory offices were physically separated from the promotional offices. Both the Joint Committee and the commission continuously discussed the question of creating a separate agency for regulation, but a final decision was postponed pending further development of the industry. By 1963, however, the commission had in place a regulatory organizational structure that remained basically intact until the inauguration of the Nuclear Regulatory Commission in January 1975.

In an important 1962 report to the President on nuclear energy, the commission concluded that nuclear power was "on the threshold of economic competitiveness." The report's prediction proved accurate, for throughout the 1960s and early 1970s, the electric power industry ordered many nuclear plants. In addition, reflecting industry's belief in economy of size, the power levels of proposed plants increased eight- to tenfold in several instances. This dynamic evolution greatly taxed the commission's regulators as they faced difficult safety questions about these larger and more advanced plants.

Because of the slim competitive margin of a nuclear plant compared to power plants using oil or coal as fuel, industry wanted rapid action on its nuclear reactor applications. Delay could mean economic loss. The agency, hoping to license reactors as quickly as possible while assuming substantial margins of safety, established what appeared as reasonable but conservative safety criteria. The regulators were successful in developing early technical criteria on such matters as urban siting and siting in seismic regions. When applied, for example, the criteria led to agency pressure on the Consolidated Edison Company to abandon plans for its 1962 proposed Ravenswood plant in New York City. Similarly, the criteria led the Pacific Gas and Electric to abandon its plans to construct the Bodega Bay facility on a site that was only 1,000 feet from the San Andreas fault in California. Furthermore, the agency was able to define its technical requirements in more specific terms. In the mid-1960s, the commission attempted a minimal level of reactor standardization by adopting a set of "General Design Criteria." The agency also instituted a somewhat standardized reactor-hazards evaluation process that included reviewing applications for key items such as quality assurance, redundancy controls, containment, and emergency-core cooling systems. In spite of this regulatory maturation, review times for power-reactor applications continued to increase. The unusual degree of uniqueness of each commercial reactor forced the regulators to rely on engineering judgment in many safety areas on almost a reactor-by-reactor basis. The process of identifying and evaluating the safety problems of individual custom-designed plants and applying the safety lessons learned from one reactor to another accounted in large part for the increasingly longer times required to license nuclear power plants.

New developments in the late 1960s and early 1970s added to the workload of the regulators. The National Environmental Policy Act of 1969 applied to nuclear power reactors, and in 1971, successful environmentalist intervention in the *Calvert Cliffs* court case forced the commission to incorporate wider environmental standards than it had done previously in its regulatory program. Until the passage of the environmental policy act, the agency had concerned itself only with the environmental consequences of radioactive effluents. The law's new requirements increased the complexity of regulating the technology.

Controversy over the safety of nuclear power mushroomed in the 1970s. Passage of the environmental act indicated a changing mood in the country and specifically signaled a growing concern for preserving environmental values. Faith in the benificence of technological advance, so common in the 1950s, no longer appeared to prevail. Queries on complex nuclear issues such as the adequacy of emergency-core cooling systems, thermal pollution, and radioactive waste disposal were more frequent, with no simple, clearcut answers forthcoming. Many citizens linked their doubts with a growing disillusionment about government objectivity in general. This feeling easily targeted nuclear regulation, housed in a federal agency historically tied to nuclear development, as a prime example of a regulatory body being compromised by the industry it regulated.

The twenty-year-old idea of completely separating the regulatory and promotional roles of the commission again surfaced and was debated. After protracted congressional hearings, the Energy Reorganization Act of 1974 abolished the Atomic Energy Commission while creating the Nuclear Regulatory Commission and the Energy Research and Development Administration.

The new commission faced two immediate tasks: to organize an adequate management structure, and to address the urgent regulatory issues it inherited from the Atomic Energy Commission. Since many of the commission's organizational units needed to carry out general administration, budget, public affairs, congressional liaison, and policy evaluation had been transferred to the Energy Research and Development Administration, the Nuclear Regulatory Commission spent much time during its first year establishing necessary support offices.

Although consuming significant resources, the organizational tasks were secondary to the ongoing work of licensing and regulation. Many additional pressing problems arose immediately, such as identifying new generic-reactor safety questions, monitoring the safety and environmental impact of the nuclear fuel cycle, safeguarding nuclear materials, reviewing Agreement State nuclear regulatory programs, undertaking an increased role in the export and import of nuclear materials and facilities, and participating in interagency efforts to support the government's program for limiting international proliferation of nuclear weapons capabilities. In addressing these issues, the new agency, just as the Atomic Energy Commission in its last years, has functioned to the present in a national atmosphere of sometimes-conflicting public concerns for development of new energy sources and protection of the environment.

FOR ADDITIONAL INFORMATION: Research in nuclear regulation must start with an understanding of the larger purposes of the Atomic Energy Commission. Three volumes of early nuclear history stand as much-acclaimed models for government history: Richard G. Hewlett and Oscar E. Anderson, Jr., *The New World* (1962); Hewlett and Francis Duncan, *Atomic Shield* (1969); and Hewlett and Duncan, *Nuclear Navy* (1974). Harold P. Green and Alan Rosenthal wrote an important book on the early work of the Joint Committee on Atomic Energy, *Government of the Atom* (1963). Objective, scholarly studies on nuclear regulation are few. The best to date include William H. Berman and Lee M. Hydeman, *The Atomic Energy Commission and Regulating Nuclear Facilities* (1961); Elizabeth S. Rolph, *Nuclear Power and the Public Safety* (1979); and David Okrent, *Nuclear Reactor Safety: On the History of the Regulatory Process* (1981).

GEORGE T. MAZUZAN

O

OCCUPATIONAL SAFETY AND HEALTH ADMINISTRATION (OSHA).

The Occupational Safety and Health Act (Public Law 91-596) became law on December 29, 1970, and took effect on April 28, 1971. Following 100 years of intensive industrial growth in the United States, OSHA was the first comprehensive nationwide attempt to insure occupational safety and health for America's workers. Prior to OSHA's organization, there had been scattered private and governmental initiatives to bring safety and health to the workplace, but these, at best, were only partially successful.

American activity in the area of safety and health began in the second half of the nineteenth century with the rapid growth of American industry. The earliest efforts to improve job safety and health were concentrated in the states, but these efforts were ineffective because of a lack of enforcement. In large measure, American society of the nineteenth century accepted occupational deaths and injuries as an integral part of the job. Most Americans viewed attempts to intervene in the operation of American business as unjustified intrusions, contrary to their belief in the free market and in individualism. Federal efforts to encourage safety and health slowly emerged by the end of the nineteenth century, but they were confined largely to individual problems in the public eye.

The growing publicity devoted to deaths and injuries on the job by muckraking reformers during the early twentieth century stimulated voluntary industry attention to occupational safety. This was part of a major industry effort to control the worst abuses of the free market in order to prevent an erosion of public support and resulting mandatory government regulation.

The second decade of the twentieth century saw the first comprehensive efforts to deal with industrial injuries and deaths. These efforts occurred on the state level in the area of compensation. Industry, government, and labor agreed that a new approach to the problem of compensation for on-the-job accidents was necessary. By 1920, the majority of the states had compensation systems that provided workers with set payments but retracted their right to sue for damages. Scientific research on occupational disease proved to be the only other serious measure undertaken to deal with workplace safety and health during the first three decades of the twentieth century. In 1914, the federal government organized the Office of Industrial Hygiene within the Public Health Service* to undertake occupational disease studies. Independent researchers, especially Alice Hamilton, also made important scientific contributions.

The years after World War I saw little legislative activity in the area of safety and health. Industry's voluntary program seemed to satisfy both government and the public. The depression and the willingness of workers to take any available job prolonged the disinterest in workplace safety and health.

In 1935, during the New Deal, however, several federal initiatives were taken, including federal funding of industrial hygiene units in state and local agencies and federal passage of the Walsh-Healey Public Contracts Act. This act required employers with government contracts exceeding $10,000 to comply with Department of Labor* health and safety standards. Lack of vigorous enforcement reduced the effectiveness of the regulations.

The first effective federal safety program applied to coal mining. Sensational calamities, the same motivation that had led to the organization of the Bureau of Mines over forty years earlier, stimulated this effort. The 1952 Federal Coal Mine Safety Act authorized development and enforcement of standards to prevent "major disasters." In 1946, the Metal and Nonmetallic Mine Safety Act was passed, regulating the minerals industry.

The evolving environmental movement and continued mine disasters were the principal stimuli for passage of the Occupational Safety and Health Act of 1970 and the agency that bears the same name. Concern over water and air pollution and a fear that America's wildlife and scenic beauty were being destroyed grew during the 1960s. Beginning in 1963, several Clear Air Acts were passed, constituting the first serious efforts to regulate environmental quality.

In January 1968, President Lyndon B. Johnson proposed the nation's first comprehensive occupational health and safety program, but the bill died in committee. President Johnson's decision to withdraw from the 1968 presidential race and the lukewarm support that organized labor gave the bill led to its failure. Organized labor's weak support stemmed from its failure to regard workplace safety and health as a key collective bargaining issue. Ignorance of health dangers in the workplace, acceptance of job-related accidents as a fact of life, and fear that improving workplace safety and health through collective bargaining might necessitate wage concessions influenced labor's attitude.

By 1969, support for a comprehensive law had increased. In November 1968, a mine explosion in Farmington, West Virginia, killed seventy-eight miners and served as the catalyst for passage of the comprehensive Coal Mine and Safety Act of 1969. Following passage of this act, Democratic congressional forces began to push for a comprehensive occupational safety and health bill. At the same time, President Richard Nixon, in an effort to win greater blue collar support for his programs, began to call for "proposals to help guarantee the health and safety of workers." Organized labor's leadership now resolved to obtain a comprehensive law. The Farmington mine disaster, a growing rank-and-file movement for safety and health, and efforts by public interest groups, especially Ralph Nader's effort, forced labor to move quickly on the issue before it became a political liability. Meanwhile, industry decided it could not win a fight to kill such a bill and resolved to work for the most unstructured bill possible.

While a consensus had emerged by 1969 that the time was right for a comprehensive bill, differences remained concerning the shape of the bill. The key issue was the location of authority to set and enforce standards. The Nixon Administration and its Republican supporters in Congress and private industry wanted to disperse these powers among several agencies, while congressional Democrats and the AFL-CIO wanted all authority to reside in the Department of Labor, which was thought to be historically sympathetic to workers. All the while, extensive lobbying by a variety of interest groups was under way. Jack Sheehan, a chief union lobbyist, noted that he and his colleagues spent day and night on Capitol Hill fighting for labor's version of the bill. The Steelworkers bussed members to Washington to intensify labor's lobbying effort. Meanwhile, business lobbyists were also highly visible.

The legislative process saw a series of bills introduced in committee in both the House and Senate. Eventually, the House accepted the Republican version, or the Steiger bill, in place of the Democratic, or Daniels bill, which had been approved in committee. The Democratic-controlled Senate passed the Williams bill, which was supported heavily by labor. The Conference Committee hammered out a compromise bill. To insure that standard setting was left to the Secretary of Labor, a key union demand, the Democrats agreed to delete a provision authorizing the Secretary of Labor to shut down a plant immediately if a life-threatening situation existed. The substituted provision allowed the Department of Labor's inspectors to cite business violations of standards but required a court order to shut down a dangerous operation.

While the Republicans, for the most part, were not pleased with the Conference Committee bill, it was approved. This was due to the Nixon Administration's decision that a comprehensive bill be passed. Jack Sheehan has noted that the administration continually gave ground as the legislative process evolved. It was committed to building a blue collar constituency, and, therefore, it would not oppose a bill that would have a direct impact on the lives and health of America's workers. President Nixon signed the bill on December 29, 1970, just before the end of the legislative session.

The final bill, the Williams-Steiger Occupational Safety and Health Act of 1970, required almost every private employer to "furnish each of his employees employment and a place of employment . . . free from recognized hazards . . . likely to cause death or serious physical harm to his employees." The act also established a process for the development of standards. For toxic substances, the act specifically required the Secretary of Labor to set standards assuring employee health regardless of length of toxic exposure.

Equally significant, the act authorized OSHA's inspectors to enter any workplace without prior notice. Both employer and employee representatives were allowed to accompany OSHA compliance officers on their inspections. The act also specified penalties for violation. Employers, however, were able to contest violations and/or penalties by appealing to the Occupational Safety and Health Review Commission, an independent body composed of three presidentially appointed members. Judicial review of penalties by the U.S. Court of Appeals was also guaranteed. While the federal government oversaw OSHA, the states were authorized to establish their own programs as long as they were as effective as the federal plan.

In addition, the act provided for the establishment of a National Institute for Occupational Safety and Health in the Department of Health, Education, and Welfare (Department of Health and Human Services*) to carry out research and related activities on occupational safety and health. Employer recordkeeping to aid in uncovering the causes of occupational accidents and illnesses was mandated, as were statistical studies to improve the effectiveness of the overall program.

OSHA's first few years were highly contentious. While the labor movement had been quick to view it as its agency, the early direction and management came from Republican administrations whose relationships with the labor movement were chilly, at best. Differences between labor and the Nixon Administration first surfaced over the issue of agency staffing. OSHA's first director was George C. Guenther, a Pennsylvania businessman who had previously served as chief of the Labor Department's Bureau of Labor Standards. He was probably chosen by several industry lobbyists, and labor resented not being consulted in the selection. The unions immediately criticized Guenther for failing to appoint union representatives to senior positions.

The adoption of 400 pages of national consensus standards almost one month to the day after the act took effect proved to be another inflammatory issue. This appeared to be both a mandate of the OSHA Act and an aggressive first step by the Nixon Administration to give OSHA a solid foundation. The national consensus standards were a collection of voluntary guidelines industry had evolved over many years. Many were irrelevant to safety and health, while others were petty or inappropriate as mandatory and enforceable standards. The adoption of the consensus standards made small business and its lobbyists, who originally had been unenthusiastic about OSHA during the legislative debate, outright enemies of the act. They considered it a dangerous and unwarranted intrusion in their affairs.

The labor movement, the natural constituent of OSHA, also was not pleased. It saw OSHA concentrating on less serious problems to avoid tackling dangerous workplace hazards. Many in the labor movement speculated that the enforcement of national consensus standards was a ploy by an uncommitted Republican administration to discredit and cripple OSHA. While the Nixon Administration had no desire to make OSHA a vigorous regulator of American workplaces, it is highly unlikely that it attempted to destroy an agency it had helped to create.

The rapid promulgation of the consensus standards was probably an attempt to present an image of a functioning and effective agency. During hearings on the OSHA bill, it was agreed that consensus standards were the most appropriate standards to launch OSHA. In large measure, this was a reasonable first step. However, a selective analysis of these voluminous, voluntary, industry guidelines was not undertaken. Selection of only the most important standards would have proved far more effective and less controversial in the long run.

OSHA's early efforts focused on safety inspections, while scant resources were devoted to the generation of health standards or to health-related inspections. In fact, between 1973 and the first half of 1975, only slightly over 10 percent of inspections were health-related, for two reasons. First, OSHA did not have the industrial hygiene expertise during its early years to conduct health inspections. In fact, there were fewer than two thousand industrial hygienists in the United States in 1970, and, as late as 1973, OSHA employed only sixty-eight of them. Second, health inspections, with their potential for heavy expenditures to upgrade facilities, would have increased industry attacks on OSHA. The Nixon Administration preferred to avoid such a situation.

OSHA eventually was forced to adopt several vigorous health standards and to announce a health hazard targeting program to appease vocal criticism from the labor movement. In December 1971, in direct response to pressure from the Industrial Union Department (IUD) of the AFL-CIO, the Secretary of Labor announced an emergency standard for asbestos followed by a permanent standard. Finding the permanent standard inadequate, the IUD filed suit (*IUD* v. *Hodgson*), claiming OSHA had given unjust consideration to economic issues in generating its final standard. The court upheld OSHA, and, for the first time, a directive to consider costs in developing standards was announced. This was a victory for business, which felt that a cost-benefit analysis should be an integral part of the standards development process.

In April 1973, John Stender, a former official of the Boilermakers' Union and a Republican loyalist, replaced Guenther as head of OSHA. Under Stender, OSHA issued permanent health standards for fourteen carcinogens and vinyl chloride. As with asbestos, the initial impetus for these standards came from union petitions for emergency standards.

By 1975, OSHA had struggled through five years of operation hampered by vocal, public dissatisfaction. While industry felt the agency had abused its authority and become a needless and expensive burden, labor felt it had never truly fulfilled its mandate to protect workers to the greatest extent possible. Congressional oversight also found OSHA lacking administrative expertise and a clear sense of direction. OSHA suffered further damage during the Watergate investigations when a memorandum was uncovered revealing George Guenther's suggestion to Nixon Administration officials that promises to relieve business from OSHA enforcement could be used to attract Republican contributions for the 1972 Nixon reelection campaign. While there was no direct evidence that this policy was ever carried out, the labor movement and its supporters repeatedly used this memorandum as proof that OSHA had never been properly administered or supported by Republicans.

In an attempt to improve OSHA's operations, the Ford Administration appointed a third director, Dr. Morton Corn, in 1975. He was the first health professional to run the agency. Almost immediately, he designed a more centralized OSHA structure to insure that policy emanated from Washington rather than from the field. He expanded OSHA's technical expertise, developed a program to attract more industrial hygienists to the agency, and placed new emphasis on health-hazard inspections. In addition, he began a vigorous effort to speed the promulgation of health standards and attempted to prune the voluminous and unpopular consensus safety standards. He also upgraded labor, business, and public participation in the development of OSHA policy by emphasizing the National Advisory Committee on Occupational Safety and Health, a committee established by legislative statute. Improved communication was also enhanced with other federal agencies.

Corn's tenure at OSHA was brief because of the Carter presidential victory in November 1976, but his efforts to improve OSHA were continued by his replacement, another health professional, Dr. Eula Bingham. For the first time, it was clear that OSHA was in the hands of policymakers sympathetic to labor. Organized labor was intimately involved in the selection of Bingham, and its advice was actively sought in policymaking decisions.

In May 1977, Bingham and Secretary of Labor Ray Marshall announced their OSHA policy of "Common Sense Priorities." While it varied little from Corn's program, it was highly publicized. The key priorities were a focus on serious dangers, a streamlining of regulations, and efforts to help small businessmen comply with OSHA regulations without undue hardship.

Under Bingham, nine major health standards, many of which were initiated by Corn, were issued. Most significantly, a generic cancer standard established a method for identifying, classifying, and regulating potential occupational carcinogens which were viewed as epidemic problems. Other standards limited exposure to benzene, the pesticide DBCP, arsenic, cotton dust, acrylonitrile, and lead. The lead standard, for the first time, provided for mandatory transfer of workers with high blood-lead levels without loss of pay or other benefits. Another standard guaranteed workers access to employer-monitored medical and toxic-exposure records.

In the compliance area, Bingham concentrated inspections on industries with the most serious health problems. By 1980, there was a significant increase in citations for serious, willful, and repeated violations. In addition, under Bingham OSHA used the courts to further its enforcement efforts. More firms were prosecuted by the Justice Department* for inspection violations than during both the Nixon and Ford years.

Industry increasingly challenged OSHA's regulations in the courts during the Carter years. In February 1980, the Supreme Court, in a unanimous decision (*Marshall* v. *Whirlpool*), upheld the right of workers to refuse a job that presented an immediate danger of death or serious injury. Also in 1980, OSHA's benzene standard was overturned on grounds that it had not been proven necessary to prevent significant health risks. OSHA's regulation requiring employers to pay employees for time spent accompanying OSHA compliance officers on inspections was vacated. Finally, the cotton dust and lead standards were on the Supreme Court's docket when the Carter Administration left office.

Of special significance were OSHA's efforts to aid small businesses and workers during Bingham's tenure. Small businesses were offered free consultation, their recordkeeping requirements were reduced, and they were more fully involved in the OSHA rule-making process. Furthermore, the "New Directions" program in 1978 provided grants to unions, employers, and nonprofit organizations to increase safety and health expertise.

Despite the reorganization of OSHA during the Carter years, the agency remained as controversial as ever. Many people in industry felt OSHA's tilt toward workers went too far during the Bingham years. Businessmen and others believed that OSHA's reluctance to weigh costs against benefits in generating standards was irresponsible, leading to excessive costs for business to achieve compliance. Others, especially in labor, argued that it was immoral to weigh costs against benefits when death and injury were potential outcomes. Equally controversial was an increasing number of studies suggesting that OSHA had not reduced injury rates significantly. These debates insured ongoing efforts to redesign OSHA. In 1980, Senator Richard Schweiker (Republican, Pennsylvania) made the most serious attempt to restructure OSHA by introducing a bill to exempt from inspection workplaces with better-than-average accident records. Labor rallied its forces in an intense national lobbying effort, and the bill, which would have eliminated from inspection a majority of workplaces, died in committee.

The Reagan Administration has initiated a major revamping of OSHA by administrative rather than legislative action. Under Thorne Auchter, a former Florida businessman, OSHA has made a major effort to become as untroubling to industry as possible. While industry complaints about the agency have fallen, labor complaints have risen dramatically. Over ten years after the OSHA act's passage, the agency is no longer threatened with extinction. However, its basic design, with emphasis on developing and enforcing standards, insures that it will always displease either industry or labor. Nevertheless, OSHA has stimulated industry efforts to protect workers on the job, spurred union bargaining on safety and health, and increased knowledge and research on occupational safety and health.

FOR ADDITIONAL INFORMATION: Research on OSHA should begin with a study of secondary literature, which includes John Mendelhoff, *Regulating Safety: An Economic and Political Analysis of Occupational Safety and Health Policy* (1979); Nicholas A. Ashford, *Crisis in the Workplace* (1976); and *The Job Safety and Health Act* (1971), an analysis of the act and its legislative history. Also useful are Robert Stewart Smith, *The Occupational Safety and Health Act* (1976); Herbert Northrup, et al., *The Impact of OSHA*

(1978); and Joseph Page and Mary-Win O'Brien, *Bitter Wages* (1973), a work sponsored by Ralph Nader. The primary sources include the eleven volumes of the *OSHA-History Project*, located in the Office of the Historian, Department of Labor, Washington, D.C.; the federal records of OSHA, located in the National Archives*; summary newsletters, for example, the *Occupational Safety and Health Reporter*; and popular accounts in the press. The relative youth of OSHA allows personal interviews with key participants in the agency's development. This author has taped oral interviews with John Sheehan, legislative director for the United Steelworkers, and with then Senator Harrison Williams (Democrat, New Jersey).

PAUL D. ADDIS

OCEAN SURVEY. See National Ocean Survey.

OFFICE OF CHILD DEVELOPMENT. See Children's Bureau.

OFFICE OF EDUCATION. See Department of Education.

OFFICE OF HUMAN DEVELOPMENT SERVICES. See Children's Bureau.

OFFICE OF MANAGEMENT AND BUDGET (OMB). Observers of American politics have long recognized the central role that the Office of Management and Budget plays through its fiscal and legislative clearance, program coordination and development, budget preparation, and, to a lesser extent, executive management functions. Indeed, the OMB is the most highly developed administrative coordinating and program review unit in the executive office and provides the central institutional mechanism for imprinting (some would say, inflicting) presidential will over the government. While OMB's primary staff responsibility is budget preparation and execution, the office is also responsible for evaluating the performance of federal programs; reviewing organizational structures and management processes within the executive branch; coordinating the President's legislative program; preparing and clearing Executive Orders and proclamations; planning and promoting the development of and coordination of federal statistical services; and advising the President on the activities of all federal departments and agencies.

The OMB has undergone several major changes since its inception (Bureau of the Budget) as part of the 1921 Budget and Accounting Act. President Warren Harding selected General Charles G. Dawes, a former chief of Supply Procurement for the American Army in France and a future Vice-President of the United States, as the first director of the Bureau of the Budget (BOB). In Budget Circular No. 1 of June 29, 1921, Dawes established certain cardinal principles for the BOB. Success of the budget system would depend on basic tenets which needed to be so firmly entrenched that they would never be questioned in the future. These commandments were that the BOB should remain impartial, impersonal, and nonpolitical, the budget director should act as an adviser to department officials on matters of business administration; and the director's request for administrative information should take precedence over competing claims of Cabinet officials.

Dawes insisted that his agency had nothing to do with policymaking, but only with economy and efficiency in routine government business. He said that "much as it loved the President, if Congress in its omnipotence over appropriations and in accordance with its authority over policy, passed a law that garbage should be put on the White House steps, it would be our regrettable duty, as a bureau, in an impartial, non-political way and non-partisan way to advise the Executive and Congress as to how the largest amount of garbage could be spread in the most expeditious and economical manner" (Charles Dawes, *The First Year of the Budget of the United States*, 1923, p. 178). Dawes was, of course, involved in policymaking. The so-called politics-administration dichotomy represented, in practice, not the separation of one from the other, but the dominance of administrative values over political ones.

This was a period of retrenchment in government spending. Dawes's enthusiasm, his excellent working relationship with the President, and his keen sense of historical mission were important in establishing the BOB as the President's primary staff agent for ensuring economy and efficiency in matters of routine business. Yet, Dawes's insistence that one could not successfully preach economy without practicing it was interpreted as a mandatory self-imposed policy for the BOB. In the final entry of his diary, Dawes wrote that of the $225,000 appropriated for the BOB for 1922, about $120,000 had been spent in the year's work; it took its own medicine. "Taking its own medicine" almost destroyed the usefulness of the BOB. The emphasis on matters of routine business was countered by Dawes's neglect of government-wide administrative reform. He viewed administrative management as part of the budget review process of identifying waste and reducing spending.

Dawes's successors, General H. M. Lord and Colonel J. Clawson Roop, showed similar patterns of leadership. Lord actually checked employees' desks for excessive use of official stationery, paper clips, and other government supplies. Lord engaged in such quaint-sounding ploys as establishing a "Two Per Cent Club" for agency heads who trimmed that amount off their estimates, a "One Per Cent Club" reserved for the less efficient, and the "Loyal Order of Woodpeckers," whose motto read: "All hail to the loyal Order of Woodpeckers, whose persistent tapping away at waste will make cheerful music in government offices and workshops the coming year." Administrative management activities were reduced to supervising travel regulations and negotiating reduced hotel rates for government employees. The bureau directed federal agencies to use the Army radio network instead of telephones, and gave commendations for taking upper berths in Pullmans and for using brooms until they were completely worn out.

This self-imposed parsimony forced key issues of administrative management to the background. By 1937, however, President Franklin D. Roosevelt was simply overwhelmed by the administrative aspects of an expanded modern government. On January 10, 1937, Roosevelt met with his Committee on Administrative Management. In no uncertain terms, he informed his guests that he needed both personal and institutional help.

The FDR Committee believed it was ludicrous for the BOB's appropriation to be less than that of any finance agency or accounting division in government; yet, with a staff of forty-five it was expected to prepare a billion dollar budget. The BOB's major failing, however, had been in administrative management. Progress had been achieved in the fiscal area, but the bureau had not even approached its fullest potential in the area of administrative management. FDR's committee looked to the bureau as a directing and controlling agency because the President needed a staff to help manage the executive branch. The "salvation by staff" theme embodied in the Brownlow recommendations was a two-pronged idea: the President would receive both personal and institutional assistance in the job of being President. These functions were by no means the same. His personal assistants (few in number) would serve the immediate political interests of the President; the institutional staff (larger in number) would provide continuity and a government-wide perspective of and for the presidency.

After much political negotiating, the basic lines of the Brownlow report were enacted into law in Reorganization Plan No. 1 of April 25, 1939, which established the new Executive Office of the President (EOP) and transferred to it the BOB (from Treasury)* and the National Resources Planning Board (from Interior)*. The reinvigorated BOB was at the center of this newly institutionalized presidency. The functions assigned to the Budget Bureau by Executive Order 8248 of September 8, 1939, illustrated the magnitude of its role. The born-again BOB needed leadership of far greater vision and administrative ability than it had received since 1921. On March 11, 1939, Harold D. Smith, budget director for the state of Michigan, was appointed by President Roosevelt as director of the reconstituted BOB. Both a strong proponent of the Brownlow recommendations for administrative reform and a personal friend of Brownlow, Smith molded the BOB into an indispensable presidential managerial staff and, in doing so, established the budget director as a key adviser to the President. Smith possessed a far broader vision of the BOB's role in the federal system than his predecessors and is truly one of the unheralded administrators in the history of American political institutions.

Between 1939 and 1970, the BOB escaped public notoriety. Aside from standard "green-eyeshade" or "abominable no-man" jokes, the BOB benefited (and in many ways earned) the image of a reasonably impartial, objective, presidential staff agency. If the budget director was sometimes used as a presidential firefighter on political issues, the Budget Bureau as an institution was rarely looked to or perceived as a source of partisan support. In 1970, the BOB was replaced by the Office of Management and Budget. The demands of the 1960s revealed certain institutional weaknesses. First, the BOB's management arm proved unable to ameliorate the many intergovernmental problems facing both President and country; second, in order to service a legislatively activist President, the bureau traded its long-run institutional perspective for short-term influence as the peddler of task force reports and unrealistic budget predictions. Moreover, over time (beginning in the Eisenhower years) the BOB career staff had rigidified. Presidential expectations surpassed bureau capabilities, and no one could turn off external demands. The 1970 reorganization provided the President with increased institutional staff capabilities in program evaluation and coordination, government organization, information and management systems, and the development of executive talent. Yet, the division of government into two interests—the Domestic Council (what) and OMB (how and how well)—assumed that policy could be separated from administration.

The most crushing blow to OMB's credibility came during the Watergate period. In the last months of the Nixon Administration, with the President's attention focused primarily on legal matters, responsibility for running the government literally fell to the OMB and Nixon loyalist Roy Ash. At the peak of Watergate, journalist John Herbers reported that the OMB had begun administering the Nixon policies, including controlling the day-to-day operations of the domestic bureaucracy and, in effect, making decisions that should have been made by Cabinet or agency officials. With John Ehrlichman and several members of the domestic council staff either under investigation or indicted, the OMB moved into the role vacated by the domestic council. In particular, Ash, Deputy Director Frederic V. Malek, and the four associate directors (Pads) replaced the domestic council as the critical link between agency heads and the White House.

The OMB's credibility as an objective staff agency remains tarnished from events of the 1970s when it was referred to as the Office of Meddling and Bumbling, an appellation characterizing this intolerable interference into the internal management processes of departments and agencies. Moreover, by the conclusion of the Nixon Administration, all perceptions of OMB's neutrality had been dispelled. President Gerald Ford's transition team accused OMB of becoming too involved in departmental policy processes and of politicizing the budgetary decision-making process. The Congressional Budget Office, House and Senate budget committees, statutory curbs on impoundment, and confirmation requirements for the OMB director and deputy director were intended by Congress to serve as mechanisms for improving OMB's responsiveness to nonpresidential clients. In its 1976 presidential transition recommendations, the National Academy of Public Administration (NAPA) concluded that, while the staff of the Office of Management and Budget "must be sensitive to the political problems of the President, [it] is essential that the President have available to him the OMB professional judgment on how best to achieve his presidential objectives. To the extent any politicizing effects of the Nixon White House remain, these should be eliminated promptly" ("The President and Executive Management: Summary of a Symposium" [1976] p. 18).

This perceived politicization disheartened those who valued OMB's predecessor, the Bureau of the Budget, as the bastion for "neutral competence" in American government—an American equivalent to the British civil service cadre at Whitehall. BOB recruits, educated by the best the civil service offered, emerged from orientation meetings believing that theirs was a select presidential mission. Few spoke in terms of personal pronouns, and those seeking individual record-building usually found employment elsewhere. Budget Bureau veterans, proud of their relatively small staff size and their location at the center of the resource allocation system in American politics, viewed themselves as the elite of the civil service, which had to protect an "institutional pride." BOB officials often told the story, for example, that if a Martian army marched on the Capitol, everybody in Washington would flee to the hills, except the Budget Bureau staff, which would stay behind and prepare for an orderly transition in government.

Contrary to popular myth and bureaucratic folklore, the OMB is neither a program administrator nor an independent policymaker—unless the President (at significant costs) desires OMB to approximate such a role. Moreover, in its staff capacity, OMB continually faces the danger of overextending its responsibilities into the political and operating levels or narrowing its role and viewpoint through concentration on routine details. This is not an apologia for OMB's lost innocence. Rather, the OMB (professional staff of budget examiners and management specialists) are convenient whipping posts for those, as William Carey observed, "who are left holding losers stubs in the budgetary sweepstakes" (William Carey, "The Roles of the Bureau of the Budget, paper [1966], p. 5)—all of which serves to illustrate the old bureaucratic adage, "where one stands depends upon when one sits." To some, OMB examiners substitute their judgment for department expertise in making budget decisions, but OMB staffers argue that theirs is but a presidential mission acting on direct instructions from the OMB director, who is *primus inter pares* among senior presidential advisers. When Hale Champion left his post as Undersecretary of Health, Education and Welfare* in June 1979, he told an interviewer for *The National Journal* that his biggest disappointment occurred in dealings with OMB, which he called "too big, too complicated and too inexperienced to run this government." Champion observed that the OMB staff "tries to get too far into the details of individual programs and individual departments that they don't understand. They say that they represent the President's interests, but, with the exception of trying to get budget control, I think they basically represent what they think about various program operations" (*National Journal*, June 16, 1979, p. 998). OMB's dilemma is that its effectiveness depends upon responsiveness to presidential needs. The President must decide whether he wants a partisan agent or a politically sensitive budget/management staff. As executors of Maurice Stan's law—"good budgeting is the uniform distribution of dissatisfaction"—OMB responds to presidential instructions. President Jimmy Carter delegated extraordinary responsibilities to Budget Director James "Dr. No" McIntyre, Jr., and David Stockman, President Ronald Reagan's director, seeks primarily to please the President.

OMB can live with this reputation as long as distinctions are maintained between the President's need for a politically sensitive OMB and the President's utilization of OMB as a partisan instrument for managing the executive branch. OMB can serve a President in many ways, but it is unparalleled for offering an analytic and reasonably impartial perspective on executive branch programs. A President who believes he no longer needs an institutional conscience loses what the OMB exists to provide. OMB must play within the game rules if it is to survive as a credible presidential staff. A President has many people telling him what to do, but he needs staff, which can perform the essential support functions effectively. So long as it is that "abominable no-man," OMB can take the heat as an occupational hazard. The OMB is still the closest thing a President has to an interest-free perspective on executive branch policies, but only if the President distinguishes institutional from personal-staff services. OMB staff at all levels can be engaged in policymaking as well as coordination—so long as it is performed without the spur of preordained partisan program decisions that set forth what, when, how, and by whom. It is otherwise impossible to make or coordinate policy—or to be objective. No OMB can protect the President and develop options when White House staff interpose themselves and their judgments between staff agency and President. Recent experience has revealed that an Office of Meddling and Bumbling gains little credibility in the executive establishment and helps neither itself nor the President.

FOR ADDITIONAL INFORMATION: Charles Dawes, *The First Year of the Budget of the United States* (1923); Herbert Emmerich, *Federal Organization and Administrative Management* (1971); and U.S. *President's Committee on Administrative Management, Report of the Committee, with Studies of Administrative Management in the Federal Government* (1937). For a fascinating look at this period, see the *Harold D. Smith Diary* in the Franklin D. Roosevelt Presidential Library, Hyde Park. Also see Larry Berman, *The Office of Management and Budget and the Presidency, 1921-1979* (1979); *The Bureau of the Budget During the Administration of President Lyndon B. Johnson*, November 1963-January 1969, 2 vols., Lyndon Baines Johnson Library. See also U.S. Congress, Senate, *Establish a Commission on the Organization and Management of the Executive Branch*, Hearings before the Subcommittee on Executive Reorganization of the Committee on Government Operations (1968), p. 2. Also see Task Forces (1966 Outside), box 4, "Outside 1966 Task Force on Government Organization"—the Heineman Task Force, Lyndon Baines Johnson Library, Austin.

Other useful citations are Aaron Wildavsky, *The Politics of the Budgetary Process*, 2d ed. (1974); John Herbers, "The Other Presidency," *New York Times Magazine* (March 3, 1974): 16; Joel Havemann, "OMBs New Faces Retain Power, Structure Under Ford," *National Journal* 7 (July 26, 1975): 1074; Philip Shabecoff, "Budget Office Withstands Moves to Cut Its Powers," *The New York Times* (November 11, 1974); Frederick Mosher, et al., *Watergate: Implications for Responsible Government* (1974), pp. 41-42. "The President and Executive Management: Summary of a Symposium" (The National Academy of Public Administration, 1976), p. 18, mimeographed; Hugh Heclo, "OMB and the Presidency: The Problem of Neutral Competence." *Public Interest* 38 (Winter 1975): 84; William Carey, "The Roles of the Bureau of the Budget," Paper delivered at the Fourteenth Annual Meeting of the Markle Scholars, Lake Placid, New York (September 30, 1966), p. 5; and Linda Demokovich, "The Rewards and Frustrations of the Federal Bureaucracy," *National Journal* (June 16, 1979): 998.

LARRY BERMAN

OFFICE OF PERSONNEL MANAGEMENT (OPM). No institution of the federal government over the past century had as much impact on the civil service of the United States as did the Civil Service Commission and its principal successor, the Office of Personnel Management. And most of the story is a very positive one. Over a span of ninety-six years, the central personnel agency was called the U.S. Civil Service Commission. Only since January 1979 has it been the Office of Personnel Management, buttressed by two related agencies, the Merit Systems Protection Board and the Federal Labor Relations Authority.

From the status of watchdog guarding against partisan machinations affecting government job appointments to that of a modern executive agency concerned with the motivation and productivity of civil servants, the central personnel establishment has, at various stages in its century-long career, been at the center of pressure and controversy, of leadership and foot-dragging, of charge and countercharge, of brilliant imagination and shallow obtuseness, of success and failure. Yet, with all its ups and downs, this agency—in its continually expanding roles—has helped shape what is undoubtedly (political candidates' strident attacks to the contrary notwithstanding) the most competent, the most effective, and the most influential civil service in the modern world. From the original civil service reform movement of the 1870s to the much-debated neo-reforms of the 1970s, the central personnel organization has been the principal mechanism through which vast changes were initiated and made operable. For this and other reasons, it is fully deserving of our intensive examination.

It has long been understood that the origins of the Civil Service Commission lay not in farsighted visions of modern personnel management but in the need to break the hold that the partisan "spoils system" had on appointments and tenure in the federal civil service. Every President from Abraham Lincoln onwards, being plagued with party henchmen scrambling for jobs, had advocated better methods of filling the posts of a growing government but had not succeeded with a reluctant, spoils-minded Congress. A rider on an appropriation bill in 1871 did provide for entry examinations, an administering agency was set up, and some examinations were actually held, but funds were discontinued just two years later. Meanwhile, reform-minded leaders kept up pressure for change. It was not until President James G. Garfield was assassinated by a disappointed office-seeker in 1881 that the nation was finally galvanized into action. Historians Charles A. and Mary R. Beard, in *The Rise of American Civilization* (1927), aptly encapsulated the country's reaction: "That cruel shot rang throughout the land, driving into the heads of the most hardened political henchmen the idea that there was something disgraceful in reducing the Chief Executive of the United States to the level of a petty job broker."

A bill to establish a merit system, drafted by the National Civil Service Reform League, was introduced by Senator George Pendleton of Ohio, in 1881, but languished until after the fall elections of 1882 had demonstrated that the people considered civil service reform a "must." It was finally passed and signed into law in January 1883. That was the basic act establishing the first durable central personnel agency and outlining the elements of a merit system for filling and retaining government jobs. It was the birthday of the U.S. Civil Service Commission—which was often reorganized and from time to time expanded in function but which was not totally revamped or superseded until 1979.

Thus established in an atmosphere of negativism—a determination to throw roadblocks in the path of making government personnel decisions under the philosophy of "to the victor belong the spoils"—the original commission focused on keeping undesirables out of government, not on positive steps to recruit the best minds and hands. Gradually, this negative purpose was transformed so that, by the late 1930s and 1940s, the emphasis was on programs that bear greater resemblance to modern personnel management.

Of special importance is the remarkable durability of the basic principles of the 1883 Civil Service Act. It was a blueprint for a civil service that America could respect and trust. Even the Civil Service Reform Act of 1978, which created the most comprehensive organizational changes in nearly a century, did not really alter the basic thrust of the original idea. It clarified organizational arrangements and other features, created new emphases, and provided greater specificity, but essentially the basic principles advocated in the 1870s and 1880s "stood both the test of time and the transition of the United States from a pioneer society to one of the most complex in the world" (U.S. Civil Service Commission, *Biography of an Ideal* [1974], p. 45).

From inauspicious beginnings, with very limited scope and budget, the commission was gradually but steadily extended in function. In the early decades, this took the form almost exclusively of greater jurisdiction in applying merit methods to government employment. Administering the merit system is the number-one function even to this day. And it is the main reason why a former official of the commission observed that the institution remains "different things to different people."

However the commission and its successors may be viewed by these or other client groups, this central personnel establishment has become a significant influence on the manner in which the bureaucracy is run through its impact on the quality and treatment of career workers. The original Civil Service Act contained a remarkably useful provision—permitting a succession of presidents to expand the proportion of government positions covered by the merit system, from a very limited body of jobs at its birth to the overwhelming bulk of the service at this day. Notable in this expansion were the substantial extensions ordered by Presidents Theodore Roosevelt (who had been one of the early Civil Service commissioners), Woodrow Wilson, and Franklin Roosevelt. There was even some modest growth during the administrations of William H. Taft, Calvin Coolidge, and Herbert Hoover. Obviously, such expansion necessitated an enlargement of the size of the Civil Service Commission and, as this maturing ensued, invited reliance on the commission to take over a continually increasing variety of activities relating to the personnel function (and on occasion some that were rather remote).

Among the early substantive additions to the commission's role were the

Retirement Act of 1920 (subsequently revised and liberalized many times), providing for deferred compensation to long-time civil servants upon leaving the service; and the Classification Act of 1923, providing an orderly system for evaluating jobs and fixing salaries (likewise amended in many respects, particularly through a complete revamping in 1949, through pay reform measures, notably in 1962 and 1970, and through revisions in its upper reaches effective in 1980). Although sometimes started under special, independent agencies of their own, these and other functions were always fairly promptly transferred to the already existing commission, as it became more and more the logical repository of responsibilities that governed the handling of personnel matters.

Even before World War II, there were signs of this central agency focusing on general oversight and decentralizing some daily personnel operations to the various departments of government. Almost from the beginning, the system for examining for entry into the service depended on the use of boards of examiners staffed by specialists from the departments where the jobs to be filled existed. The new Classification Act of 1949 later gave a new impetus to decentralization by requiring the commission to concentrate on standard-setting and by allowing agencies to classify their own jobs subject to post-audit. But both before, during, and following the war, federal managers and students of the scene roundly criticized the commission for holding too tightly to detailed controls and not letting agencies handle the daily grist of personnel operations to meet their pressing needs.

During the early years of Roosevelt's New Deal, impatience with the government's personnel policies and their centralized administration led to the creation of separate merit systems (independent of the commission) for several new agencies, notably the Farm Credit Administration, the Social Security Board,* and the Tennessee Valley Authority.* Initially, these innovating programs had a healthy influence on personnel developments and on attitudes of the commission leadership, although in most cases the commission's jurisdiction over at least portions of these systems was extended some years later. A few agencies, however, given new freedom in personnel matters but without real merit strictures, became notorious for poor management during the 1930s.

Even more important, in 1938 President Roosevelt issued Executive Orders that, not only extended the competitive merit system almost to the limits of his authority and completely revised and modernized the civil service rules for the first time since 1903, but also (significant especially to the role and status of the Civil Service Commission) (1) required the establishment of personnel management divisions in each department and major agency of the government; (2) institutionalized a system for regular consultation and participation of agency personnel directors regarding personnel policy development and application; and (3) gave support to agency in-service training programs, with commission responsibility for leadership and cooperation in those endeavors. This was a great leap forward, not only in giving further underpinning to decentralization, but also in recognizing the true scope of modern personnel administration—embracing far more than controlling entry into the service. Shortly after, the Hatch Act of 1939 greatly restricted the dangers of politicization of the career service by proscribing partisan activities either by or against civil servants.

These moves were further fortified by the emergency measures during World War II. Although the commission's more limited scope of duty had constrained its influence during World War I (though it is credited with some imaginative recruiting efforts and building up of qualified sources of scarce manpower), its adjustment to a war economy in the early 1940s was an outstanding achievement. The then War Department,* fearing it could not hire and manage civilians rapidly enough under traditional procedures, had sought authority to run its personnel system independently. But the skill and leadership of Civil Service Commissioner Arthur S. Flemming thwarted this move by adjustment of the merit system to wartime conditions. The commission not only vastly speeded up its recruiting and other services but it also greatly augmented the board of examiner method, extended training activities, and created new types of appointments which gave operating agencies greater flexibility and efficiency in personnel matters. The executive civil service, about 800,000 strong in 1938, had expanded to almost 4 million by 1945. Flemming's dramatic leadership and the response of the commission's staff are credited with "saving the merit system," thereby contributing to the effectiveness of the war effort and largely keeping political favoritism out of the career service.

Near the end of the war, in 1944, the commission's responsibilities were further increased by passage of the Veterans' Preference Act, which provided a variety of unique benefits to war veterans in employment and retention in the civil service. It was so generous that in later years many questions were raised about justification for such benefits in perpetuity, but only minor changes since then have reduced its impact.

Even though legally it had originally been established as such, by the late 1940s and 1950s the Civil Service Commission was clearly recognized as an executive agency of the President, rather than as merely an independent restraint on executive powers. During the Harry S Truman and Dwight D. Eisenhower years, many readjustment programs were undertaken, but the general processes of decentralization were elaborated rather than abandoned. Of course, the President had always been the final rule-making authority, but now he was beginning to look to the commission as his major personnel advisory and implementing arm in managing the enlarged bureaucracy.

During the postwar years, numerous developments served to expand the commission's functions. Originating with the prodding of the two Hoover Commission* reports (in 1949 and 1955), the head of the commission was given more directive authority within the commission, examining through the heretofore cited boards was further strengthened, promotions were made more systematic and equitable, training was increased, and the commission took greater initiative in guiding agencies in the conduct of their personnel programs. When the Korean

War began, with its attendant manpower shortages, the personnel system easily adapted. Both old and new devices had prepared it for almost any emergency.

The scope of merit system coverage, in proportions of the service to which it applied, actually increased during this period. In addition, new fields of emphasis were created in the early 1950s through legislation which provided for tighter security and loyalty checks on employees, for incentive awards to highly productive workers, for group life insurance coverage benefiting civil servants, and for more liberalized retirement opportunities—all administered by the still growing Civil Service Commission. Increasing reliance on consultation with employee unions and extension of the career system to fit Uncle Sam's expanding responsibilities overseas also added to the commission's chores as well as to those of the affected operating agencies. In 1954, the commission's internal organizational structure was dramatically revised, reflecting the increasing need to elevate the status of its critical functions, to concentrate its policymaking and research duties, to formalize its direct operating activities, and to strengthen its oversight of agency personnel operations.

It was also during this time that a new commission chairman, Robert Ramspeck, a former congressman, launched a "Truth Campaign" to promote greater public understanding and appreciation of the civil service and to recognize the fine contributions government workers were making to the public good. Ramspeck felt it necessary to counteract the tendency of politicians, the press, and others to criticize unduly the defenseless career people in the service. This meant much greater consciousness on the part of all commission staff not only to assume the role of defenders of the service, but also to watch out for and head off any tendencies toward administrative untidiness throughout the bureaucracy that might generate overreaction of critics. It was a new perspective on the role of the central personnel agency.

From the late 1950s through the early 1970s, there was an unprecedented surge of personnel legislation, again expanding the commission's already significant roles in managing the civil service. The Government Employees Training Act (1958), the group health insurance program (1959), the first Salary Reform Act (1962) and its major improvement in 1970, the Intergovernmental Personnel Act (1970), the Job Evaluation Policy Act (1970), the Equal Employment Opportunity Act (1972), not to mention lesser revisions in retirement and other going systems, were milestones in their respective fields. The Intergovernmental Personnel Act resulted in an entire new bureau in the commission to consolidate and oversee the administration of merit systems operating under federal grants to states and localities and generally to make personnel administration itself in those governments an object of federal assistance and leadership. This federal intergovernmental program (as distinguished from many others) has brought almost uniform praise from the lower levels of government. The commission's prestige as an executive agency was further enhanced under the brief but effective leadership of Roger W. Jones as chairman in the latter part of Eisenhower's presidency.

During the 1960s and 1970s, merit system objectives and processes were sharpened through renewed stress on equal opportunity for minority groups and women to enter and advance in the service, on updating methods of recruiting and examining, and on attention to placement in career executive levels. Salary and retirement systems continued to improve, in-service training from executive levels on down flourished, investigations of potential and existing employees for character and suitability were improved, and greater systemization of relations with employee unions took place. Of special significance was the launching of the Federal Executive Institute within the commission structure. This advanced educational facility for senior civil servants was the answer to the long-sought administrative staff college paralleling such institutions in the military services and in other countries.

The longest, and probably the most dynamic and effective, term of chairmanship of the commission was that of John W. Macy from 1961 to 1969, following Jones. In this period presidential reliance on the commission as a true central personnel agency came to its fullest flower. In addition, numerous adaptations and policy changes had to be made during this time because of the conflict in Vietnam, although the adjustments were not nearly as marked as they had been during previous wars.

A further test of the commission's responsiveness and adaptability occurred when it was given responsibility under the Voter Rights Act of 1965 to assure that registration of black citizens in the South was conducted with energy and fairness. The commission threw its elite corps of investigators into the breach to serve as observers at the polls and to adjudicate challenges made by local officials against registrants. Anomalous as it was for a personnel agency, the assignment was testimony to the commission's well-established reputation for objectivity and efficiency.

All of this continual change and elaboration of functions did not take place without some agonizing pain. Rising expectations in various segments of society, disillusionment with the Vietnam involvement, and a new degree of militancy on the part of certain groups seeking to remedy one of society's real or perceived ills created a rash of demonstrations, sit-downs, and strikes, some of which spilled over into the bureaucracy. Zeal for improving the lot of minority sectors among the populace resulted in pressure for outright favoritism for these groups, thus creating resentment that "reverse discrimination" was being practiced. Robert E. Hampton, chairman of the commission during the early 1970s, was considered a staunch defender of a genuine merit approach. For the most part, guided by the example and uprightness of the commission, the government agencies came through this period without serious scars. Most groups generally accepted the notion that achieving equity in personnel decisions, while difficult and disputable, was about as good as could be hoped for.

Not everyone, however, had been satisfied with the Civil Service Commission's role. Academic people and others had long felt that its appellate and merit protection functions were incompatible with its executive leadership responsibilities. Indeed, as far back as 1937, the Brownlow Commission had proposed to President Roosevelt and the Congress that there be a single personnel administrator, to be nominated by a Civil Service Board that would also have continuing responsibility as a watchdog in merit administration. A similar idea was pressed as recently as the 1960s. Furthermore, there had been a felt need for special personnel provisions for the upper career service (as the second Hoover Commission in 1955 had proposed), and there was dissatisfaction with the veteran preference strictures that made dismissal of nonproductive employees difficult. Having campaigned on an anti-Washington theme, President Jimmy Carter, in 1977, capitalized on negative feelings about the bureaucracy growing out of the Watergate scandals (however unjustified these feelings were) and set about getting changes along the lines suggested.

Given the receptive atmosphere for new approaches, the energies and salesmanship of Carter's new commission chairman, Alan K. Campbell, became the main force leading to passage of the Civil Service Reform Act of 1978, which was effective as to its organizational features in 1979. This comprehensive legislation may create greater expectations than it can satisfy, but it certainly deserves respect for its breadth and its several innovations. Abolishing the old commission structure, this act set up an Office of Personnel Management (OPM) parallel to the already existing Office of Management and Budget.* Campbell was made its first director. A Merit System Protection Board (MSPB) was given authority to police merit administration, largely through its hearing of appeals and protection of employee rights to report wrongdoing. A Federal Labor Relations Authority (FLRA) acquired functions concerned with union-management relations that had heretofore been shared between the old Commission and the Department of Labor.*

Equally unprecedented was the creation of a Senior Executive Service, which covered most of the jobs in the three highest grades of the service, for which unique recruitment and placement, mobility, compensation, separation, and motivation features were established—conditions that were just getting into place in 1980. The effort to minimize obstacles to firing poor workers was only partially successful, but the act for the first time did establish merit system standards for the federal service (patterned after those written in the Intergovernmental Personnel Act of 1970), reinvigorated the means of evaluating worker performance, provided greater flexibility in the middle managerial grades for salary incentives, and made possible a substantially expanded program of experimentation and research in personnel management.

Few would contend that all the human problems of running the nation's greatest administrative organization are now solved. Employee groups fear that some features of the new reform may lead to politicization of parts of the service. Conflict in policy control already appears between the new OPM and the FLRA.

Salary systems yet need consolidation and major overhauling. It will take some time for bureaucrats to get adjusted to the new emphasis on productivity and on incentives and disincentives. New decentralization moves require more clearcut standards and followup. All may be addressed in due time.

Taking the long view, a close observer is struck by several characteristics of the government's personnel organization over the years—its occasional stodginess, yes, but, more prominently, its remarkable adaptability to periods of crisis and its absolute integrity and incorruptibility throughout a century of vital activity.

When we speak of an agency concerned with the staffing and energizing of a great bureaucracy, we must remind ourselves of the great dependence the American people have on their civil service. It is in many ways a "fourth branch of government." In spite of political turmoil, of agonizing over corruption during Watergate-like episodes and other occasions, of questioned competence in political leadership, of exasperating executive-legislative relations, the great civil service machine plods along. Mail is delivered, taxes are collected, emergencies around our shores, in our forests, and in our cities are met, checks are received by millions of citizens, military establishments are kept in the ready by civilian support staffs, foreign relations are monitored, park rangers please vacationers at campfire lectures, censuses are conducted and analyzed, the airways are kept open and safe, foods and drugs are inspected—all this and much more, carried out by the most varied aggregation of occupations in the world. Indeed, during the so-called Watergate crisis, not only did all these day-to-day functions continue unabated but not one career civil servant was even accused of wrongdoing.

The career bureaucracy, for which the central personnel agency is recruiter, pace-setter, controller, and conscience, has been the great mainstay of an enormously complex array of public functions. Over the wisdom of starting or continuing public programs, the politicians and parties must contend, but those that are best administered—by able career people—can seldom be challenged. It is this "best administered" goal to which a career civil service, based on merit, contributes. Keeping the service meritorious was bolstered when the central personnel agency served as a innovative and influential force during great transitions in its century-long lifetime.

FOR ADDITIONAL INFORMATION: Donald R. Harvey, *The Civil Service Commission* (1970); *Introducing the Civil Service Reform Act* (1978); Gladys Kammerer, *Impact of War on Federal Personnel Administration* (1951); O. Glenn Stahl, *Public Personnel Administration*, 7th ed. (1976); U.S. Civil Service Commission, *Biography of an Ideal, A History of the Federal Civil Service* (1974); and Paul P. Van Riper, *A History of the United States Civil Service* (1958).

Useful as background material are Winston W. Crouch, *Guide for Modern Personnel Commissions* (1973); H. Eliot Kaplan, *The Law of Civil Service* (1958); John W. Macy, Jr., *Public Service, The Human Side of Government* (1971); David H. Rosenbloom, *Federal Service and the Constitution, Development of the Public Employment Relationship* (1971); O. Glenn Stahl, *The Personnel Job of Government Managers* (1971); and John D. Weaver, *The Great Experiment* (1965).

O. GLENN STAHL

OFFICE OF PRICE ADMINISTRATION (OPA). The Office of Price Administration was one of the largest, most publicly visible, and most influential civilian, wartime agencies in the United States during World War II. It administered the rationing programs for tires, gasoline, meat, sugar, and many other commodities. OPA also ran the rent control programs in about two-thirds of the cities and counties in the nation. Finally and most importantly, the agency developed and presided over the longest lasting and most effective system of public price controls in American history.

OPA's basic objective was to prevent the rampant inflation that had historically occurred during periods of war. Of course, the OPA was not the only, or officially even the primary, anti-inflation agency during the war. Wage stabilization was the responsibility of the National War Labor Board. The Treasury Department* had jurisdiction over the crucial tax and Savings Bond programs that were needed to divert from markets the increased spendable income from full employment and wartime wages. The War Production Board* (WPB), the Federal Reserve Board,* and the War Food Administration (WFA) also contributed to stabilization through their controls, while the coordination of all these activities rested with the Office of Economic Stabilization (and later the Office of War Mobilization and Reconversion). Throughout the war years, however, OPA was the centerpiece of the anti-inflation program, and its officials were generally the leading architects of anti-inflation policies. Wage stabilization rested on the success of price stabilization; rationing, the WPB production controls, and WFA subsidies buttressed rather than superseded price controls; and fiscal and monetary policy was inevitably able to play only an incomplete role in keeping supply and demand in balance. Accordingly, the OPA and its officials can properly claim a large share of the credit for holding the total rise in the Consumer Price Index to 27 percent from May 1941 to May 1946, despite a near doubling of the Gross National Product and serious reductions in the supply of civilian goods. Indeed, during the peak of OPA's effectiveness—from May 1943 to May 1946—consumer prices rose at an average annual rate of less than 2.3 percent.

At its peak, OPA had more than 60,000 employees and enlisted the services of nearly a quarter million volunteers. From its headquarters in Washington, the agency directed the operations of 9 regional offices, 108 district offices, more than 400 area rent control offices, and some 5,500 War Price and Rationing Boards in American towns and cities. The boards, modeled loosely on Selective Service* boards, represented probably the most significant administrative aspect of the program. They involved local citizens, aided by a few paid clerks and more voluntary assistants, in finding and resolving price control violations, allocating ration coupons, publicizing regulations and restrictions, and, indirectly, legitimating the authority of a radically new and powerful federal agency.

The OPA had its origins in the National Defense Advisory Commission (NDAC) which President Franklin D. Roosevelt set up on May 29, 1940, to coordinate the mobilization of American resources for possible war after the fall of France to Germany. The NDAC member with responsibility for economic stabilization was Leon Henderson, a New Deal economist and member of the Securities and Exchange Commission.* Henderson, a dynamic individual who had played an active role in the Roosevelt Administration's economic policies since the days of the National Recovery Administration,* promptly used this position as a base both to push for more rapid defense preparedness and to develop plans for stabilization. Recruiting a staff of bright, young attorneys and economists from New Deal agencies and universities, Henderson also began to deal with rises in particular commodity prices, holding meetings with companies, reaching informal agreements, and making similar persuasive efforts to hold down prices.

Henderson's efforts were given a stronger institutional base in April 1941, when Roosevelt at Henderson's request established the Office of Price Administration and Civilian Supply (OPACS) to complement the recently created Office of Production Management (OPM). By Executive Order, OPACS had the authority to establish price ceilings and certain vague powers to enforce them. During 1941, the agency used this authority to develop a steadily expanding network of price schedules and similar semiformal controls over the prices of about half of American manufacturing. OPACS also was assigned the task of preserving supplies of essential goods for civilians, as well as potential jurisdiction over rationing. However, in August, after a long battle between OPACS and OPM over the pace of conversion of the auto industry, civilian supply and rationing were transferred to OPM, and the resulting Office of Price Administration was left without power over production or allocation. (Operational responsibility for rationing was returned to OPA after Pearl Harbor, however.)

The law that provided a statutory authority for OPA and its price controls, the Emergency Price Control Act of 1942, was first introduced in the House of Representatives in July 1941, before the United States formally entered the conflict. Because of the administration's sensitivity to the preferences of labor, the bill did not seek authority for wage controls. Farm groups quickly sought similar lenient treatment, and prevailed on the administration and the House to prescribe legal minimums above parity levels for price ceilings on agricultural products. The House made other changes to protect businesses from the agency before a price control bill passed on November 28. That bill, while markedly weaker than the one originally sought, was still a formidable and innovative piece of legislation. (One of the most important innovations was the creation of a Temporary Emergency Court of Appeals to hear legal challenges to controls without tying the act as a whole in lengthy litigation.)

The Japanese attack on Pearl Harbor on December 7, 1941, and the resulting U.S. entry into the war shifted congressional attitudes toward acceptance of a stronger price control bill, and the Senate reversed most of the House's restrictive amendments. Still, the final bill passed by both Houses and signed by the President on January 30, 1942, provided for neither wage controls nor effective controls on the many agricultural prices that were at or below parity.

Even before the price control act was signed, OPA had reacted to the change in economic conditions after Pearl Harbor. OPA officials pushed through and assumed administrative responsibility for a tire-rationing plan to preserve rubber supplies threatened by Japanese advances. To administer the plan, the agency organized thousands of local boards with volunteer members to decide who should receive how many of the limited inventory of tires. Rationing of autos, sugar, gasoline, meat, and other goods followed, and was also delegated to the local boards. Meanwhile, rent controls had been instituted in more and more areas experiencing an influx of war workers or military personnel, and price controls were placed on many previously uncontrolled products. In early January, labor and business leaders made no-strike, no-lockout pledges for the duration, and Roosevelt created the National War Labor Board to deal with wage disputes between these parties.

Henderson and the OPA staff were convinced that these initial actions would be insufficient, and Henderson joined with a few other administration officials in urging Roosevelt to adopt a more comprehensive anti-inflation program. The OPA staff had already been forced by the growing threat of inflation to abandon its policy of selective price controls and move toward a general price freeze. To complement that policy it also wanted more explicit restraints on wages, more realistic and effective ceilings on farm prices, and tougher tax and savings policies. Roosevelt's announcement on April 27, 1942, of a seven-point anti-inflation program encompassed most, but not all, of these proposals, but key parts of the program languished as the President turned his attention to other matters.

Henderson and OPA fulfilled their responsibilities with an April 28 freeze on all but agricultural prices, but then engaged in a lonely effort within the administration to achieve better control of wages and agricultural prices. These attempts became more intense as the freeze was eroded by rising food prices and alienated labor unions and farm groups, but the clear need to bring these areas under control finally forced Roosevelt in September to seek appropriate legislation. After bruising floor fights and under the threat of independent presidential action, a disgruntled Congress, on October 2, passed the Stabilization Act of 1942. The act lowered the legal minimum for price ceilings on agricultural products, gave the President authority to control all wages, and created an Office of Economic Stabilization to coordinate the various agencies. Henderson's efforts on behalf of the bill and its implementation made him anathema to farm groups and many congressmen, however. He resigned in December after many Democrats blamed the party's losses in the November congressional elections on him and OPA.

The Stabilization Act did not immediately bring about economic stabilization, nor did Henderson's resignation end OPA's political problems. Organized labor was willing to accept wage stabilization, but only if the cost of living were kept from rising further. To accomplish that, the administration, at OPA's prompting, turned in late 1942 and early 1943 to the use of subsidies to keep legally required farm-price increases from pushing up food prices. OPA simultaneously moved to tighten up its price controls by returning to more restrictive product-specific ceilings, developing explicit controls for retail prices, requiring quality labels on products, and making the local rationing boards into agents for achieving retail compliance. The use of subsidies further aroused the anger of farm groups and their congressional representatives who acted to ban the practice. OPA's other actions alarmed small businessmen, and a more conservative Congress in the first half of 1943 launched a host of hostile investigations of OPA and its activities. Fearing a relaxation of price controls, labor threatened to withdraw its support for wage controls.

Prentiss Brown, the former Democratic Senator who replaced Henderson as OPA administrator, tried to steer the agency through the conflicting pressures with mixed success. Because of rising retail prices and the conflicting farmer, business, and labor pressures, the economic situation became so volatile in April that Roosevelt issued a "hold-the-line" order against further wage and price increases. This ended OPA's discretion to administer prices, but, with the status quo thus effectively frozen, farmers and labor unions backed off from their threats to the controls program. Aided by the extensive use of subsidies, prices then stabilized and rose only modestly for the rest of the war. Nonetheless, an unappeased Congress cut back the agency's funding, placed restrictions on its activities, and forced economists and others who lacked "business experience" out of policymaking positions.

After the crises of mid-1943 had passed, Brown resigned and was replaced by Chester Bowles, a former advertising executive and an official in OPA's Connecticut office. Bowles faced the formidable task of maintaining the "hold-the-line" policy while restoring the agency's morale, public and congressional standing, and authority. To fulfill the congressional directive to have businessmen run the agency, Bowles recruited a number of corporate executives for senior OPA positions. To meet the President's directive, he gave these officials firm and clear standards for when price ceilings should be adjusted, and he retained a staff of economic and legal advisers to monitor conformance with these standards. Simultaneously, he sought to co-opt opposition from labor, business, and farm groups by setting up advisory committees for these interests to provide administrative suggestions to OPA. Finally, he expanded the functions and membership of the local boards, both to involve the largest possible number of people in achieving compliance and to create at least an image of OPA as a citizen's rather than a bureaucrat's program. These efforts bore fruit in nearly stable price indexes from mid-1943 to mid-1946, and in relatively tranquil and routine congressional extensions of the price control acts in 1944 and 1945.

OPA faced persistent minor problems in small-scale black markets, rationing violations, and price-control attributed shortages and quality deteriorations in 1944 and 1945, but no major difficulties arose until the approaching end of the war raised the issues of reconversion and decontrol. Unlike most people, Bowles and the OPA staff were convinced that the cessation of hostilities would bring severe inflation rather than recession. Consequently, they believed that, while some of the controls on the economy could be ended or relaxed at war's end, the anti-inflation program as a whole should be kept intact until the resumption of civilian production caught up with accumulated consumer demand. The majority opinion, however, was that the immediate danger would be recession and that the best course for the government was to remove controls as soon as possible. When the Japanese surrendered on August 15, 1945, much earlier than expected, President Harry S Truman followed a compromise course between the conflicting advice. He let wage controls lapse in the fall of 1945, ended most rationing and allocation rules, reduced many subsidies, and eased fiscal policy. At the same time, Truman heeded part of Bowles's arguments and, because of their popularity with the public, retained price controls. These were left to bear the anti-inflation burden alone.

Without the support of the other programs, OPA price controls first buckled and then broke under the inflationary pressures that Bowles had predicted. The first blow came in February 1946, when Truman, in order to end a strike of the steel industry, agreed not only to wage increases but also to offsetting price increases. Bowles resigned in protest, only to be persuaded by Truman to return as Economic Stabilization director. Bowles and Paul Porter, the new OPA administrator, tried to hold a new line during the spring of 1946 but were forced to give ground in some cases to encourage production. These concessions, however, were insufficient for most farmers and businessmen who called on Congress to relax or end price controls. Despite a vigorous lobbying effort by consumers on behalf of controls, the House and Senate in June passed a price control bill that substantially eroded the effectiveness of OPA's restraints. Bowles's last act before resigning again was a letter to Truman urging a veto of the bill; to nearly everyone's surprise, Truman did so on June 29. When Congress failed to override the veto or quickly pass a new bill, price controls lapsed for a month, and prices rose sharply. In late July, Congress adopted a slightly improved bill, which Truman reluctantly signed.

OPA's renewed activity was short-lived, for cattle farmers reacted to a return of meat price ceilings in August by holding their animals from market. The resulting meat shortage quickly turned public sentiment against price controls, and Truman in mid-October gave in and removed meat price controls. The action came too late to reverse public frustration with Truman and OPA, however, and the Republicans took both Houses of Congress in the November elections. Bowing to the inevitable, Truman lifted the remaining price controls a few days later, and OPA effectively came to an end on November 9, 1946.

Despite the ignominious end to OPA and price controls, the program had been remarkably successful. Price controls in conjunction with other restraints kept inflation in check during the war years and for a critical year afterwards. OPA also earned high marks for the accuracy of its economic forecasts, sensitivity to the public, and the scandal-free and professional quality of its administration. It was, however, immersed in political controversy at all times, and political considerations had an enormous impact on the policies it pursued. The success it had in holding back inflation and dealing with the inevitable black markets and dislocations depended on its political success in winning and holding the confidence of the interest groups, Congress, and the public. That success, in turn, was largely due to the public cooperation and extraordinary powers OPA could draw on in wartime. With the end of the war, those conditions ebbed, and the program collapsed. Nonetheless, OPA's achievements from 1940 to 1946 established the legitimacy of price controls as anti-inflation measures and set a precedent for later public acceptance of related incomes policies.

FOR ADDITIONAL INFORMATION: Andrew H. Bartels, "The Politics of Price Control: The Office of Price Administration and the Dilemmas of Economic Stabilization, 1941-46" (Ph.D. dissertation, Johns Hopkins University, 1980); John Morton Blum, *V Was for Victory: Politics and American Culture During World War II* (1976); Chester Bowles, *Promises to Keep: My Years in Public Life, 1941-1959* (1971); Lester V. Chandler, *Inflation in the United States, 1940-1948* (1951); Marshall B. Clinard, *The Black Market: A Study of White Collar Crime* (1952); John Kenneth Galbraith, *A Theory of Price Control* (1952); Seymour E. Harris, *Price and Related Controls in the United States* (1945); Harvey C. Mansfield, et al., *A Short History of OPA* (1947); Richard Polenberg, *War and Society: The United States, 1941-1945* (1972); U.S. Bureau of the Budget, *The United States at War* (1946); and U.S. Office of Temporary Controls, *Historical Reports on War Administration: Office of Price Administration*, Vols. 1-5 (1947-1948).

ANDREW H. BARTELS

OFFICE OF SCIENTIFIC RESEARCH AND DEVELOPMENT (OSRD). In June 1940, when President Roosevelt approved an order establishing the National Defense Research Committee (NDRC), he began an organizational revolution that was as important to American science as was the associated revolution in military affairs represented by World War II. Seen in retrospect, the order meant that the fragmented, uncoordinated approach that had been characteristic of all earlier governmental uses of science was to be replaced by the centralized authority of an autonomous agency with ready access to the higher echelons of command. Furthermore, the centralized agency, while having military representation, was to be directed by leading members of the civilian scientific community, even though it was charged with initiating, coordinating, and supervising research on problems relating to the national defense. Deliberately conceived as a link between America's scientific leadership and the military, it was to have up to twelve members, appointed by the President, including representatives from the War Department,* the Navy Department,* and the National Academy of Sciences. In carrying out its mission, it was authorized to contract directly with educational institutions, individuals, and industrial organizations for scientific studies and reports. Among other projects, this agency took over the direction of research that demonstrated the feasibility of an atomic bomb.

A second step, broadening the committee's original mission to include medicine and extending its activities beyond research into development, was taken on June 28, 1941, with the issuance of Executive Order No. 8807, which created the Office of Scientific Research and Development and transferred the NDRC to it as its advisory council.

Both the NDRC and the OSRD emerged as a result of conferences held in early 1940 between President Roosevelt and the four leading scientists who remained as his key science advisers during the war. Vannevar Bush, an electrical engineer, at that time president of the Carnegie Institution of Washington, and James B. Conant, a chemist and president of Harvard University, headed the nation's most prestigious foundation and most prestigious university. Frank B. Jewett, an electrical engineer, headed the Bell Telephone Laboratories and was also president of the National Academy of Sciences. The fourth member of the group, Karl T. Compton, a physicist with broad experience in governmental science, was president of the Massachusetts Institute of Technology. The nation was in imminent danger of being forced into a war for which it was pathetically unprepared, the four scientists argued. Therefore, the government required an organization that could make an independent assessment of the military's science requirements and undertake the necessary arrangements to supply them. Science in the twentieth century was developing rapidly; thus, the traditional notion that military leaders would know what they needed and ask scientists to aid in its development was obsolete. Earlier agencies formed for the purpose of bringing science to the aid of a war effort had been based on this assumption. The National Academy of Sciences, formed during the Civil War, could only offer its advice in response to an explicit request, and the National Research Council of World War I worked under a similar limitation. The military attitude just prior to World War II was the same as it had been historically—questions about the strategic or tactical practicality of new weapons were for the judgment of professional soldiers. The implication that civilian scientists and engineers could be useful only if they were closely directed and controlled by military officers discouraged civilian scientists from working on military problems, and it also weakened existing organizational links between the armed services and the scientific community. The agency being created in 1940, however, was designed to reverse this relationship. It would bypass the existing governmental research apparatus (this is one reason it was created by Executive Order rather than by act of Congress) and would allow scientists as the men with the most up-to-date knowledge about what was possible, to make the critical judgments determining innovations in weaponry during World War II. Before Pearl Harbor, in fact, the OSRD had already proceeded to make these judgments.

Under the leadership of Vannevar Bush, who served as OSRD director throughout the war, the agency became directly responsible for ongoing projects being handled by more than 1,100 men for the Army,* Navy,* and other departments of government. But in the choice of new projects, Bush exercised that independent judgment the scientists had argued for, sometimes initiating projects on his own, sometimes refusing to move in directions requested by the services, sometimes, in fact, acting against the outright opposition of the armed services. But despite what often appeared to be a carte blanche, Bush continued to construe his mandate narrowly. Viewing the agency as a temporary creation to serve only for the duration of the war, the head of OSRD was lacking the empire-building aspirations normally associated with bureaucrats. Indeed, he actually contracted out as much work as possible and refused to sponsor scientifically interesting projects that seemed to have only long-range payoffs. Realizing that the agency was in competition for America's limited scientific and technical talent with war industries and with the technical branches of the armed services, Bush knew that the lack of manpower was the most significant limitation he faced. He, therefore, insisted that his agency confine its activities to those fields that seemed most likely to produce results immediately useful to the war effort. Thus, the OSRD, like the National Advisory Committee for Aeronautics (NACA), of which Bush had been chairman, and the Army Air Corps, showed no interest in jet engines for either aircraft or missiles. The payoff was too far in the future, and undertaking such research would divert too many of the limited number of engineers from the immediate task of improving the piston aircraft whose designs already existed and developing the mass fleet of such aircraft that was needed.

The role of the OSRD in the development of the atomic bomb also illustrates Bush's determination to get the most from what was available. The uranium problem had been assigned to the NDRC in 1940, and research went ahead under Bush's guidance until the summer of 1941. At that time, the decision was made to go ahead with the development of the bomb, on the assumption that it could be achieved within the duration of the war. But recognizing not only that the decision to go ahead involved a major commitment to the technology of fissionable material and the mechanics of a bomb, but also that it called for the creation of an entire industry and a military delivery system as well, Bush knew that such a commitment could well absorb the capacity of the OSRD. Thus, the decision was made, well before Pearl Harbor, to separate the bomb program from the OSRD complex and place it directly under military direction, where it became the Manhattan District of the Corps of Army Engineers.*

The major positive choice that the scientists did make was to establish the electronic background for warfare. The science of electronics by 1940 had been brought to the point of theoretical development where many useful applications could be expected after solving relatively minor technical problems, and many existing agencies in this country as well as others were already at work in the field. Electronics was thus thought to be ripe for development, and its implications for modern warfare were obvious. Radar, a device for "seeing" aircraft and ships beyond visual range, was one of the earliest applications, but a whole system of radar and radio connected to weapons actually evolved. Improved bomb sights for "blind-bombing" and the proximity fuse, which came into use during the war, as well as the early work in the development of sonar, are prominent examples.

Electronics by no means consumed all of the OSRD's energy. Its organization into relatively independent divisions and sections assured that it would have a hand in every scientific matter connected with warfare. Research in thickened fuel, for example, led to a greatly improved flame-thrower; other aids to infantrymen included the bazooka and a variety of other rocket launchers and propellants such as a chemical warfare rocket developed by the California Institute of Technology. Still other sections pioneered in the use of DDT and penicillin development. The names of some of the sections suggest the range of interests represented by the individual research projects presided over by the OSRD: Physical Explosives, Organic Explosives, Toxicity, Immunology, Aerosols, Absorbents, Metallurgy, Petroleum Warfare, Camouflage, Sound Control, and a great many others. As the names indicate, the OSRD's orientation was to specific problems or concrete needs, rather than to traditional disciplinary divisions in the physical, biological, and engineering sciences.

Before the war's end, the OSRD through its Office of Field Services had dispatched nearly 300 scientists and technicians on overseas missions, principally to accompany new equipment and explain its use. Its primary mode of operation, however, was by contract with existing laboratories in the United States. At the first meeting, the OSRD had decided to operate through contracts rather than by establishing its own laboratories or by using its own staff to conduct scientific research. This decision, never modified, had far-reaching results for the future of American science. For one thing, on the "to him that hath, it shall be given" principle, it favored the further buildup of capacity in already existing agencies. Although some thought was given to considerations of equity and geographical distribution, the natural tendency was to assign problems to those institutions with the facilities and manpower to promise the best results in the shortest time. The net result was the creation of research centers at favored institutions—Harvard, MIT, Chicago, Cal Tech, Berkeley—and the further impoverishment of those not so favored. No matter how much they tried to avoid such favoritism in some areas, such as chemistry, radar, and rocket research, the benefits of teamwork were simply too prominent to be overlooked. The pressing needs of the national emergency made it easy to justify neglecting such time-hallowed niceties as geographical distribution and other fundamentals of pork-barrel politics. Maury Maverick, a former Congressman from Texas then serving with the War Production Board,* perhaps inelegantly expressed it by saying that the job was to kill "Japs and Germans." All other considerations had to take a back seat for the duration.

A second decision—adopting the principle that research should not yield a financial profit but should be performed on an actual cost basis—had similar problems. Academic institutions, presumably not in business for profit anyway, had no difficulty here, and there were certain beneficial side-effects for the teaching mission of universities performing research. But the principle did make it difficult to work with small industrial organizations, and it favored the buildup of capacity of large industries with well-established, separate research and production departments. Thus, Bell Telephone, General Electric, Westinghouse, DuPont, RCA, and a few other giants dominated industrial research and emerged after the war with an even greater research and productive capacity than they had before.

Paradoxically, the tendency toward centralizing research in a few favored institutions was accelerated by the highly decentralized nature that was deliberately built into OSRD. Precisely defined fields of activity were assigned to more than fifty divisions or sections, and the initiative in planning contracts in each field rested with the division or section chief. In each case, the prime concern was to place contracts with institutions that the chief thought could best solve his problem; he was not concerned with how many OSRD contracts in other fields might have been placed with the same organizations. The result of these tendencies is illustrated by the fact that MIT, the single largest recipient of funds, had seventy-five contracts whose dollar value totaled $116,941,352, or well over 20 percent of the grand total. The largest industrial contractor was Western Electric, a subsidiary of AT&T, whose seventy-four contracts totaled $17,091,819.

Despite its impressive accomplishments, the OSRD's research function was carried out on a rather modest budget—just $0.5 billion had been spent by the end of fiscal 1946. Because it was conceived as a temporary wartime agency, it was not as revolutionary as it might otherwise have been. Nevertheless, its decision to operate by contract with existing universities and business firms, while it had the inevitable side-effects referred to earlier, disrupted both those institutions and the broader society far less than any scheme of direct governmental operation of the laboratories would have done. Similarly, the existence of a national emergency and the conception of the agency as temporary made it unnecessary to raise fundamental political questions. Such questions were implicit in the fact that an agency making important policy decisions and dispensing large amounts of public money was essentially under the control of men outside the ordinary governmental lines of responsibility.

Neither did the implicit conflict-of-interest issue arise as long as the national emergency persisted. Some people noticed that major contractors were represented on the OSRD, for example, MIT, Bell Laboratories, Harvard, and Cal Tech, but favoring these institutions could be justified in terms of the need for speed. By late 1944, as the war began to move toward a forseeable end, major attention began to be devoted to the question of what to do with science in the postwar world. These previously neglected questions then began to be considered.

Even as the wartime agency was being dismantled, it was generally agreed that research would remain an important responsibility of government. The utmost importance of research and development to national security had been dramatically illustrated by the events of the wartime years, and there were no serious suggestions that the *status quo ante bellum* should be resumed. Weapons research was shifted from the OSRD to the armed services, the Atomic Energy Commission* took over a great deal more, as did other operating agencies, and a Research and Development Board was established to coordinate such research and its relations with civilian scientists.

What to do about basic research, as opposed to the mission research funded by the agencies, was a matter of dispute and was not resolved quite so readily, although, once again, the war had convinced virtually everyone that it was important and should be maintained. The question had been considered in hearings arranged by Senator Harley Kilgore (Democrat, West Virginia) before a Senate subcommittee in 1942, 1943, and 1945. Kilgore and others, alarmed by OSRD's irregular status and the power it nevertheless commanded, wished to establish a regular agency of government—perhaps a bureau—with a director appointed by the President and responsible to Congress as other agencies were. The principle which OSRD clearly violated was that an agency which controls the spending of public funds in an important national program must be a part of the regular machinery of government. Kilgore visualized a central scientific and technical agency that would transcend the narrowly military aim of OSRD and could consequently include those scientists who had found no place in the war effort—the agricultural researchers, the biologists, and the geologists, for example.

Bush, speaking for the leadership of the scientific community in a report to the President, published as *Science, the Endless Frontier*, suggested another program for government research. His preference for an agency quite like the OSRD, headed by a part-time board of "disinterested experts," otherwise unconnected with the government, was embodied in a bill that was swiftly vetoed by President Harry S Truman. The proposed National Science Foundation* (NSF), said Truman, was an anti-democratic institution whose provisions radically departed from sound principles for the administration of public affairs. Five years later, when the NSF was finally established, the mission agencies had taken over so much of the responsibility for research that opposition to an agency had diminished. The $15 million ceiling on appropriations made it evident that the establishment of a "Czar of Science" was not being contemplated, and enough changes had been made in the manner of appointment of officials to calm the fears of the President.

It only remains to mention a final legacy of the OSRD. The huge, coordinated projects served as a training ground for scientific leadership and determined the power structure as well as much of the shape of postwar science for the next generation. Seven of the first eight presidential science advisers were alumni of either the Los Alamos Scientific Laboratory or the MIT Radiation Laboratory. Five came from Northeastern universities, two from the California Institute of Technology, and the other from Bell Laboratories. They guided science-government relations through that difficult period of readjustment. The patterns established by the OSRD were carried over by these men and incorporated into postwar programs sustained by the Office of Naval Research, and Air Force Research and Development Command, the Atomic Energy Commission, and the National Science Foundation. Today, despite alterations forced by budget cuts, changing national priorities, and the exigencies of pork-barrel politics, the institutional pattern of American science still bears their stamp. Thus, the OSRD's most important role in terms of permanent impact may well have been as the first step in what one careful student of the subject has termed the "permanent mobilization of science" for national purposes.

FOR ADDITIONAL INFORMATION: James Phinney Baxter III, *Scientists Against Time*

(1948); A. Hunter Dupree, "The Great Instauration of 1940: The Organization of Scientific Research for War," in Gerald Holton, ed., *The Twentieth Century Sciences: Studies in the Biography of Ideas* (1972); Daniel J. Kevles, "Scientists, the Military and the Control of Postwar Defense Research: The Case of the Research Board for National Security, 1944-1946," *Technology and Culture* 16 (1975); Carroll Pursell, "Science Agencies in World War II; The OSRD and Its Challengers," in Nathan Reingold, ed., *The Sciences in the American Context: New Perspectives* (1979); and Irving Stewart, *Organizing Scientific Research for War* (1948).

One prominent member of the group gave decentralization and flexibility major credit for OSRD's success: James B. Conant, "The Mobilization of Science for the War Effort," *American Scientist* 35 (April 1947): 196. Other useful readings include Vannevar Bush, *Science, The Endless Frontier*, reprint (1960), p. 21; *Congressional Record—Senate*, August 6, 1947 (1947), pp. 10567-10569; Kent C. Redmond, "World War II, a Watershed in the Role of the National Government in the Advancement of Science and Technology," in C. Angoff, ed., *The Humanities in the Age of Science* (1968); and Harvey M. Sapolsky, "Academic Science and the Military: The Years Since the Second World War," in Reingold, *The Sciences in the American Context*, p. 389. See also John Maddox, "American Science: Endless Search for Objectives," *Daedalus* 101 (Fall 1972):129-140.

GEORGE H. DANIELS

OFFICE OF WAR INFORMATION (OWI). The Office of War Information, the World War II propaganda agency of the United States, reflected America's often ambiguous aims in the war. In its stormy life, OWI fought over the shape of the propaganda program that mirrored the conflicts at both public and policy levels over what the war was all about. Ostensibly fought for the loftiest liberal goals, in time the war seemed to become a struggle for victory alone. Propagandists who initially tried to trumpet the democratic aims in which they believed reluctantly had to accept the new priorities as they emerged. American might and American right then became the dominant themes of their message, as OWI finally settled into a role it could effectively play.

OWI originated in the efforts of liberal interventionists to commit the United States to a necessary cause, even before the attack on Pearl Harbor brought the country into the war. Archibald MacLeish and Robert Emmet Sherwood were among those who clung to a vision of a war that would result not merely in victory but also in a stronger and more democratic world order. Both literary figures of note, both aware of the importance of words and expressions in human affairs, they were responsible for setting up the organizations that were ultimately transformed into OWI.

MacLeish, an accomplished poet as well as government official, was passionately committed to the survival of democracy in an unstable world. He had watched with horror the growth of fascism in Europe and had come to realize that the regimentation and brutalization he saw in Germany and Italy threatened the values he held most dear. Hoping to help other Americans understand their vested interests in the outcome of the war, while still Librarian of Congress, he became head of a new Office of Facts and Figures in the fall of 1941. His task was to give the public the presumably ungarnished facts about the war and the American response to it, but largely because of President Franklin D. Roosevelt's unwillingness to be too open in the anxious days before American entrance into the war, the agency met at best with a mixed response.

Sherwood, meanwhile, was engaged in a similar effort directed toward the rest of the world. A three-time winner of the Pulitzer Prize, the playwright was equally committed to the triumph of the democratic way in the war that soon threatened to engulf the United States. He, too, pleaded for the preservation of human freedom and dignity as the fundamental purpose of the war. While working as a speech writer for Roosevelt, Sherwood organized and headed the Foreign Information Service and, through the newly founded Voice of America, sought to spread the gospel of democracy to audiences abroad.

Neither organization worked particularly well, and by early 1942 the whole information program was in trouble. On both the domestic and foreign fronts there were demands for a more-focused propaganda effort, but the directions it should take were unclear. In an administrative reorganization, mandated by Executive Order on June 13, 1942, a new Office of War Information was created with news commentator Elmer Davis at its head.

Davis's appointment offered hope for the future of the propaganda program. The CBS announcer with the clear, direct delivery and dry humor seemed to convey honesty and common sense to the audience of 12.5 million people listening each night. Americans appreciated Davis, for he seemed, in one journalist's words, "solid American to the core—the sort of American that belongs to the heart of the country" (H.I. Brock, "Uncle Sam Hires a Reporter," *New York Times Magazine*, June 21, 1942, p. 8).

The new organization reflected the influence of Sherwood and MacLeish, both of whom were very much involved, and of talented men who joined the agency because they shared the same perception of an ideological battle between the forces of evil and good. Working through both a domestic branch and an overseas branch, they plunged into the struggle. They fervently believed in the "four essential freedoms"—freedom of speech and expression, freedom of worship, freedom from want, and freedom from fear—that the President had spoken of in his message to Congress on January 6, 1941. They believed, too, in the provisions of the Atlantic Charter which Roosevelt and British Prime Minister Winston Churchill had laid out in the summer of that year. To the propagandists those declarations provided a sense of purpose in the fight. From the start they sought to determine how far they could go in laying out the issues honestly and openly in the face of the demands of the war. Beginning with high hopes, they soon discovered that they could not go very far at all in pursuing their own ends. Encountering opposition at every turn, they became aware of how differently others in the administration viewed the war and how those other views affected the propaganda they wished to produce.

The State Department,* led by courtly Cordell Hull, proved to be the first stumbling block. Although Hull frequently voiced American policy, he did not always play a key role in making it, but he was, nevertheless, intensely jealous of instrusions into his domain. Cautious by nature, he was not particularly interested in functions that lay beyond the traditional scope of the State Department. Yet, he was reluctant to allow other organizations to intervene in anything that touched on foreign affairs. Hull was uncomfortable with OWI, for he and his staff considered the propaganda agency careless and irresponsible, given to using confidential material for inappropriate purposes. The Secretary sought to constrain OWI when he wrote in July 1942 that he assumed from the Executive Order that war information activities did not include information relating to U.S. foreign policy over which the department had exclusive jurisdiction. That view, Davis responded, "would appear tenable only on the hypothesis that our foreign policy had no relation to the war" (Davis to Hull, July 10, 1942, Box 5, Records of OWI, National Archives). Davis may have had the best of that interchange, but his organization still found itself hemmed in by the Department of State.

So it was with the military. Secretary of War Henry L. Stimson, seventy-four years old at the time of Pearl Harbor, was intent on winning the war and gave military necessity precedence over everything else. Concentrating all his energy on his last major task in public service, he could, as Felix Frankfurter once observed, focus on one thing like an old victrola needle caught in a single record groove. Concerned about whipping a flabby department into fighting shape, he was impatient with programs that he feared might complicate his work. Suspicious of civilians who might interfere with strategic operations or compromise security regulations, Stimson saw the war as a military engagement that Army* and Navy* could best fight. He viewed OWI and the newfangled propaganda techniques as only peripheral to that task.

High-ranking Navy officials took Stimson's side. Secretary Frank Knox, a newspaperman himself, understood the demands of the information group. But now he knew his job was to find out what the admirals needed and to respond to their demands, and he was correspondingly less sympathetic to OWI. Men like Admiral Ernest J. King knew exactly what they wanted. After the disaster at Pearl Harbor, King reputedly commented to colleagues that when leaders found themselves in trouble, "they always send for the sons of bitches" and he was the one sent for to revive the fighting fleet. Forceful and harsh, forthright and grim, he was devoted to the Navy and had a sense of naval tradition that he intended to maintain untarnished. In fighting the war, he had little use for embellishments that he felt only got in the way. Propaganda was one of those embellishments.

Aware of the constraints they faced, OWI's propagandists still hoped to work with FDR's liberal pronouncements to try to publicize and popularize the democratic order they passionately hoped would emerge as a result of the war. In their pamphlets and broadcasts, they sought to commit the United States to the vision they held, and from their own perspective, they often tried to elaborate the American aims in the war. Sometimes that involved trying to encourage thoughtful discussion of the purposes of the war rather than simply stimulating support for the struggle. Sometimes it meant offering criticisms of what the propagandists took to be the compromises that seemed to contradict the aims of the fight. Some members of OWI were outspoken in their denunciation of the agreement with Admiral Jean François Darlan, commander-in-chief of the French armed forces. As Robert Sherwood later noted, the deal with the Nazi sympathizer which followed the North African landings of November 1942 apparently reflected the Americans' ignorance about Europe. In the same way, the propagandists criticized the Roosevelt Administration's willingness to work with Italian King Victor Emmanuel III and Marshal Pietro Badoglio, who succeeded Benito Mussolini in July 1943. One OWI broadcast spoke of "the moronic little king" as it observed that fascism remained in power in Italy.

For those independent efforts, OWI found itself under attack from all sides. Its homefront activities drew criticism from Republicans who viewed the organization as little more than a public relations office generating support for a fourth term for FDR. Southern Democrats found objectionable its sympathies for black aspirations during the war. The domestic propaganda was "a stench to the nostrils of a democratic people," Representative Joe Starnes of Alabama told his colleagues in the House, and others echoed the same sentiments. Similarly, the propagandists in the overseas branch found little support for their outspoken views. Arthur Krock of the *New York Times* was highly critical of the Italian episode, and other commentators took up the attack. The War Department and State Department were irate at what was going on. Something was going to have to give.

When the Office of War Information tried to enlist the President's support as it struggled to survive, Roosevelt remained aloof. His detachment was characteristic of his whole approach to his office, especially in time of war. As commander-in-chief in a cataclysmic struggle, he had his own priorities which took precedence over all else. He assumed personal responsibility for important negotiations more than other Presidents had, and, given his fascination with the strategy and tactics of war, he carried innumerable details around in his head. Although he accepted the need for an American role in the postwar world, his view was subject to change, and, even as he allowed the development of the notion of international organization, he seemed to favor big-power domination. Yet, for all the planning behind the scenes, during the war he appeared to want victory first and foremost, as much an end in itself as a means of enforcing a measure of cooperation among allies with conflicting demands of their own. Despite the repeated requests from propagandists for specific declarations of war aims, he himself preferred to talk of the Four Freedoms and Atlantic Charter in general terms, with the assertion that anything else could wait until after the war. Uneasy about formal propaganda, unwilling to allow the power of publicity to drift from his own hands, he accepted the propaganda organization as a necessary if cumbersome addition to the war effort, but not one that demanded any more than his minimal support. OWI was left to fend for itself.

The first major attack came in mid-1943 when the Congress just about dismantled the domestic branch of the propaganda organization. The initial vote in the House of Representatives was for abolishing the homefront office entirely, but the Senate was a little less destructive. The conference committee left enough money, Elmer Davis noted, so that it would not be blamed for putting OWI out of business, and at the same time not sufficient funds to allow it to accomplish a great deal. Basically all the domestic branch could do from that time on was to provide support for the campaigns intended to boost public morale. In the foreign field, after the furor surrounding the OWI criticisms of American policy toward Italy, the propaganda leaders finally understood that, if any organized information effort was to survive, the message would have to be consonant with the real aims of the war, however nebulous those might be. The agency would have to follow the military lead and create a picture of America that would pass the scrutiny of those more highly placed in the administration of the war.

A tightly knit, psychological warfare program was one result of that realization. As Davis wrested control of his organization from the more outspoken officers who had often sought to proceed on their own, he oversaw the creation of a support program in the field that came more and more directly under military command. A Psychological Warfare Branch (PWB), assisted by OWI and attached to Allied headquarters, had already launched a leaflet program in early 1943 in the North African theater. In Tunisia, PWB dropped 20 million leaflets that contributed to the demoralization of the enemy. Leaflets with such themes as "You Are Surrounded" and "Drowning Is a Nasty Death" rained on Axis territory from Royal Air Force planes. Americans who had grumbled that "you can't kill a Heinie with a spitball" watched as the number of Axis soldiers surrendering began to rise.

Propagandists acknowledged that leaflets alone could not bring about surrender. But Davis and others argued on the basis of experience that when enemy soldiers were in a precarious situation, propaganda looms quite effective. Leaflets helped make it safe for antagonists who were already vulnerable to give up. They did not need to use surrender passes or other such materials when they found them, but could hide them away for future use. Those passes became increasingly important as the war went on.

Radio broadcasts carried proclamations from military commanders and elaborated on official announcements in other ways. Sometimes sound trucks belonging to a newly formed Psychological Warfare Division attached to Supreme Headquarters for the European campaign moved as close as possible to enemy forces and then broadcast what the GIs called *Schweinheils*—pig calls—that revealed to the Nazis their desperate plight.

In general, the military propaganda efforts met with a favorable response from the Army. There were still moments of friction, however. General George S. Patton, Jr., for example, was usually cooperative with psychological warfare programs, but at one point reacted vigorously to a suggestion that he use more leaflet warfare against enemy soldiers. He shouted that he was not there to write letters. He was there to "kill the S.O.B.'s!" (James M. Erdmann, "USAAF Leaflet Operations in the ETO during the Second World War," [Ph.D. diss., University of Colorado, 1970], p.351). Another officer complained that an issue of the tiny newspaper *Internenbanner*, which showed the treatment that prisoners-of-war received, looked like a travel folder. American soldiers under fire often resented the conspicuous sound equipment which they feared would only draw further attacks. Still, on a number of occasions propaganda did contribute to enemy desertions, which ensured that the efforts would go on.

Perhaps even more important than the military connection was the picture of America which emerged in the broadcasts and publications issued from home. That portrayal of the American way of life, all that the State, War, and Navy Departments, all that the White House would allow, was meant to persuade people abroad of the righteousness of the American cause. It sought to highlight those qualities that might describe ordinary Americans in their ordinary tasks in the optimistic assumption that such a representation would give faith and sustenance around the world. The men who headed OWI knew they had to combat a distorted image of America as a decadent, gangster-ridden society that had emerged from American film and other arts and then been embellished by Axis propaganda. In the materials they produced, the nation appeared as a mighty, dedicated, wholesome country, which somehow had the better interests of all mankind at heart.

All American virtues were visible in that general scheme. Americans were sympathetic, even sentimental, and combined idealism with common sense. A booklet entitled *Small Town, U.S.A.* told the story of Alexandria, Indiana. It was a quiet, pleasant town of 4,801, like thousands of other small towns across the country, where the people, always hard-working, dedicated, and industrious, now supported the war in the factories and armed forces. *Victory*, OWI's major propaganda publication, carried similar accounts, set against stories of Americans in action. The citizens of the United States, quiet and peaceful by nature, could compete with anyone when driven to war.

Most of the propaganda stressed American power and productivity. Despite Axis successes, the United States was creating the greatest fighting machine ever known. The first issue of *Victory* carried on the cover a color picture of an American bombardier at his controls. The caption underneath read, "Two Million Men Will Fight in 185,000 U.S. Planes." A story inside pointed out that as many as twenty-five bombers a day were already being flown to England. One factory produced a four-engine bomber every hour. The color photos of assembly lines in the centerfold depicted the country's productive might. While some readers might remain skeptical, it was an imposing message that *Victory* presented, a message conveyed, too, by other materials in a variety of ways. OWI's film *Autobiography of a Jeep* told in sixteen different languages the story of the vehicle that had come to symbolize the war effort wherever it went.

Not only was America powerful; it was committed as well to providing an example that other nations should follow. That theme, which persisted throughout the war and into the period that followed, reflected a traditional American attitude of dominance. Davis stated the case early for OWI. The basic message was that the United States was going to win and that its victory would ultimately benefit everyone. He continued to make that point throughout his tenure, as reflected in the propaganda produced.

The propaganda effort consistently aimed to engender sympathy for the Allied cause. A commitment to a "strategy of truth" led agency members to acknowledge occasional faults in American society in the materials they turned out, but in general the treatment was optimistic in the extreme. Bad news should be reported as necessary, but always with the note that progress was taking place.

OWI, in the composite picture it created, finally hit on a vision of America that reflected the ways others represented the war as well. The same virtues came through in the *Why We Fight* films which producer Frank Capra made for the War Department. They were also mirrored in American advertising for the duration of the struggle, as public relations men sketched the war as a struggle for the American way of life and stressed the components—both spiritual and material—that to them made America great. And perhaps most important of all, the general image seemed consonant with the way ordinary Americans viewed the war. Both Bill Mauldin and Ernie Pyle noted the lack of interest among soldiers in the large causes or politics of war. Civilians, in the same way, had their minds on other things. Once the information leaders came to that realization and ceased trying to publicize the war they hoped to win, their message began to enjoy more success.

Propaganda ended up serving the war well. OWI managed to play a significant role in the last year of the fight, and, although it was disbanded when hostilities came to an end, it received credit for a job well done. The pictures of America which the agency produced were frequently trite, above all noncontroversial, and yet they represented the country's dominant view of World War II. In the struggle, OWI finally came to reveal what the nation considered important as it strove to reconcile its basic values and the requirements of war, even as it demonstrated the limitations of the American vision itself.

FOR ADDITIONAL INFORMATION: For a more detailed and more documented treatment of these themes, see Allan M. Winkler, *The Politics of Propaganda: The Office of War Information, 1942-1945* (1978). Based on a variety of sources, the book draws most heavily on the OWI records at the National Archives* annex in the Federal Records Center in Suitland, Maryland. See also citations in the *Congressional Record*, hearings of Congress, and various newspapers and journals. Also useful are Robert Emmet Sherwood, *Roosevelt and Hopkins: An Intimate History* (1948). Elmer Davis, "War Information," in Elmer Davis and Byron Price, *War Information and Censorship*, American Council on Public Affairs (n.d.); James Morris Erdmann, "U.S.A.A.F. Leaflet Operations in the ETO During the Second World War" (Ph.D. dissertation, University of Colorado, 1970).

ALLAN M. WINKLER

P

PARK SERVICE. See National Park Service.

PATENT AND TRADEMARK OFFICE (PTO). The Patent and Trademark Office is one of Washington's oldest and hardiest bureaus. Its function is to implement the registration of trademarks and the issuance of invention and design patents, which give their holders the potentially important right to exclude others from using the covered subject matter. Granting inventors for a limited time an exclusive right to their discoveries is specifically sanctioned in Article I, Section 8, of the U.S. Constitution as a means of promoting "the progress of science and useful arts." The first patent law of 1790 was administered by a committee of Cabinet-level secretaries, but in 1802 the forerunner of a Patent Office was created, and in 1836 the office was reorganized to carry out its assignment in a manner closely resembling the modern patent issuance procedure. Responsibility for registering trademarks was added in 1905. In 1925, the PTO lost its independence and became part of the Department of Commerce.*

The basic idea of the patent system is to enhance incentives for invention and the development of new technology by letting inventors or their assignees have a temporary monopoly (in the United States, seventeen years from the time a patent is issued) on their inventions. The patent is in effect a right to exclude—specifically, for the patent holder to seek a court injunction against the manufacture or otherwise unauthorized use of its invention by others. Under U.S. law, the patent holder bears no obligation itself to use or "work" the invention. If there were no such exclusive property rights, it is argued, inventions could easily be imitated by competitors, leading to an early decline in prices and the inventor's inability to recoup the costs, and be compensated for the risks, incurred in creating and perfecting the invention. Lack of patent protection would therefore inhibit investment of time and money in inventive activity. Inventors might also be more inclined to keep their findings secret, whereas under the patent system, details of the invention become public when the patent (whose Latin root is "open") is issued.

To be patentable, an invention must satisfy three criteria: it must be new, it must be useful, and it must have genuine inventive content going beyond what would have been obvious to a person with ordinary skill in the relevant technology. The Patent Office ensures that these criteria are met before a patent is issued. Each application (of roughly one hundred thousand received annually) is assigned to an examiner specializing in the particular field of technology to which the application's subject matter most closely pertains. The most extensive part of the examination is a search of the "prior art"—that is, largely but not solely previous patents, domestic and foreign—to determine whether the invention is indeed "novel" or whether it had predecessors. "Utility" of the invention is normally shown by citing possible uses and evidence from experiments conducted by the applicant. Whether the application exhibits sufficient inventive content requires the examiner's subjective judgment. If all three criteria are satisfied, a patent is issued, unless two or more applications claiming essentially the same invention arrive at this stage roughly simultaneously. Then an "interference" proceeding is declared. The contending parties present evidence illuminating who was the first to conceive the invention and diligently reduce it to practice. If, on the other hand, the examiner rejects an application, various appeals can be pursued.

During the 1970s, roughly 70 percent of all applications led to the issuance of patents. About seventy thousand patents were issued per year. In December 1976, the four-millionth U.S. invention patent was issued. Roughly half of all patents issued during the 1970s were assigned by inventors to U.S. corporations, usually because the inventor was an employee of the corporation. One-fourth went to foreign corporations and 22 percent to independent or unaffiliated inventors. The share of unaffiliated inventors has been falling over time. It was 81 percent in 1901 and 42 percent in 1940.

The PTO also issues plant patents covering hybrid or mutant plant variants. Numbering roughly 150 in a typical year, they are similar in most respects to normal or "utility" patents. A few thousand design patents are also issued annually. They cover the ornamental aspects of product designs and have lives of from 3 1/2 to 14 years, depending upon the size of the fee the applicant chooses to pay.

Since 1905, trademarks have been registered with the PTO. The main social purpose of trademarks is to permit business enterprises to maintain unique identifying marks for their products, which in turn help consumers select products shown by experience or reputation to be satisfactory. Although the PTO staff examines trademark applications to screen out duplications, there is no examination comparable to the utility and inventive content tests for invention patents. The legal criteria for securing court injunctions against alleged infringers are also different; trademark registration does not confer a presumption of exclusive rights in the same way that a patent grant does. Unlike patents, trademarks do not have legally bounded lives; the life could in principle be perpetual. Approximately twenty-five thousand trademarks are registered annually. The one-millionth U.S. trademark registration occurred in 1974.

At its principal location in Crystal City near Washington's National airport, the PTO performs these and certain ancillary tasks (such as making printed patents available, maintaining records, operating a massive public "search" library, conducting statistical analyses, and sustaining the National Inventors Hall of Fame) with a staff of approximately three thousand. Its organization is relatively simple. It is headed by the commissioner of patents, a presidential appointee. There are divisions (under assistant commissioners) for patents, trademarks, administration, finance and planning, and legal matters along with quasi-judicial boards handling appeals and interferences. Although the office grants monopoly privileges that in rare cases can be worth tens or even hundreds of millions of dollars, its record is remarkably clear of the influence trading and corruption scandals experienced by some other federal grant and regulatory agencies. Not surprisingly, it and the several thousand private patent attorneys who work with it form a unified and strong coalition supporting the patent system against critics.

The PTO levies fees for patent application processing and issue, trademark registration, and the dissemination of printed patents and other publications. During the 1970s, these were sufficient to cover only about a third of the office's operating budget. The rest came from congressional appropriations. Occasional budgetary shortfalls have been met by cutting back on such avoidable expenses as outside printing, which in turn led to the deferral of patent issues and the backlogging of completed applications. Budgetary support during the 1960s and 1970s was, however, sufficiently strong that the office was able to reduce the average period of pendency (that is, the lag between application and patent issuance) from more than three years to roughly a year and a half. A 1981 law change permitting the office to charge "maintenance" fees on patents already issued and still in force (that is, at the four-, eight-, and twelve-year patent life points) may permit a greater degree of financial self-sufficiency.

A chronic problem of the PTO has been, and continues to be, how to keep afloat in the vast sea of technical information with which it must contend. With more than 4 million U.S. patents averaging seven pages each, not to mention foreign patents, there is a huge "prior art" to which the hundred thousand new applications each year must be juxtaposed. A beginning has been made toward computerized search procedures, but no real substitute has yet been developed for manual searches through sheaves of printed patents in bins organized into more than 300 subject matter classes and a huge number of subclasses. The task is enormous and will undoubtedly challenge the office for decades to come.

A more basic problem is maintaining the quality of the patents issued. The examination for novelty, utility, and inventive content is performed by fallible middle-level civil servants under a fair amount of time pressure. In 1975, the average patent application commanded an examiner's attention for nineteen hours. The examiner must make judgments based upon what the applicant has submitted, the PTO's vast files, and his or her own knowledge of the technical specialty. Oversights and factual or judgmental errors are unavoidable. When the invention is an important one and there is doubt over whether the patent examiner's decision was correct, competitors of the patent holder often choose to ignore the patent and engage in potentially infringing use. The patent holder must weigh the costs and risks of taking the infringer to court against those of ignoring the infringement or attempting to negotiate a licensing agreement on relatively weak terms. A patent, it has been said, is nothing more than an opportunity to bring a law suit. Several hundred patents end up being challenged in court each year, and of those that are litigated to a decision, from 45 to 75 percent have been declared invalidly issued. Of the 190 patents whose validity was challenged before appellate courts between 1973 and 1977, 72 percent were held invalid, most often on the ground of insufficient inventive contribution. To be sure, these invalidated patents comprise only a small fraction—less than one-half percent—of all patents in force. But because law suits are costly, they are a sample biased toward patents characterized by high economic importance and relatively great difficulty of evasion through "inventing around," which in turn implies above-average inventive content. It is not known how many patent infringement suits are never initiated because the patent holder senses the weakness of its position, but the number is undoubtedly substantial. Certainly, the high rate of judicial invalidation casts a pall on other patents in force.

One way of improving the average quality of patents might be to make the patent issuance process an open adversary proceeding rather than a closed administrative proceeding involving (except in interference cases and appeals) only the applicant and the examiner. This would be done by instituting an "opposition" procedure long used by some nations and adopted in 1973 as part of a unified European patent system. Under it, the patent application would be published, and other parties who have reason to believe a patent would not be valid are given a certain period of time to come forward, challenge the application, and present relevant evidence that the patent examiner might have lacked. Disadvantages of the opposition approach are its greater initial cost and a tendency for large companies to use opposition as a means of harassing smaller competitors into granting licenses on terms favorable to the challenger.

Still more basic is the question of whether the patent system represents the most desirable trade-off between stimulus and monopoly burdens in a world where, unlike the world for which the system was originally devised, sizable corporations rather than independent inventors carry out most invention and innovation. Indeed, independent inventors and small companies often suffer an appreciable handicap in using the patent system because of their inferior staying power relative to large corporations in a legal battle over patent rights. It is also argued that the patent grant is an unnecessary or redundant stimulus to invention by large corporations because their well-established market positions give them sufficient protection against competitive imitation and because fear of being preempted by innovative rivals forces them to support research and development.

To the extent that this is true, patent grants confer or strengthen monopoly power without a *quid pro quo* of enhanced technical progress. The most careful empirical studies reveal that much industrial inventive and innovative activity would indeed have taken place without the prospect of patent protection, but there are important exceptions in areas where the technical risks and costs are especially great and imitation is particularly easy. Pharmaceutical research and development is the most prominent of these exceptions. One proposed solution to this dilemma is to fine-tune the patent system so that exclusive rights are granted only when inventors (or their corporate sponsors) bear the burden of showing that a technical advance would have been improbable without such rights. However, the administrative complexity and cost of such a procedure would be formidable, and some inventive activity would undoubtedly be delayed or discouraged by uncertainty as to how the proceedings will turn out. Although other less drastic reforms continue to be considered, the U.S. patent system has stood largely intact for nearly two centuries because no one has been able to invent a superior substitute.

FOR ADDITIONAL INFORMATION: Useful material is available in *Journal of the Patent Office Society*, a monthly "house organ" with articles on current legal and administrative issues, including critical views; Carole Kitti, "Patent Invalidity Studies: A Survey," *Idea* 20, No. 1 (1979): 55-76, survey of the judicial invalidation problem (see also the Patent and Trademark Office's *Official Gazette* [January 1, 1980]: 129-130, for later statistics); and Fritz Machlup, *An Economic Review of the Patent System*, Study No. 15 of the U.S. Senate Committee on the Judiciary, Subcommittee on Patents, Trademarks, and Copyrights (1958), a comprehensive historical and economic survey, part of a larger set of subcommittee-commissioned studies exploring virtually all aspects of the patent system.

See also Peter D. Rosenberg, *Patent Law Fundamentals* (1975), everything you wanted to know and more about patent law and practice; F. M. Scherer, *Industrial Market Structure and Economic Performance*, 2d ed. (1980), Chapter 16, an analysis of patent system economics that is more up-to-date on theory and empirical studies than Machlup's; and C. T. Taylor and Z. A. Silberston, *The Economic Impact of the Patent System* (1973), a particularly thorough investigation (through interviews with British companies) of the patent system's effects.

F. M. SCHERER

PEACE CORPS. By the end of 1981, the Peace Corps had celebrated or marked its twentieth anniversary on four separate occasions and had held a reunion for its "alumni"—fitting for an agency that has lived in a goldfish bowl for more than two decades. Few government agencies have received more public scrutiny and evoked more emotional response, both negative and positive, in its relatively short existence than has the Peace Corps.

In its infancy, the Peace Corps made all the mistakes only a child can. It was undisciplined, a little spoiled, sometimes petulant, unsure of itself, romantic to a fault, and given to public self-criticism. During its early teens—especially under the Nixon and Ford administrations—it was seldom heard of or from. It had survived the Vietnam conflict, but just barely, and it strove quietly for maturation. As it neared adulthood under the Carter Administration, it was shaken by conflicts over policy decisions and claims that it had outlived its usefulness.

One-third of the way through its twentieth-anniversary year, the Peace Corps learned that one of its sister agencies, Volunteers In Service To America (VISTA), was being phased out of existence by order of President Ronald Reagan. Staff members at Washington headquarters were saying with justifiable realism that anyone who could kill VISTA could kill the Peace Corps as well. One troubled agency official wondered why our own poor should be ignored while we continued to serve the poor overseas. The President's decision left them shocked and upset.

The first of the twentieth-anniversary celebrations was held at the University of Michigan on October 14, 1980. Standing near the spot where presidential candidate John F. Kennedy first proposed the creation of the Peace Corps, former Secretary of State Edmund S. Muskie said that Americans had been "sobered" by a new understanding of the world in the past twenty years, but, he added, "We must reject defeatism. . . . We have made a difference." Flanking Secretary Muskie were Richard Celeste, the then-current Peace Corps director, and Sargent Shriver, the agency's first director. Noting a change in Peace Corps attitude, Celeste said, "When we began, we sought to change the world. Now we work at changing only parts of the world." Referring to the 1970s as "The Me Decade," a subdued Sargent Shriver added, "We are not in Kennedy's era, we are not on the New Frontier. . . . We are hunkered down trying to keep what we've got."

Shriver may have been remembering the abandonment and rapidity with which things were done under Kennedy. Kennedy created the Peace Corps by Executive Order on March 1, 1961, and Congress gave it permanence in late September after a relatively short debate in both houses. Kennedy signed the bill into law on September 22, 1961. By that time, Peace Corps headquarters had received some 13,000 applications for service, the Washington staff numbered 362, and more than 600 volunteers were at work in eight countries.

The early days were not easy, and some mistakes were made. A few were given worldwide attention; others remain known only to Peace Corps insiders. The first gaffe occurred less than a month after the Peace Corps Act was signed, leading to a chorus of "We-told-you-so" by critics. In October 1961, Margery Michelmore, a volunteer serving in Nigeria, lost a postcard she had written to a friend back home. In her message, Michelmore described the volunteers' "initial, horrified shock" at the squalor and unsanitary conditions in Ibadan, the capital city. The postcard was found; students at the University College of Ibadan had it duplicated and distributed, and called a rally at which a resolution was adopted condemning Michelmore and demanding deportation of all Peace Corps volunteers then serving in Nigeria. Nigerian Prime Minister Sir Abubakar Tafawa Balewa publicly demanded that the young volunteer be "unequivocally condemned." Before the incident escalated further, Michelmore wrote a letter of apology to Nigerian authorities and offered her resignation from volunteer service. Later, she worked with the agency for a brief time, counseling trainees. Then as now, politicized university students in host countries most frequently are those who agitate for the ouster of the Peace Corps.

Careful volunteers avoid being caught up in host-country politics. An incident in the Dominican Republic revealed how the less educated, host-country national, with whom the volunteer works most closely, can differentiate between the status and intentions of the Peace Corps worker and anti-Americanism in local politics. In the spring of 1965, a rebellion broke out in the Dominican Republic. During the fighting, Peace Corps volunteers were the only Americans permitted to pass safely through the battle lines. One volunteer came across a Dominican in Santo Domingo who had just finished painting "Yankee Go Home" on a wall. "Well," said the volunteer, "I guess that means me. I'll get packed." "Oh, no!" replied the Dominican, "I mean the Yankees, not the Peace Corps."

The volunteer is and always has been a private American citizen, selected, trained, assigned, and supported in the field by full-time, salaried employees of the Peace Corps and is not an employee of the Peace Corps. The Peace Corps volunteer is obviously motivated by humanitarian considerations because he or she receives a modest monthly living allowance comparable to that of those with whom he or she works. In addition, roughly $125 is set aside for the volunteer in a trust fund for every month of service. This fund provides a small nest egg that becomes available upon completion of service and the return home.

A clearer understanding of the dynamics of the Peace Corps comes with the recognition that there are actually two separate Peace Corps. The first is the Washington headquarters, which is linked to field operations through its three regional offices: the African Region, the Latin American and Caribbean Region, and the North Africa, Near East, Asia and Pacific Region. There is then the host-country Peace Corps director and his or her cadre. The second Peace Corps is the individual experience of each volunteer, past and present. The second Peace Corps is represented by the experiences of 85,000 Americans who have served as volunteers since the program began. Their remoteness from Washington—and sometimes even from the host-country bureaucracy—has caused some myopia among a few volunteers who have been prone to blame everything that goes wrong, including jungle rot and the weather, on the in-country staff and ultimately on Peace Corps/Washington.

Managerial efficiency does vary from country to country and from program to program, but the returning volunteer has most consistently criticized the training he or she received. For example, Miss Lillian Carter, the former President's mother and a former health program volunteer in India, discovered when she arrived in India that she should have been taught Hindi rather than Marathi during her language training.

When the Peace Corps headquarters opened on March 1, 1961, there was precious little expertise to draw from. In the *National Geographic* of September 1961, Sargent Shriver described how he and fifteen to twenty persons with experience in managing international student and education programs spent the month of February 1961 completing the outline of an organization.

Shriver drew genuine praise from experienced Washington hands for his salesmanship and for his willingness to make use of both government and civilian experts. Shriver ran a centralized operation with high turnover among top-level officers. This turnover was partly the result of his policy of allowing the bright young men he hired to work at cross-purposes. He would sometimes assign the same project to two or three persons without any of them knowing it. The result was constant turmoil. Freshly minted organizational charts appeared with great frequency.

In 1965, President Lyndon Johnson asked Shriver to head the newly established Office of Economic Opportunity while remaining director of the Peace Corps. In that same year, Shriver asked Congress to add a provision to the Peace Corps Act which would prohibit top staff members from serving more than five years with the agency to assure the infusion of fresh ideas and leadership. Congress acceded, specifying that the amendment was not to be retroactive. Inside the agency, the private term for the provision became known as "the five-year flush."

"The five-year flush" went largely unnoticed during the directorship of Jack Hood Vaughn. Vaughn had served with both the United States Information Agency* and the Agency for International Development* before joining the headquarters staff of the Peace Corps in 1961. He left in 1964 when he was appointed U.S. ambassador to Panama and then returned to Washington to hold simultaneously the positions of Assistant Secretary of State for Inter-American Affairs and U.S. coordinator for the Alliance for Progress before being named Peace Corps director on March 1, 1966. A pragmatic romantic, Vaughn was volunteer-oriented, and his tenure was marked by a decentralization of responsibilities. He eliminated some top-level jobs in Washington and gave to the host-country directors and their staffs a major share of managing their volunteer programs.

It was also during Vaughn's term of office that the number of programs, host countries, and volunteers burgeoned. During 1966-1967, nearly 15,000 Americans served in or were in training for service in 58 countries. Learning from past mistakes, the agency under Vaughn tightened its selection process, improved its training programs as more and more of them were moved from the United States to host countries, and more host-country citizens were hired to help conduct the training of volunteers and serve as in-country staff members. Today, all but two or three training programs are conducted overseas.

On March 17, 1969, Vaughn was replaced by a Richard Nixon appointee, Joseph Blatchford. The era of the generalist volunteer ended, and the era of the volunteer with technical expertise began. The shrinkage in the number of volunteers also began under Blatchford, who took office determined to meet what he felt were the real needs of host countries. He explained in a July 1969 hearing before the House Foreign Affairs Committee the necessity of avoiding outside technical aid by these nations.

Blatchford's tenure as Peace Corps director was perhaps stormier than that of any other director. During his two predecessors' terms of office, Congress granted most Peace Corps requests. Blatchford and his staff experienced tortuous frustration at congressional budget hearings.

Congress was not Blatchford's only problem. As director of the Peace Corps, he also saw the Washington headquarters occupied by protesters of U.S. involvement in Vietnam, many of whom were returned volunteers. He had to dismiss twelve volunteers for publishing their views of Vietnam in host-country newspapers in violation of agency policy. He presided over the dismissal of a volunteer for use of marijuana, and he watched Congress cut back on appropriations until there were less than half the number of volunteers in the field than there had been under Vaughn.

It was Blatchford, too, who watched his agency lose its independence. Under the Executive Order which President Kennedy had signed to create the temporary Peace Corps, the agency was placed under the State Department.* The Peace Corps Act giving the agency permanence placed it directly under the President, a status it enjoyed until Nixon succeeded in creating ACTION, the "umbrella" agency under which the Peace Corps, VISTA, and seven domestic volunteer programs were placed in 1971. In 1979, Richard Celeste and others were successful in convincing President Jimmy Carter of the need for some Peace Corps autonomy. Carter signed an Executive Order on May 16, 1979, that made the Peace Corps an autonomous agency within ACTION with authority to direct its own program, policy, and budget operations. Blatchford was appointed ACTION'S first director.

With Blatchford heading ACTION, the Peace Corps sought to recruit more black Americans and older, more experienced citizens. More blacks did respond but not nearly as many as had been hoped for. Much more successful was the recruiting of younger volunteers with job experience and specialized skills and older Americans at or nearing retirement age.

Blatchford also enforced the "five-year flush." Early in 1971, he announced that eighty-three Washington staffers had completed their five years of service and would be leaving. There was a hue and cry and heavy press coverage of the announcement, but Blatchford had his way. A year later, there was a wholesale firing of half of all the country directors overseas and 250 senior staff members at headquarters in Washington. To insiders it appeared that the anticipated Nixon purge had finally arrived. This and the creation of ACTION to house volunteer programs at home and abroad appeared to them to be Nixon's move to relegate the Peace Corps to obscurity and ultimate oblivion. The ploy was not successful, but the agency did have to find the means to survive the neglect of the Nixon and Ford administrations. The means were simply to hold fast to the status quo, thus postponing expansion.

Carter's election was viewed as paving the way for renewed Peace Corps vitality. After all, his mother, Miss Lillian, had served as a Peace Corps volunteer. Hopes soared when Carter appointed Sam Brown as director of ACTION.

Agency sympathizers reasoned that Brown would be people-oriented and, through his organizing ability, would streamline and improve volunteer recruitment, selection, training, and placement. They also thought he would discover and implement programs overseas that would have impact in a Third World that was no longer willing to settle for quantity over quality. Brown had been a most visible antiwar activist during the 1960s and had organized the 200,000-person anti-Vietnam War protest demonstration in Washington.

Brown's tenure was beset by battles over policy with a Peace Corps director of his own choice, congressional charges of misapplication of funds and other irregularities by Peace Corps and VISTA officers, and general sniping from conservative members of Congress. He was also disliked by a certain entrenched element within Peace Corps ranks who were horrified that Brown was at least willing to think about the possibilities of "internationalizing" the Peace Corps in concert with like programs from other industrialized nations.

Thus, Peace Corps I limped into its twentieth-anniversary year. At the end of May 1981, it was operating under a newly appointed deputy director, Everett Alvarez, Jr., and a director-designate, Loret Miller Ruppe, wife of Philip E. Ruppe, former six-term Congressman from Michigan. Mrs. Ruppe had been co-chairman of the Reagan-Bush election campaign in Michigan. While awaiting Senate confirmation of her appointmment, Ruppe spent her days learning about the Peace Corps programs in sixty-one countries and writing letters to editors in response to growing editorial comment and discussion of President Reagan's appointment of Thomas Pauken as director of ACTION.

Pauken came highly recommended and highly qualified for the top ACTION post, but those opposed to his appointment cited his connections with earlier military intelligence activities. As an Army officer in Vietnam, he had been given an intelligence-gathering assignment. While not a provision by law, since the agency's inception there has been a Peace Corps regulation that no person who has worked for an intelligence agency or has been engaged in intelligence-related activities can serve as a volunteer or staff member for at least ten years after leaving such an assignment. That regulation had never been broken. Critics of the appointment, while agreeing that Pauken was qualified for the job, argued that his intelligence experience, although behind him, could be used to place every volunteer in the field in jeopardy and intensify the long-standing charges by anti-American groups in some host countries that Peace Corps volunteers are covert agents of the CIA.* This was the reasoning of Senator Alan Cranston (Democrat, California), who in the spring of 1981 submitted a bill to remove the Peace Corps from ACTION and place it under the State Department where it began.

The story of Peace Corps II—the 85,000 separate tours of duty since the Peace Corps was founded—should not be told in terms of success or failure but in terms of what it has meant to the daily lives of desperately deprived people. There have been a few magnificent successes and a few startling failures, largely because of whom the individuals were who succeeded or failed. Ultimately, the collective Peace Corps experience will have been of more benefit to the personal lives of those volunteers who lived that experience and to America itself than to those countries that have hosted the volunteers. It is also true that the Peace Corps has meant little people helping little people—this is the real change, and the real benefit, and the real gift.

The programs that have had the greatest impact are those in public health, nutrition, agriculture, and fisheries. Community development often seems only to have worked while the volunteer was there to offer help. Some host governments have failed to reinforce gains made. Purely technical assistance has often been rebuffed by host-country nationals jealous of the intrusion or wedded to traditional ways of doing things.

Volunteers have been stoned, spat upon, reviled, raped, murdered, shot, and killed during civil disturbances and military coups, held hostage (in one instance in Colombia, for a period of three years), killed in train accidents, victimized by earthquakes and violent tropical storms, and jailed for creating their own disturbances. They have also been made honorary chiefs, acknowledged as heroes and living legends, and widely loved and respected by their hosts.

The paradigm of the magnificent success story involves a carpenter who volunteered in 1967. He served in Africa in Gabon, Upper Volta, Togo, and Sierra Leone. Evidence of his work can be found throughout Sierra Leone in the form of schools, bridges, and other construction projects that he has built or has taught Africans to build. He has had malaria twice, pneumonia six times, and dysentery once. He was once "put on loan" to the government of Togo to inventory all the primary schools and dispensaries in the country. His design of a school building to allow for maximum ventilation as well as protection from rain has become a standard design in Africa. All of these achievements are made more remarkable by the fact that this volunteer, Odilon ("Odie") Long, was sixty-five and retired when he entered Peace Corps service. In 1981, at the age of seventy-nine, he was in Washington to have a knee joint repaired before being reassigned for his eighth two-year tour—this time to Upper Volta where the Peace Corps is building 200 agricultural training centers. Sierra Leone has already conferred its Order of Rokel, its highest honor, on Odie Long. His work honors all Americans.

A recurring criticism of the Peace Corps over the past decade is that the agency and its volunteers have lost the earlier spirit of dedication and commitment to the idealism of the Kennedy era. This is not true. Volunteers, young and old, remain dedicated and committed to humanitarianism. And they do not take kindly to criticism or harassment from those who "have never been there." There was another person flanking Secretary Muskie during his commemoration speech at the University of Michigan in October 1980. During Muskie's speech, a group of students began heckling him over U.S. Middle East policy. Melvin Manthey, seventy-two, a horticulturist who had served as a volunteer in both Tunisia and Iran, was bewildered and angry. "Why are they yelling at us?" he asked. "We're the Peace Corps." In 1960, the Peace Corps was referred to as "an idea whose time has come." People-to-people programs did not begin with the Peace Corps, and they will not end even if the Peace Corps is killed.

FOR ADDITIONAL INFORMATION: The reader should consult Robert G. Carey, *The Peace Corps* (1970) a definitive history of the first nine years of the Peace Corps. This work considers problems in organization and administration at Washington headquarters, recruitment, selection, training, and assignment of volunteers, and the volunteer experience in the field. Ernest Fox, et al., eds., *Citizen in a Time of Change: The Returned Peace Corps Volunteer*, Report of the Conference for Returned Volunteers held in Washington, D.C., March 5-7, 1965 (1965), is an agonizing self-appraisal by returned volunteers and presents some evidence of what the Peace Corps experience meant to returnees as well as to America. Samuel P. Hayes, *An International Peace Corps: The Promise and Problems* (1961), is one of the first of many systematic studies to analyze the possibility of the creation and effectiveness of an international Peace Corps.

The following articles are useful: Joy Billington, "A Long Way from Home, Still Serving," *The Washington Star* (April 5, 1981): Cl, Col. 2, which tells about Odilon Long, the oldest and longest serving Peace Corps volunteer, who at the time he was interviewed had spent fourteen years in Africa; Terence Smith, "Peace Corps: Alive But Not So Well," *New York Times Magazine* (December 25, 1977): 6, a balanced but critical analysis of the status of the Peace Corps at that time containing interviews with congressmen, Washington officials, all but one of the former Peace Corps directors, former volunteers, and active volunteers in Nicaragua and Colombia; and Kathryn Tolbert, "Winner's Way: Potomac's Loret Ruppe Bones Up to Direct the Peace Corps," *The Washington Post* (March 26, 1981): 1 (Maryland Weekly), a vignette of President Reagan's choice for director of the Peace Corps.

Since 1972, ACTION has published an Annual Report, which includes a detailed and statistical account of Peace Corps programs and activities. Especially valuable for key periods of Peace Corps history are the Annual Reports for 1974 and 1980. Copies of these reports are still available upon request at ACTION, Office of Public Affairs, Washington, D.C. 20525.

ROBERT G. CAREY

PERSONNEL MANAGEMENT OFFICE. See Office of Personnel Management.

POSTAL SERVICE. See United States Postal Service.

POST OFFICE. See United States Postal Service.

POWER COMMISSION. See Federal Power Commission.

PUBLIC DEBT BUREAU. See Bureau of Public Debt.

PUBLIC HEALTH SERVICE (PHS). The Public Health Service, a part of the Department of Health and Human Services (DHHS), is the principal health agency of the federal government. Its job is to protect and advance the health of the American people. More specifically, the PHS gives leadership and direction to the nation's health programs; contributes to the advancement of health knowledge through research; disseminates that knowledge to health professionals and the general public; assures that adequate health manpower and facilities are available to all citizens; improves the organization and delivery of health services in the communities; provides direct medical services to its legal beneficiaries and to special groups in the population; controls or eradicates diseases in the United States and prevents their importation from abroad; promotes the safety and health of the nation's workforce and protects consumers against unsafe foods and drugs and against many other hazardous or ineffective products and substances; works with other nations and international agencies toward the solution of international health problems; develops policies and programs for the treatment and prevention of alcohol, drug abuse, and mental health problems; and collects, analyzes, and disseminates statistical data on the state of the nation's health.

The six major agencies that make up the PHS are responsible for carrying out these functions—the National Institutes of Health (NIH), the Food and Drug Administration (FDA),* the Center for Disease Control (CDC), the Alcohol, Drug Abuse, and Mental Health Administration (ADAMHA), the Health Resources Administration (HRA), and the Health Services Administration (HSA). The Assistant Secretary for Health heads the service, advises the DHHS Secretary on health and health-related matters, and directs the activities of the major PHS agencies.

The current missions of the major health agencies can be summarized as follows. NIH, which consists of eleven research institutes, four divisions, a research hospital called the clinical center, the National Library of Medicine, and the Fogarty International Center, is one of the largest and most prestigious medical research centers in the world. Its 1981 budget of $3.6 billion was used to conduct research in its own laboratories; to support research in universities, hospitals, and other research institutions in this country and abroad; to help nonprofit institutions build and equip biomedical research facilities; to support the training of young, promising career researchers; and to improve the communication of biomedical information to scientists, health practitioners, and the public. Nearly 90 percent of the annual budget was distributed to investigators outside the institutes. NIH thus supports about 40 percent of all biomedical research and development in this country. It certainly has come a long way from its early days as a single-room Hygienic Laboratory in a marine hospital on Staten Island. The story of its growth and development is an important part of PHS history and will be told in greater detail below.

FDA is the oldest and largest consumer protection agency of the federal government. It is responsible for enforcing laws which require that foods be safe and wholesome, that drugs and medical devices be safe and effective, that cosmetics be safe, and that all of these products be truthfully labeled. FDA also protects consumers from unnecessary exposure to radiation and has authority over the regulation of vaccines, serums, and other biological products.

The emphasis at CDC, as its name implies, is on the control and prevention of disease. CDC tracks disease incidence and trends throughout the world, administers a national quarantine program, trains health workers, studies infectious diseases, licenses clinical laboratories engaged in interstate commerce, disseminates health education materials, and conducts laboratory research and epidemiological studies to determine hazards in the workplace and how to eliminate them. CDC was reorganized in October 1980 and now consists of five smaller centers and the National Institute for Occupational Safety and Health.

ADAMHA leads the national effort to prevent and treat alcohol abuse and alcoholism, drug abuse, and mental and emotional illness. The agency conducts clinical and biochemical research in its own laboratories, but much of its work is accomplished through grants and contracts that it awards for research, prevention, training projects, and the delivery of treatment services in community-based programs.

The primary concerns of HRA are the identification, development, and utilization of the nation's health resources. HRA does health planning, supports studies of the health care system, gives aid to institutions training health professionals, and administers programs related to health care facilities, such as the monitoring of insured construction loans to hospitals.

The HSA, through its bureaus of community health services, medical services, health personnel development and service, and the Indian Health Service, works to improve the quality and availability of comprehensive health care to all citizens. This is done by encouraging health professionals to set up practice in underserved communities, by correcting inadequacies in the distribution of health services, by improving the quality of health care, by giving financial aid to medical students, and by providing hospital and clinical care, directly, to certain legally defined groups of American citizens, such as American Indians, Native Alaskans, merchant seamen, and members of the uniformed services. HSA's direct-care responsibilities can be traced back to the 1798 act of Congress which established the Marine Hospital Service, the precursor of the PHS, to provide for the "relief of sick and disabled seamen."

Through these six major agencies, fifteen offices, and the Regional Health Administration, the PHS has become involved in virtually every aspect of the United States' multi-billion-dollar health enterprise. Until now, the story of the PHS has been one of growth and expansion, of ever increasing federal responsibility for health care, and of change in response to the evolving health needs of our nation. The history of the PHS can be divided into three periods: the Marine Hospital Service (1798-1902), the Public Health and Marine Hospital Service (1902-1912), and the Public Health Service (1912-present).

The story of the PHS began in 1798 when President John Adams signed into law an act (1 Stat. L., 605-606) which furnished medical relief to merchant seamen. This was one of the earliest federal activities that was not related directly to the actual operation of the government and showed the new national government's concern that a healthy merchant marine was necessary for economic prosperity and a strong national defense. The law stipulated that twenty cents a month was to be deducted from the wage of each seaman serving on an American ship and paid to the collectors of customs, who in turn would give the money to the Secretary of the Treasury. The President was authorized to use that money to provide medical services for the seamen in existing hospitals, or to build new hospitals, and to appoint directors of marine hospitals.

Taxing American seamen to provide for their medical care was among the first direct taxes enacted by the federal government and was the first prepaid medical care program in the United States. The concept of government support for the medical care of merchant seamen originated in Britain at the end of the sixteenth century, when after the defeat of the Spanish Armada a hospital was established in Greenwich to care for the British seamen and was supported by a deduction from their wages. Seamen of the American colonies also were taxed to support this hospital.

The first marine hospitals were established in the port cities along the East Coast, such as, Norfolk, Virginia; Boston, Massachusetts; Newport, Rhode Island; and Charleston, South Carolina. As trade expanded along the inland waterways and the Great Lakes and finally reached the West Coast, the marine hospitals followed. A hospital was even erected in Hawaii.

During the early years, the Marine Hospital Service (MHS) encountered a number of problems. Too many hospitals were built; some were poorly located; and the demand for services far exceeded the funds available. Therefore, seamen with chronic or incurable conditions were excluded from medical relief, and a four-month limit was placed on hospital care for the rest. Supplemental funds had to be appropriated constantly from Congress in order to maintain the service and to build the hospitals. The biggest problem, however, was the absence of any central supervisory authority. The 1798 act had placed all authority in the President, who then delegated most of it to the Secretary of the Treasury. But the Treasury Department* had no supervisory mechanism by which to centralize or coordinate the activities of the separate service hospitals. The President at first appointed the surgeons in charge of these hospitals but later allowed the collectors of customs to make these appointments, further diluting authority. Consequently, each hospital was managed independently.

The act of June 29, 1870 (16 Stat. L., 169) formally organized the MHS as a national agency with a central headquarters and with a supervisory surgeon in charge of all the hospitals. The act also increased the hospital tax on seaman from twenty cents to forty cents per month. The money collected was placed in a separate MHS fund. The tax on seamen was abolished in 1884, and from 1884 to 1906 the cost of maintaining the marine hospitals was paid out of a tonnage tax. From 1906 until 1981, medical care for merchant seamen and other beneficiaries was supported by direct appropriations from Congress. In 1981, the eight remaining PHS hospitals and twenty-six clinics were closed or transferred to other federal agencies, state or local jurisdictions, or private organizations. Nearly two centuries of medical care for merchant seamen in government-run hospitals had come to an end.

John M. Woodward was appointed the first supervising surgeon (the title was later changed to surgeon general) in 1871 and promptly reorganized the service on a more efficient basis. Entrance examinations for medical officers were instituted. Appointments of surgeons were made to the general service rather than to a particular locality, emphasizing the national character of the service and circumventing local political pressure. Publication of Annual Reports and sanitary reports (forerunner of the present *Public Health Reports*) was initiated. The Commissioned Corps, a mobile group of medical officers who could be sent quickly anywhere in the United States or the world to fight disease, to staff marine hospitals, or to perform other health functions, was established in 1889. The corps was permitted to hire engineers and dentists in 1930, and, in 1944, this authority was expanded to include research scientists, nurses, and a range of other health specialists.

The functions of the MHS expanded greatly to include the supervision of national quarantine, the medical inspection of immigrants, the prevention of interstate spread of disease (especially yellow fever, cholera, smallpox, and plague), and general investigations in the field of public health (such as the investigation of yellow fever epidemics).

The MHS was quick to apply the newly emerging science of bacteriology to the study of disease in the United States. A small one-room bacteriology laboratory was established at the marine hospital on Staten Island, New York, in 1887. The first director of this Hygienic Laboratory, as it was called, was Joseph J. Kinyoun, a student of Robert Koch, the famous German bacteriologist. Although small, the laboratory was equipped with the best German instruments and began doing some very notable work. During its early years, the laboratory focused on the study of the etiology, pathology, and prophylaxis of such acute infectious diseases as cholera, yellow fever, smallpox, and bubonic plague—especially cholera and yellow fever, the two great scourges of nineteenth-century America. Many studies and experiments were made on different kinds of disinfectants. A special fumigation apparatus was designed. Water was chemically analyzed for the presence of disease-causing microbes. In 1891, the laboratory moved from Staten Island to larger quarters in Washington, D.C., where its sections were expanded to include pathology, chemistry, pharmacology, and zoology.

The increase in the duties of the MHS, including medical research, made it desirable to change its name and give it more specific statutory powers. This was done by the act of July 1, 1902 (32 Stat. L., 712), which designated the surgeon general as head of the service; provided a definite organization and budget for the Hygienic Laboratory; and required the surgeon general to call an annual conference of the health authorities of the states, territories, and the District of Columbia, furthering the coordination of national and state public health functions.

The Biologics Control Act, which President Theodore Roosevelt also signed into law on July 1, 1902, authorized the Public Health and Marine Hospital

Service (PHMHS), through the Hygienic Laboratory to test biologicals such as viruses, serums, toxins, antitoxins, and analogous products and to license manufacturers of these products. This was the first federal law regulating the interstate and foreign sale of a specific class of drugs in the United States and preceded by four years the first Food and Drug Act. The aim of the biologics act was to protect the public against infections from impure preparations and to establish a standard of strength and purity for various antitoxins and vaccines. The workload and the responsibilities of the Hygienic Laboratory increased significantly.

As a result of the strict enforcement of the biologics act, the quality of the biologics sold on the open market improved markedly. The act also stimulated original scientific research to establish the U.S. standard of potency for various antitoxins and vaccines, and to understand the nature of certain adverse body reactions to these preparations. Milton J. Rosenau and John F. Anderson of the Hygienic Laboratory did pioneering work in these fields.

The scientific work of the service expanded and began reaching out into the communities and workplaces through special field investigations. Studies in the South of the hookworm disease by Charles W. Stiles and later of pellagra by Joseph Goldberger clearly demonstrated the relationship between poor living conditions, meager diet, and disease, and helped stimulate the development of full-time county health work as well as focus attention on rural health problems. Epidemiological studies of typhoid fever in Washington, D.C., and elsewhere (1906-1910) by Leslie Lumsden contributed to the development of the rural sanitation movement. PHMHS scientists were sent to Missouri and Colorado to study silicosis among miners. The results of these and other studies began to be published in the *Hygienic Laboratory Bulletin*.

Following a congressionally mandated investigation of leprosy, the PHMHS opened a Leprosy Investigation Station in 1909 at Kalaupapa, Molokai, in the Hawaiian Islands. It was one of the best equipped and staffed federal research facilities of its time. Yet, it remained open for less than four years primarily because in its design and construction as an in-patient hospital and laboratory, the outdoor-oriented life-style of Kalaupapa's residents was not taken into consideration. Consequently, the patients never visited the federal hospital, and it had to close. This was an example of an opportunity lost to research and develop an effective treatment for an important infectious disease because of an emphasis on medical technology without the necessary understanding of the patient's behavioral needs. A hospital for the treatment of leprosy patients and later a research center were established in Carville, Louisiana, in 1921, and they are still active today.

The PHMHS further developed the national maritime quarantine by continuing to buy and take over the operations of local quarantine stations, and by extending their quarantine functions to Hawaii, Cuba, Puerto Rico, the Panama Canal, and the Philippine Islands.

The PHMHS also began to become involved in international health matters by actively participating in the creation of the Pan American Sanitary Bureau (1902) and the International Office of Public Health in Paris (1908).

Throughout the first decade of the twentieth century, political efforts were made to combine the public health-related work being done by various federal agencies, but they were unsuccessful in Congress. The act of August 14, 1912 (37 Stat. L., 309) merely changed the name of the PHMHS to PHS and authorized the investigations of the diseases of man and of the pollution of navigable streams. Consolidation began in June 1939 when the PHS was transferred to the Federal Security Agency, which combined certain health, education, and welfare activities of the federal government. Thus ended over 140 years of association between the PHS and the Treasury Department. In 1953, PHS, along with other units of the Federal Security Agency, became a part of the newly created Department of Health, Education, and Welfare* (HEW). Prior to this all of the laws affecting the functions of the service had been consolidated for the first time in the Public Health Service Act of 1944.

In the past seventy years, the PHS has done much to protect and improve the health of the American people. Among its accomplishments are completion of the national maritime quarantine system; development and expansion of field investigations (Frost's stream pollution studies, Lumsden's local health department demonstrations, industrial hygiene investigations, study of drug addiction problems and nutritional deficiency diseases, venereal disease, and malaria control programs); expansion of research; organization of the medical service of federal penal and correctional institutions (1930); inauguration of grants-in-aid to states as part of the Social Security Act (1935); coordination and control of programs designed to prevent environmental health hazards (the Water Pollution Control Acts of 1948 and 1956 and the Clean Air Act of 1963); allocation of resources to train health workers and to construct health facilities (the Health Professional Educational Assistance Act of 1963, the Nurse Training Act of 1964, the Hospital Survey and Construction or Hill-Burton Act of 1946); and the development of health maintenance organizations (the HMO Act of 1973).

The area of largest growth has been basic medical research. The Ransdell Act in 1930 changed the name of the Hygienic Laboratory to the National Institute of Health and further committed it to fundamental research. In keeping with the New Deal idea that the federal government had a responsibility to act in important matters affecting the nation's health, the National Cancer Act (1937), which established the National Cancer Institute, for the first time provided permanent authority to make grants in support of medical research at nonfederal institutions. Extramural support of biomedical research in the United States by NIH has grown tremendously since World War II. The National Heart Act (1948) authorized the creation of the Heart Institute and changed the name of NIH to the National Institutes of Health (plural). Over the next two decades, Congress authorized other institutes, so that now there is a total of eleven. This growth in research reflects and parallels the rise of American medicine to world preeminence. The kind of basic research that has been undertaken reflects a shift away from the study of infectious and nutritional diseases, which the PHS had fought so successfully in the past, to the chronic and environmentally induced diseases, which are the major health problems today.

The scope of the work done by the PHS continued to expand throughout the first half of the century. In 1929, Congress authorized the PHS to provide confinement and treatment for persons addicted to the use of habit-forming drugs (Narcotics Act). A Narcotics Division was created in the PHS, and two hospitals for addicts were built in Lexington, Kentucky (1935) and Fort Worth, Texas (1938). In the 1920s, federal and state maternal and child health programs were strengthened by the Sheppard-Towner Act. Venereal disease control programs were initiated during World War I and were carried forward and expanded very vigorously by Surgeon General Thomas Parran during the late 1920s and 1930s. On the whole, these programs were effective, but, at least on one occasion, they led to a questionable study—the ill-fated Tuskegee Study of the effects of untreated syphilis on black men in Macon County, Alabama. The PHS also moved strongly into the area of mental health following the passage of the Mental Health Act in 1946.

These are just samples of the historic highlights from the work of the PHS. The activities and responsibilities of the PHS are too numerous and complex to be discussed in detail in this short account. This is also true of the various pitfalls, shortcomings, and problems that the service has faced over the years. The PHS has undergone frequent organizational restructuring in HEW since 1953 and now again in the Department of Health and Human Services. The growth and expansion of the service has slowed considerably. Federal responsibility for health care is being reexamined in light of President Ronald Reagan's policy to transfer many federal programs to the states and local governments. The appropriateness of decentralizing various federal health functions should be carefully examined in light of our historical experience with such matters as quarantine, sanitation, disease control, the purity of foods and drugs, international health relations, and basic research.

FOR ADDITIONAL INFORMATION: Records of the PHS are found in Record Group 90 at the National Archives* in Washington, D.C. They include audiovisual and cartographic records. Much information about the organization, administration, and scientific work of the service is found in PHS publications, such as the *Annual Reports*, the *Hygienic Laboratory Bulletins* (later *NIH Bulletins*), *Public Health Bulletins*, and *Public Health Reports*.

Ralph Chester Williams's *The United States Public Health Service 1798-1950* (1951) remains the most comprehensive history of the PHS. A more popular, journalistic version is Bess Furman's *A Profile of the United States Public Health Service 1798-1948* (1973). Laurence F. Schmeckebier's *The Public Health Service: Its History, Activities and Organization* (1923) is a very useful administrative and legislative history of the PHS until 1920. It has an appendix listing and reprinting most of the major laws dealing with the PHS and a helpful bibliography. An updated chronology of major health legislation and several articles dealing with the history and present status of the PHS may be found in the government publication *Health in America: 1776-1976* (1976). The pamphlet, *The*

Public Health Service Today (1976), contains a nice summary of the organization and structure of the PHS and its major agencies in 1976, but now is badly in need of an update. The early history of the PHS is ably surveyed by Robert Straus, *Medical Care for Seamen: The Origin of Public Medical Service in the United States* (1950). Richard Thurm's *For the Relief of the Sick and Disabled: The U.S. Public Health Service Hospital at Boston 1799-1969* is a case study of one of the earliest marine hospitals and contains reprints of many original letters and documents dealing with the history of the Boston hospital. C. J. Simpson's *Federal Responsibility for Medical Care of Seamen* (1955) is a strong polemic, with a historical focus and many facts, for the continuance of government support of the medical care of seamen. The best summary of the scientific research work done by the PHS, especially in bacteriology, may be found in A. M. Stimson's *A Brief History of Bacteriological Investigations of the United States Public Health Service* (1938). Paul Clark's chapter on important contributions to microbiology by federal agencies in his *Pioneer Microbiologists of America* (1961) places the work of the Hygienic Laboratory in the broader context of biomedical research at the end of the nineteenth and first half of the twentieth centuries. Jeannette Barry's *Notable Contributions to Medical Research by Public Health Service Scientists* (1960) is a useful bibliographical guide to some of the major PHS scientists and their work until 1940. The history of NIH remains to be written. Nevertheless, some important insights concerning its early history and rapid rise may be gained from Victor Kramer's *The National Institute of Health: A Study in Public Administration* (1937) and Donald C. Swain's "The Rise of a Research Empire: NIH, 1930 to 1950," *Science* 138 (1962):1233-1237. The emergence of a national policy for cancer research and the establishment of the National Cancer Institute are nicely described in Stephen Strickland's *Politics, Science, and Dread Disease* (1972). A number of books have been written about specific work of the PHS, such as Thomas Parran's *Shadow on the Land: Syphilis* (1937) and Elizabeth Etheridge's *The Butterfly Caste: A Social History of Pellagra in the South* (1972). They tend to show the PHS at its best. A counterpoint would be James H. Jones's *Bad Blood: The Tuskegee Syphilis Experiment* (1981). Many important documents and studies, including those of the PHS, have been reprinted by Arno Press in the series *Public Health in America*, edited by Barbara G. Rosenkrantz.

RAMUNAS A. KONDRATAS

PUBLIC WORKS ADMINISTRATION (PWA). The Public Works Administration allocated almost $6 billion to construct significant roads, tunnels, dams, power plants, and other public projects during the Great Depression. Its projects touched virtually every county in the United States and comprised half of the school buildings and most of the municipal water and sewage disposal plants constructed in the 1930s. For these "nonfederal" projects, PWA donated 30 percent of the cost and loaned the various municipalities the remaining 70 percent, secured by appropriate municipal bonds. The PWA intended that these projects be self-liquidating and that borrowed funds be repaid to the federal government out of user fees such as water service charges. Among the larger projects was the Chicago sewage system costing $42 million. The PWA also loaned just under $200 million to thirty railroads for equipment and upgrading.

The PWA allocated $1.8 billion directly to other federal agencies, such as the

Bureau of Reclamation,* the Bureau of Roads, and the War Department.* Its funds helped build Grand Coulee Dam, many Navy vessels, Queens Midtown Tunnel, and the All American Canal from the Boulder Dam on the Colorado River to the southern California Imperial and Coachella valleys.

From 1933 to 1939, PWA actually disbursed only $4.1 billion of its allocation. This amounted to 15 percent of all construction in the United States during these years of the depression, with a high point of 33 percent in 1934. The PWA employed an average of 139,662 workers on site each year, but with an estimated cumulative primary and secondary employment of 768,141 per year. A study of the sewage systems financed by PWA showed that only 26 percent of the funds went for labor on the site, leaving 50 percent for materials and over 23 percent for profit and overhead.

The rationale for a Public Works Administration sprang from four years of vigorous discussion during the Hoover Administration. Four constituencies offered increasingly stronger reasons for a massive public works program to stem the depression. Economists, both popular and academic, were in the forefront. In 1930, William Trufant Foster and Waddill Catchings reprinted two essays under the title *Progress and Plenty*. Foster and Catchings argued that new construction of highways, public buildings, and other projects through direct or indirect borrowing put new money into circulation, money that would inevitably flow to consumers. Planning to achieve solid, valuable projects was universally considered essential, and as early as 1921 Otto T. Mallery had discussed a general reserve fund for public works in *The Long Range Planning of Public Works*. In an important article by Georg Bielschowsky in the *Quarterly Journal of Economics* in 1930, the emphasis was on careful planning.

A second constituency was a group of senators who advocated public works as a way to recovery from the depression. This public works faction was led by Robert M. LaFollette, Jr., of Wisconsin and Bronson Cutting of New Mexico, both Liberal Republicans, and Democrat Edward P. Costigan of Colorado. Advance planning for public works was passed by Congress in 1931 and approved by President Herbert Hoover. In 1932, Congress passed the Emergency Relief and Construction Act funded with more than $2 billion to promote public works construction. Congress also considered a bill by Senator LaFollette to create a Public Works Administration, with funding of $5 billion.

Two other constituencies actively supported these measures. Notable were the construction trade associations and their journals such as the *Engineering News-Record*. Likewise supporting public works were the social service organizations such as the National Conference of Catholic Charities under the leadership of the Reverend John O'Grady.

Out of the debate and discussion among and within the constituencies during the Hoover years emerged three essential reasons for a public works program— pump priming, employment, and socially useful projects. Each of these reasons can be associated with a tendency of the New Deal. Pump priming meant that, through the rapid expenditure of large sums of federal funds, private purchasing power would be increased, thus leading to "recovery." The employment of a public works program provided direct "relief" for those thrown out of work. The socially useful projects were envisioned as a method of "reform" of the industrial structure of America. These projects were to demonstrate the relevance and value of national projects such as the Tennessee Valley Authority* and the great dams. The electrification of the Pennsylvania Railroad between New York and Washington demonstrated how cooperation between big business and government could accomplish more socially useful results than either alone.

Shortly after the inauguration of President Franklin D. Roosevelt in March 1933, two members of his Cabinet came to the forefront in the renewed struggle for a public works program—Democrat and Secretary of Labor Frances Perkins, and Liberal Republican and Secretary of the Interior Harold L. Ickes. Working from the LaFollette $5 billion proposal, these Cabinet supporters were forced by administration conservatives, such as Budget Director Lewis Douglas, to compromise on $3.3 billion for public works, doled out as 30 percent grants, with the balance in secured loans. During the campaign, Roosevelt had refused to support a Public Works Administration, so PWA was made Title II of a proposed National Recovery Administration.* There the program would have been administered by General Hugh S. Johnson in a manner designed to bring recovery, that is, money would have been granted swiftly for any project on hand. But Johnson's lack of political adeptness enabled the Liberal Republicans to outmaneuver him by stressing the need for socially useful projects. Johnson was quickly replaced by Ickes, the administrator of the PWA for its duration.

Ickes initially decentralized PWA in order to provide patronage positions for loyal Democrats in all the states and to stimulate localities to submit projects for funding. A state chairman, a state advisory board, and a state engineer were provided for, all of whom were under eight regional administrators, and then a large central staff in Washington. But projects came in slowly, primarily because PWA insisted that all work be done by carefully drawn private contracts and that all loans be fully secured. Objections to these meticulous standards soon led Ickes to dismiss the state chairmen, state boards, and regional administrators. Thereafter, the state engineer screened projects, and the Washington staff scrutinized them. Of the initial appropriation of $3.3 billion, PWA finally spent only $2.8 billion, and more than half of that sum did not go to municipalities and nonfederal projects; it went to other federal agencies. When Ickes turned PWA over to its successor agency, the Federal Works Administration, PWA's central office numbered over 2,000 employees.

Congress devoted attention to PWA in every year of the New Deal, but three major acts define it. The first was the National Industrial Recovery Act, which created it. Ickes's slowness to start spending prompted Roosevelt to remove $400 million from PWA for a Civil Works Administration (CWA) under Aubrey Williams and Harry Hopkins. CWA was a model of expedition. In 1934, since Ickes still had not spent more of his appropriation, Congress merely authorized him to sell collateral for some of the nonfederal loans and to recapture the money for further lending. In 1935, Congress passed the second major act, the Emergency Relief Appropriation Act, containing almost $4.9 billion. By then PWA had amply demonstrated that it would not bring recovery, and the bulk of the money went to the new Work Projects Administration (WPA).* Substantial sums were also allocated to other federal agencies, and Ickes' nonfederal program wound up with $313 million. While the new WPA provided the direct employment that PWA could not, it also failed to bring recovery. In 1938, with unemployment steeply on the rise, PWA was given its last appropriation, $1.6 billion. The open channels of communication and the experience of the preceeding five years enabled this new program to be speedily implemented, and all the funds were put to contract within six months.

Of the achievements of PWA, three stand out. First, the agency pioneered in direct allotments between the federal bureaucracy and municipal governments, bypassing the state. It was a pattern that was to multiply in the succeeding decades. Second, the PWA initiated the federal housing program, a program institutionalized by the Housing Act of 1938 and subsequent urban renewal legislation. Third, the quality and value of the PWA projects must be recognized. Its projects are still in place, still serving America.

The PWA is also significant for its failure to bring recovery. It stands as a harbinger of the difficulties that beset the U.S. government in the post-World War II era as it attempted to modify the economic cycle.

The aspect of the PWA that deserves the most study is its role in the 1938 recovery. This last PWA program has been largely ignored. Unlike the Federal Emergency Relief Administration and the WPA, no statistical volume has been prepared on the PWA. The claims of the various commentators on the program are at variance with each other. A complete review of the project records in the National Archives* (Record Group 135, Records of the Public Works Administration) will be required.

FOR ADDITIONAL INFORMATION: Virtually all of the studies of the PWA were published during the 1930s. Harold Ickes's *Back to Work: The Story of P.W.A.* (1935) and *The Secret Diary of Harold L. Ickes*, 3 vols. (1953) contain much information on the political intrigue of PWA. The best study of PWA's economic impact was prepared by the National Resources Planning Board, *The Economic Effects of the Federal Public Works Expenditures 1933-1938* (1940). The first independent study of PWA was prepared by Jack F. Isakoff, "The Public Works Administration," *Illinois Studies in the Social Sciences* 23 (1938):190:350. Many contemporary magazine articles analyzed PWA; among the best was by David Cushman Coyle, "What About Public Works?" *Harpers Magazine* 170 (January 1935):146-158. Two scholarly studies of particular topics are J. Kerwin Williams, *Grants-in-aid Under the Public Works Administration, A Study in Federal-State-Local Relations* (1939) and Viola Wyckoff, *The Public Works Wage Rate and Some of Its Economic Effects* (1946). In 1968, William D. Reeves completed "The Politics of Public Works 1933-1935" (Ph.D. dissertation, Tulane University), and in 1973, he published "PWA and Competitive Administration in the New Deal," *Journal of American History* 60 (September 1973):357-373.

WILLIAM D. REEVES

R

RAILWAY ASSOCIATION. See United States Railway Association and Consolidated Rail Corporation.

RECLAMATION SERVICE. See Bureau of Reclamation.

RECONSTRUCTION FINANCE CORPORATION (RFC). Although the stock market mania, declines in foreign trade resulting from protectionism, poor distribution of national income, and a chronic shrinkage in farm income had all contributed to the Great Depression, no economic problem in the 1920s and early 1930s was more important than the instability in the money markets. Years of speculation, overbanking, and undercapitalization had severely strained bank reserves, while the decline in farm values and railroad bonds had frozen many bank assets. Contradictory Federal Reserve* policies had only confused the situation, and between 1920 and 1930 more than 5,000 banks had failed. The stock market crash in 1929 further eroded bank assets, and in 1930 another 1,350 banks closed their doors. Austria's largest bank, the Kredit-Anstalt, failed in May 1931, and in September the Bank of England abandoned the gold standard. Western society was in the midst of an unprecedented credit crisis.

Herbert Hoover, the Republican President, had won the election of 1928 promising peace and prosperity, as well as a limited economic role for the federal government. But the credit crisis of 1931, particularly the failure of 450 commercial banks in September, challenged his political philosophy, forcing him to consider drastic federal intervention. At first, President Hoover tried a more traditional approach, one that relied on the private sector and the voluntary cooperation of commercial bankers. Under his leadership, several prominent New York bankers organized the National Credit Corporation (NCC) in October 1931. A private revolving credit fund of $500 million, the National Credit Corporation was designed to make loans to troubled banks. But the NCC was also cautious and conservative, and in October and November it made only $10 million in loans, hardly enough to liquefy frozen bank assets. President Hoover then had to implement a government alternative, proposing the creation of the Reconstruction Finance Corporation.

For Hoover, the RFC was the prerequisite to economic recovery. The Great Depression, he believed, was largely a crisis of confidence, and employment and industrial production would not begin increasing until private bankers were more willing to make business loans. Hoover assumed that there were thousands of frustrated businessmen clamoring for bank credit and thousands of bankers unwilling to make those loans because the rash of bank failures during the 1920s and early 1930s had left them frightened and overcautious. Endowed with an initial capital of $500 million and the ability to raise another $1.5 billion, the RFC was to make low-interest loans to commercial banks, savings banks, savings and loan associations, mortgage companies, credit unions, and railroads. The power to make railroad loans was particularly important, the President believed, because so many money market institutions had invested heavily in railroad bonds since 1900. Faced with competition from long-haul trucks in the 1920s and declining freight volume, railroad revenues had decreased sharply, eroding the value of railroad bonds and compromising the investment portfolios of thousands of banks and savings banks. Through railroad and bank loans, the RFC would restore banker confidence and stimulate needed increases in business loans. Recovery would then ensue. When Congress created the Reconstruction Finance Corporation in January 1932, President Hoover thought he had turned the corner on the Great Depression.

Afraid of embroiling the RFC in political controversy, Hoover appointed a bipartisan board of directors, including Eugene Meyer, the Republican chairman of the Federal Reserve Board; Charles G. Dawes, Chicago banker and former Republican Vice-President of the United States; and Jesse Jones, the Democratic banker and newspaperman from Houston, Texas. With dramatic energy, the RFC quickly began making loans, and by July 1932 had extended more than $1 billion to more than four thousand banks, railroads, credit unions, and mortgage loan companies. And on one level, the RFC was a success, for in August only eighty-five commercial banks failed. But on another political and economic level, the agency failed. Many critics accused Hoover and the RFC of being insensitive to the suffering of the poor and unemployed. Two loans in particular—$13 million to the Missouri-Pacific Railroad and $90 million to Charles G. Dawes's Central Republic Bank of Chicago—convinced many Americans that the RFC was out to bail the rich out of their troubles. Hoover countered that the failure of the Missouri-Pacific Railroad would have devalued the bonds of thousands of banks, while the closing of the Central Republic Bank would have brought on a banking panic in the entire Midwest. He felt both loans were justified, but the public did not agree. In addition to this political failure, the RFC had not reached its ultimate goal of increasing the volume of bank credit. Although thousands of bankers had accepted RFC loans, hugh volumes of excess reserves were still on hand at Federal Reserve banks, and commercial loans were continuing to decrease. Economic recovery was not in sight.

With so many people out of work and recovery still problematical, Hoover decided to join Democratic liberals in supporting the Emergency Relief and Construction Act, which gave the RFC $300 million for relief loans to the states, $1.5 billion for public works construction, and the power to make loans to financial institutions helping farmers to store and market argicultural products. In one sense, this was the beginning of the New Deal, for although critics accused the RFC construction and relief programs of being too slow and stingy during 1932 and early 1933, the RFC office handling construction projects later became the Public Works Administration,* the relief office became the Federal Emergency Relief Administration, and the agricultural loan office became the Commodity Credit Corporation. History, however, would forget this connection between the Hoover Administration and the New Deal.

Despite all the loans and legislation, the RFC proved a failure in the winter of 1932-1933. Outstanding commercial loans continued to shrink as bankers replaced those loans with more liquid U.S. government securities, and bank failures began to increase. In August 1932, a panic spread throughout southern Idaho and eastern Oregon, and in November the Governor of Nevada declared a statewide banking holiday. Franklin D. Roosevelt swamped President Hoover in the election early that month. Securities prices slumped in October and November, further eroding bank assets, and frightened depositors began demanding their funds. With over $40 billion in deposit liabilities, the banking system dwarfed the capabilities of the RFC. In January, Iowa declared a banking moratorium, and Louisiana followed in early February. When the two largest banks in Detroit closed in mid-February, a national banking holiday ensued which led to President Roosevelt's banking holiday in March 1933. When Hoover left office in March, the RFC had loaned nearly $2 billion, but the banking system had collapsed anyway.

The Emergency Banking Act, passed by voice vote a few days after Roosevelt's inauguration, permitted the RFC to purchase preferred stock in commercial banks. Like Hoover, Roosevelt too was concerned about the decline in business loans, and he felt that the six-month term of RFC loans had made bankers too cautious; with repayment to the RFC always imminent, they could hardly afford to be too generous in their commercial loans. By permitting the RFC to invest in the banks and receive dividends, Roosevelt thought that private bankers would have more freedom to make long-term plans. By mid-1935, the RFC had purchased $1.3 billion in preferred stock from more than 6,200 commercial banks. But even that did not achieve the ultimate goal of increasing bank credit. From a high of more than $38 billion in 1930, commercial loans had dropped to little more than $20 billion in 1935, as precipitous a decline under Roosevelt as under Hoover.

President Roosevelt then decided to expand greatly the RFC's functions and authority. First, he converted the RFC into a major funding agency, the source of money for the Federal Emergency Relief Administration, the Home Owner's Loan Corporation, the Farm Credit Administration, the Regional Agricultural

Credit Corporation, the Federal Home Loan Bank Board, the Federal Farm Mortgage Association, the Federal Housing Administration, the Rural Electrification Administration,* and the Resettlement Administration. To assist the Tennessee Valley Authority* by creating a market for electricity, the RFC established the Electric Farm and Home Authority, which financed the sales of small electrical appliances. Roosevelt also had the RFC set up the Disaster Loan Corporation to extend financial assistance to victims of natural disasters. Second, to liquefy bank assets even further, the RFC established and directed the RFC Mortgage Company, the Export-Import Bank,* the Commodity Credit Corporation, and the Federal National Mortgage Association. Finally, Roosevelt succeeded in getting legislation permitting the RFC to make direct business loans as a means of stimulating commercial credit. In 1939, to supervise this vast government credit operation, President Roosevelt created the Federal Loan Agency and named Jesse Jones, head of the RFC, to direct its efforts. In the eight years since its creation, the RFC had made more than $8 billion in loans to a wide variety of financial institutions and private businesses.

On the eve of World War II, the RFC was focusing its attention on the credit problems of small businesses, but the German invasion of France in June 1940 immediately raised new concerns about shifting to war production. Between 1940 and 1945, the RFC established several government corporations to stimulate defense production. The Defense Plant Corporation* spent $9.2 billion in constructing 2,300 factories and mills in 46 states. The RFC then leased the plants to private companies engaged in the production of war goods. The Defense Supplies Corporation also spent $9.2 billion in procuring and storing scarce commodities essential to the war effort, including aviation fuel, industrial alcohol, quinine, radio parts, diamond dies, and silk. The Metals Reserve Company disbursed $2.7 billion acquiring and storing copper, scrap iron, nickel, tungsten, zinc, mercury, manganese, chromium, mica, silver, and gold. To create economic difficulties for Germany and Japan, the RFC established the United States Commercial Company to enter markets in neutral countries and purchase any commodities the Axis Powers needed, even if the Allies did not require them. The U.S. Commercial Company spent more than $2 billion purchasing wolfram, ammonium sulphate and nitrate, petroleum products, and cellulose. The Rubber Reserve Company stockpiled more than 600,000 tons of crude rubber before the Japanese attack on Pearl Harbor, and during the war founded and directed the synthetic rubber industry in the United States. To help provide housing for the millions of Americans moving near defense plants and military installations, the RFC established the Defense Homes Corporation and constructed nearly eleven thousand housing units by 1945. Finally, the RFC established the Petroleum Reserves Corporation to purchase oil concessions in Saudi Arabia. It failed to make that purchase, and in 1945, the RFC changed the Petroleum Reserves Corporation to the War Assets Corporation, using it to dispose of surplus property held by the government after the war.

Late in the 1930s, before the outbreak of war in Europe so dramatically changed American priorities, the RFC had focused some attention on the credit needs of small business. Those concerns resurfaced for a time in 1945. Congress transferred the duties of the Smaller War Plants Corporation, a government agency assisting small businesses with war contracts, to the RFC, but in 1948 also reduced RFC capital stock to $100 million. With the economic need for the RFC declining early in the 1950s, and with some kickback schemes among RFC officials revealed in 1951 and 1952, the corporation lost its credibility and fell victim to government retrenchment programs. Congress passed the RFC Liquidation Act in 1953, transferred its loan powers to the Small Business Administration* in 1954, and abolished the agency in 1957. After twenty-five years and $50 billion, the Reconstruction Finance Corporation, until then the largest government agency in American history, was dissolved.

FOR ADDITIONAL INFORMATION: Jesse H. Jones, *Fifty Billion Dollars. My Thirteen Years with the RFC (1932-1945)* (1951); Susan Estabrook Kennedy, *The Banking Crisis of 1933* (1973); James S. Olson, *Herbert Hoover and the Reconstruction Finance Corporation, 1931-1933* (1977); Herbert Spero, *Reconstruction Finance Corporation Loans to Railroads, 1932-1937* (1939); and Gerald T. White, *Billions for Defense: Government Finance by the Defense Plant Corporation During World War II* (1980).

JAMES S. OLSON

RESERVE BOARD. See Federal Reserve Board.

RESERVE SYSTEM. See Federal Reserve Board.

REVENUE SERVICE. See Internal Revenue Service.

ROADS ADMINISTRATION. See Federal Highway Administration.

RURAL ELECTRIFICATION ADMINISTRATION (REA). The Rural Electrification Administration, an agency located in the United States Department of Agriculture,* makes loans to finance electric and telephone facilities in rural areas. The REA was born of economic emergency in the depths of the depression. The distances to be traversed by transmission lines, plus the scarcity of consumers coupled with their low income, made many rural areas unprofitable ventures for private utilities. Until 1935, neither the federal nor state governments had a significant role in rural electrification.

In the $4 billion Emergency Relief Appropriation Act of April 8, 1935, Congress included rural electrification as one of eight categories and earmarked for it a sum not to exceed $100 million. Initially, it was assumed that REA would operate primarily as an agency to get people back to work and money into circulation. On May 11, 1935, President Franklin D. Roosevelt, by Executive Order No. 7037, created the Rural Electrification Administration as an independent agency and allotted $50 million (later reduced to $10 million) to the task of promoting rural electrification. Executive Order No. 7130, issued on

August 7, 1935, freed REA from work relief requirements and made it basically a lending agency. Applications for loans, which came from state rural electrification authorities, rural power districts, existing electric cooperatives, municipal plants, and commercial electric companies, were slow in coming.

The Norris-Rayburn bill, approved by Congress on May 20, 1936, established the REA as an independent government agency. The chief provisions were as follows:

1. A ten-year program of promoting rural electrification was established with the REA designated as an agency to lend funds to "persons, corporations, States, Territories and subdivisions and agencies thereof, municipalities, peoples' utility districts and cooperative nonprofit or limited dividend associations . . . on their obligations having a maturity of ten or more years." Preference in granting loans was to be given to "States, Territories, and subdivisions and agencies thereof, municipalities, peoples' utility districts, and cooperative, nonprofit or limited dividend associations."

2. Loans were to be made to provide electric energy to persons in rural areas who were not receiving central station service.

3. Loans for construction and operation of generating plants or for electric transmission and distribution lines were to be amortized over a period not to exceed twenty-five years. Loans for wiring premises or purchase and installation of electrical and plumbing appliances and equipment were to be amortized over five years. Rate of interest was to be the average rate of government long-term securities. Duration of loans and interest rate were later changed.

4. "Rural Area" was defined as "any area of the United States not included within the boundaries of any city, village or borough having a population in excess of fifteen hundred inhabitants."

5. The act provided for an administrator, appointed by the President and confirmed by the Senate, for a term of ten years. The administrator was required to certify that in his opinion the security for each loan approved was reasonably adequate and the loan could be repaid within the agreed-upon time. The administrator makes an annual report to Congress.

The REA is administered on a nonpartisan basis. Under Reorganization Plan No. 2, July 1, 1939, REA became part of the Department of Agriculture, although it still maintained its administrative integrity. Effective September 21, 1944, the interest rate on new loans was set at 2 percent, and the balance of existing loans was adjusted to the same figure. The same act extended the amortization period from twenty-five to thirty-five years.

On October 28, 1949, the Rural Electrification Act of 1936 was amended to provide for a rural telephone program. On May 7, 1971, the Rural Electrification Act was further amended to establish a Rural Telephone Account and Rural Telephone Bank. An amendment to the Rural Electrification Act, May 11, 1973 (Public Law 93-32), established the Rural Electrification and Telephone Revolving Fund in the United States Treasury for REA loan funds. This replaced the REA direct-loan program. The standard interest rate for REA loans was increased to 5 percent, and a 2-percent interest rate was continued for borrowers meeting special statutory criteria. Collections on outstanding loans and sale of borrowers' notes to the Secretary of the Treasury or money market provided funds for the Revolving Fund. The act was also amended to provide authority to guarantee loans, usually large-scale loans, by non-REA lenders. A substantial portion of this loaning comes from the National Rural Cooperative Finance Corporation Banks for Cooperatives and other financial institutions.

Although originally designed to lend money to electrify farms not receiving central-station service, by 1961, REA was primarily financing the development of an integrated rural power system organized and operated through cooperatives. In the first twenty-five years of the rural electrification program, electrified farms in the United States increased from 10.9 percent to 96.8 percent of total farms. Today, 98.7 percent of 2.3 million farms are electrified. During 1979, approximately three hundred thousand new consumers were added to the REA-financed systems.

Approximately 94 percent of REA loans are made to electric cooperatives. As of January 1, 1980, $13.9 billion in loans had been approved to 1,098 borrowers serving 9 million consumers with over 1.9 million miles of line. Approximately $12.5 billion had been advanced to borrowers. The borrowers represented 981 cooperatives, 54 public power districts, 37 other public bodies, and 26 electric companies located in 46 states, the Virgin Islands, and Puerto Rico.

Approximately 63 percent of loans approved have been for electric distribution facilities; 36 percent for generation and transmission facilities; and 1 percent for financing farmsteads' installation of wiring, plumbing, electrical equipment, and irrigation facilities.

As of January 1, 1980, REA and the Rural Telephone Bank had approved more than $4.8 billion in loans to 728 commercial companies and 252 cooperatives in 46 states for the purpose of improving or initiating telephone services by 4.5 million subscribers.

In the area of loans, REA now emphasizes loan guarantees. In fiscal 1979, the figure was $7.5 billion. Its spending for large-scale generation and transmission projects far surpasses its spending for local electric distribution. Fifty generating and transmission cooperatives now receive approximately 90 percent of all REA financing. Rural electric cooperatives in thirty-six states are involved with investor-owned utilities in fifty-eight existing and planned joint power-supply projects. At least thirty-four of these are nuclear projects. The coop share is never more than 30 percent. Since 1974, approximately 45 percent of $7.8 billion of all rural electric loan guarantees have been for joint ventures with investor-owned utilities, and approximately 30 percent or $5.3 billion for nuclear projects. Estimates indicate that, by the year 2000, REA financing may account for as much as 20 percent of all electric utility financing.

There is a drift of consumer and public power systems toward large-scale electric power generation. New and more expensive generation and transmission facilities projected for the 1980s may double or triple electric rates. The service territories of local rural electric systems cover 75 percent of the U.S. land mass and serve about 25 million people living in 2,600 of the 3,100 counties in the United States. Electric rural coops are the fastest growing segment in the electric utility industry. Many coop customers are suburban customers who use all-electric homes.

The power loads of REA borrowers are doubling every seven years. Much of the growth is in rural fringes around cities and metropolitan areas and in recreational areas where second homes are built. Rural electric systems have developed into strong business enterprises which stimulate further growth. Costs in producing electricity go up because of higher interest rates, increased fuel costs, rising labor costs, inflation, longer lead times because of more complex facilities, and higher environmental costs.

Low-interest rates on REA loans to electric borrowers have long been considered sacrosanct. Rural areas no longer include just farmers or small towns. Rural areas which included towns of less than 1,500 population were permitted by the Rural Electrification Act to receive power from REA cooperatives. These areas now include immense housing developments. Four-fifths of REA cooperatives customers are now nonfarmers.

Initially, it was anticipated that wholesale power needs would be met by investor-owned companies and federal power agencies such as the Tennessee Valley Authority and the Bureau of Reclamation.* Federal power production has not kept pace with increased demand. Rate costs from investor-owned companies have increased and, hence, electric cooperative consumers incur greater expense. Increased costs have led investor-owned companies to encourage electric cooperatives to build their own generating plants in joint ventures with investor-owned companies.

Representatives of investor-owned utilities, from the inception of REA, argued that electric cooperatives had an unfair advantage in the production and distribution of electric power. Electric cooperatives pay no income taxes. The local and state taxes of cooperatives are less, on the average, than those of private power companies. The costs of borrowed funds of REA borrowers is less than the cost of funds of privately owned companies. The 2-percent early interest charge on funds borrowed from the REA was considerably lower than the interest charges of private companies. Another charge borne by the federal government is the administrative cost of REA itself. Thus, REA provides personnel as consultants in development, legal, environmental, and finance areas. These costs are borne by the public through taxes. REA borrowers are also subsidized in that they are beneficiaries of federal agencies supplying power to cooperatives. Investor-owned utilities and other privately owned industries benefit from public power, although the private segment must pay taxes to support it. The public sector and cooperatives have prior claim on public power. The rationale for the interest subsidy has been that electric cooperatives generally have fewer customers per mile of line, and hence, receive less revenue per mile of line than do investor-owned electric utilities.

Electric cooperatives range in size from those serving 2,000 consumers to those serving over 50,000. REA is instrumental in financing electric and telephone services in rural areas, areas where industry is developing, people are building homes, resources are being exploited, and, in general, areas where population and industry continue to grow.

REA policy has been one of encouraging the furtherance of balanced rural development programs through better farming and industrial expansion to provide off-farm employment opportunities and improved education, health, and welfare activities. The REA Rural Development staff directs and coordinates rural area development; maintains liaison with other federal agencies on development; makes specialized assistance available to borrowers and their associations in promotion, stimulation, organization financing, construction, and operation of rural enterprises; and encourages consumer loans for financing electrical equipment for commercial and industrial enterprises.

The total cost of the REA program is in part conjecture as it involves an estimate of tax and interest revenues foregone as well as summation of dollars directly appropriated. The subsidy features of the rural electrification program include (1) appropriations for administrative cost; (2) loans of federal funds at less than their cost to the Treasury; (3) exemption of cooperatives from the payment of federal income taxes; (4) tax advantages granted by some states to cooperatives; (5) preference rights to federal power at rates that may reflect considerable subsidies; (6) and power contracts with private companies at rates lower than those charged other users of comparable blocks of power.

As of September 30, 1979, REA net assets amounted to $9.6 billion—$9.4 billion on loans and interest receivable, net certificates of Beneficial Ownership, and allowances for possible loss; and $0.2 billion in other assets—cash net equipment and Rural Telephone Bank Class A stock. Total salaries and expenses provided through appropriations from inception of REA to September 30, 1979, amounted to $452,454,000.

In 1979, the General Accounting Office* (GAO) made a study of REA costs. Of current REA rural utility programs (four telephone and three electric), five are direct- or insured-loan programs and two are guaranteed-loan programs. These programs are (1) telephone loans insured at a special rate of 2-percent interest; (2) electric loans insured at a special rate of 2-percent interest; (3) telephone loans insured at a standard rate of 5 percent; (4) electric loans insured at a standard rate of 5 percent; (5) Rural Telephone Bank loans; (6) telephone loans guaranteed; and (7) electric loans guaranteed.

Costs borne by the government in making direct loans are interest, default, delinquency, and administration. The interest subsidy is the difference between the cost of money to the government and what REA charges borrowers. REA rates in the past have run between 2 and 8 percent. Currently, it pays about 8.5

percent, although with higher interest rates, these interest costs will accelerate, and hence, result in more government subsidy.

In the 1979 study, the GAO estimated what a new $10 million, thirty-five-year loan would cost. It was estimated that a 2-percent telephone direct loan ($10 million) made for thirty-five years would cost $17.1 million interest subsidy, an administrative cost of $150,000, and an estimated $5,000 in delinquent costs. A direct 2-percent electric loan would cost $17.1 million of interest subsidy, $93,000 for administrative cost, and $4,000 for delinquent cost. A 5-percent electric loan would cost $9.8 million interest subsidy, $101,000 in administrative cost, and $5,000 in delinquent cost. Rural Telephone Bank loans involve no interest subsidy; administrative costs for a $10 million thirty-five-year loan were estimated to be $93,000. Guaranteed telephone loans estimated cost would be $43,000 in administrative cost. Guaranteed electric loans estimated cost would be $47,000 in administrative cost.

Federal guaranteed loans are not costless to the total economy as they tend to divert funds from private borrowers who do not have government guarantees. The REA and the Telephone Revolving Fund loans are made at subsidized rates. Loans from the Rural Telephone Bank do not involve subsidy interest rates. The Federal Financing Bank provides loan funds to rural electric and telephone systems financed with REA guarantees. Here the principal REA costs are administrative.

An indication of the magnitude of REA operations is the loan program. In fiscal year 1979, $6.8 billion was made available to telephone and electric programs. As of January 31, 1979, REA electric-distribution borrowers were required to develop energy conservation programs as a requirement for continued REA financing.

In January 1980, there was a major reorganization of the REA electric program. From 1969 to 1979, power supply loans increased from 25 percent to 87 percent of total REA financing. Thus, the five area offices were replaced with two new divisions, the Distribution Systems Division and the Power Supply Division. In addition, the Engineering Standards Division was established to develop standards and approve construction materials; an Environmental Energy Requirements Division to develop energy forecasting and environmental policies and procedures; the Electric Loans and Management Division to process distribution loans and provide management assistance to borrowers; and the Energy Management and Utilization Division to oversee the development and effective utilization of supplemental energy sources.

A thirty-year comparison of REA loans and employees indicates that, in 1950, REA administered a loan program of $375,151,456 with 1,328 employees. In 1979, REA had 729 employees, and at the end of the 1979 fiscal year loans were almost eighteen times as large. Electric projects may call for sizable power supply arrangements possible in several states with inter-ties with neighboring utilities. Environmental aspects must be considered. In the telephone field, the new telecommunication technology calls for continual updating expertise. In fiscal 1979, REA's administrative funds amounted to $24,706,010. Approximately 377 staff-years were used in the electric program, and 347 in the telephone program.

Approximately 80 percent of the 1979 loan program took the form of REA guarantee loans made by other lenders at interest rates agreed upon by borrower and lender. Furthermore, approximately $312 million in supplemental financing was made available to electric borrowers by non-REA lenders without guarantees.

In the 1970s, electric cooperatives and privately owned utilities cooperated in building power plants. Electric cooperatives have access to lower cost loans through the REA, and hence, facilities are being built that would not have been possible with higher interest rates.

The REA is a prime example of a governmental function, which has become institutionalized in the nation. The more varied and widespread a governmental function becomes, the more intently must it be made the subject of careful scrutiny. Those who turn to government agencies to redress the economic evils of competitive life see in their administrators selfless individuals devoted to the public welfare and scientifically equipped to make decisions affecting the public weal. Congress and the public are unable to keep a careful, continuous watch on all governmental activities. After the establishment of an agency, or a change or discussion of its mandate which may arouse a lively interest, the public turns its attention to other things. For the agency its original sense of an urgent public mission may decline, and, with the lapse of time and personnel turnover, it may evolve into the process of bureaucratic survival and routine-operation activities. The pressures and direction of interested parties continue and may wear away the initial purpose of the agency.

The Rural Electrification Administration is a government agency with roots that run deep. It has become a permanent part of the American scene. It has been successful in bringing electric and telephone service to rural America. Its adherents have the ability to apply great political power on a state, local, and federal level. There are about a thousand rural cooperatives and managers and fifteen thousand directors who are persons of substance in their communities. In addition, there are consultants, lawyers, supply-house owners, and others who have a vested interest in REA expansion. There is also the National Rural Electric Cooperative Association which can apply pressure to commissioners, legislatures, and the Congress of the United States.

Within the REA itself, highly skilled, career civil service employees, economists, accountants, lawyers, engineers, and a retinue of clerical workers look to the REA for employment, promotion, a way of life, and, finally, for retirement security. There is a great amount of documentation which leads to the conclusion that where governmental agencies exist long enough to gain adherents who develop vested interests in their continuance as a function, they tend to be long-lived and expansive.

REA loans have benefited rural areas that have attracted people and industry. Rural electrification has made for a higher standard of living, which, in turn, has broadened the tax base. It seems quite likely that without REA loans some isolated rural communities would not have received electricity. In the past, investor-owned utilities have opposed REA loans in the Congress and in the courts, although at the present time there are expanded areas of cooperation between investor-owned utilities and cooperatives. The issue of REA loans has been politicized, as is evidenced by the policy changes attempted by the party in power. One thing is clear: rural areas now have access to electricity.

Each person must judge for himself as to the merit of institutionalizing a government agency. It appears that the REA has become a permanent force in the electric and telephone field, even though its mission, started forty-five years ago, has been completed. Its role in the future is dependent upon voters' philosophy of governmental direction in the economy.

FOR ADDITIONAL INFORMATION: The reader should consult D. Clayton Brown, *The Fight for REA* (1980); Clyde T. Ellis, *A Giant Step* (1966); John D. Garwood and W. C. Tuthill, *The Rural Electrification Administration, An Evaluation* (1963); Walter Gellhorn, *Individual Freedom and Government Restraints* (1958); and Edwin Vennard, *The Deviation of REA* (1962). Also helpful are a number of timely articles in the journal *Public Utility Fortnightly*, especially during 1965-1970; U.S. Department of Agriculture, *REA Bulletin*; congressional hearings; and other Agriculture and REA reports and bulletins.

JOHN D. GARWOOD

S

SAFETY BOARD. See National Transportation Safety Board.

SCIENCE FOUNDATION. See National Science Foundation.

SCIENTIFIC RESEARCH OFFICE. See Office of Scientific Research and Development.

SECRET SERVICE. See United States Secret Service.

SECURITIES AND EXCHANGE COMMISSION (SEC). As in a number of social and economic reforms, the United States lagged far behind other nations in measures designed to curb fraudulent stock and investment practices. Both Great Britain and Germany, as in the 1844 and 1900 Companies Acts of the former, had early recognized the need to set up minimal standards of financial honesty if citizens were expected to bring their funds into the investment marketplace.

Like a variety of other American regulatory laws and agencies, the introduction of securities laws at the national level was preceded and influenced by the attempts in several states (such as the Kansas "Blue Sky" laws of 1911) to protect the unwary investor and regulate the sales of securities.

The need for regulation extending beyond a single state's boundaries became most glaringly evident in the prosperous days of the 1920s. Many fraudulent practices, ranging from secret pools rigged by stock exchange members to stocks and bonds offered without any substantial basis to a trusting public, were publicized in the wake of the Great Crash of 1929, which was the greatest loss to an investment public in all of financial history. The focal point was the New York Stock Exchange, which handled 90 percent of all U.S. securities transactions.

Although its socially prestigious president, Richard Whitney, continued to insist that the Exchange was a completely impersonal, laissez-faire operation moved only by a free market, it was evident to Congress and the public that the manipulations and short selling by Exchange members scarcely fitted that lofty description. More accurately, the Exchange operated under a private-club philosophy, which permitted any fleecing of the public so long as it did not result in the defrauding of a fellow-member. President Herbert Hoover remonstrated, insisting that such things as "bear raids" and short selling by insiders "did not contribute to the recovery of the nation." With his encouragement, an earlier Senate resolution to investigate short-selling practices (later expanded) got under way. The resultant investigation went beyond both his wishes and his tenure in office. It was instrumental in bringing the New York and other exchanges under strict regulation and aiding in the exposures that saw Whitney sent to Sing Sing for his usage of clients' funds.

Acts such as the Securities Act of 1933, the Securities Exchange Act of 1934 (which actually set up the commission), and the Public Utility Holding Company Act of 1935 were the earliest of the tightly drawn legislative enactments which implemented the congressional wish to deputize its administrative will in the area of securities and stock exchanges. Added to these bills at the end of the New Deal period were the Federal Bankruptcy Act and the Trust Indenture Act of 1939, and the Investment Company and Investment Advisers Act of 1940. Thus, the scope of the SEC was broadened to include everything from investigating securities frauds and recommending criminal sanctions against violators to the overseeing of mutual funds and corporate reorganizations under the Bankruptcy Act. It required the registration of securities dealers and investment advisers, and set rigid standards for both. It established regulations for stock trading by Exchange members and financial requirements for brokers. It supervised the accounting profession, and its stringent disclosure regulations not only required the publication of all pertinent management background information (even to the salaries of corporation officials) but also set forth complete corporate accountability for any stock sold to the public.

In its formative years, the SEC embodied a New Deal philosophy to save American capitalism in spite of itself—regardless of the cries of those who insisted it was "destroying business and business confidence"—through tight regulations administered with strict discipline. Self-discipline was the ideal, but it was an ideal achieved only with a regulatory body looking over the shoulder of the institution charged with its own regulation, ready to take action if the rules were not properly enforced.

In its early years, the SEC was the only government regulatory agency that consistently drew praise from the business community, usually expressed in terms of its "fairness" and its "highly practical" approach. It was also considered unique among regulatory agencies in the considerable public stature and continuing political importance of its first few chairmen.

Its first chairman—controversial among New Dealers but welcome to Wall Street—was Joseph P. Kennedy, one of the few millionaire supporters of President Franklin Roosevelt. Kennedy came from a relatively new but influential Boston Irish family, was educated at Harvard, and had quickly demonstrated a capacity for management and lone-wolf entrepreneurial opportunities. He and Roosevelt met when Roosevelt was Assistant Secretary of the Navy and Kennedy was involved in shipbuilding activities. Kennedy went on in the 1920s to make several fortunes, one turning out quickie Westerns in earliest Hollywood and another one in the stock market. He was one of the few to get out with profits intact before the Great Crash of 1929 and was thoroughly familiar with Wall Street practices and manipulations.

Kennedy served only for the important first fifteen months of the new agency, but was invaluable in cracking down on a number of shady or insubstantial securities ventures and in demonstrating with these publicized enforcement practices that the new agency meant business. He reiterated in many ways his views that uncontrolled economic individualism and shady exploits were a danger to the financial community and to the entire capitalistic structure. This business philosophy was invaluable in convincing Wall Street powers and the important brokerage firms that they had far more to gain from public confidence than from the unbridled practices of the past.

Kennedy filled several other assignments for Roosevelt, finally coming to grief because of his recalcitrant appeasement views as ambassador to Great Britain in 1939-1940. In later years, he was widely known for his efforts in aiding the successful political careers of three sons, the eldest of whom—John F. Kennedy—became the first Catholic President of the United States.

Kennedy was succeeded as chairman first by James M. Landis and then by William O. Douglas. Both men were legal scholars of repute, and each had helped draft various securities acts. Landis later was an adviser to President Kennedy. Under Douglas's stern hand, the last vestiges of unsatisfactory self-enforced regulation were swept away. All stock exchanges were reorganized, introducing such innovations as paid technical staffs for administrators to replace "Old Guard" cronyism and public participation in policy formulation. Douglas then moved to the U.S. Supreme Court, where he would hold the longest tenure as Justice on that body in history.

Thus, the agency was moved along its designated path in those all-important first half-dozen years by the experience and economic philosophy of its first three chairmen, all of them individuals of continuing political importance and influence on the national scene far beyond that of the average head of a regulatory agency. Added to this leadership was a small staff of able and zealous individuals, whose *élan* and competence were frequently considered to be superior among regulatory agencies.

By the end of World War II, the SEC had fully worked the kinks out of its governing legislative acts and had laid down its own policies and administrative procedures. As a regulatory agency, it may be said to have reached maturity. The initial decade and a half of the postwar years were largely stable and prosperous, and the securities markets benefited from strong public confidence.

For the agency, they were years of consolidation marked by little innovation or new legislation.

However, the growing complexity and sheer quantitative growth of the securities industry in the 1950s brought both new difficulties and newly added functions. By 1960, the average daily volume of shares traded had more than doubled over 1950, and the number of brokers, salesmen, and advisers had tripled. The beginning of the 1960s also saw increased speculation in a variety of new glamour stocks, together with several startling fraud cases. Both Congress and the SEC launched investigations—this time largely with Wall Street support. As a result of the investigations, the SEC expelled several brokerage firms from their exchanges and two notable individuals sought the safety of exile in Brazil. The investigations culminated in the 1964 Amendments to the Exchange Act, which further tightened the restrictions to be exercised by the SEC on smaller exchanges and their broker members.

New legislation in 1970 amended the Securities Exchange Act of 1934 by the Securities Investor Protection Corporation (SIPC). The corporation was composed of all registered brokers and dealers, with a small governing board. The member fees of this large body were used to furnish insurance to protect an investor's account up to $50,000 against fraudulent loss in much the same manner that the Federal Deposit Insurance Corporation protects each bank depositor up to a certain amount.

Structurally, the SEC remained close to its original arrangement to carry out these functions. It continues to be directed by five commissioners. These are appointed by the President, and no more than three come from the same political party. Their terms are for five years, with one member's term expiring on June 5 of each year. The President designates one member of the commission as chairman.

Like other old-line agencies such as the Federal Trade Commission* or the Federal Communications Commission,* the SEC is independent of the executive branch and is accountable only to Congress. However, both the tone and direction of the agency's influence derive in some part from the presidential appointee as chairman. He might espouse either a harder or softer regulatory line, depending on his political and economic views. Commissioners have been known to take up political posts after their SEC tenure, as well as positions within the securities industry. For example, William J. Casey, a former chairman appointed by Richard Nixon, headed the Ronald Reagan presidential campaign of 1980 and was thereafter named by President Reagan as the new director of the CIA.*

The many duties of the agency are divided among its five divisions, carried on by a central headquarters in Washington and eight regional offices. The Division of Corporate Regulation administers the Public Utility Holding Company Act of 1935 and performs advisory functions under Chapter X of the Bankruptcy Act. The Division of Corporation Finance, perhaps most important for business people and accountants, is responsible for standards of auditing and financial reporting and disclosure. For the administration of these requirements as set forth by law, it must review all corporation registration statements.

The Division of Market Regulation acts for the commission in the regulation of national securities exchanges and of all registered dealers and brokers. It carries on a continuous surveillance of the trading markets. The Divison of Investment Management Regulation administers the provisions of the Investment Company Act and the Investment Advisers Act of 1940. The Division of Enforcement supervises investigations, carries on all enforcement activities, and determines whether cases should be sent to the Department of Justice* for prosecution. It accordingly works closely with such major internal offices as the Office of General Counsel and the Office of Chief Accountant.

Opportunities for internal squabbles exist in any large institution, and the SEC has been no exception. There were always the understandable rivalries of bureau chiefs, and sometimes these were further exacerbated by the fact of numerous overlapping functions. A change of focus by a new chairman might have resulted in additional clashes. It has also been a matter of record that power devolved upon that divison or section that received the most publicity, which stimulated additional friction. This role, for example, was filled for a number of years by the Division of Enforcement, which brought a number of gaudy violators to book in publicized hearings. But before that, largely in the 1960s, the Division of Market Regulation's activities placed it in the spotlight and in a preeminent position. As the 1970s came to a close and the 1980s began, shifts in the chairman's decisions emphasizing more traditional areas of SEC concern, such as disclosure, meant a more elevated role for the Division of Corporation Finance. The shift away from dramatic enforcement cases was, like other divergences, largely a sign of the times, for as the 1980s opened, the decade brought an era of impatience with regulation in general, a Supreme Court distaste with any enforcement innovation, and a neo-conservative Republican administration.

There has evidently been much less friction among the commissioners themselves, although in recent times one of the few women commissioners resigned by virtue of her outspoken manner and continually strong disagreement with her colleagues. Generally, however, the agency—which continues to brag about being the most effective federal agency with one of the smallest staffs in government—has exhibited a high degree of internal cooperativeness.

Many of a regulatory agency's achievements or failures rest in the eye of the beholder. No one, including the industry under regulation, denies the agency's basic and major achievement of making the securities markets safe for the investing public, of providing for disclosure of corporate information to enable the investor to make his decisions, and of establishing respected guidelines for corporate auditing and accounting practices. Some of its earlier dramatic achievements, such as taming the recalcitrant stock exchanges, have been previously noted. More recently, Congress gave the agency further responsibility under the Foreign Corrupt Practices Act of 1977. Post-Watergate disclosures revealed that hundreds of American corporations had elaborate systems and slush funds for under-the-table payments to foreign officials and politicians. Although corporations insisted that they must be able to pay a kind of "corporate baksheesh" to gain contracts abroad, Congress decided that such practice violated disclosure requirements and perverted the free enterprise system, and therefore, made such bribery illegal both at home and abroad. Subsequent complaints have largely been directed at SEC leniency in dealing with the violators. The Justice Department* announced it would put a "low priority" on such cases.

More general accusations of regulatory failure have been leveled at the slowness with which SEC carried out its many congressional mandates. Others complain that fewer and fewer court actions or suspensions of trading indicated too much agency leniency, although recent chairmen have contended that the agency has relied more upon "alternative approaches" to secure compliance. These contrary views could be further explained, on one hand, by noting a new era of anti-regulation, or, on the other hand, by showing that the means for ensuring compliance have become more sophisticated and more diverse.

Too much emphasis should not be put, however, on the spirit of deregulation visible as the 1980s get under way. As in some other regulatory agencies, those businesses that are regulated and that depend on the public for their profitable existence—whether brokerage houses, airlines, or accounting firms—no longer could envision doing without agencies like the Securities and Exchange Commission which by their regulatory discipline have ensured them public confidence and public patronage.

FOR ADDITIONAL INFORMATION: Alan R. Brombert, *Securities Law: Fraud* (1973); Ralph F. de Bedts, *The New Deal's SEC: The Formative Years* (1964); Hazel E. Haining, "Federal Regulation of the Securities Industry" (Ph. D. dissertation, University of Nebraska, Lincoln, 1972); Robert L. Knauss, *Securities Regulation Sourcebook* (1972); and Securities and Exchange Commission, *Annual Reports*.

RALPH F. de BEDTS

SELECTIVE SERVICE SYSTEM. The Selective Service System, an independent agency in the executive branch of the federal government, was created in 1940 to administer the military draft instituted at that time. Except for a brief period after World War II, when the agency was replaced by the Office of Selective Service Records, it has existed continuously. Current statutory provision for the Selective Service System is the Military Selective Service Act of 1971 (50 U.S.C. App. 451 et seq.), which, together with implementing regulations (32 CFR 1600), details its structure and defines its mission.

Military conscription, although never accepted as a permanent institution in the United States, has been utilized repeatedly. The colonies and, after independence, the states drafted men for militia service. National conscription was strongly advocated and only narrowly averted during the War of 1812. Both the Union and the Confederacy conscripted men during the Civil War, the draft was utilized in World War I, and in 1940 the first peacetime national conscription law was adopted. Although permitted to expire in 1947, after World War II, conscription legislation was reenacted in 1948, and men were drafted throughout both the Korean and Vietnam conflicts and episodically at other times between 1948 and 1973.

Tragic experience with the Civil War draft was a major factor shaping later conscription policies. A draft in any form probably would have met with some resistance at the time because the war itself had become increasingly unpopular. However, antidraft sentiment was much exacerbated by provisions in the 1863 legislation authorizing registration by house-to-house canvas, investing military officials with full and direct powers at all levels of administration, and exempting prospective conscripts who furnished substitutes or paid a fee of $300 to the federal government. Opposition culminated in the New York draft riots of 1863— one of the worst civil disturbances in the history of the United States—in which over 1,000 persons died during five days of violence.

In 1866, Brigadier General James Oakes filed a report highly critical of the Civil War draft and recommending that future conscription legislation provide for local administration by civilians, registration at central locations, and imposition of a personal nontransferable obligation to serve. These recommendations were incorporated into the Selective Draft Act of 1917, which vested, subject to law and administrative regulations, broad authority in newly created local boards to classify registrants and to call those deemed available for military service. Legislation instituting the first national peacetime draft in 1940, and later wartime and postwar extensions, retained the principal administrative features of the 1917 legislation. Although conscription in the United States, whenever authorized, has been selective rather than universal, and although selection necessarily entails uneven burdens, neither the World War I nor World War II drafts encountered significant open resistance. Both wars had broad, even if not universal, popular support. Moreover, particularly during World War II, the sheer number of draftees—about 10 million, with millions more induced to volunteer to avoid the draft—assured that the military service obligation would fall upon all classes.

The postwar experience was less favorable. Relatively few inductions were needed to maintain authorized manpower levels, even in time of armed conflict, and an extraordinary proportion of both inductees and volunteers were from economically and socially disadvantaged groups. During the Vietnam hostilities, opposition to the draft flared into open resistance. The unpopularity of that conflict was an important factor in this resistance, but even some supporters of the war were highly critical of a draft, which, as a consequence of student deferments and other policies, fell amost exclusively upon the poor and disproportionately upon ethnic minorities. The inequities of the Selective Service System were canvassed, and significant reforms were proposed in a 1967 report by the National Advisory Commission on Selective Service, entitled *In Pursuit of Equity*. However, in extending the draft in 1967, Congress, unwilling to appear moved by antidraft demonstrations, rejected the commission's proposed reforms, which included elimination of student deferments and most deferments based on occupation or dependency, random selection of inductees from among the youngest current registrants, provision for classification by professionals, and reduction in the number of local boards.

The Military Selective Service Act of 1971, the most recent conscription legislation, provides a somewhat condensed and modestly reformed version of the administrative apparatus created in 1940. Under this legislation, which has not been fully operative since 1976, the Selective Service System includes (1) a national headquarters headed by a director appointed by the President and subject to Senate confirmation; (2) offices in each state, the District of Columbia, and several overseas dependencies; and (3) approximately 2,000 local boards established at the county or intercounty level. The legislation also provides for a National Appeals Board and for appeals boards in each of the federal judicial districts. At the national and state levels, both military and civilian personnel staff the agency. The five-member local boards are composed of part-time unpaid civilian volunteers, appointed by the President upon recommendation of the Governor. Local boards normally employ a civilian clerk and other personnel. Current legislation, unlike earlier versions, seeks to broaden representation on the boards, whose exclusively male membership in the past was overwhelmingly white, over fifty years of age, and upper middle class.

The mission of the Selective Service System is twofold: to deliver manpower to the armed forces in time of emergency in accordance with the requirements of the several military services as determined by the Department of Defense;* and to administer an alternative service program for conscientious objectors. Under the 1971 statute, men between nineteen and twenty-six years of age are required to register with their local boards. The registrants constitute the Selective Service pool. The local boards perform the essential task of classifying registrants pursuant to statute and administrative regulations. Deferments and exemptions for various reasons—occupational status, religious belief, dependency and hardship, physical and mental incapacity, and others—are provided. Those classified as available for military service (I-A) are subject to call to fill the monthly quotas fixed by national and state Selective Service offices to meet the manpower requirements determined by the Department of Defense.

In 1973, the induction of registrants was terminated, and in 1975, registration was suspended. Since 1976, the Selective Service System has been on standby status, and the structure provided under the 1971 legislation has been reduced drastically. Presently, the system consists of a national headquarters and six regional offices. These are staffed by approximately 115 full-time civilian employees and 20 military reserve officers on active duty. The reserve officers provide liaison with the military services and supervise the Selective Service Reserve Forces, composed of about 700 Reserve and National Guard officers who are assigned to Selective Service for weekly drills and two-week training sessions. In the event of an emergency requiring augmentation of the Selective Service staff, this pool of trained officers would be available.

The future of the agency is clouded with uncertainty. In 1980, as a response to the Soviet invasion of Afghanistan, the Carter Administration proposed resumption of registration of nineteen-and twenty-year olds, both men and women. Congress decisively rejected female registration but voted funds for registration of men. Although a federal district court ruled that male-only registration was unconstitutional, the order enjoining registration was stayed pending appeal to the Supreme Court of the United States. As a consequence, registration, accomplished by filing questionnaires at local post offices, was conducted during the summer of 1980 and continues as additional men reach the age of nineteen. In 1981, the Supreme Court, in *Rostker* v. *Goldberg*, reversed the decision of the federal district court and sustained the validity of male-only registration. This ruling removed one uncertainty, but there are others. In campaigning for the presidency, Ronald Reagan was highly critical of the Carter proposal to resume registration, and he was strongly supportive of the all-volunteer army. Since his election, President Reagan appears to have accepted registration. He continues to support the all-volunteer concept, although his administration has conceded that a draft would be necessary if adequate numbers of qualified persons could not be recruited through higher pay and other inducements. Additional legislation would be necessary in order to reinstate the actual drafting of registrants. Moreover, inasmuch as there are presently no local boards in operation, there is no mechanism for classifying registrants, which is prerequisite to resuming inductions.

Some effort on the part of the outgoing director of Selective Service, a Carter appointee, to reestablish the 2,000 local boards is presently under way, as an appeal for persons to volunteer for appointment was issued. Whether the Reagan Administration supports this endeavor, requiring an annual outlay of $20 million, is unclear.

FOR ADDITIONAL INFORMATION: The early historical background of the military draft in the United States is presented by Jack F. Leach, *Conscription in the United States* (1952), which covers the period through the Civil War. John O'Sullivan and Alan M. Meckler, eds., *The Draft and Its Enemies* (1974), is a collection of documents, papers, and addresses concerning conscription. The World War I Selective Draft Act is extensively discussed in Edward M. Coffman, *The Hilt of the Sword* (1966). For the World War II draft, the most comprehensive source is the multivolume *Special Monograph Series* of the Selective Service System (1947-1955). President Truman's ill-fated proposal to introduce University Military Training in 1947 and the subsequent reenactment of Selective Service in 1948 are considered in Clyde E. Jacobs and John F. Gallagher, *The Selective Service Act: A Case Study of the Governmental Process* (1967). Harry A. Marmion, *Selective Service: Conflict and Compromise* (1968) focuses upon the extension of Selective Service in 1967, during the Vietnam conflict. In the *Draft and Public Policy: Issues in Military Manpower Procurement 1945-1970* (1971), James M. Gerhardt provides an insightful analysis of the problems and dilemmas of providing sufficient manpower to satisfy authorized force levels during the post-World War II era. Several popular works, published during the Vietnam conflict, are Jean Carper, *Bitter Greetings: The Scandal of the Military Draft* (1967); Bruce Chapman, *Wrong Men in Uniform* (1967); and George Walton, *Let's End the Draft Mess* (1967). Although authored by writers of divergent political perspectives, all of these works are highly critical of the draft.

James W. Davis, Jr., and Kenneth M. Dolbeare, *Little Groups of Neighbors: The Selective Service System* (1968) is an important critical study of the composition and functioning of the local draft boards, particularly during the period after World War II. This study, which is based upon both national data and materials developed by the authors through field research, considers the impact of the draft and public attitudes toward it. Gary L. Wamsley, *Selective Service in a Changing America: A Study of Organizational Environmental Relationships* (1969), also based upon extensive empirical research, seeks to account for changing public attitudes toward the military draft. Various aspects of military manpower procurement and of the draft are considered in a series of essays edited by Roger W. Little, *Selective Service in American Society* (1969). In *Mastering the Draft* (1970), Andrew O. Shapiro and John M. Striker describe the personnel and functioning of Selective Service and offer a detailed commentary and guide on registration, deferments, and related matters.

CLYDE E. JACOBS

SHIPPING BOARD. See Federal Maritime Commission.

SIGNAL CORPS. See United States Army Signal Corps.

SMALL BUSINESS ADMINISTRATION (SBA). The United States Small Business Administration was created as an independent federal agency under the Small Business Act of 1953. The mission of the SBA is stated in its charter (as amended):

It is the declared policy of the Congress that the Government should aid, counsel, assist, and protect, insofar as is possible, the interests of small business concerns in order to preserve free competitive enterprise, to insure that a fair proportion of the total purchases and contracts or subcontracts for property and services for the Government (including but not limited to subcontracts for maintenance, repair and construction) be placed with small-business enterprises to ensure that a fair proportion of the total sales of Government property be made to such enterprises, and to maintain and strengthen the overall economy of the Nation.

Antecedents of the SBA include the Reconstruction Finance Corporation,* the Smaller War Plants Corporation, the Office of Small Business of the Department of Commerce,* and the Small Defense Plants Administration. The SBA became a permanent agency with the signing of the Small Business Act of 1958.

From its initiation, the SBA has been hindered in its operations by the lack of an adequate definition for its constituency. To date, no universally accepted definition of a small business has been formulated. The legal definition fails to provide adequate criteria by which to classify businesses by size:

For the purposes of this Act, a small-business concern shall be deemed to be one which is independently owned and operated and which is not dominant in its field of operations. In addition to the foregoing criteria, the Administration, in making a detailed definition, may use these criteria among others: Number of employees and dollar volume of business. Where the number of employees is used as one of the criteria in making such definition for any such purposes of this Act, the maximum number of employees which a small-business concern may have under the definition shall vary from industry to industry to the extent necessary to reflect differing characteristics of such industries and to take proper account of other relevant factors.

The SBA has found it difficult over the years to extract a satisfactory operational definition from this broad statement. The agency has established size cutoff points for firms in virtually every industry. In book printing, a firm must have no more than 250 employees to qualify for an SBA loan program, and yet can have 500 employees and still be eligible for federal small business procurement set-asides. Annual revenues in excess of $275,000 prevent a cotton producer from being classified as small, but a tires and tubes wholesaler has a cutoff of $22 million. These arbitrary standards are critical issues to businesses nationwide which seek to qualify for SBA assistance. Size limits generate considerable controversy during periods of economic hardship for specific firms or business in general. In 1966, for example, the SBA declared American Motors, then the nation's sixty-third largest manufacturer with 32,000 employees and $991 million in sales, eligible as a small business to bid on government contracts. The criterion for the classification was that American Motors was not dominant in its field of operations.

The SBA performs a variety of functions in its efforts to serve the small business community, including (1) assistance in providing venture capital, (2) financial assistance, (3) procurement assistance, (4) management assistance, and (5) advocacy.

In 1958, Congress passed the Small Business Investment Act. Under this law, the SBA is authorized to license Small Business Investment Companies (SBICs). These are privately owned and operated corporations. The purpose of an SBIC is to extend long-term loans to small businesses while earning profits for the shareholders of the SBIC. SBICs may obtain a portion of their loan funds directly from the SBA. SBIC loans must be subordinated to bank debts. Loans are unsecured, and all investors have limited liability. Only interest is payable during the term of the loan; the principal becomes due as a balloon payment at the end of the loan period. Interest is stipulated at some level below prime rate. Minority Enterprise SBICs (MESBICs) have been established to provide venture capital for businesses with strong minority group interests (again, ill-defined). A MESBIC may be established with $300,000, as opposed to $500,000 for an SBIC.

The SBA has a broad range of loan programs for businesses that are unable to obtain funds at reasonable rates from conventional lenders. The agency was intended to be the lender of last resort for many small business owners. SBA loans may be used for business construction, expansion, or conversion, for the purchase of machinery, equipment, facilities, supplies, or materials, or for working capital. Loans may be made directly, but, since demand for funds generally exceeds supply, the SBA more frequently guarantees up to 90 percent of another lender's loan or makes the loan in cooperation with a bank or other lender. The SBA also has loan programs for special categories of borrowers, including the socially and economically disadvantaged, the handicapped, and enterprises suffering from unusual circumstances such as being displaced by federally funded construction projects, damaged by natural disasters, or suffering from extraordinary economic disasters beyond their control.

SBA offices employ federal procurement specialists who help small business managers locate government purchasers and aid in preparing bids and obtaining contracts. The SBA can provide a firm with a certificate of competency (COC) attesting that the firm is capable of performing the contract. The SBA then becomes responsible for conducting on-site verifications of the firm's competency. Two procurement programs are designed to assist specific groups: (1) The 8(a) program, authorized under Section 8(a) of the Small Business Act, as amended, enables the SBA to contract with other federal agencies and departments and then subcontract to the socially or economically disadvantaged; (2) the Minority Vendors' Program refers corporations and government agencies to socially and economically disadvantaged small business owners who may be able to supply products and services. The SBA provides or sponsors two types of management assistance activities: training and counseling. Training includes workshops, conferences, specialized training courses, and problem clinics. The primary SBA counseling programs are MAO counseling, SCORE, ACE, 406 Call Contracting, SBI, and SBDC.

MAOs (Management Assistance Officers) are staff professionals on the SBA payroll, who themselves perform counseling of both existing and prospective small business firms. They also act as resource managers, selecting one of the other counseling or training "tools" for use as seems appropriate. Currently, there are about 250 MAOs.

SCORE (Service Corps of Retired Executives) consists of volunteer experts drawing on years of executive experience who visit small business firms and work with their owners/managers to find and apply solutions to their problems. They also screen clients. Currently, there are approximately 8,000 SCORE volunteers.

ACE (Active Corps of Executives) is intended to perform the same function as SCORE but uses executives who are still active in the business and professional world.

SBA's call contracting program is commonly known by the section of the Economic Opportunity Act that originally authorized it. In this program, SBA contracts with mangement consulting firms to be on "call" to provide specific counseling and technical services when requested by the issuance of "task orders." Tasks are supposed to be performed only for owners of small businesses who are "economically and socially disadvantaged" or are located in areas of high unemployment.

Under the SBI (Small Business Institute) program, teams of senior and graduate students in colleges of business throughout the country, led by business school faculty, give personal counseling to small business owners. The program frequently, but not always, provides counseling over a longer period of time than do MAOs or the 406 program.

The SBA has also provided funds to several states to initiate Small Business Development Centers (SBDCs). These university-based, extension-type programs offer counseling, education, and research services to their respective small business communities.

The Advocacy Office of the SBA was created to represent the small business community at the various levels of government. The Advocacy Office exists to identify small business problems and to bring these problems to the attention of appropriate agencies for the purpose of finding solutions. The Advocacy Office is required to insure that federal agencies adhere to the Regulatory Flexibility Act of 1981, which demands that regulatory agencies evaluate the impact of proposed regulations to determine if they will unnecessarily impede the growth and development of small business.

In the course of his congressional confirmation hearings in 1981, Michael Cardenas, President Ronald Reagan's nominee as SBA director, was both informed and quizzed about an agency described as suffering from abuse and mismanagement. Such criticism is not new to the SBA. At intervals throughout its history, the SBA has been rocked by scandals and accusations. Most of the problems have occurred within the areas of financial and procurement assistance, but other functions have not been immune.

The SBA has been characterized as corrupt, wasteful, scandal-ridden, and incompetent. Between 1969 and 1979, over 100 articles appeared in major newspapers documenting dozens of major cases of fraud and corruption. Senator William Proxmire (Democrat, Wisconsin) has been pressing for years for the abolition of the SBA because of these problems. Many business spokespersons have supported Proxmire's bill.

Numerous examples of SBA scandals can be cited. It has been estimated, for example, that no more than one-half of the dollars the SBA has loaned out over the years have ever been paid back. In fiscal 1976 alone, $130 million in loans were lost. A one-time district director in Richmond, Virginia, was arrested, convicted, and imprisoned for authorizing fraudulent loans. Minority loan programs have been particular targets of abuse. By 1979, 3,400 minority firms had received loans, yet the SBA could locate only 30 which were still in operation. More recently, a minority enterprise loan was provided to a nephew of former President Richard Nixon.

SBA problems are regularly documented by audits conducted both in-house and by external evaluators. The General Accounting Office* has declared that SBA resources are not well coordinated and has labeled as questionable the use of funds intended for the disadvantaged. The Rockville Consulting Group analyzed SBA management assistance programs and found some to have negative impacts on client groups.

Despite all these criticisms, there appears to be no imminent threat to the survival of the SBA. In fact, the agency has been expanding the scope of its operations.

There is no guarantee that the SBA will continue to grow or even exist in the years ahead. Its history, however, has been one of ever expanded activity. In 1958, for example, the SBA had $212 million in loans outstanding. By 1968, the figure was $737 million and had reached almost $5.9 billion by 1978. A change in administrative policy was announced in 1982, indicating that loan programs would receive less emphasis than in the past and that greater attention would be devoted to management assistance.

Both Presidents Jimmy Carter and Reagan espoused more concern for small businesses than their predecessors. President Carter called the first White House Conference on Small Business in January 1980. The conference was the culmination of a series of regional meetings that had been attended by over thirty thousand small business owners. Conferees proposed fifteen priority recommendations for national policy regarding the small business sector. A number of these recommendations have since been incorporated into legislative acts.

In March 1982, President Reagan presented Congress with the first President's report of *The State of Small Business*. The report contains an eight-point policy statement, which includes support for existing and proposed SBA programs. Also in 1982, Reagan's original appointee to the position of SBA administrator resigned and was replaced. Thus, the controversy persists, but the SBA remains.

FOR ADDITIONAL INFORMATION: The Small Business Administration itself produces a wealth of publications on both small business in general and itself in particular. One comprehensive report is *The Study of Small Business* (1977), which provides especially good information on small business definitions and on taxation. More recently, the President's report on *The State of Small Business* (1982) offers a thorough examination of small business on a national scale and the role played by the SBA in serving that constituency. One of the few historical views of the SBA is *The Small Business Administration* (1968) by Addison W. Parris. A topical review of the SBA and a reference for further sources is Joseph R. Mancuso's *Small Business Survival Guide* (1980). One of the best sources of some of the criticisms of the SBA is the *Wall Street Journal*, which periodically prints revealing articles on SBA activities. In addition, the *Journal* runs a column on small business on the front page of its second section in each Monday's issue.

FRANK HOY

SMITHSONIAN INSTITUTION. The Smithsonian Institution is a trust establishment of the United States supported by federal appropriations and private trust funds. Under its organic act, it is controlled by a body actually called ''The Establishment,'' composed of the President, the Vice-President, and the Cabinet. In practice, however, oversight has always been entrusted to the institution's Board of Regents, a body composed of the Vice-President, the chief justice (its chancellor), three members each from the House of Representatives and the Senate, and nine citizen members—two residents of the District of Columbia and seven residents of states, all chosen by joint resolution of Congress. A secretary, elected by the Regents and serving at their pleasure, directs the institution's operations and carries out its policies.

The Smithsonian's relationship to the government is quite unlike that of a federal agency as generally understood. The institution derives its unique character from the will of James Smithson, its founder, and the act of Congress passed in 1836 to accept Smithson's bequest. Smithson bequeathed the whole of his property "to the United States of America, to found at Washington, under the name of the Smithsonian Institution, an establishment for the increase and diffusion of knowledge among men," and he created a charitable trust under the terms of which the United States would be trustee, "for purposes not limited to the national interest but on behalf of all mankind" (9 stat. 102). In 1836, Congress accepted the trust on these terms and pledged the faith of the United States to carry out the purposes of the trust.

This unique combination of a privately endowed institution, administered by a Board of Regents independent of the government itself, and the continuing support of the United States, as trustee, in generous fulfillment of its pledge, has made possible the institution's remarkable achievements. The Smithsonian has received contributions from private donors which were inconceivable in 1836. The great national collections now consist largely of private gifts, and continuing private additions to the Smithsonian's independent trust funds have maintained the institution's central resource for initiative and integrity. The Congress, on its part, has responded with very substantial federal support, which has been essential to the institution's growth and to many of its far-reaching services to the public for over a hundred years.

In the popular mind, the Smithsonian is identified with museums. The institution's umbrella covers eleven of them: the National Museum of Natural History; the National Museum of American History; the National Air and Space Museum; the Hirshhorn Museum and Sculpture Garden; the Freer Gallery of Oriental Art; the Museum of African Art; the National Museum of American Art; the National Portrait Gallery; the Anacostia Neighborhood Museum; the Renwick Gallery; and the Cooper-Hewitt Museum of Decorative Arts and Design. These galleries combine public exhibits and research by their staffs in appropriate subject areas. In addition, the Smithsonian includes other bureaus that are largely or solely dedicated to research. They include the Chesapeake Bay Center for Environmental Studies; the National Zoological Park; the Radiation Biology Laboratory; the Smithsonian Astrophysical Observatory; the Smithsonian Tropical Research Institute, and the Archives of American Art. Finally, there are numerous other offices which support aspects of the institution's life. These include an office overseeing museum programs, an office for membership and development (producer of the highly regarded *Smithsonian* magazine), and other offices too numerous to list. Moreover, the Smithsonian is affiliated with the National Gallery of Art, the John F. Kennedy Center for the Performing Arts, and the Woodrow Wilson International Center for Scholars, all of which operate under independent boards of trustees. Although most of the bureaus are located in the vicinity of Washington, D.C., a number are to be found elsewhere. The Cooper-Hewitt Museum is in New York City; the Astrophysical Observatory, in Cambridge, Massachusetts; and the Smithsonian Tropical Research Institute, in Panama. At present, the Smithsonian's collections, spread among all its bureaus, number more than 75 million items, of which scarcely 5 percent are on exhibit at one time.

Thus, it appears that the Smithsonian is a shelter to widely divergent interests. But how did it become what it is today? To understand its growth and development, we must turn to the obscure Englishman, James Smithson, who died in Genoa, Italy, in 1829 and whose trust launched the institution. Smithson was a natural son of Hugh Percy, Duke of Northumberland. A graduate of Pembroke College, Oxford, Smithson spent most of his life traveling in Europe. He was regarded as an amateur of the sciences, particularly mineralogy and chemistry. Smithson's will made the United States his reversionary legatee for the purpose of establishing an institution in Washington, D.C., concerned with the spread of knowledge. The proceeds of his bequest amounted to $515,169.

Andrew Jackson announced the legacy to Congress, which promptly began sixteen years of arguing over the gift. The initial dispute lay between those who regarded the gift as an example of British condescension too demeaning for a sovereign state to receive, and those who, happy to accept the gift, differed over its proper use. Advocates of a spartan and republican renunciation soon lost, but the contest over how best to employ the gift continued for many years. The testator had left no clear guidance about use of his gift, and the issue soon became whether to support pure or practical learning. Those who espoused pure learning proposed creating a library or university. Partisans of practical learning supported schemes for teacher training, practical agronomy, and other interests typical of the day-to-day needs of a young nation.

Finally, in 1846, Congress approved an organic act that sought to balance the competing claims by creating an institution devoted to the general objective of creating and diffusing knowledge among men. The Regents were directed to house the national collections then in Washington, to build a library, and to support studies in science and art. The implementation of these directives was left to the Regents and the first secretary, Joseph Henry. Some of the directives were obeyed at once. In contrast, the arts received no serious attention until 1905, when the present National Museum of American Art was created.

Joseph Henry was a distinguished theoretical scientist and one of the most noted American physicists of the nineteenth century. He came to the Smithsonian from the presidency of the College of New Jersey (now Princeton), and he had devoted much thought to how one might actually increase human knowledge. Henry was not blind to the importance of diffusing knowledge and supported a program of publications and exchanges to that end, as the institution still does.

However, he gave first attention to fostering original research. Henry appreciated the value of libraries and museums, but he was anxious that the Smithsonian's resources not be diverted from the search for "new" knowledge. It seemed to him that few organizations sponsored research, while, comparatively, many were inclined to support libraries and museums. Even at its founding, the Smithsonian's resources were not great, and they were to shrink steadily in comparison to other institutions, once nineteenth-century philanthropy was well established. Ironic as it now seems, Joseph Henry opposed the accumulation of museum collections throughout his tenure.

Spencer F. Baird, who served as secretary from 1878 to 1887, had a different vision. A student of natural history rather than the physical sciences, Baird was anxious to create a national museum. Himself an indefatigable collector, Baird supported others' efforts as well. This he did quietly during his years as assistant to Joseph Henry. Even after he succeeded Henry, the resources available to him were never very great. However, Baird was a man of vast energy and personal charm. Mixing these talents with such resources as he could assemble, Baird-cultivated amateur and professional collectors throughout the nation. He used contacts with military officers to tap the resources of the expanding West. At other times, he might give or loan a few instruments; might perform a small patronage favor through his highly placed Washington friends; or might simply arrange for use of government rations on the frontier. By all these means, Baird built up a great national history collection—the real basis for our present national collections. It is important to realize that Baird was not merely a collector. His vision was of a great national museum, which would hold and care for specimens from which scholars could work to produce new knowledge. The museum as a teaching entity was Baird's goal. In his lifetime and for long afterwards, the means to do all he hoped for were not available. Staff, funds, and space were woefully inadequate. Yet, his was a beginning, on which later generations could build.

The Smithsonian took quite a different turn when Samuel P. Langley succeeded Baird, serving from 1887 to 1906. Langley was an astronomer and a pioneering astrophysicist, an investigator of solar radiation. He began programs in those fields which the Smithsonian continues today. Langley was also a student of heavier-than-air flight. In all these fields, he and the institution made substantial contributions. In addition, the Smithsonian began its zoo, the National Zoological Park, which is still one of only a few zoos devoted to research, though it is designed as well for public instruction.

Strange as it seems today when the Smithsonian is so deeply committed to the arts, the institution long neglected the field almost entirely. The organic act of 1846 expressly authorized an art gallery, but for many years the institution contented itself with copies of a few masterpieces of sculpture and art. Finally, in 1906, the Smithsonian accepted two gifts which established its role in the arts. One, by Harriet Lane Johnston, formed the nucleus of the present National Museum of American Art. The second, from Charles Lang Freer, created the

Freer Gallery of Oriental Art, a leading American center for the study of that discipline.

Charles Doolittle Walcott, director of the United States Geological Survey,* succeeded Langley in 1907 and served until his death in 1927. Walcott was a distinguished authority on Cambrian geology and paleontology. Fittingly enough, it was during his tenure that the present building of the National Museum of Natural History was occupied—chiefly as the new home of the institution's burgeoning natural history collections. While the Smithsonian remained committed to its scientific pursuits, it was much drawn into the afairs of the larger governmental and scientific community then emerging in Washington. Walcott served on the National Advisory Committee on Aeronautics (now NASA)* and on the board of the Carnegie Institution of Washington, as well as other government and private bodies. He also began efforts to improve the institution's finances. From Smithson's day to Walcott's, the Smithsonian had received only a few bequests, mostly small ones. Walcott saw that more private support was needed and began a campaign to raise funds, hoping to strengthen and expand institutional programs. Unhappily, his death, followed closely by the depression, cut short these efforts.

Charles G. Abbot, an astronomer, succeeded Walcott in 1928 and served until 1944. To him fell the difficult task of guiding the Smithsonian through the depression and most of World War II. These were largely years of retrenchment, and the hopes of the 1920s were necessarily deferred. Still, the institution helped to found the Institute for Research in Tropical America, which was later to become one of its bureaus as the Smithsonian Tropical Research Institute. During this period, too, the Smithsonian began its affiliation with the great new National Gallery of Art, a gift to the nation from Andrew Mellon.

From 1944 to 1953 an ornithologist, Alexander Wetmore, led the institution. Despite the difficulties posed by World War II and, later, Korea, the institution began to recover its momentum. The National Air Museum (now the National Air and Space Museum) was created, and the institution's exhibits program began to undergo revision. Plans were laid for an addition to the Museum of Natural History and, more tentatively, for a new museum to house historical and technological collections.

Leonard Carmichael served as secretary from 1953 to 1964. During his administration, the Smithsonian was able to secure funding for a substantial program of renovation and expansion. Staff levels were increased and exhibits modernized. In 1957, construction began on a new museum for history and technology (now the National Museum of American History), which gave collections in those fields a much-needed separate home for the first time.

S. Dillon Ripley, the present secretary, took office in 1964. During his tenure, the following bureau-level organizations have been added to the Smithsonian family: the National Portrait Gallery (1964); the Anacostia Neighborhood Museum (1967); the Renwick Gallery (1965); the Cooper-Hewitt Museum of Decorative Arts and Design (1968); the Joseph H. Hirshhorn Museum and Sculpture

Garden (1968); the Archives of American Art (1970); the National Air and Space Museum (1976); and the Museum of African Art (1980). The Woodrow Wilson International Center for Scholars (1968) has joined the National Gallery of Art (1936) and the John F. Kennedy Center for the Performing Arts (opened in 1971) as an affiliated organization controlled by independent trustees.

It is a cliché of our age that information is now growing at a rate too great for mastery. Perhaps so. The Smithsonian, like all organizations devoted to learning, certainly finds itself taxed in many ways as it endeavors to keep abreast of expanding knowledge. That may be the institution's central problem. Nevertheless, the Smithsonian has chosen to keep to its founding purpose—the increase and diffusion of knowledge among men. Research continues across a wide spectrum of endeavor, from coral reefs to human social organization, from tropical ecosystems to the stars. The institution daily lives in intimate association with the past—the stability and perspective which history gives to human thought— and the future—the uncertain and perhaps unknowable edge at which human values and institutions are always tested. How does one increase and diffuse knowledge? That question points to an unending and never quite successful pursuit. Yet, to pursue is the Smithsonian choice.

FOR ADDITIONAL INFORMATION: The records of the Smithsonian Institution are found chiefly in the Smithsonian Institution Archives. A small body of records may be found in Record Group 106, National Archives and Records Service.* A fire in 1865 destroyed most of the records prior to that date.

Secondary sources consist principally of numerous series of titles published by the institution over the years. They include the Annual Reports of the Board of Regents to Congress (now titled *The Smithsonian Year*); *Annual Reports of the U.S. National Museum*; *Bulletins of the U.S. National Museum*; and other series and individual titles too numerous to list here. For the earlier years of the Smithsonian, consult William J. Rhees, comp. and ed., *The Smithsonian Institution: Documents Relative to Its Origin and History, 1835-1899*, 2 vols. (1901). Also useful is George Brown Goode, ed., *The Smithsonian Institution, 1846-1896. The History of the First Half Century* (1897). More recent histories include Paul H. Oehser, *The Smithsonian Institution* (1970); and Geoffrey T. Hellman, *The Smithsonian: Octopus on the Mall* (1966).

JAMES A. STEED

SOCIAL SECURITY ADMINISTRATION. The Social Security Administration is one of the largest and most influential of federal government agencies. Its expenditures account for approximately one-fifth of the federal budget, and it affects nearly every American in one way or another. Yet, remarkably little is known about it. Until the 1970s, it had (apart from its many local offices) minimal public visibility. To most Americans and to most scholars, it evoked little interest and less concern. There is reason to believe that these two features of the operations of the Social Security Administration—its vast scope and low profile—are related, the products of administrative policy as much as public acceptance of the agency's tasks or the routine character of those duties.

The administrative history of the Social Security Administration reflects the evolution of federal welfare and social insurance policy. The landmark Social Security Act of 1935 created an independent three-member Social Security Board, which reported directly to the President. In 1946, Congress created a successor agency, the modern Social Security Administration. The principal innovation was the creation of a single executive, the commisioner of Social Security, to take the place of the troika. Meanwhile, in 1939, the board had become a component of the Federal Security Agency, together with federal bureaus specializing in public health, education, and other welfare matters. In 1953, Social Security was transferred to the new Department of Health, Education, and Welfare (HEW) and in 1979, to the Department of Health and Human Services.*

The original board managed the three major programs created by the 1935 act: a federal-state system of public assistance, financed by congressional and state appropriations; a federal-state, unemployment insurance plan, financed by taxes on employers; and a federal old-age pension program, financed by a payroll tax on workers and employers. Subsequent legislation transferred the unemployment compensation program to the Department of Labor* in 1949 and the public assistance program to another arm of HEW in 1963. In the meantime, Congress broadened the responsibilities of the Social Security Administration by authorizing survivors and dependent benefits (1939), disability benefits (1956), and Medicare (1966). In 1940, Social Security benefit payments totaled $35 million, less than 0.5 percent of U.S. personal income. In 1977, they amounted to more than $117 billion and 6.9 percent of U.S. personal income. Social Security payments first exceeded public assistance outlays in 1951; since that time, Social Security, including Medicare, has remained the dominant form of social insurance in the United States. For most of this period Social Security has enjoyed wide public acceptance, while public assistance and unemployment compensation have been subject to frequent political attack.

The maneuvering that led to the passage of the Social Security Act had a substantial impact on the character of the board and its administrative policies. By tradition, provisions for individual economic security in the United States had been decentralized and uncoordinated. Families, private insurance companies, and local and state governments played the preponderant role. The Social Security Act, while transferring substantial responsibility from private to public institutions, reflected this background. The act preserved the idea of "insurance" for the elderly, enlarged the authority of the states, and left health care financing to the private sector. Subsequent developments had similar effects. Republican opposition to the act during the 1936 election campaign and pressures from the Townsend movement thereafter led federal administrators to accept wide variations in state standards and procedures for public assistance. Differing conceptions of the purpose of unemployment insurance had the same impact on state unemployment compensation programs. Finally, the early administrators of Social Security were personally committed to a managerial approach that emphasized efficiency rather than organizational innovation.

More than any other individual, Arthur J. Altmeyer (1891-1972) shaped the operations of the Social Security Administration. As a board member, 1935-1946, and as commissioner of Social Security, 1946-1953, he was in a position to influence practically every facet of Social Security policy during the system's formative period. To outsiders Altmeyer was the archetypal civil servant, bland, discreet, and professionally competent. In reality, he was a shrewd politician and an aggressive manager. An early student of Social Security described him as a man who "loves and masters detail." But Altmeyer was not only a wily bureaucrat. As an undergraduate and graduate economics student at the University of Wisconsin, he had absorbed the institutionalist perspective of John R. Commons and his colleagues. The Commons group abjured abstractions, emphasized real-world problem-solving, and celebrated the role of the nonpartisan expert in public service. Altmeyer thus brought to government administration the zeal of the reformer, and to reform the expertise of the skilled manager. Their bywords were patience, dedication, and a commitment to progress, however slow. His approach in turn became the approach that Social Security administrators adhered to until the 1970s.

The extent of Altmeyer's achievement may be gauged from a brief comparison of the operations of the Social Security Board and of the National Labor Relations Board,* (NLRB), the other major federal agency created in 1935 as a consequence of the Second New Deal. First, both organizations recruited able young professional people, including many from academic life. Altmeyer kept a close watch over hiring, insuring that his type of reformer was selected. For outsiders he required an intensive training program. The NLRB, on the other hand, allowed Communists to fill influential posts. By 1940, Labor Board members and staff were subject to sweeping criticism. Second, both agencies administered controversial measures. In the late 1930s, the Social Security Board methodically and systematically diffused the conflicts that raged over the birth of the American welfare state. By emphasizing that each worker was "insuring " his own retirement, Altmeyer and his associates converted old age pensions from a despised dole to a popular government program. Conversely, the Labor Board, by its activist policies and favoritism, intensified public hostility to mandatory collective bargaining. Finally, both agencies were initially run by unwieldy boards. Altmeyer soon came to dominate Social Security, giving it strong executive leadership in fact, if not in name. The NLRB became even more divided, precipitating the Roosevelt purge and reorganization of 1940-1941.

Altmeyer and his associates unquestionably performed with distinction during the 1930s and 1940s. A summary of their achievements would likely include the following: (1) the creation of a cost-effective social insurance system that reflected the political milieu of the 1930s; (2) the establishment of an old-age pension system that satisfied the expectations of most recipients; (3) the development of a staff that included many able individuals; and (4) a public relations campaign that made the contributory feature of the pension program a lever for disarming critics and winning public acceptance of Social Security.

There was one other effect of the Altmeyer era that became more pronounced in the postwar years. The architects and early administrators of the Social Security Act viewed their handiwork as an important but limited step toward a comprehensive social insurance system. From the beginning, their intention was expansion through accretion. However, it was not until the late 1940s that they developed a successful political strategy for achieving their aims. In essence, they came to emphasize what could be done rather than what, in their view, should be done. During Robert Ball's terms as commissioner (1962-1973), this modified approach proved to be highly successful. By enlisting sympathetic politicians and interest groups and working cautiously and patiently, Social Security administrators were able to promote major extensions of their programs. Although the most important substantive extensions came in 1956 (disability coverage), 1966 (Medicare), and 1969-1972 (higher benefit levels, including cost-of-living escalators), the administrators' campaign for expansion was continuous. Among the keys to their strategy have been a large research and planning staff, an effective congressional lobbying operation, a firm alliance with organized labor, and, to a lesser degree, organized business groups. The results for the agency have included a vastly expanded budget, new career opportunities, and, eventually, unwanted and unanticipated controversy.

When Congress passed Medicare legislation in 1966, Ball and his associates immediately turned their attention to a campaign for increased pension and disability benefits. After several years of effort they succeeded, largely because of political developments that distracted or neutralized potential opponents. Benefits and taxes increased rapidly in the 1970s, and the notion of old-age "insurance," which had never been wholly accurate, became a chimera. The "new Social Security System," as Ball termed it, developed serious strains, the most notable of which was a persistent deficit. For the first time since the mid-1930s, Social Security came under attack. By 1980, the carefully devised consensus of earlier decades was in disarray, and political critics of the system became more numerous. Symptomatic of this change was the prospect of benefit reductions, an unprecedented step that had hitherto been considered politically unthinkable.

The Social Security Administration is probably the most significant institutional legacy of the reform movements of the first half of the twentieth century. By most standards it has ably reflected this heritage. The combination of efficient administration, patient, long-term expansion, and a growing economy has enabled it to enjoy remarkable success for more than four decades. Even in the 1980s, critics contemplate only minor adjustments. Nevertheless, recent problems have raised fundamental questions about the agency's future. The role of the Social Security Administration in the 1980s and 1990s will likely depend on the ability of politicians and administrators to restore the balance that served so well for so many years.

FOR ADDITIONAL INFORMATION: For the background of the Social Security Act, see Roy Lubove, *The Struggle for Social Security* (1968); Daniel Nelson, *Unemployment Insurance: The American Experience, 1915-35* (1969); and Edwin E. Witte, *The Development of the Social Security Act* (1962). Broader historical accounts of welfare policy in the United States include Edward Berkowitz and Kim McQuaid, *Creating the Welfare State* (1980); Walter I. Trattner, *From Poor Law to Welfare State* (1974); and James Leiby, *A History of Social Welfare and Social Work in the United States* (1978). Of the many technical studies of Social Security programs, Eveline M. Burns, *The American Social Security System* (1949), and William Haber and Merrill E. Murray, *Unemployment Insurance in the American Economy* (1966), are among the most useful.

Statistical information is available in U.S. Social Security Administration, *Social Security Bulletin, Annual Statistic Supplement*. See also Hacc Sorel Tisher, *Self-Reliance and Social Security, 1870-1917* (1971); John A. Garraty, *Unemployment in History* (1978); Arthur J. Altmeyer, *The Formative Years of Social Security* (1966), Chapter 2; Charles McKinley and Robert W. Frase, *Launching Social Security* (1970), Chapter 4; and Martha Derthick, *Policymaking for Social Security* (1979).

DANIEL M. NELSON

STANDARDS BUREAU. See National Bureau of Standards.

STATE DEPARTMENT. See Department of State.

T

TENNESSEE VALLEY AUTHORITY (TVA). The Tennessee Valley Authority is not a federal agency; rather, it is a largely self-financing, government-owned corporation. It has an anomolous position in American government, not because of its now much used corporate form but because of its regional focus and its broad array of programs. Within the Tennessee Valley, it has either supplemented or supplanted various services normally carried out by traditional federal agencies with national constituencies. The major TVA programs include the production and distribution of electricity, providing the needed facilities for navigation on the Tennessee River, flood control for the Tennessee, Ohio, and Mississippi River valleys, fertilizer research and agricultural improvement, and contributions to national defense (largely nitrates and power). Secondary programs include forestry, conservation, recreation, and community and industrial development. Ancillary programs are almost endless, but have included numerous plans and surveys, educational demonstrations, technical aid for local planning agencies, malaria control, the resettlement of people displaced by dams, and even one early planned community. At an administrative level, the TVA early developed its own staff recruitment and screening procedures, experimented with several forms of employee education, and devised various ingenious modes of cooperation with both state and local governments.

The roots of the TVA go back to the nineteenth century. That these roots all came together in the TVA Act of 1933 was, in part, an accident of both place and time, in part the logical outcome of a decade-long legislative struggle.

The Tennessee River has its own peculiarities. Although the main river (from the merging of the Holston and the French Broad) is just over 600 miles in length, it drains the highest rainfall area of the eastern United States. Thus, in volume, the river rivals much longer streams, and in flood stages has a major impact on the whole lower Ohio and Mississippi systems. Because of quite reliable rainfall patterns, the flow of the Tennessee varies immensely from late winter and spring flooding to a low water level in the autumn. Even when high, the Tennessee was navigable only for about halfway to Knoxville. It suffered from a series of rapids in northern Alabama, known as Muscle Shoals, an impediment that became a potentially valuable resource with the commercial development of electricity. These peculiarities all add up to the need for, and the possibility of, unified development. The two dams needed to conquer the shoals ¡for navigation promised a windfall of hydroelectric power. The up-river storage dams which needed to even out the flow at Muscle Shoals, and thus maximize electrical production and maintain a deep channel, also promised flood relief, not only for the valley but also for the lower Mississippi. These complementary relationships of navigation, flood control, and hydroelectricity were apparent early in the twentieth century, and were further documented by a series of surveys carried out by the Army Corps of Engineers.* But the corps, its work in the Tennessee Valley limited to navigational improvements, sought such unified development only through cooperation with private power companies. By 1930, the corps had completed plans for a system either of high dams with their side benefits of electricity and flood control, or of numerous low dams in order to procure a 9-foot navigable channel to Knoxville. In 1930, Congress first approved the less expensive low-dam proposal. The TVA would subsequently substitute its own high dams, and thus provide all the facilities needed by a navigational system which the corps still operates.

In effect, the first TVA act was Section 124 of the National Defense Act of 1916, which authorized government production of synthetic nitrates for defense and, in peacetime, for fertilizers. Prior to 1916, organized conservationists had blocked all leasing of Muscle Schoals to private power companies. This made the undeveloped Schoals the likely, and also the best, site for government nitrate plants. In fact, the Wilson Administration located its first two such plants at or near Muscle Schoals, and, to meet the heavy electrical demands of one of the two synthetic processes, began construction of a large hydroelectric dam (later named for Wilson), which still produces more power than any other in the TVA system. At war's end, one small nitrate plant was useless, but the larger, power-hungry, and already almost obsolete cyanamid plant was ready for production. With Wilson Administration approval, the Army Corps continued work on Wilson Dam, both as an aid to navigation and as an eventual source of power. After failing to locate any interested private lessees, the War Department* also sought congressional approval for a federal chemical corporation to operate the nitrogen plant. Won over by the possibly illusory promise of cheap fertilizers, Southern farmers joined advocates of public power to mobilize support for such a bill. It passed in the Senate but died along with the Wilson Administration in a reluctant House, leaving unsettled the ultimate disposition of the expensive Muscle Schoals project.

In 1921, the new Harding Administration decided to lease or sell the Muscle Schoals chemical plants and power facilities. At first, neither chemical companies nor local utilities seemed interested, but then Henry Ford propelled Muscle Schoals into one of the great controversies of the 1920s. He agreed to lease all the Muscle Schoals facilities, provided the corps would complete Wilson Dam and a second, smaller up-river dam (later the Wheeler Dam). In return for the power, he agreed to pay enough rent to amortize all government costs over a hundred years and to produce fertilizer to sell to farmers. In effect, he bargained a limited commitment to fertilizer for very cheap power, and added enticing promises of a vast new industrial city in the Muscle Schoals area. Ford's offer triggered counterproposals. Power companies offered a larger rent for the power but usually with weaker promises of actual fertilizer production. Chemical companies offered firmer promises of actual fertilizer production, but in return asked for access to all power sites on the upper Tennessee and its tributaries. As a counter to all leasing arrangements, Senator George Norris, chairman of the Senate Committee on Agriculture and Forestry to which the Senate referred the Ford proposals, sponsored throughout the 1920s bills providing for full public ownership and operation of all the Muscle Schoals facilities. His great concern was electricity and its developmental uses in the valley, but in his bills he made the necessary gestures toward fertilizer experiments, if not actual production. Norris at first sought public development of the whole upper Tennessee River, including storage dams at such prime sites as Cove Creek on the Clinch (the later site of Norris Dam). Given so many contending interests, the Congress refused such a large public commitment and soon floundered in a complete impasse. But by 1928, almost by default (no private companies ever met the government's terms), both houses passed a compromise bill of Norris's, one that provided for federal operation only of the Muscle Schoals properties. President Calvin Coolidge blocked it by pocket veto. In 1930, Herbert Hoover vetoed a similar bill.

The Democratic victories in the elections of 1932 assured passage of a Muscle Schoals bill. President-elect Franklin D. Roosevelt, a long-time advocate of both public power and conservation, helped to shape the final legislation. Roosevelt easily accepted Norris's older dream of a unified development of a whole watershed. Thus, after visiting Muscle Schoals in January 1933, he proposed a vast project encompassing the whole Tennessee Valley, and one committed not only to the long-debated goals of defense, fertilizer, improved navigation, flood control, and electricity, but also such conservation of resource management goals as reforestation and the planned use of marginal land. Roosevelt always used the ambiguous word "planning" to give a rhetorical unity to all the goals of his new valley project. Norris and friendly representatives met with Roosevelt for the drafting of the TVA act. The bill ended up close to earlier Norris bills in the key sections dealing with fertilizer, power, and navigation, but it included expansive, new, but not very specific, sections on planning and on the broader social purposes of the act. On April 10, Roosevelt asked Congress for such legislation, and both houses, after limited but intense debate, overwhelmingly passed very similar bills, but bills that differed on controversial power sections. The House set tighter restrictions on new dams and heavily qualified the future TVA's authority to build its own transmission lines. Roosevelt helped arbitrate these issues in behalf of the stronger Senate version and happily signed the final bill on May 18. Already he had selected Arthur Morgan of Antioch College as the first chairman of the three-member TVA board, and Morgan had already lined up several key employees.

The TVA act set broad limits to what the TVA could do. The first three directors chose among options, and in so doing they helped shape the enduring identity of a new and quite autonomous corporation. They soon did this in the midst of bitter personal conflict. The chairman, Arthur Morgan, made vital contributions even to the TVA act. For example, he secured a last minute amendment that allowed Roosevelt to take the construction of dams from the Army Corps and award it to an engineer of his choice (Morgan was his choice). Thus, the first impact of the TVA on the valley was that of a depression dam builder and employer. Morgan chose an excellent technical staff and soon achieved an enviable record for efficient construction, high worker morale, and humane concern in the purchase of needed farms or the difficult relocation of displaced families. He also emphasized a major forestry program. Morgan, an engineer with almost utopian visions for the valley, shared Roosevelt's concerns with conservation, reforestation, land-use planning, and community development, and was equally vague and elusive in describing some of his plans. He supported public power and cheap electricity, but more as a means than as an end. He reflected no deep suspicions of private utilities, and he wanted to be fair and open in seeking cooperative arrangements with them. In some ways a political innocent, Morgan struggled for an impossible standard of nonpartisanship and never had any of the skills needed to cultivate a political constituency. He desired major structural changes in the valley, and thus he did not want to tie the TVA too closely to entrenched local elites. Moralistic and stubborn as well as visionary, he proved himself almost pathetically inept in dealing with more aggressive or more tactful people.

The other two directors—Harcourt Morgan and David Lilienthal—quickly formed an alliance against Morgan. They tried to moderate his more utopian or radical policies, particularly those that faced political opposition in the Valley, and to overcome his yielding or cooperative stance toward private utilites. In short, they struggled, successfully as it turned out, to build a strong political constituency for the TVA. Lilienthal and Harcourt Morgan first forced Arthur Morgan to accept a division of responsibility, one that reflected diverse skills and experiences. Arthur Morgan was chief engineer by presidential appointment, and continued to work on conservation and planning programs. Harcourt Morgan, former president of the University of Tennessee and long-term specialist in agricultural extension, took over the fertilizer and agriculture program. He worked easily with people in the valley, and against Arthur Morgan's desires used the Extension Service to administer the farm demonstration projects. Harcourt Morgan was modest, reticent, but politically astute and best able among the directors to mobilize local support for the TVA.

Lilienthal, a lawyer and former member of the Public Service Commission in Wisconsin, assumed responsibility for legal matters and for the power program.

His assets and liabilities were almost the opposite of Arthur Morgan's. Young and ambitious, he loved partisan fights and set out from the beginning to establish TVA as a national leader in the cheap production and aggressive marketing of electricity. He shamelessly flattered Roosevelt and Norris, gathered disciples within and without the Authority, and used his prime protagonist, Wendell Willkie of the large holding company, Commonwealth and Southern, as a foil in cementing partisan loyalties. An expert propagandist, he dramatized a few early TVA electrical contracts, exploited carefully the somewhat arbitrarily low rates charged by TVA, launched a successful financing scheme to enable people to buy home appliances and increase their electrical use, and brilliantly directed two major, protracted legal battles to establish the constitutionality of the TVA power program. By the end of the 1930s, he had won his no-holds-barred fight, and by negotiation or purchase had gained a secure TVA power market approximately double the size of the Tennessee watershed. (The TVA would also market power from later corps dams on the Cumberland.)

Arthur Morgan came to hate Lilienthal, and what he believed was a one-sided emphasis upon power. Lilienthal always won, and by winning he made the TVA what it is today. Had the TVA lost the court cases, it would have been restricted to the sale of electricity from its switchboards. It could still have set the rates charged for its power and could have cultivated its own municipal customers. But it would have gained no responsibility to serve all the power needs of a growing market and would probably have remained until today a producer only of hydroelectric power, or less than one-fifth of the power now consumed in the valley. Lilienthal's aggressive tactics also gained the fervent support of public power advocates in Congress, including Norris. Arthur Morgan slowly lost any effective voice in the TVA. More critically, he so fumbled his side of the controversy that he eventually lost Roosevelt's support. FDR had shared Morgan's broader goals for the valley. But a beleaguered Morgan, by 1936, moved from quiet resistance to open warfare against his fellow directors, baring several of his charges in public print. He exaggerated hints of earlier political patronage, overstated the degree of sophistry in Lilienthal's rate structure, and came close to capitulating to positions advanced by private utilities. He soon represented a type of internal subversion, and when challenged by Roosevelt to support with the facts his verbal assaults on his fellow directors, he refused. Roosevelt, after a prolonged hearing, had no alternative but to remove him from office in 1938.

After 1938, the TVA power program grew exponentially. By 1980, TVA power sales of over 120 billion kilowatt hours (the largest for any utility in the United States) grossed over $3 billion. Congressional appropriations for all non-self-supporting TVA programs amounted to only $222 million. Defense, war, the huge Oak Ridge nuclear facility, TVA's success in expanding residential use, and the rapid growth of valley manufacturing, all helped create the fastest growth in electrical demand in the whole country. Despite the forced construction of several new dams (or an eventual total of thirty power-producing dams), the wartime demand exceeded the hydro potential of the TVA system. TVA then turned to coal-fired steam plants; by 1960, twelve large steam plants accounted for about two-thirds of TVA output. In the 1960s, the TVA directors committed themselves to the largest nuclear power effort in the world, both to supplement steam and to replace some of the older steam plants. By 1981, the TVA had two nuclear plants in operation and five more in various stages of construction.

Not only did TVA's power program outweigh all its other mandated programs, but it also continued to dominate public controversies. The first, and only, major threat to TVA's protected market came early in the Eisenhower Administration. This involved a bid by a private combine (Dixon-Yates) to take over part of the Memphis market, but its effort failed in part because of documented charges of influence peddling, in part because Congress rallied to TVA's support. But unlike the 1930s, the power program now had to be fully self-financing. In 1961, Congress expanded TVA's debt liability to $30 billion, and provided a schedule for TVA to repay all earlier costs attributable to power production. This self-financing aroused little interest until the late 1970s, when high interest rates and the ballooning costs of nuclear plants forced TVA to maintain a long-term bonded debt of over $9 billion, plus $2 billion in short-term notes issued through the Federal Financing Bank (the Reagan Administration even challenged this privilege). By 1981, interest payments made up about a third of TVA power costs. A series of necessary rate increases, adopted by the unregulated TVA board, alienated what had been the strongest TVA constituency—its consumers and the municipal or cooperative distributors of its power. The great magic of TVA had been cheap electricity; now TVA rates were no longer the lowest in the country, and given the high consumption earlier boosted by the TVA, many valley families had difficulty paying bills. The TVA board struggled to explain its policies both in the valley and in Washington, and particularly had difficulty selling its expansive nuclear program, based on its high estimates of future valley needs. Threats of tighter congressional supervision, or of an amended TVA act providing for a five-member board, evaporated by 1981, thanks to behind-the-scenes maneuvers by valley congressmen and by a symbolically significant appointment of a new TVA chairman.

Meanwhile, the TVA faced opposition to its power program from another quarter—environmentalists. Its latter-day dam building threatened endangered fish or promised to inundate scenic rivers. Its coal-fired steam plants fed on enormous quantities of high-sulphur coal, some dug by nonunion miners, some stripped from mountain hillsides. At least indirectly, TVA seemed responsible for the denudations or stripping, even as its air-borne pollutants helped create acid rain in the Northeast. The TVA struggled to achieve stonger strip-mining regulations, but it had difficulties meeting clean air standards. As most utilities, it equivocated on remedial action, in part in response to its own rate-payers. Only in the late 1970s did the TVA finally agree fully to meet the federal regulations, and for so doing it antagonized many of its own distributors. Finally, its nuclear program suffered from the growing national campaign against fission plants, from the enormous political fallout of Three Mile Island, and from the publicity it received for some lax safety standards at its own plants.

The other TVA programs declined only relatively to power, not absolutely. The TVA continued its very successful flood control efforts, and still maintains the navigational locks operated by the corps. Apart from these water management programs (closely tied to power, but financed by appropriations), the largest TVA program has remained the fertilizer development effort at Muscle Schoals. The TVA first developed new types of phosphates in the 1930s, then added nitrates during the war. This effort continues in the present National Fertilizer Development Center, the largest fertilizer research center in the world. In the 1930s, the TVA tested and demonstrated most of its fertilizer in the valley, and used free or low-cost fertilizer as the backbone of its agricultural demonstration effort. But today it tests fertilizer in all states, and makes available its own products only for experimental or educational programs. The TVA, in a sense, has become the research and development arm of the private fertilizer industry. The budget for other programs—forestry, recreation, fish and wildlife, community development, industrial recruitment, surveys, education—remains miniscule in comparison with the budget of the power program, but recent TVA directors have given new emphasis to such programs. Concerns have shifted through time. The largest efforts in forestry and land-use planning came in the 1930s, under Arthur Morgan. Recent directors have emphasized economic development. Since Morgan's departure, the TVA has generally followed a low-key, cooperative policy, one calculated to gain local support, and has emphasized education and demonstration rather than unilateral initiatives.

The TVA has had enormous impact on other countries. Foreign visitors still flock to the valley, and underdeveloped countries still find in the TVA a model or an inspiration. But the impact of the TVA upon the people of the valley is still hard to measure; it is not even possible to demonstrate any differential impact at all (changes in the valley that would not have taken place under the impetus of other government agencies). Notably, per capita incomes in the valley have risen only marginally faster than those of the Southeast as a whole. In addition, the TVA did not, despite Roosevelt's predictions and intentions, become a model for other river developments in the United States. Roosevelt's request for new TVAs, and several bills providing for such, all foundered in the New Deal Congresses, and would not be seriously revived after World War II. The reasons for this are numerous. No other valley had the unique rainfall pattern of the Tennessee, the unique heritage of an already existing Muscle Schoals project, or so many undeveloped resources. More critical politically, even by the 1930s, several old-line federal agencies, such as the Bureau of Reclamation* or the Army Corps of Engineers, had a vested interest in other watersheds. Other federal agencies now provided TVA-like service, as, for example, the Rural Electrification Administration,* the Soil Conservation Service, and the National Forest Service.* On both the Columbia and Missouri, a loosely unified development did come, but not under the auspicies of any one agency, let alone a regional corporation. In effect, the TVA remained an anomaly because it violated the normal mode of dispensing federal services, and because its regional and corporate autonomy posed a threat to regular federal agencies.

FOR ADDITIONAL INFORMATION: The books and articles on the TVA number in the thousands. Yet, no single work provides a full history of the corporation, or an adequate survey of all its programs. The largest body of material about the TVA is in the Technical Library of the TVA at its Knoxville headquarters. A still useful but out-of-date guide to this material is TVA Technical Library, *A Bibliography for the TVA Program* (1968).

PAUL K. CONKIN

TRADE COMMISSION. See Federal Trade Commission; International Trade Commission.

TRADEMARK OFFICE. See Patent and Trademark Office.

TRANSPORTATION DEPARTMENT. See Department of Transportation.

TRANSPORTATION SAFETY BOARD. See National Transportation Safety Board.

TREASURY DEPARTMENT. See Department of the Treasury.

U

UNITED STATES AIR FORCE ACADEMY. The United States Air Force Academy is the newest of the nation's military service academies. It is located on 18,000 acres of tree-covered foothills north of Colorado Springs, Colorado. Established by act of Congress in 1954, the Air Force Academy is in many respects similar to its better known sister schools, the United States Military Academy* at West Point, New York, the United States Naval Academy* at Annapolis, Maryland, and the United States Coast Guard Academy at New London, Connecticut. The primary objective of these four schools is to train career officers for service in the air, land, and naval forces of the United States. All four academies emphasize the importance of self-discipline, commitment to country, and a broad education in engineering and science. But while the four service schools share notable similarities, they also reflect the unique individual requirements and expectations of their respective services. For the Air Force Academy this means an emphasis on academic subjects related to aviation and space technology. It also means that the development of individual initiative, responsibility, and judgment—qualities that are extraordinarily important in the cockpit of a combat aircraft—is emphasized in the classroom and in the everyday routine of cadet life.

The mission of the Air Force Academy remains fundamentally unchanged from that defined when the institution was founded. That mission is to provide instruction and experience to all cadets so that they will graduate with the knowledge and character essential to leadership and the motivation to become career officers in the United States Air Force. Their education and training is the basis for continued development throughout a lifetime of service to country, leading to readiness for responsibilities as future air commanders.

The establishment of the Air Force Academy in 1954 was both an ending and a beginning in the continuing evolution of the United States Air Force. For several decades, airmen had sought independence for their service from the Army. This was finally achieved in 1947 when the American defense establishment was reorganized and the United States Air Force was established as a separate service coequal to the Army, from which it sprang, and to the Navy. But the process of establishing service independence could not be fully realized as long as much of the senior Air Force leadership was drawn from graduates of West Point or Annapolis. The goal of an Air Force Academy represented intellectual and doctrinal independence that would complete the organizational emancipation achieved in 1947. It also represented the challenge of training young men—and beginning in 1976, young women—in the skills and knowledge deemed essential for Air Force leaders.

Cadets who enter the Air Force Academy are drawn from all sections of the country and all levels of American society. Their single, common denominator is a combination of physical fitness and intellectual ability as measured on competitive entrance examinations. Typically, over 8,000 qualified candidates apply for the fifteen hundred appointments or so available in each entering class. Successful applicants arrive at the academy during the last week of June to begin an intensive summer basic military training program. In the fall, they begin a four-year academic curriculum that leads to a Bachelor of Science degree and a commission as a second lieutenant in the United States Air Force.

The student body at the Air Force Academy—the Cadet Wing—is an organization composed of some forty-five hundred cadets. In some respects, the life of a cadet at the Air Force Academy is similar to that of any undergraduate student at a major American college or university. Between September and May, the week is dominated by the academic class schedule. During the weekends, there are intercollegiate athletic events and other social activities that might be expected on any college campus. Similarly, the problems that might be expected on other American campuses occasionally manifest themselves at the Air Force Academy. Cheating incidents among cadets, though infrequent, have drawn national attention. That attention stems not from similarities between the academy and other academic institutions, but rather from the academy's professed objective of upholding the highest standards of personal integrity—standards that are important in an academic institution, but vital in a combat environment when human lives hang in the balance. The difference is important. The academy is an educational institution, but it is first a military organization with the important military mission of training future Air Force officers and leaders.

The facilities at the Air Force Academy are impressive. The entire Cadet Wing is housed in two modern dormitories. Meals are served in a large dining hall that is capable of feeding all cadets in thirty minutes. Nearby, the academic building provides classroom space ranging from large lecture halls, to complete laboratories for various science courses, to small fifteen-student seminar rooms used for social science courses. A cadet chapel, a social center, a modern field house and gymnasium, and acres of athletic fields complete the list of the most prominent physical features of the cadet area. An airfield supports instruction in flying, navigation, soaring, and parachuting.

Yet, the cadet's character is molded by the unseen features of cadet life—the sense of shared commitment, the value placed on personal integrity, and the pursuit of academic and military excellence. In its first quarter-century, the Air Force Academy produced 12,134 graduates; more than three-fourths of these were still on active duty in 1979 when the academy celebrated its twenty-fifth anniversary. Of these graduates, 20 were Rhodes Scholars, and another 50 won Guggenheim Engineering Scholarships. Many served in combat during the Vietnam War; over 150 were killed in action. One graduate, Captain Lance P. Sijan, was posthumously awarded the Congressional Medal of Honor for extraordinary heroism while on a combat mission against a target in North Vietnam.

Organizationally, the Air Force Academy functions as a direct reporting unit to the chief of staff of the Air Force. The superintendent of the academy is a general officer, and, through his staff, directs the administration, personnel, logistics, and various other functions that would be found within any major Air Force command. But the unique nature of the academy is reflected in the three areas of responsibility directly related to cadet activities: academics, military training, and athletics.

The faculty of the Air Force Academy is led by an Air Force brigadier general and is composed predominantly of active-duty Air Force officers. Competition for faculty duty at the academy is keen; selection requires both a superior military record and graduate education in an appropriate academic discipline. Many, but not all of the officers selected for this assignment, hold doctorate degrees. Most have practical experience in the application of their academic skills to current Air Force problems. Thus, these officers serve both as instructors and as role-models for the cadets in their classrooms. Most of the instructors serve three or four years on the faculty, and then return to their career specialties in other Air Force assignments. For the instructors, as well as the cadets, duty at the academy is a time of intellectual stimulation, research, and professional growth. It is a time of preparation for future challenges and responsibilities.

In many respects, the cadre of officers assigned to the commandant of cadets and responsible for cadet military training and discipline is similar to the academic faculty. Most hold advanced degrees, and all have established a record of outstanding military competence. Their influence on cadet attitudes and motivation is pronounced. Their leadership is a major component in developing cadet responsibility and judgment.

The third organization that exerts daily influence on cadet life is the Department of Athletics. Each cadet is scheduled for physical education courses as well as intramural or varsity sports throughout the four years at the academy. Nearly all of the coaches who direct and administer this program are career Air Force officers. Like the faculty and the military training staff, coaches both teach and set the example for the cadets they encounter.

The daily interaction of career officers in each of these three areas of responsibility with the young men and women of the Air Force Cadet Wing demands the best efforts of all concerned. Life-long friendships are established between cadets and officers assigned to this uniquely rewarding duty. Officers, as well as cadets, grow in this environment. Most find a renewed sense of shared commitment to the values embodied in the mission of the academy—the preparation of professional career officers for service and leadership in the United States Air Force.

FOR ADDITIONAL INFORMATION: Periodical literature on the Air Force Academy is abundant. Newspaper accounts and magazine articles have described the academy's achievements as well as its crises, and these will be of use to researchers. More useful but rarer are analytical studies of the academy, such as Grace Lichtenstein, "How Women Are Faring at the Air Force Academy," *New York Times Magazine* (September 11, 1977); and John B. Taylor, "The New Cadets," *Airman* (December 1976), which assess the progress of women during the first year they joined the Cadet Wing. Lieutenant General Thomas S. Moorman, "Basic Philosophical Concepts of the United States Air Force Academy," *Air University Review* (December 1968); and Joseph Tuso and Rolf Trautsch, "The Air Force Academy and the Total Environmental Education," *Education* (Summer 1976) provide insights into educational goals and methods.

Public documents are also valuable. See especially U.S. Department of the Air Force, Special Committee on the United States Air Force Academy, *Report to the Secretary and the Chief of Staff of the Air Force* (May 5, 1965). This report, prepared under the direction of General Thomas D. White, USAF retired, analyzes the cheating incident that occurred at the academy in early 1965 and resulted in the resignation of over one hundred cadets. See also U.S. Congress, Public Law 83-325, *An Act to Provide for Establishment of a United States Air Force Academy* (83d Cong., 2d Sess., 1954), and U.S. Congress, House, Committee on Government Operations, Legislation and National Security Subcommittee, *Problems in Administration of the Military Service Academies* (94th Cong., 2d sess., 1976).

Of the several book-length studies written on the Air Force Academy, two are particularly valuable. Ed Mack Miller's *Wild Blue U* (1972) captures the human dimension of the academy experience through the extensive use of interviews and numerous excellent photographs. It is the best single source available on the academy. *The First Twenty-Five Years* (1979), a publication sponsored by the dean of faculty at the academy, is a very useful institutional view of the academy, its progress and the challenges that remain after the first quarter-century.

DRUE L. DeBERRY

UNITED STATES ARMS CONTROL AND DISARMAMENT AGENCY

(ACDA). President John F. Kennedy signed the Arms Control and Disarmament (ACD) Act on September 26, 1961, and in so doing formally established the United States Arms Control and Disarmament Agency. Its establishment served to elevate, functionally and organizationally, the policy objectives of arms control and disarmament and, as such, symbolized a significant change in the structure of the American national security policymaking process in the post-World War II period.

Prior to 1961, both disarmament and the less ambitious goal of arms control were objectives seldom in the mainstream of policymaking. Fundamentally, the international climate and character of U.S.-USSR bilateral relations were inhospitable for either. In addition, the pronounced Soviet inferiority in nuclear weapons coupled with deep-seated Soviet security concerns doubtless militated against any willingness on the part of the Soviet leadership to discuss meaningful limitations on nuclear forces or testing.

The ill-fated Baruch Plan in 1946 notwithstanding, general and complete disarmament—as a policy objective—enjoyed only a short-lived prominence under the Eisenhower Administration after the creation of the Office of the Special Assistant to the President for Disarmament in 1955. The very creation of this office, headed by Harold Stassen, and its charter to conduct a full review of U.S. disarmament policy, served to inject the subject of disarmament into upper-level policy deliberations. Furthermore, Stassen held Cabinet rank, which gave him full access to the President. Not surprisingly, Stassen frequently found himself and his staff at odds with other bureaucratic actors—the Atomic Energy Commission,* the Joint Chiefs of Staff, and especially the Department of State.* Indeed, it appears that Secretary of State John Foster Dulles, distrustful of the general notion of negotiating with the Soviet Union, was instrumental in the reduction of Stassen's influence in 1957 and in Stassen's resignation early the following year. Arms control received even less attention than disarmament during the postwar period. Judged in contemporary perspective, it can be argued that arms control, as a field, was in its intellectual infancy during the late 1940s and throughout the 1950s.

Stassen's departure simply underscored the concerns of many within the Congress over the absence of attention being devoted to arms control and disarmament issues during the late 1950s. Particularly influential in this regard was Senator Hubert H. Humphrey, the chairman of the Senate Foreign Relations Subcommittee on Disarmament. This subcommittee issued a number of reports decrying the lack of attention to disarmament issues and the lack of focus within the executive branch on disarmament as an important facet of national security policy. By 1960, interest in creating an agency at least to conduct research on disarmament and arms control had mushroomed; there were nearly twenty bills supporting a "National Peace Agency." Further attention was focused upon the subject when Senator John F. Kennedy attacked the Eisenhower Administration's record on disarmament during the New Hampshire primary in 1960.

Proponents of a new entity to focus specifically on arms control and disarmament issues ultimately achieved their objective, but not without compromise with those highly skeptical about the wisdom of creating such an agency. Opponents in Congress were fearful that the agency would tend to pursue disarmament ends while losing sight of legitimate U.S. defense and national security interests. Those opponents who at least could acknowledge the admissibility and legitimacy of arms control as part of national security sought to make the new entity an integral part of the State Department, rather than an independent agency. In the end, ACDA emerged as neither independent nor a part of the State Department. Instead, the ACD Act specified that ACDA's director would be the principal adviser to both the Secretary of State and the President. In this capacity, he would serve under the direction of the Secretary of State. Put simply, the ACDA director had direct access to the President, in principle at least, but his effectiveness in the policy process would be vitally dependent upon the extent to which he would be able to coordinate policy positions and objectives with the State Department.

As an additional check upon the quasi-independent agency, the ACD Act provided for, although it did not require, the establishment of a General Advisory Committee on Arms Control and Disarmament (GAC). The GAC, if established, would be a fifteen-member panel drawn from opinion leaders in government, academia, and the private sector. Functionally, it would serve in an advisory capacity to ACDA's director, the Secretary of State, and the President. The legal provision for creating the GAC was intended largely to be a palliative for those who feared that arms control zealots in ACDA would run amuck. Shortly after the passage of the new act, the GAC was constituted and put under the direction of John J. McCloy, President Kennedy's special assistant for arms control. In subsequent administrations, the GAC had its ups and downs bureaucratically, but it never played an influential role in policymaking.

Under the provisions of the ACD Act, ACDA assumed four primary functions. The first involved preparing for, and then operating, any control activities that might become part of negotiated arms control accords with foreign powers. The second was principally a research-oriented function; ACDA was to assume responsibility for conducting a sizable research activity in the domain of arms control and disarmament. Third, ACDA was to play a public affairs role, disseminating information about arms control issues to the broader public. Finally, ACDA was given the charter to prepare for, and manage, the participation of the United States in international arms control negotiations.

In 1975, as a result of some congressional dissatisfaction with ACDA's involvement in defense policy formulation, these functions were augmented. Specifically, ACDA was required by law to submit an arms control impact statement (ACIS) through the National Security Council* to the Congress on (1) any program of research, development, or modernization relating to nuclear weapons; or (2) any military program with an estimated total cost in excess of $250 million or an annual cost in excess of $50 million. The ACIS would identify the range of arms control implications of pursuing particular military programs. The effect of the legislative amendment was to broaden ACDA's role in defense policy formulation to encompass weapons acquisition.

To perform these functions, ACDA historically has maintained a relatively small staff. In 1962, the agency was authorized a total of 126 personnel; the following year, this number surpassed 200 and subsequently has hovered between 200 and 250 authorized personnel. ACDA's staff has three components: civilian specialists, foreign service and foreign service reserve officers, and military personnel. The last two categories obviously are temporary assignments to the agency and contribute to personnel turnover. Even discounting for the impact of foreign service and military tours of duty, however, the agency has a relatively high rate of turnover. Civilian staff members tend to view ACDA as a stepping-stone to career advancement elsewhere in the defense community. This high turnover rate is both advantageous and disadvantageous for ACDA. On the one hand, personnel turnover leads to an influx of new ideas and perspectives. On the other, a high turnover rate undermines the creation of a dedicated cadre of specialists in arms control matters and prevents the agency from developing institutional traditions.

The relative weight ACDA has accorded to each of its primary functions over the years has varied with administrations. The least significant function, until the signing of the first Strategic Arms Limitation Talks (SALT) accords in 1972, was its responsibility for operating control activities associated with negotiated arms control accords. Throughout the 1960s, this meant that ACDA sent an inspection team to verify the implementation of the Antarctic Treaty of 1959. However, SALT I established a U.S.-USSR Standing Consultative Commission (SCC) to monitor treaty compliance, and, since then, the chief U.S. commission representative has been a member of the ACDA.

During the 1960s, ACDA maintained a sizable external research program in the realm of arms control. Unfortunately for the agency, the often questionable nature and quality of some of the research produced under this program made it a natural target when the Nixon Administration, following SALT I, sought to reduce the agency's role. Substantial budget cuts were levied on ACDA in 1973, and the volume of external research in arms control dropped significantly.

Although the ACD Act specified that ACDA would have a public affairs function, an original provision to establish an Office of Public Affairs was struck from the bill's final version. Such an office eventually was established, but its activities have tended to be cautious. Perhaps its most active period was during the consideration of the SALT II Agreement when, in concert with the Department of State, it undertook a major effort to disseminate information about the accord to opinion leaders throughout the United States.

ACDA's responsibility regarding the preparation for, and negotiation of, arms control agreements is at best ambiguous. ACDA is responsible for "managing," but not "directing," such preparations and negotiations. In practice, this has meant that ACDA is often on uncertain bureaucratic ground with the State Department, which has a traditional prerogative regarding international negotiations. In SALT I, for example, ACDA's director, Gerard Smith, was also head of the U.S. delegation, but Smith was often overshadowed by the activities of the Secretary of State. In the conventional arms transfer talks (CATT) with the Soviet Union, the head of the U.S. delegation was the director of State's Bureau of Politico-Military Affairs, and his deputy was an ACDA official.

Finally, regarding ACDA's responsibility for preparing impact statements on major weapons programs, ACDA initially struck a cautious course for itself. So cautious was it, in fact, that Congress openly criticized the quality and adequacy of many of the early ACIS. Under the Carter Administration, the agency assumed a more aggressive posture vis-à-vis the Departments of Defense* and Energy,* although this may be only a temporary phenomenon.

Like most, if not all, federal agencies, ACDA's effectiveness in the policymaking process is a function of three sets of governmental relationships: (1) the relationship between its director and the President; (2) its relationship with other agencies that are key players in the policy process; and (3) its relationship with the Congress. Historically, ACDA's director has had little direct access and influence with the President. This was true of four administrations: Kennedy's, Johnson's, Nixon's, and Ford's. Only during the Carter Administration, when Paul Warnke headed ACDA, did the director enjoy both access and influence.

With regard to the agency's relationships with other bureaucratic actors, ACDA understandably has long been regarded with suspicion by the Department of Defense generally and the military services in particular. Its ability to influence policymaking vis-à-vis Defense and the services has been vitally dependent upon the willingness of its personnel to moderate extreme arms control positions in the interest of bureaucratic compromise. ACDA's relationship with the State Department has been profoundly shaped by the coordination, and often the personal relationship, between its director and the Secretary of State. For example, when Warnke was director of ACDA, his personal friendship with Secretary of State Cyrus Vance did much to enhance ACDA's role in the policymaking process.

Ironically, if ACDA must moderate arms control positions in order to facilitate accommodation with other agencies in the national security community such as Defense and Energy and thus influence policy formulation, it is this very act of moderation that often alienates its strongest congressional constituency. Those in Congress who support ACDA in the belief that neither arms control nor disarmament issues are given a fair and full hearing in defense policy formulation are often dismayed that the agency does not go far enough in advocating arms control positions. Thus, a constant political danger for ACDA is losing congressional support because it has attempted to be influential in the policy process.

With historical hindsight, ACDA appears to have had three significant achievements. The first, and most specific, concerns its role in advocating restraints on nuclear proliferation. Throughout the 1960s, ACDA found itself on the outside of every major policy discussion with the exception of nuclear proliferation. ACDA was the first advocate of the Non-Proliferation Treaty, and many observers have argued that the treaty came into being largely as a result of ACDA's persistence and skill. Second, during the SALT process ACDA provided incisive supporting analyses for the negotiating delegation. The final, and most ambiguous, achievement has been ACDA's advocacy role. Although often the loser in bureaucratic struggles over the shape of policy, ACDA has served a valuable role in raising alternative perspectives concerning the means to the end of national security. Without ACDA, such perspectives likely would not have been weighed as carefully, if at all, in policy deliberations.

FOR ADDITIONAL INFORMATION: Duncan L. Clarke, *The Politics of Arms Control: The Role and Effectiveness of the U.S. Arms Control and Disarmament Agency* (1979), the best and most comprehensive study of ACDA to date, draws heavily upon Clarke's incisive observations; Gerard Smith, *Doubletalk: The Story of the First Strategic Arms*

Limitation Talks (1980), provides invaluable insights into ACDA's bureaucratic relationships and the problems of coordination, particularly with the State Department, in SALT I; and Strobe Talbott, *Endgame: The Inside Story of SALT II* (1979), an excellent companion piece to *Doubletalk*, illuminates bureaucratic politics and ACDA's role in SALT II.

WILLIAM D. BAJUSZ

UNITED STATES ARMY CORPS OF ENGINEERS (CE). The United States Army Corps of Engineers, a complex federal agency charged with specific military and civilian missions, is the primary construction branch of the U.S. armed forces. The CE's traditional and most fundamental function has been to support the nation's military forces in times of war and peace. On the civilian side, it has become the nation's principal water-resource development and management agency. These combined military and civilian assignments have helped make the corps the world's largest engineering agency.

Militarily, the CE has played a vital role in every war and campaign fought by the United States Army. During wartime, Army engineers have provided battlefield support by constructing roads, bridges, harbor and dock works, airfields, and water supplies. The CE has also been responsible for military demolition work, as well as for drawing, reproducing, and distributing maps throughout the Army. In addition, it has been charged with the construction of a worldwide network of military installations.

The Corps of Engineers traces its origins back to June 16, 1775, when General George Washington appointed Colonel Richard Gridley as chief engineer of the Continental Army. Congress specifically established a Corps of Engineers in March, 1779, but disbanded it in 1783 after the end of the War for Independence. In May 1794, Congress established a Corps of Artillerists and Engineers to construct new coastal fortifications. Because America lacked a body of trained engineers in 1794, early officers for the corps were recruited in Europe. In an attempt to remedy this problem, Congress, on March 16, 1802, established the United States Military Academy* at West Point, New York. The present Corps of Engineers was formally and permanently established by that same act.

West Point thus became the first engineering school in the United States and remained the only one until 1824. It continued to be the nation's premier educator of engineers throughout the antebellum period. Not until after the Civil War in 1866 was the responsibility of operating West Point transferred from the Corps of Engineers to the War Department.*

In 1824, Congress gave the Corps of Engineers its civil works mission. The General Survey Act of April 30, 1824, committed the Corps of Engineers to the survey and planning of internal improvements of national importance. Because improved waterways would benefit the entire nation by facilitating both interstate commerce and military logistics, Congress also in 1824 assigned the CE the task of snagging and clearing the Ohio and Mississippi rivers in order to provide an open channel for navigation. Besides work on navigation in the nation's rivers and harbors,the CE gradually received other civil works responsibilities, such as the provisions of surveys and plans for canals, roads, and railroads, as well as the construction of lighthouses, public buildings, monuments, bridges, and aqueducts. The corps also played an important role in the exploration and mapping of the American West. By furnishing the essential engineering talent required for such large-scale civil works, it did much to assist in the nation's early economic development and westward expansion.

The early twentieth century was a transitional period for the CE's civil works mission. Prior to 1900, navigation and harbor improvements represented the Corps' principal civil works responsibility. Although the creation of the Mississippi River Commission in 1879 gave the corps some flood-control responsibilities, such projects were justified solely by their ability to enhance navigation. Prompted by the conservation movement of the early twentieth century, multiple-purpose planning for the nation's resources gained widespread popularity. Congress gradually responded to this need by broadening the CE's involvement in water-resource planning and development. Legislation in 1909 directed the corps to consider the potential for hydroelectric power generation in all its preliminary surveys for navigational projects. Congress officially committed the federal government to assume major responsibility for the control of floods on the Mississippi and Sacramento rivers with the passage of the Flood Control Act of 1917. The act also required the corps to include flood-control recommendations in all its waterway surveys. The Flood Control Act of 1928 approved the establishment of a hydraulics laboratory by the corps near Vicksburg, Mississippi, while the Beach and Erosion Board, established in 1930, allowed the corps to improve maintenance of the banks of lakes and rivers within its jurisdiction. The seminal act in expanding the CE's civil works responsibilities during this period, however, was the Flood Control Act of 1936. This first general flood-control legislation enacted by Congress made the corps responsible for a nationwide program to protect against flooding. By incorporating the principle of multiple-purpose planning, the 1936 act broadened the criteria used in measuring the benefits of federal water projects. The Flood Control Act of 1944 further broadened the criteria. Today the corps justifies its projects not solely on the benefits of navigation, but also on flood control, water supply, hydroelectric power production, irrigation, recreation, and fish and wildlife conservation.

By the 1960s, improving water quality was another major civil works mission assigned to the Corps of Engineers. This was done in part through expansion of its regulatory authority. The CE's history as a regulatory agency dates back to 1893 when it was given the task of regulating the dumping of waste tailings from hydraulic mining operations into California's navigable streams. Sections of the River and Harbors Act of 1899 gave the corps authority to prevent the obstruction of the nation's navigable waterways. The 1899 act was applied solely to questions of navigability until 1970, at which time the federal courts reinterpreted the act more broadly to include such factors as aesthetics, pollution, and fish and wildlife conservation. The corps' responsibility for insuring water quality was furthered in 1971, when it began a nationwide program of regulating the discharge of pollutants into navigable waters. This permit-granting function was transferred to the Environmental Protection Agency* by the Federal Water Pollution Control Act Amendments of 1972. The corps maintained its responsibility of regulating the disposal of dredged and fill material under Section 404 of the 1972 amendments, while its jurisdiction was expanded beyond navigable waterways to include adjacent wetlands, tributaries, and headwaters.

The expansion in the CE's civil works mission during the 1930s and the added military responsibilities accompanying World War II hastened a trend within the corps to rely increasingly on civilian personnel for engineering and managerial expertise. The continuation of this trend after the war led to its civil works program becoming a largely civilian organization. By 1980, the CE was made up of about three hundred Army officers at the leadership level and about twenty-eight thousand civilian employees.

Following along military lines, however, the Corps of Engineers is a highly decentralized agency. At the top of the chain-of-command is the Office of the Chief of Engineers. It is from this office that policy decisions, engineering regulations, and final project review occur; it is also the office that answers to the President and to Congress. During the late nineteenth century, two regional levels of organization were created within the corps. Engineers in charge of individual projects were called district engineers. In 1884, they were placed under the supervision of division engineers who had jurisdiction over four geographical regions. In 1913, the district offices were no longer defined by their projects, but by distinct geographical boundaries. The number of division and district offices within the corps fluctuated throughout the twentieth century, reaching a peak of eleven divisions and forty-one districts during World War II. Reorganizations reduced this number to nine division offices and thirty-seven district offices by the early 1970s. As a decentralized agency, the CE grants a great degree of autonomy to its districts. It is at the district level that the planning, construction, and operation of the CE's public works projects take place.

Although the Corps of Engineers is in the executive branch of the government inasmuch as it operates within the Department of the Army (its top official is the Assistant Secretary of the Army for Civil Works), in the area of civil works it has traditionally carried out the will of Congress. Congress is the agency responsible for formulating national and regional water resource development policy. Consequently, all of the corps' surveys, improvements, construction projects, and regulatory functions must originate from specific congressional orders.

The general public opinion of the Corps of Engineers was quite favorable during its first 150 years. Economic development was viewed as a principal goal of the nation, and the contributions of the corps in providing adequate transportation and water supply were seen as highly beneficial and necessary for this growth. This is not to say that criticism of the corps was absent during this period. Criticism dating back at least to the 1870s came from some of the nation's civil engineers who opposed military engineers controlling the design, construction, and maintenance of large federal public works projects. Various special interest groups have frequently opposed specific corps projects. Because the corps works only on those projects approved by Congress and under funds appropriated by Congress, its project list has been subject to political abuse. Consequently, it has been the target of criticism related to the fact that it has been a primary vehicle for the transfer of "pork" to congressional districts in the form of large public works projects.

Widespread criticism of the CE's civil works program did not occur, however, until the late 1960s with the growth of the environmental movement. The corps' involvement with some of the major environmental alterations in the nation brought heavy criticism for many of its civil works activities. As the nation's largest developer of water resources, the Corps of Engineers came to symbolize the environmental insensitivity of a growth-oriented society. With the passage of the National Environmental Policy Act in 1969, the CE was required to consider the environmental ramifications of its projects. The decade of the 1970s was a period of rapid change for the corps, led internally by a number of policy revisions made by the Office of the Chief of Engineers and furthered by a series of environmental laws and court decisions.

FOR ADDITIONAL INFORMATION: There is no definitive history of the Corps of Engineers. For its early history, see Paul K. Walker, *Engineers of Independence: A Documentary History of the Army Engineers in the American Revolution, 1775-1783* (1981). An uncritical overview of CE history may be found in *History and Traditions of the Corps of Engineers* (1953). The organizational structure of the corps is well described in W. Stull Holt, *The Office of the Chief of Engineers of the Army: Its Non-Military History, Activities, and Organization* (1923); and Raymond H. Merritt, *Creativity, Conflict & Controversy: A History of the St. Paul District, U.S. Army Corps of Engineers* (1980). The contribution of the corps to America's westward expansion is analyzed in William H. Goetzmann, *Army Exploration in the American West, 1803-1863* (1959); Forest G. Hill, *Roads, Rails & Waterways: The Army Engineers and Early Transportation* (1957); and Frank N. Schubert, *Vanguard of Expansion: Army Engineers in the Trans-Mississippi West, 1819-1879* (1980). Official histories of the role of the corps in World War II include Blanche D. Coll, Jean E. Keith, and Herbert H. Rosenthal, *The Corps of Engineers: Troops and Equipment* (1958); Karl C. Dod, *The Corps of Engineers: The War Against Japan* (1966); Lenore Fine and Jesse A. Remington, *The Corps of Engineers: Construction in the United States* (1972). The involvement of the corps in environmental issues is the topic of Albert E. Cowdrey, "Pioneering Environmental Law: The Army Corps of Engineers and the Refuse Act," *Pacific Historical Review* 46 (August 1975): 331-349, and Daniel A. Mazmanian and Jeanne Nienaber, *Can Organizations Change? Environmental Protection, Citizen Participation, and the Corps of Engineers* (1979). Some of the major works critical of the corps include Martin Heuvelmans, *The River Killers* (1974); Arthur Maass, *Muddy Waters: The Army Engineers and the Nation's Rivers* (1951); Gene Marine, *America the Raped: The Engineering Mentality and the Devastation of a Continent* (1969); and Arthur E. Morgan, *Dams and Other Disasters: A Century of the Army Corps of Engineers in Civil Works* (1971).

JEFFREY K. STINE

UNITED STATES ARMY SIGNAL CORPS. Military signal communications have existed throughout recorded history. In earlier times, they were simple, consisting of fires, flashes from a burnished shield, trumpets, and couriers. To the best of our knowledge, however, the assignment of signal communications to a separate military organization only goes back, at least in modern history, to a series of events in the midnineteenth century: the authorization of the United States Army's first signal officer on June 21, 1860; the appointment of Assistant Surgeon Albert James Myer (1828-1880) to the new position with the rank of major; and the assignment of a signal corps to Myer's organization.

Until 1863, Myer had to depend upon temporary details of officers and enlisted men, but in that year Congress authorized a "permanent" organization of the Signal Corps for the duration of the Civil War. This change permitted direct commissioning and enlistment of signal personnel but did not entirely end the use of the detail system, which persisted for a number of years. The corps disappeared with the mustering out of troops at the end of the war, but Myer's regular commission remained in force, although he was then without a duty assignment, and Second Lieutenant Lemuel B. Norton was on duty, by detail, when Congress reestablished the corps in 1866.

In the beginning, Myer concentrated on his wigwag signaling, which he invented, to provide signal equipment that was both light enough and practicable for a signalman to carry wherever he went. Wigwag was basically a two-element system in which left and right swings of a flag or torch in particular combinations represented letters of the alphabet. Although Myer was familiar with the electric telegraph, having worked while a medical student for a company employing the Bain system, he seems to have paid no attention to its military application until forced to consider it early in the Civil War by the U.S. Military Telegraph, a rival of the Signal Corps. Before losing his position as chief signal officer in a shifting of Civil War duties in 1863, Myer attempted to improve the Beardslee magnetoelectric telegraph, a dial machine he had obtained as a portable, short-range tactical telegraph, by equipping it with a sounder, which would require skilled operators. The Beardslee had significant weaknesses, but Myer's concept of a rugged, front-line, portable electric communications device that an unskilled soldier could operate was an innovation in the U.S. Army.

The Military Telegraph disappeared at the end of the Civil War, and, in 1867, the Signal Corps, once again under Myer (who was now a colonel), became responsible for the military uses of the electric telegraph. Thereafter the corps controlled both visual and electrical signaling. Myer had to rebuild the corps from the ground up. In 1868, he opened a signal school in southeast Washington, which replaced the old wartime school in Georgetown (D.C.). The following year Myer moved the school across the Potomac River to Fort Whipple, which was renamed Fort Myer after his death. There, until 1886, signalmen gained proficiency in the duties of the Signal Corps, including those of weather observation and reporting. Years later, after various relocation, the signal school was established at Fort Monmouth, New Jersey, which was the principal Signal Corps post for many years after World War I.

In 1870, the Signal Corps became responsible for a national system of weather observation and reporting, which used both commercial and, when built, military telegraph lines for transmitting its reports to Washington headquarters. In Washington, the Signal Corps processed the meteorological reports in the Division of Telegrams and Reports for the Benefit of Commerce and Agriculture. Myer, who sought this responsibility, perhaps did not anticipate that for the next two decades the corps would be largely preoccupied with its meteorological work. Dissatisfaction and criticism that surfaced under Myer's able successor, Brigadier General William B. Hazen, chief signal officer, 1880-1887, led to legislation in 1890 that transferred the weather service to the Department of Agriculture* where it became the United States Weather Bureau* in 1891.

With the Signal Corps (Signal Service, as it was called for many years) solely responsible for military telegraphy after 1867, Myer organized flying or field telegraph trains equipped with conventional battery-powered instruments. In 1869, the Signal Corps linked its Washington office with Fort Whipple by telegraph, and in the 1870s became responsible for building and operating an electric telegraph line along a portion of the East Coast as an aid to the Life-saving Service in reporting shipwrecks. This coastal line remained under Signal Corps control until 1891. The corps also built and operated thousands of miles of military telegraph lines across the Southwest and Northwest. These western lines linked military posts, became a part of the weather-reporting system, and served the commercial and other needs of private citizens.

During the 1870s, the Signal Corps tested and adopted the heliograph, which it used into the early years of the present century. In 1878 the corps began experimental work with messenger pigeons, a project it continued until after the Korean War. The corps phased out its breeding and training of pigeons in 1955 and its academic work on the subject in 1957.

It was also in 1878 that the Signal Corps installed telephone instruments on the Fort Whipple telegraph line and built a forty-mile experimental line at that post. Although the Signal Corps used the telephone in the Spanish-American War, development of the telephone into an important instrument for military communications, especially in tactical situations, was generally slow until the early years of the twentieth century. In the years down to the Spanish-American War, the Signal Corps experimented with signal lamps and, over the turn of the century, with electrical fire-control equipment for the Coast Artillery. In the 1890s, the corps also resumed the use of observation balloons, which the Army had discontinued during the Civil War.

The Signal Corps, much reduced when it lost the weather service in 1891, included only eight officers and fifty enlisted men at the approach of the Spanish-American War. Brigadier General Adolphus W. Greely, chief signal officer, 1887-1906, one of Myer's most remarkable successors, placed the work on a wartime footing through legislation authorizing a volunteer signal corps. In Cuba,

Puerto Rico, and the Philippines, signalmen acquitted themselves well. Notable was the repair of the French cable in Guantanamo Bay that enabled the Army in Cuba to communicate with Washington via Haiti and New York in twenty minutes. The Signal Corps also provided signal communications for the troops in Cuba itself. In the Philippines, Greely observed in 1900, the Signal Corps initiated, constructed, and maintained an unsurpassed network of telegraph and telephone lines for the war there. During the Boxer Revolt that same year, Greely sent a detachment of signalmen to China.

In the succeeding years, the Signal Corps was caught up in the new technical developments of the era and in the construction of a cable and telegraph system for Alaska that Congress authorized in 1900. Among the young officers in charge of the Alaskan work under Greely were George S. Gibbs and William Mitchell. Gibbs later served as the chief signal officer, 1928-1931, and Billy Mitchell became a controversial exponent of air power. The Alaskan lines should be regarded as the last of the frontier telegraph lines of the Signal Corps, which, by 1900, had discontinued most of its old western lines. Over the years, the telegraph gave way to radio and to the radiotelephone, which was universal in the Alaska Communications System after July 1937. This system, commercially indispensable and located in Seattle, remained under military control for over sixty years.

Radio, called "wireless" at the beginning, was one of the most significant technical developments in signal communications that occupied the Signal Corps in the years between the Spanish-American War and World War I. Early Signal Corps radio work went forward under such officers as James Allen who, as a brigadier general, succeeded Greely as chief signal officer, 1906-1913, and George O. Squier, chief signal officer, 1917-1924. In 1917, Squier became the first major general in Signal Corps history. The Signal Corps in 1899 opened experimental radio communication between Fire Island and Fire Island Lightship, a distance of twelve miles. The corps established an electrical division with laboratory facilities in 1902. Thereafter, the corps continued to expand its radio research and, in 1917, established a radio division. Major Charles McK. Saltzman, later chief signal officer, 1924-1928, admitted in 1909 that interference was a "great hindrance" to extending wireless telegraphy to the field, but asserted that "no modern army" could dispense with either the wireless telegraph or the telephone.

Concurrently with its efforts to adapt electronics to military uses, the Signal Corps moved beyond ballooning and became involved in the development of heavier-than-air flight. In 1907, Allen established in the Signal Corps an aeronautical division (later the Aviation Section), which procured the U.S. Army's first airplane in 1909. As World War I broke out, Brigadier General George P. Scriven, chief signal officer, 1913-1917, thought that the airplane might be too terrible a weapon for attack and might therefore become anathema to the public.

With the technical advances of the Signal Corps in the new century, development in the organization of signal units increased in both number and variety.

In 1914, the Signal Corps established the Army's first aero squadron. New tables of organization that year also provided for separate wire and radio units.

As a result of World War I, the Signal Corps expanded from 42 officers and enlisted men in 1916 to 10,336 officers and 150,120 enlisted men in 1918. Over 200 uniformed, bilingual American women served as telephone operators in Army headquarters in France without military status. In 1979, the survivors of these women received formal military discharges.

Wire, both telegraph and telephone, was the mainstay of signal communications in World War I. American signal communications across the Atlantic were primarily by cable. In its early stages, the American Expeditionary Force was completely dependent upon French administrative and strategic wire facilities; by the war's end, the Signal Corps had established a remarkable record of the construction and use of wire communications both behind the lines and in the trenches. Radio carried little of the war's communications load, but it came of age in World War I through the efforts of Squier and young radio engineers such as Edwin H. Armstrong. Visual signals played a relatively minor role. Pigeons proved useful but saw only limited service. Cryptography, meteorology (the Signal Corps had retained military responsibility in this field), and photography assumed new importance.

With only fifty-five antiquated airplanes in service in 1917, American airmen had to fly French aircraft during the war. In May 1918, the Signal Corps lost aviation, but for a number of years remained responsible for the design and procurement of the radio apparatus required by Army aviation.

Of great importance after World War I was the establishment by the Signal Corps of the War Department Radio Net in 1922. This grew out of the provisions of War Plan White, which called for a military communications network that would be safe during the extreme, even revolutionary, civil disorders that military planners of the day envisioned. This was the beginning of an Army radio system that grew in the ensuing years into the Army Command and Administrative Network, as it was known in World War II. The Signal Corps also developed a separate worldwide system for the Army Air Forces called the Army Airways Communications System.

Important advances in wire and radio that also helped set the stage for signal communications in World War II included improved wire, a lightweight field teletypewriter, a standard battery-powered field telephone, and a lightweight field telephone powered by the speaker's voice. During the 1930s, infantry, armor, and aviation required communications with new mobility, range, and reliability. Out of these needs came such new Signal Corps equipment as the "handie-talkie," the "walkie-talkie" and a vehicular set with a 100-mile voice range in motion and a Morse-code range of hundreds of miles. Among wartime radio items developed for Army aviation were devices for long-range airborne liaison, short-range command, and aerial navigation.

Important among the radio developments of the 1930s were Armstrong's invention of frequency modulation (FM) and, with Armstrong's close collaboration, of push-button, crystal-controlled FM radios, at the Signal Corps Laboratories, under the direction of Colonel Roger B. Colton. The advantages of these new voice radios were their freedom from static and from dial-tuning, which enabled unskilled soldiers in moving vehicles to communicate at the push of a button. Frequency modulation proved to be a major contribution to vehicular, tactical radio in World War II. For various reasons, however, it found no application in the air during World War II; the short-range radios of the Signal Corps, such as the handie-talkie, did not become frequency-modulated and integrated with the radios of the armored and artillery arms until after the war.

Perhaps the most remarkable of all the radio developments of the period before World War II was radar. It was by no means an exclusively Signal Corps or even an exclusively American invention, for its parentage was truly international. Nevertheless, Lieutenant Colonel William R. Blair carried on radar work at the Signal Corps Laboratories at Fort Monmouth that led to the wide use of radar equipment in World War II. Some of this work was in the field on Sandy Hook and on the New Jersey Highlands where Myer had experimented with his wigwag signaling seventy-five years earlier. In 1946, Signal Corps radar helped usher in the space age by bouncing radar signals off the moon.

World War II was a war of production and technology involving the use of both wire and radio. The Signal Corps grew to a strength of about 350,000 officers and enlisted personnel stationed in theaters all over the world. In the wartime year of 1943, its budget was over a billion dollars, considerably more than the $528,906.330 that the Signal Corps had spent, on the average, for each of the first three years of the Civil War. Major General Dawson Olmstead served as chief signal officer from 1941 to 1943; Major General Harry C. Ingles succeeded him in 1943 and served until 1947.

Following World War II, the Signal Corps had to respond to the greatly increased mobility of warfare and the greater range and lethality of weapons, which increased the need for even more sophisticated communications for all purposes—administrative, logistic, strategic, and tactical. The needs of the times led to automatic switching; to electronic data processing; to multimodal communication using voice, teletype, and digital data; to facsimile and video signals; and to satellite communication, which played an important role in the Vietnam War.

The chief signal officers of the 1950s were Major General Spencer B. Akin, 1947-1951; Major General George I. Back, 1951-1955; Lieutenant General James B. O'Connell, 1955-1959, the highest ranking of all the chief signal officers; and Major General Ralph T. Nelson, 1959-1962. The corps had hardly celebrated its centennial, under Nelson, before it was enmeshed in the historic departmental reorganization of 1962, in which it lost responsibility for such important functions as training, research and development, and procurement.

Also in 1962, the Army combined certain signal agencies into the Army Strategic Communications Command (STRATCOM) and placed it under the command of Major General Earle F. Cook, chief signal officer, 1962-1963. In

1964, however, the Army made STRATCOM a major command, responsible to the chief of staff, and redesignated the chief signal officer (in 1963-1964, Major General David P. Gibbs, the son of George S. Gibbs) the chief of communications-electronics (CC-E). General David Gibbs was thus the last of the chief signal officers.

Meanwhile, in 1960, the Department of Defense* created the Defense Communications Agency (DCA) to improve and regulate the strategic, long-distance communications of all the armed services, each service becoming responsible for a part of what was called the Defense Communications System (DCS). After having become responsible for operation of the Army's part of the DCS, STRATCOM formed the First Signal Brigade in 1966. Thereafter, under operational control of the U.S. Army, Vietnam, the brigade played a major role in the Vietnam War. The First Signal Brigade grew larger than a division, which made it the largest signal unit in the history of the Army up to that time. It operated the huge. mostly fixed communications facilities of the DCS in Southeast Asia and was responsible for the area communications systems. Its subordinate units, within particular geographical regions, provided signal support to all military units in a given area—Army, Navy, Marine Corps,* Air Force, or Coast Guard*— that required signal communications in addition to their own. The brigade also provided communications in the base camps of the tactical zones. Combat signaling was the responsibility of signal battalions organic to divisions and corps-equivalent field forces. Signalmen at remote communication sites provided for their own defense and, in some instances, fought off attackers. The U.S. military signal communications of the Vietnam War were among the most sophisticated in the world, with as many as 250 to 300 sites in Southeast Asia and approximately 120,000 signal personnel from 1962 through 1970.

By redesignation in 1973, STRATCOM, with headquarters at Fort Huachuca, Arizona, became the Army Communications Command. Meanwhile, in 1967, the CC-E was called the assistant chief of staff for communications-electronics (ACSC-E). In 1974, the Army abolished this position and transferred its responsibilities to the head of a directorate under the deputy chief of staff for operations and plans. There they remained until designation in 1978 of the assistant chief of staff for automation and communications with general staff responsibility for Army-wide policies within the two areas of his mission.

Over the course of almost a century and a quarter, the Signal Corps has made very significant military and civil contributions to our national life. Through all the changes of these years, which saw the demise of the corps as a distinctive headquarters agency of the Department of the Army,* the Signal Corps has continued to serve as a branch and technical service of the Army. It continues to have responsibility for installing and operating all kinds of modern signal communications equipment, including satellites in space, while also fighting as combat infantry when necessary. Today its men and women still wear the crossed-flags-and-torch insignia, a stylized representation of Myer's wigwag equipment, wherever the U.S. Army is found.

FOR ADDITIONAL INFORMATION: *Quadrennial Report of the Chief Signal Officer, U.S. Army, May 1951-April 1955; Quadrennial Report...May 1955-April 1959*, Office of the Chief Signal Officer, Department of the Army (1955-1959); Thomas Matthew Rienzi, *Communications-Electronics, 1962-1970*; Paul J. Scheips, ed., *Military Signal Communications*, 2 vols. (1980), a compilation of historical material on the U.S. Army Signal Corps and on the military signaling of other countries, together with a list of suggested additional readings, for the period through World War II; and Christopher H. Sterling, Advisory Editor, *Historical Studies in Telecommunications*, 13 vols. to date (1977-1981).

See also Major General Thomas M. Rienzi, "Vietnam Studies" (1972). The author of this preliminary study was a commander of the First Signal Brigade. A detailed history of the U.S. Army signal communications in the Vietnam War, by Lieutenant Colonel John D. Bergen, is in press. For a biography of Myer, see Paul J. Scheips, "Albert James Myer, Founder of the Army Signal Corps: A Biographical Study" (Ph.D. dissertation, American University, Washington, D.C., 1966), Facsimile No. 66-3393, University Microfilms International, Ann Arbor, Michigan, 1977. Donald R. Whitnah, *A History of the United States Weather Bureau* (1961, paperback edition, 1965), has two excellent chapters on the Signal Corps weather service.

PAUL J. SCHEIPS

UNITED STATES COAST GUARD. The history of the Coast Guard may be approached through many avenues, none of which is easily traveled because the service has had many missions. The best approach is to study the service through the evolution of its organization. This evolutionary process has paralleled the changes in functions and activities.

Today's service is an amalgamation of five predecessors. On January 28, 1915 (38 Stat. 800, 802), the service acquired its current name when the Revenue Cutter Service and the Life-saving Service were merged. Three decades later, the Lighthouse Service was absorbed on July 1, 1939 (53 Stat. 1432). On February 28, 1942 (Ex. Ord. 9083), the Bureau of Navigation and Steamboat Inspection, which itself had been formed by a recent merger of two agencies, was added to the Coast Guard.

The Coast Guard traces its primary root to the Revenue Cutter Service. From the beginning, the Revenue Cutter Service was a "military" organization, an element that has molded the character of the Coast Guard probably more than any other factor. At first, the service had masters, mates of three grades, mariners, and boys comprising the cutters' personnel. Pay was fixed by statute, and subsistence allowances were made the same as those prevailing for captains, lieutenants, and privates in the Army. When, in 1799, the cutters were made available for cooperation with the Navy, the President was authorized to place officers and crews on the Navy basis of pay and allowances. This was the beginning of assimilation to Navy personnel.

Decentralization was the rule during the early years of the service, the revenue cutters being placed under the immediate direction of the local collectors of customs who were subject to little administrative control from Washington. It was not until 1843, after more than fifty years, that a central control was attempted. In that year, the Secretary of the Treasury, with the approval of the President, detailed a captain from the field to take charge of a "Revenue Marine Bureau" in his office. The results of this innovation appear to have been favorable with regard to efficiency and discipline, but in 1849, when a change in administration took place, the Revenue Marine Bureau disappeared, and control of the cutters reverted to local collectors of customs.

In 1869, a commission appointed by the Secretary of the Treasury, charged with considering primarily the matter of equipment, pointed out the need for centralized administration. It was soon recognized that successful operation of the system required the establishment of the strictest regulations which only the highest authority could lift. In consequence, a Revenue Marine Division was set up in the Secretary's office, and on February 1, 1871, Sumner I. Kimball, a civilian, was made chief. Kimball continued as chief until 1878 when the Life-saving Service was given separate status, of which he became general superintendent.

In 1894, the Revenue Marine Division became the Division of Revenue Cutter Service, and the position of chief was entrusted to a uniformed man, Captain Leonard G. Shepard, from the service. This was a reversion to the type of organization attempted between 1843 and 1849. Captain Shepard is considered the first commandant of the service, even though he did not have that title. A law in 1908 authorized the President to appoint a captain commandant from among the active captains of the line to act as chief of the division, for a renewable period of four years. The tile of "commandant" for head of the service came into existence, in 1923. The rank of the commandant has evolved to one of four stars. The Revenue Cutter Service, however, still remained (after 1908) a division in the office of the Secretary of the Treasury, and the Secretary was still its statutory head. It was not until the drastic reorganization of 1915 that the service, now to become the Coast Guard, attained bureau status in the department.

The reorganization act of 1915 effected a merger of services, one of which was military (the Revenue Cutter Service) and the other civilian (the Life-saving Service); for a time the resulting organization carried the effects of a necessary compromise. The captain commandant of the Revenue Cutter Service became the sole executive, and, while the personnel of the former Life-saving Service were for the most part given military status, supervisory management continued in some degree to be in the hands of men who were civilians, and civilian methods were still somewhat in evidence. There were, however, almost continuous developments in the organizational setup, tending toward complete military control and supervision. The various steps were substantially completed by 1937, when an organization was set up that was not basically different from that which exists today. The principal changes that have since occurred have been those resulting from adding two additional agencies, the Lighthouse Service and the

Bureau of Marine Inspection and Navigation. At headquarters these two agencies were assimilated without any drastic organizational changes.

In the field, somewhat more apparent changes occurred. For example, from 1915 through 1939, the field service was organized into nine divisions and thirteen districts; these two groups of organizational units corresponded generally to the setup according to functions that belonged to the former Revenue Cutter Service and Life-saving Service, respectively. With the acquisition of the Lighthouse Service in 1939, which was organized in seventeen field districts, the field organizational units were consolidated, removing all distinctions based on functional activities. As a result, out of nine divisions and thirteen districts of the Coast Guard and seventeen districts of the Lighthouse Service, there emerged a field organization of thirteen districts, each named from the city where the headquarters was located: Boston, New York, San Juan, Norfolk, Jacksonville, New Orleans, Cleveland, Chicago, Saint Louis, San Francisco, Seattle, Juneau (later Ketchikan), and Honolulu.

On November 1, 1941, the Coast Guard began operating as part of the Navy. The number of districts was increased to sixteen, and they were numbered in order to facilitate cooperation with naval districts. In this increase, new districts were set up with headquarters at Charleston and Key West (with the Jacksonville District eliminated); district offices were also set up at Philadelphia and Los Angeles. The field organization has changed little since World War II.

The first concerted life-saving efforts in this country were undertaken on a volunteer basis and at private expense. The first such organization was the Massachusetts Humane Society, founded in 1785 and modeled on an English society dating from 1774. Its policy included the relief of persons on vessels in distress. Several small huts were built on exposed parts of the coast, and rewards were offered to anyone making "signal exertions" to save life. In 1807, the society established at Cohasset a station equipped with the first lifeboat ever used in the United States. All of this activity was shore based and was distinct from assistance by cruising cutters undertaken, in 1837, by the Revenue Cutter Service.

The field of life-saving was further explored, and action was agitated both privately and publicly. One suggestion was that lighthouse keepers perform this service. The first appropriation for rendering assistance to the shipwrecked from the shore was made in an item of $5,000 added to the lighthouse appropriation for 1848. However, it was not used until two years later when it was turned over to the collector of customs at Boston to provide boathouses and appliances on Cape Cod for use of the Massachusetts Humane Society. Gradually, other appropriations were made, for boathouses and apparatus, chiefly along the coasts of Long Island and New Jersey, but there was no organization or personnel to look after the property or supervise the activity. The idea was that they would be utilized by local residents when the occasion arose. From 1850 to 1854, about $82,500 were appropriated, but there was still the same volunteer method for rendering service, and neglect and vandalism were the common experience. An act of December 14, 1854, marked a more systematic effort, by providing for additional stations on the Long Island and New Jersey coasts, but more especially for the appointment of a keeper at a maximum salary of $200 per year at each new station and a superintendent for Long Island and one for New Jersey, all under the Secretary of the Treasury. Officers of the Revenue Marine Service rendered service in this undertaking from time to time on detail. Employment of surfmen followed in 1870. In 1871, when the chief of the Revenue Marine Division, Sumner I. Kimball, caused an inspection to be made of the life-saving stations, larger appropriations were obtained and a life-saving unit was set up within the Revenue Marine Service. Thenceforth, material improvement took place in this service, culminating in the Organic Act creating the Life-saving Service in the Treasury Department* with full bureau status.

The act provided for the appointment of a general superintendent, to which Kimball was appointed by the President, and he was given general administrative charge of the service under the direction of the Secretary of the Treasury. The act also provided for an assistant to the general superintendent. The open season for stations was fixed, and a district superintendent for the Gulf Coast was authorized. Crews were required to reside at stations during the active season, and keepers were at all times to reside in the vicinity of their stations. Keepers were responsible for salvaged and for public property, but their primary duty was to use their utmost endeavors to save life. The general superintendent was directed to cause an investigation to be made of shipwrecks attended with loss of life. A law of May 2, 1882, made fitness for their duties the test of appointments, and the rules of the classified civil service were not applied until April 1, 1897. Under another provision of the Organic Act, the Secretary, on January 3, 1882, appointed a Board on Life-saving Appliances, consisting of seven members, to investigate plans, devices, and inventions for the improvement of life-saving apparatus. A representative of the Revenue Marine Service was a member of this board.

The field organization of the Life-saving Service developed a high degree of efficiency in part because of good management and methods of selecting and promoting personnel. The service developed and progressed normally, with no changes in basic functions, but with improvement in method with advances in mechanical and technical knowledge and invention. The advent of the motorboat was of great importance in facilitating life-saving operations. The telegraph, telephone, and radio increased efficiency. But the prime objective was still the saving of lives and property from shipwreck, which involved maintaining patrols and lookouts, manning and operating surfboats, boarding vessels in distress, transporting the rescued to the shore, and care, shelter, and first-aid attention to those in need, as well as the operation of breeches-buoys and other shore rescue apparatus and signals. During the spring of 1913, crews from stations at Louisville, Cleveland, Lorain, and elsewhere on the Great Lakes engaged in rescue work for flood victims in Kentucky, Ohio, Indiana, and Illinois. This appears to have been the first of such flood-rescue undertakings on the great interior rivers which are now a regular part of Coast Guard work. Under the auspices of the Life-saving Service, statutory provision was made for awarding medals for hazardous service in the saving of lives from the perils of the sea, within the United States or upon any American vessel. These awards are still given and are not restricted to Coast Guard personnel.

The Life-saving Service was perhaps unique among government agencies in that it had only one man as administrative head throughout its entire history. Sumner I. Kimball, who was appointed general superintendent in 1878 when the service was created, continued in that capacity until the merger with the Coast Guard in 1915, an incumbency of thirty-seven years, in addition to prior service. As a reward, the act of January 28, 1915, provided for his retirement on three-fourths pay, which was an unusual provision for a civilian. The Life-saving Service merged with the Revenue Cutter Service in 1915 to become the United States Coast Guard.

The Lighthouse Service, begun in 1789, is the oldest forefather of the Coast Guard. The United States accepted title to and jurisdiction over the existing lighthouses and other aids to navigation on the coasts of the several states, erected by the colonial governments, and provided for the support, maintenance, and repair of all lighthouses, beacons, buoys, and public piers, to be defrayed out of the Treasury of the United States.

The colonies had established and operated twelve lighthouses down to the year 1789, the oldest of which was Boston Light, Massachusetts, 1716. Of these twelve, six were in Massachusetts and one each in New Hampshire, Rhode Island, Connecticut, New York, Delaware, and South Carolina. In addition, four other lighthouses were commenced by the states, but they were not completed until after the federal government had been inaugurated.

The Secretary of the Treasury and even the presidents personally intervened in the early administration, which was chiefly under the commissioner of the revenue from 1792 to 1802 and from 1813 to 1820. In 1820, the care and superintendence of the lighthouse establishment were assigned to the fifth auditor of the Treasury; the incumbent for nearly thirty-three years was Stephen Pleasanton. For local administration and supervision, the collectors of customs were appointed superintendents of lights, receiving as extra compensation a small commission on the disbursements. In 1854, there were sixty-three such superintendents. In 1938, by act of Congress, the Atlantic Coast was divided into six districts and the Great Lakes into two districts.

For several years in the midnineteenth century, there were a number of surveys, studies, and reports concerning the lighthouses and administration of the system, indicating the need for improvement or change. The last of these was conducted by a board appointed, in 1851, by the Secretary of the Treasury. After a study also of European lighthouse systems, the board recommended a complete reorganization, with administration by a permanent board instead of by a single executive. This approach was adopted in 1852, when Congress created the Lighthouse Board as its governing head. The board was to consist of two high-ranking Navy officers, one officer each from the Corps of Engineers* of the Army and the Corps of Topographical Engineers of the Army, and two civilians with advanced scientific credentials. A Navy officer and an officer of Engineers of the Army were to serve as secretaries. An additional officer of the Corps of Engineers of the Army later took the place of the officer of the Corps of Topographical Engineers. In the field, the Atlantic, Gulf, Pacific, and Lake coasts were divided into twelve districts, to each of which were assigned an officer of the Navy as inspector for operation and supervision and an officer of the Corps of Engineers of the Army to superintend construction and repair. In 1870, jurisdiction was extended to include the Mississippi, Missouri, and Ohio rivers, with the addition of two administrative districts. In 1886, the number of districts was increased to sixteen. As the several outlying islands and territories were taken over by the United States, the board's jurisdiction was extended to them by including them in subdistricts. By a number of subsequent special acts, other inland or nontidal waters were included.

The Lighthouse Board administered the service from 1852 to 1910. During this period, especially the early years, it instituted many important improvements in methods and equipment, and the service had a substantial growth in keeping pace with the rapidly expanding maritime commerce of the nation. There were occasional proposals to transfer the service to the Navy Department,* or for other transfers or consolidations, but these all came to naught.

In 1903, when Congress created the Department of Commerce and Labor,* the Lighthouse Service was transferred from the Treasury Department to the newly created department (known after 1913 as the Department of Commerce). The form of organization represented by the Lighthouse Board had become less effective as the service had grown. Problems were caused by a lack of an executive head with definite authority and responsibility; the division of authority in each lighthouse district with its dual heads; and the brief period of detail of Army and Navy Officers who lacked the opportunity to master conditions. On June 17, 1910, Congress provided for a more direct administration, abolishing the Lighthouse Board and creating the Bureau of Lighthouses. As administrative head of the bureau, there was provided a commissioner of lighthouses, assisted by a deputy commissioner, a chief constructing engineer, and a superintendent of naval construction, all four to be appointed by the President. The first commissioner was George R. Putnam, who had previously served in the Coast and Geodetic Survey*; he held the office for twenty-five years, retiring in May 1935.

The new law also changed field administration. A single official, called a lighthouse inspector, was provided for, instead of two officers for each district. This change resulted in economy of administration and more direct responsibility to headquarters. All lighthouse inspectors were civilians except in the three river districts where officers of the Corps of Engineers of the Army were retained. The number of districts rose to nineteen, the three new ones embracing Puerto Rico and adjacent waters, Alaska, and the Hawaiian Islands.

Administrative improvements were instituted, consisting of a systematic inspection by headquarters' representatives of vessels, equipment, stations, business methods, property accounts, and clerical organization. A uniform system of cost-keeping, as well as a revision of keeping the general accounts at headquarters and in the field, was introduced. Periodical conferences, held about every two or three years commencing in 1914, brought the heads of the field districts to headquarters for discussion and interchange of ideas and practice. Minutes of the meetings were kept and copies sent to the inspectors.

The service grew rapidly after the reorganization in 1910. The number of aids to navigation increased about 200 percent from that date to 1939—from about 11,000 to about 30,000, or nearly double the number in the previous 120 years. Technical improvements included the extensive introduction of automatic lighting apparatus, as well as the replacement of a considerable number of lightships by fixed structures and improved buoys. Both of these measures resulted in substantial economy.

On July 1, 1939, the Bureau of Lighthouses was transferred to and consolidated with the Coast Guard, in accordance with President Franklin Roosevelt's Reorganization Plan No. II and pursuant to the provisions of the Reorganization Act of 1939. This consolidation resulted in the transfer to the Coast Guard of approximately 30,000 aids to navigation, 5,200 personnel, 64 buoy tenders, 30 depots, and 17 district offices.

The law of June 28, 1938, "authorizing the appointment of persons to test the usefulness of inventions to improve and render safe the boilers of steam engines against explosions," was the beginning out of which the Steamboat Inspection Service developed. Another law of the same year provided for regulation of steam vessels by requiring masters or captains to be licensed and for regular inspections of hulls and boilers to be made by competent persons who should issue certificates of such inspections. Later statutes strengthened the powers and expanded the functions of this agency.

Originally, the Bureau of Navigation was established in 1884 in the Treasury Department under the direction of a commissioner of navigation, who was charged with the general superintendence of the commercial marine and merchant seamen of the United States, who were not then subject to any existing laws. When the Department of Commerce and Labor was established in 1903, the Steamboat Inspection Service and the Bureau of Navigation were transferred to its jurisdiction; they remained in the Department of Commerce when the Labor section was separated in 1913. In 1932, they were consolidated into one bureau as the Bureau of Navigation and Steamboat Inspection, but without otherwise affecting their status and functions. The name was changed, in 1936, to the Bureau of Marine Inspection and Navigation. This change effected a material reorganization in the service, looking to a stricter and more far-reaching performance of the duties pertaining to the safety of vessels and preventions of casualties at sea.

The principal functions of the Bureau of Marine Inspection and Navigation included:

(1) Administration of the laws concerning the construction, equipment, manning, inspection, and admeasurement of commercial vessels of the United States.

(2) Assignment of official numbers to commercial vessels.

(3) Supervision of the shipment, discharge, and living conditions of seamen.

(4) Administration of the navigation laws of the United States, including the collection of tonnage taxes and other navigation fees.

(5) Issuance of registers, enrollments, and licenses to merchant vessels.

(6) Enforcement of laws pertaining to the equipment and operation of motorboats.

(7) Investigation of marine casualties.

The Bureau of Marine Inspection and Navigation had a multiplicity of laws to enforce and to be governed by, more extensive than those of any other Coast Guard predecessor.

Largely as a wartime measure, for the better coordination and direction of functions related to maritime activity, President Roosevelt, in 1941-1942, transferred the larger part of the functions of the Bureau of Marine Inspection and Navigation to the Coast Guard.

A new Coast Guard was born out of World War II. The service had entered 1939 as an amalgamation of two agencies and emerged from the war as a unified service, encompassing five agencies. By 1945, the Coast Guard had assumed its present character.

In 1967, the Coast Guard was transferred from the Treasury Department to the newly created Department of Transportation.* This administrative change reflected the shift in priorities that had occurred within the service.

FOR ADDITIONAL INFORMATION: There is no general reference work on the U.S. Coast Guard. The best single work for the nineteenth and early twentieth centuries is Stephen H. Evans, *The United States Coast Guard 1790-1915* (1949). During the 1920s, the Brookings Institution's Institute for Government Research prepared a series dealing with the history, activities, and organization of various government agencies. Four of these provide valuable data on the early Coast Guard and its predecessors: No. 8 *Steamboat—Inspection Service*, No. 15 *Bureau of Navigation*, No. 40 *Lighthouse Service*, and No. 51 *The Coast Guard*. Most literature concerning the Coast Guard since World War I is mission-oriented and of narrow focus. The best single source for this later time period is the Annual Report.

ROBERT L. SCHEINA

UNITED STATES COMMISSION ON CIVIL RIGHTS (CCR). The U.S. Commission on Civil Rights is an independent commission created in 1957 when Congress passed the 1957 Civil Rights Act (Public Law 85-315, as amended). The six person, bipartisan agency was directed to: (1) investigate complaints alleging that citizens are being deprived of their right to vote by reason of their race, color, religion, sex, age, handicap, or national origin, or by reason of fraudulent practices; (2) study and collect information concerning legal developments constituting discrimination or a denial of equal protection of the laws under the Constitution because of race, color, religion, sex, age, handicap, or national origin, or in the administration of justice; (3) appraise federal laws and policies with respect to discrimination or denial of equal protection of the laws; (4) serve as a national clearinghouse for information in respect to discrimination or denial of equal protection of the laws because of race, color, religion, sex, age, handicap, or national origin; and (5) submit findings, reports, and recommendations to the President and the Congress.

Since 1957, the commission has had five chairpersons. Dr. John A. Hannah, president, Michigan State University, was the initial chairman and served from 1957 to 1969. The Reverend Theodore Hesburgh, a member of the commission since 1957 (and president, Notre Dame University), served as the second chairman, 1969-1972. Stephen Horn was the third, temporary or acting chairman, 1972-1974. Arthur Flemming, appointed in 1974 by President Gerald Ford, served from 1974 to 1982 when, under intense pressure from the Ronald Reagan Administration, he stepped down. The present chairman of the CCR, nominated by President Reagan and recently confirmed by the Senate, is Clarence Pendleton, Jr., formerly with the New Coalition for Economic and Social Change and associated with the Urban League in California.

Congress created the CCR in 1957 when pressure grew for the national government to act positively with respect to discrimination, particularly voting discrimination, as it appeared in our society. The first civil rights act was a fairly weak piece of legislation that essentially placed the burden of eradicating vestiges of slavery by taking the case to the federal district courts in the jurisdictions that discriminated. In the beginning, the CCR's task was to monitor voting activities, especially in the South, and to prepare Annual Reports on the condition of civil rights in America. It very soon became the nation's "in-house conscience" regarding the state of civil rights in America.

Concerned with discrimination based on race, color, religion, sex, national origin, age, and handicap, primarily in the areas of voting, education, employment, housing, and administration of justice, the CCR consists of the six commissioners, staff director, general counsel, and staff directors of the following bureaus: Program Policy Review, Federal Civil Rights Enforcement, Congressional and Public Affairs, Program Planning and Evaluation, Administration, and Regional Programs. In addition to the staff in Washington, D.C., the CCR does have state advisory boards, that is, citizens within each of the fifty states who comprise the state advisory board and participate in the activities of the CCR when the agency is involved in findings of fact for its reports.

Although the CCR has no enforcement authority, its evaluations of federal laws and the effectiveness of governmental, equal opportunity programs, voting rights, sex discrimination, and equal-education programs have played a major role in bringing to light discrimination and in bringing about changes in the affected areas. In addition to examining the effectiveness of federal programs instituted to end various forms of discrimination, the CCR serves as a clearinghouse for information on the state of civil rights.

The CCR's clearinghouse reponsibility is directly to the public at-large. Through its clearinghouse publications such as its civil rights quarterly, *Perspectives*, publication of the *Civil Rights Directory*, and the publication of various reports on reverse discrimination (*Bakke*), sex discrimination (*More Hurdles To Clear: Women and Girls in Competitive Athletics*), and so on, the agency provides the interested public with detailed analyses of major issues in the area of civil rights.

The CCR's statutory responsibilities involve the development and distribution of reports to the President, president of the Senate, and speaker of the House of Representatives. The Annual Report is entitled *The State of Civil Rights: (year)*. This Annual Report to the political actors examines housing, education, employment, and additional civil rights concerns such as voting rights, police practices, and immigration policies.

In addition to the Annual Report, the CCR very often focuses on specific areas such as voting rights and has its staff, through the use of the state advisory panels, and informal hearings in Washington, D.C., and the regional CCR offices, prepare extensive studies for use by the Congress and the executive branch. For example, in the area of enforcement of voting rights, the CCR, years before the passage of the 1965 Voting Rights Act, called for the Congress to move from a litigative voting-rights strategy to a direct-action strategy by which the national government would move to register black voters in areas of discrimination and would set up a mechanism to protect the voting rights of newly enfranchised blacks. Its 1961 report on *Voting* and its report on *Voting in Mississippi* were spurs to action. After the passage of the 1965 Voting Rights Act, the CCR staff put together a number of watershed reports that supported the extension and the expansion of the Voting Rights Act: *Voting Rights Act—First Months* (1966); *Political Participation* (1968); *Voting Rights Act: Ten Years Later* (1975); and *Voting Rights Act: Unfulfilled Goals* (1981). These reports, focusing on the problems that confronted minorities in maintaining voting rights and on the problems the Department of Justice* has had in implementing the Voting Rights Act (as well as commenting on the political interferences perceived by the CCR staff in the course of field surveys and hearings), were instrumental in developing legislative support for extension of the act. The intense and extensive attention to civil rights issues has been seen in the voluminous study made of *Desegregation of the Nation's Public Schools: Status Report*, 1980, and in the 1970-1975 multivolume report on *Federal Civil Rights Enforcement Effort*, in which the CCR staff evaluated the civil rights activities of federal agencies with the responsibility for ensuring nondiscrimination in federally assisted programs under Title VI of the 1964 Civil Rights Act.

FOR ADDITIONAL INFORMATION: Since 1957, the CCR has served as the conscience of the nation in the area of civil rights for all persons in our society. It has been extremely critical, at various times, of less than aggressive conduct by public agencies in support of civil rights. Through hearings, field studies, and close examination of voting data, the

CCR has encouraged federal and state agencies to improve the quality of civil rights for their employees and their constituents. Many volumes have been written about civil rights that examine the role and functions of the CCR. Howard Ball, Howard G. Krane, and Thomas P. Lauth, *Comprised Compliance: Implementation of the 1965 Voting Rights Act* (1982), carefully traces the growth and the activities of the CCR in the area of voting rights. Charles F. Wilkinson, *From Brown to Bakke* (1981), illustrates the role of the CCR in the effort to end school segregation in America. Almost every monograph that has as its focus an issue of civil rights will invariably have reference to the CCR. Without any doubt, review of CCR Clearinghouse Publications as well as review of Annual and Special Reports of the CCR to the President and the Congress are indispensable aids for those interested in the activities of the CCR. All this information is available through the Public Affairs Office, U.S. Commission on Civil Rights, Washington, D.C. (202-254-6697).

HOWARD BALL

UNITED STATES COMMISSION ON INDUSTRIAL RELATIONS (CIR). During the years 1913 to 1915, the United States Commission on Industrial Relations, through public hearings and research, conducted a nationwide investigation into the causes of industrial strife. Hundreds of witnesses testified before the federal panel, while members of its research staff produced important special studies. In its *Final Report* the commission analyzed the contemporary state of labor-management relations and provided guidelines for the future. Its eleven volumes of hearings and its research records presented a panoramic view of American industrial society on the eve of World War I.

Impetus for creation of the commission came when James B. McNamara, a member of the International Association of the Bridge and Structural Iron Workers (BSIW), admitted that he had blown up the building of the vehemently anti-union *Los Angeles Times*, thereby causing the deaths of twenty people. At the same time his brother, John J. McNamara, Secretary-Treasurer of the BSIW, pleaded guilty to the charge of conspiracy in the dynamiting of the Llewellyn Iron Works in the same city. Up until this time, John McNamara had ranked among the most respected, conservative union leaders in the country. Shocked by these confessions, *Survey*, a magazine dedicated to social work and socio-economic problems, devoted almost an entire issue to "The Larger Aspects of the McNamara Case." Several distinguished scholars, businessmen, journalists, educators, lawyers, and social workers contributed their views. Most agreed that the case clearly demonstrated that industrial strife had now reached such an intensity that it threatened to tear the nation apart. Soon afterward a group of reformers and the editors of *Survey* petitioned President William Howard Taft to institute a federal investigation into the causes of industrial unrest.

On February 2, 1912, in his State of the Union message, Taft asked Congress to establish a United States Commission on Industrial Relations. After some debate, both houses of Congress passed the legislation, which received the signature of the chief executive on April 23, 1912. The act called for a commission comprised of three representatives each from business, labor, and the public. Congress gave it extensive power to hold public hearings and to pursue research into all areas pertinent to its task.

Several groups, including the National Civil Federation (NCF), the American Federation of Labor (AFL), the National Association of Manufacturers (NAM), and the original *Survey*-reformer faction, tried to influence Taft in his selection of commissioners. Reacting to these pressures, the President named as his labor choices: John B. Lennon, treasurer of AFL; James O'Connell, third vice-president of AFL; and Austin B. Garretson, president of the Order of Railway Conductors. For the business panel Taft selected NAM Vice-President Ferdinand Schwedtman; copper magnate Adolph Lewisohn; and Frederic A. Delano, president of the Wabash Railroad. As a representative of the public and chairman of the commission, Taft nominated conservative Republican Senator George B. Sutherland of Utah. Taft's other nominees for the public section included Charles S. Barrett, president of the Farmer's Union, and George B. Chandler, one-time chairman of the Connecticut state legislature's Committee on Labor. Taft's slate satisfied all of the interested parties except the social reformers who attacked it for failing to provide representation for radical labor or for working women. With the defeat of Taft in the presidential election, however, the Senate refused to confirm any of his appointees, leaving the matter open to his Democratic successor, Woodrow Wilson.

Wilson accepted Taft's labor panel but dislodged Schwedtman and Lewisohn from the business side, replacing them with California businessman and public servant Harris Weinstock and Kentucky mill-owner S. Thurston Ballard. Delano remained on the panel, but, when he later resigned, his place was taken by Richard H. Aishton, president of the Chicago and Northwestern Railroad. Wilson also removed Chandler and Barrett as representatives of the public, naming in their stead Professor John R. Commons, labor historian from the University of Wisconsin, and Mrs. J. Borden Harriman, New York social work leader. Most importantly, Wilson replaced Senator Sutherland with Frank P. Walsh, labor lawyer and reformer from Missouri. Wilson's selections proved a change from those of Taft in that the NAM's influence evaporated when the President replaced Schwedtman and Sutherland with liberal businessman Ballard and outspokenly pro-labor Walsh. The appointments of Mrs. Harriman and Professor Commons mollified the social reformers. In general, Wilson's new commission took on a more progressive hue while still representing small business and conservative unionism. Historian James Weinstein asserts that the difference between Taft's appointees and those of Wilson was minor. While he agrees that Wilson's panel did not include any representatives from big business, he feels that ultimately it proved of greater benefit to the large corporations. By excluding the radical right of business and the radical left of labor, Weinstein believes that the commission, in effect, endorsed the NCF viewpoint, which promoted a partnership between responsible corporations and conservative unions within a capitalist framework.

For the next year and a half the commissioners crossed the continent taking several million words of testimony. In pursuing their work, they investigated most of the major industrial trouble spots in America. While in the East, the commissioners probed the open warfare that had erupted between striking silk workers, led by the Industrial Workers of the World (IWW), and mill owners in Paterson, New Jersey. This violent upheaval in 1913 also produced the dramatic "Pageant of Paterson," held in Madison Square Garden, directed by radical journalist John Reed, and featuring workers as the chief actors. In New York City, the commissioners examined the massive fight by men and women workers of the garment industry for union recognition and improved conditions. After considerable turbulence, the struggle subsided with acceptance of a Protocol of Peace, which for a short time provided the machinery for the peaceful settlement of disputes.

Moving westward, the commissioners held hearings on the long and bitter strike between 1911 and 1915, which plagued the sprawling Illinois Central and Harriman railway lines. Physical assault, property destruction, and bloodshed marked this battle, which spread through several states including Illinois, Mississippi, and Kentucky. Moving to Dallas, Texas, in their sole investigation of agricultural labor, the commissioners listened to testimony, which clearly revealed the class tensions which in part had accounted for the substantial growth of Socialist party membership in the Southwest.

In California, the federal inquiry explored the background of the McNamara case, which had led to establishment of the commission. A twenty-year history of rancorous labor relations in Los Angeles had culminated in the destruction of the *Times* building. The McNamara confessions also robbed the Los Angeles Socialist party, strongly supportive of the brothers, of almost certain victory in the mayoral election. Later attempts to soften the animosity between capital and labor came to naught. While still on the West Coast, the commissioners also investigated several further incidents of violence, including the infamous Wheatland Hops riot in northern California.

Of all of the commission's hearings, the one dealing with the Ludlow Massacre in Colorado attracted the most attention and provoked the greatest controversy. Striking coal miners of the Rockefeller-controlled Colorado Fuel and Iron Company (CFI), having been forced to vacate their company-owned houses, had established tent colonies for themselves and their families. Members of the National Guard, believing that the miners were about to attack them, launched a frontal assault on a major colony and ignited a fire that swept through the entire community causing catastrophic results. Soon afterward, open warfare exploded throughout Colorado, subsiding only with the entry of U.S. Army troops. In his interrogation of John D. Rockefeller, Jr., Walsh set out to prove, by the use of Rockefeller's own correspondence, that the millionaire had been in close communication with company executives and had given his approval to their harsh anti-union tactics both before and during the strike. Rockefeller insisted that he had dealt only with company finances, not with day-to-day management. Walsh's vigorous grilling of the industrialist aroused the ire of some who felt that he unfairly mauled Rockefeller; others declared that his investigation had clearly revealed the dangers of concentrating too much economic power in too few hands.

In the midst of the commission's work, a bitter internal dispute erupted over the status of the Research Division. Research Director Charles V. McCarthy, originator of the Wisconsin Legislative Reference Library, had assembled a staff of talented young people, several of whom later rose to scholarly prominence. In addition to gathering information preparatory to each public hearing, the division had also embarked on an ambitious program of special studies related to industrial relations. McCarthy and Professor Commons regarded the Research Division's work as of greater importance than that of the hearings; they hoped to produce a comprehensive plan for the reformation of industrial relations in America. When budgetary difficulties threatened to impede the commission's work, McCarthy suggested curtailment or elimination of the hearings. Instead, Walsh decided to diminish the Research Division's activities and to fire McCarthy.

Commons and McCarthy struck back at a full executive session of the commission; they proposed reinstatement of the director and a redirection of funds into research. Walsh retorted by demonstrating that the Research Division had not completed a single one of some six to eight major reports that had fallen due. In addition, the chairman produced correspondence between Rockefeller and McCarthy, which he claimed clearly revealed that the director had tried to maintain a close personal friendship with Rockefeller while he was conducting an investigation of the millionaire's activities. In defense of McCarthy, Professor Commons declared that Walsh had distorted and misrepresented the facts. After considering all of the evidence, the commission by a vote of 7 to 1 (only Commons in opposition) approved Walsh's budget and even granted the chairman additional fiscal powers; the Research Division continued to function but with a considerably smaller staff. Author Rhodri Jeffreys-Jones declares that the Research Division's work faltered because its members wasted time trying to document the existence of violence in labor-management disputes. He claims that much of the violence in American history, including that investigated by the CIR, is either exaggerated or mythical.

Dissension further rent the commission during preparation of its *Final Report*. Eventually, it issued a document divided into three main sections. A statement signed by the three labor representatives and by Chairman Walsh became known as the majority report. It placed the blame for labor unrest squarely on the shoulders of capital, declaring that an unjust distribution of wealth lay at the base of industrial strife. Noting that only 2 percent of the population owned 60 percent of the wealth, they advocated a steeply graded inheritance tax. Their report also favored prosecution of fraudulent monopolists, revision of land laws, and a tax on all nonproductive land. It further supported severe restrictions on private detective agencies and called for additional safeguards of trial by jury. Finally, their *Report* strongly endorsed the protection of labor's right to collective bargaining.

In a separate statement, Commons and Harriman recommended establishment of joint labor-capital agencies to work with state and federal commissions to centralize and administer industrial relations policies. Those on the commission who represented business stressed the wrongdoing of labor. While they accepted the principle of collective bargaining, they decried sympathetic strikes, the closed shop, contract abrogation, restriction of output, and irresponsible union politics.

All commissioners agreed that deep-rooted social tensions and violence threatened American society. The majority *Report* blamed capital's refusal to negotiate and its employment of strikebreakers as major incitements to unrest. While the business commissioners agreed that some employers exploited women and children and had hired thugs who committed reprehensible crimes, they also stressed that some union leaders both advocated and practiced violence. Agreeing that the struggle between capital and labor had so overrun the bounds of civil restraint that it might lead to revolution, Commons and Harriman placed their faith in the settlement of these conflicts through arbitration agencies and special industrial commissions.

Other long-range influences emanated from the commission's work. Experts on the Research Division eventually produced studies, among which Robert Hoxie's *Scientific Management and Labor* (1915) ranked as the most important. Other significant works included George West's *Report on the Colorado Strike* (1915) and Luke Grant's analysis of the Bridge and Structural Ironworkers union, also in 1915. Some of the ideas in the *Final Report* found expression in the policies of the War Labor Board. Later, New Deal programs such as the National Recovery Administration,* graduated income tax, strengthening of collective bargaining, minimum wage scales, and the eight-hour day all resembled *Report* suggestions. In its own time, the commission had demonstrated the formative part which industrial unrest and violence played in shaping the Progressive era. Concern that the forces unleashed by modern industrialism might destroy society had stimulated a commitment to social reform.

FOR ADDITIONAL INFORMATION: Many collections and primary sources contain material pertinent to the CIR, but among the more important are the Papers of Frank P. Walsh, New York Public Library, New York City; the Papers of the United States Commission on Industrial Relations, National Archives,* Washington, D.C.; the Papers of William Howard Taft and the Papers of Woodrow Wilson, Library of Congress, Washington, D.C.; and the Papers of Charles V. McCarthy, State Historical Society, Madison, Wisconsin. Indispensable for any study of the commission is U.S. Senate, *Industrial Relations: Final Report and Testimony Submitted to Congress by the Commission on Industrial Relations Created by the Act of August 23, 1912. Document No. 415, 64th Congress, 1st Session (1916)*. 11 vols.

Some relevant unpublished studies are Edward T. Gibbons, "Frank Walsh and the United States Commission on Industrial Relations" (Master's thesis, History Department, University of Notre Dame, South Bend, Indiana (1958); Sister Maria Eucharia Meehan, "Frank Walsh and the American Labor Movement" (Ph.D. dissertation, New York University, 1962); and Leonard Rapport, "The United States Commission on Industrial Relations" (Master's Thesis, History Department, George Washington University, Washington, D.C., 1957).

Published works that deal with the CIR include Graham Adams, Jr., *Age of Industrial Violence, 1910-1915: The Activities and Findings of the U.S. Commission on Industrial Relations* (1966); Rhodri Jeffreys-Jones, *Violence and Reform in American History*, (1978); and James Weinstein, *The Corporate Ideal in the Liberal State, 1900-1918* (1968).

GRAHAM ADAMS, JR.

UNITED STATES CUSTOMS SERVICE. The United States Customs Service, created by an act of July 31, 1789, established customs districts and authorized customs officers to collect duties imposed by the Tariff Act of July 4, 1789. The service became part of the Treasury Department* when that department was established on Septemberr 2, 1789. The Secretary of the Treasury and later the Division of Customs administered the service until March 3, 1927, when the division acquired bureau status and assumed the functions of the Special Agency Service. Effective August 1, 1973, the Bureau of Customs was redesignated the United States Customs Service by Treasury Department Order 165-23, dated April 4, 1973.

Today the service administers and enforces customs laws, assessing and collecting customs duties, fees, and penalties on imported merchandise, and interdicting and seizing contraband, including narcotics and dangerous drugs. It processes persons, carriers, cargoes, and mail entering and leaving the United States, and protects American business and labor by enforcing statutes and regulations governing antidumping, countervailing duties, copyright, patent, and trademark provisions, commodity quotas, and the marking of country of origin. It collects trade statistics and assists more than 40 other government agencies by enforcing over 400 regulations and statutes to protect international trade.

The service is supervised by the commissioner of customs appointed by the Secretary of the Treasury. The 50 states plus Puerto Rico and the Virgin Islands are divided into 9 customs regions with 45 subordinate district area offices under which are 300 ports of entry, supervised by collectors of customs. There are also foreign field offices at Montreal, Mexico City, London, Paris, Rome, Hong Kong, and Tokyo, and a dog detector-training center near Front Royal, Virginia,

To accomplish its varied missions, the service is a member of the Customs Cooperation Council (CCC) (with headquarters at Brussels), the Cabinet Committee to Combat Terrorism, and the International Narcotics Control Program. It supports programs of several international organizations such as the General Agreement on Tariff and Trade (GATT), International Civil Aviation Organization, and the Organization of American States.

The Act of July 31, 1789, created customs districts in more than 100 ports. Each district was in charge of a collector, a naval officer, a surveyor, and other officers as needed. The collector, the chief officer, was responsible for collecting duties and fees, keeping records, and reporting his financial transactions; the admeasurement and documentation of American vessels engaged in foreign and domestic trade; the protection of American seamen and marine passengers; and forwarding basic data for reports on immigration and imports and exports. He also imposed fines, penalties, and forfeitures for violations of laws. The naval officer was required to keep all manifests and entry papers, estimate all customs duties, keep separate records, and countersign certain accounts of the collector. Under the Tariff Act of 1922, the title of naval officer was changed to comptroller of customs. The surveyor, under the supervision of the collector, kept a daily record of vessel arrivals and clearances, and, assisted by inspectors, weighers, and gaugers, collected duties on imports, tonnage duties, and fees. He supervised lading for drawbacks, the collection of bounty allowances, and the admeasurement of foreign vessels for tonnage duties. Customs officials were compensated for their services by a percentage of the proceeds of specified fees fixed by law and of the total receipts deducted from monies received before the receipts were deposited in the Treasury.

From time to time, Federal legislation, Executive Orders, or Treasury regulations changed the district boundaries, assigned new duties to the service or transferred functions from it to other federal agencies, and changed the method of compensating officials. An act of August 4, 1790, provided for the construction of ten cutters to secure the revenue. The cutters were assigned to the principal ports and were supervised by the collectors until 1878, when supervision was transferred to the Revenue Marine or Revenue Cutter Division of the Office of the Secretary of the Treasury. In 1915, this division was combined with the Life-saving Service to form the United States Coast Guard.* The Coast Guard was transferred in 1967 to the newly created Department of Transportation,* but it continues to cooperate with customs to fulfill its original mission, the prevention of smuggling.

The activities of the Barbary pirates and the wars between England and France from the mid-1790s through the early nineteenth century occasioned the passage of several laws to protect American seamen and shipping from seizure on the high seas. The laws were implemented by the issuance by collectors of Mediterranean passports and seamen's protective certificates, and the requirement, by an act of February 28, 1803, that masters of vessels bound for a foreign port file with the collector at their port of clearance a crew list and a bond to produce the crew upon the vessel's return. A copy of the crew list, documenting the loss or defection of any crew member and certified to by an American consul at the foreign port of call, was to be filed by the master with the collector at the first U.S. port of entry.

Seamen sometimes required hospitalization after a long sea voyage. Marine hospitals were maintained in some districts, and hospital monies were collected by masters of vessels from their crew members to defray the cost of hospitalization. Today, the marine hospitals are administered by the Public Health Service.*

On March 2, 1819, an act providing for the protection of marine passengers and the collection of immigration statistics was adopted. Masters of vessels entering U.S. ports from a foreign port were required to file a passenger list with the collector at their port of entry. Through 1874, copies of these lists were sent to the State Department* whence quarterly reports by port were sent to the

Congress and were published in the Serial Set of Congressional Documents. The keeping of immigration statistics became the responsibility of the Immigration and Naturalization Service* founded in 1882. The use of modern technology has returned to the Customs Service prime responsibility for accounting for persons entering the country. Computerized records kept by the service, however, are available to the Immigration and Naturalization Service.

The Constitution provided that no act prohibiting the slave trade could be passed until after December 31, 1807. Several laws governing this trade were passed between 1794 and 1820. A law of 1820 declared slaving an act of piracy and authorized the execution of anyone convicted of participating in the trade. Section 8 of this law prohibited the transportation of slaves in any vessels under forty tons except on rivers of the United States. Section 9 of the same act required all vessels of over forty tons carrying slaves in the coastwise trade to file with collectors at their ports of clearance and entry manifests showing the name and age of each slave, the names and residences of exporter and consignee, and a pledge that the slaves had not been imported after 1807.

An act of February 10, 1810, specified a method for determining commodity value and required the deposit of inward and outward cargo manifests with collectors. Trade statistics supplied to the Treasury by the collectors, and reported to Congress, first by the Register of the Treasury and then by the Bureau of Statistics, founded in 1866, are published as congressional documents.

During the war of 1812, an act of June 26, 1812, regulated the granting of letters of marque, and an act of July 6, 1912, provided penalties for trading with the enemy. The enforcement of these acts was assigned to the collectors. The advent of steam navigation also increased the collectors' duties. No documents could be issued for a steamboat until steamboat inspectors had certified that provisions for safety had been complied with.

Special regulations governing exports were issued during the Civil War. In some Southern ports where control had been regained from the Confederacy, collectors sometimes performed duties for the Treasury special agents. These duties comprised issuing trade permits and keeping records of seized Confederate property. In some instances, collectors also collected excise taxes on tobacco and alcoholic products for the Internal Revenue Service,* recreated in 1863.

To provide greater uniformity in the appraisal of imports, a Board of General Appraisers was created in 1890. So great were the number of cases referred to the board and the delays involved that the Tariff of 1909 provided that the Court of Customs Appeals under the Justice Department* have exclusive jurisdiction to review the examiners' decisions. The provision of the 1890 act for referral of important cases to the Supreme Court, however, was retained.

An act of August 24, 1912, authorized the President to reorganize the Customs Service. An Executive Order of March 3, 1913, redefined district boundaries by establishing one district in each state and territory. It also abolished the system of paying collectors a percentage of fees and other emoluments. All collectors were now salaried.

Between 1914 and 1917, the service was responsible for detecting and prosecuting violations of neutrality laws. Customs officials acted as agents for War Risk Insurance that insured vessels, cargoes, and seamen against risks due to the state of war. With the entrance of the United States into the war, customs seized enemy vessels in American ports. Imports and exports were licensed to conserve shipping space and to retain needed commodities at home. The War Trade Board issued the licenses; customs enforced the regulations and checked shipments. Personnel of merchant ships were issued seamen's protective certificates. Passengers and baggage leaving the country were examined to detect violations of regulations that prescribed the amount of currency and specie that could be taken out of the country.

During World War II, customs seized German and Italian vessels in American ports. By an Executive Order of February 28, 1942, certain marine functions including the registry, enrolling, licensing, and admeasurement of merchant vessels, previously performed by customs before the establishment of the Department of Commerce and Labor* in 1903, were returned to customs from the Bureau of Marine Inspection and Navigation of the Department of Commerce. These functions were transferred to the Department of Transportation upon its creation on October 15, 1966. Throughout the war, customs cooperated with the War* and State departments, the Immigration and Naturalization Service, the War Shipping Board, and the Office of Price Administration* to protect American ports from sabotage; to prevent enemy aliens from entering the United States; and to keep statistics on the import and export of strategic war materials. It also assisted the Foreign Funds Control by preventing the export of funds, securities, and property in excess of amounts authorized by the Secretary of Treasury.

During the fighting in Vietnam, an office of the Customs Service in Saigon assisted the South Vietnamese government in establishing and improving its customs service. In 1978, the service provided technical, managerial, and personnel training to the Saudi Arabian customs service.

Increased activities and rising costs of administration necessitated a reform of customs procedures that led to the adoption of modern business methods including modern technology. A reorganization of the headquarters office, begun in 1979, was completed in June 1980. Progress was made establishing uniform procedures, including a monitoring system to achieve uniformity in applying penalties. Updated communications and screening systems speed up passenger processing, and the use of the Treasury Department Enforcing Communication System (TECS), a computerized information and communication network, provides immediate information to detect violations and collect trade statistics. Consolidation of all automation under one program was implemented nationwide in 1980, and 100 percent of all collections in seventy-three locations was processed under the Independent Collection Subsystem (ICS).

The Customs Service administers Orderly Marketing Agreements (OMA), whereby foreign governments voluntarily agree to restrict their imports to the

United States. OMAs with Japan, Korea, and Taiwan covering color TV sets and with meat-supplying countries expired in 1980; quotas were imposed on color TV sets from Korea and Taiwan and on meat products from Australia, New Zealand, and several Central American countries.

The Office of Investigations, the investigative branch of the service, evolved from the use of special agents to investigate wrongdoing of customs officials and fraud by importers. The "Spoils System," whereby politics dominated appointments and the practice of compensating collectors with percentages of their collections, deductible before placing the remainder in the Treasury, led to corruption. The "Tariff of Abominations" and other high tariffs contributed to fraud. So great was the alleged corruption in the New York Customhouse when Chester A. Arthur was collector that a special commission was appointed in 1877 to investigate it. The findings of this commission and those of similar investigations were published in the Serial Set of Congressional Documents. Nineteen volumes of letters received by the Treasury Department concerning charges against customs officials exist for the years 1833-1861. Far greater is the volume of extant correspondence or "case files" concerning the attempts of importers and tourists to defraud the government. Customs officials today are concerned more with identifying and interdicting large-scale fraud than with harassment of tourists. By agreement with the Immigration and Naturalization Service and the Agriculture Animal and Plant Health Inspection Service, passenger clearance at selected international airports is expedited by the "One Stop" system whereby a customs inspector, alone, examines baggage and stamps the passports of American citizens returning from abroad.

The Customs Service, in cooperation with other government agencies and with the international community as well, is intensifying its efforts to interdict illicit traffic in drugs and exotic birds and to prevent the entrance of known terrorists into the United States. The use of covert aircraft-tagging beacons, unattended alert-surveillance systems, infrared search lights, night-vision goggles, and long-range night vision systems have contributed to the success of several joint missions, including the breakup of a multimillion dollar oil theft ring in the Houston area.

A radar net, an airborne camera that detects and films hidden airfields, a cargo x-ray system, and an ultrasound device to detect narcotics in sealed cans are some of the devices in use to detect smugglers and illegal aliens. Detector dog teams have made many drug seizures with a great saving in man-hours.

Through participation in the Customs Cooperation Council, the service promotes international trade and goodwill. Working with the State Department's Bureau of International Narcotics Matters, it provides enforcement training to foreign customs officials, including training with detector dogs. It has also conducted enforcement courses in Peru, Pakistan, Turkey, the Philippines, and the Caribbean nations, and continues to provide technical aid to the Department of Customs of Saudi Arabia.

In fiscal 1980, customs collected over $8 billion in revenue and made 21,598 dangerous-drug seizures valued at $3.5 billion. With the continued use of improved business methods and modern technology, the service strives to improve its operations, reduce the cost of its administration, and promote the prosperity, health, and security of the United States.

FOR ADDITIONAL INFORMATION: Laurence F. Schmeckebier, *The Customs Service, Its History, Activities and Organization* (1924), contains an excellent, extensive, annotated bibliography of official government publications and of secondary works about the Customs Service through 1923. *Annual Report of the Secretary of the Treasury on the State of the Finances*, Fiscal Year 1979, is useful, as are earlier Annual Reports; for a listing of reports for the period 1790-1909, see *Checklist of U.S. Public Documents, 1789-1909* (1911); ''Customs USA, A Special Report on the Activities of the United States Customs Service during fiscal 1979,'' (1980), which is also the basis for the portion of the Secretary of the Treasury's Annual Report that pertains to the Customs Service. *Guide to the National Archives of the United States* (1974),* p.p. 168-173. It contains a brief administrative history of the Customs Service and a description of records of that service found in the National Archives*. Kenneth Munden and Henry P. Beers, *Guide to Federal Archives Relating to the Civil War* (1962), includes descriptions of pertinent customs records. Forrest R. Holdcamper, comp., ''Preliminary Inventory of Records of the Bureau of Customs (Record Group 36)'' (1968), unpublished. Carmelita S. Ryan and Hope K. Holdcamper, comps., ''Preliminary Inventory of the General Records of the Department of the Treasury (Record Group 56)'' (1977), includes correspondence of the Secretary's office relating to customs through 1968 and records of the Division of Customs and of the Special Agency Service before the Bureau of Customs was formed in 1927.

HOPE K. HOLDCAMPER

UNITED STATES FISH AND WILDLIFE SERVICE. The Fish and Wildlife Service was formed on July 1, 1940, by a merger of the Bureau of Fisheries and the Bureau of Biological Survey. The two bureaus had been transferred to the Interior Department* in 1939 from the Departments of Commerce* and Agriculture,* respectively.

Many of the major programs administered by the Fish and Wildlife Service originated with the two bureaus and their predecessors. The older of the bureaus, the Bureau of Fisheries, was successor to the independent United States Fish Commission, which had been established by a Joint Resolution of Congress on February 9, 1871. Spencer F. Baird, assistant secretary of the Smithsonian Institution, was appointed the first commissioner of fisheries. He served in that capacity until his death in 1887.

An act of February 14, 1903, placed the United States Fish Commission in the newly established Department of Commerce and Labor,* and renamed it the Bureau of Fisheries. When the department was divided in 1913, the Bureau of Fisheries was assigned to the Department of Commerce.

The duties of the Fish Commission and the Bureau of Fisheries comprised five general areas. The primary function of the commission, specified in the 1871 act creating the agency, concerned the scientific investigation of the causes for the decrease of commercial food fish and aquatic animals, such as mussels, oysters, and sponges, in the coastal and inland waters of the United States. Later related activities included studying the effects of river impoundment projects on fish migration patterns, determining the feasibility of using fishways to direct fish around obstructions, and investigating the effects of red tides and water pollution in coastal and inland waters on commercial fish and shellfish. This work was largely conducted in the field at biological laboratories such as the facility established by Baird at Woods Hole, Massachusetts, and by Fish Commission vessels.

In 1872, the Fish Commission undertook the propagation and distribution of fresh-water food fishes into the inland waters of the United States. This work, which included the development of techniques to propagate and maintain fish outside their natural environment, resulted in the establishment of federally operated fish hatcheries and aquaria. Later legislation extended this work to include marine fish, shellfish, and lobsters.

In 1879, Congress directed the Fish Commission to collect and publish statistical data bearing on the commercial fishing industry. The work later included investigating methods of storing and processing fish, establishing standards of quality, and recommending improvements in fishing gear and methods.

The Fish Commission had also been involved in scientific investigations in Alaska in the 1890s. These included using the Fish Commission Steamer *Albatross* to transport Treasury Department* agents to investigate the fur seal herds of the Pribilof Islands and Bering Sea, and later to transport fishery biologists surveying the fishery resources of streams in southern and southeastern Alaska.

On February 15, 1905, and December 28, 1908, the administration of Alaskan salmon fisheries and fur seals, respectively, was transferred from the Office of the Secretary of Commerce and Labor to the Bureau of Fisheries. The regulation of these industries had been the responsibility of the Treasury Department from 1868 to 1903.

The Alaska Fisheries Act of 1906 clarified existing fishery laws and made the bureau responsible for the regulation of commercial fish, in addition to salmon and shellfish, and authorized the inspection of private fish hatcheries, the study of the habits of commercial migratory fish, and the collection of statistics on the amount canned or salted.

The work in Alaska was expanded by an act in 1924 that authorized the bureau to undertake fishery-management programs, including the operation of fish hatcheries, regulation of fishing gear and methods, and collection of data on spawning salmon.

In 1910, the bureau was made responsible for the protection of certain Alaskan fur-bearing animals. This work was tranferred to the Bureau of Biological Survey in 1920. Also in 1920, responsibility for the protection of sea lions and walrus was transferred from the Bureau of Biological Survey to the Bureau of Fisheries.

Other regulatory functions included enforcement of the Federal Black Bass Law of 1930, which provided for the regulation of interstate commerce in black bass. The bureau was also charged with the collection of statistical and biological whaling data under the provisions of the Whaling Treaty Act of 1936.

The Bureau of Biological Survey originated with a clause in the Agricultural Appropriation Act of 1885, which authorized the Division of Entomology in the Department of Agriculture to conduct investigations into the interrelationships of birds and agriculture. On July 1, 1886, the work was transferred to the newly created Division of Economic Ornithology and Mammalogy and extended to include the investigation of mammals and their relationship to agriculture and forestry. In 1896, the division was renamed the Division of Biological Survey and subsequently designated the Bureau of Biological Survey in 1905. Clinton Hart Merriam was placed in charge of the work in 1886 and remained chief until 1910.

The work of the Bureau of Biological Survey was organized into four general areas: wildlife research, regulatory duties, refuge management, and predator and rodent control.

Wildlife research, a continuation of the original duties of the survey's predecessors, grew to include investigations concerning commercial fur production; studies of the diseases, parasites, and grazing habits of reindeer and other stock in Alaska; and research concerning bird and animal diseases.

The regulatory duties of the survey fell into three general categories. First, under the Lacey Act of May 25, 1900, the survey undertook the compilation and publication of state game laws and regulations, issued regulations governing the importation of mammals and birds, and cooperated with state game authorities in enforcing laws regarding the interstate shipment of birds killed in violation of state game laws. The "Egg Act" of June 3, 1902, extended the regulation of imports to include the eggs of game birds.

Second, under the Alaska Game Law of 1902, the survey was charged with the protection of game, primarily trophy animals, in Alaska. An act in 1908 amended the Alaska Game Law and transferred responsibility for its enforcement to the Governor of Alaska. In 1920, jurisdiction over certain islands in Alaska leased for fox farming purposes, and responsibility for protecting land fur-bearing animals in Alaska were transferred from the Bureau of Fisheries.

A Joint Resolution of Congress in 1924 returned the authority to administer the Alaska Game Law from the Governor of Alaska to the survey. In 1925, the Alaska Game Law was amended to provide for the protection of both game and fur-bearing animals in cooperation with the newly formed Alaska Game Commission.

The third regulatory area concerned the protection of migratory birds. The Federal Migratory Bird Law of March 4, 1913, authorized the survey to promulgate and enforce regulations to fix the closed seasons on migratory game birds. That law was superseded by the Federal Migratory Bird Treaty Act of 1918, which was the result of a treaty with Great Britain concerning the protection of birds migrating between the United States and Canada, and, as amended in 1936, in accordance with the provisions of a treaty with Mexico.

The survey maintained and operated the federal refuge system. It administered the first bird refuge, which was established by Executive Order on March 14, 1903, on Pelican Island in Florida. Its management duties later included big game preserves when the National Bison Range was transferred from the Forest Service* in 1909. Refuge areas administered by the Biological Survey before 1929 were acquired by Executive Order, Act of Congress, gift, or cession. The Migratory Bird Conservation Act of 1929 authorized the purchase or rental of lands and marsh areas suitable for bird refuges as recommended by the Secretary of Agriculture, with the approval of the newly established Migratory Bird Conservation Commission. That act was supplemented by the Migratory Bird Hunting Stamp Act of 1934, which provided for the establishment and maintenance of migratory waterfowl refuges using emergency funds allotted by Congress and the disposition of proceeds from the sale of migratory bird hunting stamps.

The work of the survey also included the operation of predator and rodent-control programs. An act of 1914 authorized the survey to conduct experiments and demonstrations in the eradication of predatory animals injurious to livestock, and rodents that hindered the cultivation and storage of grains. Other legislation enlarged the survey's predator and rodent-control programs to include work on the public domain, the eradication of rabies, cooperation with the Forest Service, and the negotiation of cooperative agreements with the states to finance and undertake control activities.

When the Fish and Wildlife Service was created in 1940, the management and administrative units of the two former bureaus were merged, but the program units remained virtually intact throughout the sixteen-year existence of the Fish and Wildlife Service.

The former Bureau of Biological Survey had administered provisions of the Federal Aid in Wildlife Restoration Act of 1937, also known as the Pittman-Robertson Act. In 1950, the Federal Aid in Fish Restoration Act, also known as the Dingell-Johnson Act, expanded the program making the Fish and Wildlife Service responsible for administering grants-in-aid programs to the states for wildlife and fish-restoration projects and related management research.

An area of growing importance concerned international fisheries. An Office of Foreign Activities was established in 1945 to administer international fishery activities. The office coordinated the assignment of technical experts from research units of the service to foreign countries to conduct fishery research and organize assistance programs; maintained liaison with the State Department* regarding U.S. commitments under fishery agreements; and assisted in drafting and negotiating international fishery agreements. The office was also responsible for U.S. representation at international conferences and meetings concerning fisheries, and on regional and international fishery commissions.

Two new major programs were begun under the Fish and Wildlife Service. The first, started in 1944 and administered by the Office of River Basin Studies, concerned the investigation of the effects of federal water development projects and private projects begun under federal permits on fish and wildlife resources.

The second, the Columbia River Fishery Development Program, was authorized by an act in 1946. It was designed to encourage closer cooperation between the states of Idaho, Oregon, and Washington by facilitating cooperative use of the facilities of the conservation agencies of those states to conserve the salmon fisheries of the Columbia Basin.

The Fish and Wildlife Service was reorganized under the provisions of the Fish and Wildlife Act of 1956 and renamed the United States Fish and Wildlife Service. The service, as reorganized, consisted of a Bureau of Commercial Fisheries and a Bureau of Sport Fisheries and Wildlife.

The functions of the Bureaus of Commercial Fisheries and Sport Fisheries and Wildlife corresponded closely to the functions of the former Bureaus of Fisheries and Biological Survey, respectively.

The Bureau of Commercial Fisheries was made responsible for commercial fishery investigations, including research relating to anadromous and inland commercial fish, and commercially important marine fish and shellfish; and activities associated with industrial research, which included the collection of fishery statistics, fishing-gear investigations, exploratory fishing, and other areas related to advising the fishery industry in developing markets and utilizing modern technology to capture and process fish.

The Bureau of Commercial Fisheries was also assigned responsibility for the Columbia River Fishery Development Program, management of Alaska fisheries, and certain functions relating to fur seals, sea otters, whales, and other sea mammals.

In 1966, functions concerning international fisheries, largely the same as those administered by the former Office of Foreign Activities, were transferred from the Office of the Commissioner of the United States Fish and Wildlife Service to the Bureau of Commercial Fisheries.

The Bureau of Sport Fisheries and Wildlife was made responsible for program areas similar to those under the jurisdiction of the former Bureau of Biological Survey. These were the direction of wildlife research, enforcement of federal statutes and regulations applying to migratory birds, operation of the national refuge system, management of predator and rodent control work, and administration of federal aid programs. The bureau was also assigned functions relating to river-basin studies, the Federal Black Bass Law, and the national fish hatchery system.

Soon after the 1956 reorganization, a new program area relating to studies and surveys of the production and utilization of marine and fresh-water sport fisheries evolved in the bureau. Later, the work was expanded to include the establishment of fishery cooperative units in cooperation with state agencies and universities.

In 1970, the Bureau of Commercial Fisheries was transferred to the Department of Commerce and renamed the National Marine Fisheries Service. On July 1, 1974, the Bureau of Sport Fisheries and Wildlife, which had remained in the Interior Department, was renamed the United States Fish and Wildlife Service.

In the 1970s, three major programs reflecting concern with the impact of environmental changes on fish and wildlife were initiated or expanded within the Bureau of Sport Fisheries and Wildlife and its successor. Under the authority of the Endangered Species Acts of 1966 and 1973, the service was directed to maintain an official list of threatened and endangered species, to acquire habitat for such species, and to undertake the restoration of those species. Beginning in 1975, the service became responsible for evaluating the impact on fish and wildlife of offshore development.

In 1976, in response to increasing problems with oil spills, the service was charged with responsibility for developing programs to protect fish and wildlife and coordinate the efforts of individuals and states to rescue and rehabilitate oiled birds.

FOR ADDITIONAL INFORMATION: It is heartening to note the recent upsurge of critical interest in the role of the Fish and Wildlife Service as the nation's wildlife conservation agency. Two books based on extensive research in primary source materials offer useful insights into the philosophical and practical origins of two Fish and Wildlife Service predecessors: Keir B. Sterling, *Last of the Naturalists: The Career of C. Hart Merriam* (1974), and Dean Conrad Allard, *Spencer Fullerton Baird and the U.S. Fish Commission: A Study in the History of American Science* (1978). These volumes are especially valuable for their informative bibliographies. An older, yet durable, study of the Bureau of Biological Survey is Jenks Cameron's *The Bureau of Biological Survey: Its History, Activities, and Organization*, Institute for Government Research, Brookings Institution, Service Monographs of the United States Government No. 54 (1929). A bibliography by Ronald J. Fahl titled *North American Forest and Conservation History* (1977) is an exhaustive work that includes many references to manuscript and published studies of the Fish and Wildlife Service and its predecessors.

RENEE M. JAUSSAUD

UNITED STATES GEOLOGICAL SURVEY (USGS). Founded in 1879, the United States Geological Survey has ever since been investigating the metals, minerals, and mineral fuels of the American continent. It maps geology and topography, measures the supply of water and assesses its quality, and manages mineral extraction on public and Indian lands, and on the outer continental shelf.

In his brief tenure from 1879 to 1881, Clarence King ratified the intention of Congress at the founding and organized scientific parties for work in centers of gold and silver mining—in Virginia City and Eureka, Nevada, and in Leadville, Colorado. The first director set a course that would be followed for decades by Survey geologists as they researched both precious and common minerals all over the mountain West from Colorado to the Sierra Nevada. Bulletins and monographs helped miners to extend their discoveries of valuable ores, and led to an important theoretical advance: geologists learned more about classifying ore deposits according to the physical and chemical conditions of their origin. King also initiated Annual Reports on the statistics and technology of minerals.

John Wesley Powell. director from 1881 to 1894, ran a much more diversified Survey than King had. First, he broadened its geographical base by persuading Congress in 1882 to authorize operations in the Eastern states. He then launched a national program in topographical mapping, which gave geologists a base on which to inscribe their formations. Powell also permitted mining studies to take a new direction in the Appalachian coalfields, in Southern phosphates, and in the iron ores of the Great Lakes. And staff geologists were free to begin on the Atlantic coastal plain. In the Grand Canyon and in the Yellowstone, Powell inspired the practice of doing the geology of striking landscapes, while urging their preservation; in the future, Rainier and Yosemite would come under purview. Economic geologists out West learned to leaven their intensive studies in mining camps with larger, regional topics—mountain building, for example, and the structural stresses and faulting that accompanied it. In paleontology Powell organized the largest force in the country, with dinosaurs, trilobites, and insects receiving attention first.

The rapid growth of the Geological Survey in the 1880s made it an obvious target for Democratic congressional leaders who had two reasons for disliking the bureau: it grew more expensive every year and was harvesting strange knowledge. These Democrats were of the Grover Cleveland variety, who reacted against the growth of government by urging a return to the scale of the federal establishment before the Civil War. They talked nostalgically of simpler times and used the language and symbols of pre-Darwinian, biblical-minded America. Republican leaders, on the other hand, accommodated themselves to larger government and its services; progress, they said, could not be stopped nor the clock turned back. The method that Congress used to investigate the Geological Survey (and several other post-Civil War scientific agencies) was a joint commission, which met on and off over an eighteen-month period between December 1884 and May 1886. After the hearings and the widespread publicity that accompanied the report of the commission, it was clear that Powell had won a strong vote of confidence for himself and the Survey. The point upon which the favorable result had largely hinged was the merit of the chemical and statistical analyses which the Survey was making annually on the raw materials and metallurgical processes of American industry. In the political crunch, mineral science proved the core strength of the Survey.

Having secured for the Survey an accepted place in the government, Powell soon involved himself and the bureau in a visionary program of land reform for the Western arid regions, which ruined him as director and gravely endangered the Survey. By 1888, sentiment for irrigation in the Rocky Mountain West had developed far enough to induce Congress to employ the Survey in locating irrigable lands and reservoir sites. Congress also provided that all located lands be reserved from sale or occupation. For two years Powell supervised topographical mapping, selection of reservoirs, and stream measurement in the arid West. At every opportunity, he also urged the partition of the arid region into self-contained geographical districts occupied and organized by separate groups of settlers for the purpose of practicing irrigation. The climax and end of Powell's irrigation survey came in 1890 when the enforcement of the reservation clause threatened to shut down all the land offices in the arid West, pending the selection of the lands valuable for irrigation. Angry, Western Republican senators seized the initiative, abolished the irrigation survey, and in 1892 joined with economy-minded Democrats in both House and Senate to reduce severely the money for geology, paleontology, and chemistry. Powell's resignation was inevitable.

The new director, C. D. Walcott, (1894-1907), first repaired the damage done by Powell's policies. He rededicated the Survey to the geology of minerals, and he also stressed Western coal, as the national use of that fuel was nearing a climax. He raised the standards of the topographical mapping, where Powell had tolerated poor science in his haste for a national map. Walcott was the first director to secure a million dollars in direct appropriations from Congress, and he channeled some of this money in new directions. Reconnaissance and exploration began in the mining camps of Alaska at the turn of the century; for decades, this territory epitomized the Western, frontier spirit of the Survey. A contribution to the rising conservation movement was topographical mapping for eight years of the forest reserves which Presidents Benjamin Harrison and Grover Cleveland had been accumulating. Furthermore, Walcott emphasized the measurement of flowing streams, started by Powell, and, defining underground water as a mineral resource, he encouraged studies of this valuable, but hidden reserve. Beginning briefly in 1902, Congress established reclamation under the aegis of the Survey.

The directorships of George Otis Smith (1907-1930) and Walter Curran Mendenhall (1930-1943) constitute the long "middle period" of Survey history. The feeling for continuity prevailed with these two directors, and gradual, slow change characterized the course of the Survey. During the Progressive Era, Smith led the bureau into land classification on the public domain. In the name of science and efficiency, geologists and engineers began to survey and map federal lands that had coal, oil or oil shales, natural gas, sodium, and phosphates. Water-power sites were also selected. After 1925, the Survey administered these valuable categories, framing lease terms, regulating prospecting and mining, proposing royalites, and receiving payments. In the mid-1920s, Smith organized the activities of classification and supervision for public minerals, fuels, and other materials into a division of conservation. Both directors secured rising appropriations for the investigation of water resources, as flood, drought, and competition for supplies among industry, agriculture, and municipalities made America increasingly water-conscious. Papers on water-bearing formations and their thickness, on the chemistry of water, and on artesian conditions became a standard part of the output. Scientists measured low, mean, and flood discharges for thousands of streams, with predictive knowledge as the ultimate goal.

Another significant trend was the growing involvement of the bureau with state, municipal, and private organizations, and with other federal agencies. In 1927, the Survey published the first complete geological map of the state of Oklahoma; the parties cooperating with the Survey were the National Research

Council, the Oklahoma Geological Survey, oil companies, and individual geologists. The same year (1927), Smith reported that the contribution to the annual budget by states and other local units constituted 40 percent of that budget; this contribution went mostly for work in topography and water resources. During the 1930s, Director Mendenhall announced three collaborations in economic geology. One occurred for several years in Colorado through two state agencies: the Geological Survey Board and the Metal Mining Fund Board. The Arizona Bureau of Mines cooperated at Tombstone, and geological maps were published for Texas and Colorado. Late in the Mendenhall administration, federal agencies were contributing a million dollars a year to the Survey for studies in water resources.

In technology, the two directors presided over the development of aerial photography for mapping, or photogrammetry as it is now called. First used extensively in southeastern Alaska in the 1920s and then for the Tennessee Valley Authority* in the 1930s, photogrammetry advanced greatly during World War II, when the Survey and the Army Air Force developed an assembly of three cameras, two of them aimed obliquely for shooting the ground. Plotting techniques also advanced, so that increasingly the mapmaker could obtain through aerial observations the scientific detail that once could be secured only through painstaking field observations.

Smith and Mendenhall were the Survey directors during the world wars. Both times the concept of strategic minerals prevailed, which meant Survey scientists sought to increase the supplies of minerals vulnerable to restrictive action by foreign governments. Manganese, tungsten, petroleum, chromium, and high-grade clays were sought during each conflict. In World War I, exploration at Searles Lake, California, made the country independent of foreign potash, but there was no success in finding nitrate to offset the dependence on Chile. In World War II, reserves were added to in tungsten, mercury, copper, and, above all, in bauxite, the ore of aluminum. Army, Navy, and civilian administrators found the Survey's knowledge indispensable when they sought sites and water supply for cantonments, naval stations, munitions plants, and testing grounds.

The waning of pure research after the strong start in the nineteenth century frustrated the Survey leadership for decades. The best that Smith seemed able to do was to reaffirm in his Annual Reports the faith in theoretical science. Mendenhall saw an actual opportunity when Herbert Hoover, the celebrated mining engineer, became President. In 1930, with the friendly interest and support of executive and Congress, he secured an appropriation of $100,000 for fundamental research in geological science. Survey geologists moved into such subjects as California batholiths, the San Andreas fault zone, glacial geology in the northern Rockies, and stratigraphy and paleontology on the Atlantic and Gulf coastal plain. But the practice of economy during the Great Depression and New Deal set back this promising change. Only in 1939 could Director Mendenhall report that programs had returned to their level at the beginning of the decade.

Under Directors William E. Wrather (1943-1956) and Thomas B. Nolan (1956-

1965), the Survey entered a period of rapid expansion and innovation. By the 1960s, total appropriations had passed $100 million. Originally a territorial organization in western United States, it now worked near the North and South Poles, and its staff ranged from the Atlantic seaboard to the Pacific islands. After World War II, Director Wrather launched the largest exploration in the Survey's history as scientists began drilling for uranium ore on the Colorado plateau, which soon became the center for the nation's production of that metal. In 1960, during Nolan's directorship, the Survey established an astro-geology program to map the surface of the moon. After the Alaskan earthquake on Good Friday, 1964, Survey scientists showed their understanding of this event in some twenty-eight papers or articles; clearly, they were looking for data and methods to predict this type of catastrophe. An interest common to both directorships was engineering geology, wherein geologists advised civil engineers about geological formations and processes that affected the stability of building sites or offered hazards to them. Bedrock, landslides, and mud flows are the subjects of this recent branch of geoscience.

Statements by these two later directors showed a confidence and candor, which reflected, no doubt, the increasing importance and strength of the natural sciences in the government and the nation. Every year they communicated new discoveries in minerals and other natural resources, and they knew that miners and prospectors consulted Survey publications all the time. They said without hesitation that taking inventory of natural resources was a recurring task; that programs must be long-term; that immediate returns were not likely to occur; that the distant future must be attended to as well as the ongoing present; and, finally, that scientific research led to discoveries with practical results only when accompanied by the interplay of curiosity and chance.

A consciousness of the increasing force and effectiveness of geology's affiliated sciences informed the purposes of these two men. In 1948, Director Wrather announced a program in radioactive age determination, one part of which would be the measurement of the isotopic variation of lead in nature and the finding thereby of better dates for geological materials, and improved correlation of worldwide geological events. Wrather also promised the expansion of a Survey unit to study trace elements. Geologists had been learning through more refined chemical analysis to identify minute quantities of metallic elements, which aggregate sometimes as halos near ore bodies, or migrate into nearby water, vegetation, and soil. From such traces, said Director Nolan, prospectors could move back, even several miles, to the ore body they sought. Both leaders wrote continually about several kinds of geophysical surveys, strengthened now by new instrumentation. Magnetic surveys depended heavily upon the magnetometer, a World War II invention of the Geological Survey and the Naval Ordnance Laboratory. According to Director Wrather, this instrument, when airborne, took in iron ranges, lead mineralization, atolls, volcanic phenomena, and buried igneous materials. Earth resistivity surveys used an electric current to probe layers of rock and other materials for ore bodies, ground water, and gravel deposits—all concealed. Geothermal surveys measured heat flow, and there were also radioactive, gravitational and seismic surveys. In 1964, Director Nolan cited another technical trend: the use of the computer for retrieving and analyzing data. Using technology, yet also trying to curb its effects, during Nolan's regime the Survey began assuming more responsibility for the quality of the natural environment.

The eighth director, William T. Pecora (1965-1971), is remembered for his success in urging surveys by satellite through remote-sensing Landsat. Pecora's successor, V. E. McKelvey (1971-1978), worked hard for the conservation division, which had—and still has—the serious task of supervising oil and gas exploitation on the continental margins of the Atlantic, Pacific, and Arctic oceans.

FOR ADDITIONAL INFORMATION: Thomas G. Manning, *Government in Science: The U.S. Geological Survey, 1867-1894* (1967); John C. Rabbitt and Mary C. Rabbitt, "The U.S. Geological Survey: 75 Years of Service to the Nation, 1879-1954," *Science* 119 (1954); and F. L. Ransome, "Historical Review of Geology as Related to Western Mining," *Ore Deposits of the Western States* (1933); Annual Reports of the USGS.

THOMAS G. MANNING

UNITED STATES INFORMATION AGENCY (USIA). During both World War I and World War II, the United States attempted to bolster morale through propaganda. The well-learned lessons of wartime later stimulated both informational and cultural overseas activities sponsored by the federal government. The Office of War Information* (OWI) carried out the propaganda functions during 1941-1946, while the Department of State* conducted the duties as the Cold War developed right after World War II. A movement for independent status culminated in the establishment in 1953 of the United States Information Agency (USIA), which in 1978 was renamed the International Communication Agency (ICA), and, early in 1983, changed back to USIA. From the wartime beginning, its overseas operations were called the United States Information Service (USIS).

In 1946, OWI left to State information staffs at seventy-six overseas missions, a daily, 7,000-word wireless bulletin to forty locations; a motion picture service in twenty-four languages; sixty-seven information libraries; a Russian-language magazine called *America* with a circulation of 50,000; twenty-six cultural centers with forty-five branches; and the popular Voice of America (VOA) radio service, begun in 1942, which then operated via thirty-six transmitters in twenty-five languages. At its peak in World War II, the VOA used forty languages. Perhaps the most important aspect of the total USIA program, the VOA's policy stressed using both favorable and unfavorable news, stating clearly U.S. policy and arguing for it, and placing on the air only those news items it could gain from a minimum of two independent sources.

Despite its earlier promises, VOA unveiled an overriding theme of anticommunism, but Congress passed Public Law 402 in 1947, which again stressed the VOA and total informational programs as providing a better understanding of

America, telling the truth and explaining our motives, presenting a clear picture of American life, bolstering the morale of foreign population, while supporting American foreign policy and selling America. The reader will readily discern the incongruity of these goals. For example, what stance should be assumed when two friends, India and Pakistan, start a war? How do you explain the Russians shooting down our famous U-2 spy plane?

VOA came to be envied by various Soviet authorities, much as the American GIs preferred the German Axis Sally broadcasts in Europe during World War II to the colorless offerings of the BBC. The Peoples' Republic of China authorities also monitored VOA. But the Soviet Union quickly reacted to VOA influence in 1948 by inaugurating a massive and expensive attempt to jam its broadcasts, especially those in foreign languages. One immediate cause of the jamming was the reporting of Mrs. Anna Kasenkina's leap for freedom from the Russian Consulate in New York City.

Although Secretary of State Cordell Hull apparently paid little heed to the OWI, by the end of the war this thriving organization employed approximately 13,000 persons with a budget of $70 million. The United States was the last major power to assume governmental broadcasting (VOA) on a permanent basis.

William Benton supervised the successor to OWI, now named the Office of International Information (OII), within the Department of State. He stressed the need to emphasize the truth. In 1948, the informational duties were retained by the OII, while cultural exchanges became the domain of the new (also in State) Office of Educational Exchange. Following drastic postwar budget cuts, the appropriation figures stood at $24 million in 1948, $33 million in 1949, $47 million in 1950, and, because of the Korean War, $120 million in 1951. Personnel rose from 2,500 in 1948 to 4,370 in 1951.

By midcentury, the propaganda wing of State had definitely become a political football. The first Hoover Commission* had offered a compromise over the heated debate as to whether to move the activities into an independent agency. Though ideal to separate it from State, the commission suggested naming a general manager for the informational and exchange programs. State then organized the International Information Administration in 1952.

Nevertheless, in 1953 Congress separated the entire program from State by creating the United States Information Agency. One extremely awkward administrative decision at the time continued to plague USIA and ICA to date. Control and assignment of exchange persons remained in State, even though USIA was designated to administer this program overseas. The independent status undoubtedly proved to be a wise move, because Congress, amidst all of its bickering with State during 1951-1952 over anticommunism, had slashed the fiscal 1952 budget to $85 million and personnel by approximately 25 percent.

Just as OWI and State leaders could imbue their emphases on the programs, often the subsequent USIA directors guided the volatile organization in various directions. Theodore Steibert, a former New York radio executive, became the initial director in 1953 and strenuously moved to increase the number of VOA transmitters on the air in an effort to become as competent as the BBC. Arthur Larson, a labor law expert and former speech writer for President Dwight D. Eisenhower, served for one year in 1956 and was included in regular sittings of the National Security Council.* George V. Allen, career diplomat and lawyer, served during 1957-1960 and persistently urged increases in the areas of teaching English abroad, translation of American books, English broadcasts by VOA, participation of Americans in foreign trade fairs, and partaking of American experts (business and professional) lecturing and visiting their counterparts overseas. Abbott Washburn, as deputy director, capably administered daily operations under all three directors.

Under President John F. Kennedy, the extremely popular and effective Edward R. Murrow, famous for his wartime broadcasts and twenty-five years with the Columbia Broadcasting System (CBS), directed USIA. His major accomplishment included gaining regular contacts between the White House and USIA and relating better our media programs to foreign policy. Because of failing health, Murrow later delegated a large portion of the duties to his deputy, Donald W. Wilson, a veteran of eleven years with *Life*, who at the outset of their regime, handled most of the intra-agency doings. On February 28, 1964, Carl T. Rowan became director under President Lyndon B. Johnson. Former Deputy Assistant Secretary of State, ambassador to Finland, an author, and a newspaper reporter, Rowan managed to continue the cordial agency relations with the President before resigning in the summer of 1964. Leonard Marks, LBJ's radio lawyer, then became director (1965-1968) and Robert Akers his deputy. Marks had been Time-Life International general manager and soon quietly and effectively instigated better control of media programming under Akers, tailoring the cultural thrust to individual posts abroad. For example, USIA no longer persisted in preaching about the United States in Berlin and Vietnam to individual Third World nations which might be uninterested.

Through these early directors, by the late 1960s the USIA had appreciably strengthened its role among these foreign affairs organizations: the Departments of Defense* and State, and the Agency for International Development.* In 1966, President Johnson announced the establishment of a coordinating system, the Senior Interdepartmental Group, to be chaired by the capable Undersecretary of State George Ball. Ball held regular meetings, but his successors did not always do so.

Meanwhile, other key developments highlighted the important 1960s. A perennial fight on policy between USIA and VOA apparently disgruntled at least three veteran broadcasters who directed VOA. Henry Loomis, after seven years at the helm, resigned in 1965. He was succeeded, in turn, by John Chancellor (1966-1967), and John Daly (1967-1968), both of whom complained of the same interference. Nevertheless, VOA improved and streamlined its offerings, for example, increasing the broadcasts of the popular American jazz complete with slang and interpretive notes, a magazine, and jazz clubs—1,600 of them, 709 in Europe in 1967 including 31 in Communist Czechoslovakia. American forums were begun, discussing issues, for example, urban development, news, music, and comedy. Chancellor substituted the theme music of "Yankee Doodle" for "Columbia, the Gem of the Ocean." Also presented were excerpts from summer music festivals, opera, symphony and orchestra concerts, church music, and music saluting American composers. VOA, in recording sixty-three programs simultaneously, reportedly could reach about 70 percent of the world's population and was heard by an average of 42 to 43 million listeners each week. VOA estimated that the USIA staff reviewed about 10 percent of all material before each broadcast.

The jamming of VOA programs continued sporadically. The Soviets discontinued it during Premier Nikita Khrushchev's American visit in 1959 but resumed this interference until 1963 when Romania also quit it. Russia jammed VOA in 1968 during the crisis in Czechoslovakia but generally has not done so since except briefly during unrest. The Polish crisis in 1980 marked its first interference in seven years against VOA, BBC, and West Germany's Deutsche Welle. Ironically, in 1967, Svetlana Stalin requested that VOA inform the Russians of her successful defection into Switzerland.

Budget-wise, the USIA's overall programs rebounded enough to gain $173 million in 1967 with 10,512 on the payroll, over 50 percent of whom were non-Americans hired locally overseas. Another 3,500 were American citizens working at headquarters in Washington, D.C. Over 200 libraries and reading rooms in eighty-three countries held 1.9 million books and were visited by 23 million persons a year. One-fourth of the books were in local languages. In addition, sixty-six magazines existed in twenty-seven languages, while a 10,000-word radio transmission carried material six times every week. VOA used 19 million watts of power to broadcast 932 hours weekly in thirty-seven languages. Films to millions of viewers went to approximately 2,000 television stations in over ninety countries.

The Richard Nixon Administration brought an abrupt change in philosophy at the top in the leadership of Director Frank Shakespeare (1969-1972), a former executive at CBS and a conservative. Shakespeare apparently had to deal with Security Adviser Henry A. Kissinger and Secretary of State William P. Rogers instead of directly with Nixon. He was scored by the American press for being far more anti-Communist than Nixon's administration and for not coordinating policy with the State Department. James Keogh, former executive editor of *Time*, became director in 1972, focusing his attention on USIA's efforts to increase trade and tourism for the United States.

By the mid-1970s, the USIA operations flourished again in a more balanced manner in both policy and effectiveness. Its 1972 budget of $251.8 million constituted 1 percent of the U.S. annual budget compared with almost 2 percent for Egypt and approximately 9 percent each for both France and West Germany in their propaganda efforts. However, experts cautioned that, considering inflation, the dollar value of its appropriations for 1973 just equaled the 1954 total of $84 million. In a sheer flair for the spectacular, USIA changed its address for the coming U.S.A. bicentennial from 1778 to 1776 Pennsylvania Avenue. VOA, still attempting to rival BBC, accounted for almost one-fourth of the entire USIA expenditures.

The largest portions of USIS spending in 1973 were incurred in Japan, with West Germany second. In 1975, fifteen new positions were slated for inaugurating operations in East Germany and increasing them in the People's Republic of China, bringing the total personnel in Communist nations to thirty. Overseas, non-U.S. citizens employed by the USIA may emigrate to the United States after fifteen continuous years with the agency; they ranged in totals (1973) from 1 each in Barbados, Ruanda, and Switzerland, to 494 in India.

Violence against the United States overseas, begun earlier, continued to plague USIS installations after the early 1970s, sometimes ending in death or injury. For example, USIS Director Alfred A. Laun III was kidnapped at Cordoba, Argentina, but he recovered and returned to his post; a hand grenade exploded at the USIS office in Asmara, Ethiopia; a warehouse was momentarily seized in Laos; headquarters were stoned in Nigeria; two aides were captured but later released at Beirut, Lebanon; Charles Jones, with USIA in Iran, was held captive in the famous detention of American officials in Tehran, Iran (1979-1980). In March 1982, a student visitor at the mission in Pusan, South Korea, was killed in a fire started by a group of arsonist youths who poured gasoline on the floor and ignited it. Officials in Taiwan broke up a plot to kidnap the USIS director in Taipei and blow up American buildings.

The usual friction and name-calling persisted with the USSR. The Soviets denied that they slowed the visa application until too late for an American reporter to attend a book fair; Andrei Gromyko, in 1980, charged the VOA with provocative and instigatory broadcasts interfering with Polish affairs; and, in 1982, the Russians ridiculed as dull and subversive our television special domestic production on the Polish Solidarity Front. Once on another occasion the Soviets actually complimented our VOA as more objective than Canada's broadcasts (1975).

Whether guilty or innocent, USIA activities occasionally drew foreign and U.S. internal criticism for Central Intelligence Agency* involvement. The most blistering and continuing attack pertained to our manipulations over the Allende regime in Chile ending in 1973. Zambia expelled our director for alleged CIA activities in 1981.

In 1953, the USIA commissioned a study to find out the operating assumptions that guided the agency. Completed in 1954, the twenty-two-page report, based on 174 interviews, was rejected by USIA leadership because the quotes were not attributed to specific persons and no percentage data indicated exact agreement or disagreement with agency policies. The report, published twenty-two years later, clearly indicated the existing confusion: susceptibility to external pressures, especially with Congress, maneuvering for a favorable position in relation to other agencies, constant preoccupation with budget concerns which subordinated program needs, and conflicts of interests among cooperating divisions within the agency. Relatively new, the agency in 1954 contained a rare mix of foreign service officers, media specialists, and linguists, all of whom were difficult to squeeze into the conventional hierarchy of civil service.

The infamous late Senator Joseph McCarthy, Republican from Wisconsin, particularly slashed morale and damaged the agency. He sent his hatchet men, G. David Schine and Roy Cohn, to Europe to investigate USIS centers, whose personnel became panicky. Books were burned, personnel fired, and McCarthyism led directly to significant budget cuts. USIS also feared the many visits of Senator Allen J. Ellender, Democrat of Louisiana. Congress demanded excessive publicity on U.S. foreign aid, scorned USIS art exhibits, and pressured against the use of Communist contacts. Numerous employees wondered how they could fight communism on the one hand and yet attempt to reflect objectivity on the other.

During 1963-1968, another massive set of interviews was conducted on the USIA. Experts believed it took until 1968 to recover from the McCarthy attacks which allegedly sought Communists and sexual perverts, and even then, USIA excessively argued the cause of the United States versus the USSR. For years Congress also turned a deaf ear to pleas for a career service.

Other investigators discerned additional problems. For example, lack of continuity among directors plagued the agency: there were seven directors in the first sixteen years. In the field, a country public affairs officer, press attaché, or information officer often left several months before the replacement arrived. Continuity annd local contacts were lost. In Thailand, considered one of our best programs by one evaluator, the mission had to endure four investigations during 1966-1969 by Senator J. William Fulbright (Democrat, Arkansas). During the Vietnam struggle, liberals in Asia worried that the United States might withdraw, and they criticized us for not saying what we might do. The program (1969) in Iran drew great praise for our cultural efforts there. VOA broadcasts to the People's Republic of China brought up the question of using pure Mandarin Chinese, although the majority of Chinese speak a corrupted form of Mandarin or another type of Chinese, the Cantonese.

Pressures from within USIA and State persisted; VOA at times considered other USIA interference worse than from State. The State Department, through its ambassadors (who wanted the United States to be liked), could exert tremendous pressure on USIA policy in the field. One former ambassador to Pakistan and lawyer in State would abolish USIA and let private firms carry out the informational duties; he believed that USIS was hated abroad as badly as the CIA. Informational and cultural experts fought within State and the USIA.

Internal discord among U.S. officials included the U.S. Embassy in Tel Aviv which prevented VOA's Charles Weiss, in 1976, from using a new contact, a Palestine Liberation Organization official in Cyprus. In the same year our ambassador to Uruguay, Ernest Siracusa, denounced the VOA broadcast about torture there as full of exaggerations and distortions. U.S. diplomats in Cuba have emphatically opposed President Ronald Reagan's plan to establish a separate radio station, MARTI, for propaganda against Fidel Castro. It is hoped that the Senate Foreign Relations Committee's cool reception of the idea will kill it. Castro vowed he would jam the station, which would hurt other U.S. stations on the same frequency.

One journalist has pointed out how easy it is to miss a golden opportunity to impress the foreign press and the public. Gathered in 1969 at the Normandy Beachhead for the twenty-fifth anniversary of the invasion, twenty-two correspondents noticed that the USIA had failed to cover the event. Finally, several of those reporters attending carried the news back to a French newspaper.

Not all congressmen have reacted adversely to the USIA. Senator Jacob Javits (Republican, New York) wondered why we could spend $47 billion a year on defense but only $130 million on the war of ideas. Congressman Dante B. Fascell (Democrat, Florida), chairman of a House subcommittee report on international groups in the late 1960s, lauded the USIA and its potential to combat the negative foreign image of the United States as a violent, racist, crime-ridden society also plagued by the war in Vietnam. The Fascell Committee discovered a still strong pro-U.S. sentiment in the world, which could be nurtured by careful definition and implementation of goals within the USIA.

By 1975, another form of criticism, this one involving technology, emerged. For example, 94 percent of VOA broadcasts were then via shortwave, but one-half of the world's radio receivers did not have shortwave, many in the Communist and poorer nations. Perhaps increased medium-wave transmission will be necessary. Television and satellite transmission might prove of greater importance, but many of the emerging nations had nationally controlled television, for example, Zanzibar.

In South Africa, USIS officials rallied to the defense of a colleague, who accompanied American black poet Michael Harper to a reading at one of the schools, and to the support of a U.S. commercial attaché's wife, who participated in a protest there. Spying entered the scene in 1978 as the Federal Bureau of Investigation* arrested one USIA official and a Vietnamese citizen living there. Convictions and jail terms resulted.

ICA and its predecessors approached the thirtieth anniversary of independent existence facing the perennial issue: how to remain objective and yet please Congress, the military, and foreign nations, and at the same time receive adequate funds to conduct varied programs of both an informational and cultural nature. On balance, a perusal of the documents and literature on this agency suggests that its record, basically sound, probably rates equally with those propaganda antics of its friends and supposed foes. Its successful future rests heavily on cooperation, not antagonism, from within the federal hierarchy as well as on the best available personnel and leadership.

FOR ADDITIONAL INFORMATION: The researcher will find a voluminous amount of congressional and other federal documents on the USIA—hearings, Annual Reports, special investigations, and USIA's own records. The most detailed secondary literature is on the period through the 1960s. Interpretative accounts include Leo Bogart, *Premises for Propaganda, The United States Information Agency's Operating Assumptions in the Cold War* (1976), which concentrates on numerous interviews conducted at the end of 1953 and early 1954; Robert E. Elder, *The Information Machine: The United States Information Agency and American Foreign Policy* (1968), a thorough, fair, and penetrating analysis, which uses interviews over the period of 1963-1967; John W. Henderson, *The United States Information Agency* (1969), also full of critiques and one of the very best of the Praeger series on U.S. agencies; and Edward L. Bernays and Burnet Hershey, eds., *The Case for Reappraisal of U.S. Overseas Information Policies and Programs* (1970), a provocative collection of essays from governmental and outside critics as of 1969. Of the other articles and books mentioning the USIA, the best single citation is in John H. Esterline and Robert B. Black, *Inside Foreign Policy: The Department of State Political System and Its Subsystems* (1975), Chapters 5-7, evaluating the performance of USIA within our total policy, the USIA in Washington, D.C., and overseas functions.

DONALD R. WHITNAH

UNITED STATES INTERNATIONAL TRADE COMMISSION. The United States International Trade Commission has existed under its present title only since 1975 when it succeeded the United States Tariff Commission. Congress decided to transform the tariff commission into an international trade commission in an effort to increase the agency's independence from the executive branch and its effectiveness in defining the nation's trade relationships. From its earliest days, the commission has been at the heart of a heated controversy over whether the nation should pursue a protectionist policy or a free-trade approach. This controversy had existed long before the Tariff Commission was created as an attempt to relieve some of the political and ideological emotionalism that surrounded the development and implementation of the nation's foreign trade policies.

Early attempts to establish nonpartisan tariff boards or commissions proved to be short-lived and unsatisfactory. The Progressive reform sentiments that swept the nation early in the twentieth century made the commission mechanism both popular and possible. A major Progressive goal was to take complex technical questions out of the hands of uninformed politicians and turn them over to panels of experts. They had already revived and strengthened the Interstate Commerce Commission,* developed the Federal Reserve System,* and created the Federal Trade Commission.* A tariff commission was viewed as the final agency needed to regulate the nation's affairs wisely and apolitically. As the last of the four to be created, the Tariff Commission in many ways also remained the least effective of the four.

President Woodrow Wilson asked Congress to create a tariff commission in February 1916. Bolstered by the support of such divergent groups as the American Federation of Labor, the United States Chamber of Commerce, and a dedicated Tariff Commission League, the Progressives drafted legislation that was signed in September. The commission's chief duty was to provide Congress with all sorts of trade information and statistics to help individual senators and representatives make rational decisions regarding tariff revisions.

The commission was to have no particular partisan or ideological bent. To that end, the legislation authorized the President to appoint six commissioners, no more than three of whom could be members of the same political party. Because the Republicans had traditionally favored high protective rates and the Democrats lower tariffs, it was hoped that this provision would produce a balanced, independent, and unbiased agency. Unfortunately, the commission's experience over the succeeding years has shown that the party restriction has not had the desired result. The rules have never been changed, however, and the commission is still unique in the federal structure in that it must, by law, never have a majority of members from any one political party.

The commission got off to a slow start because the United States entered World War I just one week after it commenced operations. In its first years, it confined its attention to data gathering; it had no direct input on rate-setting decisions. For the first time, the United States was systematically collecting and compiling exhaustive statistics about imports, exports, revenue trends, and a number of related topics. The commission gradually accumulated the evidence essential either to support or undermine the contentions of the protectionists and the free traders who had been debating trade policy for decades without really knowing the effects of their decisions. Consequently, the commission was fully prepared to provide Congress with information when President Warren G. Harding urged it to consider revisions of the U.S. tariff structure in 1921. The degree to which this information was read or understood is doubtful, however, since the resulting Fordney-McCumber Tariff Act of 1922 resembled nothing so much as a reversion to the standard protectionist tariff schedules that had prevailed since the Civil War.

One supposed advantage of the new legislation, however, was that it included provisions for a "flexible" tariff. The Tariff Commission was authorized to investigate the effects of the new rates. If it found any of them to be inconsistent with the costs of production in the United States and abroad, it could recommend to the President that the rates be raised or lowered as much as 50 percent on particular commodities. The two major functions that the commission has consistently performed throughout its existence had thus been established. The present-day commission is still engaged in collecting and compiling all sorts of trade data, and it still conducts investigations of particular tariff rates in order to assess their impact.

Whereas the commission's data-gathering activities had provoked little concern, its flexible-tariff investigations aroused considerable controversy. At no time in its history was the Tariff Commission the subject of more debate, discussion, and criticism than in the 1920s. One area of concern which still figures in the commission's operations is that the investigatory process takes so much time. The commission holds lengthy hearings, seeks out expert witnesses, and examines all types of data before concluding whether a particular rate should be adjusted up or down.

Much more important than the time factor in the 1920s was the politicization of the commission. The notorious sugar case revealed that the President himself was deliberately intruding directly into the commission's operations. The tariff on sugar produced from one-fourth to one-third of all the revenue generated under the Fordney-McCumber Act. Congress had set it high in response to pressures from the sugar-growing regions, and the Tariff Commission began investigating the rate in March 1923. President Harding had just filled a vacancy on the commission with a conservative Democrat from Louisiana named Henry G. Glassie. Because his wife's family grew and processed sugar, it was expected that Glassie would remove himself from the commission's investigation. When he did not, other commissioners requested Calvin Coolidge to order him to stand aside. The President staunchly defended Glassie's refusal to do so. The discontented commissioners then appealed to Congress, which did pass special legislation to prevent Glassie from voting. The commission could then recommend, on a 3 to 2 vote, that the sugar tariff be reduced by 40 percent. President Coolidge sat on this recommendation for more than a year before rejecting it summarily. Hoping to avoid such problems in the future, he carefully selected new commissioners who shared his own ultraconservative philosophy.

Both Democratic and Republican Progressives who had agreed to high rates in 1922 only because they felt the commission would be able to modify them were furious with Coolidge. The Senate created a special committee to examine the politicization of the commission. Progressive Senator Robert La Follette led the congressional attack on the administration, keeping the commission at the center of public attention. Some suggested that the commission be abolished altogether, but most felt that, with certain modifications, it might yet function effectively and usefully. When the Smoot-Hawley Tariff Act passed in 1930, it contained provisions that slightly revised the commission's investigative duties. Furthermore, it canceled the terms of all the sitting commissioners and altered the length of future terms from twelve years to six. President Herbert Hoover had lobbied hard to save the commission because he needed it to counter the widespread criticism of the high rates in the new law. The commission would continue to have the authority to adjust rates as it had under the flexible-tariff provision.

The cumbersome and time-consuming nature of the investigations which the commission conducted made it doubtful that it could have altered the Smoot-Hawley Tariff in any significant way even if the world's economy had not collapsed in the early 1930s. The wholesale decline in world trade that accompanied the international depression made the consideration of particular tariff rates irrelevant. A whole new trade structure needed to be created. President Franklin D. Roosevelt faced this crisis squarely by calling for the negotiation of reciprocal trade agreements. In 1934, Congress granted the President authorization to carry out bilateral negotiations with other nations aimed at reducing barriers to trade. The minor adjustments possible under the flexible-tariff procedures were of no significance in the face of these general, broad-ranging reductions.

The tariff commissioners and their staff proved highly useful in the ensuing negotiations, however. Their experience and the data they had collected were extraordinarily helpful in developing a new set of trade relationships through the reciprocity process. Individual commissioners and staff members participated directly on the negotiating teams on an equal basis with State* and Treasury Department officials. The commission's data-gathering activities remained important, but now the commissioners had a much more direct role in tariff-setting than ever before. The incorporation of commission members into the executive branch was even more comprehensive once the United States entered World War II.

As that conflict drew to a close, statesmen considered the wisdom of developing a common trade policy for all the members of the United Nations. The bilateral, reciprocal trade agreements the United States instituted beginning in 1934 had far-reaching effects due to the inclusion of most-favored-nation provisions in the various trade agreements. Concessions made to one country were thereby extended to all regular trading partners. Multinational negotiation was the next logical step. The Tariff Commission again participated actively in the exhaustive round of discussions that produced the General Agreement on Tariffs and Trade (GATT) in 1947.

The GATT included within it an "escape clause" permitting individual countries to withdraw negotiated concessions if they either injured or might injure domestic producers. The Tariff Commission was the natural choice to conduct escape-clause investigations for the United States. From 1947 on, the commission has continually been responsible for looking into charges that particular tariff rates may be injuring American producers.

The year 1948 proved to be a milestone for the Tariff Commission. The Eightieth Congress was particularly wary of President Harry Truman, so it altered the commission's role considerably. Since 1934, commissioners and staffers had routinely served as members of trade negotiation teams. Congress now specifically forbade this practice, intending to make the commission completely independent of the executive branch. This move resembled the 1930 legislation in that Congress was once again concerned about the President's influence on what was supposed to be an independent agency. Even though the explicit prohibition was shortly revoked, then passed and revoked yet again, the commissioners have generally abided by the spirit of this congressional directive ever since. Commission members do not participate directly in the setting of tariffs, although they continue to provide the negotiating teams with abundant data and advice. They have become increasingly jealous of their independent position in recent years and have tried to avoid falling under the sway of either branch of the federal government.

The 1948 legislation also ordered the commission to review all concessions that the President's negotiators might propose and indicate the points at which the concessions might imperil domestic producers. The "peril point" procedure resembled the escape-clause determinations the commission was already handling except that they were designed to head off possible harm before final agreements had been reached. The peril-point restraint remained in force through much of the 1950s but was dropped in 1962 when President John F. Kennedy convinced Congress to give him an expanded authorization to negotiate new trade agreements. The 1962 legislation ordered the commission to look into the "probable economic effects" of proposed concessions, but no specific peril point was to be designated.

By the early 1970s, serious ideological differences had developed between the executive and legislative branches. Republican President Richard Nixon had assigned the trade negotiations to his Special Trade Representative, and the Democratically controlled Congress intended to define sharply the distinction between the commission's activities and those of the executive branch. The agency's new name, the International Trade Commission, symbolized its thorough restructuring. The Trade Act of 1974 sought to reinforce the commission's independence. For example, it stipulated that seniority alone, rather than a presidential appointment, would determine who should be chairman of the commission. Commissioners' terms were extended to nine years. They were never to participate directly in any decision-making on the setting of tariff rates. The legislation granted the commission an independent authorization so that the Office of Management and Budget* could not tamper with its budget requests. In these structural ways, the International Trade Commission had finally achieved the truly independent status it was originally intended to have, insulated from presidential interference at all levels. The complete emancipation of the commission is clearly evident in the 1974 legislation, which allows the commission itself, rather than the President, to apply the remedies for which its investigations call. No longer can a Coolidge delay action on a commission finding and then ignore it without explanation.

Even so, the commission has not necessarily thrived under its new mandate. Political pressures from the White House, Capitol Hill, and the nation's business community have intensified in the face of unfavorable trade balances and import competition. The emotional and political content of the commission's decisions in recent years has kept it controversial and has interfered with its performance.

FOR ADDITIONAL INFORMATION: Little of a historical nature has been published on the commission itself. The only book that examines the development and activities of the agency over time is John M. Dobson, *Two Centuries of Tariffs: The Background and Emergence of the United States International Trade Commission* (1976). Commission activities can best be traced through its Annual Reports which contain descriptive listings of all of its publications. Two books that study the political pressures the commission faced in its early years are Thomas Walker Page, *Making the Tariff in the United States* (1924) and E. E. Schattschneider, *Politics, Pressures and the Tariff* (1935). The switch to the reciprocity approach aroused considerable interest in the 1930s as evidenced by William S. Culbertson, *Reciprocity: A National Policy for Foreign Trade* (1937) and Francis Bowes Sayre, *The Way Forward: The American Trade Agreements Program* (1939). Howard S. Piquet, *Aid, Trade, and the Tariff* (1953) and Don D. Humphrey, *American Imports* (1955) discuss the GATT. Two books relating to recent developments are Ernest H. Preeg, *Traders and Diplomats* (1970) and John W. Evans, *The Kennedy Round in American Trade Policy* (1971).

JOHN M. DOBSON

UNITED STATES MARINE CORPS. The United States Marine Corps, one of the two separate services within the Department of the Navy,* can field combat forces possessing a full range of weaponry from bayonets to nuclear-capable aircraft. The National Security Act of 1947 established the corps' present roles and missions, providing that it be organized, trained, and equipped primarily to provide Fleet Marine Forces (infantry, artillery, and so on, with supporting aviation components) to serve with the fleet and to seize and defend advanced bases. In addition, this act charges the Marine Corps to act in concert with the Navy and Army in order to develop tactics, techniques, and equipment to be employed in amphibious landings on a hostile shore. Miscellaneous provisions within the act give the corps the added mission of providing detachments for service in ships of the United States Navy and ashore at naval stations and bases, to protect naval property, and to perform whatever duties the president of the United States may direct.

A 1952 amendment to the National Security Act assured the organizational structure of the Marine Corps, providing that the corps be organized into not less than three active divisions and air wings. A fourth division and air wing serve as a ready reserve. The Fleet Marine Forces—roughly half of the corps' total strength—thus provided for are balanced, with land and air elements integrated within the Atlantic and Pacific fleets. In addition, the 1952 amendment gave the commandant of the Marine Corps a permanent place on the Joint Chiefs of Staff.

Presently, three active division/wing teams are organized for combat into Marine Amphibious Forces (MAFs): one in the Atlantic and two in the Pacific. These teams, formed into Marine Air Ground Task Forces (MAGTFs) for combat operations, consist of command and control, ground, air, and support elements. They are deployable by sea (in amphibious shipping) or by air (aircraft or helicopter), and the mission assigned and the capability of the opposing forces govern their size.

The three basic types of MAGTFs are the Marine Amphibious Unit, (MAU); the Marine Amphibious Brigade (MAB); and the Marine Amphibious Force (MAF). The MAU is regarded as the smallest (2,700 men) and most responsive of the MAGTFs, and is usually viewed as the forward element of a larger force that can be brought to bear if the situation demands it; MAUs are deployed in the Mediterranean, Western Pacific, and, occasionally, in the North Atlantic region. The MAB is built around a regimental landing team (two to five infantry battalions, and artillery battalion, tank, combat engineer, reconnaissance and amphibious assault vehicle companies—some 15,800 men) and a Marine Aircraft Group (MAG). The MAB can be embarked in sixteen to twenty-one amphibious ships, and is capable of amphibious operations to secure a beachhead and subsequent operations ashore; it may be deployed afloat for an extended period of time to provide an immediate response. The largest and most powerful of the MAGTFs, the MAF, consists of some 51,900 men in a division/wing team capable of a wide range of amphibious operations.

All of the above units are organized for rapid deployment as part of the Navy/ Marine Corps team and, when deployed in a timely fashion, can provide a continuous presence in international waters as well as expand quickly, support themselves, and project varying degrees of combat power ashore. Most recently, the pre-positioning of supplies at strategic points has been projected to support the "Rapid Deployment Force" established as a result of the 1979 Near Eastern crisis.

The corps, established as the "Marine Corps" in 1798, in an act approved by President John Adams, traces its antecedents back to the two battalions of "marines" authorized by the Continental Congress on November 10, 1775, for service in the war with Great Britain. Immediately after the United States had gained her independence, the American armed forces dwindled in size to practically nothing. The ratified Constitution, however, allowed for the buildup of an Army and Navy; with the Navy came the "Marine Corps." The corps came into being on July 11, 1798, and William Ward Burrows became major commandant the following day. The post of "commandant" has remained in existence to this day.

Initially, the Marines existed to police the ship in which they served, to keep order among the polyglot crews. In battle, Marines manned the "fighting tops" providing musket fire to harass enemy cannoneers. In addition, the marine's training as a soldier fitted him eminently to serve in an incipient "expeditionary" capacity in ships' landing parties—the first significant example of this occurring in March 1776 at New Providence, in the Bahamas. Marines were also employed in this capacity, most notably, at Derna, Tripoli, during the Tripolitan War (1801-1805).

Marines served at sea, in seventy ships, during the War of 1812—as they had done during the Quasi-War with France (1799-1800)—and in land campaigns, notably at Bladensburg (1814) and New Orleans (1815). Five years after the last war with Great Britain came to a close with the Treaty of Ghent, Archibald Henderson became commandant (1820). He served in that post until his death on January 6, 1859, introducing high standards of training for his officers and men and fostering the corps' unique *esprit de corps*. During Henderson's commandantcy, Marines not only aided in the suppression of piracy and the slave trade in the West Indies, but also fought Indians (Seminole Wars, 1835-1842) and Mexicans (the Mexican War, 1846-1847), took part in the joint Anglo-American operations against the Chinese (at the Canton Forts, 1856), and performed ceremonial duties with Commodore Matthew C. Perry in Japan (1854). In addition, during Henderson's time as commandant the corps saw its status clearly defined: the "Act for the Better Organization of the Marine Corps" (June 30, 1834) established without doubt that, except when the President of the United States ordered Marine units to cooperate with the Army, the Marine Corps constituted a part of the naval establishment at all times.

During the Civil War, each side, North and South, had Marines. They served primarily in the ships of their respective navies, performed guard duties at naval bases and stations, and took part in an occasional action ashore.

Shortly after the War between the States, Marines began to take on a new duty, foreshadowed by their duty with Perry at the opening of Japan—that of protecting American diplomats abroad. Marine guard detachments were established at Tokyo, Japan (1868), and Seoul, Korea (1888), beginning what has become a two-century tradition of cooperation with the Department of State.*

During that same period, however, the advent of steam propulsion and modern gunnery caused some to question the need for Marine detachments in ships of the fleet, since one function of Marines, doing battle at close quarters as sharp-shooters in the "tops," had been rendered an anachronism. In addition, some Navymen felt that using Marinse as "police" was an affront to the "New Navy" sailor.

The controversy extended into the twentieth century, and a movement developed to get the Marines off the ships and to base them ashore, where they could engage in their "soldierly" pursuits (which some felt duplicated Army missions) to serve as a readily transportable expeditionary force. On numerous occasions, however, shipboard Marine detachments had proved their worth, particularly in situations where civil strife in a far-off land required the presence of armed Marines to protect American lives and property.

Congress assigned the Marine Corps the mission of providing "fleet infantry" to establish and defend advanced bases for the Navy in 1894. The bases extended the range of the fleet in allowing it to move further from its home ports and yards and still be able to coal, provision, and take on water and other vital necessities. The comparative speed with which an expeditionary force of Marines was formed, transported, and landed to take and defend such a position as Guantanamo Bay, Cuba (June, 1898) validated Congress's decision. The War with Spain saw the United States emerge as a world power, and thrust upon it a colonial empire of its own. Around the turn of the century, Marines participated in consolidating that empire (the Philippine Insurrection, 1899-1903) and protecting American diplomats in China (the Boxer Rebellion, 1900).

The Marines, having proved their prowess in combat to their enemies abroad, found it necessary to continue to fight for a part of their mission at home. The controversy over removing Marines from ships of the fleet came to a head during the administration of President Theodore Roosevelt, who succeeded, for a time, in getting the Marines taken off. Roosevelt's successor, President William H. Taft, reversed that decision, and the Marines returned to their shipboard duties in major warships of the fleet, a task they fulfill to this day.

In the years immediately preceding World War I, the Marine Corps participated in a number of "police type" actions in Latin American and Caribbean climes, supporting American foreign policy in the Western Hemisphere. In so doing, they gained valuable experience in counterinsurgency warfare, laying the groundwork for the establishment of units of reinforced infantry that operated integrally with the fleet. In addition, command doctrine to utilize that infantry was formulated.

Japan's emergence as a world power following its defeat of Russia (1906) caused many to fear its expansion in the Far East and western Pacific. Nevertheless, World War I brought a temporary shift in thinking from Pacific to Atlantic. A swiftly mobilized Marine brigade deployed overseas for service in France and distinguished itself in combat, earning the respect of its enemies, who dubbed them *"Teufel Hunden,"* or "Devil Dogs." The war also saw the establishment of Marine air components that operated on the Western Front (the Northern Day Bombing Group) and in the Azores.

After the Armistice, Marines took part in the occupation of Germany before returning home to "peacetime" duties. World War I had proved that the corps could function successfully on a European battlefront. The changes wrought by the war, however, in terms of the expansion of the service, brought about a significant change. Heretofore, the commmandant, assisted by a handful of aides, administered the corps' programs. The number of men in the corps had grown from 27,495 (June 1917) to 75,101 (December 1918) and had rendered that system obsolete and inadequate. On December 1, 1920, during the commandantcy of Major General John A. Lejeune, the staff system was established, allowing for better administration and coordination of the activities of the post-World War I Marine Corps.

In 1921, the Advanced Base Force was established at Philadelphia in keeping with the corps' mission, this was later broken down (1923) into East-and West-Coast Expeditionary Forces. A decade later (1933), the newly established Fleet Marine Force embraced those two forces, the forerunners of the modern Fleet Marine Force, Atlantic, and Fleet Marine Force, Pacific. The Marine Corps schools and training programs established in the wake of the world war allowed the corps to concentrate almost single-mindedly on the development of amphibious-assault techniques and the fortifying of advanced bases. Not about to rest on their laurels won on the battlefields of France, the Marines spent the decades of the 1920s and 1930s perfecting the tactics they would test on Pacific shores during World War II.

Also during that time, the Marines continued to support American foreign policy in such areas as Haiti, the Dominican Republic, and Nicaragua, learning new tactics in counterinsurgency warfare, air support, casualty evacuation, and the like. They also protected American lives and property in China during the Chinese Civil War (1927) and Sino-Japanese hostilities at Shanghai (1931 and 1937).

The Marines' unique status, as a force that could be used as the President would direct, enabled it to carry out the occupation of Iceland (1941), a landing that proved to be the corps' last before the United States actually entered World War II. The Japanese' simultaneous attack on American, British, and Dutch colonial outposts and possessions in the Far East and Western Pacific in December 1941 found Marines on duty from the Philippines to Pearl Harbor. Although overwhelmed at Guam and Wake (December 1941), and Corregidor (May 1942), Marines participated in the epic defense of Midway (June 1942) and carried out the first major assault landing of the Pacific campaign, at Guadalcanal (August 7, 1942).

Marines figured prominently in the Pacific theater, in a succession of landings: the Solomons (1942-1943); Russells, Tarawa, and Cape Gloucester (1943); the Marshalls, Marianas and Pelews (1944); and Iwo Jima and Okinawa (1945). During World War II, the number of Marines (including women and, for the first time, blacks) grew to a peak strength of 485,053 by V-J Day (August 15, 1945), in six divisions, five air wings, and support forces of every description. Aviation had assumed a major role, and Marines continued to develop tactics and weaponry to meet the challenge. Among the equipment tested in the crucible of war was the amphibian tractor. The concept of "combat unit loading" (the items needed first on the beachhead being loaded last to allow quick off-loading) and tactical units such as the shore-party battalion to expedite the unloading of vital supplies on the beach were also adopted. After World War II, Marines spearheaded the occupation forces in Japan and China, remaining committed to such duties until 1946 and 1949, respectively.

Although the Marine Corps, as the other services, saw its ranks thinned by demobilization after V-J Day, it responded decisively when duty called in the Korean War. In response to General Douglas MacArthur's request for a regimental combat team to assist in the defense of South Korea, the First Provisional Marine Brigade was activated and on its way to the Far East within two weeks' time. Subsequently, a requested Marine Division was formed and entered the fray in a daring landing at Inchon, North Korea, on September 15, 1950. This landing demonstrated that the division-sized amphibious assault was not a thing of the past.

The Korean War proved the testing-ground for the concept of "vertical envelopment" developed at Quantico in 1947. The employment of the helicopter in reconnaissance, supply, transport, communication, and casualty-evacuation functions foreshadowed an even wider use of this type of craft in the future. In addition, the Korean War proved again the qualities of close air support for ground troops, a tactic particularly refined by Marine aviation units during World War II.

In the late 1950s and early 1960s, the Marine Corps' standard of readiness enabled its quick response during a crisis in Lebanon (1958) and in the tense days of the Cuban Missile Crisis (1962). In addition, Marines helped protect and evacuate Americans caught in Santo Domingo, Dominican Republic, in 1965.

That same year, 1965, witnessed the commitment of the Ninth Marine Expeditionary (later, Amphibious) Brigade to South Vietnam in early March, the beginning of large-scale Marine involvement in the Vietnam War. That conflict saw Marines used throughout as mobile forces capable of striking from land, sea, or air, supported by Marine aircraft and other forces, until the withdrawal of American ground forces in 1970-1971, and the subsequent "Vietnamization."

After the Vietnam War, Marines still found employment in crisis situations. When a coup threw the island of Cyprus into turmoil and Greek and Turkish forces clashed on that isle, Marines of the Thirty-fourth MAU evacuated American citizens and foreign nationals (1974). The following year, incident to the fall of the South Vietnamese and Cambodian governments, Marines executed Operations "Eagle Pull" (April 1975) and "Frequent Wind" (May 1975), evacuating American diplomatic personnel from Pnomh Penh, Cambodia, and Saigon, South Vietnam, respectively. Later, Marines from the Thirty-first MAU recaptured the American containership *SS Mayaguez* (May 1975). Four years later, a small detachment of Marine Security Guards at the American Embassy at Islamabad, Pakistan, protected the embassy staff trapped there by a fanatical mob. In addition, during the prolonged Iranian Hostage Crisis (1979-1981), Marines participated in the abortive rescue attempt (April 1980). The last-named crisis spawned the creation of the Rapid Deployment Force (RDF) to enable the United States to react quickly to situations in the Near East. Significantly, the first commanding general of the RDF was a Marine, Lieutenant General P. X. Kelley.

For over two hundred years, the Marine Corps has resisted attempts to strip it of its missions, to amalgamate it into the Army, or to take away its sea-going function aboard major warships of the fleet. It has triumphed over its enemies, both at home and abroad, and zealously defended its assigned mission. With a present strength of 185,000 active-duty Marines and 33,000 reserves, the corps of today provides a force-in-readiness, to perform whatever is required of it.

FOR ADDITIONAL INFORMATION: Perhaps the best institutional history of the United States Marine Corps is that written by Allan R. Millett, *Semper Fidelis: The History of the United States Marine Corps* (1980), which should supersede all other books on the subject. Nevertheless, the general histories by Robert D. Heinl, Jr., *Soldiers of the Sea: The U.S. Marine Corps, 1775-1962* (1962), and Edwin H. Simmons *The United States Marines: The First Two Hundred Years, 1775-1976* (1974), are highly readable, lively accounts. An earlier work by Clyde H. Metcalf, *A History of the United States Marine Corps* (1939), is still valuable, being a good, sound study of the corps. Two official histories very much worth consulting are William D. Parker, *A Concise History of the United States Marine Corps, 1775-1969* (1970), and Kenneth J. Clifford, *Progress and Purpose: A Developmental History of the United States Marine Corps, 1900-1970* (1973).

ROBERT J. CRESSMAN

UNITED STATES MILITARY ACADEMY. The United States Military Academy was founded in 1802 during the second year of President Thomas Jefferson's first administration. The enabling federal statute authorized a corps of engineers of seven officers and ten cadets and directed that they be stationed at West Point, New York, to constitute a military academy. This new organization, with its prime emphasis on military education, replaced the older Corps of Artillerists and Engineers, which had previously garrisoned Fortress West Point.

For some years, the national leadership of the United States had been contemplating such a step. Their experience in the American Revolution with the lack of military engineering and technical skills available among patriot officers had convinced them that a better solution could be found than hiring and commissioning qualified foreign officers. The domestic unrest of the Confederation period, the continuing necessity to mount a military force along the Western frontiers, and the international instability resulting from the French Revolution supported those whose judgment favored a better trained armed force. On the need for a national military academy, George Washington, Thomas Jefferson, John Adams, and Alexander Hamilton were all agreed.

The first superintendent of the new school was Jonathan Williams, a grand-nephew of Benjamin Franklin. He established a curriculum heavy in mathematics and sciences that emphasized practical field surveying and measurement. In addition, Williams founded, and secured Thomas Jefferson's patronage for, an organization known as the United States Military Philosophical Society, established along lines similar to those of the older American Philosophical Society. His purpose was to encourage cadets to continue their studies and scientific inquiries after graduation; he knew that the education provided at West Point did not produce professional artillerymen and engineers of the caliber found in the regular armies of Europe. This experiment ended with the War of 1812 and the assignment of many officers of the fledgling Corps of Engineers* to wartime duties.

A new law of 1812 expanded the Corps of Cadets to 250 and specified their organization into companies. Their military training was to be a three-month annual encampment plus instruction in all the duties of the private soldier and the noncommissioned and commissioned officers. In addition, admission standards were set that required all prospective candidates for cadetship to be competent in reading, writing, and arithmetic. Finally, the legal basis for the Academic Board, composed of the department heads (tenured professors who were the equivalent of department chairmen) with the superintendent as presiding officer, was set forth. This governing body deliberated on passes and failures, recommendations on newly graduating cadets for the various branches of the Army, dismissals of cadets for a variety of reasons, and any matters on which the superintendent might wish their advice.

During the War of 1812, the academy came under the direction of Alden Partridge, later founder of Norwich University. As a military drillmaster and teacher of mathematics and engineering, Partridge was a success. However, his administration of the academy was flawed by his own poor judgment and by personal conflict between Partridge and his professorial colleagues. In 1817, President James Monroe directed that Partridge be replaced by Sylvanus Thayer, an 1807 graduate of Dartmouth College and an 1808 graduate of West Point.

This change was accomplished with no little difficulty. Partridge tried to wrest command of West Point from Thayer, requiring the direct intervention of General Joseph G. Swift, chief of engineers, who had the next immediate responsiblity for oversight of the military academy. Ultimately, Partridge was convicted by a court-martial and was allowed to resign from the Army. His bitterness, extended to everyone associated with West Point, fueled the later criticisms of the academy and its graduates that began in earnest during the Jacksonian era and were echoed for years past the last battles of the Civil War, even into the twentieth century.

Once firmly in charge, Thayer single-mindedly set about making West Point a prominent national institution. The broad outlines of the "Thayer system" continue as the foundation of the educational and pedagogical philosophy of the contemporary academy. In essence, all classroom sections were small enough for daily recitation and grading. The curriculum was prescribed. The cadets were required to develop rigorous study habits as well as an ability to speak and think on one's feet regularly. Competition was encouraged by placement in class sections by order of merit according to grades; resectioning occurred often to account for the effect of frequent marks. Accompanying policies included mandatory weekly attendance at chapel religious services (eliminated by federal court action in the 1970s) and insistence on high standards of appearance, discipline, and personal moral conduct.

Thayer's method was not typical of its day. The emphasis he gave to thorough grounding in mathematics and natural and experimental philosophy, and especially the required study of a modern language, French (rather than classical Latin and Greek), did not become standard practice in American higher education for some years. West point was thus the first American engineering college and, along with the French Ecole Polytechnique, among the first anywhere.

The faculty that came to West Point during the Thayer years played a prominent role in innovative engineering education and in advancing scientific knowledge, in part through their work at West Point but also through widespread contacts with the growing civilian education and scientific community. They were young, energetic men, each of whom had taken charge of an academic department within ten years of his own graduation from West Point. One of them, Dennis Hart Mahan, was the father of the noted naval theorist, Alfred Thayer Mahan. The elder Mahan began the work that eventually evolved into the current required course in the history of the military art and the elective program in the history and theory of warfare.

Sylvanus Thayer departed the military academy because of the intrusion of the Jacksonian "Spoils System" into West Point: a cadet dismissed for indiscipline or academic failure was readily reinstated either as a result of direct appeal to the President or through the intervention of politically important friends. Nevertheless, Thayer's contributions to the educational system at West Point— and to American higher education elsewhere—survived.

Certain characteristic aspects of cadet life began to develop during these early years. With the exception of those who could summon political power to overturn a dismissal, cadets were accorded scrupulously equal treatment. Each received the same pay, wore the same uniforms, lived two or three to similar rooms, and had the same opportunity to excel in studies. Written regulations governed cadet life.

As late as the last years before the War with Mexico, the survival of the military academy appeared questionable to its friends, graduates, and faculty. Sectionalism played a role. Southerners, for example, sometimes felt that West Point was too far away, too far North, too devoted to the national (as opposed to state) interests. Others saw West Point as fostering an undesirable aristocratic tradition. Some felt that the academy should be abolished and that the funds then made available should be devoted to improving the state militia systems. The national need for civil engineers attracted graduates to resign from the Army, a cause of additional criticism. The contribution of West Point during the long Seminole Wars was largely overlooked. The war with Mexico—and the role of officers from West Point in it—provided a respite from the debate. In the following years, the nation was more concerned with westward expansion and the increasingly bitter feeling over slavery than with the affairs of an institution that had proved its value.

Despite pressures that worked to forge unity among the cadets and faculty, the bitter sectional feeling that had developed throughout America was reflected at West Point, as it was in the Army at large. The disparity in academic preparation between Northern and Southern cadets before coming to West Point was but one matter between the two groups that highlighted the differences between the sections; Northern cadets seemed generally better prepared to undertake the rigors of the curriculum. The sectional issues raised by political campaigns were followed with interest and emotion. John Brown's raid electrified people at West Point as it did the rest of the United States. The election of 1860 similarly increased tensions among the faculty and cadets. After the election of Abraham Lincoln to the firing on Fort Sumter, many Southern cadets began to resign and return to their seceding home states, as did many Army officers from the South. The national institution had failed to replace sectional loyalty with national fealty.

Although the course of the Civil War was closely followed at West Point, instruction generally continued as usual, with several classes graduating early to meet the needs of a rapidly expanding Army. Graduates served with distinction in both Union and Confederate armies; they also participated in disasters.

Despite the fact that almost three-fourths of the West Point graduates who were on active military service remained in the Union Army, the controversial debates over the academy were rekindled. Such resignations as had occurred among the cadets and officer corps led to accusations of treasonable teachings at the institution. The critics included Simon Cameron, Secretary of War. Political generals, some of them men of ability, such as John A. Logan, attacked the institution because of a perceived preference for West Pointers in high command in the Union Army. The controversy did not end with Robert E. Lee's surrender; critics continued to speak out during the rest of the nineteenth century, while the academy's defenders tended to overreach themselves in their zeal to prove the value of West Point to the nation.

During the first century of its existence, the academy had flourished as a result of the reforms instituted by Sylvanus Thayer. In the years after the Civil War, however, the faculty assembled by Thayer had grown older and less energetic. They and their successors were no longer innovators in educational method or curricular content. To them the Thayer system had become sacred; the ferment then characteristic of American higher education was resisted by the conservativism that pervaded the permanent faculty. Superintendents came and departed; few were inclined to innovation themselves, and those found themselves relatively helpless in the face of the experience and long tenure of the department heads. The department heads were the only permanent faculty assigned to West Point and thus provided the only continuity through the years. Other faculty members, the instructors, came for relatively brief tours of several years and then returned to Army service in the field. (Gradually, the faculty situation changed in the twentieth century, so that at the present time, permanent faculty, with the academic ranks of associate professor and professor, constitutes 15 percent of some departments.) The reluctance of the Academic Board to change the curriculum caused West Point to lag behind better colleges and universities in teaching engineering and science.

The pressures for change could not be resisted indefinitely; even the most conservative members of the Academic Board realized that the institution had become little more than a school to provide officers for the small peacetime Regular Army. Several factors aided the transition, which was accomplished slowly and undramatically over the course of the twentieth century. The construction of a new physical plant from 1891 onward permitted the laboratory method of teaching science and engineering; physical education took on new life in a modern gymnasium. The permanent faculty of the nineteenth century was gradually replaced by more progressive men. In addition, reform-minded officers assumed the superintendency after each of the major American wars of the twentieth century: Douglas MacArthur after World War I, Maxwell Taylor after World War II, Garrison H. Davidson after Korea, and Andrew J. Goodpaster after Vietnam. To be sure, the prime purpose of West Point remained the education and training of future Regular Army officers, but the education itself was once again of respectable quality.

Largely because the academy believed that fledgling officers should have the same education, coupled with the desire to treat all cadets scrupulously alike in providing a common bonding experience, the curriculum remained prescribed until recently. Each cadet took the same course as his classmates; there were no elective choices until the late 1950s. Once the idea of the prescribed curriculum was abandoned, curricular reform in the last twenty years was sweeping. Cadets in the 1970s were able to concentrate in various disciplines and subject areas through eight elective choices; the prescribed curriculum was shrunk to a core curriculum to make room for the elective offerings. In the early 1980s, an academic majors program was being readied in certain disciplines for those cadets who wished to specialize further.

Military training, always a part of West Point instruction, had not been treated as conservatively as the academic education. As the doctrine, tactics, and weaponry of the Army had changed, the military training of cadets to prepare them for active service had kept pace. Following World War II, cadets began to spend part of their summer military training period away from the academy in junior officer positions with active Army units. They were also permitted to undergo parachute, jungle warfare, and other specialized training while still cadets.

The institution responded to the social currents of the country, though not always successfully. Following the Civil War, the first black cadets were admitted at government direction. Although the academy authorities sought to treat these young men as equal members of the Corps of Cadets, white cadets of the late nineteenth century often exhibited racial prejudices prevalent in many parts of America. In the first half of the twentieth century, only one or two black cadets entered with each class, except for the war years. By the 1970s, however, the number of black cadets graduating with each class became more proportional to the percentage of the black population of the United States as a whole.

In 1976, the first women cadets were admitted. The major adjustment required was in the realm of attitudes; the women lived in rooms adjacent to those of their male cohorts, and certain shower and restroom facilities were set aside for their use. One other concession alone was made: physical conditioning standards were adjusted to compensate for the differences in upper body and physical strength between males and females. Other standards remained the same.

A valued aspect of life at the Military Academy is its honor code: "A cadet will not lie, cheat, or steal, nor tolerate those who do." Developing out of the nineteenth-century officer's code, the honor system came under severe pressure from the midtwentieth century onward. Major cheating scandals in 1951 and 1976 dismayed the institution, ultimately leading to an intensive reexamination of the academy's mission and methods in the late 1970s. This review was conducted by both the staff and faculty and by external groups appointed by the Department of the Army.* The conclusion, reached independently by each and confirmed several years later by the accreditation process, was that the institution was essentially sound, but certain changes and reforms would assist the academy in carrying out its program. West Point is now implementing some of these suggestions. The stagnation characteristic of the last half of the nineteenth century is long gone. Although the U.S. Military Academy still holds to many traditional virtues, it is modern in its most important aspects.

FOR ADDITIONAL INFORMATION: Research material on the academy is most voluminous in the archives of the academy library and in pertinent holdings in the National Archives.* Sidney Forman, *West Point: A History of the United States Military Academy* (1950), is the best single published secondary historical source; the works by Stephen E. Ambrose and Thomas J. Fleming are of limited value. The most comprehensive scholarly historical treatment of the academy is found in four doctoral dissertations: Edgar Denton III, ''The Formative Years of the United States Military Academy'' (Syracuse University, 1964); James L. Morrison, ''The United States Military Academy, 1833-1866: Years of Progress and Turmoil'' (Columbia University, 1970); Walter Scott Dillard, ''The United States Military Academy, 1865-1900: The Uncertain Years'' (University of Washington,

1972); and Roger H. Nye, "The United States Military Academy in an Era of Educational Reform, 1900-1925" (Columbia University, 1969). John P. Lovell, *Neither Athens Nor Sparta? The American Service Academies in Transition* (1979), and Joseph Ellis and Robert Moore, *School for Soldiers: West Point and the Profession of Arms* (1974), provide contemporary appraisals of the modern academy.

WALTER SCOTT DILLARD

UNITED STATES NAVAL ACADEMY. The United States Naval Academy opened at Annapolis, Maryland, on October 10, 1845. From that date until the inauguration of a service-obligated Naval Reserve Officers Training Corps in 1946, it was virtually the sole source of line officers for the Navy, except during the war years 1861-1865, 1898, 1917-1918 and 1941-1945, when the Navy's need of officers far exceeded the number the academy could produce. As of 1980, it has graduated more than 47,000 midshipmen; beginning with the Civil War, 887 have been killed in action or died of wounds; and 27 have won the Medal of Honor, 14 of them posthumously. Even the most summary list of its graduates would comprise a who's who of American naval leaders over the last hundred years, including the four fleet admirals of World War II (King, Leahy, Nimitz, and Halsey), every chief of naval operations and seven commandants of the Marine Corps,* as well as the father of the nuclear Navy, Admiral Hyman Rickover, and the philosopher of sea power, Rear Admiral Alfred Thayer Mahan. Among alumni who have achieved prominence outside the naval service are President Jimmy Carter; Nobel Prize-winning physicist Albert A. Michelson, whose measurements of the speed of light helped provide the foundation for Einstein's theory of relativity; and the Polar explorer, Rear Admiral Richard E. Byrd. Today, the academy contributes approximately 10 percent of the Navy's annual intake of ensigns.

Although John Paul Jones pointed out the desirability of providing for the education of midshipmen as early as 1783, for the first five decades of its existence the United States Navy followed the British practice of relying solely on at-sea apprenticeship for midshipmen, generally aged from twelve to sixteen upon entry. During the War of 1812, Congress authorized the employment of sea-going schoolmasters to give instruction in the Navy's larger ships. In the 1820s and 1830s, eight-month cram courses were established at several shore installations to prepare midshipmen for the examination required for promotion to the rank of lieutenant, but neither of these expedients represented a coherent educational experience.

Between 1814 and 1844, more than twenty bills calling for the establishment of a naval academy were introduced in Congress; none was successful, although two passed the Senate only to die in the House. The objections raised to an academy were three: that it would constitute an unacceptable drain on the public purse; that it would produce a naval aristocracy disdainful of republican institutions; and that the notion of training naval officers at a shore school was absurd.

Repeated rebuffs notwithstanding, Progressives continued to advocate the foundation of an academy, asserting that such an institution was needed to increase both the general culture and the professional competence of the Navy's officers. The introduction of steam propulsion into the Navy in 1839 gave them another argument in favor of technical education, as it was clearly desirable for an officer to have some understanding of the machinery that moved his ship. They also pointed out that the Army had possessed a military academy at West Point* since 1803.

Officer selection and training briefly became the object of national attention in December 1842, when nineteen-year-old Midshipman Philip Spencer, the delinquent son of Secretary of War John C. Spencer, was hanged at the yardarm of the *Somers* for conspiring to mutiny. In the wake of this sensational event, William Chauvenet, a brilliant young Yale graduate in charge of the cram school housed in the Philadelphia Naval Asylum, submitted a plan for establishing a naval academy without reference to Congress. Postulating that, if the Secretary of the Navy had the authority to order midshipmen to attend the school for one year, he must also have the authority to order them for two, Chauvenet proposed concentrating all the midshipmen ashore and the schoolmasters already in service at Philadelphia and developing a comprehensive, two-year curriculum. Secretary of the Navy* David Henshaw approved the plan, but his successor, John Y. Mason, reversed the decision.

Undaunted, in the spring of 1845, Chauvenet resubmitted his plan to a new Secretary, George Bancroft, himself an educator by profession, who proceeded to put it into effect. The only major change Bancroft made was to locate the U.S. Naval School, as it was originally named, at Annapolis, where he persuaded the War Department* to transfer an obsolete Army post, Fort Severn, to the Navy. In August 1845, he directed Commander Franklin Buchanan, whom he had selected to be the school's first superintendent, to begin organizing it.

The school commenced operation in October, with a faculty of seven and a student body of fifty-six. Three of the faculty members, including Chauvenet, were civilians. This civil-military faculty mix, which came into existence simply because the academy descended from the schoolmaster system, has been retained ever since and is one of the features that distinguishes the Naval Academy from the other service academies, where, except for distinguished visiting professors, instruction is conducted solely by military personnel. Today the faculty is almost equally divided between civilian professors, 286 of whom were present at the commencement of the academic year 1980-1981, and officer instructors. The academy is convinced that this combination is ideal to perform its dual mission of education and training.

Initially, newly warranted midshipmen spent their first year in service at Annapolis, after which they were detailed to thirty months' sea duty, returning to the school for a final year of study in preparation for their lieutenants' examinations. In 1850, the curriculum was expanded to four years, still punctuated by sea duty, and the institution was officially renamed the United States Naval Academy. A year later, the academy program assumed its modern form when the decision was made to have the midshipmen spend four consecutive years at the academy and provide them with shipboard experience by means of an annual summer cruise.

The orderly evolution of the academy was disrupted by the outbreak of the Civil War in April 1861. Southern sentiment was strong in tidewater Maryland, and, in view of the troubled conditions in the Annapolis area, the superintendent, Captain George S. Blake, convinced Secretary of the Navy Gideon Welles that the academy should remove to a more tranquil setting. It took up temporary quarters at Newport, Rhode Island, where a lease was taken on the Atlantic House, a resort hotel in the heart of town. At Annapolis, the academy grounds were used as a Union supply depot and, later, a military hospital.

The academy's four years at Newport were probably the most frustrating in its history. Suitable facilities were never obtained, the upper classes were graduated early, and the officer faculty turned over almost annually, so that the plebe (freshman) classes, individually as large as the entire student body had been a few years earlier, lacked both role-models and adequate supervision. Morale, academic standards, and discipline declined.

Fortunately, when the academy returned to Annapolis in October 1865, it was under the dynamic leadership of Rear Admiral David Dixon Porter. During his superintendency, 1865-1869, he established what was almost a new Naval Academy, encouraging the development of athletics and extracurricular activities, fostering school spirit, emphasizing the technical aspects of the curriculum, improving the physical plant by a major construction and acquisition program, and transforming the academy into the showplace it has remained. The only negative feature of his reforms was the elimination of the civilian faculty from the academy's policymaking process, in which it had previously played an important part.

Conditions at the Naval Academy at all times reflect the situation of the Navy, and the effects of the post-Civil War naval decline were strongly felt at Annapolis. Between 1881 and 1887, considerably less than half of the academy's graduates were commissioned to join the shrunken fleet. Despite these grim circumstances, high academic standards were maintained, and, in 1878, the academy was awarded a gold medal by the Paris Universal Exposition for "the best system of education in the United States."

The Spanish-American War of 1898 ushered in a new era at the academy. Although the naval renaissance had begun quietly with the construction of the ABC cruisers in the 1880s, the victories at Manila Bay and Santiago rekindled America's pride in its Navy, while the acquisition of an overseas empire helped clench the country's commitment to sea power. The authorized strength of the student body was doubled, and, between 1898 and 1911, the academy was completely rebuilt in imposing, Beaux Arts style according to a comprehensive master plan developed by the noted architect Ernest M. Flagg. Most important of all, the academy gained a place in the national consciousness.

The tempo of naval expansion continued without interruption into World War

I. In 1916, the strength of the regiment of midshipmen was increased from 1,094 to 1,746, and in 1918 it was raised another 40 percent. Coupled with the rapid expansion of the student body, the war had an unsettling effect on the academy, at which the upper classes were graduated ahead of schedule, and a series of crash courses were established for reserve officers who were quartered in the yard.

The academy was returned to normal during the landmark superintendency of Rear Admiral Henry B. Wilson, 1921-1925, who combined a strict approach to disciplinary offenses with a desire to make the academy "more human, more livable" and liberalized many outmoded regulations governing midshipman life and conduct.

In institutional terms, for the academy World War II was largely a replay of World War I. Once again, classes were graduated early; the strength of the regiment, which had been cut back after the first war, was expanded; and the consequent problems persisted into the postwar period. And once again, they were overcome by a vigorous superintendent, Rear Admiral J. L. Holloway, Jr., between 1947 and 1950.

At the end of the war, serious thought was given to the possibility of increasing the annual output of ensigns needed by a global Navy either by curtailing the academy curriculum to two years or by founding a second naval academy, presumably in California. In the outcome, the Navy adopted the recommendation of a board headed by Admiral J. L. Holloway (prior to his appointment as superintendent) to establish a paid, "regular" Navy ROTC program and retain a single academy in its traditional format at Annapolis. Proposals to create a common academy for the three armed services were rejected by the Stearns-Eisenhower Board, of which Holloway was an active member, in 1949.

Aside from a period in the late nineteenth century, when a special program was established for prospective engineers, and a brief offering of advanced electives around the same time, the academy had always maintained a fixed curriculum, in which every midshipman took the same courses throughout his four years of study, the only option being in the choice of a foreign language. This and much else was changed by a series of reforms that came to be known as the "Academic Revolution." The process began in 1958 with the decision that midshipmen could exempt courses in which they were already competent by means of validating examinations and fill the openings with elective offerings which would also be accessible to midshipmen who wished to "overload" the standard curriculum. A minors program of 15 percent elective courses was inaugurated during the superintendency of Rear Admiral Charles S. Minter, Jr., in 1964, and five years later an accredited majors program was introduced by Rear Admiral James F. Calvert. In 1964, Rear Admiral Charles C. Kirkpatrick established an independent studies program, the Trident Scholarships, for outstanding first-classmen (seniors).

During this same decade, steps were taken to give the civilian faculty a voice in the administration of the academy. The post of academic dean was created in 1962; departmental chairmanships were opened to civilians; and a Civilian Faculty Affairs Committee, a Faculty Forum, and a series of civilian-staffed curriculum review boards were organized.

The academy also underwent significant social change. Only six blacks had ever been appointed to the academy when Wesley A. Brown became the first to be graduated in 1949, and minority representation remained low for years thereafter. An aggressive minorities' recruitment program, launched in 1965, soon eliminated the imbalance. The first women instructors, both civilian and military, joined the staff in the early 1970s. The admission of women to the service academies was authorized by Congress in 1975, and the academy's first eighty-one female midshipmen entered in the summer of 1976.

Through all these changes, the mission of the academy has remained the same: to prepare midshipmen, morally, mentally, and physically to be professional officers in the naval service. Graduates incur a five-year, active-duty obligation, and more than half make the service their career.

At present, around 4,400 midshipmen, including some 330 women, attend the academy. They may choose from eighteen majors, ranging from naval architecture to English, the only restriction being that at least 80 percent must major in the sciences, engineering, or mathematics. The cost of their education to the government is approximately $80,000, the lowest at any of the service academies. In recent years, independent surveys have consistently ranked the academy among the fifty best colleges and universities in the nation.

FOR ADDITIONAL INFORMATION: There have been five histories of the Naval Academy: Edward Chauncey Marshall, *History of the Naval Academy* (1862); Lieutenant Commander Edward P. Lull, USN, *Description and History of the Naval Academy from Its Origin to the Present Time* (1869); James Russell Soley, *Historical Sketch of the United States Naval Academy* (1876); Park Benjamin, *The United States Naval Academy* (1900); and Jack Sweetman, *The U.S. Naval Academy: An Illustrated History* (1979); plus a pictorial, John Crane and Lieutenant James F. Keiley, USNR, *United States Naval Academy: The First Hundred Years* (1945). Numerous other works describe life and customs at the academy, and useful historical articles may be found in the U.S. Naval Institute *Proceedings*, especially in the anniversary years 1935 and 1945, and *Shipmate*, the publication of the United States Naval Academy Alumni Association, Inc. The alumni association also publishes the annual *Register of Alumni*, which lists every alumnus and provides brief biographical data on almost every graduate. For the history of the civilian faculty, see Jack Sweetman, "The Civilian Faculty: 1845-1960," *Shipmate* 44, Nos. 1 and 2 (January-March 1981). Consult also Admiral J. L. Holloway, Jr., U.S. Navy (Ret.), with Jack Sweetman, "A Gentlemen's Agreement," U.S. Naval Institute *Proceedings* 106, No. 9 (September 1980): 71-77.

JACK SWEETMAN

UNITED STATES POSTAL SERVICE. The foundations of the American Post Office were established in the nation's colonial period. Following several unsuccessful attempts to develop a postal system in the colonies in the seventeenth century, the British government in 1692 gave Thomas Neal the exclusive right to establish a postal system throughout the American colonies. Beginning in 1693, Neal's mail service operated with indifferent success until 1707 when the British government purchased the rights to the system and began developing it as part of the empire's postal system.

Under the new direction, the colonial postal system became self-supporting in the 1720s, but it did not produce a profit, as it was expected to do, until 1761. By that time, partly because of the management of Benjamin Franklin, who became Co-Deputy Postmaster General in 1753 and because the British government had established a packet service from England to the colonies, the colonial mails were moving profitably and with regularity and safety from Maine to Charleston, South Carolina.

The improved colonial postal service, which, incidentally, enhanced England's ability to govern her American colonies at the very moment when the ties between colonies were loosening, was soon deeply enmeshed in the controversy between the mother country and her colonies. In the furor over taxation without representation, many Americans came to regard the high postage rates as an unconstitutional tax and, in the 1770s, began sending their letters outside the mails with postmen who were willing to carry them for less than the colonial Post Office charged. The necessity for doing this, however, ended in 1774 when William Goddard, a Maryland newspaper publisher, developed an independent postal system, which he called the "Constitutional Post." The next year the Second Continental Congress took control of Goddard's Constitutional Post and operated it successfully through the Revolutionary War. In 1782, acting under the authority given it by the Articles of Confederation to establish post offices and regulate the postal service between states, the Confederate Congress wrote a new postal law giving the Post Office a monopoly of carrying the mail, establishing the office of Postmaster General, setting postage rates, and stipulating the regulations under which the postal service was to operate.

This was the nation's first major postal law, and the system it established remained in effect until 1792. By that time the new Constitution, giving Congress the right to establish post offices and post roads, had gone into effect, and Congress wrote a new postal law creating a new American Post Office. Like its predecessor, the new law provided for the office of Postmaster General, set new postage, provided for the creation of post offices and post roads, and established the general rules for managing the postal service.

At the time Congress created the new American Post Office in 1792, it also established the principles around which the nation's postal policy was to be formed. According to these principles, the Post Office was to be self-supporting; it was to use whatever profits it made to extend the postal service; and in a historic departure from British practice, the Congress, not the Postmaster General, was to establish post offices and post roads. This meant, in effect, that Congress, acting in response to its constituents' demands for service, would control the expansion of the postal system.

These principles set the stage for numerous conflicts between Congress and the Postmaster General and within Congress itself. For, as Congress established an ever-increasing number of post roads and ordered the Postmaster General to begin mail service over them, it soon became apparent that the Post Office could not continue to extend its services as rapidly as Congress desired and pay its way too.

Moreover, Congress itself was torn between its urban and rural wings over the postal policy. Urban representatives, often representing business interests, argued through the years for reduced postage rates, which, until 1851, were based upon the weight of the letter and the distance it was to go. They pointed out that reduced postage for their letters was no more than fair since the cities' postal business accounted for whatever profits the Post Office made. But rural representatives, fearing that reduced postage rates would produce larger postal deficits and threaten the ability of the Post Office to extend mail service over the nonpaying and costly post roads of the rural South and West, opposed reduced postage rates and postal innovations.

Arguments over the proper postal policy continued until the 1850s when Congress changed the policy. Forced by the illegal competition of those who carried letters outside the mails for less than the regular postage rates to make drastic changes, Congress, in 1851, reduced the postage rates and declared at the same time that postal service was not to be diminished if postal deficits resulted from the lower postage rates. From that time until 1971, when Congress relinquished control of the Post Office and established the United States Postal Service with the understanding that it was to pay its own way, service rather than the principle of a self-supporting Post Office dominated the nation's postal policy. Annual postal deficits, always offset by congressional appropriations, became the rule, but under this policy the postal service was modernized and rapidly expanded.

The reduced postage of the 1850s, which virtually eliminated distance as a factor in determining rate, led, as its advocates had predicted, to greater use of the mails. The trend toward further postage reductions continued until 1885 when it cost only two cents to mail a letter. The increased use of the mails was also facilitated by the modernization of the postal service. In the 1850s, the prepayment of postage and the use of adhesive stamps were made mandatory, thereby measurably increasing the efficiency of the service. Largely for the benefit of businessmen, Congress approved a registered letter service in 1855, and followed this service with a city free-delivery system in 1863 and a postal money order service in 1864. In the same period, the mails were divided into various classes and the postage on these was again reduced. Then, as the Civil War gave way to the age of big business, the definition of second-class mail was broadened, and the postage on such mail was reduced to a penny a pound. This brought into the mails a flood of paperback books and a variety of magazines which businessmen used for advertising purposes.

Rural America was not entirely forgotten in the improvements in the mail service. By 1891, star routes running more than 230,000 miles through the countryside and connecting with more than 60,000 small, fourth-class post offices brought the mails, including packages weighing no more than four pounds, to rural America. In 1896, an experiment began in delivering the mails to farm homes. With its success in the early 1900s came demands for the creation of a parcel service that would admit to the mails packages larger than four pounds and make it possible for farmers to have goods from mail-order stores mailed directly to their farms. This new service began in 1913, three years after the postal savings bank system in which farmers and others might invest their savings had been authorized by Congress.

Meanwhile, the Post Office Department was taking advantage of the most rapid means of conveying the mails as the nation's transportation system developed. In 1813, Congress authorized the Post Office Department to use steamboats to carry the mails, and by 1838, when the nation still possessed only a few miles of railroads, it declared them to be post roads. In 1864, the first railroad post office was developed. These post offices revolutionized the way the mails were handled, for they made it possible for postal employees to sort the mails as they traveled along and eliminated the necessity for the clumsy distributing post office to which regional mails had been sent to be sorted and rerouted. In the early 1900s, rural mail carriers were turning from their horses and buggies to the automobile to deliver the mail to the farmers, and in 1918, the first regular airmail service began between Washington and New York. By this time, the Post Office Department in Washington had grown from a handful of employees to the nation's largest bureaucracy.

The law of 1792 establishing the Post Office placed upon the Postmaster General the responsibility for managing the postal service. His most important duties were to appoint postmasters for the post offices Congress created; to contract for carrying the mail over the post roads Congress had established; to collect the postal revenues, pay all postage expenses, and account to Congress for all money collected and spent; and to prescribe such regulations for postmasters and mail contractors as were necessary to conduct the postal business.

To do all this Congress provided the Postmaster General with only one assistant. Two years later, however, it permitted him to employ four postal clerks, and through the years as the business increased, the employment of more postal clerks was authorized. By 1799, nine persons were employed in the Post Office Department, and by 1810, fifteen. That year Congress authorized the appointment of two assistants to the Postmaster General and such clerks as were needed to conduct the business. Over the next two decades the postal service expanded dramatically, and its importance was reflected in the elevation of the Postmaster General to the President's Cabinet in 1829. In 1831, the department had thirty-eight permanent and sixteen extra or temporary clerks, and the work of the department had been divided into three divisions: the first to handle the postal finances, the second to appoint postmasters, and the third to provide for the safety of the mails.

So rapidly did the number of post offices and post roads increase, as the Post

Office attempted to keep pace with westward-moving Americans, that by the early 1830s postal revenues failed to pay for the service. Ostensibly to find the causes of the deficits but also to embarrass President Andrew Jackson's Administration, Congress began one of its periodic investigations of the department in the early 1830s. This investigation was followed in 1836 by a postal law that reorganized the Post Office Department.

In accordance with the new law, all money collected by the Post Office Department was to be deposited in the United States Treasury. Each year the Postmaster General was to prepare a budget estimating the needs of the department, and Congress was to appropriate the money necessary to operate the postal system from the general funds. To oversee the department's finances, an auditor in the Treasury Department* was to be established for the Post Office.

Moreover, Congress authorized the appointment of a third assistant to the Postmaster General, and by the next year, 1837, the Post Office Department had been reorganized. Three principal bureaus were created under the three assistant postmasters general as they were now called. The First Assistant Postmaster General was charged with the responsibility of making contracts with mail carriers. The appointment of postmasters became the duty of the Second Assistant Postmaster General, and the primary function of the Inspection Office, headed by the Third Assistant Postmaster General, was to insure the safety of the mails.

As time passed an imposing array of divisions, each designed to manage an important postal service such as the registered mail service, foreign mails, railway mail service, postal salaries and allowances, and the postal money order system, to name but a few, grew up within the three bureaus. In 1891, Congress provided for the appointment of a Fourth Assistant Postmaster General and a new bureau was created. By 1900, it had within it three divisions: appointment of postmasters; bonds and commissions; and post office inspectors and mail depredations.

The four bureaus with their many divisions formed the basic organization of the Post Office Department until 1949 when Congress approved and effected the President's Reorganization Plan No. 3. This plan eliminated the four bureaus, but the four Assistant Postmasters General remained to head four new departments: post office operations, transportation, finance, and facilities. This structure was still basically intact when the Post Office Department was replaced by the United States Postal Service in 1971.

Because it was virtually the only arm of the national government to perform a visible service for the people throughout the nineteenth century, of all government departments the Post Office Department was the closest to the public, and it reflected in remarkable ways the attitudes and desires of the American people and of special interests. Special interests and the American embrace of free enterprise, for example, prevented the Post Office Department from developing a postal telegraph, even though the government had sponsored Samuel Morse's famous experiment in 1844. Postal savings banks and a parcel post system were long delayed by banks and the railway express companies. Middle-class American attitudes were also reflected in the efforts to ban obscene, lewd, lascivious, and indecent writings from the mails.

Moreover, the Post Office was always deeply involved in politics as senators and congressmen sought to bring postal services to their constituents. Indeed, it was politics that prevented curtailment of postal services and caused postal deficits; but it was also politics that promoted postal innovations, inspired postal reforms, and made the Post Office the servant of the people. Politics also played a major role in the appointment of the department's personnel. Each postmaster in the communities scattered across the nation, for example, was a political appointee and formed the nucleus of a political machine for the Congressman or Senator whose influence had led to his appointment.

Postmasters represented their party in their local areas and stirred interest in their candidates. Their growing political influence was apparent as early as 1836 when Congress, in order to strike at President Jackson's use of postmasters, decreed that postmasters in the largest post offices must be appointed by the President *with the advice and consent of the Senate* rather than by the Postmaster General alone.

As political appointees, the postmasters could be held accountable by the people for the kind of postal service they gave, and politics tended to make them responsible civil servants. But civil service reformers of the 1870s viewed virtually all political appointees as inefficient, incompetent, or corrupt, and pushed through Congress the Pendleton Civil Service Act in 1883 to reform the civil service. By World War I, the appointment of most postal employees was controlled at least to some extent by civil service regulations, but as long as the Post Office remained an arm of Congress, it was never completely depoliticized.

The Post Office Department played an important part in the development of the American nation. As the principal means of communication through most of the nation's past, it served as a bond of union linking scattered Americans together, creating and promoting communities, and reminding Americans constantly of the national government's presence in their midst. Cheap postage rates and improved mail delivery sped the growth of newspapers, magazines, and books, and helped make Americans among the best informed people in the world. The franking privilege that brought government documents and political speeches through the mail free of charge heightened the American's interest in politics and nurtured democracy at the same time that it served the interests of the election officials. Postal employees, promoting the fortunes of those who appointed them, created an interest in politics and helped build the two-party system at the expense of the government rather than that of private business.

The Post Office's contributions to American business were among its most important. It subsidized stage coach lines, ships at sea, the railroads, and airlines, and hastened the growth of each of these methods of transportation. It made possible the development of a gigantic mail-order business, and it provided businessmen with their cheapest means of advertising. And if it also encouraged the development of fraudulent businesses, it helped advance the science of criminal detection in attempting to find those who abused the mail privilege. It was, in its own way, a mirror reflecting the progress of the American civilization and an agent serving to promote that progress.

FOR ADDITIONAL INFORMATION: Carl Scheele, *A Short History of the Mail Service* (1970), traces the development of the American postal system, as does Wayne E. Fuller, *The American Mail: Enlarger of the Common Life* (1972). On the postal power given to Congress by the Constitution, see Lindsay Rogers, *The Postal Power of Congress: A Study in Constitutional Expansion* (1916). The development of postal policy may be followed in Clyde Kelly, *United States Postal Policy* (1931). Wesley Everett Rich, *History of the United States Post Office to the Year 1829* (1924) is an old but thorough work on the postal service's colonial period.

The relation between the postal service and stage coaching may be found in Oliver Wendell Holmes, *State-Coach and Mail from Colonial Days to 1820* (1956). An important work on the relation between the government and the railroads in the early days is Lewis Henry Haney, *A Congressional History of the Railways in the United States to 1850* (1908).

Some aspects of the connection between the Post Office and politics may be found in Dorothy Fowler, *The Cabinet Politician* (1943) and Carl Fish, *The Civil Service and the Patronage* (1905).

For the development of some of the postal services, see Clark E. Carr, *The Railway Mail: Its Origin and Development* (1909); Dorothy Fowler, *Unmailable: Congress and the Post Office* (1977); Wayne E. Fuller, *R. F. D.: The Changing Face of Rural America* (1964); Carrol V. Glines, *Saga of the Air Mail* (1968); Edwin Walter Kemmerer, *Postal Savings* (1917); and John N. Makris, *The Silent Inspectors* (1959).

WAYNE E. FULLER

UNITED STATES RAILWAY ASSOCIATION AND CONSOLIDATED RAIL CORPORATION (CONRAIL). Conrail, the Consolidated Rail Corporation, is technically a private corporation, though financed by and effectively controlled by the U.S. government's Railway Association. It absorbed the bankrupt wreckage of the Penn Central and five other railroads on April 1, 1976, and operates them as a consolidated railroad.

American railroads began to decline after 1910 as a result of regulation and often uninspired management, and in the 1920s as a result of the rise of rival forms of transportation. Even in the depression, however, the New York Central and the Pennsylvania Railroads, traditionally the nation's largest in terms of gross revenues and volume of traffic, earned profits and paid dividends and stood like corporate rocks of Gibraltar. But after World War II, even as railroads in the West and South began to adjust to the rise of nonrailroad competition, problems seemed to descend on the railroads of the Northeast, including the New York Central and the Pennsylvania, with a vengeance. The sizable traffic of lightweight finished manufactured goods, moving over the Northeast's relatively short distances, was especially vulnerable to truck competition. The Northeast's early development of toll roads and the opening of the government-sponsored Saint Lawrence Seaway in 1959 took away a lot of railroad traffic. The growing preference for oil and gas as fuel for home heating kicked the props from under five railroads built primarily to carry anthracite coal—the Lackawanna, the Lehigh Valley, the Jersey Central, the Reading, and the Delaware & Hudson. Compared with railroads in other regions, Eastern lines always had a proportionately greater commitment to passenger transportation (traditionally about 25 percent of the gross income of the New York Central and Pennsylvania) and, thus, had further to fall when travelers turned en masse to other forms of transportation.

Most Eastern roads were weighed down with an extraordinary amount of debt. Some of it had been borrowed for legitimate reasons, to build elaborate multitrack rights-of-way which were now redundant with the decline of passenger traffic and the development of electronic signal systems. Some of it was due to the profligacy of past managements. Four reorganizations of the Erie Railroad, for example, had failed to wring out the debt incurred by the nineteenth-century "Erie Ring," which some characterized as swashbuckling, and others as crooked. By the mid-twentieth century, there was little swashbuckling in railroad leadership. Many Eastern roads suffered from entrenched and often mediocre managements. Evidence was strewn throughout the region, though it was usually buried at lower and midmanagement levels. Most serious, although it remained well hidden until the late 1960s, was the crippling traditionalism of the top management of the Pennsylvania Railroad, which seemed to respond more to the social ethos of Philadelphia than to changes in the economics of transportation. By the early 1960s, virtually the only Northeastern railroads making enough money to maintain their physical plant properly were the major haulers of bituminous coal, the Norfolk & Western and the Chesapeake & Ohio.

Caught in a dilemma partly of their own making, partly of government support for competing modes of transportation, and partly of economic and technological forces out of their control, management's answer in the 1960s was to merge. The public rationale was to consolidate duplicate services and concentrate traffic on fewer routes. Some of that, though not a lot, was actually accomplished. Private reasons included tax write-offs and the ability to market services over a wider area. From a public interest point of view, it was hoped that the strong roads, like the bituminous coal roads, might be able to pump money, talent, and traffic into the weaker ones and create a genuinely balanced system within the framework of private enterprise. But, as should have been expected, the strong roads called the merger tune, and they went after medium-strong roads, not the weak ones. The Chesapeake & Ohio took the Baltimore & Ohio, and the Norfolk & Western took two lean freight lines west of Buffalo, the Nickel Plate and the Wabash. These mergers enabled the strong roads to divert traffic from the weaker lines, leaving the weaker lines worse off than before.

The most important of the weaker lines were the New York Central and the Pennsylvania. The two had talked about merger with each other in the late 1950s and, because of their immense size, terrified other roads in the region into what may have been precipitous mergers. Central and Pennsylvania had backed off from merger themselves, primarily because of incompatible managements, and then were forced to reconsider as the other mergers put on the pressure. The Pennsylvania Railroad had stock control of the Norfolk & Western, and probably dreamed of keeping the rich coal road with its newly merged empire and taking over the New York Central, thus winding up as the dominant force in Eastern railroading. But the Supreme Court forced the Pennsylvania to give up the Norfolk & Western as a precondition to merger with the Central. The Pennsylvania and New York Central became the Penn Central on February 1, 1968.

The operating plan of the Penn Central merger was to route all traffic from the west bound for New York City or New England via the New York Central's Selkirk Yard near Albany, and all traffic bound for Philadelphia and south via the Pennsylvania's Enola Yard near Harrisburg, and thus coordinate and stream-line the operation of both roads. But for a decade, the two roads had been able to show a modest profit only by failing to maintain their facilities properly. By the time the merger took place, both roads were already suffering from decaying track and locomotive breakdowns. In the confusion following merger, operations were plunged into total chaos.

To make matters worse, the managements of the two roads held opposite views on the marketing of railroad services and, hence, on the operation of trains themselves. Forced to work with each other after the merger, they came to hate each other. Most frustrated were the young and aggressive marketing-team members of the former New York Central who were forced into subservient roles because of the financial dominance of the Pennsylvania. The determination of the Pennsylvania's management to get the merger through, no matter what, had prompted it to sign contracts with labor that were probably more generous than the unions ever expected to get. The result was to burden the merged railroad with unnecessary labor costs.

In addition, the Interstate Commerce Commission* (ICC) and the courts re-quired Penn Central to absorb the bankrupt New York, New Haven & Hartford Railroad. All the problems of Northeastern railroading, notably short-haul freight traffic and declining passenger traffic, were magnified in southern New England, especially on the New Haven Railroad. The road was in such a shabby state of disrepair by the late 1960s that even the safety of its high-speed passenger operations between New York and Boston was questionable. Throwing it in with the Penn Central was the only solution the ICC could find within the framework of private enterprise. The alternative would have been state or federal operation, a route no one was prepared to go in the mid-1960s.

The Penn Central was one of the great business fiascos of all time. Manage-ment, which had been none too savvy before, failed utterly in itstheir efforts to combine operations. Cars were misrouted or lost. Customers were presented with no bills, or wrong bills, or were dunned for bills they had already paid. They deserted in droves. In addition, it now came to light that the Pennsylvania Railroad had, for the past decade, used deceptive accounting methods to make its financial position look stronger so that it could continue to borrow money.

It borrowed money to pay dividends on its common stock, and it borrowed to invest, not in the undermaintained railroad, but in nonrailroad properties, notably Sun Belt real estate and a dubious, commuter airline venture. The nonrailroad investments may have enmeshed certain company officials in a sex scandal. By early 1970, the railroad was losing money at the then incredible rate of $1 million a day and on June 21, filed for reorganization.

For the next four years cashflow stopped in an orgy of litigation while the bankruptcy court tried in vain to reorganize the railroad. Its work was complicated by the fact that the trustees had put the company's money-making nonrailroad assets beyond the reach of the court's jurisdiction so they could not be used to balance the railroad's losses. The physical plant continued to decay, employee morale was nil, service deteriorated, customers deserted, deficits mounted, and the railroad was kept bailed together by emergency infusions of cash from the government.

In the meantime, five other railroads in the region, the ones excluded from mergers because of their financial weakness, were also plunged into bankruptcy. These included the Reading, the Jersey Central, the Lehigh Valley, the Lehigh & Hudson River, and the Erie Lackawanna, whose own weak-sister merger in 1960 had failed to save it. By 1973, the trustees of the Penn Central demanded liquidation of the railroad's property. It was thought that some individual routes might be sold off to solvent carriers—the Chesapeake & Ohio or the Norfolk & Western, or perhaps the Canadian roads. None of them seemed interested. For a time, it appeared the railroad might be sold piecemeal and service discontinued, leaving Northeastern industry and all the massive private investment it represented in ruins.

The plan that was finally adopted for a government-sponsored solution originated with Frank Barnett, president of the Union Pacific Railroad. The Union Pacific's legal counsel supplied a draft of the law. The First National City Bank supplied the financial data. The United Transportation Union wrote the essential labor contracts. Two congressmen, Richard G. Shoup of Montana and Brock Adams of Washington, introduced the bill, the Rail Reorganization Act of 1973 (the 3R Act) in the House of Representatives.

The act called for the establishment of a nonprofit, federally chartered corporation called the United States Railway Association whose directors would consist of government representatives, creditor banks, solvent railroads, and shippers. Its job was to plan a radically slimmed down Northeastern rail system out of the carcasses of the bankrupt lines and to arrange for government financing. This buffer agency was created because it could issue government loans and loan guarantees without being subject to the national debt ceiling and was thus beyond the veto power of the Office of Management and Budget.*

When the planning was done, operation of the railroad was to be turned over to Conrail, the Consolidated Rail Corporation, a private corporation chartered in a state and headquartered in Philadelphia. Its stock would be owned by the creditors of the bankrupt railroads, and they would elect Conrail's directors, except that as long as more than 50 percent of Conrail's outstanding debt was either owed to or guaranteed by the government, a majority of the directors would be appointed by the President with the advice and consent of the Senate.

The plan calculated that $2.1 billion would be sufficient to rehabilitate the railroad's decrepit physical plant. Part of the plan called for the drastic elimination of many branch lines that carried a relatively small amount of traffic. Indeed, this "rationalization" of the route structure, reducing Conrail to its lean, essential core, was supposed to make it a profitable operation within five years, even though some observers predicted this would not happen. The plan was optimistic on just about every point and, as such, was a political document, designed to show that there was an easy solution that would not cost a lot of money.

Unhappily, the plan was too optimistic and Conrail's problems too intractable to be solved cheaply and quickly. It was forced to use $285 million of its government funding merely to cover operating deficits in its first year of operation, and operating deficits continued, though at a diminished rate, once repairs began on the physical plant. However, the orginal $2.1 billion appropriation was not enough, and in 1980, an additional $1.2 billion was required. Studies made in 1980 predicted that Conrail would need to rely on government loans for most of its capital expenditures for the foreseeable future.

By 1980, Conrail's management felt that its basic physical plant was restored at least for adequate freight operations. Of course, it was a far cry from the finely manicured rights-of-way of the traditional New York Central and Pennsylvania Railroads. Less successful was the railroad's effort to "rationalize" its route structure. Route mileage was reduced by about 6,000 miles between 1976 and 1980, mostly branches, though including some major amputations of former Erie Lackawanna and Lehigh Valley mainlines. There was political opposition to line abandonments as communities often felt their future potential for economic growth depended on retaining rail service. Mostly, however, Conrail's problem was that its predecessor roads were built with many branches according to nineteenth-century needs; the branches were essential to feed traffic into the mainlines. Studies made in 1980 and 1981 seriously questioned whether it was possible to pare the railroad down to its "essential core," or if done, whether it would significantly help to make the railroad viable. There were some, of course, who still longed for the easy panacea.

Some of Conrail's problems were beyond its control. Brutal winter weather ravaged its decrepit physical plant during the first two winters of its operation. Coal shipments, which initial plans predicted would increase, actually declined, largely because of environmental restrictions on Eastern high-sulphur coal. The decline of the American steel industry after 1976 and the American automobile industry after 1979 drastically reduced shipments by some of the railroad's most important customers. Beyond that, the Northeast experienced a general business decline in those years. Asked in 1981 if he thought the Northeast's economy would ever catch fire again, with auto plants running three shifts, steel mills that lit up the night skies, and so forth, Conrail President Stanley Crane could not be optimistic.

Conrail's labor agreements, as mandated in the 3R Act, left the railroad with excessive labor, and because workers were virtually guaranteed protection for life, they had little incentive to do a good job. As a result, while wages consumed 48 percent of the gross revenues of railroads generally, they took 56 percent on Conrail. Had Conrail's average been the same as the industry's average, it could have saved $300 million in 1980. Conrail management insisted that, unless it could get relief from these labor contracts, relief that would probably have to come from Congress, it could never be a viable railroad. It was noteworthy also that Conrail's management costs rose faster than industry averages and that the number of managers increased even as the workforce that they managed shrank.

Since Conrail had failed to become self-sustaining according to the original projections, various plans were offered for its disposition. One held that, using the Penn Central's basic plan of operation, it was as sound as a rail system could be in a region of declining industry. With minor corrections, it should be left intact, with the acknowledgment that government aid may be required, perhaps forever. Another view held that Conrail preserved the immense size and operating inefficiencies that wrecked the old Penn Central. They recommended pulling Conrail apart into roughly the configurations of the former New York Central and former Pennsylvania, relying on the vigor that would supposedly come from the renewal of strong rail competition to pull the systems through. Others thought Conrail should be sold off to solvent railroads, perhaps even lines from other regions, and perhaps with some strong government incentives. Although solvent lines had not been interested before, it was believed that the improved condition of Conrail's physical plant might make it more attractive.

In authorizing an extra $1.2 billion for Conrail capital improvements, the Staggers Rail Act of 1980 required further studies and projections to be made. Conrail management and the United States Railway Association concluded that, with relief from labor contracts and with continued funding for capital improvements, the present structure of Conrail was the best. However, the Reagan Administration, which took office in January 1981, wanted all aid to Conrail stopped as part of its effort to balance the budget. It was determined to sell Conrail routes to solvent railroads (the so called private enterprise solution) and intimated that it was prepared to provide a great deal of incentive to solvent carriers. Critics suggested that, since the government would almost certainly have to pay for a settlement of Conrail's labor problems and subsidize its commuter passenger operations before the solvent carriers could move, the private enterprise solution could be more expensive than to continue the operation as it was.

FOR ADDITIONAL INFORMATION: The reports and studies on the creation of, and continuing debate on, Conrail are available at the Interstate Commerce Commission Library. For a secondary account, see Richard Saunders, *The Railroad Mergers and the Coming of Conrail* (1978).

RICHARD SAUNDERS

UNITED STATES SECRET SERVICE. Today, the Secret Service performs a function that is "vital" in the real sense of the word, the protection of the President and his entourage. For this reason, among others, the service has escaped much of the recent criticism directed against police and clandestine agencies. Yet, the service is by no means divorced from problematic and potentially controversial issues. There is, for example, the problem of whether the President should, in the interests of his own safety and of national stability, cut himself off from the very people of whom he is the elected democratic champion. To do so would be to cooperate with the Secret Service in its task of shielding him from potential assassins. If the President decides, as he usually has done, to mingle as much as possible with the people, where does this leave the Secret Service? Should the service passively accept the heightened risk, or cooperate with other intelligence agencies and exchange information with them concerning dangerous, or allegedly dangerous, citizens? The latter policy might help to forestall tragedy, but at the same time it could endanger the cherished ideals of civil liberty, and of the individual's right to privacy.

There are historical dimensions to the Secret Service that must be considered if its functions and present reputation are to be understood. First, there is a comparative dimension. Exploiting their access to privileged information, and the fact that their secret actions are necessarily accepted on trust even by their employers, undercover agencies have periodically resorted to illegal and ruthless methods, and undermined civil liberty. Has the record of the Secret Service been relatively good in this regard? Second, the service needs to be considered as a pioneer of professionalism: in the fight against crime, in the furtherance of undercover aspects of national defense, and in counterespionage. Finally, it should be noted that the Secret Service at one time occupied a central position in the American espionage network. Today, that position is occupied by the Central Intelligence Agency (CIA), with the Secret Service on the periphery mainly as a consumer, rather than producer, of information. The causes of the rise and bureaucratic eclipse of the Secret Service throw light on its present place in the intelligence and security establishment of the United States.

On July 1, 1790, Congress voted the President funds to be used secretly in the national interest, and in 1793, the national legislature formally established an executive contingency fund. From time to time over the next seventy years, the President used agents for "secret service" jobs. In the process, he incurred mounting suspicion and hostility from Congress. The denizens of the Capitol were at the time torn, as they still are, between the imperatives of decisive executive leadership and congressional privilege, secret action and open government. Between 1860 and 1865, both the Union and the Confederacy nevertheless employed numerous secret agents. The Union's most effective operative was General Lafayette Baker, who entitled his memoirs *History of the United States Secret Service* (1867). Baker's agency, which was particularly effective in its war against counterfeiting, was officially called the National Detective Bureau (NDB).

The United States Secret Service, as presently constituted, was established on July 5, 1865. The decision was taken at Lincoln's last Cabinet meeting. The service's first chief was William P. Wood, who, like many of his operatives, had served under Baker for the Union. His men failed to prevent Lincoln's assassination. They did, however, help to track down his assassin, John Wilkes Booth. Their prime duty, like that of the NDB, was the detection of counterfeiters. That is why the Secret Service was a division of the Treasury Department,* as it is today.

The newly constituted Secret Service did well in the first year of its existence, arresting over two hundred counterfeiting suspects. Building on this success, it expanded its criminal investigations. Organized crime and the Ku Klux Klan were but two of its targets. It became, in effect, a nineteenth-century precursor to the FBI,* and in 1870-1879 actually operated from within the Justice Department.* This was a period when the nation's burgeoning cities were only just beginning to adopt uniformed police forces, and when criminal detection was in danger of being left to the haphazard arts of the Pinkerton detective. The Secret Service, therefore, expanded to meet a real need. Its expansion provoked criticism nevertheless. During the Johnson impeachment hearings, it had been revealed that Baker had ruthlessly ignored people's civil liberties and had even spied on the occupants of the White House. Congress began to balk at further appropriations. The Secret Service's assumption of additional responsibilities was, in the long run, to provoke the resentment and jealousy that led to its bureaucratic eclipse.

In 1898, however, when these problems were still in their infancy, the Secret Service was to cover itself with glory. Upon the outbreak of the Spanish-American War, two Spanish diplomats—Ramon de Carranza and Juan du Bose— left Washington for Canada. They established a spy ring in Montreal. Its objectives were to recruit agents among America's Spanish-speaking immigrants, sabotage military and naval installations, betray military and naval dispositions, and identify financial and other strategic areas in coastal cities that might be within range of naval bombardment. With brilliant efficiency, the Secret Service swiftly destroyed this potent threat to U.S. national security.

In 1898, the Secret Service pursued suspected spies with indiscriminate ruthlessness. Its agents were experts on forgery and were accused of manufacturing evidence. All who spoke a Latin tongue, even Italians or Spanish-speakers who supported the Cuban revolution, were subject to arbitrary search, harassment, and detention without trial. On the other hand, Spanish assertions that the service resorted to murder were almost certainly unfounded, and the service has never indulged in barbarism on the Russian scale.

John E. Wilkie, the Secret Service chief appointed at the start of the Spanish-American War, brought Chicago business methods to the agency. Investigative techniques were systematized. Daily reports, set out according to a strict format, were required. Claims for expenses were scrutinized. Wilkie utilized recent developments in office technology. Notably, paper work was typed, and carbon copies were circulated. This facilitated liaison with other branches of government, and the centralization of information. Agents were handpicked from thousands of volunteers and subjected to the rigorous training that is still insisted upon by the service. Wilkie left an indelible print not only on the Secret Service, but also on U.S. police and security work generally.

After 1898, the Secret Service declined from its position of solitary preeminence in the world of investigative intelligence. One reason for this decline was its bureaucratic rivalry with other domestic agencies, some of which were able to capitalize on the service's uneasy relationship with Congress. In 1907, for example, President Theodore Roosevelt authorized the service to investigate a western land fraud. As a result of the investigation, a congressman and a U.S. senator were convicted. Congress thereupon restricted the investigative powers of the service. The Attorney General responded by establishing the Bureau of Investigation (the future FBI) during a congressional adjournment. At first, the bureau could only operate by borrowing Secret Service agents, but it soon grew to be a bureaucratic threat to the parent organization.

During World War I, Treasury Secretary William G. McAdoo attempted to restore the Secret Service to its former position as the central agency for domestic counterespionage, criminal investigations, and intelligence. Given new authorization by Congress, his men achieved some real success, including the breakup of a German spy ring. Their conservative adherence to constitutional principles, however, set them apart from other contemporary organizations that were willing to disregard civil liberties and whip up public hysteria. Under the leadership of William J. Flynn and William J. Burns, both former Secret Service men, the FBI in particular gained in strength. The FBI's arrest record during the Red Scare of 1919 was unimpressive, but the Secret Service was still fated to bow out from the wider field of criminal investigation. However, this was not before it had conducted another major investigation with typical disregard for political consequences. Its agents helped to uncover the Teapot Dome oil reserve scandal of the 1920s that led to the resignation of Interior Secretary Albert B. Fall.

The Secret Service was knocked from its pedestal not only by the jostling of domestic rivals, but also by the growth of foreign espionage. The Army and Navy had undertaken some of this work from the 1880s on. With the emergence of the United States as a great power in World War I, the State Department* took on the central direction of all intelligence, including the counterespionage activities of the Secret Service and FBI. In 1927, Secretary of State Frank B. Kellogg abolished central intelligence on the ground that it was inefficient. Thereafter, when Presidents Franklin D. Roosevelt, Harry Truman, and Jimmy Carter devised new formulas for centralizing intelligence, the Secret Service found itself very much on the periphery.

A further factor impelling the Secret Service toward the periphery of the intelligence establishment was, paradoxically, its assumption of an important new responsibility. In 1901, President William McKinley died of gunshot wounds inflicted by one Leon Czolgosz. Coming as it did in the wake of the assassinations of Presidents Lincoln and Garfield, this sorry event highlighted the need for a presidential protective agency. There was also the puzzle of Czolgosz himself. In spite of theories prompted by his foreign-sounding name and by his own implausible assertion that he was an anarchist, his personality and motive remained unexplained, a circumstance that foreshadowed the puzzles posed by future assassins and would-be assassins. There was a clear need, not just for brave men to guard the President, but also for a preemptive detective service. In 1901, the Secret Service was the only agency in a position to supply that need.

In 1902, the Secret Service was, for the first time, assigned the duty of protecting the President on a regular basis. Congress voted special funds for this purpose in 1906 and, in 1951, made the assignment permanent. Following various threats and attempts against members of the President's entourage, the Secret Service was successively required to protect the President-elect (1913), the President's family (1917), the Vice-President (1951), the Vice-President elect (1962), the widows and children of former presidents (1968), major presidential candidates (1968), and, at the President's discretion, visiting heads of state and other dignitaries (1971). As time went by, the service had to concentrate more and more on these ever-expanding protective duties, and for that reason encountered less congressional resistance and less opposition from other police and intelligence agencies.

The Secret Service succeeded in its task for more than sixty years before losing its first President, to an assassin every bit as enigmatic as Czolgosz. John F. Kennedy's death in 1963 provoked considerable criticism of the Secret Service. The service had not only failed to protect the President but also was unable to shed light on the motive of the assassin, Lee Harvey Oswald, or on the question of whether Oswald had acted alone. Under the chairmanship of Chief Justice Earl Warren, a presidential commission investigated Kennedy's assassination. FBI Director J. Edgar Hoover reacted so furiously to the commission's admonitions concerning his own agency that many people at the time lost sight of the fact that the Secret Service had been criticized with even greater severity. According to the Warren Commission, the Secret Service lacked the men and facilities to do its job properly. For example, it had to rely on local police forces to screen would-be assassins in cities the President was scheduled to visit. Yet, it gave no proper guidance to these forces or to other agencies on how to identify risk situations. There was not enough liaison within the intelligence community to ensure the efficient reporting of possible risks.

As a result of the Warren findings, and in a climate made more tense by the shootings of Martin Luther King, Robert F. Kennedy, and George Wallace, the Secret Service was expanded. Within ten years of the publication of the Warren Report (1964), the number of agents had increased from 361 to 1,200 and its budget from $7.6 to $62.6 million. The service screened 20,000 potential threats per annum, and kept revolutionaries and emotionally disturbed suspects under constant surveillance in cities the President was visiting. It cooperated with other agencies, exchanging lists of foreign suspects with the CIA and domestic suspects with the FBI. Its undercover work took on a further new dimension in 1971, when it began to recruit women.

The attempt on President Ronald Reagan's life in 1981 failed only by the narrowest of margins and showed that the Secret Service still faced considerable problems. The Warren Commission had recognized a principle in which Reagan himself was a firm believer: the public's right of access to the President. Congress had, in the same spirit, turned down a proposal made in 1969 by the National Commission on the Causes and Prevention of Violence: that, in order to minimize the necessity for risky public appearances, presidential candidates should be given free time on television for the period leading up to election day. Turning to another security problem, Congress has also turned down proposals to limit the sales of guns. This reticence becomes more and more serious as guns continue to increase in sophistication and ease of use. There is little that the Secret Service can do about guns or, indeed, about the nature of American society. America's rising crime rate poses two problems. First, it suggests that there will be an increasing number of assassination attempts in the future. Second, it has become necessary for the Secret Service to supervise the protection of Washington's 117 embassies. Since it also retains its anti-counterfeiting responsibilities, one might argue that its resources and powers of concentration are being stretched to the limit. On the other hand, some may harbor the suspicion that further Secret Service expansion would be a step in the direction of a police state.

The Warren Commission's findings did little permanent damage to the Secret Service's reputation and actually helped to enlarge its resources. The service escaped virtually unscathed from the intelligence "flap" of 1975-1976, when the CIA and other agencies were subjected to so much criticism. The service's good reputation is based on its past achievements, on its progressively easier relationship with other intelligence agencies and with Congress, on its now peripheral position in the intelligence community, and on the palpable and continuing danger to the life of the President. Its secret files and activities are accepted on trust, and that trust is likely to endure unless it is, one day, betrayed.

FOR ADDITIONAL INFORMATION: There are several popular memoirs and histories that deal with the exciting aspects of the Secret Service's past, notably, Michael Dorman, *The Secret Service Story* (1968), John P. Jones, *The German Spy in America* (1917), Harry E. Neal, *The Story of the Secret Service* (1971), Michael F. Reilly and William J. Slocum, *Reilly of the White House* (1947), and Rufus W. Youngblood, *20 Years in the Secret Service: My Life with Five Presidents* (1973). On the Secret Service and the problems of presidential protection, see the *Report of the President's Commission on the Assassination of President Kennedy* (1964), and William Manchester, *The Death of a President* (1967). Rhodri Jeffreys-Jones's *American Espionage: From Secret Service to CIA* (1977), discusses the counterespionage achievements of the Secret Service, its civil liberties record, and its place in the intelligence community. For additional information on the Secret Service's feuds with other agencies, see William R. Corson, *The Armies of Ignorance: The Rise of the American Intelligence Empire* (1977).

RHODRI JEFFREYS-JONES

URBAN DEVELOPMENT DEPARTMENT. See Department of Housing and Urban Development.

— V —

VETERANS ADMINISTRATION (VA). On July 21, 1930, President Herbert Hoover established the Veterans Administration by Executive Order, under authority of a congressional act passed earlier that month. The presidential order consolidated under the administrator of veterans affairs the duties and personnel of the Veterans Bureau, the Bureau of Pensions, and the National Homes for Disabled Volunteer Soldiers. The consolidation represented the final adminstrative adjustment to the problems created by World War I and provided a bureaucratic structure that still functioned half a century later. Charged with administering the benefits Congress bestows upon the nation's veterans, the VA's responsibilities expanded markedly after 1940 as a result of new benefits and because of the millions of veterans added to society during World War II, the Korean Conflict, and the Vietnam intervention. Although founded in the twentieth century, the VA is the lineal descendant of an administrative unit that dates from 1789.

Government concern about veteran care, pensions, and bonuses predates the founding of the nation and constitutes one of the legacies of colonial legislatures and British parliaments. The United States, under the Continental Congress, the Articles of Confederation, and the Constitution of 1787, continued the practice of granting veteran benefits. Few persons ever opposed necessary medical care and pensions for disabled servicemen, but the benefit demands for healthy veterans provoked an enduring political controversy as old as the nation. The types of benefits which able-bodied veterans won—pensions, cash bonuses, and land grants—reflected the conditions during and after particular military actions. Postwar veteran groups campaigned for such benefits, especially the Sons of Cincinnati, established after the Revolutionary War; the Grand Army of the Republic (GAR), organized after the Civil War; and the American Legion, founded after World War I.

The size and type of federal effort required to administer veteran benefits varied in proportion to the number of veterans and the nature of their benefits. Under the Continental Congress and the Articles of Confederation, administration rested with the individual states. In 1789, the first Congress under the new Constitution assumed from the states the responsibility for payment and administration of Revolutionary War pensions. Congress failed, however, to specify any administrative procedure except that the President had the authority to establish regulations. George Washington assigned the administrative duties to his Secretary of War. The clerk who maintained the pension records, therefore, functioned as an eighteenth-century forerunner of the VA.

During the following decades, Congress broadened eligibility for Revolutionary War pensions and added veterans of the War of 1812 to the pension rolls. The workload within the War Department* increased. In 1833, Congress authorized the first identifiable administrative unit concerned with veterans, the Bureau of Pensions, under a commissioner of pensions. The authorization merely formalized a situation that had evolved over a period of years.

In March 1849, Congress established the Department of the Interior* and transferred the Bureau of Pensions from the War Department to Interior. The workload shot up after Union forces during the Civil War suffered casualties of more than 600,000 soldiers killed or wounded. For almost half a century, the Union veterans exerted a major influence in politics as the GAR maintained a public liaison with the Republican party. The GAR's successful drives for generous pensions and liberal interpretation of regulations became important political issues, and the Bureau of Pensions, with its expanded workforce, became an agency staffed with political appointees. During the presidency of Benjamin Harrison, two bureau commissioners resigned because of scandals. As late as 1913, President elect-Woodrow Wilson believed he could not appoint a Southerner as Secretary of the Interior because of the post's jurisdiction over the Bureau of Pensions and its rolls of Union veterans.

U.S. participation in World War I added 4.75 million veterans to the population and exposed the inadequacy of the four agencies that shared makeshift responsibilities for veteran services. The United States Employment Service, which attempted to provide clearinghouse and coordinating functions, asked the newly formed American Legion to take over these tasks. The Public Health Service,* meanwhile, bore the major responsibility for hospitalized veterans, but had only a woefully inadequate 7,200 beds. The responsibility to retrain disabled veterans rested with the Federal Board for Vocational Education. Established by Congress in February 1917 to study, supervise, and retrain persons disabled in industry, the board accepted with reluctance the assignment of veteran rehabilitation. By December 1918, the board's veteran division had rehabilitated thirty-two veterans and employed two full-time workers. When the board expanded in 1919, the vocational rehabilitation of veterans suffered from excessive costs, poor planning, and mismanagement.

The fourth, and most important, agency responsible for veterans was the Bureau of War Risk Insurance. Created by Congress in September 1914, a month after World War I erupted in Europe, the bureau insured merchant ships against the hazards of war. After the United States entered the war, Congress extended the coverage to ship crews. Then, in October 1917, Congress established an allotment payment plan for dependents of military personnel; governmental insurance policies against total disability or death; and a compensation payment schedule and medical treatments for disabled ex-service personnel. Under the jurisdiction of the Secretary of the Treasury, the insurance bureau ran months behind in its payments, despite having 13,771 employees in July 1919, double the number of a year earlier. Moreover, some of its regulations, such as a soldier having to prove his tuberculosis originated in service, were unjust.

After the war, the American Legion, founded in Paris in March 1919 by American soldiers still in Europe, dramatized the shabby treatment accorded veterans. By 1920, the American Legion counted 843,013 dues-paying members and had established itself as a nonpartisan political pressure organization of importance. President Warren G. Harding responded to the legion and to the state of veteran care. Eight days after taking office in March 1921, he appointed a citizens committee headed by Charles G. Dawes to examine the administration of veteran care. The Dawes committee quickly concluded that conditions were "deplorable" and recommended the creation of an independent agency combining the responsibilities from the four agencies. As a result, Congress, in August 1921, abolished the Bureau of War Risk Insurance and established the Veterans' Bureau (VB).

The VB started poorly. For its director, Harding selected an unqualified friend, Charles R. Forbes. Graft, waste, and inefficiency characterized his directorship. Eventually, the Senate investigated and Forbes served a term in prison for his dishonesty.

General Frank T. Hines, whom Harding named as successor to Forbes in March 1923, transformed the VB into a model federal agency. He demanded and obtained honesty and efficiency. Able, hard-working, austere, and quiet, he conceived of his position as nonpartisan, advisory, and service-oriented toward veterans and his superiors. With noteworthy success, he worked hard to maintain favorable relations with Congress and veterans organizations.

Because of his reputation, Hines contributed to the establishment of the VA in 1930. Early that year, President Hoover, with strong encouragement from the legion, recommended the consolidation of the VB, the Pension Bureau, and the National Homes for Disabled Volunteer Soldiers. The Pension Bureau was located in the Interior Department, and the National Homes had been under the jurisdiction of the Secretary of War since Congresss incorporated the first home in 1866. Complaints about the divided responsibility for medical treatment reinforced Hoover's belief that the consolidation would promote efficiency at a savings of perhaps $20 million a year. Hines worked with Hoover, and together they enjoyed the support of veterans groups. The first decade of the VA produced little change, other than the launching of a hospital-building program and the 1936 payment of the World War I bonus.

World War II brought profound change. Sixteen and one-half million Americans donned military uniforms, and in June 1944, while the war still raged,

Congress enacted the G.I. Bill of Rights granting able-bodied veterans the most generous list of benefits in the nation's history. Hines and the VA failed to prepare for the inevitable administrative demands the veterans and the new benefits would bring. They failed partly because the government refused to classify the VA as a war agency and thereby entitled to priorities of personnel and materials, partly because of the Hines tradition of cautious management, and partly because Hines lacked enthusiasm for the employment and education benefits of the G.I. Bill. As a result, President Harry S Truman named Hines ambassador to Panama, and in August 1945 appointed as his successor General Omar N. Bradley, a distinguished military commander.

Bradley's quick and decisive actions, especially regarding reorganization of the medical corps and decentralization of functions, changed the VA's image from staid to dynamic, from an agency serving World War I veterans to an organization focusing on World War II veterans. The peak of the postwar action came in February 1947 with the VA operating thirteen branch administrative offices and over one thousand local offices.

In June 1953, acting upon the recommendations of a sixteen-month study by the consultant firm of Booze, Allen, and Hamilton, President Dwight D. Eisenhower authorized the VA to reorganize itself along "major purpose" lines rather than the "functional" lines that had been the case since 1930. The VA, therefore, established a Department of Insurance; a Department of Medicine and Surgery; and a Department of Benefits, which administered benefits for education, readjustment, and disabilities. In addition, in June 1953, Eisenhower named a new administrator of the VA and started the practice that the administrator changes each time a President of a different party takes office.

By 1980, events had reinforced the developments of 1945 to 1953. During the twenty-two years between the departure of Hines in August 1945 and the arrival of Joseph M. Cleland in February 1977, eight different administrators headed the VA. Hines, by way of contrast, directed the VA and its predecessor, the VB, for a total of twenty-two years. President James E. Carter's appointment of Cleland, who lost both legs and his right arm in Vietnam, helped make Vietnam veterans feel the VA knew about their special needs, much the same as Bradley had done for World War II veterans.

The VA in 1980 still consisted of three administrative departments. Medicine and surgery continued as before. Veterans' benefits also continued but included insurance, which in 1953 had been a separate department. The new department was memorial affairs, with cemetery service its major concern.

In 1980, the VA, with 226,000 employees and a budget of $22 billion, remained the big business it had become following World War II. The VA, with its 172 medical centers, 49 clinics, 92 nursing homes, and 15 domiciliaries, operated the most extensive health care system in the country. Through its insurance benefits, the VA provided coverage for almost 8 million persons with policies exceeding $105 billion, making the VA the nation's third largest life insurance company. The VA also has guaranteed over 10 million home loans.

Well into the twenty-first century, the VA will continue as a major federal agency. Based upon life-expectancy statistics, the last World War II veteran will live until the year 2030; the last Vietnam veteran will survive until the year 2060. Their widows push the final year of VA obligation even further into the future. Of the nation's 30 million veterans in 1980, more than 16 million earned their status since the end of World War II. A second factor guaranteeing the VA a major function in the next century is that the VA will eventually disburse an estimated trillion dollars to World War II veterans and even more to the Korean and Vietnam veterans. The cost of veteran benefits for a war easily exceeds the direct cost of the war.

On balance, the operation of the VA and its predecessors is meritorious, considering the number and type of constituents it serves and the emotions society exhibits toward these constituents. By adhering to its service role, the VA has remained outside controversies that have arisen among politicians, veterans, and taxpayers. Moreover, the VA's record of responsible service, combined with generous veterans benefits, has contributed substantially to integrate veterans into society and to mitigate possible negative political influences of veteran groups.

FOR ADDITIONAL INFORMATION: Historians have neglected the VA as a subject of research. The only history of the agency is "wholly descriptive" and appeared in 1934: Gustavus A. Weber and Laurence F. Schmeckebier, *The Veterans' Administration: Its History, Activities and Organization* (1934). Of the three works that present broad coverage of veteran benefits, one is outdated and the other two are governmental reports: William H. Glasson, *Federal Military Pensions in the United States* (1918); "The Historical Development of Veterans' Benefits in the United States," Staff Report No. 1 (165 pp) of the President's Commission on Veterans' Pensions (1956); and "Medical Care of Veterans," House Committee Print No. 4 (411 pp), 90th Cong., 1st Sess. (1967).

Three examples of specialized studies that deal with veterans and the administration of veteran benefits in the broader setting of politics and society are: Mary R. Dearing, *Veterans in Politics: The Story of the G.A.R.* (1952); Keith W. Olson, *The G.I. Bill, The Veterans, and The Colleges* (1974); and Davis R.B. Ross, *Preparing for Ulysses: Politics and Veterans During World War II* (1969).

In addition to an administrative history of the VA, scholars have neglected such potentially rewarding topics as the attitude and actions toward and the relationships between the VA and insurance and home mortgage companies, and the American Medical Association. The titles of the books by Dearing, Ross, and Olson suggest other types of studies that deserve historical examination.

KEITH W. OLSON

_W_

WAR DEPARTMENT. See Department of the Army.

WAR INDUSTRIES BOARD (WIB). The War Industries Board was one of the emergency agencies erected by the Wilson Administration during World War I. Created on July 28, 1917, as a subsidiary of the Council of National Defense (CND), the WIB was informally separated from the parent body on March 4, 1918, and operated under the chairmanship of Bernard M. Baruch to coordinate and facilitate wartime production for the armed forces of the United States. It was disbanded by Executive Order 3019-A on December 31, 1918, and finally liquidated on July 22, 1919.

One of the great themes in twentieth-century American history is the expansion of central power and organization. The 1917-1919 war effort alerted the country, to some extent, to the potential of national planning. The American government expanded pragmatically and incrementally during the war, spinning off new agencies as conditions demanded. Ultimately, shipping, food, fuel, transportation and communication, trade, labor, and war production were controlled to some degree by emergency boards. Unlike other war governments, however, the heads of the American agencies were not brought into the regular Cabinet. The Allied governments, for example, met their supply problems through independent ministries of munitions and supply. Organized vertically according to the conventional wisdom of the day, their chiefs held ministerial rank and were politically accountable. The American government kept most emergency agencies entirely separate from the regular administration. More by accident than by design, a horizontal, functionally organized national war administration emerged.

The War Industries Board was only one part of a broad organization, and its effectiveness grew from its facilitating relationships with other agencies rather than from some position at the apex of a pyramid of power. It was established as a temporary subordinate agency of the CND on July 28, 1917. It was formed in part to meet charges of conflict of interest among businessmen who occupied emergency positions in government that had arisen during the early months of the war and in part to rationalize and make more efficient the stumbling industrial mobilization of the first summer of the conflict. Its roots lay in the debates over the relation of munitions-makers and the national government in peace and war which had gone on since the days of Alexander Hamilton and Thomas Jefferson. The Kernan Board of the War Department in 1916 had reaffirmed the traditional mixed system of supply by government facilities and limited, private contracts, in peace and by an expanded private sector in war. The first two years of the Great War had shown, however, that some method had to be found to control war expansion if complete chaos were to be avoided. President Woodrow Wilson, Secretary of War Newton D. Baker, and Secretary of the Navy Josephus Daniels were committed to traditional policies but saw the need for such planning and coordination. During the summer of 1916, the administration pressed for a council of national defense to play that role. It was hoped that the council, composed of appropriate Cabinet members and assisted by an advisory committee of technical experts, would encourage national contingency planning and, at the same time, quiet traditional American fear of political domination by crisis-spawned special interest groups. The CND had just begun to meet when the country entered World War I on April 5, 1917.

Controversy immediately erupted between those who hoped traditional practices would be disturbed as little as possible by the war and those who wanted a centralized "modern" system created to control civilian war production and to direct government purchasing. President Wilson at first held the former position. Secretary of War Baker and his colleagues at the War Department, fearing that control of Army requirements, priority, and procurement would be taken out of their hands, supported the President. Secretary of the Treasury William G. McAdoo and Bernard M. Baruch, a Wall Street speculator who had recently entered the government as an expert on raw materials, among others, held the latter view. They urged Wilson to appoint one man with full authority to direct the supply side of the war. The conflict between "traditionalists" and "modernizers" continued throughout the war. The emergence of the WIB, its peculiar structure and its relationships with other emergency agencies and the regular national authorities, represented a significant part of that broader conflict.

The story began in June 1917, when Secretary of War Baker, in an effort to head off the "modernizers," had CND Director Walter Gifford devise a plan to link the military effectively with industry in such a way as to assure the War Department direct access to vital war supplies. There was real cause for concern. By June, the CND had generated over 150 supply committees composed of businessmen who served without pay and put the military into contact with the business and industrial communities. Industry in turn created "War Service Committees" which linked chambers of commerce and trade associations with the supply committees. Businessmen, in violation of conflict-of-interest legislation, were contracting with their own companies. The Army* and the Navy* were vying with each other and within their own supply bureaucracies for war material. The railroads, the shipping industry, civilian consumers, and the other

Allied governments were all competing for scarce resources. Prices skyrocketed and profits soared while essential products either disappeared or went to inappropriate buyers. Market conditions were approaching anarchy.

Gifford was no "traditionalist," but he did have the War Department* interest at heart. His proposal, the Baker Plan, as it came to be called, was circulated in the administration in late June and early July 1917. It suggested that five separate boards—production, raw materials, priority, finished products, and Allied purchasing—be created. The production board would be known as the War Industries Board. All would be subordinate to the CND, which, of course, was chaired by Secretary Baker. The military would determine the war program and control contracting. An organizational nucleus already existed in the General Munitions Board of the CND chaired by Frank Scott, a Cleveland, Ohio, engineer and industrialist; the board was advising the services on weapons procurement. President Wilson thought the plan was crude and clumsy and, in late July, rejected the multi-limbed monster proposed by Baker and Gifford. Wilson retained the title War Industries Board, but he brought the Army, Navy, and key civilian elements in production and distribution into that one agency. Frank Scott moved over from the defunct General Munitions Board to chair the WIB; Baruch became raw materials commissioner; Robert Lovett of the Union Pacific Railroad became priorities commissioner; Robert Brookings, a well-known business magnate, handled finished products; and, on the advice of Secretary of Labor William B. Wilson, Hugh Frayne of the AFL was added to represent labor. A purchasing commission composed of Baruch, Brookings, Lovett, and Herbert Hoover, who was about to become food administrator, acted for the Allies. The new WIB did solve, to an extent, the problem of conflict of interest, and it gave an illusion of coordination to the war effort, but its creation was a victory for the War Department "traditionalists" who wanted a less powerful coordinating agency rather than a central authority to direct economic mobilization.

The WIB was still the creature of the CND. Frank Scott had no independent grant of power like Herbert Hoover, the new food director, or James Garfield, the fuel director, and insisted that, as a result, he could have little effect on the war program. All the procurement agencies went their separate ways during the autumn and winter of 1917-1918, and they might have muddled through if not for the Allied military reverses which resulted in Italian military collapse and Russian withdrawal from the war. As the timetable for American participation was advanced and the sheer size of the American war effort multiplied, the need for effective coordination increased. The worst weather in a generation snarled rail and water transportation, and by January 1918, freight cars and barges were stalled as far west as Saint Louis and Chicago. Ports were clogged with merchantmen waiting for coal and cargo, and it appeared that the administration's war effort was a humiliating failure. Meanwhile, Scott had resigned in September 1917, and it was not until December that a successor was found in Daniel Willard, president of the Baltimore and Ohio Railroad. Willard immediately joined the critics of the administration who were calling for a ministry of supply or an economic "czar." On March 4, 1918, with Baker still recalcitrant and against the advice of important leaders in the business and financial communities, Wilson appointed Bernard Baruch chairman of the WIB, gave him an independent grant of power, and separated the WIB informally from the CND. It was a real victory for the "modernizers," but even then it was not until the Overman Act of May 1918 gave Wilson authority to reorganize the executive branch for war that the agency's legal status was confirmed (Executive Order 2868, May 28, 1918).

The WIB under Baruch was an unconventional organization. It was staffed by young "dollar-a-year" men like George Peek of the Moline Implement Company, who replaced Brookings as commissioner of finished products, and its task was to locate production facilities, link consumers with producers, and negotiate priorities of production among the numerous consumers. It divided the country into twenty-one production districts with representatives in each district. Influential businessmen were named to district advisory committees, usually with the advice of local chambers of commerce, thus completing the linkage between the local and national WIB organization. The most important work of the WIB was done in commodity committees composed of representatives from all the using agencies. The number of commodity committees expanded as new items came into short suppy and required allocation. There the competing demands of the procurement agencies were compromised. Any issues that could not be worked out were referred to the priorities division. The actual contracting was left to regular procurement agencies.

Baruch was a lone wolf. Financially independent and a Democrat with few corporate connections, he ran his own office out of the top of his hat. He preferred facilitation to overt coercion. He retained at least the illusion of voluntarism and only as a last resort did he use the commandeering prerogative available through the presidential war powers. Commandeering was an ineffective tool, or so Baruch believed, because it consumed time and money, resulted in litigation and business resentment, and interrupted production. As he said later, he preferred firmness administered gently. His greatest success was curtailment of civilian production. In the summer of 1918, motor car and truck manufacturing was stopped, and the industry converted completely to war production. Civilian construction was cut back, and attempts were made to conserve raw materials by standardizing and redesigning various products ranging from claw hammers to women's corsets.

Baruch's greatest failure was his inability to control the Army. During the fall of 1917, the War Department incorporated most of the old CND supply committees into the Ordnance and Quartermaster Bureaus. In early 1918, Secretary Baker tried to centralize requirements and procurements in the War Department and in the General Staff under Peyton C. March. Necessity, as he saw it, drove Baker the "traditionalist," to become a reluctant "modernizer." Ultimately, most of the War Department's purchasing was carried on by the Purchase Storage and Traffic Division of the War Department General Staff (the

PS and T) under Major General George W. Goethals, the "Conquerer of the Panama Canal."

Assisted by able soldiers like Hugh Johnson and civilians like Gerard Swope of General Electric and Willard Thorne of Montgomery Ward, Goethals moved to assure the military uncontested access to the production facilities of the nation. The Army captured the WIB's regional advisory committees, and, by midsummer 1918, it was obvious they were working directly with the Army rather than with the WIB. Military requirements multiplied and culminated in a fantastic plan to equip and transport to France by the summer of 1919 an army of 4 million men. When the war ended, shipping was still in crisis, the supply and munitions programs were in disarray, and civilians were questioning whether the military had been allowed to expand beyond any realistic need. Ironically, Baker and the War Departmennt, still fearing outside civilian control as they had the previous summer, were moving to concentrate in their own hands the total effort of the nation behind the Army in France. Baruch and the WIB, still trying for broader national direction, were struggling to gain some realistic perspective on what was necessary and what was unnecessary to win the conflict. The situation was moving toward a crisis. On November 11, 1918, just when it was becoming clear that Baruch's style of voluntarism and persuasion would not work much longer, the war ended.

Many knowledgeable and astute participants were ambivalent about the wartime organizational experience in general and the WIB in particular. Certain traditionalists questioned the wisdom of the whole process. Single entrepreneurs saw it simply as a nasty episode outside the American business tradition—bad enough while it was going on—which certainly should not be allowed to set any precedents for the future. Political critics charged that members of the WIB, despite their dollar-a-year status as government employees, represented the great national corporations and could not see the public interest except through the lens of their own particular interest. These commentators claimed that a powerful, self-serving, and self-regulating business organization, potentially damaging to American institutions, seemed to be growing beyond public control with the help of the American government. Ideological "modernizers" like Walter Gifford, later president of AT and T, saw it as an exercise in national voluntary cooperation and international engineering, the harbinger of a new world of efficiency and prosperity. Less dogmatic advocates like Baruch, McAdoo, and General Hugh Johnson, a late convert to the WIB, saw it as a successful example of crisis management, which stored in public memory lessons that would be helpful in future emergencies. Their postwar legacy was improved War Department planning and the Army Industrial College.

Unfortunately, in defending themselves during postwar congressional investigations, Baruch and his supporters perpetuated a most misleading myth. They claimed that the WIB was a kind of "giant hand" which had directed the war effort with great success. Baruch, or so the "WIB myth" went, had been a czar who had allocated the industrial might of the nation to the Army, the Navy, the

Allies, and other supplicants in order of need. The whole thing had been done through voluntary cooperation with great goodwill from all. That simply was not true. When the war ended, the military controlled the supply process. The PS and T under Goethals was moving to dominate the whole industrial scene. Limits would soon have to be set to the Army's demands for shipping, railroad space, and other critical elements in the war effort. Perhaps, if the war had gone on, the WIB might have become the great directing agency that Baruch later described. Possibly another organization might have been devised to which the existing agencies would have been subordinated. But the war ended. In a later war emergency, the administration of Franklin D. Roosevelt would manage the crisis in a quite different manner.

FOR ADDITIONAL INFORMATION: The classic "WIB myth" is contained in Bernard Baruch *American Industry in the War* (1921); Grosvenor B. Clarkson, *Industrial America in the World War: The Strategy Behind the Line, 1917-1918* (1923); and Benedict Crowell and Robert F. Wilson, *How America Went to War*, 6 vols. (1921). Revisionist views can be found in Daniel R. Beaver, "The Problem of Military Supply," in B.F. Cooling, ed., *War, Business and American Society* (1977); Robert D. Cuff, *War Industries Board, Business-Government Relations During World War I* (1973); James E. Hewes, Jr., *From Root to McNamara: Army Organization and Administration 1900-1963* (1975); and James A. Huston, *The Sinews of War: Army Logistics 1775-1953* (1966).

DANIEL R. BEAVER

WAR INFORMATION OFFICE. See Office of War Information.

WAR MANPOWER COMMISSION (WMC). Fighting a modern world war requires the manipulation of millions of men into companies, battalions, and divisions in the armed forces, and into vital jobs on the home front. During World War II, the United States did a magnificent job of organizing men in uniform for fighting the war. Franklin Roosevelt, however, came only reluctantly to realize that men also had to be organized for the home front. This delay reflected the idea of abundance, which had always characterized the American mind, whether dealing with mineral resources or manpower. Equally misleading was the recent experience of the depression. With 8 million men still unemployed in 1940, few leaders expected shortages in manpower to play a role in wartime mobilization. The Army* insisted that no conceivable military adventure could lead to such a shortage. Besides assumptions of abundance, thoughts of civilian labor mobilizations ran counter to the conviction that the worker and the manager could solve all problems through the normal operations of the market mechanism. Faith in the mechanical behavior of classical laws of employment remained strong despite the depression and the New Deal.

Such assumptions insured that the question of mobilizing manpower would receive only cursory attention from the Roosevelt Administration. Most leaders felt that the major problem of manpower had been settled with the passage of a Selective Service Act in October 1940, providing a peacetime draft to fill the ranks of the armed forces. The various planning agencies erected by Roosevelt in the months before Pearl Harbor, including the National Defense Advisory Commission, the Office of Production Management, and even the War Production Board,* paid little attention to civilian manpower.

Expansion of the defense industry proceeded with little worry over manpower. New munitions industries were located on the basis of strategic reasons which included everything from security to the availability of raw material, but ignored the local labor market. New plants recruited workers without much trouble into 1941, although a few shipbuilding centers did begin to report shortages. For the most part, manpower needs could be satisfied by interregional recruitment. The unemployed rushed without guidance to the new jobs.

After the attack on Pearl Harbor, things began to change. New production schedules went into effect, drastically increasing goals for most war industry. Production schedules went through turmoil as cuts and shifts in targets resulted from technical and strategic considerations. Massive labor-recruiting drives began with little attention to the housing and community services needed within a community. Some 5.5 million workers entered the defense industry in 1941. But Harold Smith, the director of the Bureau of the Budget,* could not get President Roosevelt even to talk about manpower.

The Selective Service System* was drafting huge numbers of workers into the armed forces. By early 1942, the draft and expansion of war production had largely erased the unemployed surplus of manpower. Reluctantly, Roosevelt finally allowed Smith to present plans for some type of federal direction to manpower.

Developing an acceptable plan proved difficult. Several government agencies had different ideas about manpower. The War Production Board, under Donald Nelson, was still convinced that nothing was needed. Secretary of Labor Frances Perkins felt the same way. The armed forces remained confident that the civilian economy could be squeezed much tighter without any manpower crisis.

Roosevelt finally appointed Samuel Rosenman, William Douglas, Anna Rosenberg, and Harold Smith to draft a plan, which would please everyone. Although the plan was soon finished, the selection of a man to head the new War Manpower Commission proved ticklish. Perkins wanted to run things from her department. At the urgings of Rosenberg, supported by representatives from the AFL and the CIO, Roosevelt finally turned to Paul McNutt, a committed New Dealer with some experience in federal administration.

On April 18, 1942, the President issued an Executive Order creating the War Manpower Commission with McNutt as chairman. The new agency and chairman received an impressive mandate on paper. The commission had representatives from the following departments: War*, Navy*, Agriculture*, Labor*, Selective Service, Civil Service*, and the War Production Board. McNutt, as chairman, was authorized to formulate national plans and programs to assure effective mobilization and utilization of manpower to fight the war. Before the year was out, Roosevelt had transferred to McNutt's control the United States Employment

Service (USES), the major federal job-training programs, and the Selective Service.

Although McNutt's power appeared impressive, appearances were deceptive. Congress provided no statutory support for the program and viewed the politically ambitious McNutt with undisguised suspicion. While providing implicit endorsement through appropriations, Congress consistently warned McNutt against assuming dictatorial authority over the labor force. The warning was hardly needed. Both Roosevelt and McNutt preferred a voluntary and decentralized approach to the manpower mobilization problem. Neither man saw any need for a national service law until late in the war, despite the pleas of Grenville Clark and Henry Stimson. The manpower program would be pursued with a respect for localism.

The organizational scheme of the WMC clearly reflected this decentralism and voluntarism. The basic operational unit of WMC was the local United States Employment Office, over fifteen hundred of which were spread around the country. It was at these local centers that workers received information on jobs and placements were made, all on a voluntary basis. National manpower policy was formulated by the WMC and implemented through an array of twelve regional manpower directors across the nation. Below the regional offices were area directors, appointed to handle special problem areas. These area directors numbered up to two hundred at one time. Each state also had a manpower director, who was responsible for the coordination and direction of USES offices. The local USES office made job placements, but an appeal system was also organized to allow workers to challenge local decisions. The entire system was analogous to the Selective Service System, which functioned through the largely independent county draft boards.

On the national level the WMC had several departments. The Management-Labor Policy Committee provided guidance from those two interest groups. More operational in function were the following offices: Planning and Review, Placement, Training, Utilization, Reports and Analysis. After December 1942, the Selective Service became a nominal office of the WMC. With the increased significance of women workers during 1943, a special Women's Advisory Committee was also established, although it possessed little power.

During the war, the WMC engaged in a wide variety of manpower activities. The primary task was to find labor—the right worker for the right job. To accomplish this task, the WMC established lists of essential activities and occupations, which were to guide local USES offices in placement and local draft boards in occupational deferments. To insure proper utilization of labor, the WMC researched information on the labor market and had experts analyze jobs in plants. In addition, the WMC assumed control over a massive government-sponsored training program for workers conducted in schools and in factories. The WMC also established employment stabilization plans, involving hiring ceilings and freezing workers in their jobs.

American war production became one of the greatest success stories in the history of industrial society. Besides providing the thousands of tanks, planes, and guns needed for the American Army, domestic industry also produced huge quantities for the Allies, and simultaneouly maintained a domestic living standard well above that of most of the world. From July 1940 to July 1944, the labor force in war-expanded activities in the United States jumped by 19.4 million. Some 12 million of these individuals helped to swell the ranks of the military, but the total civilian labor force also grew while these young men were being drafted. From 1941 to 1945, the industrial workforce grew by almost 4 million. Some 9.7 million new workers entered the economy, including 5.5 million women. One study has estimated that the workforce grew by 6.5 million over normal expectations during the war.

The WMC kept busy trying to deal with this enormous growth of the labor force. Some fifteen hundred manning tables were drawn up to improve worker utilization. Over 16 million workers received job training under government sponsorship. The USES made over 35 million job placements from 1942 to the end of the war. Some 2 million workers were recruited successfully for interregional job transfers. In 1942 alone, over 3.3 million farm-work placements were made. There were a few critical labor shortages during the war, primarily on the West Coast, but no evidence emerged of labor shortages leading to significant strategic or tactical setbacks for the United States.

McNutt would have been less than human not to claim credit for these manpower achievements. Yet, the WMC was only a modest factor in manpower mobilization during World War II. Without question, the most important force in mobilizing men for war industry was the operation of the market system. The vast numbers of unemployed flocked to new jobs in war industry. After this surplus had been eliminated, workers came from other occupations, attracted by the higher pay and chances for overtime. Women entered the workforce in unprecedented numbers. Most of this movement occurred with only modest help from the WMC. But this market movement also created serious problems. Labor pirating led to shortages in one war industry even as another war industry benefited. Agricultural labor had to be protected from the enormous appeal of working conditions in industry. Cities became overcrowded as workers rushed in to find jobs. Job discrimination continued against women and blacks, despite the halfhearted efforts of the government.

The WMC never achieved total control over the labor movement in the United States because it never intended such control. The agency suffered from a variety of problems which insured that its impact on manpower mobilization would always be marginal. Some of these problems were of an internal nature. McNutt had definite limitations as a leader. His forceful personality irritated Cabinet members, and his political ambitions worried congressmen. His staff seemed incompetent in dealing with manpower problems. Fowler V. Harper, the deputy chairman, did not get along with A.J. Altmeyer, the executive director. Lewis B. Hershey, head of Selective Service, went his own way and, after one year, succeeded in becoming independent of the WMC. The Management-Labor Policy

Committee assumed more and more authority as the spokesmen for powerful interest groups. At a lower level, the staff was strapped by stiff budget cuts. In several USES offices, the turnover of personnel ran over 75 percent.

Another major weakness of the WMC was the totally inadequate coordination with other government agencies. The major procurement agencies looked upon WMC as a mere feeder of labor. Neither the War Production Board nor the armed services saw fit to allow WMC a role in determining procurement or strategic questions. The armed services considered McNutt's work merely window dressing and constantly worked for a national service law.

Fundamentally, the WMC suffered from inadequate authority for enforcing its programs and rules. Depending upon an Executive Order rather than a statute, McNutt could not force compliance. Indeed, by trying to make a virtue out of this defect through emphasis upon voluntarism, McNutt contributed to his own trouble. Instead of demanding more power from the President and Congress, he labored ineffectively to make cooperation work. As a result, his inspection and enforcement programs were limited. Utilizations inspections were too few to have much effect. Attempts at enforcement were met with indifference or hostility by management secure in the support of procurement agencies. When McNutt attempted a compulsory transfer of workers in New Bedford, Massachusetts, during 1944, organized labor quickly forced him to back down.

Given the absence of an effective law and President Roosevelt's general indifference to the problem of manpower, the WMC did well to achieve anything of significance. Yet, it did promote community involvement in manpower mobilization. Thousands of USES offices did make millions of placements. Thanks to the WMC, a body of up-to-date information on the national labor market was created for the first time. This information allowed other war agencies to identify manpower problems. The various training programs did help thousands of youths, women, and others to obtain new skills. By publicizing the dangers of labor hoarding and malutilization, the WMC did contribute to ending labor piracy. Beyond these achievements, the WMC could not go, given the President's attitude and the Congress's suspicions. The war had no sooner ended in Asia than President Harry Truman announced the end of the WMC by transferring its remaining functions to the Department of Labor.*

FOR ADDITIONAL INFORMATION: The most recent study of manpower mobilization during World War II, which includes more than the history of the WMC, is George Q. Flynn, *The Mess in Washington: Manpower Mobilization in World War I* (1979). An official history of the WMC is U.S. Employment Service, *A Short History of the War Manpower Commission* (1948). See Leonard P. Adams, *Wartime Manpower Mobilization* (1951), for a study of mobilization in the Buffalo-Niagara Falls area. Byron Fairchild and Jonathan Grossman, *The Army and Industrial Manpower* (1959), offers the view of the armed services. Albert A. Blum, *Drafted or Deferred: Practices Past and Present* (1967), explains the impact of conscription on general manpower problems. Herman M. Somers, *Presidential Agency: OWMR, The Office of War Mobilization and Reconversion* (1950), reveals how the WMC fit into the overall direction of mobilization by Washington.

The official records of the WMC are in Record Group 211 at the National Archives,*
Washington, D.C. Paul McNutt's papers can be found at the Lilly Library, Indiana
University, Bloomington, Indiana.

GEORGE Q. FLYNN

WAR PRODUCTION BOARD (WPB). The War Production Board, the principal agency of the U.S. government for direction and control of the U.S.
economy in World War II, was established by Executive Order on January 16,
1942. The agency was, in fact, a continuation and expansion of predecessor
agencies created during the eighteen-month "Defense Period" (June 1940-De-
cember 1941) between the fall of France and the bombing of Pearl Harbor. The
problems, activities, and accomplishments of these predecessor agencies are thus
an integral part of the experience of the WPB, and the nation as a whole, in its
economic mobilization activities for World War II.

Throughout the 1920s and the depression years of the 1930s, neither the
American public nor successive Congresses had felt the need to maintain the
nation's military establishment even at minimum levels of preparedness for actual
combat. Although the Navy,* as the nation's "first line of defense," was kept
in a state of readiness in peacetime, the United States Army* on June 30, 1939,
was only a skeleton, numbering a mere 174,000 men and less than 15,000
officers. Its lack of equipment was even more serious. In mid-1940, after Adolf
Hilter had completed his conquest of Norway, the Low Countries, and France
in a period of less than two months, there was not enough powder in the entire
United States to last the Army at wartime strength for as much as a day's fighting.
Even worse, according to later revelations by Secretary of War Henry L. Stimson,
the United States lacked plants and other facilities which had been dismantled
after World War I. Similar shortages existed throughout the whole category of
military equipment.

This precarious situation resulted in large part from policies based on the
nation's geographical insularity, its traditional posture of isolation, and its neutrality laws designed to minimize the possibility of involvement in future wars.
In theory, the nation's ocean barriers and naval protection were sufficient to give
the United States time to rearm if and when an emergency arose. To insure a
timely and successful program of rearmament in the event of a serious threat of
war, the Army and Navy under the National Defense Act of 1920 had prepared
the Industrial Mobilization Plan (IMP). The IMP spelled out the various steps
to be taken upon declaration of an emergency, including establishment of an all-
powerful War Resources Board to mobilize the nation's economy. This wartime
governmental superagency, operating under a chairman with great powers, would
have full authority to establish and enforce priorities, allocate industrial facilities,
commandeer plants, and otherwise control the economy, while a selective service
system would provide the necessary manpower for expansion of the armed forces.

On September 8, 1939, following Hitler's invasion of Poland and the outbreak
of war in Europe, President Franklin D. Roosevelt proclaimed a "limited"

national emergency. He felt, probably correctly, that the country was not yet ready for the establishment of an all-powerful War Resources Board, which might attempt to proceed too vigorously, for a nation still at peace, with a program of mandatory priorities, curtailment of peacetime goods and services, and forced conversion to war production. Instead, he planned to reactivate the Advisory Commission to the Council of National Defense used early in World War I. This could be done quickly under existing legislation and would provide him with a small but distinguished group of commissioners who would use their expertise, prestige, and contacts to expedite the nation's rearmament under a voluntary program of economic mobilization.

On May 16, 1940, four days after the German invasion of France, Roosevelt appeared before Congress and requested greatly expanded military appropriations, indicating his desire for a program to produce 50,000 military planes annually. While Congress was considering these appropriations, Roosevelt carried out his plan to reactivate the National Defense Advisory Commission (NADC), which met in Washington for the first time on May 30, 1940. Shortly thereafter, the new commissioner for production, William S. Knudsen (president of General Motors Corporation), conferred with Assistant Secretary of War Louis Johnson to determine the overall industrial capacity required to meet the military program. As a result, the huge War Department program, known as the munitions program of June 30, 1940, was launched and financed by Congress under a series of supplemental appropriations. Early in July, a request for an additional 1,325,000 displacement tons of naval combatant vessels, amounting to the creation of a "two-ocean" Navy, was approved by Congress. It was now up to the NDAC to insure the availability of materials, manpower, and facilities to implement the program.

The NDAC initially consisted of seven advisers or "commissioners," responsible, respectively, for production, materials, labor, transportation, agriculture, prices, and consumer interests. One month later, Donald M. Nelson, executive vice-president of Sears-Roebuck, was appointed coordinator of National Defense Purchases with status equivalent to the others. The commission immediately began a vigorous program of activity, endeavoring to anticipate and provide for all the numerous shortages, bottlenecks, and other problems certain to occur in the implementation, at short notice, of a vast industrial mobilization effort.

The defense and war production programs included not only ships, planes, tanks, guns, ammunition, and other weapons of war but also transportation and communication equipment, medical supplies, fuel, food, clothing, maintenance, and countless other items essential to the operation of both the Army and the Navy and their air arms. It also included even more urgently required construction programs, military receiving camps, stations, barracks, airfields, navy yards, and operating bases of all kinds, as well as arsenals, ammunition plants, depots, and other storage and service facilities. The vast bulk of this production and construction activity would be accomplished by private industry under contracts financed by the U.S. government and placed by the established procurement offices of the Army and Navy with firms capable of meeting specifications and delivery schedules. It soon became apparent that exising manufacturing facilities in the United States, despite idle capacity still remaining after years of depression, would be insufficient for the purpose. This necessitated a program of private-plant expansion of huge but unpredictable dimensions.

With an initial appropriation of only $1 million, the NDAC quickly recruited an outstanding staff composed largely of leaders in American industry. Most of them served on a "dollar-a-year" basis, and they were supplemented by specialists from government agencies and the academic world. With no statutory operating powers at the time of its creation, the NDAC assumed the role of adviser, persuader, and gadfly, not only to the armed services and to industry, but also to Congress and the American public. It urged the armed forces to improve their requirements estimates for both military end-items and their essential components and materials. It translated military requirements into required productive capacity, developed programs for government financing of plant construction, and endeavored to persuade industry to undertake immediate expansion of capacity. It reviewed estimates of requirements for strategic and critical materials obtainable only or largely from abroad, and cooperated with other agencies in arrangements for importation and stockpiling. These activities extended to preclusive buying and the devleopment of export controls as instruments of economic warfare in addition to their function of augmenting U.S. supplies.

In the field of procurement policy, the NDAC assisted the procuring agencies to obtain from Congress relief from many crippling statutory provisions not appropriate to emergency or wartime procurement. These included time-consuming requirements for advertising and competitive bidding which precluded rapid and flexible contract negotiation; provisions requiring liquidated damages for delayed deliveries which prevented application of a system of priorities; and the "Buy-American Act' which hampered or prevented importation and stockpiling of strategic materials from abroad. New positive powers were also obtained from Congress: the tax amortization law permitting rapid write-off of new wartime facilities, provision for assignment of claims by contractors to obtain financing, and authorization of advance payments by procurement agencies, assisting contractors to expand plant, hire labor, and purchase essential supplies to complete their contracts. In addition, the NDAC developed broad principles of contract placement and distribution in order to minimize the economic and social costs of excessive migration of labor, undue geographic concentration of defense industries, and concentration of defense contracts in a limited number of large firms.

In the fundamental area of material-control systems, the NDAC influenced the character of the priorities system established by the Army and Navy Munitions Board in August 1940. The system was initiated on a voluntary basis, and by the end of the year NDAC had obtained delegation of presidential powers granted by legislation earlier in the year to authorize application of priorities on a mandatory basis. This designation to NDAC, rather than to the armed services, set the pattern for civilian control of this fundamental power. Finally, through its Office of Information, the NDAC kept the American public informed of developments on the economic mobilization front, interpreted their significance, and helped to enlist the understanding and support of the public in carrying out programs certain to require growing inconveniences and sacrifices for all concerned.

By the end of 1940, the rearmament program had been effectively launched. But shortages and bottlenecks were appearing throughout the economy, and growing problems were calling for firm decisions and more effective controls. President Roosevelt came under increasing criticism for failing to appoint a chairman to NDAC who could effectively coordinate the work of the several commissioners and their rapidly increasing staffs. This was becoming more imperative since the NDAC had now been given, by statute or Executive Order, a number of operating powers.

As a result, on December 20, 1940, Roosevelt announced the impending establishment of a new agency, the Office of Production Management (OPM), which would focus on the task of expanding defense production. Established by Executive Order on January 7, 1941, the OPM took over most of the functions and staff of the NDAC, including the entire production, materials, purchasing, and labor divisions, the bureau of research and statistics, administrative services, and others, totaling approximately a thousand employees. The important price-control function under Leon Henderson, along with the consumer protection division, was transferred from NDAC to a new independent agency, the Office of Price Control and Civilian Supply. NDAC's Office of Information eventually became the influential Office of War Information,* and, in late 1941, the transportation division became the Office of Defense Transportation. Although the information and price-control functions had been given separate agency status under the Industrial Mobilization Plan, the splintering of important production functions, such as those involving transportation, rubber, petroleum and manpower, away from the principal production-control agency was later to create problems for the War Production Board. By the fall of 1941, virtually all of NDAC's personnel and functions had been absorbed by other agencies, and the commission held its final meeting on October 22, 1941.

The new OPM organization was headed by a director general (Knudsen) and an associate director general (Sidney Hillman, NDAC commissioner for labor), operating under a policymaking OPM Council, consisting of Knudsen, Hillman, and the secretaries of War and Navy. This arrangement enabled the Army and Navy as the principal consumers of defense production to share, *Ab initio,* in basic decisions affecting production. It also answered, in part at least, criticisms that under the NDAC the program lacked central direction and had given labor an insufficient voice in its conduct. Initially, OPM was organized along functional lines, with each of the three principal operating divisions—production, purchases, and priorities—bearing the name of its function. This inevitably meant duplication of staff and dissipation of control, since important decisions in any of the functional areas required intimate knowledge of the specific industries involved. Each of the three major divisions, therefore, soon had branches or sections composed of specialists representing each of fifty or more important materials or commodities essential to production. This duplication and the resulting confusion were largely eliminated by a reorganization on June 24, 1941, which gave primary responsibility for each product or material to a single division.

The year 1941 saw the defense program moving into high gear, with total requirements growing far more rapidly than either capacity or output. In January, the British Supply Council, in response to earlier NDAC requests, presented total British purchase requirements of military items in the United States for 1941 and 1942. The numbers of required planes, merchant ships, tanks, and other items were enormous, and England, in her second year of a costly war, had virtually exhausted her supplies of dollar exchange. This situation led to the Lend Lease Act of March 11, 1941, authorizing the President, in the interest of national defense, to supply foreign governments with defense materials on such terms as he deemed satisfactory. After the German attack on Russia on June 22, the Soviet Union became a major claimant of Lend Lease assistance, which eventually totaled some $50 billion; of this amount England alone received $31 billion, while $11 billion went to Russia.

Faced with these new commitments, OPM now found it necessary to determine, for the visible future, total requirements from all sources matched against total productive capacity. This became possible for the first time, although in highly tentative form and figures, when the President, in the summer of 1941, directed the armed forces to estimate the magnitude of a total program adequate to defeat the potential enemies of the United States. This led to the gigantic Victory Program of September 1941, which dwarfed the Munitions Program of 1941 and included the requirements not only of the Army, Navy, and merchant shipping, but of all Lend Lease countries as well. This program became the basis for the expanded war production program after Pearl Harbor.

To expedite the increasing needs of the defense program,the OPM in 1941 initiated many of the familiar control devices used in World War II to channel and expedite production. Before the end of 1940, the excessive issuance of high preference ratings for machine tools and other critical items had required modification of the rating system, and by the following spring priorities in many areas could no longer guarantee timely delivery. Four days after the President's declaration, on May 27, 1941, of an Unlimited National Emergency, Congress extended the President's priority powers to include any orders deemed necessary for national defense, thus permitting the application of priorities on a mandatory basis for essential nonmilitary as well as military items, and for materials, components, and supplies at all levels of production. But this could not resolve the fundamental problem of insufficiency of basic materials and components to fill both the defense program and rapidly rising civilian demands growing out of greatly increased employment and incomes after a decade of depression. In

1941, the American automobile industry was experiencing the greatest volume of sales in its history and was extremely loath to make major cutbacks in production and sales. Organized labor, in the early months of 1941, moved aggressively to increase its membership and influence throughout industry as employment and profits increased, and a number of prolonged strikes contributed to production slowdowns and bottlenecks in industries beyond those of the strike-bound plants.

In order to bring a greater sense of urgency and increased authority to the defense effort, President Roosevelt, on August 28, created the Supply Priorities and Allocations Board (SPAB) and transferred to it the priority powers formerly delegated to OPM. Headed by Vice-President Henry A. Wallace, SPAB included the four OPM Council members, plus Leon Henderson, Harry Hopkins (Roosevelt's personal assistant), and Donald Nelson, as executive director. The Civilian Supply functions and staff formerly attached to OPACS were transferred to OPM, which now served as the operating arm of SPAB in carrying out a mandatory program of priorities and conversion to defense production.

The bombing of Pearl Harbor on December 7, 1941, brought the United States fully into the war and put an end to all questions of whether and how soon to complete the conversion of American industry to war production. Soon thereafter the major labor organizations voluntarily gave a no-strike pledge for the duration of the war, and Congress, in the First and Second War Powers Acts, conferred virtually unlimited powers upon the President to conduct the war. On January 6, 1942, Roosevelt in his important State of the Union message to Congress announced the heroic production goals of key items which he had set for the nation: for 1942, 60,000 planes, 45,000 tanks, 20,000 anti-aircraft guns, and 6 million tons of merchant ships; for 1943: 125,000 planes, 75,000 tanks, 35,000 anti-aircraft guns, and 10 million tons of merchant ships. The President went on to state: "Let no man say it cannot be done. It must be done—and we have undertaken to do it." Ten days later he ordered the replacement of OPM and SPAB with a new, all-powerful economic-mobilization-control agency, the War Production Board, headed by a single director, Donald Nelson.

WPB's initial organization included six major divisions—Purchases, Production, Materials, Labor, Civilian Supply, and Industry Operations—supplemented by a Requirements Committee, a Planning Committee, and an Office of Progress Reports. Its staff of some 7,000 employees inherited from OPM grew rapidly to 18,000 by July 1, and reached a peak of 23,000 in February 1943, of which nearly 8,000 were employees in the twelve regional offices throughout the country. The policymaking War Production Board itself consisted of the former SPAB members, but their role was limited to "advice and assistance" to the chairman, who had final responsibility both for operations and policy determination.

Nelson moved immediately to place the nation's economy on a full wartime basis and to prepare his own organization for the tasks that lay ahead. On January 24, he delegated to the Office of Price Administration* general responsibility for rationing scarce consumer goods to the civilian economy, reserving to WPB the determination of the goods, and the amounts thereof, to be rationed. On March 3, he made mandatory the placement of all war contracts by direct negotiation, in accordance with stated criteria, and raised from $500,000 to $5 million the size of individual contracts requiring advance clearance by WPB. As counseled by elder statesman Bernard Baruch, director of the highly successful War Industries Board* in World War I, Nelson refrained from attempting to take over and assimilate into the WPB organization the specialized procurement arms of the Army, Navy, and other agencies. Nevertheless, later he was often criticized for "delegating" to the armed services essential functions which they had always possessed and which were unnecessary to WPB's function of supervision and control.

Three major tasks faced WPB in the dark weeks and months after Pearl Harbor, and neither the problems nor their solutions were clearly visible in the early months of 1942. The first of these tasks was the development of a balanced program of war production, which would be feasible in terms of the nation's productive capacity and adequately responsive to the needs of the armed forces and the civilian economy. The mammoth objectives of the President's "must" program, designed to inspire the nation to maximum effort, would strain productive capacity to the utmost in the specific industries concerned. When combined with all the complementary items in the supply programs of the armed forces, the resulting program, according to estimates of WPB's Planning Committee, was dangerously in excess of the nation's capacity. Such excesses could result in seriously imbalanced and reduced output. All through the spring and summer of 1942, the issues in "the feasibility dispute" were explored and debated, culminating in an explosive meeting of the War Production Board in September. As a result, the Joint Chiefs of Staff agreed to pare down the military programs substantially to WPB's estimates of feasibility.

The second major problem was how to channel the flow of scarce materials to their most urgent uses in the war program. By early 1942 the priorities system, the simplest and most widely used control system, was in serious difficulty. Rampant "priorities inflation," created by continued overissue of high ratings, had reduced many of them to virtual worthlessness. To minimize the volume of paper work involved in applications by individual firms, the OPM early in 1941 had issued a number of "general preference orders" assigning priorities to entire industries. In May, it introduced the Defense Supplies Rating Plan (DSRP), permitting approximately a thousand firms to apply only once each quarter for standard "off-the-shelf" items required in defense production. This was followed in December by the Production Requirements Plan (PRP), under which a manufacturer could apply once each quarter for all scarce materials required by his defense contracts. The resulting across-the-board type of allocation was known as "horizontal" allocation. Late in the second quarter of 1942, under great pressure to replace the priorities system with more effective procedures, WPB made PRP mandatory beginning in the third quarter for some eighteen thousand metal users accounting for 90 percent of the nation's metal consumption. Unfortunately, PRP did not provide a tight system of material control since it relied on applicants' estimates of future material needs, including those for contracts not yet received, on the basis of past consumption experience rather than on specific bills of materials for items in approved programs.

In the meantime, the Army and Navy as well as various sections of WPB had been working to devise a budgetary type of material-control system, which would insure that all available supplies of covered materials would be delivered on schedule to approved programs. The result of these efforts was the adoption of the Controlled Materials Plan (CMP), announced by WPB on November 2, 1942. This was a vertical system of controlled allocation, under which the Army, Navy, and other claimant agencies would compute their quarterly requirements of controlled materials on the basis of bills of materials or engineering estimates for all end-products in their approved programs. Steel, copper, and aluminum were the principal controlled materials, reflecting their primary importance in the war production program. Each claimant agency would distribute its quarterly allotment among its prime contractors who would, in turn, redistribute appropriate amounts to subcontractors down the vertical chain of production. Since the warrants thus distributed were limited in quantity to total scheduled production, all warrant holders were guaranteed timely delivery of the needed materials. The new system was carefully introduced, after elaborate preparations by all concerned, in the second quarter of 1943 and became fully operative on July 1, 1943.

The third major problem, the need for central control over production scheduling, not only for programmed end-products but also for critical common components, moved to the foreground after the adoption of CMP. By this time shortages of vital components, such as motors, generators, compressors, heat exchangers, electrical-measuring instruments, and anti-friction bearings, were seriously threatening the scheduled completion of such important items as aircraft, destroyer escorts, merchant vessels, and facilities for producing aviation gasoline and rubber. Moreover, unbalanced production was locking up huge quantities of scarce materials in unusable inventories of some end items, while equally important complementary items could not be produced for lack of the same materials. To address all such problems, Nelson on September 18, 1942, apointed Charles E. Wilson, president of General Electric Company, as vice-chairman of WPB and chairman of a new Production Executive Committee (PEC), which included high-ranking representatives of the armed forces and other agencies. By the end of the year, PEC had obtained a basic agreement on scheduling policies from the Army and Navy, and in February WPB issued General Scheduling Order M-293 establishing detailed scheduling procedures for thirty-six classes of components. The following month, it was stated in a WPB meeting that of thirty-four critical components only four would be short of requirements by July.

By the end of 1943, the major problems of organizing the nation's economy for war had been brought under control, and war production in the United States had reached its peak. Overseas theaters of operation had been successfully established and logistical pipelines well filled. Stocks of many items, especially small arms ammunition, had reached unprecedented levels, and a War Department Procurement Review Board, appointed at the request of the newly established Office of War Mobilization (OWM), recommended a sober reexamination of military requirements. Contract completions and terminations were becoming numerous, and determining when and how fast to resume civilian production, with the nation still at war, involved fundamental questions of national policy.

Roosevelt had created OWM, later to become the Office of War Mobilization and Reconversion (OWMR), in May 1943 in the midst of many uncertainties over the course and direction of the war effort. He felt the need for a top-level superagency, free from the pressures of operating responsibilities, which could resolve major policy questions, conduct forward planning, and coordinate the activities of the various war agencies, many of them now beyond the jurisdiction of WPB. In the fall of 1943, the OWM director, James F. Byrnes, appointed Bernard Baruch and his associate, John Hancock, to review the whole field of contract termination and settlement and to recommend policies and machinery designed to liquidate the war production effort and smooth the transition to a peacetime economy. This resulted in the Baruch-Hancock Report of February 15, 1944, whose recommendations were adopted and became the basis for the highly successful contract-termination and settlement program for World War II.

Thus, by mid-1944, partly as a result of WPB's own achievements and shortcomings and partly because of external developments, the status of the War Production Board as the center of power in the economy had declined. Manpower shortages had now replaced material shortages as the critical bottleneck, and the resolution of current issues in war production depended more and more on decisions of the War Manpower Commission. Within the WPB Wilson had become, under successive reorganizations and delegations of authority, executive vice-chairman directly under Nelson and second in command of the entire WPB organization. As chairman of the Aircraft Production Board as well as of the powerful Production Executive Committee, he was actively involved in all major production decisions and was closely associated with military officials responsible for the successful prosecution of the war program. Nelson, on the other hand, was now less involved with the administration of current programs and for some months had been increasingly concerned with the need to formulate and develop reconversion policies and programs. In June 1944, aware of growing excess capacity and availability of materials, Nelson determined that the time had come to allow production, on a limited scale, of civilian items deemed in wartime to be "nonessential." To this end on June 18, over the objections of the armed services and the WMC, he announced to the press plans to issue reconversion orders permitting limited resumption of civilian production. Although the successful landings in France on D-Day and the progress of the war in the Pacific gave assurance of ultimate victory, the war was still far from over, and Nelson's actions became highly controversial. Although Nelson was supported by the Truman and Small Business Committees of Congress as well as the press, the military agencies and the War Manpower Commission continued their opposition. Many of the WPB staff, including Wilson, also felt the reconversion orders to be premature. Compounding the problem were press reports that Wilson's objections to the reconversion orders stemmed from his affiliation with big business and an unwillingness to allow small plants to gain a competitive advantage by resuming peacetime production in advance of large corporations tied up by war contracts.

In this situation Byrnes, as head of OWM, on August 4 issued an order giving the War Manpower Commission authority to approve or disapprove expansion of civilian production in each local area. Two weeks later, President Roosevelt announced that Nelson was being sent on a confidential mission to China. On August 24, in a final meeting with Nelson and key WPB officials, Wilson announced his resignation, stating that, as a result of insinuations in the press, his usefulness to WPB was over. When Nelson returned from China a month later, he too resigned. Although much work remained to be done before the war was over, the ending of the Nelson-Wilson era accelerated what had already begun—the gradual liquidation of WPB's organization and activities. By the end of 1944, WPB's staff had shrunk to less than 13,000 employees, and after VJ-Day in August 1945, this figure fell to 5,400 by the end of October and to 2,700 at year's end under WPB's successor. Effective November 3, 1945, an Executive Order of President Harry S Truman formally abolished the War Production Board and replaced it with the Civilian Production Administration, whose task it was to complete, in an orderly manner, the transition to peacetime production.

Historians may differ over many aspects of WPB's organization and leadership, but there can be no doubt as to the success of the war production program guided and directed by WPB and its predecessors. Although President Roosevelt's spectacular production objectives for 1942 and 1943 were eventually revised, their role as incentive goals helped to produce the total of 300,000 planes, 51 million tons of merchant ships, and countless other items which proved to be decisive in winning the war. At the end of his campaign in Europe, General Dwight D. Eisenhower paid tribute to the war production achievement.

The record would be incomplete without reference to fundamental conditions which made the production achievement possible and which may never recur. These included (1) a year and a half of "borrowed time," between the outbreak of war in Europe and the bombing of Pearl Harbor, which enabled the United States, while still at peace, to launch and vigorously prosecute its rearmament program; (2) the impregnability, in the midtwentieth century, of the continental United States and its productive machinery from attack and devastation of the kind suffered by other combatants in World War II; and (3) a condition of abundant idle resources and deflation at the beginning of the defense program, which minimized economic dislocations and both the money and the real costs of war production.

FOR ADDITIONAL INFORMATION: The basic source of information on the War Production Board is the official volume *Industrial Mobilization for War: History of the War Production Board and Predecessor Agencies, 1940-45* (1945), pp, xviii, 1010, prepared and published by WPB's successor agency, the Civilian Production Administration (reprinted by Greenwood Press, Westport). This comprehensive and carefully written volume contains a detailed list of sources, providing virtually unlimited opportunities for further investigation and research on all aspects of WPB's organization and activities.

For further description of the U.S. economic mobilization effort for World War II, including prewar planning and the wartime relationships between the WPB and the principal procurement agency, see R. Elberton Smith, *The Army and Economic Mobilization* (1959), pp. xxv, 749, in the official historical series *U.S. Army in World War II*.

For valuable personal testimony, insights, and specific details concerning the defense and war production programs of the United States for World War II, see Donald M. Nelson, *Arsenal of Democracy* (1946).

R. ELBERTON SMITH

WEATHER BUREAU. See National Weather Service.

WEATHER SERVICE. See National Weather Service.

WEST POINT. See United States Military Academy.

WILDLIFE SERVICE. See United States Fish and Wildlife Service.

WOMEN'S BUREAU. Since colonial times, women in America have been working outside the home for wages, and they have often worked under poor conditions and for wages far lower than those of their male counterparts. In 1920, the same year the Nineteenth Amendment giving women the right to vote was ratified, Congress established the Women's Bureau within the Department of Labor.* It is not coincidental that both of these women's issues—the vote and working conditions—were addressed the same year. Bettering the conditions of working women was an important part of the feminist movement beginning already in the nineteenth century. Suffragists such as Harriot Stanton Blatch equated working women with independent women.

The specific duty of the Women's Bureau (1920) was "to formulate standards and policies which shall promote the welfare of wage-earning women, improve their working conditions, increase their efficiency, and advance their opportunities for profitable employment" (41 Stat. 987).

A permanent bureau to deal with the problems of working women was not established without a great deal of effort on the part of women's organizations. In 1905, three women, including Jane Addams, representing the National Women's Trade Union League (WTUL) asked Congress to investigate the working conditions of women and children. Two years later, after pressure from a variety of groups and from President Theodore Roosevelt himself, Congress passed a bill authorizing the Secretary of Commerce and Labor to undertake this investigation and issue a report. The results of this study appeared over four years in nineteen volumes and documented such working conditions as long hours, lower pay than what men were paid for the same work, ill-lit, dirty, and dangerous work areas, as well as appalling sanitary conditions.

The report demonstrated the need for continued investigations. A Women's Division was formed in the Bureau of Labor Statistics, but so many problems soon developed that it ceased to exist. The women's salaries were extremely low, and the Women's Division's funds were frequently diverted to other inquiries. The situation completely deteriorated when the Commission of Labor Statistics so altered the statistics collected by the Women's Division that the investigators refused to sign the study and all the women in the division resigned.

As a result, a number of women's organizations such as the WTUL and the YWCA demanded the creation of a permanent and independent Women's Bureau. Their argument was strengthened by the creation of the Children's Bureau;* however, while efforts for a Women's Bureau continued, only a national crisis impelled its actual creation. U.S. participation in World War I—and the subsequent need for women in the labor force—focused attention on women workers and their problems. To deal with these issues, Congress established the Women-in-Industry Service of the Department of Labor.* The primary function of the service, with Mary Van Kleeck as director and Mary Anderson as assistant director, was to monitor the needs of women working in war factories.

Women-in-Industry was a wartime agency, and the end of World War I threatened its existence; it had to be adapted if it were to become permanent. In June 1920, Congress passed a bill to create a permanent Women's Bureau, but its potential effectiveness was hampered by a serious lack of funding. The $75,000 appropriated ($30,000 operating costs, the rest salaries) was only one-half of what the Secretary of Labor had recommended. In addition, the salary scales were far lower than those in comparable agencies. Except for the director and an assistant director, whose salaries were to be $5,000 and $3,500, respectively, the top salaries of experts at the Women's Bureau were limited to $2,000—one-third less than the same position commanded at the Bureau of Labor Statistics.

Problems of adequate funding for the Women's Bureau have continued throughout its existence. Writing in 1975 in a paper for the Women's Bureau itself, Linda Rugg reports that since its beginning the bureau has grown very little, in either amount of appropriations or number of personnel. The reason may lie not only in the hostility and indifference of Congress but also in the narrow focus of the bureau itself, and its resultant battles with feminist organizations. Irene Murphy, in her work *Public Policy and the Status of Women*, suggests that with a wider outlook, the bureau might have related sooner than it did to other major problems confronting women. A larger constituency might have meant increased power and budget.

The first director of the Women's Bureau was Mary Anderson, a Swedish immigrant factory worker who had come up through the ranks of trade unionism.

A decade earlier, she had given up working as a shoe stitcher in Chicago to take a salaried position as a WTUL organizer. This position had eventually led to her appointment as assistant director and then director of the Women-in-Industry Service, culminating in 1920 with her appointment as director of the Women's Bureau. The rest of the Women-in-Industry Service personnel and data were also taken over by the newly established Women's Bureau.

As director, Anderson saw the basic mission of the bureau to be fact-finding, coordinating, and acting in an advocacy role on behalf of women workers. In 1921, she wrote that, while the Nineteenth Amendment had given women citizenship, they still did not have many of their economic rights. She saw her agency as one that would gain those rights and promote the general status of all women. Part of this gain would be accomplished through information gathering that could be used to influence government policy. The techniques of investigation were established early; this was the collection of detailed factual data that was later analyzed by the statistical division. Field agents supplemented this information with home visits. The studies published were very carefully prepared. Anderson later stated that the conclusions were never challenged during the period in which she was the director. Eventually, the data collection by the Women's Bureau itself had to cease. As the functions of the bureau expanded while its limited resources did not, the bureau found it more valuable to discontinue original research and to rely on facts gathered by other agencies such as the Census Bureau* and the Bureau of Labor Statistics.

Anderson used much of this information to pressure for changing laws. With her connections to the WTUL, it is not surprising that as bureau director she advocated industrial standards similar to those called for by the League. These included equal pay, a six-day work-week, an eight-hour day, no night work for women, minimum wage, the prohibition of women working in industries more dangerous for them than for men, and improved working conditions.

While Anderson was the best known and most popular woman in the federal service, she was not without her detractors. These ranged from groups who perceived the Women's Bureau as un-American and un-patriotic for encouraging women to work, to feminist groups who felt that the Women's Bureau did not truly support women's needs. Indeed, for many years after its founding, one of the most bitter enemies of the Women's Bureau was Alice Paul's Women's party, and the bone of contention was the bureau's refusal to support the Equal Rights Amendment because it would do away with protective legislation for women. The Women's Bureau did not alter this position until 1970.

In the 1920s, two conferences which the Women's Bureau sponsored on Women in Industry were disrupted by the Women's party, which sought to use these conferences as forums to discuss the Equal Rights Amendment. The tactics of the Women's party at the second conference in 1926 led to special bitterness. After Anderson had refused to devote a session to the topic, the Women's party held a rally two days before the conference opened and sent a delegation to President Calvin Coolidge. They deliberately conveyed the impression that their activities were part of the conference and thus sanctioned by the Women's Bureau. At the conference itself, the Women's party—its members shouting and demonstrating—broke up the meeting with demands for consideration of the proposed amendment.

The Women's Bureau in the 1920s was also criticized by conservative women's groups. In 1922, the Woman Patriots—a reorganized remnant of the National Association Opposed to Woman Suffrage—charged that the Women's Bureau and its allies were attempting to Bolshevize the United States by its proposed destruction of the family through encouraging women to work. Their evidence was slim. In a Women's Bureau's pamphlet on maternity benefits in fourteen countries, the bibliography listed a 1916 book by Alexandra Kollontai on how the system was handled in Russia.

In 1930, there were rumors that Herbert Hoover would appoint Anderson as Secretary of the Department of Labor; this appointment would have increased the prestige of the bureau enormously. It was not to be. A few years later, Franklin Roosevelt did appoint a woman, Frances Perkins, Secretary of Labor. At first, Anderson was delighted with Perkins's appointment, believing that a woman as Secretary would be very helpful to the bureau. Anderson found, however, that the two of them were not able to work well together. Some people believed that Perkins, as the first woman to hold Cabinet rank, felt she had to be especially careful not to show preference to other women.

With the depression, the 1930s proved a difficult time for working women and for the Women's Bureau in its attempts to support them. Many women were losing their jobs because they had husbands. A Women's Bureau report of 1933 charged that qualifications, not marital status, should determine employment or dismissal. Throughout this decade, the bureau was generally in a holding pattern, attempting not to lose the ground it had already gained.

With the U.S. entry into World War II, there was again an enormous need for women workers. Anderson's work at the bureau had to expand to match the influx of new women workers. The bureau had to establish procedures to assure proper access to jobs and training, as well as maintain high work standards. Yet, with all these new duties, there were still problems over adequate funding. In 1944, after nearly a quarter of a century, Anderson resigned as director because of Perkins's failure to support an increase in the bureau's budget to match its new responsibilities.

Perkins appointed Freida Miller the new director. Miller's major goal as director was to deal with the problems of postwar employment for women, and she directed the bureau to examine job opportunities. In 1945, she created the Labor Advisory Committee of the Women's Bureau. Until 1950, representatives of fifteen unions met at the bureau each month to discuss labor problems and issues concerning working women.

In 1946, Miller organized a series of conferences with union leaders and representatives of national women's groups to discuss postwar employment problems. She asked them to develop a plan to secure equal opportunity and pay for women. Until she resigned in 1952 at the request of the incoming Republican administration, her emphasis was on equal pay and equal access to jobs for women.

Yet, Miller also had serious problems with funding and with allegations of subversive activity. After the 1946 election, the Department of Labor became the number one target of Congress. Congressman Frank Keefe, chairman of the House Appropriations Committee, was convinced that some of the people in the Department of Labor were Communists. He tried to cut entirely the $300,000 budget for the Women's Bureau, but feminists raised such an uproar that he backed down.

By the early 1950s, the issue of women's status in the workplace was not in general attracting a great deal of attention. This was after all the age of the feminine mystique, and bride, wife, and mother were the roles that were glorified for women. Yet, women remained in the workforce in much larger numbers than was anticipated, and they continued to be concerned about their position. Their concern was largely ignored, however. During this period, there was a slight but steady drop in appropriations for the bureau.

This situation changed with the election of John F. Kennedy in 1960. In the 1960s, the Women's Bureau experienced its most significant growth in terms of appropriations, personnel, and involvement in policy decisions affecting women workers. In 1961, Kennedy established a Commission on the Status of Women, an idea that originated from Esther Peterson, a member of his campaign staff and a long-time labor lobbyist whom he had appointed as director of the Women's Bureau. Thus, the bureau was intimately connected with the commission. Fifteen staff members were added to the bureau to work exclusively on programs relating to the commission, and, in 1963, the bureau's annual appropriation was enlarged to $930,000.

Peterson herself was executive vice-chairperson of the commission, which completed its work in October 1963. The commission report identified a number of problem areas for women workers, such as continuing education, child care services, job counseling, and equal pay. The bureau demonstrated its concern by publishing reports specifically on these issues and also encouraged states to set up their own commissions on the status of women.

Many people speculated as to why Kennedy had set up the commission; some believed the President had motives other than interest in the basic rights of women. Judith Hole and Ellen Levine suggest it was a means by which Kennedy could pay his political debts to women so that they would again support him in 1964, and that it would also ease the pressure on his administration to support the Equal Rights Amendment. Peterson explained a decade later that the "awful" Equal Rights Amendment was indeed a consideration, which shows that, even in the 1960s, the Women's Bureau had not shifted its position on the proposed amendment.

The bureau did not change its stand until 1970 under the leadership of Elizabeth Duncan Koontz, the former president of the National Education Association.

Although she was a Democrat, Richard Nixon appointed her as director in 1969. Koontz held bureau staff meetings to discuss the amendment, and then, not only officially announced her support, but also pressured the Department of Labor to endorse it.

Koontz believed that the Women's Bureau had not kept in touch with the varying philosophies throughout the women's movement. To attempt to remedy this failing, she held a conference to celebrate the bureau's fiftieth anniversary and invited more than a thousand women of widely varying political persuasions to attend and brainstorm. Koontz attempted to change directions in other areas as well. She hoped to aid poor women in obtaining job training, was very concerned over day care, and wanted to restructure the "entire household industry." Her attempts to achieve a larger mandate and budget for the bureau were unsuccessful, however, and Koontz resigned during the reorganization period of Nixon's second administration. Referring to the early 1970s, Irene Murphy suggests that the bureau had lost ground overall in recent years.

Most recently, the Women's Bureau has been shifting some of its focus toward low-income and minority women. The bureau has been especially concerned with nontraditional job training for them, and over twenty-one model outreach programs for job training have been developed. The bureau, hoping these programs will be duplicated by other groups, has prepared how-to manuals for this eventuality.

At present, the Women's Bureau is directed by Lenora Cole-Alexander, former teacher and university administrator. She has found that the Women's Bureau has always been a small agency with low-priority funding. Its position and scope have been changing in the last decade, and attempts have been made to heal some of the divisions between it and areas of the women's movement. The bureau's influence has ebbed and flowed depending on the economy and on the friendliness of Congress and the administration. Some critics wonder if the Women's Bureau is not cooption; they ask whether an organization can effectively work for change for women within the system. As the second wave of feminism comes of age, the future will show just what role the Women's Bureau may play in the status of working women.

Directors of the Women's Bureau

Mary Anderson	1920-1944
Freida S. Miller	1944-1953
Alice K. Leopold	1953-1961
Esther Peterson	1961-1964
Mary Dublin Keyserling	1964-1969
Elizabeth Duncan Koontz	1969-1973
Carmen R. Maymi	1973-1977
Alexis M. Herman	1977-1981
Lenora Cole-Alexander	1981-

FOR ADDITIONAL INFORMATION: The Women's Bureau itself provided a great deal of information, including Linda Rugg's 1975 study, "The Women's Bureau of the Department of Labor: A Brief History." Other useful material includes: Mary Anderson, *Woman at Work: The Autobiography of Mary Anderson as told to Mary Winslow* (1951); William Chaffe, *The American Woman: Her Changing Social, Economic, and Political Role, 1920-1970* (1972); Jo Freeman, *The Politics of Women's Liberation* (1975); Jonathan Grossman, *The Department of Labor* (1973); Judith Hole and Ellen Levine, *The Rebirth of Feminism* (1971); Marcia Hovey, "A Doughty Lady Turns 50," *Manpower*, official publication of the Department of Labor (March 1970): 14-18; Edward T. James, "Mary Anderson," in Barbara Sicherman and Carol Hurd Green, eds., *Notable American Women: The Modern Period* (1980), pp. 23-25; J. Stanley Lemon, *The Woman Citizen, Social Feminism in the 1920's* (1973); Dee Ann Montgomery, "Freida Miller," *Notable American Women: The Modern Period* (n.d.), pp. 78-79; Irene Murphy, *Public Policy on the Status of Women* (1973); Judith Sealander, "The Women's Bureau, 1920-1950" (Ph.D. dissertation, Duke University, 1977); and John Terrell, *The United States Department of Labor: A Story of Workers, Unions, and the Economy* (1968).

CAROLE LEVIN

WORKS PROGRESS ADMINISTRATION (WPA). The Works Progress Administration was created by President Franklin D. Roosevelt (Executive Order No. 7034, May 6, 1935) to administer $4.8 billion appropriated by the Emergency Relief Appropriation Act (Pub. Res. No. 11, 74th Cong., H. J. Res. 117). It was continued on a year-to-year basis under similar joint resolutions until June 30, 1943, when it was abolished by presidential letter. Under the Reorganization Act of 1939, it was placed under the Federal Works Agency and renamed the Works Projects Administration.

The WPA grew out of the Roosevelt Administration's efforts to combat unemployment during the Great Depression. The President at first established the agency to develop and coordinate a program of work relief for various other federal agencies. The President favored work relief as a substitute for "direct relief," which he believed state and local governments should provide. Thus, he announced that after 1935 the federal government would no longer provide funds for direct relief and would discontinue the Federal Emergency Relief Administration (FERA), which had been established in 1933 to aid state relief programs with grants-in-aid. At the same time, he gave the FERA staff the responsibility for administering the WPA.

Within a short time, the WPA had emerged as the dominant agency in federal work relief. This happened in part because of the experience its staff had gained in administering work relief projects in the FERA and the Civil Works Administration (CWA), which had operated federal work projects during the winter of 1933-1934. By transferring many FERA projects to WPA and by using its rapport with state and local officials, the WPA was able to move more rapidly than other federal agencies in developing projects that employed large numbers of relief recipients. Employing as many persons as possible was a natural objective for the WPA staff, which was dominated by social workers who wanted to provide maximum assistance to the needy. In its first year, WPA spent 60 percent of the congressional appropriation but employed 70 percent of the workers.

The WPA also benefited from the leadership of its chief administrator, Harry Hopkins. Raised in Iowa and a graduate of Grinnell College, where he had been exposed to the ideas of Progressive reform politics and the Social Gospel, Hopkins had held several high administrative positions in private social work and had directed New York's Temporary Emergency Relief Administration before becoming head of the FERA in 1933. In the FERA he had recruited an able group of assistants, including Jacob Baker, Corrington Gill, Aubrey Williams, and Ellen Woodward, whom he used as a general staff and upon whose judgment he relied. Seemingly at home in the helter-skelter atmosphere of improvising to meet emergencies, Hopkins lived by the words, "Damn it, find a way to do it." Under his inspiration the FERA and WPA operated with a minimum of formality as their staff members worked long hours, shared each others' problems, and kept themselves open to novel ideas for putting the unemployed to work. Hopkins was also a canny bureaucratic politician, able to use his contacts with local political bosses to build his stock with the President and Congress and to compete successfully with other federal agencies for work-relief funds. In the fall of 1935, the President endorsed WPA's high employment projects, which he realized would most rapidly take the federal government out of giving direct relief, and in following years Congress allocated WPA the overwhelming share of work-relief funds.

WPA'S work program was quite decentralized. In consultation with state and district WPA officials, local sponsors submitted project proposals to the Washington office. Washington approved the projects, authorized funds, and issued directives to the state and district offices. The WPA required sponsors to pay part of their projects' cost but had poor results until 1939 when Congress required sponsors to contribute at least 25 percent. In order to handle troublesome situations and to interpret Washington's directives, the WPA established nine (later eight) regional offices. Hopkins supplemented reports from these offices with reports from outside observers, such as Lorena Hickock, journalist and close friend of Eleanor Roosevelt. By 1937, WPA had adopted stable and regular administrative procedures. Perhaps because of this and because he was developing higher political ambitions, Hopkins resigned in 1938 to become Secretary of Commerce. President Roosevelt replaced him with Colonel F. C. Harrington, who headed WPA until his death in 1941, at which time the President appointed Howard Hunter and, after Hunter's resignation in 1942, Major General Philip B. Fleming.

WPA's employment and wage policies reflected its ambiguous status as both a work program and a relief program. Except for an allowance of 10 percent to hire workers with necessary skills, WPA drew its employees exclusively from the relief rolls. It hired workers under "force account," paying them with a government check instead of dealing with contractors, who, WPA feared, would not hire persons on relief. It paid workers a "security wage," an amount above the relief stipend and less than the wage for private employment but calculated to provide an adequate standard of living in return for continuous work. In practice, then, WPA wages were salaries with deductions for time lost because of absence or unfavorable working conditions. In 1936, Congress required WPA to pay wages at the hourly rates prevailing in private industry. This forced WPA to adjust its workers' hours so that their total pay remained at the security wage level and resulted in literally hundreds of time schedules for projects. In 1939, Congress reestablished the security wage and set a standard of 130 hours per month for employees. At the same time, Congress limited continuous employment on WPA to eighteen months while allowing a person to be rehired after one month's unemployment.

The WPA carried out an astonishing variety of projects, all but a tiny fraction of which were sponsored by state and local governments. Construction projects headed the list with the repair and building of streets and highways, hospitals, schools, libraries, sewer and water systems, and airport facilities taking over 60 percent of its funds. In addition, WPA undertook projects in recreation, pest control, engineering survey, child care, home economics education, and the conservation of natural resources. Attracting particular attention were its federally sponsored projects in writing and the arts, which followed Hopkins's observation that, like everybody else, artists had to eat. The Federal Music Project established local symphony orchestras, bands, choirs, and glee clubs that performed both standard works and new works by American composers. The Federal Writers' Project produced the American Guide Series for tourists and others interested in local Americana as well as studies of America's ethnic, racial, and regional cultures. The Federal Art Project decorated public buildings with murals, mosaics, paintings, and sculptures and held classes for aspiring local artists. The Federal Theater Project performed live drama for over 30 million Americans and experimented with such techniques as the "living newspaper." In 1939, Congress, put off by the social and economic radicalism of some theater productions, cut off funds for the Federal Theater and reduced the other arts projects by requiring them to have local sponsorship.

Administratively, WPA operated with a nice balance between federal and local authority. The inflexibility and restrictions on state and local finances and the fact that many areas of high unemployment were too poor to provide adequate relief dictated a federally financed work-relief program, while initiative and planning of local sponsors produced projects of real local value and encouraged popular support for the work-relief program.

In other areas, WPA's record was more mixed. By employing more persons than other federal work programs, it helped to relieve the immediate sufferings of the depression but perhaps at the expense of contributing to economic recovery. Spokesmen for federal programs of heavy construction pointed out that every job on the Public Works Administration* created one or two jobs in private industry, while it took six WPA jobs to create one private job. In addition, because of the administration's fiscal conservatism WPA never met its own goal of employing 3.5 million workers (its average was 2.3 million) and had to set its security wages so low that they often failed to provide what WPA itself called an "emergency standard of living." Many social workers attacked the WPA for this and for damaging its workers' morale by requiring them to undergo investigation by local relief agencies and assigning them to low-status jobs as unskilled laborers. Such criticism, however, needs to be set alongside WPA's serious and innovative efforts to find suitable jobs for its workers, reports that showed high levels of worker satisfaction, and the evidence from the rise of the labor movement during these years of widespread discontent with working conditions in private employment.

During its early years, WPA was heavily involved in politics, as Congress saddled the agency with many state and district political appointees and congressmen and local bosses tried to pressure workers for their votes. Hopkins fought these efforts with varying results, while at the same time using WPA projects to build support for the agency with the politicians. By 1939, Congress had restricted political activity by WPA workers and officials through the sweeping restrictions of the Hatch Act. As a result, WPA was never incorporated into the patronage structure of the Democratic party. The effect of WPA employment on voting behavior, however, remains to be investigated, as do charges that the administration manipulated WPA rolls to influence elections in 1936 and 1938.

Because of the peculiar circumstances that produced the WPA, it may well stand as a unique feature of America's response to the problems of unemployment. Yet, it seems clear that WPA's influence carried beyond that of the agency itself. Not only did WPA projects produce things of lasting value to American life, but its flexible administrative style, as represented by Harry Hopkins, again served the nation during the second great crisis of the Roosevelt years. As the President's chief assistant, Hopkins employed his talents for improvising and for crisis management in organizing Lend-Lease aid to Britain and the Soviet Union and in managing key elements of the American war effort after Pearl Harbor. Indeed, historians could well investigate how much the management of the crises of war owed to the management of the crises of the Great Depression.

FOR ADDITIONAL INFORMATION: There is no general history of the Works Progress Administration. The annual *Report on the Progress of the WPA Program* provides both general and detailed descriptions of WPA programs and valuable statistical information. Donald S. Howard, *The WPA and Federal Relief Policy* (1943) is the most comprehensive treatment of the agency. Searle F. Charles, *Minister of Relief: Harry Hopkins and the Depression* (1963) treats Hopkins's administration of the WPA. Useful books on specific WPA programs include Jane D. Matthews, *The Federal Theatre, 1935-1939: Plays, Relief, and Politics* (1973); Richard D. McKinzie, *The New Deal for Artists* (1973); and Monty Penkower, *The Federal Writers' Project* (1977). Arthur W. MacMahon, John D. Millett, and Gladys Ogden, *The Administration of Federal Work Relief* (1941) focuses on the administrative procedures worked out by WPA's Washington Office. Robert E. Sherwood, *Roosevelt and Hopkins* (1948) traces the career of Harry Hopkins from his early life through his wartime service.

GEORGE T. McJIMSEY

Y

YOUTH ADMINISTRATION. See National Youth Administration.

CHRONOLOGY

This appendix presents a chronological compilation of agencies and the dates of their establishment. It should be used in conjunction with the appendix on Genealogy as well as the Contents. Each distinct name of an individual agency, former or present, is listed by year. The reader will notice the bunching of new entities during various eras of increased federal government activity and expenditures. Moreover, reorganization plans, those of either the executive or Congress, often caused a flurry of activity. Sometimes the duties later assumed by a separate agency were performed under an existing department or agency. Only the distinct, individual agencies are listed in this appendix.

1776

Board of War and Ordnance

1779

Corps of Engineers

1781

Department for (of) Foreign Affairs
Secretary of War

1789

Department of State
Department of the Treasury
Department of War
Lighthouse Service
Office of the Attorney General
Post Office Department
United States Customs Service

1790

Revenue Cutter Service

1794

Corps of Artillerists and Engineers

1798

    Department of the Navy
    Marine Corps
    Marine Hospital Service

1802

    Corps of Engineers
    Military Academy
    Patent Office

1807

    Coast Survey

1812

    General Land Office

1824

    Bureau of Indian Affairs

1845

    Naval Academy

1846

    Smithsonian Institution

1849

    Department of the Interior

1860

    Army Signal Corps

1862

    Bureau of Internal Revenue
    Department of Agriculture

1863

    First Division, National Currency Bureau

1865

    Bureau of Refugees, Freedmen, and Abandoned Lands
    Secret Service

1867

    Office of Education

1869

    Bureau of Engraving and Printing

1870

    Army Signal Corps, later Army Signal Service

    Department of Justice

1871

    United States Fish Commission

1878

    Coast and Geodetic Survey

    Life-saving Service

1879

    United States Geological Survey

1881

    Division, later Bureau, of Forestry

1883

    United States Civil Service Commission

1884

    Bureau of Education

    Bureau of Labor

    Bureau of Marine Inspection and Navigation

1885

    Bureau of Biological Survey

1887

    Interstate Commerce Commission

1891

    Bureau of Immigration

    United States Weather Bureau

1893

    Office of Road Inquiry

1901

    National Bureau of Standards

1902

    Bureau of the Census

    Bureau of Reclamation

    Public Health and Marine Hospital Service

1903

 Bureau of Fisheries
 Department of Commerce and Labor

1905

 Forest Service

1906

 Bureau of Chemistry
 Bureau of Immigration and Naturalization
 Department of Agriculture

1908

 Bureau of Investigation

1910

 Bureau of Mines

1912

 Children's Bureau
 Public Health Service

1913

 Commission on Industrial Relations
 Department of Commerce
 Department of Labor
 Federal Reserve Board

1914

 Federal Trade Commission

1915

 National Advisory Committee for Aeronautics
 United States Coast Guard

1916

 National Park Service
 Shipping Board
 United States Tariff Commission

1917

 War Industries Board

1918

 Air Service

1919

 Public Debt Service

1920

    Federal Power Commission
    Women's Bureau

1921

    Bureau of Public Roads
    Bureau of the Budget
    General Accounting Office

1924

    National Capital Park Commission

1926

    Aeronautics Branch
    Air Corps
    National Capital Park and Planning Commission

1927

    Drug and Insecticide Administration
    Federal Radio Commission

1929

    Office of Education

1930

    Food and Drug Administration
    Veterans Administration

1932

    Bureau of Navigation and Steamboat Inspection
    Reconstruction Finance Corporation

1933

    Civilian Conservation Corps
    Federal Civil Works Administration
    Federal Emergency Relief Administration
    Immigration and Naturalization Service
    National Labor Board
    National Recovery Administration
    Public Works Administration
    Tennessee Valley Authority

1934

    Bureau of Air Commerce
    Export-Import Bank of Washington
    Federal Communications Commission
    National Archives and Records Service

National Labor Relations Board (old one)
Securities and Exchange Commission

1935

Federal Bureau of Investigation
National Labor Relations Board (new one)
National Youth Administration
Resettlement Administration
Rural Electrification Administration
Social Security Board
Works Progress Administration

1936

United States Maritime Commission

1937

Farm Security Administration

1938

Air Safety Board
Civil Aeronautics Administration
Civil Aeronautics Authority

1939

Federal Works Agency
Works Projects Administration

1940

Bureau of the Public Debt
Civil Aeronautics Board
Defense Plant Corporation
National Defense Research Committee
Selective Service System

1941

Army Air Forces
Committee on Fair Employment Practices
Office of Price Administration
Office of Scientific Research and Development

1942

Office of Strategic Services
Office of War Information
War Manpower Commission
War Production Board

1946

Atomic Energy Commission

Bureau of Land Management
Council of Economic Advisers
Social Security Administration

1947

Central Intelligence Agency
Commission on Organization of the Executive Branch of the Government
(First Hoover Commission)
Department of Defense
Department of the Air Force
National Security Council

1948

Economic Cooperation Administration

1949

General Services Administration
Patent and Trademark Office

1950

Maritime Administration, Federal Maritime Board
National Science Foundation

1951

Mutual Security Agency

1952

Internal Revenue Service
National Capital Planning Commission

1953

Commission on Organization of the Executive Branch of the Government
(Second Hoover Commission)
Department of Health, Education and Welfare
Foreign Operations Administration
Small Business Administration
United States Information Agency

1954

Air Force Academy

1955

International Cooperation Administration
Office of the Special Assistant to the President for Disarmament

1957

United States Commission on Civil Rights
Federal Highway Administration

1958

National Aeronautics and Space Administration

1959

Federal Aviation Agency

1961

Agency for International Development
Arms Control and Disarmament Agency
Federal Maritime Commission
Peace Corps

1962

Army Strategic Communications Command (STRATCOM)

1964

Job Corps

1965

Department of Housing and Urban Development
Equal Employment Opportunity Commission
National Endowment for the Arts
National Endowment for the Humanities
National Ocean Survey
National Weather Service

1966

Department of Transportation
Federal Aviation Administration

1967

National Transportation Safety Board

1968

Export-Import Bank of the United States

1969

Office of Child Development

1970

Environmental Protection Agency
Office of Management and Budget

1971

National Railroad Passenger Corporation (AMTRAK)
Occupational Safety and Health Administration
Postal Service

1973

Army Communications Command

1974

Energy Research and Development Administration
Federal Energy Administration
Nuclear Regulatory Commission

1975

United States International Trade Commission

1976

Railway Association and Consolidated Rail Corporation (CONRAIL)

1977

Department of Energy
Federal Energy Regulatory Commission

1978

International Communication Agency

1979

Department of Education
Department of Health and Human Services
Office of Personnel Management

1983

United States Information Agency

GENEALOGY

The material below is intended to provide the reader with the evolution of agency names from the beginning to the present. It should be utilized along with the listing of agencies in the Contents. An effort has been made to include alphabetically all former names, whenever a separate entity existed, especially since the establishment of federal government under the present Constitution in effect as of 1789. Only several entries clearly date from the period 1776-1788.

The main item in each case indicates the agency name as used in this book. Sublistings then point out any variations in name and the pertinent dates for such name designations. For example, the entry, 1862- tells us that the agency was established in 1862 and continued in existence as this book went to press. Sometimes portions of the duties subsequently performed by an agency were carried out within another department or agency and without a specific name. Only distinct agency listings are included.

In compiling this appendix, I have leaned heavily on all the contributors to *Government Agencies* and have referred also to Office of the Federal Register, National Archives and Records Service, General Services Administration, *The United States Government Manual, 1981/82* (U.S. Government Printing Office, May 1, 1981).

Agency for International Development
    Economic Cooperation Administration, 1948-1951
    Mutual Security Agency, 1951-1953
    Foreign Operations Administration, 1953-1955
    International Cooperation Administration, 1955-1961
    Agency for International Development, 1961-

Bureau of Engraving and Printing
    First Division, National Currency Bureau, 1863-1869
    Bureau of Engraving and Printing, 1869-

Bureau of Indian Affairs
    Bureau of Indian Affairs, 1824-
    (Office of Indian Affairs was the unofficial term often used until 1947.)

Bureau of Land Management
    General Land Office, 1812-1946
    Bureau of Land Management, 1946-

Bureau of Mines
    Bureau of Mines, 1910-

Bureau of Public Debt
    Public Debt Service, 1919-1940
    Bureau of Public Debt, 1940-

Bureau of Reclamation
    Bureau of Reclamation, 1902-

Bureau of Refugees, Freedmen, and Abandoned Lands
    Bureau of Refugees, Freedmen, and Abandoned Lands, 1865-1872

Bureau of the Census
    Bureau of the Census, 1902-
    (The first twelve censuses before 1910 were taken by temporary federal organizations.)

Central Intelligence Agency
    Coordinator of Information, 1941-1942
    Office of Strategic Services, 1942-1945
    National Intelligence Authority, 1945-1947
    Central Intelligence Agency, 1947-

Children's Bureau
    Children's Bureau, 1912-1969
    Office of Child Development, 1969- (HEW), now Health and Human Services

Civil Aeronautics Board
    Civil Aeronautics Authority and Air Safety Board, 1938-1940
    Civil Aeronautics Board, 1940-

Civilian Conservation Corps
    Civilian Conservation Corps, 1933-1940

Committee on Fair Employment Practices
    Committee on Fair Employment Practices, 1941-1946

Council of Economic Advisers
    Council of Economic Advisers, 1946-

Defense Plant Corporation
    Defense Plant Corporation, 1940-1945

Department of Agriculture
Department of Agriculture, 1862-

Department of Commerce
Department of Commerce and Labor, 1903-1913
Department of Commerce, 1913-

Department of Defense
Department of War, 1789-
Department of the Navy, 1798-
Department of Defense, 1947-

Department of Education
Office of Education, 1867-1884
Bureau of Education, 1884-1929
Office of Education, 1929-1979
Department of Education, 1979-

Department of Energy
Atomic Energy Commission, 1946-1974
Energy Research and Development Administration, 1974-1977
Nuclear Regulatory Commission, 1974-1977
Federal Energy Administration, 1974-1977
Department of Energy, 1977-
(DOE assumed all the above functions.)

Department of Health and Human Services
Department of Health Education and Welfare 1953-1979
Department of Health and Human Services, 1979-

Department of Housing and Urban Development
Department of Housing and Urban Development, 1965-

Department of Interior
Department of the Interior, 1849-

Department of Justice
Office of the Attorney General, 1789-1870
Department of Justice, 1870-

Department of Labor
Bureau of Labor, 1884-1903
Department of Commerce and Labor, 1903-1913
Department of Labor, 1913-

Department of State
Department of Foreign Affairs, 1781-1789
Department of State, 1789-

Department of the Air Force
  Air Service, 1918-1926
  (Since 1892, the Signal Corps had sections working on military aviation.)
  Air Corps, 1926-1941
  Army Air Forces, 1941-1947
  Department of the Air Force, 1947-

Department of the Army
  Board of War and Ordnance, 1776-1781
  Secretary of War, 1781-1789
  Department of War, 1789-1947
  Department of the Army, 1947-
  (under the Department of Defense)

Department of the Navy
  Department of the Navy, 1798-
  (under Department of War, 1789-1798; since 1947 under Department of Defense)

Department of the Treasury
  Department of the Treasury, 1789-

Department of Transportation
  Department of Transportation, 1966-

Environmental Protection Agency
  Environmental Protection Agency, 1970-
  (Duties were previously conducted by various units in the Departments of Health, Education and Welfare, Agriculture, and Interior.)

Equal Employment Opportunity Commission
  Equal Employment Opportunity Commission, 1965-

Export-Import Bank of the United States
  Export-Import Bank of Washington, 1934-1968
  Export-Import Bank of the United States, 1968-

Farm Security Administration
  Farm Security Administration, 1937-1946

Federal Aviation Administration
  Aeronautics Branch, 1926-1934
  Bureau of Air Commerce, 1934-1938
  Civil Aeronautics Administration, 1938-1959
  Federal Aviation Agency, 1959-1966
  Federal Aviation Administration, 1966-

Federal Bureau of Investigation
    Bureau of Investigation, 1908-1935
    Federal Bureau of Investigation, 1935-

Federal Communications Commission
    Federal Radio Commission, 1927-1934
    (Since 1912, the Department of Commerce has issued radio licenses.)
    Federal Communications Commission, 1934-

Federal Highway Administration
    Office of Road Inquiry, 1893-1921
    Bureau of Public Roads, 1921-1957
    Federal Highway Administration, 1957-

Federal Maritime Commission
    Shipping Board, 1916-1936
    United States Maritime Commission, 1936-1950
    Maritime Administration Federal Maritime Board, 1950-1961
    Federal Maritime Commission, 1961-

Federal Power Commission
    Federal Power Commission, 1920-1977
    Federal Energy Regulatory Commission, Department of Energy, assumed the FPC
    duties, 1977-

Federal Reserve Board
    Federal Reserve Board, 1913-

Federal Trade Commission
    Federal Trade Commission, 1914-

Food and Drug Administration
    Bureau of Chemistry, Department of Agriculture, 1906-1927
    Food, Drug, and Insecticide Administration, 1927-1930
    Food and Drug Administration, 1930-

Forest Service
    Division, later Bureau of Forestry, 1881-1905
    Forest Service, 1905-

General Accounting Office
    General Accounting Office, 1921-

General Services Administration
    General Services Administration, 1949-
    (Duties had previously been carried out in several other bureaus and departments:
    Bureau of Federal Supply, Office of Contract Settlement, Federal Works Agency,
    Public Buildings Administration, National Archives, and the War Assets
    Administration.)

Hoover Commissions
> (First) Commission on Organization of the Executive Branch of the Government, 1947-1949
> (Second) Commission on Organization of the Executive Branch of the Government, 1953-1955

Immigration and Naturalization Service
> Bureau of Immigration, 1891-1906
> Bureau of Immigration and Naturalization, 1906-1933
> Immigration and Naturalization Service, 1933-

Internal Revenue Service
> Bureau of Internal Revenue, 1862-1952
> Internal Revenue Service, 1952-

Interstate Commerce Commission
> Interstate Commerce Commission, 1887-

Job Corps
> Job Corps, 1964-

National Aeronautics and Space Administration
> National Advisory Committee for Aeronautics, 1915-1958
> National Aeronautics and Space Administration, 1958-

National Archives and Records Service
> National Archives and Records Service, 1934-

National Bureau of Standards
> National Bureau of Standards, 1901-

National Capital Planning Commission
> National Capital Park Commission, 1924-1926
> National Capital Park and Planning Commission, 1926-1952
> National Capital Planning Commission, 1952-

National Endowment for the Arts
> National Endowment for the Arts, 1965-

National Endowment for the Humanities
> National Endowment for the Humanities, 1965-

National Labor Relations Board
> National Labor Board, 1933-1934
> National Labor Relations Board (old NLRB), 1934-1935
> National Labor Relations Board, 1935-

National Ocean Survey
> Coast Survey, 1807-1878
> Coast and Geodetic Survey, 1878-1965
> National Ocean Survey, 1965-
> (Since 1965, NOS has also contained the National Geodetic Survey.)

National Park Service
> National Park Service, 1916-

National Railroad Passenger Corporation (AMTRAK)
> National Railroad Passenger Corporation (AMTRAK), 1971-

National Recovery Administration
> National Recovery Administration, 1933-1935

National Science Foundation
> National Science Foundation, 1950-

National Security Council
> National Security Council, 1947-

National Transportation Safety Board
> Civil Aeronautics Authority and Air Safety Board, 1938-1940
> Civil Aeronautics Board, 1940-1967
> Interstate Commerce Commission, 1887-1967
> National Transportation Safety Board, 1967-
> (The NTSB assumed the accident investigations of the Civil Aeronautics Board and the Interstate Commerce Commission. It also relied on assistance from the Coast Guard, Federal Highway Administration, and the Federal Railroad Administration.)

National Weather Service
> Army Signal Corps, later service, 1870-1891
> United States Weather Bureau, 1891-1965
> National Weather Service, 1965-

National Youth Administration
> National Youth Administration, 1935-1943

Nuclear Regulatory Commission
> Atomic Energy Commission, 1946-1974
> Nuclear Regulatory Commission, 1974-

Occupational Safety and Health Administration
> Occupational Safety and Health Administration, 1971-

Office of Management and Budget
> Bureau of the Budget, 1921-1970
> Office of Management and Budget, 1970-

Office of Personnel Management
United States Civil Service Commission, 1883-1979
Office of Personnel Management, 1979-

Office of Price Administration
Office of Price Administration and Civilian Supply, 1941
Office of Price Administration, 1941-1946
(to Office of Temporary Controls, 1946-1947)

Office of Scientific Research and Development
National Defense Research Committee, 1940-1941
Office of Scientific Research and Development, 1941-1947

Office of War Information
Office of War Information, 1942-1945

Patent and Trademark Office
Patent Office, 1802-1949
Patent and Trademark Office, 1949-

Peace Corps
Peace Corps, 1961-

Public Health Service
Marine Hospital Service, 1798-1902
Public Health and Marine Hospital Service, 1902-1912
Public Health Service, 1912-

Public Works Administration
Public Works Administration, 1933-1939

Reconstruction Finance Corporation
Reconstruction Finance Corporation, 1932-1957

Rural Electrification Administration
Rural Electrification Administration, 1935-

Securities and Exchange Commission
Securities and Exchange Commission, 1934-

Selective Service System
Selective Service System, 1940-
(Briefly after World War II known as the Office of Selective Service Records.)

Small Business Administration
Small Business Administration, 1953-

Smithsonian Institution
    Smithsonian Institution, 1846-

Social Security Administration
    Social Security Board, 1935-1946
    Social Security Administration, 1946-

Tennessee Valley Authority
    Tennessee Valley Authority, 1933-

United States Air Force Academy
    United States Air Force Academy, 1954-

United States Arms Control and Disarmament Agency
    Office of the Special Assistant to the President for Disarmament, 1955-1961
    United States Arms Control and Disarmament Agency, 1961-

United States Army Corps of Engineers
    Corps of Engineers, 1779-1783
    Corps of Artillerists and Engineers, 1794-1802
    United States Army Corps of Engineers, 1802-

United States Army Signal Corps
    Army Signal Corps, 1860-1865 and 1866-1962
    Army Strategic Communications Command, 1962-1973
    United States Army Communications Command, 1973-

United States Coast Guard
    Revenue Cutter Service, 1790-1915
    Lighthouse Service, 1789-1939
    Life-saving Service, 1878-1915
    Bureau of Marine Inspection and Navigation, 1884-1932
    Bureau of Navigation and Steamboat Inspection, 1932-1942
    United States Coast Guard, 1915-
    (Merger of the Revenue Cutter Service and the Life-saving Service)

United States Commission on Civil Rights
    United States Commission on Civil Rights, 1957-

United States Commission on Industrial Relations
    United States Commission on Industrial Relations, 1913-1915

United States Customs Service
    United States Customs Service, 1789-

United States Fish and Wildlife Service
    United States Fish Commission, 1871-1903
    Bureau of Fisheries, 1903-1940
    Bureau of Biological Survey, 1885-1940

Fish and Wildlife Service, 1940-1956
United States Fish and Wildlife Service, 1956-

United States Geological Survey
United States Geological Survey, 1879-

United States Information Agency
United States Information Agency, 1953-1978
International Communication Agency, 1978-1983
United States Information Agency, 1983-

United States International Trade Commission
United States Tariff Commission, 1916-1975
United States International Trade Commission, 1975-

United States Marine Corps
United States Marine Corps, 1798-

United States Military Academy
United States Military Academy, 1802-

United States Naval Academy
United States Naval Academy, 1845-

United States Postal Service
Post Office Department, 1789-1971
United States Postal Service, 1971-

United States Railway Association and Consolidated Rail Corporation (CONRAIL)
United States Railway Association and Consolidated Rail Corporation (CON-RAIL), 1976-

United States Secret Service
United States Secret Service, 1865-
(Beginning in 1790, Congress voted the President funds for individual "secret service" jobs.)

Veterans Administration
Veterans Administration, 1930-
(The VA replaced various, temporary earlier units known as the Veterans Bureau [1921-1930], the Bureau of Pensions [1833-1930], and the National Home for Disabled Volunteer Soldiers, Bureau of War Risk Insurance [1914-1921].)

War Industries Board
War Industries Board, 1917-1919

War Manpower Commission
War Manpower Commission, 1942-1945

War Production Board
> War Production Board, 1942-1945
> (WPB took over from these predecessors covering 1940-1941: Advisory Commission to the Council of National Defense, Council of National Defense, National Defense Advisory Commission, and the Office of Production Management.)

Women's Bureau
> Women's Bureau, 1920-

Works Progress Administration
> Federal Emergency Relief Administration, 1933-1938
> Federal Civil Works Administration, 1933-1934
> Works Progress Administration, 1935-1939
> Works Projects Administration, 1939-1942
> Federal Works Agency, 1939-1949

UMBRELLA AGENCIES

This appendix contains a listing of umbrella agencies, under which a number of the entities in *Government Agencies* were housed as of 1983. Citations are grouped under the appropriate Cabinet department, executive office, or independent agency in an effort to familiarize the reader with the recent organization of the many agencies written about in this book. Several former agencies are the subject of articles, and a separate compilation of these entries is also included below.

CABINET DEPARTMENTS

Agriculture

Forest Service
Rural Electrification Administration

Commerce

Bureau of the Census
National Bureau of Standards
National Oceanic and Atmospheric Administration
   National Ocean Survey
   National Weather Service
Patent and Trademark Office

Defense

Air Force
Air Force Academy
Army
Army Corps of Engineers
Marine Corps
Navy
United States Military Academy
United States Naval Academy

Education

Energy

Federal Energy Regulatory Administration (assumed many duties of former Federal Power Commission)

Health and Human Services

Food and Drug Administration
Office of Child Support Enforcement (assumed many duties of former Children's Bureau)
Public Health Service
Social Security Administration

Housing and Urban Development

Interior

Bureau of Indian Affairs
Bureau of Land Management
Bureau of Mines
Bureau of Reclamation
National Park Service
United States Fish and Wildlife Service
United States Geological Survey

Justice

Federal Bureau of Investigation
Immigration and Naturalization Service

Labor

Job Corps
Occupational Safety and Health Administration
Women's Bureau

State

Agency for International Development
Foreign Service

Transportation

Federal Aviation Administration
Federal Highway Administration
United States Coast Guard

Treasury

Bureau of Engraving and Printing
Bureau of Public Debt
Internal Revenue Service

United States Customs Service
United States Secret Service

EXECUTIVE OFFICE OF THE PRESIDENT

Council of Economic Advisers
National Security Council
Office of Management and Budget

LEGISLATIVE BRANCH (CONGRESS)

General Accounting Office

INDEPENDENT AGENCIES, BUREAUS, COMMISSIONS, CORPORATIONS

ACTION
    Peace Corps
Central Intelligence Agency
Civil Aeronautics Board
Environmental Protection Agency
Equal Employment Opportunity Commission
Export-Import Bank of the United States
Federal Communications Commission
Federal Maritime Commission
Federal Reserve Board (System)
Federal Trade Commission
General Services Administration
    National Archives and Records Service
Interstate Commerce Commission
National Aeronautics and Space Administration
National Capital Planning Commission
National Foundation on the Arts and Humanities
    National Endowment for the Arts
    National Endowment for the Humanities
National Labor Relations Board
National Railroad Passenger Corporation (AMTRAK)
National Science Foundation
National Transportation Safety Board
Nuclear Regulatory Commission
Office of Personnel Management
Securities and Exchange Commission
Selective Service System
Small Business Administration
Smithsonian Institution
Tennessee Valley Authority
United States Arms Control and Disarmament Agency
United States Commissiion on Civil Rights
United States Information Agency

United States International Trade Commission
United States Postal Service
United States Railway Association and Consolidated Rail Corporation (CONRAIL)
Veterans Administration

FORMER AGENCIES, BUREAUS, COMMISSIONS IN *GOVERNMENT AGENCIES*

Bureau of Refugees, Freedmen, and Abandoned Lands
Civilian Conservation Corps
Committee on Fair Employment Practices
Defense Plant Corporation
Farm Security Administration
Hoover Commissions: Commissions on Organization of the Executive Branch of
    Government, 1947-1949 and 1953-1955
National Recovery Administration
National Youth Administration
Office of Price Administration
Office of Scientific Research and Development
Office of War Information
Public Works Administration
Reconstruction Finance Corporation
United States Army Signal Corps
United States Commission on Industrial Relations
War Industries Board
War Manpower Commission
War Production Board
Works Progress Administration

CATEGORIES OF AGENCY SERVICE

Students of government are often puzzled about the relationship between the organization within a government agency and the actual services it provides to the public. Moreover, the numerous executive and congressional reorganization plans throughout our history have not resolved the puzzle. As just one additional attempt to stimulate reader interest regarding the categorization of services, this appendix offers an arbitrary listing of twelve broad areas of duties with the seemingly appropriate agencies therein. It is entirely unofficial and, even within this list, possible consolidations or inconsistencies exist; nonetheless, it might serve as a guide. As a matter of interest, former agencies are included within parentheses.

COMMUNICATIONS

Federal Communications Commission
Federal Power Commission
Federal Trade Commission
United States Postal Service

DEFENSE

Military

Department of Defense
Department of the Air Force
Department of the Army
Department of the Navy
United States Air Force Academy
United States Army Signal Corps
United States Marine Corps
United States Military Academy
United States Naval Academy

Civilian

(Defense Plant Corporation)
National Security Council
(Office of Price Administration)
(Office of War Information)
Selective Service System
Veterans Administration
(War Industries Board)
(War Manpower Commission)
(War Production Board)

DOMESTIC PROTECTION

Bureau of Engraving and Printing
Bureau of the Census
Bureau of Public Debt
Department of Justice
Department of the Treasury
Federal Bureau of Investigation
Internal Revenue Service
Patent and Trademark Office
United States Customs Service
United States Secret Service

ECONOMY AND EMPLOYMENT

(Civilian Conservation Corps)
Council of Economic Advisers
Department of Commerce
Department of Labor
(Farm Security Administration)
Federal Reserve Board
Job Corps
National Labor Relations Board
(National Recovery Administration)
(National Youth Administration)
(Public Works Administration)
(Reconstruction Finance Corporation)
Rural Electrification Administration
Securities and Exchange Commission
Small Business Administration
(United States Commission on Industrial Relations)
(Works Progress Administration)

EDUCATION AND THE ARTS

Department of Education
National Endowment for the Arts
National Endowment for the Humanities

ENVIRONMENTAL GROWTH AND RESOURCES

Bureau of Land Management
Bureau of Mines
Bureau of Reclamation
Department of Agriculture
Department of Energy
Department of Interior
Environmental Protection Agency
Forest Service
National Park Service
Nuclear Regulatory Commission
Tennessee Valley Authority
United States Army Corps of Engineers
United States Fish and Wildlife Service

GOVERNMENTAL HOUSEKEEPING

General Accounting Office
General Services Administration
(Hoover Commissions)
National Archives and Records Service
National Capital Planning Commission
Office of Management and Budget
Office of Personnel Management

HEALTH AND WELFARE

Department of Health and Human Services
Department of Housing and Urban Development
Food and Drug Administration
Occupational Safety and Health Administration
Public Health Service
Social Security Administration

INDIVIDUALS AND GROUPS

Bureau of Indian Affairs
(Bureau of Refugees, Freedmen, and Abandoned Lands)
(Children's Bureau)
(Committee on Fair Employment Practices)
Equal Employment Opportunity Commission
Immigration and Naturalization Service
U.S. Commission on Civil Rights
Women's Bureau

INTERNATIONAL SCENE

Agency for International Development
Central Intelligence Agency

Department of State
Export-Import Bank
Peace Corps
United States Arms Control and Disarmament Agency
United States Information Agency
United States International Trade Commission

SCIENCE AND TECHNOLOGY

National Aeronautics and Space Administration
National Bureau of Standards
National Ocean Survey
National Science Foundation
National Weather Service
(Office of Scientific Research and Development)
Smithsonian Institution
United States Geological Survey

TRANSPORTATION

Civil Aeronautics Board
Department of Transportation
Federal Aviation Administration
Federal Highway Administration
Federal Maritime Commission
Interstate Commerce Commission
National Railroad Passenger Corporation (AMTRAK)
National Transportation Safety Board
Unites States Coast Guard
United States Railway Association and Consolidated Rail Corporation (CONRAIL)

INDEX

Page numbers in *italic type* indicate the location of the main entry.

About the Editor

DONALD R. WHITNAH is Chairman of the Department of History at the University of Northern Iowa in Cedar Falls. His previous works include *A History of the United States Weather Bureau* and *Safer Skyways: Federal Control of Aviation*.